LANCHESTER LIBRARY
3 8001 00560 3000

D0102169

EQUALITY LAW

EQUALITY LAW

Monaghan

OXFORD
UNIVERSITY PRESS

OXFORD
UNIVERSITY PRESS
Great Clarendon Street, Oxford OX2 6DP

Oxford University Press is a department of the Univeristy of Oxford.
It furthers the University's objective of excellence in research, scholarship,
and education by publishing worldwide in

Oxford New York

Auckland Cape Town Dar es Salaam Hong Kong Karachi
Kuala Lumpur Madrid Melbourne Mexico City Nairobi
New Delhi Shanghai Taipei Toronto

With offices in

Argentina Austria Brazil Chile Czech Republic France Greece
Guatemala Hungary Italy Japan Poland Portugal Singapore
South Korea Switzerland Thailand Turkey Ukraine Vietnam

Published in the United States
by Oxford University Press Inc., New York

First published 2007

British Library Cataloguing in Publication Data
Data available

Library of Congress Cataloging in Publication Data
Typeset by Cepha Imaging Pvt Ltd., Bangalore, India
Printed in Great Britain
on acid-free paper by
Antony Rowe Ltd., Chippenham

ISBN 978–0–19–927795–7
1 3 5 7 9 10 8 6 4 2

To Lesford

PREFACE

Until fairly recently, discrimination law was, and could safely be, dealt with as a subset of employment law. Whilst the legislation has always covered other activities, litigation was rare outside the employment field. The position has changed. Litigation is common now in all the areas covered by the legislation. The amount of law has also increased exponentially. In its early years, the law was concerned with protecting against sex and race discrimination. To that was then added disability and, in the past few years, religion and belief, sexual orientation, and age. It is impossible to understand fully what law we have without a firm grasp of relevant EC and Convention law. If the complexity of the law, its differences, as between statutes, and its peculiarities are to be fully grasped and its purposes understood, its origins and the contexts in which these laws were enacted need to be appreciated.

This book aims to address all these things. Some time is spent on the historical and, where relevant, political context of our law because that is increasingly relied upon as an aid for interpreting law. Relevant EC and ECHR law is covered, and the anti-discrimination legislation is considered in depth. I hope that it will be useful not only to employment lawyers but also to public lawyers, police lawyers, education lawyers, and discrimination lawyers who practice across the areas caught by the legislation.

The book is a year late. It was more difficult than I had thought, and I paid the price for delay; the law changed, and its scope increased during that year. It is now up-to-date to September 2006 (and law coming into force later but enacted by then has been dealt with). Significant legislative change is unlikely now until 2010 when we can expect a Single Equality Act, if the Government comes through on its promise. In this book I have tried to highlight some of the strengths and weaknesses of our existing schemes in the knowledge that the Government is now considering what approach it should take to equality and non-discrimination law in any new Single Equality Act. I hope that, if I do write another book after 2010, I will be writing about a much-improved scheme.

Thanks are due to many, many people. Thank you to Baroness Hale for kindly writing the Foreword to this book. Thank you too to Ulele Burnham, Barbara Cohen,

Tessa Hetherington, Sanchita Hosali, Urfan Khaliq, James Laddie, Aileen McColgan, and Hugh Tomlinson for their help with research, reading, and generally. Thank you too to Sarah McGrath, Roxanne Selby, and all at OUP for their patience and support. Thanks in particular are due to all my clients who have contextualized the law for me.

The law is stated as on 1 October 2006, but I have been able to include some later developments at proof stage.

Karon Monghan
October 2006

FOREWORD

Equality, says Rabinder Singh QC, is the 'neglected virtue'. If so, we can neglect it no longer. The Equality Act 2006 not only makes important changes to our already complex anti-discrimination laws but brings us the new Commission for Equality and Human Rights with the noble task of 'encouraging and supporting the development of a society in which –

(a) people's ability to achieve their potential is not limited by prejudice or discrimination.
(b) there is respect for and protection of each individual's human rights,
(c) there is respect for the dignity and worth of each individual,
(d) each individual has an equal opportunity to participate in society, and
(e) there is mutual respect between groups based on understanding and valuing of diversity and on shared respect for equality and human rights.'

But this only goes to show what a very complex virtue this is. If we start from the Aristotelian precept that like cases must be treated alike, how are we to tell which cases are alike? It is not so long ago that it was taken for granted that men and women, boys and girls, were sufficiently different to justify treating each group differently. My mother, a trained teacher, was obliged to leave her job when she got married. So were all other women teachers at the time, whether or not they were in fact the breadwinner in the family. My university had only one place for a young woman student for every nine places it had for young men. All the married women, and all the would-be women students, were equally disadvantaged. All the married men and all the would-be men students were equally advantaged. But today we would not see this as equal treatment because we would regard their sex as an irrelevant consideration. And we would do this even if statistics showed that married women were less likely than married men to be the family breadwinner, or that women students were less likely than men to devote their whole lives to the career for which their university studies might equip them. This is because we now see that it is wrong to judge any individual man or woman according to statistically based generalities.

But that realisation only takes us so far. Only a limited number of characteristics is automatically suspect in this way. Other characteristics, for example habitual residence, may be accepted as material distinctions without the need for specific justification. Even when the characteristic is to be disregarded, decisions still have to be made about what is and is not a like case. Is pregnancy a relevant difference between a man and a woman in the same job? Are the complaints made by men who may resent the authority of a woman superior a relevant difference or are they not? Deciding what is and is not a like case can easily slide into a justification for different treatment.

Even then, treating like cases alike does not redress systemic disadvantage. It may produce a certain sort of equality of opportunity but it does not produce equality of respect and esteem still less equality of outcome. We do not expect equality of outcome for everyone. Our society is premised on individual differences. We cannot and do not expect everyone to turn out the same. Some are bound to do better than others. So how far our laws should progress from equality of opportunity to equality of outcome or esteem is a difficult issue. Some disadvantages can be combated by equality laws and others cannot but which are which?

It follows that those of us who believe that we share a commitment to equal treatment and non-discrimination may hold very different views on some of the key questions in the debate. I am not to be taken to endorse all of the opinions expressed in this book. But of the importance and complexity of the subject, especially now that the impugned grounds are being extended far beyond the comfort zones of race and sex, there can be no doubt. The issues will get more difficult before they get easier.

That is why the virtue can no longer be neglected and texts such as this are a vital contribution to our understanding of this complex area of the developing law.

Brenda Hale

29 January 2007

CONTENTS—SUMMARY

CONTENTS

IV STRATEGIC ACTION, STATUTORY DUTIES, AND COMMISSIONS

TABLE OF CASES

TABLE OF LEGISLATION

Abortion Act 1967 . . . . 4.71
s 1(1) 4.70
Access to Justice Act 1999. . . . . 8.26
Act of Sederunt (Interest in Sheriff Court Decrees or Extracts) 1975 . . . . 14.30, 14.33
Act of Sederunt (Interest in Sheriff Court Decrees or Extracts) 1993 . . . . 14.30, 14.33
Act of Settlement 1701. . . . . 1.03
Anti-terrorism, Crime and Security Act 2001
s 23 . . . . 2.08, 15.139
Asylum and Immigration Act 1996
s 8 . . . . 2.47, 4.71
Asylum and Immigration Act 1999
s 95 . . . . 1.01, 2.47
Asylum etc Act 2006 . . . . 1.30
s 19 . . . . 4.98

Bill of Rights 1689 (1 Will & Mar Sess 2 c2) 1.03, 2.01
British Nationality Act 1948. . . . . 5.54

Canada Act 1982 . . . . 6.08
Child Support Act 1991 . . . . 2.94, 2.101
Children Act 1972
s 1(2) 2.104
Children Act 1989 . . . . 2.101
Children and Young Persons Act 1933
s 18 . . . . 2.101
s 18(1)(a) 2.104
Civil Liability (Contribution) Act 1978 . . . . 14.01
Civil Partnership Act 2004 . . . . . . 1.03, 1.08, 1.46, 2.92, 2.93, 2.94, 2.95, 2.96, 2.97, 4.76, 4.81, 5.43, 5.48, 5.140, 8.48
Part 5 . . . . 2.92
s 1 . . . . 2.92, 5.46
s 1(1) 5.47
s 1(1)(b) 5.46
s 2(3) 2.92
s 6(1) 2.92
s 251(1) 5.46
s 251(2) 5.46
Commonwealth Immigrants Act 1962 . . . . 2.16, 2.24
Commonwealth Immigrants Act 1968 . . . . 2.24, 2.25, 2.26, 2.49
Constitutional Reform Act 2005
s 61 . . . . 2.13
Sch 12 . . . . 2.13
County Courts Act 1984
s 69 . . . . 14.30, 14.33

Disability Discrimination Act 1995(DDA). 1.02, 1.08, 1.09, 1.10, 1.14, 1.21, 1.22, 1.23, 1.25, 1.26, 1.27, 1.29, 1.54, 2.12, 2.42, 2.62–2.80, 3.01, 3.18, 5.72–5.132, 6.02, 6.03, 6.04, 6.18, 6.20, 6.21, 6.23, 6.76, 6.102, 6.152, 6.157, 6.159, 6.162, 6.165, 6.192, 6.193, 6.194, 6.228, 6.229, 7.03, 8.02, 8.11, 8.14, 8.15, 8.34, 8.52, 9.01, 9.02, 9.10, 9.32, 10.01, 10.07, 10.13, 10.23, 10.25, 10.26,

Statutory Instruments

EUROPEAN UNION

REGULATIONS

UNITED STATES OF AMERICA

TABLE OF TREATIES AND CONVENTIONS

LIST OF ABBREVIATIONS

ADA	Americans with Disabilities Act 1990
CA	Court of Appeal
CBI	Confederation of British Industry
CEDAW	International Convention on the Elimination of all forms of Discrimination Against Women
CEHR	Commission for Equality and Human Rights
CERD	International Convention on the Elimination of all forms of Racial Discrimination
CRC	Convention on the Rights of the Child
CRE	Commission for Racial Equality
DCS	Disability Conciliation Service
DDA 2005	Disability Discrimination Act 2005
DDA	Disability Discrimination Act 1995
DfES	Department for Education and Skills
DRC	Disability Rights Commission
DRCA	Disability Rights Commission Act 1999
EA	Equality Act 2006
EAT	Employment Appeal Tribunal
EC Treaty	Treaty Establishing the European Community
EC	European Community
ECA	European Communities Act 1972
ECHR	European Convention on Human Rights
ECJ	European Court of Justice
ECNI	Equality Commission for Northern Ireland
ECtHR	European Court of Human Rights
EEC	European Economic Community
EOC	Equal Opportunities Commission
EPA	Equal Pay Act 1970
EU	European Union
FETO	Fair Employment and Treatment (Northern Ireland) Order 1998
HRA	Human Rights Act 1998
HSE	Health and Safety Executive
ICCPR	International Covenant on Civil and Political Rights
ICESCR	International Covenant on Economic, Social and Cultural Rights
ICESCR	International Covenant on Economic, Social and Cultural Rights 1966
ICTA 1988	Income and Corporation Tax Act 1988
ILO	International Labour Organization

JCHR	Parliamentary Joint Committee on Human Rights
NHS	National Health Service
OJEC	Official Journal of the European Union
RRA	Race Relations Act 1976
RRAA	Race Relations (Amendment) Act 2000
SDA	Sex Discrimination Act 1975
SENDA 2001	Special Educational Needs and Disability Act 2001
SENDA	Special Educational Needs and Disability Act 2001
SENDIST	Special Educational Needs and Disability Tribunals
Street Report	H Street, G Howe, and G Bindman, Street Report on Anti-Discrimination Legislation (1967) Political and Economic Planning
TEU	Treaty on European Union
TUC	Trades Union Congress
UDHR	Universal Declaration of Human Rights
UN	United Nations
UPIAS	Union of the Physically Impaired against Segregation
WHO	World Health Organization
WHOICD	World Health Organization's International Classification of Diseases

Part I

INTRODUCTION

1

INTRODUCTION

A. Introduction

There is no general prohibition against discrimination in Great Britain.[1] Constitutional law provides for the principle of legality, makes all equally subject to law, and provides for some limited scrutiny of the acts of public authorities to ensure 'rationality' is measured in part by a requirement for 'equal treatment'.[2] However, there is no general 'equality' obligation to be found in the law and inequality remains largely unregulated.[3] Instead, legislation regulates particular and closely defined forms of discrimination where that discrimination is connected to membership of a particular class or due to the possession of certain personal characteristics. 1.01

1 The position in Northern Ireland is somewhat different and is discussed below.

2 *Kruse v Johnson* [1998] 2 QB 91, *per* Lord Hoffmann; *Matadeen v Pointu* [1999] 1 AC 98, 109; J Jowell, 'Is Equality a Constitutional Principle?' [1994] 7 CLP 1; PG Polyviou, *The Equal Protection of the Laws* (1980) 1–24. The concept is discussed further in Chap 2.

3 There are, of course, specific forms of protection afforded certain disadvantaged groups in the sphere of general welfare law (housing, education, welfare benefits etc). However, these are not predicated on the assumption that 'inequality' is to be guarded against, but to ensure that a basic standard of living is maintained—and the most base consequences of inequality are avoided only insofar as they fail to do this. Indeed, such welfare has even been afforded along discriminatory lines. For example, asylum seekers are excluded from entitlement in certain circumstances (Asylum and Immigration Act 1999 s 95; Nationality, Asylum and Immigration Act 2002, s 55; *R v Secretary of State for the Home Department, ex p Limbuela; R v Secretary of State for the Home Department, ex p Tesema (Conjoined Appeals)* [2005] UKHL 66). There is also now the prohibition in the Human Rights Act 1998, Sch 1 Art 14 but this provision operates only within specific spheres (see Chap 4 below).

1.02 Presently, discrimination is regulated where it is connected with sex, gender reassignment, married or civil partnership status (but not unmarried or non-civil partnership status), race, colour, ethnicity, national origins, nationality (though not usually immigration status[4]), disability, sexual orientation, religion, belief, and age.[5] Discrimination connected with other characteristics, in particular social or birth status,[6] wealth, social class, place of residence,[7] or 'immigration'[8] status, is not so regulated. So poverty, both abject and relative, remains a feature of UK life, notwithstanding our collective wealth. 'Asylum seekers' and 'immigrants' are hounded and vilified by the press, and teenage mothers remain a constant and public measure of society's moral and other failings.

1.03 Historically, legal inequality has been a significant feature of British life, and it remains so. Examples of inequality can be found, of course, in colonial law and the English courts' decisions affecting slavery,[9] and the laws regulating the civil and political rights of women.[10] More recently the laws criminalizing homosexuality were repealed only in 1967,[11] with an unequal age of consent persisting until 2001,[12] and a prohibition on same-sex marriage continuing, causing significant disadvantage until 2005 when the Civil Partnership Act 2004 came into effect.[13] There also remains much legislation and custom entrenching apparently otherwise objectionable discrimination (eg institutionalizing male primogeniture, requiring the monarch to be a Protestant, prohibiting the monarch from

---

4 *Dhatt v McDonalds Hamburgers Ltd* [1991] 1 WLR 527; [1991] ICR 238.

5 The Sex Discrimination Act 1975, the Race Relations Act 1976, and the Disability Discrimination Act 1995 regulate sex, race, and disability discrimination and discrimination on the grounds of married or civil partnership status in Great Britain. To this trio of Acts has been added (in consequence of Council Directive (EC) establishing a general framework for equal treatment in employment and occupation 2000/78/EC [200] OJL 303) the Employment Equality (Religion or Belief) Regulations 2003 SI 2003/1660, the Employment Equality (Sexual Orientation) Regulations 2003 SI 2003/1661, and the Employment Equality (Age) Regulations 2006 SI 2006/1031 (in force 1 Oct 2006) which add religion or belief, sexual orientation, and age respectively to the grounds addressed by statutory regulation. In addition, the Equal Pay Act 1970 (EPA), which came into force in 1975, regulates discrimination in pay and other contractual employment-related benefits as between men and women, and the Equality Act 2006 extends the protections against discrimination by the measures just described in relation to certain of the grounds protected.

6 Little wonder, perhaps, particularly in the context of a State headed by a constitutional monarchy.

7 Unless connected to nationality, national or ethnic origins.

8 Unless connected to nationality, national or ethnic origins.

9 A Lester and G Bindman, *Race and Law* (1972, Penguin) 27–34.

10 S Fredman, *Discrimination Law* (2002, OUP) 27–31.

11 Sexual Offences Act 1967.

12 Sexual Offences (Amendment) Act 2000.

13 For example, the issues raised in *Fitzpatrick v Sterling Housing Association Limited* [2001] 1 AC 27 and *Ghaidan v Godin-Mendoza* [2004] 2 AC 557.

entering into marriage with a Catholic,[14] and a continuing bar on same-sex partners marrying[15]).

Notwithstanding that it has been observed that '[t]he concept of equality is . . . a hallowed virtue of the English legal system',[16] the courts have not always shown consistent deference to Parliament's efforts to give effect to the principle in social and economic life. Examples can be found splattered across the common law, and include Lord Denning's notorious observation,[17] when describing the circumstances surrounding a claim brought by a man complaining of sex discrimination in having to work in a colour bursting shop in which women did not (a man whom, according to Lord Denning, had 'little regard for chivalry or for the women's hair-dos'), that '[a] woman's hair is her crowning glory . . . She does not like it disturbed: especially when she has just had a "hair-do"'.[18,19] Lord Denning evinced even more irritation when holding that there was no sex discrimination in a case brought by a man complaining of sex discrimination in relation to a rule which allowed female workers to leave a factory five minutes earlier than male workers. According to Lord Denning, though the Sex Discrimination Act 1975: **1.04**

> . . . applies equally to men as to women, . . . it would be very wrong . . . if this statute were thought to obliterate the differences between men and women or to do away with the chivalry and courtesy which we expect mankind to give womankind. The natural differences of sex must be regarded even in the interpretation of an Act of Parliament . . . Instances were put before us in the course of argument, such as a cruise liner which employs both men and women. Would it be wrong to have a regulation 'Women and children first'? Or in the case of a factory in case of fire? As soon as such instances are considered, the answer is clear. It is not discrimination for mankind to treat womankind with the courtesy and chivalry which we have been taught to believe is right conduct in our society.[20]

More subtle resistance is found in the later case law interpreting the concepts of discrimination protected by law and this is discussed in later chapters.

Whilst the public law principle of 'rationality' incorporates a requirement for equal treatment, this has been within limits. Prior to the enactment of the Equal **1.05**

---

14 Bill of Rights 1689 (1 Will & Mar Sess. 2c.2); 1701 Act of Settlement; Union with Scotland Act 1706; Union with England Act 1707.

15 Matrimonial Causes Act 1973, s 11(c), though there is an attempt at equivalence in the Civil Partnership Act 2004.

16 A Lester and G Bindman, *Race and Law* (1972, Penguin), 23. And see Lady Hale in *Ghaidan v Godin-Mendoza* [2004] 2 AC 557 para 132: 'Such a guarantee of equal treatment is also essential to democracy. Democracy is founded on the principle that each individual has equal value'. See further Chap 2.

17 See his observations too in *Science Research Council v Nassé* [1979] QB 144 at 172.

18 *Jeremiah v Ministry of Defence* [1980] QB 87 at 96.

19 Ibid, 97.

20 *Peake v Automotive Products Ltd* [1978] QB 233, 238.

Pay Act 1970, the courts' view was that such a principle did not sanction a council's decision to secure equal pay as between men and women for the same work. Such policy, according to Lord Atkinson, demonstrated '[t]he vanity of appearing as model employers of labour' and showed that 'the council [had] become such ardent feminists as to bring about, at the expense of the ratepayers whose money they administered, sex equality in the labour market'.[21] Nor is there much evidence that any common law principle of equality has extended to promoting race equality at home or abroad.[22]

1.06 Such statutory protections as are now afforded are notoriously complex and inconsistent. Their complexity and their inconsistencies have been compounded by the amendments made to the legislation from time to time, sometimes by regulations under the European Communities Act 1972.[23] Any review of UK anti-discrimination law cannot assume a consistent underpinning theme or principle. A proper explanation of the law, as opposed to a mere account of it, will recognize that its origins lie in historically specific conditions and political choices which have not produced comprehensive protections against inequality and discrimination.[24]

1.07 The Human Rights Act 1998 has now given effect to Article 14 of the European Convention for the Protection of Human Rights and Fundamental Freedoms[25] (ECHR). As will be seen in later chapters,[26] Article 14 has proved to be an important tool in addressing inequality particularly in the context of public law, but the provision also has its limits. Protocol 12 to the ECHR offers more potential in the struggle against inequality, but the UK has not signed or ratified this Protocol and has expressed no intention to do so.[27]

---

21 *Roberts v Hopwood* [1925] AC 592.

22 For example, *Wheeler v Leicester CC* [1985] AC 1054; *R v Lewisham BC ex parte Shell* [1988] 1 All ER 938. Even the promise shown by their Lordships' response to some of our more repressive recent anti-terrorist legislation (*A and Others v Secretary of State for the Home Department* [2004] UKHL 56, [2005] 2 AC 68) has been undermined by later decisions: *R (on the application of Gillan) & Anor v Commissioner of Police for the Metropolis & Anor* [2006] UKHL 12 (especially, paras 40–7 *per* Lord Hope; para 68 *per* Lord Scott; and paras 83–92 *per* Lord Brown). See further Chap 2.

23 See B Hepple, C Coussey, and T Choudhury, *Equality: A New Framework, Report of the Independent Review of the Enforcement of the UK Anti-discrimination Legislation* (2000, Hart) for a review and discussion of the inconsistencies which then existed and which with the new regulations, described in later chapters, have increased in number.

24 See Chap 2.

25 [1950] ETS No 005.

26 See Chap 4.

27 Written Answer 37, Lord Bassam of Brighton, 11 Oct 2000, Parliamentary Question, 27 Sept 2001 (available at <http://www.publications.parliament.uk/pa/ld199900/ldhansrd/vo001011/text/01011w01.htm#01011w01_sbhd1>). This is further discussed in Chap 4.

B. Protection against Inequality and Discrimination and Concepts of Discrimination

1.08 In the main, protection against discrimination in Great Britain[28] is afforded in five statutes and in regulations made thereunder: the Equal Pay Act 1970 (EPA); the Sex Discrimination Act 1975 (SDA); the Race Relations Act 1976 (RRA); the Disability Discrimination Act 1995 (DDA); and the Equality Act 2006 (EA). Regulations made under the European Communities Act 1972 now also regulate discrimination in connection with religion, belief, sexual orientation, and age.[29] Together I describe these as the 'main anti-discrimination enactments'. These main anti-discrimination enactments regulate certain discrimination connected with sex; married status; civil partnership status; gender reassignment; colour; race; nationality; ethnic or national origins; disability; sexual orientation; religion; belief; and age ('the protected classes').[30] Each of the enactments has been amended, some significantly.[31] The histories of these enactments and of the main amendments to them are considered in Chapter 2. There is also a plethora of ad hoc anti-discrimination measures found in a diverse range of domestic,[32]

---

28 The particular conditions in Northern Ireland are considered briefly below.

29 The Employment Equality (Religion or Belief) Regulations 2003 SI 2003/1660, the Employment Equality (Sexual Orientation) Regulations 2003 SI 2003/1661, and the Employment Equality (Age) Regulations 2006 SI 2006/1031 enacted to give effect to EC Directive 2000/78/EC.

30 Each of these expressions is closely defined and they are considered in detail in Chap 5.

31 See in particular, Equal Pay (Amendment) Regulations 1983 SI 1983/1794; the Race Relations (Amendment) Act 2000; the Disability Discrimination Act 2005; the Race Relations Act 1976 (Amendment) Regulations 2003 SI 2003/1626; the Sex Discrimination Act 1975 (Amendment) Regulations 2003 SI 2003/1657; the Disability Discrimination Act 1995 (Amendment) Regulations 2003 SI 2003/1673; the Employment Equality (Sex Discrimination) Regulations 2005 SI 2005/2467.

32 In diverse a range as, for example, (1) the Civil Partnership Act 2004, abolishing many of the discriminatory distinctions, based on sexual orientation, provided for in other laws; (2) the Orders made under s 4 of the Local Government Act 1999 (introducing the 'Best Value' regime) which include in the case of the 'general corporate performance indicators' the 'equality standard' found in 'Equality Standard for Local Government' (2001) which is to be used as one of the measures of performance of specified Best Value authorities including District Councils, London Borough Councils, County Councils, and a number of others (Local Government (Best Value) Performance Indictors and Performance Standards (England) Order 2005 SI 2005/598); (3) Building Regulations 2000, SI 2000/2531 and Building (Amendment) Regulations 2000, SI 2003/2692, and 'Part M: Access to and Use of Buildings' of Schedule 1 to the Regulations. In addition, there is a large amount of regulation in the employment field addressing arrangements and conferring rights which relate to protection against discrimination: see, eg, the Part-Time Workers (Prevention of Less Favourable Treatment) Regulations 2000 SI 2000/1551; the Maternity and Parental Leave etc Regulations 1999 SI 1999/3312 and ss 80F–I of the Employment Rights Act 1996 and the Flexible Working (Eligibility, Complaints and Remedies) Regulations 2002 SI 2002/3236.

regional, and international instruments,[33] and, to a limited extent, the common law.[34]

1.09 With the exception of the DDA, the main anti-discrimination enactments share a common structure. They each define discrimination in Part 1 and then, in subsequent parts, create a series of unlawful acts (statutory torts), enforceable through the courts and tribunals. As will be seen, the RRA gives the widest coverage, making discrimination by a range of bodies, including public and planning authorities, in respect of a wide number of activities, unlawful, and, importantly, creating a series of statutory duties upon certain specified public authorities.[35] The DDA operates somewhat differently with definitions of discrimination dependent on whether the impugned act occurs within the employment sphere or in the context of the provision of goods, facilities, or services, etc.[36] The EPA provides a complicated route to conferring equal pay rights between men and women, by the statutory implication of an 'equality clause' into employment contracts.[37]

1.10 Each of the main anti-discrimination enactments, except the DDA, are symmetrical so that they protect men as well as women; white people as well as black people; straight people as well as gay people, etc against unlawful discrimination. The DDA operates differently, focusing instead on discrimination against disabled, and not non-disabled, people.[38]

1.11 Article 14 does not define discrimination, but application of this provision by the European Court of Human Rights (ECtHR) and increasingly by domestic courts and tribunals reflects some of the same concepts found in the main anti-discrimination enactments. However, these concepts developed under Article 14 are more fluid than those found in domestic legislation and, as will be seen in later chapters, offer both potential and dangers.[39]

---

33 For example, Art 14 of the ECHR [1950] ETS No 005; Art 26 of the International Covenant on Civil and Political Rights; the International Convention on the Elimination of all Forms of Racial Discrimination; and the International Convention on the Elimination of all Forms of Discrimination Against Women. These are considered further in Chap 4.

34 See Chap 2.

35 RRA, ss 19A and 19B and 71 and 71A–B. Similar duties in the DDA and the SDA will soon come into effect in consequence of the DDA 2005 (December 2006) and the EA 2006 (expected 2007), respectively.

36 See, eg, DDA, ss 3A, 4A, 20–21, 21D, 21G, 21H, 24, 24A 28B, 28C. The RRA and SDA also define discrimination differently depending on the activity concerned, but the differences are relatively minor and all of the definitions are to be found in the same part of the Acts, namely Part 1.

37 EPA 1970, s 1(1).

38 Save that the victimization provisions protect both disabled and non-disabled people: DDA, s 55. See Chap 6.

39 See Chap 6. Note, in particular, that the courts have introduced into the concept of discrimination under Art 14 many of the flaws found in the case law under the domestic statutory schemes relating to comparators: See, eg, *R v Secretary of State for Work and Pensions ex p Carson and another* [2005] UKHL 37; [2006] 1 AC 173 and the approach to comparators (paras 3, 31–3, 63–4).

In summary[40] the main anti-discrimination enactments define the principal[41] forms of 'discrimination' as: 1.12

- direct discrimination (less favourable treatment on grounds connected to one of the protected characteristics);
- indirect discrimination (formally 'equal treatment' in circumstances where such treatment disadvantages certain protected classes);
- disability-related discrimination;
- a failure to comply with the duty to make adjustments (formally 'equal treatment' in circumstances where a duty arises to make adjustments to accommodate disabled people); and
- victimization (less favourable treatment connected with a person having taken action referable to the anti-discrimination enactments).

In addition, the main anti-discrimination enactments expressly define and proscribe 'harassment' connected with the protected grounds.

These concepts and the case law relating to them are explored in depth later in the book.[42] However, in summary, direct discrimination embraces the fundamental commitment and aspiration found in all modern liberal thought—that all human beings are equal and, accordingly, should be afforded equal treatment. In the UK, this concept was first given statutory force in the field of anti-discrimination law in the Race Relations Act 1965[43] which provided that in respect of 'places of public resort':[44] 1.13

> . . . a person discriminates against another person if he refuses or neglects to afford him access to the place in question, or any facilities or services available there, in the like manner and on the like terms in and on which such access, facilities or services are available to other members of the public resorting thereto.

Direct discrimination is now formulated more generally in each of the main anti-discrimination enactments by a standard model which proscribes treatment which is 'less favourable' than that which is, or would be, afforded another on racial grounds,[45] on grounds of religion, belief,[46] or sexual orientation,[47] or on the 1.14

---

40 The details are considered in the following chapters.

41 The Employment Equality (Age) Regulations 2006 SI 2006/1031 also define 'instructions to discriminate' as a form of discrimination. Others of the enactments address 'instructions' as a discrete unlawful act; see Chap 6.

42 See Chap 6, in particular.

43 Discussed further in Chap 2.

44 RRA, 1965, s 1(1).

45 Ibid, s 1(1)(a). This is the widest meaning of direct discrimination in the anti-discrimination enactments, see Chap 6.

46 Regulation 3(1)(a) of the Employment Equality (Religion or Belief) Regulations 2003 SI 2003/1660. This is a wider formulation than is found in the SDA, DDA, and the Age Regulations.

47 Regulation 3(1)(a) of the Employment Equality (Sexual Orientation) Regulations 2003 SI 2003/1661. This is a wider formulation than is found in the SDA, DDA, and the Age Regulations. See further Chap 6.

grounds of the complainants' sex,[48] disability,[49] or age.[50] In recognition that in the USA a mere prohibition on 'unequal' treatment was not sufficient to outlaw racial segregation,[51] the RRA 1968 expressly outlawed racial segregation,[52] and that prohibition is also now found in the RRA 1976.[53]

1.15 With the exception of age discrimination,[54] direct discrimination under the main anti-discrimination enactments cannot be defended on the general ground of 'justification'. Instead, narrowly drawn exemptions exist in relation to some activities.[55] This is generally a strength. However, the approach to the comparator question that is, whether the treatment complained of is *less favourable* than that which was, or would have been, afforded another[56] in a *comparable situation* has, arguably and controversially, allowed for the justification of directly discriminatory treatment and so withered away the sharp edges of what otherwise might have been a strict liability in certain fields. This is discussed further in Chapter 6.

1.16 The concept of indirect discrimination derives from US jurisprudence and, in particular, the case of *Griggs v Duke Power* (*Griggs*).[57] In *Griggs*, black employees brought an action under title VII of the Civil Rights Act 1964 ('discrimination in employment'), challenging the respondent's requirement that its employees have a high school diploma or pass an intelligence test as a condition of employment or as a condition for a transfer to particular jobs. These requirements were not directed at or intended to measure ability for a particular job and, prior to the enactment of the Civil Rights Act, the company had openly discriminated on the basis of race in hiring and transferring employees. Accordingly questions were raised about the respondent's motives. However, the Court of Appeal concluded that as no discriminatory purpose was found the requirements were permitted. This was so notwithstanding that, as a consequence of the requirements, a disproportionate number of black employees were rendered ineligible for employment or transfer.

---

48 SDA, s 1(1)(a) and 1(2)(a). This is a narrower formulation than that found in the RRA and in the Employment Equality (Religion or Belief) Regulations 2003 SI 2003/1660, and the Employment Equality (Sexual Orientation) Regulations 2003 SI 2003/1661.

49 DDA, s 3(A)(5). This is a narrower formulation than that found in the RRA and in the Employment Equality (Religion or Belief) Regulations 2003 SI 2003/1660, and the Employment Equality (Sexual Orientation) Regulations 2003 SI 2003/1661.

50 Regulation 3(1)(a) of the Employment Equality (Age) Regulations 2006 SI 2006/1031.

51 *Plessy v Ferguson* 163 US 537 (1896).

52 RRA 1968, s 1(2).

53 RRA 1976, s 1(2).

54 Regulation 3(1), Employment Equality (Age) Regulations 2006 SI 2006/1031.

55 See for example SDA, s 7 and RRA ss 4A and 5. See Chaps 8–13.

56 RRA, ss 1(1)(a) and 3(4); SDA, ss 1(1)(a) and (2)(a) and 5(3); and DDA, s 3A(5).

57 401 US 424, 91 SCt 849.

On appeal, the US Supreme Court concluded that the Civil Rights Act required 'the removal of artificial, arbitrary, and unnecessary barriers to employment when the barriers operate invidiously to discriminate on the basis of racial or other impermissible classification'. To this end, it was necessary 'that the posture and condition of the jobseeker be taken into account'. Thus, the Act proscribed 'not only overt discrimination but also practices that are fair in form, but discriminatory in operation'. According to the Supreme Court's decision, to determine whether or not a practice is unlawful, 'the touchstone is business necessity . . . [i]f an employment practice which operates to exclude negroes (*sic*) cannot be shown to be related to job performance, the practice is prohibited'. In this instance, the completion of a high school diploma and a general intelligence test did not bear any demonstrable relationship to successful performance of the jobs and was unlawful. The Court concluded that: **1.17**

> [G]ood intent or absence of discriminatory intent does not redeem employment procedures or testing mechanisms that operate as 'built in headwinds' for minority groups and are unrelated to measuring job capability.

This concept of indirect discrimination expounded in *Griggs* found its way first into the SDA and then the RRA, despite the decision post-dating the influential *Street Report*[58] that laid much of the ground work for both Acts. The authors of the *Street Report* did not appear to have in their contemplation any concept of indirect discrimination. Indeed, as will be seen in Chapter 2, the text of the report suggests that the authors disavowed any prohibition on treatment which was not either based on race or intended to discriminate on grounds of race.[59] **1.18**

By the time the SDA was drafted,[60] *Griggs* had been decided,[61] and the statutory device of indirect discrimination was introduced into UK law. The indirect discrimination provisions have proved important. They acknowledge that disadvantage is not gender, race, or disability neutral, and that we do not all start at the same place when measuring the impact of particular rules or provisions. For instance, a requirement that all staff work full time could formally be categorized **1.19**

---

58 H Street, G Howe, and G Bindman, *Street Report on Anti-Discrimination Legislation* (1967) Political and Economic Planning (*Street Report*). The *Street Report* was commissioned by the Race Relations Board, the predecessor of the Commission for Racial Equality and is discussed further below in Chap 2.

59 Ibid, paras 28.1 and 185.3.

60 *Equality for Women* (1974) Home Office, Cmnd 5724.

61 And discovered, following a trip by Roy Jenkins to the US with his then special adviser Anthony Lester (D Pannick, *Sex Discrimination Law* (1985, OUP), 39) probably through discussions with Lou (now Judge) Pollak, then Dean of Yale Law School or via a lecture given by Lou Pollak whilst he was in London around this time (author's information), or quite probably both.

as equal treatment, and, however disadvantaged a woman with childcare responsibilities felt by such a requirement, she would have no claim in direct discrimination. However, the indirect discrimination provisions might offer some redress, acknowledging as they would that such rules are still likely to disadvantage women who remain the primary child carers in our society. Indirect discrimination, unlike direct discrimination, is capable of being 'justified', sometimes allowing dominant interests to prevail. The test of justification is discussed further in Chapter 6.

1.20 Disability-related discrimination is unique to the DDA and is a form of discrimination which outlaws less favourable treatment of a disabled person for a reason relating to the disabled person's disability.[62] It is a wide enough concept to capture incidents of direct discrimination and, in its original enactment, provided the only form of protection against direct disability discrimination. In addition, some forms of indirect discrimination are protected by this concept. For example, the dismissal of a disabled person for a long-term absence due to his or her disability would constitute disability-related discrimination and, without justification, would be unlawful.[63] As with indirect discrimination, disability-related discrimination can be justified in certain circumstances.

1.21 The concept of 'reasonable adjustments' is also found only in the DDA and is arguably the most progressive concept of discrimination in any of the main anti-discrimination enactments. The concept acknowledges diversity and requires those caught by its terms to recognize difference and take positive steps to accommodate it, thereby offering a real opportunity to tackle structural disadvantage. However, both the DDA and the concept of 'reasonable adjustments' have their limitations.[64]

1.22 As mentioned, the concept of discrimination 'reasonable adjustments' is not found in any of the other main anti-discrimination enactments, though in other jurisdictions it can be seen operating more broadly in the equality law sphere.[65] The 'reasonable adjustments' duties in the DDA derive from a concept of disability discrimination which focuses on society's obstruction of equal access to disabled people, rather than the disabled person's particular impairment. This 'social model' regards disability as a social construct and places the focus on 'how society (consciously or otherwise) compounds a person's impairment by constructing social and economic processes that fail adequately to take account of the disability

---

62 DDA, ss 3A(1), 20(1), 21D, 21G, 24(1), 28B(1), and 28S(1).

63 *Clark v TDG Ltd t/a Novacold* [1999] ICR 951; [1999] IRLR 318.

64 See, for a full discussion, Chap 6.

65 See by way of example, ss 7(e), 8(h), and 9(c) of South Africa's Promotion of Equality and Prevention of Unfair Discrimination Act 2000.

in question. In other words, the focus is . . . on how society disables by failing to provide equal opportunities for participation'.[66] There have been many campaigns by disability rights groups seeking recognition of a social model of disability and pushing a civil rights agenda for disabled people. The Union of the Physically Impaired against Segregation (UPIAS), a group of disabled people formed as long ago as 1975, regarded disability in these terms and aimed to have all segregated facilities for physically impaired people replaced by arrangements allowing disabled people to participate fully in society.[67]

As is discussed in later chapters,[68] the emphasis in the definition of 'disability' in **1.23**
the DDA upon a medical diagnosis undermines any aspiration that the DDA will successfully address disability discrimination as a social phenomenon. However, the duty to make reasonable adjustments goes some way to doing so and reflects the aspirations of those commentators who regard disability in such terms.

There is little written about the origins of victimization. It most likely derives **1.24**
from New York State law and the US 'Model Act',[69] both of which contained provision making it unlawful to retaliate or discriminate against a person because he had opposed a discriminatory practice, made a complaint, or given evidence or assisted or participated in any investigation or proceedings or hearing under the Act.[70] The *Street Report* referred to these laws and recommended that domestic anti-discrimination law should cover 'retaliating against a person who has opposed discrimination'.[71] Given the influential effect of the report[72] it is likely that it was that which led to the victimization provisions in the SDA and then the RRA and the other parts of the main anti-discrimination legislation that followed in later years.

With the exception of the DDA, none of the main anti-discrimination enact- **1.25**
ments require positive discrimination or action and only allow it in certain circumstances. There are limited exceptions. For example, the indirect discrimination provisions may require the positive accommodation of certain protected groups if

---

66 G Quinn 'Human Rights for People with Disabilities', in Alston (ed), *The EU and Human Rights* (2000, OUP), 287.

67 See 'Policy Statement' adopted 3 Dec 1974 and amended 9 Aug 1976 at <http://www.leeds.ac.uk/disability-studies/archiveuk/UPIAS/UPIAS.pdf>.

68 See Chaps 2 and 5.

69 Drafted on behalf of the National Conference of Commissioners on Uniform State Laws, with the object of harmonizing the legislation across states.

70 *Street Report*, para 42.1.

71 Ibid, Summary: at para 127.2.

72 The *Street Report* was expressly referred to in the White Paper preceding the SDA, *Equality for Women* (1974) Home Office, Cmnd 5724.

unlawful discrimination is not to occur.[73] Otherwise the only provisions which allow for any form of positive action are certain limited provisions of the SDA,[74] RRA,[75] the Employment Equality (Sexual Orientation) Regulations 2003,[76] the Employment Equality (Religion or Belief) Regulations 2003,[77] and the Employment Equality (Age) Regulations 2006,[78] which address training and—in the case of the RRA only—education and welfare.[79] These provisions allow for (but do not require) limited arrangements for providing opportunities to particular protected groups only in relation to the provision of training or encouragement to take advantage of opportunities for doing particular work where certain conditions are met. In addition, the RRA allows for the provision of services directed at meeting the 'special needs' of members of particular racial groups in relation to education, training, or welfare.[80] These provisions provide little scope for remedying under-representation and, in any event, have been under-used.[81]

1.26 The DDA operates quite differently; it protects only 'disabled' persons.[82] It requires certain steps to be taken to secure substantive equality for disabled people and is less focused on the 'formal equality' which might be afforded through the direct discrimination provisions. Indeed, in its original enactment the DDA did not protect against direct discrimination in the same way as the other main anti-discrimination enactments. As discussed, to the extent that it protected against direct discrimination it did so by outlawing less favourable treatment for a reason relating to a disabled person's disability which was both a much wider and in some respects a narrower approach to addressing incidences of less favourable treatment.[83] Whilst it would not be right to describe the DDA in its original enactment as providing for positive discrimination generally, it did require positive action to secure equality and remedy some of the more extreme forms of disadvantage experienced by disabled people. The 'reasonable adjustments' duties represent a form of mandatory 'positive action' which acknowledge that formal

73 See Chap 6.

74 SDA, ss 47–8.

75 RRA, ss 35, 37–8.

76 SI 2003/1661, Regulation 26.

77 SI 2003/1660, Regulation 25.

78 SI 2006/1031, Regulation 29.

79 RRA, s 35.

80 RRA, s 35.

81 A search on the Equal Opportunities Commission's website reveals no evidence of the provisions' use though the Commission for Racial Equality does produce guidance explaining the possibilities for innovative action using the positive action provisions. See further Chap 13.

82 As defined within the DDA (see Chap 5), outside the protection afforded by the victimisation provisions, see Chap 6 below.

83 See Chap 6.

equal treatment alone would do little to address the disadvantages faced by disabled people in a society that organizes itself around a non-disabled norm. As Lady Hale has observed:

> According to its long title, the purpose of the 1995 Act is 'to make it unlawful to discriminate against disabled persons in connection with employment, the provision of goods, facilities and services or the disposal or management of premises . . .'
>
> But this legislation is different from the Sex Discrimination Act 1975 and the Race Relations Act 1976. In the latter two, men and women or black and white, as the case may be, are opposite sides of the same coin. Each is to be treated in the same way. Treating men more favourably than women discriminates against women. Treating women more favourably than men discriminates against men. Pregnancy apart, the differences between the genders are generally regarded as irrelevant. The 1995 Act, however, does not regard the differences between disabled people and others as irrelevant. It does not expect each to be treated in the same way. It expects reasonable adjustments to be made to cater for the special needs of disabled people. It necessarily entails an element of more favourable treatment.[84]

1.27 It is not right to observe without qualification that men and women and 'black' and 'white' people are '*opposite sides of the same coin*'. This might be so in a society where men and women and black and white people are equally placed, but it is not so in the UK where patterns of disadvantage and discrimination continue. Nevertheless, only the DDA requires positive measures to be taken to remedy disadvantage caused by structural and other barriers.

1.28 What constitutes unlawful 'discrimination' in the main anti-discrimination enactments is tightly defined and focuses on addressing specific and individualized incidents of wrongdoing linked to the protected characteristics. Although the enactments are intended to tackle structural disadvantage, they were not originally directed at it.[85] The concept of 'institutional discrimination'[86] offered some promise in recognizing that entrenched disadvantage is just as likely to be caused by practices, policies, and organizational barriers as by individual acts of hostility. The Stephen Lawrence Inquiry Report defined 'institutional racism' as:

> the collective failure of an organisation to provide an appropriate and professional service to people because of their colour, culture or ethnic origin. It can be seen or detected in processes, attitudes and behaviour which amount to discrimination

84 *Archibald v Fife Council* [2004] UKHL 32, [2004] ICR 954, [2004] IRLR 651, at para 47.

85 The indirect discrimination provisions may be regarded as a limited exception to this and also, to a greater extent, the reasonable adjustment duties in the DDA.

86 See, S Carmichael and CV Hamilton, *Black Power: the Politics of Liberation in America* (1967, Penguin Books) 20–1.

> through unwitting prejudice, ignorance, thoughtlessness, and racist stereotyping which disadvantage minority ethnic people.[87]

This definition has its strengths in refocusing attention from individual wrongs to collective failures but it is not unproblematic. As Paul Gilroy observed in *There Ain't No Black in the Union Jack*:

> The learned judge's well-publicised adjustments to the concept of institutional racism acknowledged that prejudice was present but emphasized the idea that it was 'unwitting'. He identified institutional racism with collective organisational failures but provided a definition of what counted as racist that was so narrowly and tightly drawn that it excluded almost everybody and left the sources of these mysterious failures inaccessible to all but the management consultants.[88]

1.29 For the same reasons identified by Gilroy, the concept adopted by the Inquiry is also difficult to underpin with any legal force.[89] However, the Stephen Lawrence Inquiry Report did lead directly to the outlawing of race discrimination by public authorities, and its influence on the law has been significant. In particular, it has led to the introduction of statutory duties on identified public authorities to take action to promote equality. Given the context of the Inquiry, it is no surprise that the RRA was the first of the main anti-discrimination enactments to be amended to include such provision. The RRA now imposes general duties on identified public authorities when carrying out their functions to 'have due regard to the need to eliminate unlawful racial discrimination and to promote equality of opportunity and good relations between persons of different racial groups'.[90] Specific duties are imposed by regulations made under the RRA.[91] Amendments have been made to similar effect to the DDA and SDA.[92]

C. Formulating the Proper Approach to Equality Law

1.30 The main anti-discrimination enactments have, without doubt, worked to stop some of the more explicit acts of discrimination. Some black and ethnic minority

---

[87] *Report of an Inquiry by Sir William McPherson of Cluny* (1999 Cmnd 4262), paragraph 6.34, available on the Home Office website at <http://www.archive.official-documents.co.uk/document/cm42/4262/4262.htm>.

[88] Introduction to the 1992 publication of P Gilroy, *There Ain't No Black in the Union Jack* (first published 1987, Unwin Hyman) (1992, Routledge) xxiii.

[89] *Commissioners of Inland Revenue v Morgan* [2002] IRLR 776, para 38.

[90] RRA, s 71(1).

[91] Ibid, s 71(2)–(3).

[92] See DDA, ss 49A and 49D as inserted by the Disability Discrimination Act 2005 (in force in Dec 2006) and SDA, s 76A–B as inserted by the EA 2006 (in force in April 2007).

workers, women, and disabled people may still be physically and verbally abused at work, be underpaid, excluded from clubs, and suffer other social and economic disadvantage, but the extent of open hostility has reduced, and the social and political culture has shifted so that open expressions of prejudice are regarded as less acceptable. We no longer see signs proclaiming 'no blacks, no Irish and no dogs', as were prevalent in the 1950s and 1960s. The 'no travellers' signs seen regularly in some British cities in the 1990s are also much less common. We have to thank in large part the main anti-discrimination enactments for this. The Acts reflect changes in society but they have also caused a shift in mores, and this normative function has proved as important as their remedial role. That is not to say that disadvantage and prejudice do not remain (witness the fall-out from the London bombings of July 2005).[93] History shows that the anti-discrimination enactments have not succeeded in eliminating widespread discrimination and disadvantage, and this should be the real measure of their success. To a large extent this failure reflects the limits of the law as formulated and the limited objectives of government in enacting those laws. The Race Relations Board,[94] in its first annual report,[95] identified the role of legislation in tackling racial discrimination as follows:

> A law is an unequivocal declaration of public policy.
>
> A law gives support to those who do not wish to discriminate, but who feel compelled to do so by social pressure.
>
> A law gives protection and redress to minority groups.
>
> A law thus provides for the peaceful and orderly adjustment of grievances and the release of tensions.[96]

These are limited aspirations. Though the report recognized the existence of widespread disadvantage and made recommendations that the law be amended to

---

93 July 2005. See, the suggestion by Ian Johnston, Chief Constable of the British Transport Police, that his officers would be concentrating on particular racial groups, and would not 'waste time searching old white ladies' reported in The Times, 2 August 2005 <http://www.timesonline.co.uk/article/0,,2087-1724531,00.html> (a judgment apparently endorsed by the House of Lords in *Gillan v Commissioner of Police for the Metropolis and another* [2006] UKHL 12, paras 41–7, 67–8, 91–2); the proposals by Tony Blair PM, 2005 to 'strip citizenship from those individuals with British or dual nationality who act in a way that is contrary to the interests of this country'; 'consult on extending these powers, applying them to naturalised citizens engaged in extremism and making the procedures simpler and more effective' and increase the use of deportation orders even to countries known to use torture where they give 'the necessary assurances, against [the deportees] being subject to torture or ill-treatment contrary to Article 3', if necessary amending the Human Rights Act 1998. See also the Asylum etc Act 2006.

94 Established under s 2 of the Race Relations Act 1965 '[f]or the purposes of securing compliance with the provisions of . . .[the] Act and the resolution of difficulties arising out of [its] . . .provisions' and continued in existence by s 14 of the Race Relations Act 1968. See Chap 2.

95 *Report of the Race Relations Board for 1966–67* (1967) Race Relations Board, London.

96 Ibid at para 65.

provide wider coverage,[97] the aims of the law were not said to extend beyond those described above. These aims raise as many questions as they answer.

1.31 In fact the main anti-discrimination enactments, with their peculiar meanings of discrimination, do not generally address the causes of disadvantage, nor do they challenge the *advantages* associated with being a member of a protected class. Outside limited circumstances,[98] they do not require a 'levelling up' to secure any particular advantage for members of a protected class. They start from the fiction that all classes start from the same level and measure 'discrimination' against that norm. As discussed, the positive action provisions are too weak and narrow to have had any real impact, and otherwise, the provisions in the main anti-discrimination enactments protect the white, straight, non-disabled, Christian man with equal enthusiasm as they protect the disadvantaged and marginalized.

1.32 In addition, the main anti-discrimination enactments require any person seeking their protection to identify herself or himself mono-characteristically. They do nothing to protect a black, pregnant, disabled woman from disadvantage suffered as such unless she can prove that *either* her race, disability status, or sex is causally connected to the disadvantage complained of.[99] This fails to recognize that we are not mono-characteristic and does little to tackle 'intersectional' or 'multiple' discrimination.[100]

1.33 In the usual case, the main anti-discrimination enactments rely on comparisons with a white and/or straight and/or Christian and/or full-time employed, male and/or non-disabled norm representing the pinnacle to which we are all assumed to aspire.[101] They have only limited redistributive aims. The main anti-discrimination enactments will not ask an employer to explain why it is paying its workforce less than the minimum wage, but will rather look at whether it is paying all the same equally low wage. Similarly, it will not address the quality or cost of accommodation a landlord rents to the poor, but only whether he or she is willing to rent accommodation on equal terms to all.[102] This is so even where women or black

---

[97] Ibid at para 66.

[98] Sometimes to grant the non-disadvantaged the same rights as the disadvantaged who may acquire rights through the indirect discrimination provisions, as where, eg, a woman obtains the right to part-time work through the application of the indirect discrimination provisions which may then have to be afforded a male worker in the same work, at risk otherwise of falling foul of the direct discrimination provisions. See Chap 6.

[99] See, eg, the experience of black women and pregnancy at work: *Pregnancy General Formal Investigation, BME Consultation in Wales* (2004). EOC: <http://www.eoc.org.uk/EOCeng/EOCcs/AboutEOC/bme%20group%20report.pdf>.

[100] See Chap 5 for further discussion.

[101] The comparator problem is dealt with at Chap 5.

[102] Nor does it prohibit 'mere' 'unreasonable' treatment: *Zafar v Glasgow County Council* [1998] ICR 120, [1997] 1 WLR 1659, [1998] IRLR 36.

and ethnic minority people are concentrated amongst these groups of workers and tenants.[103] It should come as no surprise then that disadvantage, linked to membership of a particular class or the possession of certain characteristics, remains very much a feature of life in the UK.[104]

The object of the anti-discrimination legislation has been identified. As mentioned above, the Race Relations Board gave a summary of the role of law in tackling race discrimination, and those modest objectives are regarded as essentially of similar significance in other fields.[105] The focus is on addressing incidence of prejudice which, whilst a cause of disadvantage, is not the only cause. Nor is the elimination of it by itself necessary or enough to remove disadvantage. This appears to be recognized by the White Paper that preceded the SDA which stated:[106] **1.34**

> It is important to recognise the inevitable restraints on what can be achieved by legislation, so that it is seen in proper perspective, without arousing false expectations or encouraging a sense of complacency. An anti-discrimination law is relevant only to the extent that economic and social conditions enable people to develop their individual potential and to compete for opportunities on more or less equal terms. A woman will obtain little benefit from equal employment opportunity if she is denied adequate education from training because economic necessity or social pressures have induced her to enter the labour market at an early age. Some mothers will derive as little benefit if there is inadequate provision for part-time work or flexible working hours, or for day nurseries . . . Legislation is a necessary precondition for an effective equal opportunities policy but it is not a sufficient condition.[107]

Much can be learnt from other jurisdictions in formulating any new equality laws. South Africa and Canada both treat the elimination of 'disadvantage' and the protection of 'dignity' as key measures in addressing unfair discrimination.[108] This approach recognizes the structural nature of disadvantage associated with membership of a particular class, and the relationship between disadvantage and human dignity. It also respects human rights and civil rights—deferring as appropriate to collective and individual interests. The stated objects of South Africa's Promotion of Equality and Prevention of Unfair Discrimination Act 2000 are inspirational in this respect: **1.35**

> This Act endeavours to facilitate the transition to a democratic society, united in its diversity, marked by human relations that are caring and compassionate, and guided

103 See below.

104 See the findings in, *The Equalities Review: Interim Report for Consultation* (2006) *The Equalities Review.*

105 See, eg, *Equality for Women* (1974) Home Office, Cmnd 5724 (the White Paper that preceded the SDA 1975).

106 Ibid.

107 Ibid, para 21.

108 See, eg, South Africa's Promotion of Equality and Prevention of Unfair Discrimination Act 2000 and see *Law v Canada (Minister of Employment and Immigration)* [1999] 1 SCR.

by the principles of equality, fairness, equity, social progress, justice, human dignity and freedom . . . [109]

The objects of this Act are—

(a) . . .

(b) to give effect to the letter and spirit of the Constitution, in particular—
  (i) the equal enjoyment of all rights and freedoms by every person;
  (ii) the promotion of equality;
  (iii) the values of non-racialism and non-sexism contained in section 1 of the Constitution;
  (iv) the prevention of unfair discrimination and protection of human dignity as contemplated in sections 9 and 10 of the Constitution;
  (v) the prohibition of advocacy of hatred, based on race, ethnicity, gender or religion, that constitutes incitement to cause harm as contemplated in section 16(2)(c) of the Constitution and section 12 of this Act;

(c) to provide for measures to facilitate the eradication of unfair discrimination, hate speech and harassment, particularly on the grounds of race, gender and disability;

(d) to provide for procedures for the determination of circumstances under which discrimination is unfair;

(e) to provide for measures to educate the public and raise public awareness on the importance of promoting equality and overcoming unfair discrimination, hate speech and harassment;

(f) to provide remedies for victims of unfair discrimination, hate speech and harassment and persons whose right to equality has been infringed;

(g) to set out measures to advance persons disadvantaged by unfair discrimination;

(h) to facilitate further compliance with international law obligations including treaty obligations in terms of, amongst others, the Convention on the Elimination of All Forms of Racial Discrimination and the Convention on the Elimination of All Forms of Discrimination against Women.[110]

1.36 The *unfairness* of any discrimination is determined by reference to a number of criteria, including the extent to which any discrimination 'is likely to impair human dignity' and 'the position of the complainant in society and whether he or she suffers from patterns of disadvantage or belongs to a group that suffers from such patterns of disadvantage'.[111]

1.37 The Act's focus is on outcomes (eg the promotion of equality; to set out measures to advance persons disadvantaged by unfair discrimination), and the remedial scheme it adopts reflects this. There are wide-ranging duties imposed on public and private actors,[112] and wide powers are given to the courts to remedy existing

109 Preamble.

110 Section 2.

111 Section 14(3). A 'dignity' model is considered further in Chap 6.

112 Chapter V of the Promotion of Equality and Prevention of Unfair Discrimination Act 2000.

discriminatory practices and to require that special measures are taken to address inequality.

As will be seen in later chapters,[113] the remedies provided for under our main anti-discrimination enactments are individually focused and do little to address collective disadvantage, reflecting as they do the individualized nature of the unlawful acts provided for under each of the enactments. 1.38

D. Statistics and Disadvantage

Statistical data continues to demonstrate that there remains widespread disadvantage amongst those classes protected by the anti-discrimination enactments. 1.39

Gender remains a significant cause of disadvantage and, in general terms, being a woman carries with it a ticket to low pay, unskilled work, and prejudicial stereotyping. There is still a significant gap between male and female hourly earnings—women working full time earned only 83 per cent of the average full-time earnings of men in 2005, and the gap between the hourly earnings of women working part time and men working full time is even wider.[114] Further, 30,000 of the 45 per cent of working women who become pregnant each year will lose their employment due to pregnancy discrimination.[115] There is also significant job segregation, which is replicated in the take-up of further education so that, for example, 90 per cent of learners in construction and engineering, technology, and manufacturing are men, whilst 91 per cent in hairdressing and beauty therapy are women.[116] The most female-dominated subjects in higher education are subjects allied to medicine such as nursing, physiotherapy, and other health sciences, in which 81 per cent of students are female.[117] 1.40

113 See Chap 14 in particular.

114 *Shaping a Fairer Future* (Feb 2006) Women and Work Commission, 1–2, available at http://www.womenandequalityunit.gov.uk/women_work_commission/, which recorded the data in 2005 as showing, in relation to full time work, a 13% pay gap measured using *median* hourly pay rates and 17% measured using *mean* hourly pay rates and in relation to the difference between full time male earnings and part time female earnings, a 41% pay gap using *median* hourly pay rates and a 38% pay gap using *mean* hourly rates. And see reasons for the same: Working Paper Series No.17: W Olsen and S Walby, *Modelling Gender Pay Gaps* available at <http://www.eoc.org.uk/cseng/research/modelling%20gender%20pay%20gaps%20wp%2017.pdf>.

115 *Greater Expectations, Final Report of the EOC's Investigation into Discrimination Against New and Expectant Mothers in the Workplace* (June 2005, Equal Opportunities Commission) VII.

116 *Facts About Women and Men in Great Britain* (2005, Equal Opportunities Commission), 6.

117 Ibid 7. It may be noted that the Equal Opportunities Commission does not publish similar research on women outside of the labour market, eg women in prison and, save in respect of those in the labour market disabled women, asylum seekers, and other women unable by law to work. This raises questions about the focus of the gender equality agenda itself and to whom it is assumed to apply.

1.41 Current statistics indicate that one woman in four will experience domestic violence at some point in their lives. Two women each week are killed by violent partners. A 1991 survey indicated that a quarter of women had experienced rape or attempted rape and that the most common perpetrator was a current or former partner. Only 12 per cent of victims who contact the Rape Crisis Federation make any complaint at all. Of the small number of reported rapes, only 5.8 per cent result in conviction.[118] Women in prison are put at particular risk of self-harm and suicide.[119]

1.42 As to ethnic minority communities, care has to be taken about generalizations because the experience of disadvantage varies between black and ethnic minority communities.[120] However, research demonstrates that across a broad range of measures, black and ethnic minority people suffer a greater degree of disadvantage than non-minority groups. Research indicates that:

- on average, employment rates amongst almost all ethnic minorities are lower than those of the white population;
- ethnic minorities are disadvantaged in the labour market on a broad range of measures of achievement, including earning levels, progression/occupational attainment in the workplace, and levels of self-employment; and
- the extent and nature of this disadvantage differs significantly by ethnic group.[121]

1.43 The most recent results of the National Census[122] indicate that people from ethnic minorities are disproportionately represented among the unemployed, low-waged, and socially excluded. The Trades Union Congress (TUC) has recently published research confirming that, whilst some real progress has been made over the past 10 years in combating race discrimination at work, racism persists, often in a disguised form. Thus, in-depth interviews revealed more subtle forms of racism, including being passed over for promotion, putting up with racist language, and management only paying lip service to equal opportunities policies.[123] Certain ethnic minority communities are becoming increasingly segregated from the majority of the community, so that 'ghettos' now exist, in which more than two-thirds of the residents belong to a single ethnic group. This residential isolation is increasing for many minority groups, especially South Asians. The number

---

118 *Interim Report on Victims and Witnesses, Commission on Women and the Criminal Justice System* (2003, Fawcett Society).

119 *Commission on Women and the Criminal Justice System, One Year On* (2005, Fawcett Society), 1, 16.

120 *The Equalities Review: Interim Report for Consultation* (2006) *The Equalities Review*.

121 *Ethnic Minorities and the Labour Market, Final Report* (March 2003) Cabinet Office Strategy Unit.

122 The census is undertaken every 10 years. The results of the most recent census, conducted in 2001, became available in Feb 2003. It is the most reliable as well as the main source of information on the social make up of the UK. This census was more detailed than the 1991 census. It is available at <http://www.statistics.gov.uk>.

123 *Black Voices at Work* (2003) TUC, reported in the *Equal Opportunities Review* No 117, 3.

of people of Pakistani heritage living in what are described as 'ghetto' communities trebled between 1991 and 2001. In Leicester 13 per cent of people with Pakistani heritage live in such communities (this figure was 10.8 per cent in 1991), as do 13.3 per cent living in Bradford (this figure was 4.3 per cent in 1991).[124] In 2002, nearly one in four of the 71,000 prisoners in England and Wales was from an ethnic minority,[125] compared with one in 11 of the whole population, and that differential is increasing. Thus, between 1999 and 2002 the total prison population grew by just over 12 per cent, but the number of black prisoners increased by over 51.4 per cent. It is a shocking fact that more young black men enter prison each year than enter university.[126] In the words of Trevor Phillips, Chair of the Commission for Racial Equality:

> Imprisonment is becoming a defining experience for some ethnic minority groups. The possession of a degree and three years of campus life has offered new opportunities and fresh horizons to an increasingly large proportion of the British people. For my community, however, incarceration is now shaping our collective experience . . . It's a scandal that no reasonable nation should tolerate . . .[127]

There is now widespread recognition of the disadvantages faced by disabled people. However, significant prejudice and misunderstanding still exist about the nature of 'disability' and its impact on the potential of disabled people to engage fully in society. It is now understood that 'disadvantage' arising out of disability is largely the result of civil society constructing its arrangements for engagement on the basis of a 'non-disabled' norm. Thus, there are physical barriers to buildings, making access for disabled people difficult or impossible; communication modes are adopted which are inaccessible to certain parts of the community; and there are attitudinal barriers which obstruct the proper and fair engagement of disabled people in social life. Individual assumptions too can become part of organizations' **1.44**

124 *After 7/7: Sleepwalking to Segregation* (2005), speech by Trevor Phillips, Chair of the Commission for Racial Equality, made on 22/9/2005, available at <http://www.cre.gov.uk/Default.aspx.LocID-0hgnew07s.RefLocID-0hg00900c002.Lang-EN.htm#hard>.

125 According to the *Equalities Review*, of UK nationals in prison in 2005, one in five males belonged to an ethnic minority (10% Black, 5% Asian, and 3% Mixed), as did about one in eight female prisoners (8% Black, 1% Asian, and 4% Mixed). Of the foreign nationals in prison, nearly three in four were non-white: *The Equalities Review: Interim Report for Consultation* (2006) The Equalities Review, 25.

126 In 2002 there were more African Caribbean entrants to prisons in England and Wales (over 11,500) than there were to UK universities (around 8,000). For every African Caribbean male on campus, there were two Black Britons in jail. And even taking all ethnic minority communities into account, a non-white Briton was about three times more likely to enter jail rather than higher education than a white Briton: Trevor Phillips, *Waking from the Dream* (2004) 17th Annual Martin Luther King Memorial Lecture, 17 Jan 2004, available at <http://www.cre.gov.uk/Default.aspx.LocID-0hgnew042.RefLocID-0hg00900c002.htm>.

127 Ibid.

policies and practices, and result in institutional discrimination.[128] The impact of these barriers is evident in statistical evidence which indicates that disabled people are twice as likely as non-disabled people to be unemployed or have no formal qualifications.[129] Disabled people are also disproportionately concentrated in low paid and vulnerable atypical work. For example, 15 per cent of home workers are disabled, even though disabled people make up 12.7 per cent of the employed population.[130] The barriers to employment faced by disabled people are compounded when they have additional responsibilities as parents. Disabled parents are significantly more likely to be unemployed than non-disabled parents, and less than one-third of disabled lone parents are in work.[131] Research also demonstrates that around 42 per cent of disabled people still have problems accessing goods and services.[132]

1.45 All three groups are under-represented in civil and political life, with a disproportionately low number of women Members of Parliament (19.8 per cent),[133] and very few black and ethnic minority or visibly disabled Members of Parliament. Only 8.44 per cent of judges at High Court level or above are women.[134] Only 15 MPs elected to Parliament in May 2005 are from ethnic minorities—and this is a record.[135] There is only one black High Court judge, and there are no black or ethnic minority judges in more senior posts.[136] Only 3.5 per cent of councillors in office after the May 2004 elections were from an ethnic minority background.[137]

1.46 Gay men and lesbians have experienced the disadvantages associated with not being permitted to marry. Though many of these disadvantages are mitigated by the impact of the Civil Partnership Act 2004, they continue to suffer prejudice.[138]

---

128 *From Exclusion to Inclusion, Final Report of the Disability Rights Task Force* (1999) Final Report of the Disability Rights Task Force.

129 Ibid, para 8.

130 Disability Rights Commission submission to the Department for Trade and Industry's review of the Employment Relations Act 1999, s 23, cited in *Achieving Equality at Work* (2003, IER), 69.

131 J Ballard, *Disabled Parents and Employment* (2004, EOR), 126, 20.

132 Government's final response to Task Force recommendations, March 2001, para 1.2. See too The Analytical Report *Improving the Life Chances of Disabled People* published by the Prime Minister's Strategy Unit: <http://www.strategy.gov.uk/output/Page5046.asp>.

133 *Women's Representation in British Politics* (2005) Fawcett Society, available at <http://www.fawcettsociety.org.uk/index.asp?Pageid=95>.

134 At 1 October 2005, Department for Constitutional Affairs at <http://www.dca.gov.uk/judicial/womjudfr.htm>.

135 <http://www.cre.gov.uk/media/publicaffairs/index.html>.

136 The one black judge is Ms Justice Linda Dobbs.

137 Notwithstanding that 8.4% of the adult population is from an ethnic minority: *National Census of Local Authority Councillors in England 2004* Employers Organisation for Local Government (2004), 6.

138 According to the *Equalities Review*, lesbian and gay adults reported that over four in five (82%) had been subject to name-calling at school, while well over half (60%) reported being hit or kicked; over half (53%) had contemplated self-harm as a result of the bullying, and two in five

Homophobic bullying is still widespread in schools and was institutionalized by section 28 of the Local Government Act 1988, until its repeal in 2000 in Scotland and 2003 in England and Wales.[139]

Religious discrimination is different to the forms of discrimination already discussed because the extent of disadvantage varies considerably as between faith groups and generalizations are difficult. For example, the experience of being Muslim in Great Britain is quite different to the experience of being Christian. We still have an established church and, in doing so, institutionalize social and political advantage for its members. On the other hand, religious minorities report widespread discrimination in education, employment, and the media.[140] Religion is also, on occasion, used as a proxy for race, so that discrimination characterized or manifesting as religious discrimination sometimes has racism underpinning it. **1.47**

Many of the disadvantages associated with gender reassignment have arisen because of a failure to recognize a person's changed sex.[141] The Gender Recognition Act 2004 attempts to ameliorate that situation.[142] However, protection against discrimination based on prejudice, stereotyping, and general antipathy towards transpeople remains largely unregulated by our anti-discrimination scheme,[143] and there is evidence of widespread discrimination which will not be addressed by recognizing a change in gender alone.[144] **1.48**

(40%) had attempted suicide on at least one occasion; and a Stonewall survey of secondary school teachers found that four in five (82%) of them were aware of incidents of verbal homophobic bullying, one in four (26%) knew of physical homophobic bullying: *The Equalities Review: Interim Report for Consultation* (2006) The Equalities Review, 26.

139 Local Government Act 1988, s 28 inserted s 2A into the Local Government Act 1986 and read that 'a local authority shall not—(a) intentionally promote homosexuality or publish material with the intention of promoting homosexuality; (b) promote the teaching in any maintained school of the acceptability of homosexuality as a pretended family relationship.'

140 *Religious Discrimination in England and Wales* Home Office Research Study 220, available at <http://www.homeoffice.gov.uk/rds/pdfs/hors220.pdf>. See too, *The Equalities Review: Interim Report for Consultation* (2006) The Equalities Review.

141 *Bellinger v Bellinger* [2003] 2 AC 467; *KB v National Health Service Pensions Agency and Another* (Case C-117/01) [2004] ICR 781, [2004] IRLR 240; *Chief Constable of the West Yorkshire Police v A and Another (No.2)* [2004] UKHL 21, [2005] 1 AC 51.

142 See Chap 2.

143 The SDA, which is the only enactment which addresses in terms discrimination based on gender reassignment, covers only discrimination in the employment and related fields (Part II SDA), though this may change with the enactment now of an EC Directive addressing sex discrimination outside the employment fields (Council Directive 2004/113/EC), see Chap 4, and the fact that in EC law discrimination on the grounds of gender reassignment is treated as discrimination on the grounds of sex, see Chap 4.

144 See, *The A to Z of Transpeople's Discrimination* Press for Change at <http://www.pfc.org.uk/campaign/a-z.htm>.

1.49 Age discrimination must necessarily be regarded as a different form of discrimination. Unlike the other protected grounds, age is something experienced by all of us. We will all be young and, if we are fortunate enough, will all be old. Indeed, age discrimination is the most commonly experienced form of discrimination, with 29 per cent of adults reporting experiences of age discrimination.[145] There is well-understood discrimination and prejudice towards, and stereotyping of, different age groups which disadvantage members of those groups. As has been observed:

> Images of older people as dependant, burdensome and of no further use to society provided support for detrimental practices, such as early retirement and redundancy, rationing of health care, poorer quality social services, and social exclusion. Similarly, detrimental treatment of young people is frequently justified as being in their 'best interests'. Lawful parental chastisement, exclusion from the minimum wage and lack of participation in decision-making on issues closely affecting their lives are just a few examples.[146]

1.50 The highest unemployment rates are in younger age groups. At the other end of the age spectrum, more than one in five pensioners lives in relative poverty. As with other disadvantaged groups, disadvantage is not experienced in the same way amongst all older and younger people. Social class, amongst other things, is a key determinant so that, for example, the health of a 65-year-old from a routine or manual occupational background is estimated to be equivalent to the health of a 75-year-old from a professional background.[147]

1.51 Age discrimination raises particular challenges for the legislature and these are addressed later in the book.[148]

E. Conclusions

1.52 This Government has a manifesto commitment to a Single Equality Act. With this in mind, in early 2005 it established a 'Discrimination Law Review'[149] to:

> assess how our anti-discrimination legislation can be modernised to fit the needs of Britain in the 21st Century. This work will consider the approaches that are effective in eradicating remaining discrimination but avoid imposing unnecessary, bureaucratic burdens on business and public services.[150]

---

145 *The Equalities Review: Interim Report for Consultation* (2006) The Equalities Review, 25.

146 S Fredman, 'The Age of Equality' in, Fredman and Spencer (ed), *Age as an Equality Issue, Legal and Policy Perspectives* (2003, Hart) 21, 22.

147 *The Equalities Review: Interim Report for Consultation* (2006) The Equalities Review, 25.

148 See Chaps 2 and 6.

149 See Joint DTI and Cabinet Office Release at <http://www.gnn.gov.uk/environment/detail.asp?ReleaseID=148053&NewsAreaID=2&NavigatedFromDepartment=False>.

150 Ibid.

To run parallel to this review, an 'Equalities Review' was established (chaired by Trevor Phillips, Chair of the Commission for Racial Equality) to undertake 'a root and branch review to investigate the causes of persistent discrimination and inequality in British society'.[151] This offers the possibility of real progressive change. However, the emphasis on avoiding 'unnecessary, bureaucratic burdens on business and public services' sets a worrying tone. Recommendations for change have come and gone before, and have sometimes been scuppered by an over-anxious Government concerned about its relations with the business community and the wider electorate.[152]

Much can be learnt from previous reviews (including the recognition of a reluctance in Government to take firm measures to address discrimination in the private sector). In April 1998, the Commission for Racial Equality presented its proposals for change to the Home Secretary, in a paper entitled 'Reform of the Race Relations Act 1976: Proposals for Change'. These proposals included a positive right to be free from discrimination in the areas protected by the RRA. Whilst receiving these submissions, the Government's 'Better Regulation Task Force'[153] undertook a review of the anti-discrimination legislation. That review was published in May 1999 and the task force concluded that it was 'not persuaded of the need for major legislative overhaul at this stage'.[154] The only significant recommendation made in relation to increasing the scope of the RRA was that 'legislation may be needed to . . . simplify and clarify complex areas; and with regard to the public sector (*sic*)'. The task force supported the recommendation, 'in the Macpherson report, that the Race Relations Act should be extended to fully cover the public sector'.[155] It also excluded the possibility of further legislation in the private sector by concluding that 'our analysis clearly suggests that imposing additional statutory burdens on business would be counter-productive at this stage'.[156] As a result of these findings, the Race Relations (Amendment) Act 2000[157] was enacted imposing statutory duties on listed public authorities. The private sector, however, consistent with the demands of the business lobby, remained untouched by any positive duties to secure change. **1.53**

151 Ibid.

152 See Chap 2.

153 Appointed in Sept 1997 to advise Government on improving the quality of government regulations, the working group who produced the review of anti-discrimination legislation was identified in their report as chaired by Ram Gidoomal, of Winning Communications, and included Sue Slipman of Camelot Plc and Hugh Field of BCB International. See <http://www.brc.gov.uk/downloads/pdf/antidisc.pdf>.

154 Ibid, 19.

155 Ibid, 19.

156 Ibid, 23.

157 See Chap 15.

1.54 The statutory duties to make adjustments found in the DDA and the 'fourth generation'[158] statutory duties on public authorities[159] represent a move towards a 'social model' of discrimination which recognizes that we socially construct barriers which disadvantage certain groups, and intervention in the form of positive action is required if real equality is to be achieved.[160] As has been seen, there is still widespread disadvantage amongst certain communities. Tackling that is a political and human rights issue. Awaiting the goodwill of the more advantaged, or the identification of a 'business case'[161] for promoting equality, has not to date proved adequate, and further legislation is now required.

158 S Fredman, *Discrimination Law* (2002, OUP), 176.

159 See Chap 15.

160 For a further discussion, see Chap 15.

161 See, eg, *Equality at Work? Workplace Equality Policies, Flexible Working Arrangements and the Quality of Work* (2005) Equality Authority in Ireland, which sets out quantitative data in support of the business case for the first time in an Irish context (the study finds that where there is a formal equality policy, it impacts positively on employees' perceptions of fairness at the workplace), available at: http://www.equality.ie/index.asp?locID=105&docID=269. And see, for example, *Equal Pay Briefing. The Business Case*, the Equality Commission for Northern Ireland, available at <http://www.equalityni.org/uploads/pdf/TheBusinessCase.pdf>. And see, for example, *The Business Case for Diversity* (2005) Home Office, which sets out race and diversity as a business imperative, and outlines the importance of a diverse police service that is able to engage more effectively with communities.

2

THE HISTORY AND CONTEXT OF PROTECTION AGAINST DISCRIMINATION IN UK LAW

A. Introduction

The absence of a comprehensive written constitution in the UK has deprived those within its jurisdiction of a fully formed constitutional equality guarantee.[1] As mentioned in Chapter 1, constitutional law through the principle of legality operates to guard against the more repugnant instances of arbitrary treatment 2.01

[1] Magna Carta and the Bill of Rights provide very little so far as any equality commitment is concerned. In the first place, the arrangement with the King (King John, in 1215, from whom various guarantees were extracted by the property-owning classes and entrenched in Magna Carta) embraced and entrenched class distinctions, anti-Semitism, and misogyny ('Heirs may be given in marriage, but not to someone of lower social standing. Before a marriage takes place, it shall be made known to the heir's next-of-kin; if a man dies owing money to Jews, his wife may have her dower and pay nothing towards the debt from it; if anyone who has borrowed a sum of money from Jews dies before the debt has been repaid, his heir shall pay no interest on the debt for so long as he remains under age, irrespective of whom he holds his lands; no one shall be taken or imprisoned on account of the appeal of a woman concerning the death of another than her husband'). In the second place, the Bill of Rights, 'An Act Declaring the Rights and Liberties of the

and makes all equally subject to law. It also provides for some limited scrutiny of the acts of public authorities in particular so as to ensure that 'rationality' is measured by, amongst other things, a requirement for 'equal treatment'.[2] However, these guarantees focus on process rather than substance. The traditional public law obligations manifested in these duties are not principally concerned with the substantive content of law but rather guard against its wrongful application.[3]

2.02 This might be contrasted with the position in those jurisdictions that have more developed constitutional equality guarantees where there is at least the opportunity to tackle structural and legislative inequalities by reliance on constitutional settlements. Such settlements allow for challenges to law and other State measures but also, at least in theory, provide a rich context for interpreting law and social policy and for their formation. Constitutional equality guarantees are usually multi-faceted, including guarantees of 'equality before the law' and 'equal protection and benefit of the law'[4] (see South Africa,[5] Canada,[6] and, differently expressed, the US[7]). They are capable of functioning so as to afford equality under the law not merely in a formalistic sense but in a substantive sense. This means that they operate so as to allow for the scrutiny of any measure for its

---

Subject and Settling the Succession of the Crown' (importantly entrenching what we now describe as the principle of parliamentary sovereignty) institutionalized anti-Catholicism ('And whereas it hath been found by experience that it is inconsistent with the safety and welfare of this Protestant kingdom to be governed by a popish prince, or by any king or queen marrying a papist, the said Lords Spiritual and Temporal and Commons do further pray that it may be enacted, that all and every person and persons that is, are or shall be reconciled to or shall hold communion with the see or Church of Rome, or shall profess the popish religion, or shall marry a papist, shall be excluded and be for ever incapable to inherit, possess or enjoy the crown and government of this realm and Ireland and the dominions thereunto belonging or any part of the same, or to have, use or exercise any regal power, authority or jurisdiction within the same; and in all and every such case or cases the people of these realms shall be and are hereby absolved of their allegiance').

2 *Kruse v Johnson* [1998] 2 QB 91; per Lord Hoffmann; *Matadeen v Pointu* [1999] 1 AC 98, 109. See too J Jowell, 'Is Equality a Constitutional Principle?' [1994] 7 CLP 1. For a discussion, see PG Polyviou, *The Equal Protection of the Laws* (1980, Duckworth), 1–24. Also the common law regulated the obligations of Innkeepers and common carriers and rendered void certain discriminatory conditions on testamentary dispositions (A Lester and G Bindman, *Race and Law* (1972, Penguin), 63–69) but these are of little contemporary relevance.

3 J Jowell, in 'Is Equality a Constitutional Principle?' [1994] 7 CLP 1, 13 points to some limited and exceptional case law indicating that a substantive equality scrutiny has taken place in some older cases.

4 For example, s 15 of the Canadian Charter of Rights and Freedoms (Part 1 of the Constitution Act 1982); art 9 of the South African Constitution; and, differently expressed, the Fourteenth Amendment to the US Constitution.

5 South African Constitution, art 9.

6 Canadian Charter of Rights and Freedoms, s 15.

7 US Constitution, Fourteenth Amendment.

(discriminatory) impact, its breadth (over-inclusiveness and under-inclusiveness), and its substantive content:

> In other words, the equal protection of the laws is invariably treated as a substantive constitutional principle which demands that laws will only be legitimate if they can be described as just and equal.[8]

Such an approach makes equality norms fundamental, providing important protections and, whilst formally binding only State organs, can affect private persons.[9] Much depends on the judges' willingness to interpret law progressively, but Canada and South Africa, in particular, have progressively developed a modern and substantive concept of equality under their constitutional equality provisions, discussed further in Chapter 6. **2.03**

Presently, the UK's constitutional arrangements, and the concept of Parliamentary sovereignty in particular, leave little room for 'supreme' or constitutionally entrenched equality provisions. European Union (EU) law, exceptionally, confers some constitutional-level equality guarantees and this is discussed further in Chapter 4. In addition, an equality guarantee with 'quasi-constitutional' status may be available by extending the protection of the Human Rights Act 1998 by ratifying Protocol No 12 to the European Convention on Human Rights (ECHR), which again is discussed further in Chapter 4; but this has not happened yet and every indication is that it will not.[10] Instead, in the UK legislative reform has progressively led to the repeal of sexually and racially discriminatory measures and, more recently, hetero-normative laws stigmatizing gay men and lesbians[11] and the enactment of ground-specific (race, sex, etc) legislation. **2.04**

In the absence of a written constitutional equality guarantee, a principle of equality has developed at common law, though this is still no more than at embryonic stage and its life is very much in danger. Professor Jeffrey Jowell has argued that equality is a 'constitutional principle'[12] such that: **2.05**

> Just like free speech it is a principle that derives from democracy itself. Basic to democracy is the requirement that every citizen has an equal vote, and therefore an

8 See PG Polyviou, *The Equal Protection of the Laws* (1980, Duckworth) 4.

9 In particular, they can have 'horizontal' effect when addressing legislation affecting private persons; see, for example, *Romer v Evans* 517 US 620 (1996), available at: <http://laws.findlaw.com/us/000/u10179.htm> (in which the court struck down a Colorado constitutional amendment which sought to deny homosexuals minority status, quota preferences, protected status, or a claim of discrimination: '[T]hat laws of the kind now before us raise the inevitable inference that the disadvantage imposed is born of animosity toward the class of persons affected. [I]f the constitutional conception of "equal protection of the laws" means anything, it must at the very least mean that a bare . . . desire to harm a politically unpopular group cannot constitute a legitimate governmental interest.' *Department of Agriculture v Moreno*, 413 US 528, 534 (1973).

10 See further Chap 4.

11 See some referred to in Chap 1.

12 J Jowell, n 2 above, citing, amongst other things, *Kruse v Johnson* [1998] 2 QB 91.

equal opportunity to influence the composition of the government. The notion of equal worth is thus a fundamental precept of our constitution. It gains its ultimate justification from a notion of the way individuals should be treated in a democracy. It is constitutive of democracy . . . [13]

Our constitution rests upon an assumption that government should not impose upon any citizen any burden that depends upon an argument that ultimately forces the citizen to relinquish her or his sense of equal worth. This principle is deeply embedded in our law, although it is rarely made explicit.[14]

2.06 Some support for such a contention can be found in recent case law. In *Ghaidan v Godin-Mendoza*[15] Baroness Hale observed that:

Democracy is founded on the principle that each individual has equal value. Treating some as automatically having less value than others not only causes pain and distress to that person but also violates his or her dignity as a human being. The essence of the Convention, as has often been said, is respect for human dignity and human freedom: see *Pretty v United Kingdom* (2002) 35 EHRR 1, 37, para 65. Second, such treatment is damaging to society as a whole. Wrongly to assume that some people have talents and others do not is a huge waste of human resources. It also damages social cohesion, creating not only an under class, but an under class with a rational grievance. Third, it is the reverse of the rational behaviour we now expect of Government and the State. Power must not be exercised arbitrarily. If distinctions are to be drawn, particularly upon a group basis, it is an important discipline to look for a rational basis for those distinctions. Finally, it is a purpose of all human rights instruments to secure the protection of the essential rights of members of minority groups, even when they are unpopular with the majority. Democracy values everyone equally even if the majority does not.[16]

2.07 Such an approach reflects the express rationale for equality measures in other jurisdictions including South Africa.[17] It also reflects the earlier US constitutional case law that provided the juridical basis for modern equal protection jurisprudence in the US under the Fourteenth Amendment.[18]

---

13 J Jowell, n 2 above, 7.

14 Ibid, 18.

15 [2004] UKHL 30, [2004] 2 AC 557, 605, para 132.

16 See too, *Matadeen v Pointu & O'rs* [1999] 1 AC 98 *per* Lord Hoffman (giving judgment for all their Lordships on the committee) at 109.

17 See, for example, the Promotion of Equality and Prevention of Unfair Discrimination Act 2000, preamble.

18 'All persons born or naturalized in the United States, and subject to the jurisdiction thereof, are citizens of the United States and of the State wherein they reside. No State shall make or enforce any law which shall abridge the privileges or immunities of citizens of the United States; nor shall any State deprive any person of life, liberty, or property, without due process of law; nor deny to any person within its jurisdiction the equal protection of the laws.' See, *United States v Carolene Products Co.* (1938) 304 US 144, available at: <http://laws.findlaw.com/us/304/144.html> providing 'the most celebrated footnote in constitutional law'(LF Powell Jr, 'Carolene Products Revisited' [1982] 82 Colum L Rev 1087, 1087), as follows: 'There may be narrower scope for operation of the presumption of constitutionality when legislation appears on its face to be within a specific prohibition of the

Perhaps the high point, in so far as discerning any constitutional-level equality guarantee in the UK is concerned, is found in the important case of *A v Secretary of State for the Home Department*.[19] In *A* the House of Lords were required to consider the lawfulness of measures which allowed for the indefinite detention of terrorist suspects who were not nationals of the UK. The House of Lords declared the relevant measures incompatible with Articles 5 and 14 of the ECHR and quashed the derogation order[20] made by the Government under the Human Rights Act 1998, which purported to derogate from the UK's obligations under Article 5 of the ECHR. In considering the measures in issue and their lawfulness, Lord Bingham apparently approvingly referred to commentary asserting the right to equality as 'a fundamental right'.[21] However, the House of Lords have not proved consistent in their approach to inequality and discrimination. In particular, in cases where the equality issues do not touch so closely on 'the instincts and traditions'[22] of the people of the UK the results have been less equality-sensitive. In *Secretary of State for Work and Pensions v M*,[23] the House of Lords relied upon the historical existence of hostility towards gay men and lesbians and institutionalized discrimination against them as reasons in themselves for not holding certain existing sexual orientation discrimination in child support law unlawful.[24] **2.08**

'Equality' itself, therefore, is not regarded as so embedded in our social and political norms as to yet require the law's unwavering support,[25] and this no doubt **2.09**

Constitution, such as those of the first ten Amendments, which are deemed equally specific when held to be embraced within the Fourteenth . . . It is unnecessary to consider now whether legislation which restricts those political processes which can ordinarily be expected to bring about repeal of undesirable legislation, is to be subjected to more exacting judicial scrutiny under the general prohibitions of the Fourteenth Amendment than are most other types of legislation . . . . . . Nor need we enquire whether similar considerations enter into the review of statutes directed at particular religious . . . or racial minorities . . . whether prejudice against discrete and insular minorities may be a special condition, which tends seriously to curtail the operation of those political processes ordinarily to be relied upon to protect minorities, and which may call for a correspondingly more searching judicial inquiry . . .' *per* Justice Stone.

19 [2005] 2 AC 68. The context was the Government's conclusion that there was a public emergency threatening the life of the nation within the meaning of Art 15 of the ECHR and its making of the Human Rights Act 1998 (Designated Derogation) Order 2001 designating the UK's proposed derogation, under Art 15, from the right to personal liberty guaranteed by Art 5(1) of the ECHR, scheduled to the Human Rights Act 1998. Section 23 of the Anti-terrorism, Crime and Security Act 2001 then provided for the detention of non-nationals if the Home Secretary believed that their presence in the UK was a risk to national security and he suspected that they were terrorists who, for the time being, could not be deported because of fears for their safety or other practical considerations.

20 Human Rights Act 1998 (Designated Derogation) Order 2001.

21 Para 46.

22 *A v Secretary of State for the Home Department* [2005] 2 AC 68, 129, para 86, *per* Lord Hoffman referring to 'liberty' rights.

23 [2006] UKHL 11.

24 See particularly para 6, *per* Lord Bingham.

25 Though see the convincing dissenting speech of Baroness Hale particularly at paras 113–14.

in part reflects the judiciary's own lack of experience in equality law and the principles underpinning it and their own lack of experience of *inequality*. As is well known, the senior judiciary is predominantly male, almost exclusively white, and almost exclusively *out* only as heterosexual and, almost by definition, not otherwise disadvantaged by reason, for example, of social class. That these characteristics bring a particular perspective would seem difficult to doubt. Lord Bingham has given us a contemporary clue to the experience of a senior judge when observing:[26]

> An English judge may have, or think that he has, a shrewd idea how a Lloyd's broker, or a Bristol wholesaler, or a Norfolk farmer, might react in some situation which is canvassed in the course of a case but he may, and I think should, feel very much more uncertain about the reactions of a Nigerian merchant, or an Indian ship's engineer, or a Jugoslav banker. Or even, to take a more homely example, a Sikh shopkeeper trading in Bradford.[27]

2.10 The task of addressing complaints of equality and discrimination is especially liable to be affected by personal perspective. The oft-repeated suggestion that gender, race, class, and other defining personal characteristics are irrelevant is wrong. These factors inform the life experiences and world-views of judges no less than they do society at large. In a modern diverse democracy it might be said that no one experience or view of the world should be allowed pride of place in the judicial process. The preponderance of one set of views and experiences will invariably have an adverse effect on central aspects of the notion of justice such as fairness and equality. It is bad for justice and for law. Without a diverse judiciary, special care must be taken to secure justice in discrimination and equality cases. In *Secretary of State for Work and Pensions v M*,[28] for example, the approach Lord Bingham considered right for determining whether a complaint fell within the 'ambit' of the ECHR's non-discrimination guarantee in Article 14, having regard to Strasbourg case law, involved the making of a 'value judgment'.[29] 'Value judgments' are, of course, inherently likely to reflect one's own view of the world—how else is a value to be put on the impact of a discriminatory measure except by asking oneself how oneself, or one's friends and relations, would feel about it? In the context of discrimination and equality 'value judgments' must be recognized and made with particular care as they carry the danger of entrenching the judge's prejudices and outlooks. In *M*, the 'value judgment' made was such that the State stigmatizing of a same-sex relationship (by failing to recognize the relationship as constituting a single unit for the purposes of calculating child support as would

26 In discussing the value of 'demeanour' in assessing the evidence before a court.

27 T Bingham, *The Business of Judging, Selected Essays and Speeches* (2000, OUP), 14.

28 [2006] UKHL 11, para 14.

29 See too, Lord Hoffman in *R v Secretary of State for Work and Pensions ex p Carson and another* [2005] UKHL 37; [2006] 1 AC 173 at para 15.

have been the position had the relationship been an opposite-sex relationship) was not sufficiently close to the right to respect for private life under ECHR, Article 8 to fall within its ambit and attract the protection of Article 14. This is so notwithstanding the pernicious effect of such penalties on gay and lesbian people.

It can be noted that the consistent voice for the disadvantaged in the House of Lords is Baroness Hale—the only woman member and the only member who comes from a background that is not judge-typical.[30] **2.11**

However, the answer to an unrepresentative judiciary does not lie in removing from judges any significant role in addressing inequality, as is sometimes suggested. Conor Gearty,[31] for example, whilst acknowledging Parliament's sometimes poor history on protecting minorities (asylum seekers and suspected 'terrorists' in particular), argues that there are advantages in the courts 'in the British constitutional tradition' taking 'second place to Parliament in the definition of human dignity and in its promotion through law' 'which lawyers may be slower than others to understand. An explicit legislative intervention is a more effective way of achieving change than is the isolated case, both in terms of enforcement and consciousness-raising'.[32] This, of course, may or may not be true depending on the constitution of Parliament and, in particular, the case or the law concerned. Many laws, including those on asylum and 'terrorism', suggest otherwise, as Conor Gearty himself acknowledges. In addition, many progressive 'dignity' measures have been introduced through Private Members' Bills, as Conor Gearty again himself suggests. He puts this down (inexplicably) to 'permitting the legislators the luxury—and the onerous responsibility—of voting in accordance with their consciences rather than the relevant central office dictate'.[33] The rather more compelling explanation—and the one that reminds us of the need to aspire to and cherish a rigorous, diverse, and independent judiciary—is that the protection of minorities, the disadvantaged, and marginalized is too often regarded as unpopular with the electorate and so is sacrificed for political expediency.[34] **2.12**

In a modern liberal democracy—perhaps most especially one like the UK's which is principally based on a 'first past the post' electoral system—judges must have the power and the duty to protect the disadvantaged and minorities against both **2.13**

---

30 She spent many years in academia, then in the Law Commission before taking up a judicial post.

31 C Gearty, *Principles of Human Rights Adjudication* (2004, OUP) 88–91.

32 Ibid, 90.

33 Ibid, 88–90.

34 In this respect it can be noted that several Private Members' Bills, described below, preceded the enactment of both the RRA and DDA; and other anti-discrimination enactments came only when compelled by European law.

procedural and substantive legal inequalities.[35] The opportunity for so doing exists through the embryonic common law principle of equality, considered by Jowell and heralded by Baroness Hale, amongst others, and through Article 14. Protocol 12 would serve as a further measure of protection, were it to be implemented. However, hope for a radicalization of equality law depends in large part on a commitment to fundamentally changing the constitution of the judiciary.[36] The establishment of a Judicial Appointments Commission offers some promise in this respect.[37]

B. The History of the Main Anti-Discrimination Enactments

(1) The Race Relations Acts

2.14 The Race Relations Act (RRA) 1976 currently in force was the third Race Relations Act to be enacted in the UK. The RRA 1965 and the RRA 1968 preceded it. The first Act followed a number of Private Members' Bills seeking to outlaw race discrimination to a greater or lesser extent, many of which were introduced by Fenner Brockway MP. To understand the history of the Act, it is important to know something of the history of race relations in the UK more generally.

2.15 Britain's dominant political institutions have historically demonstrated an attitude to black and ethnic minorities which can, at best, be described as ambivalent and at worst as plain racist. It is difficult to analyse effectively the approach to race relations in Britain without scrutinizing the legislature's parallel approach to immigration law. The law of immigration is outside the scope of this work but the 'problem' of immigration continues to have prominence in the political arena and as such affects race relations generally. The history of race relations legislation shows that there has been a 'twin track approach' to racism so that when non-discrimination rights have been conferred by legislation, immigration rights have been removed (often with attendant hostility towards 'immigrants').

2.16 Britain has a history of poor treatment of immigrants. In this respect, there is little between the dominant political parties. Modern immigration law, as it affects black and ethnic minority communities in particular, can be traced back to the Commonwealth Immigrants Act 1962—a Conservative Act—which for the first time extended immigration control to certain categories of British subjects

---

[35] See the observations of Arden LJ in *Secretary of State for Defence v Elias* [2006] EWCA Civ 1293 at para 267.

[36] See the comments of S Fredman, 'Scepticism under Scrutiny: Labour Law and Human Rights' in Campbell, Ewing, and Tomkins (ed), *Sceptical Essays on Human Rights* (2001, OUP), 197 at 207.

[37] Established under s 61 and Sch 12 of the Constitutional Reform Act 2005.

('coloured immigra[nts] from the New Commonwealth'[38]). In 1965, under a Labour Government, the first RRA was enacted. By this time, however, 'a profound change occurred in the Government's attitude towards coloured immigration from the New Commonwealth'.[39] Though Labour had, when in opposition, resisted the Commonwealth Immigrants Bill, principally on the ground that attempting to limit entry into Britain of 'coloured' (*sic*) immigrants was 'blatantly discriminatory',[40] the Labour Party's position changed when in government. Increasingly they were seen to adopt racist immigration policies and embrace racially discriminatory measures. It is likely that this shift came about at least in part because of perceived electoral unpopularity which was believed to result from the passing of the RRA 1965.[41]

In fact the first RRA was very limited in its scope, and this was a deliberate device **2.17**
by Sir Frank Soskice, Home Secretary and promoter of the Bill, to ensure its successful passing in the face of considerable opposition. The Act did not include measures addressing employment, housing,[42] or education and only outlawed direct discrimination. The Act outlawed discrimination 'in places of public resort', namely hotels, restaurants, cafes, public houses, theatres, cinemas, dance halls, sports grounds, swimming pools and other places of public entertainment or recreation, public transport, and any other places of public resort maintained by a local authority or other public authority.[43] Compliance with the Act was to be secured through a 'Race Relations Board', established under section 2 of the Act. The Board was obliged to constitute local conciliation committees which were under a duty to consider any complaints of discrimination addressed to them by the general public, make such inquiries as were necessary, and, where appropriate, use their best endeavours to secure a settlement of any difference between the parties involved and a satisfactory assurance from the discriminating party against further discrimination.[44] Where conciliation was not achieved, the local conciliation committee was required to prepare a report for the Board which could in turn report the matter to the Attorney-General.[45] The Attorney-General could then bring injunction proceedings against the discriminating party to enforce the terms of the Act. Where a court was satisfied on such an application that a person had engaged in conduct made unlawful by the Act, and that, unless restrained, he or she was likely to persist in such conduct, it was empowered to grant an injunction

38 A Lester and G Bindman, *Race and Law* (1972, Penguin) 120.
39 Ibid.
40 Ibid.
41 Ibid, 121.
42 Save in respect of the disposal of tenancies, s 5.
43 S 1.
44 S 2.
45 Or the Lord Advocate as the case may be.

restraining such a person from committing or causing or permitting acts of discrimination outlawed by the Act.[46]

2.18 Even these modest measures, however, met with considerable resistance, not just from the avowedly right wing but also from the Labour movement. As mentioned, Fenner Brockway, a long-time anti-racist campaigner and MP, had, on numerous occasions, introduced racial discrimination Bills containing prohibitions on racial discrimination in a variety of areas of public life. His later Bills excluded reference to discrimination in the employment field. This omission he has explained as follows:

> because of trade union opposition. I wanted to get the *principle* of non-discrimination accepted and was prepared not to go the whole way in the first instance. I am not sure that I was right, because employment, with housing, is now proving the severest sphere of discrimination.[47]

2.19 A similar strategy was adopted by Sir Frank Soskice[48] who, it appears, did not have much enthusiasm for the legislation which, by then, the Government had committed itself to.[49] He was also in the very difficult position of having responsibility for a Bill which was not universally popular, in the context of a divided Parliament with a tiny Government majority and 'an atmosphere of growing racial intolerance among the general public'.[50] Anthony Lester and Geoffrey Bindman suggest that it is likely that, in the context of those difficulties:

> soon after the Bill was published he decided to seek a wider consensus in support of the Bill. He would do so by making a substantial concession to the lobbyists and to the Opposition by substituting conciliation for criminal sanctions; and at the same time he would try to secure Opposition approval by defending the Bill against the attempts of his own back benchers to widen its scope or strengthen its enforcement.[51]

In just the same way as Fenner Brockway had sought to establish the principle of racial discrimination legislation, so Sir Frank Soskice, though with less enthusiasm, sought to have enacted something that would give effect to the Government's manifesto commitment by embracing the *principle* of anti-racial discrimination law.

2.20 In any event, it very soon became clear that the 1965 Act was inadequate, both in tackling racial discrimination and in meeting the aspirations of those campaigners

46 Ss 2–3. In addition, incitement to racial hatred was criminalized under the Act; s 6.

47 F Brockway, *This Shrinking, Explosive World: A Study of Race Relations* (1967, Epworth Press), 81, cited in A Lester and G Bindman, *Race and Law* (1972, Penguin), 109.

48 16 July 1965, Hansard (HC) Vol 716 cols 1055–6.

49 The Labour Party's general election manifesto for 1964 contained a commitment to legislate against racial discrimination and incitement in public places.

50 A Lester and G Bindman, *Race and Law* (1972, Penguin) 114.

51 Ibid.

who had struggled to get anti-race discrimination laws on the statute books.[52] That further legislation was enacted appears to be in significant part due to the efforts and commitment of Roy Jenkins who replaced Sir Frank Soskice at the end of 1965 and quickly committed himself to achieving further change.[53] His efforts were assisted by the publication of two important reports almost simultaneously: the *Report of the Race Relations Board for 1966/67* and the Political and Economic Planning *Report on Racial Discrimination* (1967).

The *Report of the Race Relations Board for 1966/67*[54] identified a number of deficiencies in the Act, including the delay inherent in the two-stage procedure requiring first that conciliation had been attempted before a report could be made to the Attorney-General and any consequent injunction proceedings instigated. As was observed, this 'in some circumstances [may] reduce the effectiveness of the sanction of the law'.[55] In addition, the Board noted that 70 per cent of the complaints received by the local conciliation committees were 'about matters which [fell] outside the scope of the Act and the two largest categories [were] employment and housing'.[56] The Board 'were left in no doubt, especially by immigrant groups, that though legislation to tackle discrimination in places of public resort was welcome, it was in employment and housing that discrimination most seriously affected the day to day existence of coloured *(sic)* people'.[57] Importantly too, the Board noted the existence of *de facto* segregation whereby new non-white communities were concentrated in particular geographical and occupational areas,[58] and advised that 'the growth of ghettos' should be avoided to prevent the development of racial tension.[59] The Board noted that: **2.21**

> There are . . . three elements that can in combination make *de facto* segregation permanent: the fact that colour makes the immigrant identifiable: the fact that it will not disappear over the generations: and the existence of colour and racial prejudice. None of these elements will disappear by refusing to admit they exist or by refusing to take steps to counteract prejudice and its consequences.[60]

52 Including the important Campaign against Racial Discrimination (CARD)—a multi-racial campaign group to which other groups were affiliated and with which other groups (including the Indian Workers' Association (Southall) and the West Indian Standing Conference) worked on campaigning for race discrimination law.

53 A full and informative history is found in A Lester and G Bindman, *Race and Law* (1972, Penguin) 122 *et seq.*

54 (1967) HMSO made pursuant to RRA 1965, s 2(4) and laid before Parliament pursuant to that sub-section.

55 Ibid, para 38(xi).

56 Ibid, para 39.

57 Ibid, para 39.

58 Ibid, para 42.

59 Ibid, para 42.

60 Ibid, para 45.

2.22 However, significantly, the Board recognized that a policy of assimilation was not appropriate. The Board noted that the Home Secretary had confirmed that assimilation was not the policy of Government and that they sought 'integration which he said was not a flattening process of assimilation, but equal opportunity, accompanied by cultural diversity, in an atmosphere of mutual tolerance'.[61] There were good reasons for holding that 'assimilation' was not the right approach. It does not in fact work as was very soon discovered. The influential report of Political and Economic Planning,[62] *Report on Racial Discrimination* (1967),[63] disclosed widespread racial discrimination and, contrary to popular myth, that black people who had been in Great Britain the longest experienced racial discrimination the most. Other indicators against 'assimilation' being any answer to racism came with the findings that, for example, experience of discrimination was highest amongst people with the highest qualifications, including those with English trade, professional, and school leaving qualifications, and that experience of discrimination was highest amongst people who had spoken only English as a child and lowest amongst those who had spoken no English.[64]

2.23 There was thus a social and statistical foundation for pursuing further legislation in the field of race discrimination and, notwithstanding opposition to legislation from the two sides of industry, the Government made plain its intention to enact further legislation to deal with racial discrimination in employment following the publication of these two reports.[65]

2.24 Shortly thereafter, UK citizens of Asian origin began to arrive in Britain in increasing numbers from Kenya because of the Kenyan Government's 'Africanization' policies. A racist campaign began in Britain with its aim being to deprive these UK citizens of the right to enter and settle in Britain. In November 1967 James Callaghan became Home Secretary, replacing Roy Jenkins, and it was decided fairly quickly to introduce legislation removing the right of entry into the UK from those UK citizens who had not been born in Britain or whose parents and grandparents had not been born here. The Commonwealth Immigrants Act 1968, as it became, respected the precedent set by the 1962 Act in marching alongside increasing calls for anti-racial discrimination legislation.

---

61 Ibid, para 44.

62 The forerunner to the Policies Study Institute.

63 Political and Economic Planning, *Report on Racial Discrimination* (1967).

64 Cited in A Lester and G Bindman, *Race and Law* (1972, Penguin) 81.

65 26 July 1967, Statement of Roy Jenkins in the Commons, Hansard (HC) Vol 761 Col 744 indicating that the Government had decided in principle to extend the Act to deal with racial discrimination in employment, housing, insurance and credit facilities and that public places would be given a wider definition.

The second Commonwealth Immigrants Act was enacted to restrict the immigration of East African Asians—citizens of the UK—on the grounds of colour. It restricted the immigration of holders of UK passports issued outside the UK. Very shortly after the enactment of the second Commonwealth Immigrants Act, the Race Relations Bill 1968 was published. This was designed to extend the scope of the 1965 Act by regulating discrimination on racial grounds in employment, housing, and the provision of commercial and other services. The Bill proposed to extend the functions of the Race Relations Board, permitting it to bring proceedings where it formed an opinion that an act of unlawful discrimination had occurred and where they had not succeeded in obtaining a settlement and appropriate assurances. The Bill also proposed the establishment of a Community Relations Commission with responsibility for establishing 'harmonious community relations', amongst other things. The Bill was finally passed in an atmosphere 'charged with emotion'[66] and racism.[67] **2.25**

The paradox of introducing racist immigration laws at the same time as anti-race discrimination measures is obvious and the inadequacy of such an approach is perhaps best reflected in the events that followed the publication of the 1968 Race Relations Bill which, as mentioned, followed swiftly after the second Commonwealth Immigrants Act. On 20 April 1968, three days before the second reading debate of the 1968 Race Relations Bill and about two months after the passing of the Commonwealth Immigrants Act 1968, Enoch Powell delivered his notorious 'Rivers of Blood' speech.[68] The engendering of racist antipathy by the introduction of laws which stigmatize and target certain minority groups is inherently antithetical to 'harmonious community relations' and the promotion of racial equality. The approach is explicable only by political weakness and the desire to pander to a racist electorate which, certainly in the 1960s, included a powerful Trade Union lobby whose votes the Labour Party relied on and which could not be relied upon to support legislative measures outlawing racial discrimination. **2.26**

66 A Lester and G Bindman, *Race and Law* (1972, Penguin) 134.

67 The RRA 1968 did not repeal in its entirety the RRA 1965 (s 28(8)). It repealed those provisions outlawing discrimination in places of public resort, establishing the Race Relations Board and the conciliation committees, and addressing proceedings by the Attorney-General or Lord Advocate as the case may be. The provisions addressing the disposal of tenancies which provided that where the licence of consent of a landlord or of any other person was required for the disposal of premises comprising a tenancy, such licence or consent was to be treated as unreasonably withheld if and so far as it was withheld on the ground of colour, race, or ethnic or national origin, save where the person required to give licence or consent occupied part of the premises (RRA 1965, s 5) was not repealed. Nor was the provision creating an offence of incitement to racial hatred (s 6 and see s 7 which was also not repealed and which amended the Public Order Act 1936). The 1965 and 1968 Acts were, after the enactment of the 1968 Act, together to be cited as the RRAs 1965 and 1968 (RRA 1968, s 29(1)).

68 Referred to in A Lester and G Bindman, *Race and Law* (1972, Penguin) 134.

2.27 The enactment of the early RRAs were, then, not without resistance. The context was one of racial hostility and civil unrest caused by widespread racism reflected in the race riots in Nottingham and Notting Hill in 1958 and threatened again by the US civil rights movement in the early 1960s. This created a real political imperative to take action to prevent the most overt and violent forms of racial discrimination and not withstanding their weaknesses, the RRAs were a significant achievement. As Geoffrey Bindman and Anthony Lester note:

> The RRAs [1965 and 1968] were passed despite powerful opposition and with little public support[69] [and were] . . . won against formidable odds. Like much legislation, they were the product of skilful lobbying by interested pressure groups. However, there was something unusual in the process by which the Race Relations legislation came to be enacted: the legislators yielded to a pressure group which was urging them to give a lead before the problem of racial discrimination grew worse; they did not merely legislate against existing problems or in defence of legitimate existing interests.[70]

2.28 They were bold measures but would have been bolder still if they were not compromised by racist immigration measures which at their worst deprived UK citizens of the benefits which they would ordinarily enjoy on grounds of colour alone.

2.29 The 1968 Act outlawed racial discrimination for the first time by employers,[71] trade unions and employers' and trade organizations,[72] and in housing,[73] as well as in the provision of goods, facilities, and services to members of the public.[74] It also outlawed discriminatory advertisements[75] and made provision for the continuation of the Race Relations Board.[76] The 1968 Act also expressly declared that 'segregating a person from other persons on any [of the protected] grounds is treating him less favourably than they are treated'.[77] This recognized the US experience where the doctrine of 'separate but equal' had had a long and ugly history, embraced as it was by the Supreme Court.[78]

2.30 There were two features of the 1968 Act which were of particular significance. Firstly, and most importantly, the enforcement mechanisms provided for by the 1968 Act proved especially problematic to its effectiveness. Secondly, the 'racial balance provisions', which could have allowed for the promotion of greater racial diversity, had a quite different effect.

---

69 Ibid, 15.
70 Ibid, 149.
71 S 3.
72 S 4.
73 S 5.
74 S 2.
75 S 6.
76 S 14.
77 S 1(2).
78 See, eg, *Plessy v Ferguson* (1896) 163 US 537 referred to in the *Street Report* at para 22.1.

In the first place, the enforcement mechanisms provided for by the 1968 Act depended entirely on action by the Race Relations Board. As with the 1965 Act, the Board was required to constitute committees, known as conciliation committees, for the purpose of discharging the functions of the Board which included the 'resolution of differences'.[79] Further, unlike under the 1965 Act, the Race Relations Board could bring proceedings but only they (and not individuals) were empowered to do so.[80] **2.31**

In the second place, the 1968 Act included a controversial 'racial balance' provision. By section 8(2) it was provided that: **2.32**

> It shall not be unlawful by virtue of either of [sections 2 or 3[81]] to discriminate against any person with respect to the engagement for employment in, or the selection for work within, an undertaking or part of an undertaking if the act is done in good faith for the purpose of securing or preserving a reasonable balance of persons of different racial groups employed in the undertaking or that part of the undertaking, as the case may be.

'Racial group', for these purposes, meant 'a group of persons defined by reference to colour, race or ethnic or national origins and for the purposes of that subsection persons wholly or mainly educated in Great Britain [were to] be treated as members of the same racial group'. As was observed fairly early on, this provision was capable of having a remarkable effect. It allowed for employers to decline to employ, for example, black Caribbean workers because it already had a proportionate number of Pakistani workers and thus had a 'reasonable balance' of white and non-white workers employed in the workplace. It would also permit an appropriate 'balance' to be achieved by the employment of those educated in Ireland and Australia, for example, with those educated in Great Britain.[82] The 'racial balance' provision was enacted, apparently, as a result of negotiations with the Confederation of British Industry (CBI) and the Trades Union Congress (TUC) so as to protect employers who already employed substantial numbers of non-white workers.[83] It was a racist measure designed to ensure that there were not 'too many' non-white workers employed in a particular workplace and that there was no real threat to the racial preference that had been afforded white workers historically. It could, of course, have been used to promote equality but that was neither its aim nor its effect.[84]

---

79 Ss 4 and 15.

80 Under the 1965 Act such proceedings could only be brought by the Attorney-General, s 3.

81 Those being the provisions outlawing discrimination in the field of the provision of goods, facilities and services, and employment.

82 See A Lester and G Bindman, *Race and Law* (1972, Penguin) 165.

83 Ibid, 140.

84 Ibid, 175.

2.33 In 1967 the well-known and influential *Street Report*[85] had been published. This report, prepared by Harry Street, Geoffrey Howe, and Geoffrey Bindman, considered the race discrimination laws in Great Britain and in the US and made recommendations for further legislative action in Great Britain. The *Street Report* recommended that the 'racial imbalance' provisions of the US model Anti-Discrimination Act be included in our domestic anti-race discrimination scheme. The US model Anti-Discrimination Act provided that the state commissions responsible for giving effect to its provisions had the power 'to sanction programmes to eliminate racial imbalance, even where these may involve positive discrimination in favour of the minority group'.[86] This would permit plans designed to address disadvantage reflected in 'racial imbalance' but was quite different from the 'racial balance' provision finally enacted in the 1968 Act. The recommendation in the *Street Report* was not accepted.

2.34 Very soon, problems were identified with the 1968 Act, in particular in relation to its enforcement provisions. As mentioned, the *Street Report*[87] had made a number of recommendations for amending the 1965 Act, including that the anti-race discrimination scheme should focus on achieving conciliation.[88] Many of the recommendations of the *Street Report* were not taken up in the 1968 Act,[89] but its recommendation that 'conciliation should continue to be regarded as the most important part of the legislation'[90] was reflected in the 1968 Act. However, the recommended conciliation-focused approach adopted by the 1968 Act proved to be problematic.

2.35 As the White Paper which preceded the 1976 Act observed:[91]

> . . . [T]he requirement that all complaints should be investigated [by the Race Relations Board] may create resentment and hostility among those it is designed to assist. The process may seem cumbersome and protracted. The complainant may feel aggrieved at being denied the right to seek legal redress while his complaint is being processed. If his complaint is not upheld, he is likely to resent the fact that he is denied direct access to legal remedies. Even if it is upheld, he may feel aggrieved because, in his view, the Board or conciliation committee has accepted a settlement or assurance which he regards as inadequate; or, worse still, because after conciliation has failed, the Board has decided not to bring legal proceedings, whether because it considered that it had insufficient prospects of proving the case in court or for some other reason.

---

85 H Street, G Howe, and G Bindman, *Street Report on Anti-Discrimination Legislation* (1967, Political and Economic Planning).

86 Ibid, para 47.1.

87 Ibid.

88 Ibid, chap 16.

89 Including, for example, the establishment of a fact finding body (see Chap 17) amongst other things.

90 Para 156.

91 *Racial Discrimination* (1975) Cmnd 6234, paras 40–41.

> Thus the requirement that all complaints should be investigated by the Race Relations Board or its conciliation committees and that the alleged victim of racial discrimination (unlike the victims of almost all civil wrongs) should be denied direct access to legal remedies suffers from a double disadvantage. It distracts the statutory agency from playing its crucial strategic role whilst leaving many complainants dissatisfied with what has been done on their behalf by means of procedures which may seem cumbersome, ineffective or unduly paternalistic.[92]

The White Paper, therefore, was concerned to identify not only the weaknesses in the complaints system but also the impact of a focus on individual complaints on the strategic role and work of the Board. The White Paper recommended an increase in the strategic powers of a newly established Commission and a direct right of access to the courts for individuals affected by unlawful discrimination.[93]

By the time of the publication of the White Paper, *Racial Discrimination*,[94] the Government had already published its White Paper on sex discrimination—*Equality for Women*[95]—and what would become the Sex Discrimination Act (SDA) 1975 was very close to enactment.[96] Many of the recommendations in the White Paper on racial discrimination therefore reflected the recommendations already contained in the White Paper, *Equality for Women*, which stated that it was the Government's ultimate aim 'to harmonise the powers and procedures for dealing with sex and race discrimination so as to secure genuine equality of opportunity in both fields'.[97] It expressly acknowledged the learning derived from the experience of the RRA, and in the drafting of the proposals for sex discrimination law the Government 'attempted to avoid a number of weaknesses which experience has revealed in the enforcement provisions of the race relations legislation'.[98] **2.36**

92 It is interesting to note that the recent Canadian experience has been similar. The Canadian Human Rights Act 1977 also adopts an enforcement process which depends upon action by a Commission (the Human Rights Commission) which is responsible for investigating and conciliating and thereafter the instituting of proceedings to a Human Rights Tribunal. The Canadian Human Rights Act Review Panel, chaired by Justice LaForest reported in 2000 (*Promoting Equality: A New Vision* available at: <http://canada.justice.gc.ca/chra/en/toc.html>) and made a number of recommendations for change to the existing enforcement mechanisms, including the reform of the complaints system so as to allow claimants the right to bring their cases directly to the Tribunal themselves and empowering the Commission to join in cases where significant issues are raised but without providing it with any exclusive enforcement role. As with the White Paper referred to above, the report of the Canadian Human Rights Act Review Panel considered that the Commission's activities should be enlarged to include more strategic work (including the making of codes of practice, policy statements, research, information gathering, and inquiries on specific issues arising under the Act etc, see recommendations 16–25) (as to the recommendations regarding the reform of the complaints system, see recommendations 28–29).

93 Paras 40–41 and 38.

94 *Racial Discrimination* (1975) Cmnd 6234, Sept 1975.

95 *Equality for Women* (1974) Cmnd 5724.

96 Enacted on 12 November 1975.

97 *Equality for Women* (1974) Cmnd 5724, para 24.

98 Ibid.

2.37 Therefore, the White Paper *Equality for Women* was responsible for setting the framework for new law in the field of both sex discrimination and race discrimination. In so doing, it drew heavily[99] on the *Street Report*[100] referred to above. Indeed, a number of the measures found within the SDA 1975 and subsequently within the RRA 1976 can be traced back to the *Street Report*, including, for example, protection against victimization[101] and against those who aid discriminators.[102]

2.38 However, neither the *Street Report* nor the *Equality for Women* White Paper referred to the important concept of indirect discrimination. Indeed, legislation addressing anything that might be capable of constituting indirect discrimination was not countenanced as appropriate by the authors of the *Street Report*; in Chapter 22 they remarked that:

> It should be made plain that nothing in the Act is intended to prohibit selection that is based upon factors *other* than race, colour or ethnic or national origin. This general declaratory statement of the law seems preferable to some American provisions which permit discrimination in favour of, for example, certain named relatives—with the possible implication that discrimination of more remote relatives would be unlawful. For the general principle is that discrimination is only unlawful when it is shown to be based upon racial grounds. There can in these circumstances be no harm in stating in plain terms the right to 'discriminate' on any *other* ground that can be legitimately established as having been effective.[103]

Similarly, in the *Equality for Women* White Paper, the concept of unlawful discrimination was described as referring to situations 'where one person is accorded less favourable treatment on grounds of sex or marriage than is or would be accorded to other persons'.[104] It was made clear that:

> It will not apply to differences of treatment made for any other reason, eg, because a potential employee is not suitably qualified for a particular job, or because a potential borrower lacks sufficient financial standing or credit worthiness.[105]

Indeed at the stage of drafting the *Equality for Women* White Paper, it was intended that motive or intent (proved actually or inferred) would be required to establish unlawful discrimination.[106] This reflected the provisions of the RRA 1965 and 1968, both of which outlawed only direct discrimination and apparently

---

99 *Equality for Women* (1974) Cmnd 5724, para 23.

100 H Street, G Howe, G Bindman, *Street Report on Anti-Discrimination Legislation* (1967) Political and Economic Planning.

101 As discussed in Chap 1.

102 See H Street, G Howe, G Bindman, *Street Report on Anti-Discrimination Legislation* (1967), Political and Economic Planning, paras 42.1 and 125.1.

103 Ibid, para 185.3(e), internal footnote reference removed.

104 *Equality for Women* (1974) Cmnd 5724, para 33.

105 Ibid.

106 Ibid.

required some intent[107] though that intent was capable of being inferred.[108] The history of the inclusion of the concept of indirect discrimination has already been referred to in Chapter 1[109] and followed the discovery of the decision in the US case of *Griggs v Duke Power*.[110]

Thus, the RRA 1976 included new concepts of discrimination, abolished the Community Relations Commission and the Race Relations Board, and in their place established the Commission for Racial Equality (CRE)[111] which was itself given broad powers to take strategic action[112] and gave individuals for the first time the right of access to a court in their own name to seek redress for unlawful racial discrimination. As with previous legislation, it too was introduced by a Labour Government following their acceptance that the 1965 and 1968 RRAs were ineffectual in tackling racial discrimination. The White Paper, *Racial Discrimination*, which set out the principles to which the Act was meant to give effect, identified the social mischief the RRA 1976 was designed to tackle as follows: **2.39**

> Despite the RRAs, substantial discrimination continues to occur at work[113] . . .
>
> The possibility has to be faced that there is at work in this country, as elsewhere in the world, the familiar cycle of cumulative disadvantage by which relatively low-paid or low-status jobs for the first generation of immigrants go hand in hand with poor and overcrowded living conditions and a depressed environment. If, for example, job opportunities, educational facilities, housing and environmental conditions are all poor, the next generation will grow up less well-equipped to deal with the difficulties facing them. The wheel then comes full circle, as the second generation finds themselves trapped in poor jobs and poor housing. If, at each stage of this process, an element of racial discrimination enters in, then an entire group of people are launched on a vicious spiral of deprivation. They may share each of the disadvantages with some other deprived group in society; but few other groups in society display all their accumulated disadvantages.[114]

The 1976 Act remains in force, though it has been amended several times since its original enactment. Whilst the RRA 1976 was, without doubt, an important **2.40**

---

107 A Lester and G Bindman, *Race and Law* (1972, Penguin), 167.

108 Ibid.

109 Para 1.16.

110 401 US 424, 91 SCt 849.

111 The CRE inherited some of the Board's and the Commission's staff and the RRA 1976 provided for transitional arrangements. The origins of the CRE in the Community Relations Commission and the Race Relations Board explains the CRE's closer connection to community activity as compared to the Equal Opportunities Commission which was a novel creature of the SDA, without any community roots.

112 Though some of these were construed more narrowly than intended by the courts, as again referred to in Chap 1 as will be discussed in Chap 15.

113 *Racial Discrimination* (1975) Cmnd. 6234, para 7.

114 Ibid, para 11.

stride forward in the protection against racial discrimination, there are real doubts about whether its design has been sufficient to tackle the 'wheel of disadvantage' identified as the mischief it was seeking to address. It would be wrong to say that the RRAs have had no effect. As set out in Chapter 1, they plainly have had an impact on very overt forms of discrimination, in particular. However, as referred to in Chapter 1, there is ample evidence suggesting that race discrimination remains prevalent in all important areas of life in the UK.

> Judged in terms of the aims expressed in the White Paper on racial discrimination—to reduce discrimination and by so doing to help break the 'familiar cycle of cumulative disadvantage'—the ineffectiveness of the RRA 1976 is irrefutable.[115]

Further, the RRA 1976 did not come without a price, namely the Immigration Act 1971 and the Nationality Act 1981 which again served to enshrine racially discriminatory laws.[116]

(2) The Race Relations (Amendment) Act 2000

2.41 Further change came again under a Labour Government, elected in May 1997 on a manifesto which included a commitment to ending 'unjustifiable discrimination wherever it exists'.[117] In fact such change resulted directly from the recommendations made in the *Stephen Lawrence Inquiry Report*[118] (and which were, because of their context, politically irresistible).

2.42 Two major statutory reviews had been conducted by the CRE in 1985 and 1992 (both under Conservative Governments), recommending wide-ranging changes to the 1976 Act. The first received no response at all from the Government. The second, in 1992, was considered by the Government, but its recommendations were not proceeded with. In announcing the Government's response to this second review,[119] the Home Secretary Michael Howard emphasized that it was the Government's view that the way forward for equal opportunities and good race relations lay more with promotion, education, and voluntary action than with 'quick-fix legislation'. In his (or the Government's) view, the introduction of compulsory ethnic monitoring would impose 'significant additional cost and

---

115 B Hepple, 'Have 25 years of the RRAs in Britain been a failure?' in Hepple and Szyszczak (ed), *Discrimination: The Limits of Law* (1992, Mansell), 19.

116 Ibid, 28.

117 Labour Party Manifesto, 1997, available at <http://www.labour-party.org.uk/manifestos/1997/1997-labour-manifesto.shtml>.

118 *The Stephen Lawrence Inquiry: Report of an Inquiry by Sir William Macpherson of Cluny*, advised by Tom Cook, the Rt Rev Dr John Sentamu, Dr Richard Stone, Cm 4262-I.

119 Government's response to the CRE's second review, July 1995 reported at 'Government rejects key CRE proposals for reforming RRA' (1994) *Equal Opportunities Review*, No 57, 5. Even this took well over a year to provide.

administrative burdens on businesses' which 'would not help businesses to be competitive as we emerge from recession'. Notwithstanding the history of voluntary action in the field of discrimination, which had been singularly unsuccessful,[120] Michael Howard added that he was 'strongly committed to encouraging more effort in monitoring, but on a voluntary basis, helping employers to see the benefits in making sure they recruit and promote the best candidates, whatever their colour'.[121]

A third review by the CRE did lead to legislative change. However, the recommendations made by the CRE were proceeded with only insofar as they matched the recommendations of the *Stephen Lawrence Inquiry Report*,[122] the resulting public pressure from which secured such change.[123] **2.43**

As explained in Chapter 1, the Race Relations (Amendment) Act 2000 (RRAA) reflects the recommendations made by the *Stephen Lawrence Inquiry Report*, most significantly by outlawing discrimination by public authorities in the carrying out of their functions and introducing general statutory duties upon scheduled public authorities to 'have due regard to the need to eliminate unlawful racial discrimination and to promote equality of opportunity and good relations between persons of different racial groups'.[124] These provisions represented an important step in addressing the institutional discrimination that the *Stephen Lawrence Inquiry Report* found in the police force and in many other institutions and organizations;[125] they are discussed further in later chapters. **2.44**

---

120 See, for example, the Equal Pay Act (EPA) 1970 and the position in relation to the employment of disabled people before the enactment of the DDA 1995, discussed below.

121 The Government did endorse the recommendation that the CRE should be able to accept a legally binding undertaking from employers that they would change practices which disadvantage a particular group. According to the Home Secretary, this represented 'a simple way of resolving a dispute without going through the costly—and contentious—process of a formal investigation under the Act or a tribunal hearing'. He added that: 'taking firms to court does little to encourage sensible cooperation and much to set in concrete ill-feeling between the parties'. No change was made, however, to the RRA (cf DDA 1995, s 5 and now Equality Act 2006, s 23, see Chap 15).

122 *The Stephen Lawrence Inquiry: Report of an Inquiry by Sir William Macpherson of Cluny*, advised by Tom Cook, the Rt Rev Dr John Sentamu, Dr Richard Stone, Cm 4262-I.

123 See *Reform of the RRA 1976, Proposals for Change* (1998) CRE, 6 and *Fairness for All: A New Commission for Equality in Human Rights, a Response* (August 2004) CRE, 40, available at <http://www.cre.gov.uk/downloads/ffa_cre_response.doc>.

124 Ss 19B and 71. The Act also amended the RRA 1976 so as to introduce a power upon the Secretary of State to introduce by order 'such duties as he considers appropriate for the purpose of ensuring the better performance' by persons scheduled of their general duty under s 71: RRA 1976, s 71(2). Importantly too, the RRAA amended the 1976 Act to make Chief Constables vicariously liable for the acts of their police officers (RRA 1976, s 76A as amended).

125 *The Stephen Lawrence Inquiry: Report of an Inquiry by Sir William Macpherson of Cluny*, advised by Tom Cook, the Rt Rev Dr John Sentamu, Dr Richard Stone, Cm 4262-I, paras 46.27, 321.

(3) European Community Law

2.45 More recent amendments to the RRA 1976 have been driven by the requirements of European Community (EC) law.[126] This is discussed further in Chapter 4.

(4) Conclusion

2.46 The main enactments addressing racial discrimination have, therefore, been driven through by Labour Governments, sometimes forced by political pressure, sometimes bravely, and sometimes compelled by EC law. Notwithstanding the importance of Labour Governments in the progression of anti-racial discrimination law, Labour's position on racial minorities has continued to be ambivalent. As mentioned above, its approach to the management of immigration has sometimes been racist. The present Labour Government continues to view immigration as a 'problem'. Within months of their election in 1997, Mike O'Brien, then Home Office Minister, announced the re-launch of the 'Customs Coastwatch', designed, amongst other things, to enlist the public's help in catching 'illegal immigrants', with the comment that 'illegal immigration is a very real problem'.[127]

2.47 Further, and to their great discredit, the Labour Government decided not to repeal section 8 of the Asylum and Immigration Act 1996 which requires employers to check their workers' immigration status and in particular their entitlement to work, or to face the risk of criminal sanctions.[128] This is despite the fact that in opposition the Labour Party opposed its introduction; that the United Nations Committee on the Elimination of Racial Discrimination[129] expressed its concern that most of those affected by the new legislation and regulations would be persons belonging to ethnic minorities;[130] and the recommendation of Labour's own Better Regulation Task Force that section 8 be repealed.[131] Other discriminatory measures based on immigration status, litter statute, and case law, and have not been repealed.[132]

---

126 See, the Council Directive 2000/43/EC (the Race Directive) and the RRA 1976 (Amendment) Regulations 2003 SI 2003/1626.

127 *Legal Action*, July 1997, 5.

128 Though the Immigration, Asylum and Nationality Act 2006, ss 26, 61, Sch 3 will repeal s 8, it is not yet in force and in any event will put in its place substantially the same provision (see s 15), albeit with the power to introduce a code of pratice on avoiding discrimination (s 23).

129 After reviewing the UK's report on its record of discrimination in March 1996.

130 Runnymede Trust Bulletin, March 1996, No 293, cited in S Spencer, 'The Impact of Immigration Policy on Race Relations' in T Blackstone, B Parekh, and P Saunders (ed), *Race Relations in Britain; a Developing Agenda* (1998, Routledge), 79.

131 See, Better Regulation Task Force, *Anti-Discrimination Legislation* (May 1999), 28.

132 By way of example only, see *R (Baiai & Ors) v SSHD* [2006] TLR, 14 Apr 2006; Asylum and Immigration Act 1999, s 95 and Nationality, Asylum and Immigration Act 2002, s 55; *R v Secretary of State for the Home Department ex p Limbuela; R v Secretary of State for the Home Department ex p Tesema (Conjoined Appeals)* [2005] UKHL 66.

Further still, the summer of 1999 saw the then Labour Home Secretary, Jack Straw, characterize 'the so-called travellers' as burglars, thieves who 'caus[e] all sorts of trouble, including defecating in the doorways of firms and so on'. He sought to distinguish this group from 'law abiding Gypsies' so reinforcing the stereotype of Gypsies as—commonly—not law abiding.[133] These comments came within months of the racist attacks against eastern European Romany Gypsies in Dover (dubbed, amongst other things, 'Giro Czechs' by the local papers[134]) and followed the issuing of a good practice guide by the CRE to the media aimed at preventing racist coverage of stories relating to Travellers and Gypsies.[135] **2.48**

This hostility towards immigrants by a Government purportedly committed to equality and human rights is a further reflection of the dichotomy in attitude to race in the dominant political institutions in Britain, as previously starkly illustrated by the enactment of both the 'positive' RRA and the racist Commonwealth Immigrants Act in the same year (1968). It also goes some way to explaining the failure of legislation to combat racist antipathy in the UK. As has been observed: **2.49**

> If our immigration laws racially discriminate in their aims and effect, it becomes difficult to persuade employers, workers, property developers and house-owners to treat people on their merits, regardless of race. If our nationality laws create a pseudo-citizenship, imposing the obligations of allegiance and loyalty to the British Crown upon a group of citizens, while denying to them, as 'non-patrials' or 'non-belongers' the same rights as their fellow citizens, even the wisest and most vigorous policies for racial equality are likely to lack credibility both with [the] majority and minority.[136]

It would be quite wrong, however, to assume that immigration and Government reaction to it explains racial discrimination. Whilst it may reflect deeply entrenched racism in British society, it does not explain its existence: **2.50**

> The large scale immigration of black people into Britain in the fifties and sixties . . . offers no satisfactory causal explication of racial discrimination in Britain. Yet most political and social commentators on race relations in Britain choose not to go beyond the fifties in search of explanation, and the main reason . . . is that the history beyond that epoch is too barbaric for them to confront.[137]

---

133 BBC Radio West Midland, 22 July 1999; reported in the *Guardian* 20 August 1999.

134 *Connections* (1998, CRE), Autumn.

135 *Travellers, Gypsies and the Media: A Good Practice Guide from the Commission for Racial Equality* (December 1998, CRE).

136 A Lester and G Bindman, *Race and Law* (1972, Penguin), 14.

137 S K Yeboah, *The Ideology of Racism* (1988, Hansib) 31: 'Indeed Dr Stuart Hall, then Director of the Centre for Cultural Studies, University of Birmingham, . . . was driven to comment in a public talk . . . : " . . . the development of an indigenous British racism in the post-war period begins with the profound historical forgetfulness—what I want to call the loss of historical memory, a kind of historical amnesia, a decisive mental repression—which has overtaken the British people about race and empires since the 1950s. Paradoxically, it seems to me, the native, home-grown variety of racism begins with this attempt to wipe out and efface every trace of the colonial and imperial past." To understand the origin and development of racial prejudice, it is imperative to go back into . . . history.'

As Geoffrey Bindman and Anthony Lester note:

> In several senses post war immigration from the new Commonwealth has transplanted to the old mother country prejudices and patterns of behaviour which could conveniently be ignored or righteously condemned so long as they flourished only within an Empire beyond our shores.[138]

2.51 Race discrimination is embedded in Britain's colonial past. The opportunity to address its continuation will only arise by recognizing the disadvantage that it has caused to many black and 'immigrant' communities. Without significant change in the political priorities of Government, positive leadership engendering a culture of respect for black and ethnic minority people, and radical measures addressing disadvantage, there is little to suppose that entrenched attitudes to racial minorities will change. The opportunity for so doing is presented by the *Discrimination Law Review* referred to in Chapter 1.

(5) The Equal Pay Act 1970 and the Sex Discrimination Act 1975

2.52 The origins of the Equal Pay Act 1970 (EPA) and the Sex Discrimination Act 1975 (SDA) are quite different from the RRA.

2.53 The Treaty of Rome 1957 contained express provisions addressing equal pay. In Article 119 it provided that: 'Each Member State shall . . . maintain the principle that men and women should receive equal pay for equal work.'[139] The EPA was enacted, albeit before accession to the European Economic Community, in the expectation that it would give effect to Article 119 (now Article 141), though as later cases proved, this expectation was unmet by the actual terms of the EPA. Nevertheless its enactment took skilled lobbying by Barbara Castle in particular, then Secretary of State for Employment and Productivity in a Labour Government. It seems that she had very little support.[140]

2.54 The enactment of the EPA came less than three weeks before the Labour Government was ousted from office in the May 1970 General Election. However, it was not intended to be brought into force for some five years and nor was it.[141] It appears that the reason for this delay was the expectation that employers would use the time in between the enactment of the EPA and its coming into force to

---

138 Ibid, 13.

139 See Chap 4 for its detailed provisions.

140 See, P Toynbee, '30 years of Women's Rights in the Workplace' (2006) *Spotlights 2006*, Economic and Social Research Council, available at, <http://www.esrc.ac.uk/ESRCInfoCentre/about/CI/CP/Our_Society_Today/Spotlights_2006/work.aspx?ComponentId=13396&SourcePageId=13442>.

141 Enacted 29 May 1970, in force 29 December 1975 (see s 9).

take voluntary measures to secure equal pay between men and women. As it happened, the 'hope that employers would voluntarily remove sex discrimination in pay and the other contractual terms of employment by that date' was in vain.[142] In the meantime a European Council Directive was enacted providing substance to the Treaty guarantee. The 'Equal Pay Directive',[143] to which Member States were required to give effect by 19 February 1976,[144] made express provision for the principle of equal pay for work of equal value, as well as equal pay for the same work. In addition, the European Court of Justice decided in the case of *Defrenne v SABENA (No 2)*[145] in 1976 that Article 119 was directly effective. As such, in the courts of Member States it could be relied upon directly in claims brought against both private and State parties.[146] The impact of European law made the bringing into force of the EPA inevitable.

The EPA dealt with contractual terms and conditions of employment. At an early stage, it was proposed that complementary provision would be made through another enactment addressing non-contractual conditions and other employment-related issues.[147] With the, albeit slim, Labour majority returned after the 1974 general election, more radical proposals were introduced for addressing gender inequality in those areas not covered by the EPA. The Labour Party's manifesto before the February 1974 elections contained a commitment to achieving equality between men and women, promising that: **2.55**

> women and girls must have an equal status in education, training, employment, social security, national insurance, taxation, property ownership, matrimonial and family law. Women at work, whether wives and mothers or those otherwise caring for dependent relatives, must receive more consideration from the community. We shall create the powerful legal machinery necessary to enforce our anti-discrimination laws.[148]

The absence of an overall majority led to a second general election in October 1974,[149] by which time the White Paper that preceded the SDA—*Equality for Women*[150]—had been published. As observed above, the White Paper adopted many of the recommendations of the *Street Report* and sought to 'harmonise the powers and procedures for dealing with sex and race discrimination so as to secure

---

142 D Pannick, *Sex Discrimination Law* (1985, Oxford), 92.

143 Directive 75/117/EEC.

144 Article 8.

145 Case 43/75 [1976] ECR 455.

146 Discussed in Chap 4.

147 See the White Paper preceding the SDA, *Equality for Women* (1974) Cmnd 5724, para 22.

148 *Let Us Work Together—Labour's Way Out of the Crisis* (1974) The Labour Party, para 15, available at <http://www.psr.keele.ac.uk/area/uk/man/lab74feb.htm>.

149 The first election in 1974, in February, did not produce an overall majority for the Labour Party, with the Liberals holding the balance of power.

150 *Equality for Women* (1974) Cmnd 5724.

genuine equality of opportunity in both fields'.[151] The Labour Party returned with a bigger majority in October 1974 and enacted the SDA in November 1975.

2.56 Shortly after the enactment of the SDA a further European Council Directive was enacted addressing gender discrimination. The Equal Treatment Directive[152] required Member States to introduce measures outlawing sex discrimination in the employment and related fields by the middle of 1979.[153] This is discussed further in Chapter 4.

2.57 Regular amendments have been made to the EPA and the SDA since and these have, in the main, effected the changes necessary to secure compliance with European law. There are many examples of these changes which will be addressed in detail in the following chapters as they arise. They include early amendments to the EPA to give a right to equal pay for work of equal value[154] and amendments to the SDA to give effect to the Equal Treatment Directive and the amended Equal Treatment Directive[155] so as to include, amongst other things, express provision addressing gender reassignment discrimination,[156] harassment and sexual harassment, and a more liberal concept of indirect discrimination than that originally enacted.[157] Other amendments have been introduced with the aim of creating parity between the rights afforded under the RRA 1976 and those afforded under the SDA. With amendments made from time to time over the years, the gaps between the protections afforded under the SDA compared with the RRA had increased. This was particularly striking after the amendments made by the RRAA. The Equality Act 2006 has brought the SDA broadly back into line with the RRA. The Equality Act amends the SDA so as to outlaw sex discrimination by public authorities[158] and introduces duties on public authorities to have 'due regard to the need to eliminate unlawful discrimination and harassment, and to promote equality of opportunity between men and women'.[159] Some differences remain, however; for example, there is no equivalent to the EPA in relation to race discrimination (see Chapter 6).

2.58 As with the RRA in relation to race discrimination, the SDA and, to a lesser degree, the EPA have addressed many of the overt instances of discrimination, though by no means all of them. Pregnancy-related discrimination, for example, remains overt

151 *Equality for Women* (1974) Cmnd. 5724, para 24.
152 76/207/EEC.
153 Article 9(1).
154 Equal Pay (Amendments) Regulations 1983 SI 1983/1794.
155 These being amendments made by Directive 2002/73.
156 Sex Discrimination (Gender Reassignment) Regulations 1999, SI 1999/1102.
157 Employment Equality (Sex Discrimination) Regulations 2005, SI 2005/2467.
158 New s 21A of the SDA 1975, to be introduced by the Equality Act 2006, s 83.
159 New s 76A of the SDA 1975, to be introduced by the Equality Act 2006, s 84.

and common. As the Equal Opportunities Commission's formal investigation into pregnancy discrimination found in 2005, each year almost half of the 440,000 pregnant women in Great Britain experience some form of disadvantage at work, simply for being pregnant or taking maternity leave, and as many as 30,000 women are forced out of their jobs.[160] Unequal pay remains a feature of being a woman and in large part the law simply does not address its causes. Unequal pay for women is attributable in the main to job segregation, women's patterns of work (including part-time work and breaks in service to care for children and other relatives), and the undervaluing of 'women's work'. As the Women and Work Commission have found:[161]

> Women and men tend to do different jobs, a pattern which is usually referred to as 'occupational segregation'. Women tend to work in lower paid occupations, in particular dominating the five 'c's—caring, cashiering, catering, cleaning, and clerical. The occupations which are regarded as 'women's work' are under-valued.
>
> . . . Women have less labour market experience than men and more interruptions to their work experience. Women tend to take more time out of work to care for children. Experience is one of the factors that employers reward and it is often difficult for women to return to work at the same or a higher level after taking time out . . . Women work part time much more than men, earning lower hourly pay rates than their full-time counterparts and suffering a long-term negative impact on their earnings even if they return to full-time work. The lower rates of pay for part-time work are linked to general lower rates of pay in those sectors offering the most part-time opportunities. Travel to work issues can also be a factor. Women, particularly women with children, tend to have shorter commuting times than men which limits the range of jobs available to them. This potentially leads to the crowding of women into those jobs available locally, and in either case, depresses wages.

Although some inequality in pay experienced by women arises from straightforward discrimination,[162] much arises from social patterns which disadvantage women and this remains unaddressed by the EPA.

In addition, the EPA's and the SDA's insistence on the identification of a comparator, real or hypothetical, has served to compound certain forms of gender discrimination. This is discussed further in Chapter 6. In outline, both the EPA and the SDA require a woman to compare herself to a similarly positioned man if she is to show that the treatment afforded her was unlawfully discriminatory. This requirement can serve to entrench some forms of gender discrimination. Much discrimination occurs because public life, for example, is organized around a male norm. **2.59**

160 *Greater Expectations: Final report of the EOC's investigation into discrimination against new and expectant mothers in the workplace* (2005) Equal Opportunities Commission, 7, available at <http://www.eoc.org.uk/PDF/pregnancy_gfi_final_report.pdf>.

161 *Shaping a Fairer Future* (Feb 2006) Women and Work Commission, 4, available at <http://www.womenandequalityunit.gov.uk/women_work_commission/> (internal references removed).

162 Ibid, 5.

Requiring a woman to compare herself to a similarly situated man merely means that women are unprotected against gender discrimination unless they live their lives like men. In relation to work, for example, it has been said in the Australian context[163] that:

> 'work' is a fundamentally gendered construct. The arrangements for work in industrialised societies were made by and for the benefit of a 'male breadwinner', even though this model may well fit uncomfortably for significant numbers of women and men today. The construction of 'worker' presupposes that he is a man who has a woman, a (house) wife to take care of his daily needs . . . the sturdy figure of the 'worker', the artisan, in clean overalls, with a bag of tools and a lunch box, is always accompanied by the ghostly figure of his wife.[164]
>
> The factors that define and separate men and women are the different constructions of their sexuality[165] and their relationship to family and home. Women enter the workforce defined as sexualised and family oriented people. Men, despite the fact that they also possess sexuality and have families, are not defined in this way.[166]
>
> Women's bodies—female sexuality, their ability to procreate and their pregnancy, breastfeeding and child care . . . —are suspect, stigmatised and used as ground for control and exclusion.[167]
>
> It is argued that the adverse practical consequences to women of pregnancy and motherhood are not the result of chance but
>
> '. . . rather a reflection of the various perceptions of what it means to be a Pregnant Woman . . . The law constructs its own notion of Woman and in particular of Pregnant Woman, which is at odds with the way in which real women wish to lead their lives. As a consequence, women are forced by the law into behaving in certain ways and making certain choices.'[168]
>
> The law has a central role in maintaining and reinforcing these perceptions. As one commentator has noted, '. . . not only do these rules *reflect* a notion of the worker that is based on the full-time male model . . . these rules actually construct this notion'.[169]

163 *Pregnant and Productive: It's a Right not a Privilege to Work while Pregnant, Report of the National Pregnancy and Work Inquiry* (1999) Human Rights and Equal Opportunity Commission, ISBN 0 642 26964 5.

164 C Pateman, *The Sexual Contract* (1988, Polity Press), 131. See also R Hunter, 'Representing Gender in Legal Analysis: A case/book study in labour law' (1991) 18 *Melbourne University Law Review* 305.

165 See also S Fitzpatrick (Submission no 12).

166 See J Wajcman, *Managing Like a Man: Women and Men in Corporate Management* (1999, Allen & Unwin); Pateman, n 165 above; C Cockburn, *In the Way of Women: Men's Resistance to Sex Equality in Organisations* (1991, Macmillan); Hunter, n 164 above.

167 J Acker Hierarchies, 'Jobs, Bodies: A Theory of Gendered Organizations' (1990) 4 *Gender and Society* 139.

168 A Morris and S Nott, 'The Law's Engagement with Pregnancy' in J Bridgeman and S Millns, *Law and Body Politics: Regulating the Female Body* (1995, Dartmouth Publishing Co), 55.

169 R Lifschitz, *The Artisan and the Ghost: Rewriting the subject of labour law*, Faculty of Law McGill University Masters Thesis (unpublished) Montreal, November 1998, 16. See also R Owens, 'Women, Atypical Work Relationships and the Law' (1993) 19 *Melbourne University Law Review* 399; Hunter, n 164 above.

In the Australian context, this is most clearly embedded in the *Harvester* judgment which awarded a wage based on the 'normal needs of the average employee regarded as a human being in a civilised society', that is, a man with a wife and three children to support.[170] This case, decided in 1907, formally informed judicial decision making until 1974.[171]

The gender neutral language of parental leave and other family-friendly policies '... obscures the fact that present social arrangements for care benefit men'.[172]

Family-friendly policies primarily focus on allowing women to combine family and labour market responsibilities. Their purpose is to enable women to enter and remain in a workforce constructed by men for men without family involvement. The fact that men are also parents is incidental to these reforms ... Policies that increase support for women's mothering role help to perpetuate the domestic definition of women workers.[173]

Rights associated with maternity leave are often dependent on length of service, a concept that reflects traditional male working patterns. This means that many women do not have access to these provisions because of their casual status or interrupted service. The very employees intended to benefit from those policies are less likely to be able to take advantage of them.[174]

Some argue that the terminology associated with pregnancy also has negative workplace connotations. One submission to the inquiry pointed out that the term 'falling pregnant' '... makes pregnancy sound like an unfortunate and regrettable condition, and makes the person who "finds" herself in this position to be a "fallen" woman'.[175]

Effecting flexible reforms that address the realities of the current workforce demographic, rather than perpetuating traditional paradigms based on male models of previous generations, is the challenge facing industrial relations and anti-discrimination policy makers and legislators. Turning these reforms into active and normal workplace practice is the challenge for employers, both large and small.

Policies and laws that promote the harmonisation of work, pregnancy and family responsibilities must apply and be seen as applying equally to men and to women. In the context of pregnancy and work, it is essential that policies and laws treat pregnancy and family responsibilities as neither a disability nor a liability, rather as part of the normal life cycle encountered by many workforce participants.[176,177]

---

170 *Ex p HV McKay* (1907) 2 CAR 1. See also S Deery and D Plowman, *Australian Industrial Relations* (3rd ed, 1991, McGraw-Hill Book Company), 353; Hunter, n 164 above.

171 Hunter, n 164 above.

172 J Wajcman, *Managing Like a Man: Women and Men in Corporate Management* (1999, Allen & Unwin), 26.

173 Ibid.

174 See *Parental Leave Case* (1990) 36 IR 1 sub nom *Federated Miscellaneous Workers Union v Angus Nugent & Son Pty Ltd*; Lifschitz, n 170 above, 18; Hunter, n 164 above.

175 S Fitzpatrick (Submission no 12).

176 Australian Council of Trade Unions, Queensland Branch (Submission no 50).

177 Para 2.11 *et seq*.

2.60 As a generality, women's lives are not like men's; rather work and other aspects of social life are organized around men, excluding and disadvantaging women. Requiring women to compare themselves with men and measuring unequal treatment against the male norm can normalize, rather than challenge, those discriminatory patterns. Thus a woman disadvantaged because she does not work late into the night, or network in clubs and bars, may be treated the 'same' as any similarly situated man (that is, a man who does not work late into the night, or network in clubs and bars) and so is not directly discriminated against. However, such an analysis ignores the fact that women and men are not similarly situated and pays no regard to the social realities of women's lives. Indirect discrimination does address some discriminatory patterns at work and in other areas of life but this has been slow in fundamentally altering work and social norms. This is addressed further in Chapter 6.

2.61 As with race discrimination, tackling gender discrimination will require a brave political commitment to radical reform of the law.

(6) The Disability Discrimination Acts 1995 and 2005

2.62 Protection against disability discrimination in the UK did not arrive until 1995[178] with the enactment of the Disability Discrimination Act 1995 (DDA), a total of 16 Private Members' Bills introduced by disability rights campaigners having previously been rejected. Even then, and despite widespread disability discrimination, it took significant lobbying on the part of disability rights organizations for the DDA to be enacted.[179]

2.63 Prior to the enactment of the DDA, disabled people had no enforceable rights against disability discrimination. Instead disability was seen principally as a 'welfare' issue, to be addressed through social security schemes and, on occasion, tort law.[180] The Disabled Persons (Employment) Act 1944, introduced to address the concerns about returning wounded service men, provided a quota system for the employment of disabled people. However, the Act was enforceable only by criminal sanction rather than by individuals; furthermore, it allowed for employer-wide exemptions and was honoured more in the breach than in the observance. Its ineffectiveness as a protection against disability discrimination is starkly illustrated by the fact that, despite widespread non-compliance, there was not a single criminal prosecution under it.[181]

---

178 And indeed most of its more important provisions were not brought into force until the end of 1996 and some much later, see below.

179 S Fredman, *Discrimination Law* (2002, OUP), 58–59; and see M Stacey, 'Eradicating Disability Discrimination At Work' in A McColgan (ed), *Achieving Equality at Work* (2003, IER) 69–70.

180 Fredman, n 179 above, 58.

181 C Palmer, T Gill, K Monaghan, G Moon, and M Stacey, ed A McColgan, *Discrimination Law Handbook* (2002, LAG), 133.

The apparently successful enactment of the Americans with Disabilities Act 1990 (ADA) provided increased impetus for legislation in the UK. The ADA prohibits discrimination on the basis of disability in a similar way to the US Civil Rights Act 1964 (in respect of race) and covers similar areas, namely: employment, State and local government, public accommodations, commercial facilities, transportation, and telecommunications. It followed the publication of the National Council on Disability's report *Toward Independence*[182] in February 1986, which first recommended the enactment of a comprehensive law requiring equal opportunity for individuals with disabilities, and provided an outline of what is now the ADA. The Council Bill was initially introduced in Congress in 1988, supported by the Congressional Task Force on Rights and Empowerment of Americans with Disabilities.[183] The Bill was reintroduced in May 1989 and amended and passed by the Senate on 7 September 1989.[184] Following scrutiny in five separate House Committees, the House of Representatives passed the Bill on 22 May 1990; and after two conferences between the House and Senate to resolve differences over the Bill, the ADA was passed by Congress and signed into law on 26 July 1990.[185] **2.64**

'Disability' is defined by the ADA in section 3(2), as meaning 'with respect to a person (a) a physical or mental impairment that substantially limits one or more of the major life activities of such individual; (b) a record of such an impairment; or (c) being regarded as having such an impairment'. It therefore, importantly, covers *perceived* disability as well as actual disability, importing a social model of disability, as is discussed further later.[186] Importantly too, the ADA introduced the concept of 'reasonable accommodations' by defining discrimination as including 'not making reasonable accommodations to the known physical or mental limitations of an otherwise qualified individual with a disability who is an applicant or employee, unless [the] covered entity can demonstrate that the accommodation would impose an undue hardship on the operation of the business of such covered entity'.[187] **2.65**

---

182 The National Council on Disability is an independent federal agency established by Title IV of the Rehabilitation Act of 1973 (29 USC 780 *et seq*) as amended. It makes recommendations to the President and Congress 'to enhance the quality of life for all Americans with disabilities and their families'. It is composed of 15 members appointed by the President and confirmed by the US Senate: <http:www.ncd.gov>.

183 For an extensive history of the ADA see further <http://www.adata.org/whatsada-history.aspx>.

184 Ibid.

185 Ibid. ADA, s 2 comprehensively sets out the aims and purposes of the Act, and in particular notes the 'findings' of Congress which led to the introduction of the Act.

186 Chapter 5.

187 ADA, s 102(b)(5)(A). And see also s 201 (State and local governments' activities); s 302(2).

2.66 The British (Conservative) Government's consultation paper preceding the DDA referred in terms to the ADA. It also revealed the Government's reluctance to enact a rights-based scheme. The document opened with the following words:

> The Government's strategy for tackling discrimination is through education and persuasion, backed by practical help . . . The current legislative framework is established by the quota scheme.

The paper identified three alternatives to the then existing scheme under the Disabled Persons (Employment) Act 1944, namely a strengthened quota scheme; a voluntary approach based on education and persuasion; and, lastly, a new statutory anti-discrimination right. As to the latter, the Government conceded that the 'Government does not consider that voluntary action on its own would satisfy the reasonable aspirations of disabled people or provide sufficient assurance that acts of unjustified discrimination would be adequately resolved'. Nevertheless, the consultation document suggested that the Government was prepared to countenance something other than that which would 'satisfy the reasonable aspirations of disabled people':

> The Government would welcome views on these options. While there would appear to be particular advantages in establishing a new statutory right . . . the Government would be prepared to reconsider the position if there was substantial support for a workable alternative.

2.67 Notwithstanding the palpable reluctance of the Government to enact rights-based legislation,[188] the DDA was finally enacted in 1995. In its original enactment the DDA regulated disability discrimination in employment and related fields;[189] in the access to and provision of goods, facilities, and services;[190] and in the management, buying, or renting of land or property.[191] However, many of its important provisions were not brought into force for some time, in respect of some provisions not until 1999,[192] and, in the case of the important duties on service

---

188 See the observations too of M Stacey, 'Eradicating Disability Discrimination At Work' in A McColgan (ed), *Achieving Equality at Work* (2003, IER) 70.

189 DDA, ss 4–18.

190 DDA, ss 19–21, excluding education and transport, s 19(5) and (6).

191 DDA, ss 22–24.

192 In October 1999, see the provisions making it unlawful for service providers to fail to comply with the duty to make reasonable adjustments for disabled people where the existence of a practice, policy, or procedure makes it impossible or unreasonably difficult for disabled persons to make use of a service they provide; so as to provide a reasonable alternative method of making the service in question available to disabled persons where the existence of a physical feature makes it impossible or unreasonably difficult for disabled persons to make use of a service they provide and the failure to comply with the duty to take reasonable steps to provide auxiliary aids or services to enable or facilitate the use by disabled people of services which the service provider provides (unless that would necessitate a permanent alteration to the physical fabric of a building or unless such failure is justified) (DDA, ss 19, 20(2), 21(1), 21(2)(d), 21(4)): DDA 1995 (Commencement Order No 6) Order SI 1999/1190; Disability Discrimination (Services and Premises) Regulations 1999 SI 1999/1191, Reg 4.

providers to make adjustments to the physical features of their premises,[193] not until 2004. In addition, though in its original enactment the DDA made provision in the fields of education and transport, it did not outlaw discrimination in these fields or provide any individually enforceable rights.[194] Further, no Commission (comparable to the CRE and the Equal Opportunities Commission) was established to address disability discrimination and promote the DDA. Instead, the DDA created the National Disability Council with very limited powers which did not include powers to assist litigants in claims under the DDA or to take enforcement action in their own name. The primary function of the National Disability Council[195] was to advise the Secretary of State on, amongst other things, matters relevant to the elimination of discrimination against disabled people and people who have had a disability.[196] It also had responsibility for preparing proposals for codes of practice.[197]

Shortly after the Labour Government came to office in 1997, it established the Disability Rights Task Force to give effect to its manifesto commitment to deliver 'comprehensive and enforceable civil rights for disabled people'.[198] Its formal terms of reference were: **2.68**

> To consider how best to secure comprehensive, enforceable civil rights for disabled people within the context of our wider society, and to make recommendations on the role and functions of a Disability Rights Commission. To provide the latter by March 1998 and to provide a full report of its recommendations on wider issues no later than July 1999.
>
> The Task Force will take full account of the costs as well as the benefits of any proposals, so far as is quantifiable and practicable, and in particular ensure that its recommendations for a Disability Rights Commission achieve value for money for the taxpayer.[199]

193 In October 2004, see the provisions making it unlawful for service providers to fail to comply with the duty to make reasonable adjustments for disabled people where the existence of a physical feature (for example, one arising from the design or construction of a building or the approach or access to premises) makes it impossible or unreasonably difficult for disabled persons to make use of a service, when the service provider will be under a duty to take reasonable steps to remove the feature; alter it so that it no longer has that effect; provide a reasonable means of avoiding the feature and to take reasonable steps to provide auxiliary aids or services to enable or facilitate the use by disabled people of services which the service provider provides even such steps as would necessitate a permanent alteration to the physical fabric of a building sections (DDA, ss19, 20(2), 21(2), and 21(4)): Disability Discrimination (Services and Premises) Regulations 1999 SI 1999/1191, Reg 4.

194 DDA, ss 29–31, 32–49.

195 Created by DDA, s 50 in its original enactment.

196 DDA, s 50(2)(a).

197 Which would be subject to approval by the Secretary of State and then by each House of Parliament pursuant to the negative resolution procedure (DDA, s 52).

198 *From Exclusion to Inclusion, Final report of the Disability Rights Task Force* (1999), The Disability Task Force para 2, available at <http://www.dft.gov.uk/stellent/groups/dft_mobility/documents/page/dft_mobility_611415-01.hcsp#P26_625>.

199 Ibid.

2.69 In April 1998 the Task Force produced an interim report on the role and functions of a Disability Rights Commission and the main difficulties with the DDA as mentioned above. In response to the Task Force's first report, made to Government in March 1998, the Government issued a White Paper consultation in July of the same year: *Promoting disabled people's rights—creating a Disability Rights Commission fit for the 21st Century.*[200] This in turn led to the Disability Rights Commission Bill which received Royal Assent in July 1999 and as such became the Disability Rights Commission Act 1999. This established the Disability Rights Commission (DRC) from April 2000[201] and abolished the National Disability Council.[202]

2.70 The Task Force made a number of further recommendations for change in its final report, *From Exclusion to Inclusion, Final Report of the Disability Rights Task Force.*[203] Many of these have been implemented. The Task Force, in particular, recommended that there be major extensions to the coverage of the DDA. As mentioned above, the DDA as enacted in 1995 excluded education from the scope of the unlawful acts it created.[204] This was a significant flaw which the Task Force recommended should be remedied by the creation of new rights for disabled people not to be discriminated against by schools and local education authorities and in further, higher, and adult education.[205] The Task Force recommended that the partial exclusion of transport from the DDA[206] should be remedied.[207] Importantly too, the Task Force recommended that 'the public sector should have a duty to promote the equalization of opportunities for disabled people'.[208] The Task Force also recommended that the definition of disability should be extended to cover people with HIV from diagnosis and people with cancer from when it had significant consequences on their lives.[209]

200 ISBN 0101397720.

201 The Commissions and their powers are addressed in Chap 15.

202 Disability Rights Commission Act 1999, s 1. And see SI 2000/880, Art 2, Sch 2 for the bringing into force of the relevant provisions of the Disability Rights Commission Act 1999.

203 (1999), The Disability Task Force, available at <http://www.dft.gov.uk/stellent/groups/dft_mobility/documents/page/dft_mobility_611415-01.hcsp#P26_625>.

204 DDA, s 19(5)(a) and (6).

205 *From Exclusion to Inclusion, Final Report of the Disability Rights Task Force* (1999) Chap 2, para 4.

206 DDA, s 19(5)(b).

207 *From Exclusion to Inclusion, Final Report of the Disability Rights Task Force* (1999) Chap 2, paras 15–16 and Chap 7, para 7.2.

208 Ibid, Chap 2, para 7.

209 Ibid, Chap 2, para 11. Amendments to the DDA and the enactment of the DDA 2005 has remedied many of the deficiencies identified. See Chap 5 for the meaning of 'disability' and Chaps 7 onwards for the acts now made unlawful by the DDA 1995.

In November 1999, the Government acknowledged the inadequacies of the DDA in its published Equality Statement, in which it also set out its approach to tackling disability discrimination. It stated that: **2.71**

> eliminating unjustified discrimination where it exists and making equality of opportunity a reality is at the heart of the Government's agenda . . . It is not only inherently right, it is also essential for Britain's future economic and social success . . . We will ensure that the right legislative framework and institutional arrangements are in place . . . to challenge discrimination and deliver fair treatment to allow everyone to develop and contribute to their full potential.
>
> . . .
>
> The DDA lags behind sex and race legislation in the protection it provides for disabled people. The establishment of a Disability Rights Commission . . . will address one of the Act's major weaknesses but there are other gaps in coverage . . . we are committed to improving the rights of disabled people.[210]

The Government provided an interim response to the Task Force's recommendations in March 2000.[211] In that response the Government confirmed its commitment to introducing legislation to address the recommendations on rights for disabled children and adults in education. It also addressed those aspects of the Task Force's recommendations which required non-legislative action, for example its recommendation that Government should do more to raise awareness amongst owners of premises of the benefits of physical adaptations that increase accessibility for disabled people,[212] amongst other things. In its final response to the Task Force's final report, *Towards Inclusion*, the Government invited views from disabled people, their representative bodies, employers, service providers, and public bodies on the recommendations made by the Task Force which required legislation.[213] The Government also made proposals itself regarding those legislative changes that it intended to make. Thereafter the Special Educational Needs and Disability Bill was put before Parliament on 7 December 2000 and enacted to become the Special Educational Needs and Disability Act 2001 (SENDA 2001). In addition, and in the meantime, the Council of Ministers agreed the terms of the Council Directive 2000/78/EC (the Framework Directive), which imposed obligations on Member States to regulate disability discrimination in certain fields.[214] Both of these measures proved very significant, as will be seen in later chapters. **2.72**

---

210 Equality Statement, November 1999 cited in the Government's final response to the Task Force recommendations, March 2001 at paras 1.1 to 1.3.

211 *Interim Government Response to the Report of the Disability Rights Task Force* (2000).

212 Recommendations 6.28 and 6.29.

213 Government final response to Task Force recommendations, *Towards Inclusion*, March 2001, Foreword by Margaret Hodge, MP, Minister for Disabled People.

214 See Chap 4.

2.73 In January 2003 the Government announced its intention to introduce a draft Disability Bill later in the year[215] to implement those recommendations of the Disability Rights Task Force accepted by the Government in its response, *Towards Inclusion*. In April 2003, the DRC published its first review of the DDA, *Disability Equality: Making it Happen*.[216] In that review, the DRC called upon the Government to include in the draft Disability Bill those proposals made in the DRC's review in addition to those made by the Disability Rights Task Force. It observed that:

> Civil rights legislation for disabled people needs to be comprehensive. This is necessary both to establish a clear public principle of equality, and to ensure that all the barriers to disabled people's full participation are removed.[217]

2.74 The DRC also recommended 'consistency' across the different parts of the DDA and where possible between disability and other anti-discrimination legislation.[218] Further, and importantly, the DRC acknowledged that proposals were needed which 'promote[d] systemic change' and that the legislative scheme needed to 'move from relying on individual enforcement towards a proactive approach to disability equality'.[219] By the time of the review, draft Regulations had been published amending the DDA to give effect to the Framework Directive, amongst other things.[220] Further, a Private Members' Bill had been introduced (though eventually unsuccessful) by Bridget Prentice which included a statutory duty upon public authorities to promote equality of opportunity for disabled people.[221] A further Private Members' Bill, sponsored by Neil Gerrard, was passed in November 2002—the Private Hire Vehicles (Carriage of Guide Dogs etc) Act 2002—which had the effect of implementing the Task Force's recommendations that private hire vehicles should not be allowed to refuse to carry service animals.[222]

2.75 Many of the recommendations for change made by the DRC in its review were given effect to by the Disability Discrimination Act 1995 (Amendment) Regulations 2003[223] and the Disability Discrimination Act 2005. The Disability

215 *Disability Equality: Making it Happen* April 2003, Disability Rights Commission, 8.
216 April 2003, Disability Rights Commission.
217 Ibid, 10.
218 Ibid, 10.
219 Ibid, 10.
220 See *Disability Equality: Making it Happen* April 2003, Disability Rights Commission, 13, 14.
221 Ibid, 14.
222 See recommendations 7.3 and 7.4.
223 SI 2003/1673. In addition, the DDA 1995 (Pensions) Regulations 2003 SI 2003/2770 make provision in relation to pensions. They give effect to the provisions of the Framework Directive that address 'pay' (Art 3(c)). The Pensions Regulations create a number of unlawful acts in relation to the provision of pension benefits. They came into force on 1 October 2004. The issues arising from the regulations are discussed in the following chapters.

Discrimination Act 1995 (Amendment) Regulations 2003 were enacted to give purported effect to the Framework Directive. The 2003 Regulations amended the DDA by introducing new concepts of disability discrimination (direct discrimination and harassment) and by extending the scope of the employment-related provisions of the DDA 1995. The most important provisions of the DDA 2005 outlaw discrimination by public authorities,[224] and impose new and wide duties upon public authorities to have due regard to the need to eliminate discrimination of, and harassment against, disabled people; to promote equality of opportunity between disabled persons and other persons; to take steps to take account of disabled persons' disabilities, even where that involves treating disabled persons more favourably than other persons; to promote positive attitudes towards disabled persons; and to have due regard to the need to encourage participation by disabled persons in public life.[225] In addition, the definition of disability is extended for the purposes of the DDA 1995 so as to treat people with HIV infection, cancer, or multiple sclerosis as 'disabled' from the point of diagnosis (going somewhat further than the Task Force's recommendations referred to above), and by the removal of the requirement in the original Act that any mental illness be clinically well-recognized if it is to be regarded as a 'disability' for the Act.[226]

However, not all recommendations on disability law reform have been carried forward. The Government rejected a number of the recommendations made by the Joint Parliamentary Committee established for the purpose of scrutinizing the Bill which eventually became the DDA 2005.[227] For example, the Government rejected[228] the recommendation by the Joint Committee that all progressive conditions should be deemed a disability for the purposes of the DDA from the point of diagnosis, rather than the point at which they begin to have an effect (as required by the DDA),[229] not least because the evidence suggested that the inclusion of some progressive conditions and not others was inconsistent and **2.76**

---

224 DDA 1995, s 21B as amended by the 2005 Act. In force on 4 December 2006: see SI 2005/2774, Art 4(a).

225 DDA 1995, s 49A as amended by the 2005 Act. In force on 4 December 2006: see SI 2005/2774, Art 4(a). The other amendments made, including those affecting clubs and councillors are addressed in later chapters as they arise.

226 Sch 1, para 1(1) of the unamended DDA 1995.

227 *Joint Committee on the Draft Disability Discrimination Bill—First Report* (2004), available at <http://www.parliament.uk/parliamentary_committees/dddb.cfm>. And *The Government's Response to the Report of the Joint Committee on the Draft Disability Discrimination Bill* (15 July 2004), available at, <http://www.parliament.uk/parliamentary_committees/dddb.cfm>.

228 *The Government's Response to the Report of the Joint Committee on the Draft Disability Discrimination Bill* (15 July 2004), available at, <http://www.parliament.uk/parliamentary_committees/dddb.cfm>, at R11.

229 *Joint Committee on the Draft Disability Discrimination Bill—First Report* (2004), para 63.

itself discriminatory.[230] The Government has indicated that whilst they accepted the 'principle' of the recommendation, they were not persuaded that there were any additional progressive conditions where protection would be inadequate after the DDA 2005 was enacted. This does not meet the concerns expressed and identified in the evidence to the Joint Committee. However, the Government did ensure that there were sufficient powers in the DDA to enable the definition of disability to be amended should this prove necessary so as to allow further progressive conditions to be covered more effectively and to address any concerns that might arise from case law, which suggested that the definition was not working in the way intended.[231]

2.77 The Joint Committee also recommended that the DDA be amended so as to protect persons associated with disabled people against discrimination and harassment and to protect persons who are perceived to be disabled against such discrimination and harassment.[232] This would have brought the protection in line with the protection afforded, for example, under the RRA (section 1(1)(a))[233] and would have made it compliant with EC law, in particular with the requirements of the Framework Directive. It is highly likely that the failure to protect people against less favourable treatment 'on grounds of disability' (which would include discrimination by association or a misperception that a particular person is disabled) violates the requirements of the Framework Directive.[234] However, the Government has rejected this recommendation relying on the asymmetrical nature of the protection afforded by the DDA:

> The DDA is unique because it does not generally prohibit discrimination against non-disabled people. Indeed, it actively requires positive action to be taken to ensure a disabled person has equality of access or outcome. This contrasts with the approach taken in other anti-discrimination legislation . . . extending the Act to cover people who associate with disabled people or people who are perceived to be disabled would fundamentally alter the approach taken in the DDA.[235]

This rather misses the point. As research has demonstrated, persons associated with disabled people, for example carers and parents, themselves suffer disadvantage.[236] The DDA does nothing to address this.

2.78 The definition of 'disability' remains controversial. One of the main criticisms from disability campaigners about the model adopted by the DDA is that it,

---

230 Ibid, paras 56–57.

231 Ibid. And see the regulation-making power enacted in Sch 1 para 5 given general effect following the amendments made by s 18 of the 2005 Act.

232 *Joint Committee on the Draft Disability Discrimination Bill—First Report* (2004), available at <http://www.parliament.uk/parliamentary_committees/ddb.cfm.>, para 109.

233 See, for example, *Weathersfield (t/a Van and Truck Rentals) v Sargent* [1999] IRLR 94.

234 Art 2. See discussion in Chaps 4 and 6.

235 R16.

236 J Ballard, *Disabled Parents and Employment* (2004, EOR) 126, 20.

principally,[237] adopts a medical rather than a social concept of disability. As will be discussed in Chapter 5, a social model acknowledges that there is a 'close connection between the limitations experienced by individuals with disabilities, the design and structure of the environments and the attitudes of the general population'.[238] The medical model, on the other hand, addresses disability by regarding it as relating solely to the individual person and their particular impairment. The idea of disability as a social construct places the focus on 'how society (consciously or otherwise) compounds a person's impairment by constructing social and economic processes that fail adequately to take account of the disability in question. In other words, the focus is . . . on how society disables by failing to provide equal opportunities for participation'.[239] The emphasis in the definition of 'disability' in the DDA upon a medical diagnosis undermines any aspiration that it will successfully address disability discrimination as a social phenomenon.

The DRC has recently launched a consultation[240] on the meaning of 'disability'. It **2.79** is expected that the results of the consultation will inform the DRC's position in any discussion in the *Discrimination Law Review*[241] on the contents of a Single Equality Act. The consultation document notes that because of the definition of discrimination, the focus of many disability cases is not whether discrimination has occurred, and indeed sometimes apparently discriminatory behaviour will be admitted, but on whether the claimant is 'disabled' for the purposes of the DDA.[242] The consultation asks for views on the desirability or otherwise of a change to the DDA definition of disability, in particular by a broadening of it to afford legal protection against discrimination on the grounds of impairment, regardless of the level or type of impairment.[243] The DRC has not taken any position at this stage on the desirability of change but highlights a number of advantages and disadvantages in such an approach.[244]

237 Exceptions are the coverage of past disabilities and severe disfigurements in particular, see Chap 5.

238 United Nations Standard Rules on the Equalisation of Opportunities for Persons with Disabilities, para 5, cited by B Doyle, 'Disabled Workers Rights, the DDA and the Un Standard Rules' [1996] 25 ILJ 1, 11; and see, Disability Rights Commission website: <http://www.drc-gb.org/citizenship/howtouse/socialmodel/index.asp>, in its citizenship and disability pages.

239 G Quinn, 'Human rights for people with disabilities', in P Alston (ed), *The EU and Human Rights* (2000, OUP) 287.

240 Definition of disability: Consultation Document (2006) Disability Rights Commission.

241 See Chap 1.

242 Definition of disability: Consultation Document (2006) Disability Rights Commission, para 8.

243 Ibid, para 6.

244 Ibid, paras 7 and 49–67 and paras 49–53, 58, 59 *et seq*.

2.80 The key provisions of the DDA are the reasonable adjustment duties. They have proved very significant indeed. They are discussed further in Chapter 6.

(7) Religion and belief discrimination laws

2.81 Religious discrimination is institutionalized in Britain. The Church of England occupies a privileged space in Britain's constitutional arrangements; 26 Bishops of the Church of England sit in the legislature's upper house, the House of Lords. The position of these 'Lords Spiritual' is unique; no representatives from other religious organizations are entitled as of right to membership of the House of Lords. It is difficult to understand why, in a modern pluralistic liberal democracy, such a position is tolerated. Notwithstanding the wide-ranging constitutional reforms effected and proposed by this Labour Government, the right of senior Church of England Bishops to sit in the Lords is to be retained.[245]

2.82 Other forms of religious discrimination have been addressed. Until recently there was no legal protection against discrimination on the ground of religion and belief in Great Britain.[246] However, as will be seen in Chapter 5, certain 'religious' groups have been characterized as constituting 'ethnic groups'. This coincidence between ethnicity and religion meant that certain religious groups were protected by the RRA 1976 against discrimination connected with their religion; thus, according to case law, both Jews[247] and Sikhs[248] constitute 'racial groups' for the purposes of the RRA 1976. This recognizes the relationship between culture and religion: many people belonging to particular racial groups see their religion as occupying more of a cultural or political space in their lives and may see their 'faith' as less significant to their identity. In Northern Ireland, therefore, where there has been compelling protection against discrimination connected with religion and belief in employment and related fields for some time,[249] it is well understood that this is to address the political and cultural rather than the theological divides between the Catholic and Protestant communities.

2.83 However, the protection afforded to Sikhs and Jews under the RRA was held not to extend to other religious groups, such as Muslims or Rastafarians whose religions have a social and political as well as a theological dimension and yet have not been defined as constituting 'ethnic groups'. Accordingly, there has been a

245 Department for Constitutional Affairs Consultation Paper: Constitutional Reform: Next steps for the House of Lords (September 2003) paras 29 and 70, available at <http://www.dca.gov.uk/consult/holref/index.htm>.

246 The position has been somewhat different in Northern Ireland, as described below.

247 *Seide v Gillette Industries Limited* [1980] IRLR 427.

248 *Mandla (Sewa Singh) v Dowell Lee* [1983] 2 AC 548.

249 The Fair Employment and Treatment (Northern Ireland) Order 1998 SI 1998/ 3162 (NI 21).

distinction between the protections afforded to different religious groups by the anti-discrimination legislation. This has caused a good deal of controversy. Thus, when promoting new law addressing religious discrimination,[250] the Lord Chancellor observed that this 'remedie[d] the anomaly whereby members of some religions are protected against discrimination in the provision of goods, facilities and services, but members of other religion or belief groups are not'.[251]

A similar distinction as between religious groups arose from the outlawing of incitement to racial hatred but not religious hatred[252] and the common law offence of blasphemy. Blasphemy is an indictable offence at common law consisting of the publication of 'contemptuous, reviling, scurrilous or ludicrous matter relating to God, Jesus Christ, the Bible or the formularies of the Church of England' (only).[253] **2.84**

The distinction in protection afforded to different religious groups has been mitigated by a series of legislative measures. Firstly, the Employment Equality (Religion or Belief) Regulations 2003[254] make discrimination connected with a person's religion and belief unlawful in employment and related fields. Secondly, Part 2 of the Equality Act 2006 outlaws discrimination and makes related provision connected to religion and belief in the provision of goods, facilities, and services; in the disposal and management of premises; in education; and by public authorities.[255] Thirdly, the Racial and Religious Hatred Act 2006 criminalizes 'threatening words or behaviour, or displays [or] written material which is threatening . . . if [such is] . . . intend[ed] thereby to stir up religious hatred'.[256] The latter provision was highly controversial and led to a campaign by well-known comedians[257] concerned about the censoring of religious criticism. However, the difficulty they faced was that religious criticism was in fact already outlawed, but only in relation to certain religions. This discriminatory distinction had a pernicious effect on non-protected religious groups and was plainly difficult to justify. In the present environment of increased hostility towards Muslims, in particular, a position where the law protected Christians, Sikhs, and Jews but left Muslims as such unprotected was simply unsustainable. **2.85**

The trigger for the first non-discrimination measures, found in the Religion or Belief Regulations, was the impact of EC law. As will be discussed in Chapter 4, **2.86**

250 The Equality Act 2006, discussed below.
251 Lord Falconer, cited in M Rubenstein, 'Equality Act 2006: A Guide' [2006] EOR 151, 25.
252 Public Order Act 1986, s 18.
253 'Criminal Law, Evidence and Procedure' in *Halsbury's Laws of England*, para 348.
254 SI 2003/1660, Reg 25.
255 At the time of writing, it is expected that these provisions will be brought into force in April 2007.
256 Racial and Religious Hatred Act 2006, Sch 1, which amends the Public Order Act 1986.
257 <http://news.bbc.co.uk/1/hi/uk_politics/4073997.stm>.

new EC legislation in the form of the Framework Directive has compelled action by Member States and created a context for driving forward broader measures.

2.87 The new protections against religious discrimination reflect the schemes adopted to address other forms of discrimination, particularly race discrimination,[258] albeit in a more limited way.[259] Accordingly the comments above about the schemes are equally applicable. The Human Rights Act 1998 also provides key protection against religious discrimination and this is addressed in Chapter 4.

(8) Sexual orientation discrimination laws

2.88 Protection against sexual orientation discrimination comes late in the history of UK equality law. Discrimination and prejudice against gay men and lesbians, and against others who have challenged society's perceptions of 'normal' sexual identities and relations (such as transgendered people), have been institutionalized and historically widespread. Feminists and queer theorists have argued that 'sexuality' and supposed norms, and therefore 'differences', around sexuality are socially constructed and exist within a broader social framework. Such norms have a cultural and historic place and:

> heterosexuality is a complex matrix of discourses, institutions, and so on, that has become normalized in our culture, thus making particular relationships, lifestyles, and identities, seem natural, ahistorical, and universal. In short, heterosexuality, as it is currently understood and experienced, is a (historically and culturally specific) truth-effect of systems of power/knowledge. Given this, its dominant position and current configuration are contestable and open to change.[260]

2.89 Society is structured around a heterosexual ideal, with its related assumptions about monogamy and children, and gay people are regarded as 'different' therefore. Law forms part of those structures. Heterosexualized and hetero-normative law is seen in obvious places like the law of marriage and in the criminalizing of some forms of sexual conduct[261] but in less obvious places as in the legal construct of 'family' (which usually has at its centre a presumed monogamous, and, at least until recently, opposite-sex relationship).[262]

---

258 The Employment Equality (Religion or Belief) Regulations 2003 define direct discrimination as less favourable treatment 'on grounds of religion or belief' (Reg 3). This is somewhat different to the meaning of direct discrimination provided for in the SDA and the DDA, as to which see Chap 6.

259 For example, there are no statutory duties on public bodies applicable to religion, as such, as compared to, for example, race (see RRA 1976, s 71A).

260 N Sullivan, *A Critical Introduction to Queer Theory* (2003, Edinburgh University Press), 39–40.

261 In addition, sexual discrimination against gay men and lesbians has a long history with gay sex criminalized until 1967 and in Northern Ireland until later: *Dudgeon v UK* (1981) 4 EHRR 149.

262 See, for example, the situation in *Secretary of State for Work and Pensions v M* [2006] UKHL 11.

Institutionalized discrimination against gay men and lesbians has been in some ways more resistant to change than some other forms of discrimination. That resistance can be seen, for example, in the case of *Secretary of State for Work and Pensions v M* discussed above. It may be that this is because any undermining of the ideal of heterosexuality and all of its constructions, including patriarchy, the oppression of women and children in families, and the dominance of men, is more challenging to society than, for example, the formal equal treatment of women and ethnic minorities in public spaces, like work. **2.90**

As mentioned in Chapter 1, much recent discrimination against gay men and lesbians arises from the absence of a right to marry and a broader failure to recognize their unions. This has meant that all the social protections afforded to partners, married or otherwise, were until recently denied to gay men and lesbians. These included, for example, the absence of a right to inherit the tenancy of a partner on the same terms as a straight partner.[263] Respectable political arguments can be made that the extension of marriage and the replicating of features of heterosexuality should not be sought by progressive gay men and lesbians because of all the baggage that heterosexuality brings, as described above. However, from an equality perspective, depriving gay and lesbian couples of the benefits enjoyed by persons in straight unions would seem plainly unjustified. The stigmatizing of gay relationships by their non-recognition has increasingly been seen as incompatible with fundamental rights. The enactment of the Human Rights Act 1998, addressed in Chapter 4, provided an imperative for removing discrimination between gay and straight unions. In consequence of that and of skilled lobbying by organizations such as Stonewall, as well as a sympathetic Labour Government, a consultation paper was issued by the Department of Trade and Industry in 2003 proposing arrangements for the formal recognition of gay unions. In the foreword to the paper, *Civil Partnership: a framework for the legal recognition of same-sex couples*, Jacqui Smith, Minister of State for Industry and the Regions and Deputy Minister for Women and Equality, observed that: **2.91**

> Today there are thousands of same-sex couples living in stable and committed partnerships. These relationships span many years with couples looking after each other, caring for their loved ones and actively participating in society; in fact, living in exactly the same way as any other family. They are our families, our friends, our colleagues and our neighbours. Yet the law rarely recognizes their relationship. Many have been refused a hospital visit to see their seriously ill partner, or have been refused their rightful place at their partner's funeral. Others find themselves unable to access employment benefits reserved only for married partners. Couples who have supported each other financially throughout their working lives often have no way of gaining pension rights. Grieving partners can find themselves unable to stay in their

[263] *Fitzpatrick v Sterling Housing Association Ltd* [2001] 1 AC 27.

shared home or to inherit the possessions they have shared for years when one partner dies suddenly without leaving a will. In so many areas, as far as the law is concerned, same-sex relationships simply do not exist.

That is not acceptable.[264]

2.92 Following the consultation document, the Civil Partnership Act 2004 was enacted. The Act creates a structure for the establishment and formal recognition of 'civil partnerships'. These are defined by section 1 of the Act as follows:

(1) A civil partnership is a relationship between two people of the same sex ('civil partners')—
 (a) which is formed when they register as civil partners of each other,
 . . .
 (b) which they are treated under Chapter 2 of Part 5 as having formed (at the time determined under that Chapter) by virtue of having registered an overseas relationship.

As can be seen from section 1, a civil partnership is created by a civil registration process or by the automatic recognition of certain overseas same-sex relationships as civil partnerships. The Act provides the bureaucratic mechanisms necessary for the purposes of the civil registration process. There are express distinctions between this process and marriage. Thus, a civil partnership may not be effected on religious premises or in a religious ceremony.[265]

2.93 The consultation document, *Civil Partnership: a framework for the legal recognition of same-sex couples*, made it plain that marriage would not be available for same-sex couples[266] and nor would civil partnerships be available for opposite-sex couples[267] thus maintaining the impression and legal reality of *difference*. In excluding gay couples from marriage and straight couples from civil partnerships, the Civil Partnership Act creates a *separate but equal* fiction. A *separate but equal* doctrine which sustains distinctions between disadvantaged and advantaged classes is one which had found favour in the context of race in the US prior to the US Supreme Court decision in *Brown v Board of Education of Topeka* (1954).[268] It is one which

---

264 *Civil Partnership: a framework for the legal recognition of same-sex couples* (2003) Women and Equality Unit, 9.

265 Civil Partnership Act 2004, ss 6(1) and 2(3).

266 *Civil Partnership: a framework for the legal recognition of same-sex couples* (2003) Women and Equality Unit, para 1.3 ('It is a matter of public record that the Government has no plans to introduce same-sex marriage').

267 Ibid, para 1.4.

268 347 US 483. Available at: <http://laws.findlaw.com/us/347/483.html> ('To separate [children] from others of similar age and qualifications solely because of their race generates a feeling of inferiority as to their status in the community that may affect their hearts and minds in a way unlikely ever to be undone . . . in the field of public education the doctrine of "separate but equal" has no place. Separate educational facilities are inherently unequal', p 494).

is difficult to reconcile with a liberal concept of equality. Indeed it suggests a concession to those lobbies which consider that gay and lesbian unions should be accommodated but do not see them as equally socially valuable as compared with straight unions and thus not worthy of recognition through marriage. This was reflected recently in some judicial observations. Thus in *Ghaidan v Godin-Mendoza*[269] Lord Millett observed:

> Persons cannot be or be treated as married to each other or live together as husband and wife unless they are of the opposite sex. It is noticeable that, now that Parliament is introducing remedial legislation, it has not sought to do anything as silly as to treat same sex relationships as marriages, whether legal or de facto. It pays them the respect to which they are entitled by treating them as conceptually different but entitled to equality of treatment.[270]

Notwithstanding the legislatively mandated distinction between gay and straight couples, the Civil Partnership Act has made a very significant difference to the rights of gay and lesbian people. The Act repeals the provisions found in other statutes which define families and couples (for the purpose of imposing burdens or granting benefits) around a heterosexual norm so as to exclude gay couples. An example of such a provision could be seen in *M* which concerned the Child Support Act 1991 and regulations made under it.[271] The regulations defined 'couple' and 'family' for the purposes of calculating child support, as follows: **2.94**

> In these Regulations unless the context otherwise requires—
>
> . . .
>
> 'couple' means a married or unmarried couple;
>
> . . .
>
> 'family' means
>
> (a) a married or unmarried couple (including the members of a polygamous marriage);
> (b) a married or unmarried couple (including the members of a polygamous marriage) and any child or children living with them for whom at least one member of that couple has day-to-day care;
> (c) where a person who is not a member of a married or unmarried couple has day-to-day care of a child or children, that person and any such child or children;
>
> . . .
>
> 'married couple' means a man and a woman who are married to each other and are members of the same household;

269 [2004] 2 AC 557.
270 Para 82.
271 Child Support (Maintenance Assessment and Special Cases) Regulations 1992, SI 1992/1815.

. . .

'partner' means—

(a) in relation to a member of a married or unmarried couple who are living together, the other member of that couple;

(b) in relation to a member of a polygamous marriage, any other member of that marriage with whom he lives;

. . .

'unmarried couple' means a man and a woman who are not married to each other but are living together as husband and wife.[272]

Accordingly, a same-sex partner was not to be regarded as a member of the absent parent's family or a 'partner'. That position, which reflected the provision made in other legislation including in the social security sphere, has now changed. Thus, for example, the Civil Partnership Act (and in particular regulations made under it[273]) has amended the definition in the child support regulations described above so as to define a 'couple' as:

(a) a man and woman who are married to each other and are members of the same household;

(b) a man and woman who are not married to each other but are living together as husband and wife;

(c) two people of the same sex who are civil partners of each other and are members of the same household; or

(d) two people of the same sex who are not civil partners of each other but are living together as if they were civil partners.

2.95 The regulations therefore now recognize gay and lesbian partnerships (whether formally registered or not) like opposite-sex relationships, and their definitions of 'family' are centred on the new definition of couple.[274] The Civil Partnership Act (and regulations under it) makes similar amendments to other legislation containing discriminatory definitions of 'couples', 'families', and the like.

2.96 In addition, the Civil Partnership Act provides for the breakdown of a civil partnership in much the same way as marriage; it also amends laws relating to children, the succession of tenancies, wills, and inheritance, social security, child support, taxation, and domestic violence[275] to provide gay and lesbian partners with

---

272 Regulation 1(2).

273 Civil Partnership (Pensions, Social Security and Child Support) (Consequential, etc Provisions) Order 2005 SI 2005/2877, Sch 4, para 2(2).

274 See Civil Partnership (Pensions, Social Security and Child Support) (Consequential, etc Provisions) Order 2005 SI 2005/2877, Sch 4, para 2(2).

275 For a summary see N Gray and D Brazil, *Blackstone's Guide to the Civil Partnership Act 2004* (2005, Oxford).

much the same rights as straight partners. There remains some discrimination in occupational pensions, with any rights afforded having only limited retrospective effect so continuing some discrimination in relation to partnership benefits.[276]

The Civil Partnership Act has, therefore, remedied much discrimination found in other statutory schemes. As to non-discrimination *rights* for gay men and lesbians, these are found in the Employment Equality (Sexual Orientation) Regulations[277] (the Sexual Orientation Regulations). As with the Religion or Belief Regulations, and as discussed further in Chapter 4, this legislation against sexual orientation discrimination, in the employment and related fields only, was driven by EC law and reflects the schemes adopted to address other forms of discrimination, particularly race discrimination,[278] albeit in a more limited way.[279] Accordingly the comments above about the schemes generally are equally valid. **2.97**

In addition, a late amendment to the Equality Bill (which became the Equality Act 2006), at its third reading in the House of Lords, introduced a regulation-making power which allows the Secretary of State to make provision outlawing discrimination and harassment on grounds of sexual orientation in wider fields and, in particular, in the provision of goods, facilities, and services, in housing, in education, and in the exercising of public authority functions.[280] Unlike in the case of religious discrimination, the Equality Act does not itself create any unlawful acts connected with sexual orientation in these fields. This reflects the lateness of the amendment to the Bill which followed a well organized campaign led by the gay and lesbian campaigning group Stonewall.[281] The Government has now issued a consultation paper,[282] and regulations outlawing sexual orientation discrimination across a wider range of activities are expected to be brought into force in April 2007. **2.98**

---

276 Civil Partnership (Contracted-out Occupational and Appropriate Personal Pension Schemes) (Surviving Civil Partners) Order 2005 SI 2050/2005; Civil Partnership (Miscellaneous and Consequential Provisions) Order 2005 SI 3029/2005.

277 SI 1661/2003.

278 The Employment Equality (Religion or Belief) Regulations 2003 define direct discrimination as less favourable treatment 'on grounds of religion or belief' (Reg 3). This is somewhat different to the meaning of direct discrimination provided for in the SDA and the DDA, as to which see Chap 6.

279 For example, there are no statutory duties on public bodies applicable to religion, as such, as compared to, for example, race (see RRA 1976, s 71A).

280 Equality Act 2006, s 81.

281 *Give us the Goods* (2005–06), Stonewall website, <http://www.stonewall.org.uk/campaigns/605.asp>.

282 *Getting Equal: Proposals to Outlaw Sexual Orientation Discrimination in the Provision of Goods & Services* (2006) Women and Equality Unit.

2.99 As to transgenderism, the law has responded more quickly to discrimination against transpersons. As will be seen in Chapter 4, domestic law was first required to respond because at the European level the concept of 'sex' found in the sex equality Directives[283] was held to be a broad enough concept as to embrace transgenderism, and accordingly discrimination against transsexual people as such was unlawful under EC sex equality law.[284] This was at a time when the European Court of Justice was declining to give a meaning to the concepts of sex discrimination which would embrace sexual orientation discrimination, as is further discussed in Chapter 4, suggesting that gender norms are more amenable to *changing* genders than to non-conforming within a gender. This idea is reflected in the views of some feminists who argue that the phenomenon of gender reassignment is profoundly conservative in that it reinforces gender norms rather than challenging them.[285] Germaine Greer, in her derisorily entitled chapter 'Pantomime Dames', argues that:

> As sufferers from gender role distress themselves, women must sympathise with transsexuals but a feminist must argue that the treatment for gender role distress is not mutilation of the sufferer but radical change of gender roles . . .
>
> Sex-change surgery is profoundly conservative in that it reinforces sharply contrasting gender roles by shaping individuals to fit them.[286]

In any event, as discussed further in Chapter 4, as a result of EC law, the SDA was amended to provide some limited protection against discrimination on the grounds of gender reassignment.[287] The Gender Recognition Act 2004 now provides a framework for recognizing a change in sex.[288]

2.100 The Human Rights Act 1998 also provides key protection against sexual orientation discrimination and discrimination against transgendered persons, and this is addressed in Chapter 4.

(9) Age discrimination laws

2.101 As mentioned in Chapter 1, protection against age discrimination as such has come last in the history of the UK's anti-discrimination enactments—'age

---

283 As to which see Chap 4 below.

284 *P v S and Cornwall County Council* Case C-13/94 [1996] ICR 795; [1996] ECR I-2143, ECJ; [1996] IRLR 347; *KB v National Health Service Pensions Agency and Anor* Case C-117/01 [2004] ICR 781; [2004] IRLR 240; *Richards v Secretary of State for Work and Pensions* Case C-423/04 [2006].

285 However, for a critique, see S Whittle, 'Gender Fucking or Fucking Gender?' in I Morland and A Willox (ed.) *Queer Theory* (2005, Palgrave) 115.

286 G Greer, *The Whole Woman* (1999, Anchor), 71.

287 SDA 1975, s 2A applicable to employment and related fields only, reflecting the scope of then EC law (see Chap 4 for further discussion). The position will have to change when the UK implements the Gender Goods and Services Directive described in Chap 4.

288 Discussed in Chap 5.

discrimination is a relative newcomer to the equality arena'.[289] There has, on the other hand, been much protective legislation addressing groups of people who are vulnerable by reason of age. In the UK this has been so particularly in the case of children, in respect of whom for many decades there has been legislation against exploitation through work,[290] sex,[291] and social welfare law.[292] In addition, the other main anti-discrimination enactments protect all persons irrespective of age, and therefore a black or disabled child, for example, discriminated against at school will have a claim under the RRA or DDA as the case may be. Further, some 'age' discrimination might constitute indirect sex or race discrimination. A rule, for example, that persons retire at a certain age might disadvantage men or women depending upon the occupational pool affected[293] and may be indirectly sexually discriminatory. Other upper age limits may be both indirectly sexually[294] and racially[295] discriminatory. However, until recently there was no explicit anti-age discrimination legislation. This may be contrasted with the position elsewhere.

In the US for example, the Age Discrimination in Employment Act was passed by Congress in 1967 and protected workers between the ages of 40 and 65. It appears 65 was chosen as the upper limit because at that time it was the usual or at least a very common retirement age.[296] In 1986 the age cap was removed altogether, effectively abolishing mandatory retirement, but the lower age limit has been retained. As well as this Federal law, every state now has some sort of age discrimination law of its own[297] and some do not specify any particular age for the purposes of acquiring the protection of the anti-age discrimination legislation.[298] In addition to the Age Discrimination in Employment Act, the Age Discrimination Act, another Federal statute, was enacted in 1975 and this applies to all programmes and activities that receive support from Federal Government. Such are not allowed to discriminate 'on the basis of age'—and that includes any age. However, the Age Discrimination Act does not apply to actions that 'reasonably take into **2.102**

---

289 S Fredman and S Spencer, *Age as an Equality Issue, Legal and Policy Perspectives* (2003, Hart), 1.

290 Children and Young Persons Act 1933, s 18 (no child may be employed under the age of 14 years old).

291 See Sexual Offence Act 2003, ss 47 and 49 (paying for sexual services of a child and controlling a child prostitute or a child involved in pornography).

292 Children Act 1989 and Child Support Act 1991, for example.

293 *British Airways plc v Starmer* [2005] IRLR 862.

294 *Rutherford and anor v Secretary of State for Trade and Industry (No 2)* [2004] EWCA Civ 1186; [2004] IRLR 892.

295 *Perera v The Civil Service Commission* [1983] ICR 428; [1983] IRLR 166 (though unsuccessful on its facts).

296 L Friedman, 'Age Discrimination Law; some remarks on the American experience' in S Fredman and S Spencer (eds), *Age as an Equality Issue, Legal and Policy Perspectives* (2003, Hart) 175.

297 Ibid, 176.

298 Ibid.

account age as a factor necessary to the normal operation . . . of the programme or activity'; or 'benefits or assistance'. This has resulted in the Age Discrimination Act having limited effect.[299] The Age Discrimination in Employment Act has been more influential in addressing age discrimination, notwithstanding its limitations. The groups most likely to be protected by the Act are men in general, then men in their 50s, and then men in their 50s from the professional/managerial grades.[300] This is important because history shows such a group to be disadvantaged by age stereotyping. However, they are not the only group affected by age discrimination. This is so particularly where age combines with other characteristics, like gender (with women more likely to take gaps during their working years so making them older than some of their peers), race (arising from the fact that newly arrived communities often have to start from a lower level in the labour market at an older age and/or re-qualify), and disability. Further, young people are often disadvantaged by stereotyping and other discriminatory practices directed at them.

2.103 In addition, the US anti-age discrimination statute applies only in the context of employment. Ireland has adopted a more comprehensive model. Its Employment Equality Acts 1998 and 2004 and the Equal Status Acts 2000 and 2004 protect against discrimination connected with age not only in the employment context but also in relation to the provision of goods, services, accommodation, and clubs (as indeed does Australia's Age Discrimination Act 2004, mentioned below). Notwithstanding the wide scope of the protection against age discrimination, the provisions have 'proved relatively unproblematic'.[301] Most of the age discrimination cases outside the employment field have arisen in the context of the provision of goods and services 'indicating the ongoing existence of many prejudicial age-based assumptions that are discriminatory in effect and yet will remain unchallenged if equality legislation is confined to the employment context'.[302] However, there are criticisms of the Irish model. The exemptions were 'exceptionally broad'[303] and this reduced the efficacy of the legislation giving it a minimalist impact.[304]

---

299 Not, however, no effect. It would, it appears, prohibit a medical school, eg, which gets money from the Federal Government, from adopting a blanket age bar: L Friedman, 'Age Discrimination Law; some remarks on the American experience' in S Fredman and S Spencer (ed), *Age as an Equality Issue, Legal and Policy Perspectives* (2003, Hart) 177.

300 Ibid, 182.

301 C O'Cinneide, 'Comparative European Perspectives' in S Fredman and S Spencer (eds), *Age as an Equality Issue, Legal and Policy Perspectives* (2003, Hart), 207.

302 Ibid.

303 Ibid, 208.

304 This might be contrasted with the Dutch model which adopts a general objective justification test. This may be said to introduce less certainty but allows sufficient flexibility to have regard to particular circumstances and developing conditions.

In addition, the Employment Equality Act applies only 'in relation to persons above the maximum age at which a person is statutorily obliged to attend school',[305] and an employer may set a minimum age, not exceeding 18 years, for recruitment to a post.[306] Thus, again, young people are not protected against age discrimination as such. The ceiling age, however, of 65 which was in the original enactment has been removed (by the 2004 Act), removing a key and important exclusion. There are exemptions too in the Equal Status Act including: those applicable to age requirements for a person to be an adoptive or foster parent, where the requirement is reasonable having regard to the needs of the child or children concerned; in the treatment of persons in respect of the disposal of goods, or the provision of a service, which can reasonably be regarded as goods or a service suitable only to the needs of certain persons;[307] and differential treatment in respect of the allocation of places to mature students.[308] Nevertheless the Ireland model does provide for broad protection against age discrimination.

An important consideration in addressing age discrimination is whether a lower or upper age bar is appropriate. In the employment field, a lower age bar is unlikely to be controversial or indeed necessary because of the bar on employing children.[309] However, it may be highly relevant outside the employment field. The Australian Age Discrimination Act 2004 applies to persons of all ages and describes its objects as including: **2.104**

> to allow appropriate benefits and other assistance to be given to people of a certain age, particularly younger and older persons, in recognition of their particular circumstances; and
>
> to promote recognition and acceptance within the community of the principle that people of all ages have the same fundamental rights . . . [310]

Protecting young people against disadvantage associated with being young has not been an aim of the UK's anti-discrimination scheme but 'young age' discrimination cases are increasingly seen in the human rights context.[311] As has been observed, 'the majority of commentators appear to accept that the vulnerability of children and their dependency on adults (usually their parents) to meet their needs and desires mean that children cannot be granted exactly the same rights **2.105**

---

305 Employment Equality Act 1998, s 6(3).

306 Ibid.

307 A generic exception.

308 Equal Status Act, s 7(3)(e).

309 Children and Young Persons Act 1933, s 18(1)(a) (substituted by the Children Act 1972, s 1(2); and amended by the Children (Protection at Work) Regulations 1998, SI 1998/276, reg 2(2)(a)).

310 Australian Age Discrimination Act 2004, s 3.

311 For example, *A v UK* (1999) 27 EHRR 611; *R v H* [2002] 1 Cr App R 59.

as adults'.[312] Such acceptance needs some careful scrutiny. As has been noted, groups of adults or specific adults (including old people) in certain situations may also be vulnerable and the law will step in to protect them.[313] Thus:

> Those arguing for equality of rights between children and adults tend to play up the autonomy of children and downplay their vulnerability and dependency . . . [A] stronger case for equality of rights can be based on recognizing the dependency and vulnerability of adults, rather than seeking to prove the competence and self-sufficiency of children. A system of rights that recognizes the fundamental role that mutually dependent cooperative relationships play in the lives of adults and children; that respects and upholds those relationships; and that protects people who are exploited by inappropriate relationships is a good system of human rights; not just for a few powerful autonomous individuals, but for the majority of dependent and vulnerable people, be they adults or children.[314]

2.106 The recent focus on elder abuse highlights the absence of an obvious explanation for a different approach to respecting the rights of children and adults, based on age alone. It is therefore difficult to justify excluding children from rights-based age equality legislation.

2.107 In the UK, however, protection against age discrimination as such applies only in employment and related fields and so necessarily principally affects adults. Such protection as there is flows from the requirements of the Framework Directive, discussed further in Chapter 4, addressing age discrimination. Thus the Employment Equality (Age) Regulations 2006[315] (the Age Regulations) address age discrimination only within employment and related fields. Unlike provision made in the other anti-discrimination enactments, all direct discrimination on grounds of age is capable of being objectively justified. In addition, the Age Regulations contain wide exemptions including in relation to retirement ages,[316]

---

312 J Herring, 'Children's Rights for Grown-ups' in S Fredman and S Spencer (ed), *Age as an Equality Issue, Legal and Policy Perspectives* (2003, Hart), 170.

313 Ibid, 170, citing illustrations from the case law, including *Barclays Bank v O'Brien* [1994] 1AC 180; *R v Hinks* [2000] 4 ALL ER 833.

314 J Herring, 'Children's Rights for Grown-ups' in S Fredman and S Spencer (ed), *Age as an Equality Issue, Legal and Policy Perspectives* (2003, Hart) 173.

315 SI No 2006/1031. The Regulations came into force on 1 October 2006.

316 Considered in Chap 8. At the time of writing, the High Court has just decided to refer the lawfulness of the exclusion in relation to retirement ages to the European Court of Justice, reportedly without objection by the Government, on an application by Age Concern. At the time of writing no official reports have been published, but see <http://www.heyday.org.uk/wps/portal/!ut/p/kcxml/04_Sj9SPykssy0xPLMnMz0vM0Y_QjzKLN4g3cjMESYGZrsH6kRhiphhijgiRIH1vfV-P_NxU_QD9gtzQ0IhyR0UAH5joqA!!/delta/base64xml/L0lDU0lKQ1RPN29na21BISEvb0VvUUFBSVFnakZJQUFRaENFSVFqR0VBLzRKRmlDbzBlaDFpY29uUVZHaGQtc0lRIS83XzBfOU4xLzI2MzE1Mg!!?PC_7_0_9N1_WCM_CONTEXT=/content/home/community/community_campaigns_mra_6+dec+announcement&bodyfield=2&WCM_DOC_ID=com.ibm.workplace.wcm.api.WCM_Content/community_campaigns_mra_6%20dec%20announcement/e57b66457284cdf>.

the lawfulness of which must be doubted having regard to the terms of the Framework Directive.[317] Age discrimination as such, therefore, remains largely unregulated. There are no present plans to extend the protection afforded, though the *Discrimination Law Review* provides an opportunity for revitalizing discussion around age discrimination law.

C. Conclusion

Each of the main anti-discrimination enactments has very different and idiosyncratic histories. Understanding the history of the enactments is important in making sense of their contents. The ad hoc nature of the statutory developments has resulted in a disjointed set of laws and a hierarchy of protection, as observed in Chapter 1. **2.108**

The classes protected by our existing laws, the unlawful acts created, and the broader schemes promoting strategic change under the enactments are dealt with from Chapter 5 onwards. **2.109**

317 *Mangold v Helm* [2006] IRLR 143.

3

INTERPRETING THE ANTI-DISCRIMINATION LEGISLATION

A. Legislative Goals

3.01 As is discussed below, case law on the scope of the main anti-discrimination enactments indicates that a 'purposive' interpretation should be given to its terms. One consequence of such an approach is that it is necessary to identify the purpose or goals of the legislation and these are somewhat obscure. Their provisions make it clear that their formal purpose is to outlaw certain forms of discrimination in certain activities, but that is of little assistance in identifying their broader social purpose or the mischief they seek to address. Some clues can be gleaned from the history and context of the main anti-discrimination enactments, discussed in Chapter 2 and further below, but there is no express purpose identified in the statutes beyond that found in their long titles. The long titles give little away. The long title of the Equal Pay Act 1970 (EPA) reads that the Act is 'An Act to prevent discrimination, as regards terms and conditions of employment between men and women'; the long title of the Sex Discrimination Act 1975 (SDA) reads that it is 'An Act to render unlawful certain kinds of sex discrimination and discrimination on the ground of marriage, and establish a Commission with the function of working towards the elimination of such discrimination and promoting equality of opportunity between men and women generally, and for related purposes'; the long title of the Race Relations Act 1976 (RRA) reads that it is 'An Act to make fresh provision with respect to discrimination on racial grounds . . .'; and the long title of the Disability Discrimination Act 1995 (DDA) reads that it is 'An Act to make it unlawful to discriminate against disabled persons in connection with employment, the provision of goods, facilities and services or the disposal or management of premises; to make provision about the employment of disabled persons'.[1]

3.02 There are provisions in the main anti-discrimination enactments identifying the general duties or obligations imposed on the statutory Commissions[2] which help to illuminate the purposes of the legislation overall. The Equality Act 2006 (EA), in particular, identifies what will be the duties of the Commission for Equality and Human Rights (when established[3]) in broad and purposive terms, as follows:

> The Commission shall, by exercising the powers conferred by this Part—
> (a) promote understanding of the importance of equality and diversity;
> (b) encourage good practice in relation to equality and diversity;
> (c) promote equality of opportunity;
> (d) promote awareness and understanding of rights under the equality enactments;
> (e) enforce the equality enactments;
> (f) work towards the elimination of unlawful discrimination; and
> (g) work towards the elimination of unlawful harassment.[4]

'Diversity' and 'equality' are defined.[5] 'Diversity' means the fact that the individuals are 'different' and 'equality' means equality between individuals. The existing anti-discrimination legislation, however, does not expressly define its *own* purpose. As observed above, the nearest it gets to doing so is by the long titles but these do not identify the broad social objectives of the legislation or identify any underpinning principles.

3.03 Purpose clauses are unusual in the UK.[6] The absence of a purpose clause or clauses in the UK's anti-discrimination enactments might be compared to the position in other jurisdictions. The important purpose clause in South Africa's Promotion of Equality and Prevention of Unfair Discrimination Act 2000 has already been referred to in Chapter 1.[7] In other jurisdictions, international human rights treaties are sometimes identified explicitly as the inspiration for statutory measures.[8] The Australian Sex Discrimination Act 1984 identifies its 'objects' in section 3

---

1 There are no long titles in the Religion or Belief Regulations 2003 and the Sexual Orientation Regulations.

2 See, eg, SDA, s 53; RRA 1976, s 43; and Disability Rights Commission Act 1999, s 2(1).

3 Expected in Oct 2007. See Chap 15.

4 EA, s 8 and see s 2 for the Commission's general duty.

5 EA, s 8(2).

6 Examples can, however, be seen in the Health and Safety at Work, etc Act 1974, s 1 and the Income and Corporation Taxes Act 1988, s 488(1).

7 Para 1.36.

8 Eg, the Preamble to the Australian Racial Discrimination Act 1975.

and these include 'to give effect to certain provisions of the Convention on the Elimination of All Forms of Discrimination Against Women'. The relevant international human rights instruments for the UK are identified below.[9] The Canadian Human Rights Act 1977 identifies its aims at section 2 as including:

> the principle that all individuals should have an opportunity equal with other individuals to make for themselves the lives that they are able and wish to have and to have their needs accommodated, consistent with their duties and obligations as members of society, without being hindered in or prevented from doing so by discriminatory practices.[10]

Certain jurisdictions, then, expressly identify the goals sought to be realized by their equality legislation. This has the obvious advantage of guiding judicial interpretation and contextualizing the provision made for those needing to implement it. The value of identifying the purpose of equality legislation has been the subject of some consideration by the Canadian Human Rights Act Review Panel.[11] They referred to section 2 of the Canadian Human Rights Act set out above and noted the importance of this 'in the interpretation of the protection provided by the Act, its remedial focus and the concept of discrimination itself'.[12] They concluded that 'a purpose provision in the Act is necessary'[13] and recommended that the Act should in addition contain a preamble referring to various international agreements to which Canada was a party and identifying 'the broad aims of the Act, including the relevance of Canada's commitment to achieve equality' with a purpose section identifying more precisely the principles underlying the Act.[14] **3.04**

As to the goals of the UK's main anti-discrimination enactments, the long titles suggest that they are modest. As to what the goals of a fully functioning statutory equality scheme should be, Sandra Fredman has argued that: **3.05**

> equality ought to encompass four central aims. First, it should break the cycle of disadvantage associated with out-groups. Second, it should promote respect for the equal dignity and worth of all, thereby redressing stigma, stereotyping, humiliation and violence because of membership of an out-group. Third, it should entail positive affirmation and celebration of identity within community, and, finally, it should facilitate full participation in society.[15]

---

[9] Chap 4.

[10] Canadian Human Rights Act 1977, s 2.

[11] Chaired by Justice LaForest, *Promoting Equality: A New Vision* (2000) The Canadian Human Rights Act Review Panel (ISBN 0-662-84622-2), available at: <http://canada.justice.gc.ca/chra/en/toc.html>.

[12] Ibid, 7.

[13] Ibid, 9.

[14] Ibid,12.

[15] S Fredman, 'The Future of Equality in Britain' (2002) Working Paper Series No 5, Equal Opportunities Commission (ISBN 1 842060384), 10.

As seen above, some of these aspirations are reflected in the goals identified by equality legislation in other jurisdictions. Identifying the goals of any equality legislation is principally a political issue and the political history of each of the main anti-discrimination enactments has been specific and sometimes tense, as described in Chapter 2. A number of different aims have been identified in the equality discourse. These include achieving *equal treatment* or *equal opportunity*; supporting a *business case* or participation on *merit*; *respect for diversity* or *dignity*; *democratic participation* and *redistribution and social justice*.

3.06 An *equal treatment*[16] objective is generally understood to embrace a requirement that the same treatment be afforded to 'like' cases. This approach informed the early anti-discrimination enactments and the formulation of direct discrimination. It is an important aim but inadequate by itself to address disadvantage and the focus on the 'same-ness of treatment' and 'like' cases sometimes frustrates the achievement of substantive equality, as will be discussed in Chapter 6.

3.07 A commitment to *equal opportunity* is usually[17] concerned to 'equalise the starting point'[18] and so recognizes that existing disadvantage has the effect that merely treating people in the same way will not achieve equality. This has driven the indirect discrimination model. It is an important aim but inadequate by itself to address disadvantage. This is because, as has been famously said, it is 'not enough to open the gates of opportunity. All our citizens must have the ability to walk through those gates'.[19] Whilst the concept of indirect discrimination can capture some incidents of disadvantage, it has not gone far enough in addressing disadvantage, as the statistics in Chapter 1 demonstrate, in part at least because, as is discussed in Chapter 6, the 'justification' defence allows for dominant interests to prevail.

3.08 Arguments have also been made that anti-discrimination law should, and does, meet a *business case* and promote achievement on *merit*. Such an approach requires that individuals are treated according to their 'abilities' and not according to their status or group membership, and in recent years that has formed part of a 'business' case for equality. It holds that equality policies and laws bring 'efficiency and productivity by facilitating recruitment on merit rather than on the

---

16 Or 'equality of process', as the *Equalities Review* refers, to it, *The Equalities Review: Interim Report for Consultation* (2006) *The Equalities Review*, 71.

17 As the *Equalities Review* notes, the expression is sometimes given a 'meritocratic interpretation' ie that benefits should depend 'only on your talents and the efforts you make' (much like the 'equal treatment' and sometimes the 'business case' models): *The Equalities Review: Interim Report for Consultation* (2006) *The Equalities Review*, 72.

18 S Fredman, *The Future of Equality in Britain* (2002) Working Paper Series No 5, Equal Opportunities Commission (ISBN 1 842060384) 5.

19 President Lyndon Johnson, cited in S Fredman, *The Future of Equality in Britain* (2002) Working Paper Series No 5, Equal Opportunities Commission (ISBN 1 842060384) 6.

basis of prejudice'.[20] It is an important aim, but again inadequate by itself to address disadvantage. This is because, firstly, 'merit' concepts may be underpinned by discriminatory assumptions; secondly, it does nothing to address the position of people who do not qualify on a merit assessment because of entrenched social disadvantage or physical characteristics like pregnancy or disability; and thirdly, 'a focus on "merit" assumes that the individual should fit the job, rather than that the job should be adjusted to fit the worker'.[21] Indeed, the concept of 'merit' really lacks any substantive content—it might encompass discriminatory requirements, but it might just as well repel them. So in the context of judicial appointments, for example, whilst the present Lord Chancellor has observed that '[j]udicial diversity is central to merit, and to the maintenance of merit',[22] others will assert that qualifications that depend upon studying at 'old' universities and an ability to work full time in different locations (which might disadvantage certain minority groups and women respectively) are 'central to merit' in so far as certain posts, including judicial posts, are concerned. The 'merit' and 'business' case is therefore an uncertain basis for securing fundamental rights.

In a similar way to a 'business case', sometimes the 'economic case' is presented. **3.09**
This holds, much like the 'business case', that discrimination is too economically expensive for society to tolerate. The *Equalities Review* has spent time considering the economic cost of discrimination[23] but observed:

> Whilst the economic case is a powerful one, it can easily skew the sorts of strategies we pursue, by appealing to the economic forces which contribute significantly to generating patterns of inequality in the first place. Too much emphasis on the economic costs of inequality as the most compelling case for change can have the unintended consequence of placing an economic value on an individual's right to equality. This can re-affirm uneven patterns of investment in resolving inequalities, based not on social value but solely on economic value and in doing so perpetuate the exclusion of those most marginalised.[24]

As with the 'business case', the 'economic case' is too uncertain a foundation for securing equality as a fundamental right.

---

20 S Fredman, *The Future of Equality in Britain* (2002) Working Paper Series No 5, Equal Opportunities Commission (ISBN 1 842060384) 6.

21 Ibid, 8.

22 'Increasing Judicial Diversity: the next steps', Speech by the Constitutional Affairs Secretary and Lord Chancellor, Lord Falconer, to the Commission for Judicial Appointments Diversity Summit, 2 November 2005 cited in 'Black and Minority Practitioners in the Legal Profession and the Judicial Appointments Process' (2006) Commission for Judicial Appointments discussion paper, available at <http://www.cja.gov.uk/files/Discussion_Paper-Black_and_Minority_Practitioners_in_the_Legal_Profession.doc>, 1.

23 *The Equalities Review: Interim Report for Consultation* (2006) *The Equalities Review*, chap 4.

24 *DRC Statement on the Equalities Review Interim Report* (2006), Disability Rights Commission, available at <http://www.drc-gb.org/newsroom/news_releases/2006/drc_responds_to_equalities_rev.aspx>.

3.10 *Respect for diversity* might be a key aspiration for substantive equality laws. Such an approach is sometimes argued as part of a 'business case'[25] and sometimes a human rights case. The business case says that diversity should be strived for because of the benefits it brings to business through the breadth of experience thereby obtained. Such a view is expressed in the Lord Chancellor's comments above. The human rights case holds that we should respect all humanity in its diversity.

3.11 A case which rests on respect for dignity is a more certain foundation for a concept of equality which promotes and embraces 'diversity'. *Respect for human dignity*, and the valuing of each human being as deserving of respect by virtue of their humanity, embraces the notion that each person has value deriving from their status as human beings. It 'ensures that equality has a universal application'[26] and is reflected in most human rights instruments. Thus:

> Since all persons are entitled to human dignity and freedom and to that extent are equal, the principle of equal treatment is an obvious postulate for free democracy.[27]

'Dignity' also introduces substantive protection—it does not allow for a levelling down (that is, that there is no objectionable discrimination where all are treated equally badly[28]). It provides a principled basis for determining *who* should be protected—a dignity model will protect a person or group of persons if the distinction complained of is based on attributes or characteristics that objectively have the potential to impair the fundamental human dignity of persons as human beings.[29] A 'dignity' model is discussed further in Chapter 6 when the meanings of 'discrimination' contained in law are explored, but it is increasingly recognized that it is a helpful way to address inequality in a diverse community, with the potential to protect all against arbitrary interferences—recognizing as it does the inherent value deriving from our status as human beings and therefore accommodating difference and addressing disadvantage.

3.12 *Promoting participation* is sometimes said to be an important basis for equality law. Such an approach holds that democracy requires the full participation and inclusion of everyone, including minorities (measured numerically and by the distribution of power), in all important social and political institutions.[30] This has

---

25 Ibid, 9–10.

26 S Fredman, *Discrimination Law* (2002, OUP), 17.

27 'Communist Party' 5 BverfGE 85 (1956), cited in S Fredman, *Discrimination Law* (2002, OUP) 18.

28 A thesis which underpins the UK's anti-discrimination legislation with its emphasis on comparatively less favourable treatment (aside from that addressing disability).

29 LWH Ackermann 'Equality and the South African Constitution: The Role of Dignity' Bram Fischer Lecture (2000), cited in S Fredman, 'Discrimination Law' (2002, OUP), 18.

30 It is seen referred to in the 'the most celebrated footnote in constitutional law' (L Powell 'Carolene Products Revisited' [1982] Colum L Rev 1087, 1087, cited in G Stone, L Seidman, C Sunstein, and

the effect of mitigating the harsher consequences of majoritarian democracy. Democracy is already seen as an important basis for discerning the scope of discrimination law (in the human rights context) in domestic law: '[I]t is a purpose of all human rights instruments to secure the protection of the essential rights of members of minority groups, even when they are unpopular with the majority. Democracy values everyone equally even if the majority does not.'[31]

A *redistributive or social justice*[32] model aims to achieve fairer distribution; a commitment to social justice requires the morally proper distribution of social benefits and burdens among society's members.[33] As can be seen, there is an overlap between such a driver and the 'participative' aims described above. The aim of all anti-discrimination schemes is to an extent driven by a commitment to social justice, but that only truly works as an aim if that which is to be distributed is identified and measures are taken to support fair distribution. In the context of economic redistribution or social justice, an example in the UK's anti-discrimination legislation can be seen in Northern Ireland and the requirements of the Fair Employment and Treatment Order 1998 at Article 55 which provides that: **3.13**

(1) In the case of each registered concern, the employer shall from time to time review the composition of those employed in and ceasing to be employed in the concern in Northern Ireland and the employment practices of the concern for the purposes of determining whether members of each community are enjoying, and are likely to continue to enjoy, fair participation in employment in the concern.
(2) In a case where it appears to the employer in the course of the review that members of a particular community are not enjoying, or are not likely to continue to enjoy, such participation, he shall as part of the review determine the affirmative action (if any) which would be reasonable and appropriate.

The *Equalities Review* referred to in Chapter 1, and which it is intended will inform new equality laws, has identified a further approach. In its interim report for consultation it suggests that a 'capabilities' model may be appropriate: **3.14**

> [A] 'capabilities' approach, a version of equality of opportunity which focuses less on the assets of an individual (income, socio-economic status) or special characteristics

M Tushnet, *Constitutional Law* (4th edn 2001, Aspen), 507, as follows: 'Prejudice against discrete and insular minorities may be a special condition, which tends seriously to curtail the operation of those political processes ordinarily to be relied upon to protect minorities, and which may call for a correspondingly more searching judicial inquiry' (*United States v Carolene Products Co* [1938] 304 US 144, available at: <http://laws.findlaw.com/us/304/144.html>).

[31] *Ghaidan v Godin-Mendoza* [2004] AC 605, para 132, *per* Baroness Hale.

[32] Sometimes used to promote a more formal 'equality of outcome' goal: *The Equalities Review: Interim Report for Consultation* (2006) The Equalities Review, 71.

[33] LM Young 'Justice and the Politics of Difference' [1990] Princeton University Press, 16 cited in S Fredman, *Discrimination Law* (2002, OUP), 17.

> such as gender or race, and concentrates more on what people are able to do or be in their lives. What someone is able to do or be in their lives depends not only on their personal resources, but also, crucially, on the context in which they live—the economic, political, legal, social, cultural, and even physical conditions which shape the freedom an individual has to pursue his or her goals in life. We need to acknowledge that people can be held back from fulfilling their potential by the prejudice of others.
>
> The important advantage of this approach for us is that on the one hand it does not simply assert that once all discriminatory barriers are down we leave the rest to competition. It also recognizes that often people make choices that are constrained by cultural or other pressures. But on the other hand, it does not ignore the fact that individuals may be trying to achieve different things in their lives: not everyone wants the same. And for the most part, it should not be the business of public policy and certainly not of law, to correct for such a difference.
>
> So, to summarise, 'capability' has a number of attractive features:
>
> - it recognises the diversity of values and preferences among individuals, by focusing on the substantive opportunity individuals have to lead the kind of life they want to lead. This avoids the paternalism or authoritarianism which is sometimes associated with policies framed in terms of achieving equality of outcome.
> - It acknowledges variations in need. An individual who has greater needs, perhaps because she/he has children to look after, or because she/he is disabled, will need more flexible arrangements and greater material resources, in order to have access to the same opportunities—for employment, good health, and so on—as an individual without those additional needs.
> - It reflects the potential for advantage and disadvantage to accumulate over a lifetime, by emphasising the way in which social institutions and policies tend either to enhance or stunt the development of an individual's life chances (for example through education).
>
> This way of thinking about equality is widely used in international policy and in academic research, which means there is a solid base of evidence and practice on which the Review can draw.[34, 35]

This approach presents some difficulties. Firstly, it begs the questions it seeks to answer, as the interim report makes clear: 'what capabilities matter, and when?'[36]

[34] See G Brown, Annual UNICEF Lecture, 29 June 2005 (<http://www.hm-treasury.gov.uk/newsroom_and_speeches/press/2005/press_60_05.cfm> accessed 9 Jan 2006); European Commission (2003) *Strategies to enhance social integration: National Action Plan against poverty and social exclusion 2003–2005, Germany*, Directorate-General for Employment, Social Affairs and Equal Opportunities (<http://www.europa.eu.int/comm/employment_social/social_inclusion/docs/nap_03_05_en_fassung.pdf> accessed 9 Jan 2006); United Nations Development Programme (2005) *Human Development Report 2005*, New York, UNDP; *Human Development and Capability Association* (2005) (<http://www.fas.harvard.edu/~freedoms/index.cgi> accessed 9 Jan 2006).

[35] *The Equalities Review: Interim Report for Consultation* (2006) *The Equalities Review*, 73–4.

[36] Ibid, 74.

It does not provide a framework for answering those questions. This might be compared to a *dignity* model, which, as mentioned above, provides a substantive basis for affording equality. Secondly, the 'capabilities' model advocated by the *Equalities Review* carries the danger of refocusing responsibility for disadvantage onto individuals and so de-prioritizing the structural factors. Thirdly, it risks frustrating a human rights driven equality goal.

A 'capabilities' model does nevertheless have a grounding in modern political and philosophical thought. The approach taken by academics in this field, however, is rather different to that apparently taken by the *Equalities Review*. A capabilities model, in modern philosophical thought, does not impose a *threshold* for full social engagement or the enjoyment of certain benefits, as the *Equalities Review* would have it, but instead confers a series of *entitlements*. Recognizing the problems in Rawlsian social contract theory, particularly in seeking to do justice to disabled people and in seeking to do justice to all people irrespective of national barriers,[37] Martha Nussbaum has developed a 'capabilities' theory.[38] In describing her work she has said: **3.15**

> I . . . have used the ['capabilities approach'] . . . to provide the philosophical underpinning for an account of core human entitlements that should be respected and implemented by the governments of all nations, as a bare minimum of what respect for human dignity requires . . . I argue that the best approach to this idea of a basic social minimum is provided by an approach that focuses on *human capabilities*, that is, what people are actually able to do and to be, in a way informed by an intuitive idea of a life that is worthy of the dignity of the human being. I identify a list of *central human capabilities*, arguing that all of them are implicit in the idea of a life worthy of human dignity.
>
> . . .
>
> These . . . capabilities are supposed to be general goals that can be further specified by the society in question as it works on the fundamental entitlements it wishes to endorse . . . Here is the current version.
>
> *The Central Human Capabilities*
>
> (1) *Life*. Being able to live to the end of a human life of normal length; not dying prematurely, or before one's life is so reduced as to be not worth living.
> (2) *Bodily Health* . . .
> (3) *Bodily Integrity* . . .
> (4) *Senses, Imagination and Thought* . . .
> (5) *Emotions* . . .
> (6) *Practical reason* . . .

[37] And in the treatment of non-human animals which I do not address in this book because of a lack of experience, knowledge, and space.

[38] Along with Amartya Sen (an economist) she is the leading capabilities theorist, both having developed the model although each with a different focus.

(7) *Affiliation*...
(8) *Other species.* Being able to live with concern for and in relation to animals, plants and the world of nature.
(9) *Play*...
(10) *Control over one's environment*...[39]

3.16 Each of these 'capabilities' is expanded upon and explained by Martha Nussbaum but together they read as a list of fundamental elements of human existence that are basic entitlements for all persons and which are inextricably linked to the concept of human dignity. The approach adopted by the *Equalities Review* appears to depart radically from this academically produced and well grounded 'capabilities model' developed by Martha Nussbaum and others. In particular, the *Equalities Review* seems to suggest that 'capabilities' are determined to a greater or lesser extent by individualized variables such as personal resources, context, values, and choices, and accordingly they do not attempt to set out fundamental entitlements that should apply to everyone.

3.17 As mentioned, it is difficult to discern the goals of our anti-discrimination legislation as they are presently framed. The Equalities Review offers the opportunity for new ways of thinking about the aims of new anti-discrimination law, but great care must be taken in so doing. An individualized model secures important civil rights, but, as history shows, without acknowledging the structural causes of disadvantage little progress will be made. A 'dignity' model may offer a framework for responding to the social causes and effects of disadvantage whilst respecting diversity and all individuals' inherent worth. Much can be learnt from other jurisdictions and this is discussed further in Chapter 6.

B. Purposive Construction

3.18 As mentioned, case law holds that the UK's main anti-discrimination enactments should be given a *purposive* interpretation. In addition, there are compelling interpretative obligations arising in EU law and under the Human Rights Act which are addressed in Chapter 4. According to Francis Bennion a 'purposive' interpretation 'is one which gives effect to the legislative purposes by':

(a) following the literal meaning of the enactment where that meaning is in accordance with the legislative purpose ...;
(b) applying a strained meaning where the literal meaning is not in accordance with the legislative purpose ...[40]

[39] M Nussbaum, *Frontiers of Justice, Disability, Nationality and Species Membership* (2006, Belknap), 70, 75, 76–7.

[40] F Bennion, *Statutory Interpretation* (4th edn 2002, Butterworths), 810.

It might be said that each of the aims identified above has been progressively incorporated into UK law to a greater or lesser extent, starting with the 'equal treatment' guarantees which led to legislation repealing legally entrenched differences between the sexes and races and between gay and straight people (by, for example, the extension of the franchise to women, the abolition of slavery, the repeal of laws criminalizing same-sex activity) and moving to 'equal opportunity' and 'merit' laws (seen first in the RRA and then the SDA). 'Diversity' has been further embraced by an indirect discrimination guarantee and, more particularly, by a reasonable accommodation model (as seen in the DDA). However, as mentioned above, the difficulty in identifying the *legislative purposes* of the main anti-discrimination enactments in the UK is that it is now not possible to discern any consistent underpinning theme. As has been discussed in Chapters 1 and 2, discrimination is defined differently in the Acts, their scope varies, and each of their histories is very distinct. There are no purpose clauses, therefore identifying the purposes is no easy task. Earlier case law, as described in Chapter 1, suggested that some judges considered that the purpose of the SDA, for example, was not 'to obliterate the differences between men and women or to do away with the chivalry and courtesy which we expect mankind to give womankind' so that '[t]he natural differences of sex must be regarded even in the interpretation of an Act of Parliament', thus entrenching gender stereotyping.[41]

In fact a *purposive* interpretation of the main anti-discrimination enactments has **3.19**
usually meant in practice that a broad meaning is given to the scope of its protections[42] and a broad reach given to its liability provisions. According to Lord Justice Waite in *Jones v Tower Boot Ltd*:

> The legislation now represented by the race and sex discrimination Acts currently in force broke new ground in seeking to work upon the minds of men and women and thus affect their attitude to the social consequences of difference between the sexes or distinction of skin colour. Its general thrust was educative, persuasive, and where necessary coercive. The relief accorded to the victims, or potential victims, of discrimination went beyond the ordinary remedies of damages and an injunction introducing, through declaratory powers in the court or tribunal and recommendatory powers in the relevant Commission, provisions with a pro-active function, designed as much to eliminate the occasions for discrimination as to compensate its victims or punish its perpetrators. These were linked to a code of practice of which courts and tribunals were to take cognizance. Consistently with the broad front on which it operates, the legislation has traditionally been given a wide interpretation: see eg *Savjani v Inland Revenue*

41 *Peake v Automotive Products Ltd* [1978] QB 233, 238.

42 Except where to do so would promote racial hostility for example; *Redfearn v SERCO* [2006] EWCA Civ 659; [2006] IRLR 623.

Commissioners [1981] QB 458, 466–467, where Templeman LJ said of the Race Relations Act 1976:

'the Act was brought in to remedy a very great evil. It is expressed in very wide terms, and I should be slow to find that the effect of something which is humiliatingly discriminatory in racial matters falls outside the ambit of the Act'.[43]

3.20 Examples of a *purposive* interpretation being given to the main anti-discrimination enactments include cases giving a wide meaning to *facilities* for the purposes of the provisions outlawing discrimination in the provision of goods, facilities, and services[44] and a wide meaning to the concept of secondary liability including 'aiding'.[45] EU and ECHR law also create a very important context for interpreting and applying domestic anti-discrimination law and this is discussed in Chapter 4.

C. Consistency and Coherence

3.21 There is much case law indicating that the main anti-discrimination enactments should be read consistently. This is so even where an interpretation is given to a particular enactment in consequence of mandatory EU law which does not impact on another enactment directly.[46] If the language in the enactments is the same or broadly similar, it should be given the same meaning.

3.22 Moreover, in interpreting the enactments coherence should be strived for. This means that, for example, the SDA and EPA should be read as achieving, together, the implementation of Article 141, the Equal Pay Directive and the Equal Treatment Directive:[47] 'The cases establish that the Equal Pay Act 1970 has to be construed so far as possible to work harmoniously both with the Sex Discrimination Act 1975 and Article [141]. All three sources of law are part of a code dealing with unlawful sex discrimination'.[48] And the EPA and the SDA: '. . . should be construed and applied as a harmonious whole and in such a way

43 *Jones v Tower Boot Ltd* [1997] ICR 254 at 262, [1997] IRLR 168 at para 31, *per* Waite LJ.

44 *Savjani v Inland Revenue Commissioners* [1981] QB 458, 466–467.

45 *Jones v Tower Boot Ltd* [1997] ICR 254 at 262, [1997] IRLR 168; *Anyanwu and another v South Bank Student Union and another (Commission for Racial Equality intervening)* [2001] UKHL 14; [2001] 1 ICR 391; [2001] WLR 638; [2001] IRLR 305. There are also examples of non-purposive interpretations being given to the main anti-discrimination enactments, in particular in the older cases, some of which have been referred to in Chap 1; but recent examples include the decision of the EAT in *Redfearn v SERCO* [2005] IRLR 744, now overturned by the Court of Appeal, adopting a purposive construction at [2006] EWCA Civ 659; [2006] IRLR 623.

46 *Rhys-Harper v Relaxion Group Plc; D'Souza v London Borough of Lambeth; Jones v 3M Healthcare Ltd; Kirker v British Sugar plc; Angel v New Possibilities NHS Trust; BOND v Hackney Citizens Advice Bureau* [2003] UKHL 33; [2003] IRLR 484; *Anyanwu and another v South Bank Students' Union and others* [2001] UKHL 14; [2001] ICR, 391; [2001] IRLR 305, HL; *per* Lord Bingham at para 2.

47 See Chap 4.

48 *Strathclyde Regional Council v Wallace and Others* [1998] ICR 205.

that the broad principles which underlie the whole scheme of legislation are not frustrated by a narrow interpretation or restrictive application of particular provisions'.[49] This is not always easy.

Similarly, the other main anti-discrimination enactments constitute the domestic implementation of the Race Directive, the Framework Directive, the Equal Treatment Amendment Directive, and the Gender Goods and Services Directive,[50] and a meaning consistent with these Directives should therefore be aspired to.[51] **3.23**

49 *Shields v E Coomes (Holdings) Ltd* [1978] ICR 1159, 1178.
50 See Chap 4.
51 See Chap 4.

4

EU LAW AND FUNDAMENTAL RIGHTS

A. European Union Law

(1) Introduction and the fundamental principle of equality

European Community (EC) and now European Union (EU) law have been responsible for many progressive changes to the UK's equality law. The main European enactments are addressed below, but their impact on domestic law, particularly through case law, is dealt with throughout the following chapters as and when particular issues arise. The system of legal rules that flows from the UK's accession to the European Economic Community (EEC) is addressed at paragraph 4.58 below. It is of considerable importance to both the interpretation and application of domestic anti-discrimination law. 4.01

4.02 The Treaty of Rome 1957, creating the EEC, contained some equality provisions. The Treaty and its subsequent amendments have now been consolidated, forming the Treaty Establishing the European Community[1] (EC Treaty), and its original Articles have been renumbered. The new numbering is referred to in this chapter. The Treaty's prime function, of course, was to create a common market by the eventual abolition of tariff barriers and the securing of the free movement of people and goods within it, and it therefore essentially comprised a trade agreement. The original equality provisions must be understood in that context. Gradually, however, equality has been seen as a fundamental right and this has informed both the content of the Treaty and the parameters of Community law more generally, 'transcending' the specific provisions of the Treaty.[2] It applies therefore in the context of any activity covered by EC law, irrespective of any specific legislative measure and whether the activity concerned arises in the State or private sphere.[3]

4.03 The principle of equality embraces an obligation not to discriminate for reasons connected with status (including sex, race, disability, sexual orientation, religion or belief, and age). A number of international instruments and the constitutional traditions of Member States are the source of this principle.[4] It seems clear now, having regard to recent European Court of Justice (ECJ) case law, that a national court, faced with a domestic legislative measure operative in an activity covered by EC law that is in breach of the principle of equality, must disapply it[5] so as to ensure primacy is given to EC law.[6] This is necessary to 'guarantee the full effectiveness of the general principle of non-discrimination'.[7] As such the fact that there is no specific legislative measure in place, or the transposition date for a specific measure in the field of equality and non-discrimination has not yet expired, does not relieve a Member State of the obligation to conform to the principle of

---

1 OJ C 340, 10 November 1997.

2 T Takis, *The General Principles of EU Law* (2006, Oxford) 61–2.

3 *Mangold v Helm* [2006] IRLR 143, see Advocate-General Tizzano's opinion, paras 83–4, 101 and ECJ judgment, paras 74–6; *Ángel Rodríguez Caballero v Fondo de Garantía Salarial* C-442/00 [2002], paras 30–32.

4 See, for example, Recitals (2), (3), (5), (9), (11), Council Directive 2000/43/EC 'implementing the principle of equal treatment between persons irrespective of racial or ethnic origins' (the Race Directive); Recitals (1), (4), Council Directive 2000/78/EC 'establishing a general framework for equal treatment in employment and occupation' and Recitals (1), (2), (4), Council Directive 2002/73/ EC 'amending Council Directive 76/207/EEC on the implementation of the principle of equal treatment for men and women as regards access to employment, vocational training and promotion and working conditions'.

5 *Rodríguez Caballero v Fondo de Garantia Salarial* [2003] IRLR 115.

6 *Mangold v Helm* [2006] IRLR 143, ECJ judgment, paras 77–8; *Simmenthal* [1978] ECR 629, para 21.

7 *Mangold v Helm*, ibid, para 78.

equality[8] in relation to any matter falling within the broadly defined activities of the Community.[9] This principle is of very great importance to the development of equality law domestically. The principle of equality (and its reflection in certain specific Treaty provisions discussed below) extends beyond those areas in which specific non-discrimination legislation has been enacted by Council Directives. This is discussed fully below, but many of the grounds protected are covered by specific legislative measures addressing employment and occupation only.[10] The Community's competence extends beyond such activities[11] and the principle of equality must be understood as applying across them all.

Further, where specific legislative measures are in place in the form of Council Directives, Member States, including courts, are obliged to desist from taking action which frustrates their objectives from the date of their publication and therefore before the transposition date.[12] Member States are under a duty to refrain from doing anything 'liable seriously to compromise the attainment of the result prescribed by the Directive' during this period.[13] **4.04**

EC law also requires that Member States guarantee the 'effectiveness' of EC rights.[14] This means that in respect of any right conferred by EC law, Member States must secure access to effective judicial process and the availability of effective remedies for a breach.[15] This requires sanctions which are such as to guarantee real and effective judicial protection and that have a real deterrent effect.[16] In the context of discrimination, this principle will require that full monetary compensation is available and any rule limiting the availability of the same must be disapplied.[17] This principle is reflected in the non-discrimination Directives as is described below. **4.05**

[8] Ibid.

[9] EC Treaty, Arts 2–3.

[10] See paras 4.06 onwards below.

[11] EC Treaty, Arts 2–3, and see the scope of certain of the non-discrimination Directives described below which go much wider, paras 4.33 and 4.47.

[12] *Mangold v Helm* [2006] IRLR 143, paras 66–70.

[13] Ibid, para 67. Such duty derives from EC Treaty, Arts 10 and 249.

[14] EU Charter of Fundamental Rights, Art 47.

[15] *R v Secretary of State, ex p Factortame Ltd (No 5)* [2000] 1 AC 524; *Brasserie Du Pecheur SA v Federal Republic of Germany*; *R v Secretary of State for Transport ex p Factortame Ltd and O'rs (No 4)* [1996] QB 404.

[16] *Von Colson and Kamman v Land Nordrhein-Westfalen* [1984] ECR 1891.

[17] Ibid; *Marshall v Southampton and South West Area Health Authority II*, Case C-271/91 [1993] ECR I-4367; [1993] ICR 893; [1993] IRLR 445. Remedies for a breach of the principle of equality which are dependent upon proof of fault or some other mental element are therefore inconsistent with EC law: *Dekker v Stichting Vormingscentrum Voor Jonge Volwassen (VJV-Centrum) Plus*, Case 177/88 [1992] ICR 325).

B. The Treaty of Rome and Relevant Directives

(1) Free movement

4.06 The Treaty has always contained provisions prohibiting nationality discrimination. Article 12[18] of the EC Treaty provides:

> Within the scope of application of this Treaty,[19] and without prejudice to any special provisions contained therein, any discrimination on grounds of nationality shall be prohibited.

In addition, provision was made prohibiting restrictions on freedom of establishment (of business) within the Community[20] and restrictions on freedom to provide services within the Community,[21] in both cases in respect of nationals of Member States only. Article 39[22] also provides that:

> 1. Freedom of movement for workers shall be secured within the Community.
> 2. Such freedom of movement shall entail the abolition of any discrimination based on nationality between workers of the Member States as regards employment, remuneration and other conditions of work and employment.
> 3. It shall entail the right, subject to limitations justified on grounds of public policy, public security or public health:
>   (a) to accept offers of employment actually made;
>   (b) to move freely within the territory of Member States for this purpose;
>   (c) to stay in a Member State for the purpose of employment in accordance with the provisions governing the employment of nationals of that State laid down by law, regulation or administrative action;
>   (d) to remain in the territory of a Member State after having been employed in that State, subject to conditions which shall be embodied in implementing regulations to be drawn up by the Commission.
> 4. The provisions of this Article shall not apply to employment in the public service.

4.07 Article 39 was given added force by Regulation 1612/68/EEC on the free movement of workers within the Community. In its Recitals, the Regulation recognizes the fundamental nature of the right to free movement and that mobility is one means by which a worker is guaranteed the possibility of improving his living and working conditions. It guarantees the right to workers of Member States to take up employment in another Member State without discrimination and the right to the same assistance afforded to nationals of that Member State in

18 Ex Art 6.

19 Therefore protecting only nationals of Member States.

20 Art 43 (ex Art 52).

21 Art 49 (ex Art 59).

22 Art 39, like its predecessor Art 48, had direct effect: *Van Duyn v Home Office*, Case 41/74 [1974] ECR 1337. For its domestic impact in the field of discrimination law, see *Bossa v Nordstres Ltd* [1998] ICR 694; [1998] IRLR 284.

seeking employment.[23] The Regulation also guarantees such workers the right not to be treated differently in respect of conditions of employment including remuneration, dismissal, reinstatement, and re-engagement; the right to the same social and tax advantages as national workers (and the concept of 'social advantage' is given a wide meaning[24]); and the same right under the same conditions to access to training in vocational schools and centres.[25] It also requires Member States to afford equal treatment to such workers in relation to the membership of trade unions and in relation to the benefits afforded workers in respect of housing; and it guarantees rights to their families, irrespective of nationality.[26] Although the Regulation does not provide any definition of nationality 'discrimination', case law from the ECJ indicates that its meaning includes 'direct' as well as a rather liberal concept of 'indirect' discrimination. Thus, for example, in *Commission v Greece*[27] the ECJ held that a rule or practice which rendered it impossible for employment in the public service of another Member State to be taken into account for the purposes of determining a public service employee's entitlement to a seniority increment, when periods of employment completed in the national public service were taken into account, breached Article 39 and the Regulations. The Court held that the rule plainly operated to the detriment of migrant workers who had spent part of their working life in the public service of another Member State and therefore contravened the principle of non-discrimination enshrined in the Regulations. And in *Commission v Greece*[28] a challenge was brought to the payment of special allowances by the State to 'large' families but only where their habitual residence was in Greece and subject to certain conditions concerning in particular the (Greek) nationality or (Greek) origins of family members. This was held to be discriminatory and in contravention of Article 39 and the Regulations. In *O'Flynn v Adjudication Officer*[29] the ECJ concluded that a rule which made the grant of a social fund payment to cover funeral expenses subject to the condition that burial or cremation take place within the territory of that Member State was prohibited by Regulation 1612/68, holding that:

> Unless objectively justified and proportionate to its aim, a provision of national law must be regarded as indirectly discriminatory if it is intrinsically liable to affect

23 Arts 1 to 5.

24 Covering, for example, social grant payments to cover funeral costs, discount rail cards, guaranteed minimum incomes, interest-free loans following childbirth, and some forms of student grant: *O'Flynn v Adjudication Officer* [1996] ECR 1-2617; *Fiorini v SNCF*, Case 32/75 [1975] ECR 1085; *Reina v Landeskreditbank Baden-Wurttemberg*, Case 65/81 [1982] ECR 33; *Scrivner Centre Public d'Aide Sociale de Chastre*, Case 122/84 [1985] ECR 1027, respectively. And see: *Secretary of State for Defence v Elias* [2006] EWCA Civ 1293, para 56.

25 Art 7.

26 Arts 8, 9 and 10, and may confer other derivative rights on spouses in certain circumstances; *Carpenter v Secretary of State for the Home Department*, Case C-60/00 [2002] ECR I-6279.

27 Case C-187/96, [1998] ECR I-1095. And Art 3a(4) has very limited reach, as this case demonstrates.

28 Case C-185/96 [1998] ECR I-6601.

29 Case C-237/94 [1996] ECR I-2617.

migrant workers more than national workers and if there is a consequent risk that it will place the former at a particular disadvantage.

It is not necessary to find that the provision in question does in practice affect a substantially higher proportion of migrant workers.[30]

(2) Gender discrimination and equal pay

4.08 Article 141[31] of the EC Treaty provides that:

1. Each Member State shall ensure that the principle of equal pay for male and female workers for equal work or work of equal value is applied.
2. For the purpose of this Article, 'pay' means the ordinary basic or minimum wage or salary and any other consideration, whether in cash or in kind, which the worker receives directly or indirectly, in respect of his employment, from his employer.

Equal pay without discrimination based on sex means:

(a) that pay for the same work at piece rates shall be calculated on the basis of the same unit of measurement;

(b) that pay for work at time rates shall be the same for the same job.

3. The Council, acting in accordance with the procedure referred to in Article 251, and after consulting the Economic and Social Committee, shall adopt measures to ensure the application of the principle of equal opportunities and equal treatment of men and women in matters of employment and occupation, including the principle of equal pay for equal work or work of equal value.
4. With a view to ensuring full equality in practice between men and women in working life, the principle of equal treatment shall not prevent any Member State from maintaining or adopting measures providing for specific advantages in order to make it easier for the under-represented sex to pursue a vocational activity or to prevent or compensate for disadvantages in professional careers.

Article 141 looks like, and indeed has been in practice, a social justice measure. However, its aims reflect the common market objectives of the EC Treaty. Thus:

Article [141[32]] pursues a double aim.

First, in the light of the different stages of the development of social legislation in the various member states, the aim of article [141] is to avoid a situation in which undertakings established in states which have actually implemented the principle of equal pay suffer a competitive disadvantage in intra-community competition as compared with undertakings established in states which have not yet eliminated discrimination against women workers as regards pay.

---

30 Paras 20–1.

31 Ex Art 119. The original text read: 'Each Member State shall during the first stage ensure and subsequently maintain the application of the principle that men and women should receive equal pay for equal work. For the purpose of this Article, "pay" means the ordinary basic minimum wage or salary and any other consideration, whether in cash or in kind, which the worker receives, directly or indirectly, in respect of his employment from his employer. Equal pay without discrimination based on sex means: (a) that pay for the same work at piece rates shall be calculated on the basis of the same unit of measurement; (b) that pay for work at time rates shall be the same for the same job'.

32 Ex Art 119.

> Secondly, this provision forms part of the social objectives of the community, which is not merely an economic union, but is at the same time intended, by common action, to ensure social progress and seek the constant improvement of the living and working conditions of their peoples, as is emphasised by the preamble to the Treaty. This aim is accentuated by the insertion of article [141] into the body of a chapter devoted to social policy whose preliminary provision, article [136[33]], marks:
>
> > 'the need to promote improved working conditions and an improved standard of living for workers, so as to make possible their harmonisation while the improvement is being maintained'.[34]

According to the ECJ, '[t]his double aim, which is at once economic and social, shows that the principle of equal pay forms part of the foundations of the community.'[35] Article 141 has indeed proved very significant to the development of equality law. Its scope is wide, covering all remuneration, whether contractual, non-contractual, made pursuant to a collective agreement[36] or otherwise, in respect of work, including: concessionary travel;[37] elements of maternity pay (including statutory maternity pay);[38] sick pay;[39] bonuses and other one off or ad hoc payments whether for retrospective performance or future loyalty;[40] occupational pensions[41] and related benefits;[42] and compensation for loss of a job (including redundancy pay[43] and unfair dismissal compensation[44]). Article 141 also embraces a wide concept of equality so that it protects against direct and indirect discrimination.[45] It is now clear that a hypothetical comparator may be relied upon to support at least a claim of indirect 'pay' discrimination.[46] This is important in considering domestic law on equal pay which, as far as the Equal Pay **4.09**

---

33 Ex Art 117.

34 *Defrenne v Sabena*, Case 43/74 [1976] ICR 547, paras 8–11.

35 Ibid, para 12.

36 *Kowalska v Freie und Handestadt Hamburg*, Case C33/89 [1990] ECR I-2591; [1992] ICR 29; [1990] IRLR 447.

37 *Garland v British Rail Engineering Ltd* [1983] 2 AC 751; [1982] ICR 420.

38 *Gillespie and o'rs v Northern Health and Social Services Board and o'rs*, Case C-342/93 [1996] ICR 498; *Alabaster v Woolwich and A'or*, Case C-147/02 [2005] ICR 695; [2004] IRLR 486.

39 *Rinner-Kuhn v FWW Spezial-Gebaudereinigung GmbH & Co KG* [1989] ECR 2743; [1989] IRLR 493.

40 *Lewen v Denda*, Case C-333/97 [2000] ICR 648.

41 *Bilka-Kaufhaus GmbH v Weber Von Hartz*, Case 170/84 [1987] ICR 110; [1986] IRLR 317.

42 *Ten Oever v Stichting Bedrijfspensioenfonds voor het Glazzenwassers-en Schoonmaakbedrijf*, Case C-109/91 [1993] ECR I-4879; [1995] ICR 74; [1993] IRLR 601; *KB v National Health Service Pensions Agency and another*, Case C-117/01 [2004] IRLR 240 (survivors pensions).

43 *Burton v British Railways*, Case 19/81 [1982] ECR 555; [1982] IRLR 116; *Barber v Guardian Royal Exchange Assurance Group*, Case 262/88 [1990] ECR I-1889; [1990] IRLR 240.

44 *R v Secretary of State for Employment ex p Seymour-Smith and Perez*, Case C-167/97 [1999] 2 AC 554; [1999] IRLR 253.

45 See, for an example, *Bilka-Kaufhaus GmbH v Weber Von Hartz*, n 42 above.

46 *Allonby v Accrington and Rossendale College and others*, Case C-256/01 [2004] ICR 1328; [2004] IRLR 224.

Act 1970 (EPA) is concerned, precludes reliance on hypothetical comparators. This is addressed further below and in more detail in Chapter 6. In addition, pools for comparison may be widely drawn. Article 141 allows for comparisons to be made between a woman and her predecessor[47] and between women and men employed at different establishments so long as there is a 'single source' regulating terms and conditions, whether that is a single legislative or quasi-legislative source, or a collective agreement or some other cross-establishment agreement.[48] Article 141(4), which addresses positive action, is considered in Chapter 13.[49]

4.10 The existence of Treaty measures addressing discrimination led the ECJ to conclude that equality is one of the fundamental principles underpinning Community law so that disparity in treatment by measures falling within the competence of the Community must be objectively justified by being shown to depend on legally relevant and significant differences.[50] This is discussed above.[51] However, social measures addressing discrimination across a wide range of grounds have come only recently. Prior to the amendments made to the Treaty of Rome by the Amsterdam Treaty, there was little basis for enacting anti-discrimination legislation, and such that there was emerged very much from the 'market' imperatives reflected in the Treaty.

4.11 As discussed in Chapter 2, Article 141 provided the impetus for the enactment of the EPA. It also provided the inspiration and competence for the enactment of the Equal Pay Directive[52] which in turn inspired the Equal Treatment Directive[53] (and then the Equal Treatment Amendment Directive[54]) which in turn inspired

---

47 *Macarthys Ltd v Smith*, Case 129/79 [1980] ICR 672; [1980] IRLR 210.

48 *Lawrence v Regent Office Care Ltd and others*, Case C-320/00 [2003] ICR 1092; [2002] IRLR 822. *Allonby v Accrington & Rossendale College and others*, Case C-256/01 [2004] ICR 1328; [2004] IRLR 224.

49 As to EU measures directed at mainstreaming gender equality, see 'Commission of the European Communities, Incorporating Equal Opportunities for Women and Men into all Community Policies and Activities' (COM(96)final).

50 *Les Assurances de Credit SA and others v Council and Commission*, Case C-63/89 [1991] ECR I-1799, [1991] 2 CMLR 737; *P v S and Cornwall County Council* Case C-13/94 1996] ICR 795; [1996] ECR I-2143, ECJ; [1996] IRLR 347, para 18 describing the principle of equality as 'one of the fundamental principles of Community law'.

51 Para 4.02 onwards.

52 Council Directive 75/117/EEC of 10 Feb 1975 on the approximation of the laws of the Member States relating to the application of the principle of equal pay for men and women (OJ L 45, 19 Feb 1975, 19).

53 Council Directive 76/207/EEC of 9 Feb 1976 on the implementation of the principle of equal treatment for men and women as regards access to employment, vocational training and promotion, and working conditions (OJ L 39, 14 Feb 1976, 40).

54 Council Directive 2002/73/EC amending Council Directive 76/207/EEC on the implementation of the principle of equal treatment for men and women as regards access to employment, vocational training and promotion, and working conditions (OJ L 269, 5 Oct 2002, 15–20).

the Social Security[55] and the Occupational Social Security Directives.[56] The Equal Pay Directive places flesh on the bones of Article 141. In particular, in its original enactment (prior to the amendments made by the Treaty of Amsterdam[57]), Article 141 did not address discrimination in pay as between men and women doing work of equal *value*. This was addressed by the Equal Pay Directive, together with discrimination in job classification systems, by providing at Article 1 that:

> The principle of equal pay for men and women outlined in Article [141] of the Treaty, hereinafter called 'principle of equal pay', means, for the same work or for work to which equal value is attributed, the elimination of all discrimination on grounds of sex with regard to all aspects and conditions of remuneration.
>
> In particular, where a job classification system is used for determining pay, it must be based on the same criteria for both men and women and so drawn up as to exclude any discrimination on grounds of sex.

Soon after the UK's accession to the Treaty and its joining of the EEC, and notwithstanding its belief that the EPA gave effect to its obligations on equal pay, the Commission brought infringement proceedings against the UK relying on the absence of a right in the EPA to bring equal value claims.[58] This led directly to the first significant amendments to the EPA made by the Equal Pay (Amendment) Regulations 1983[59] which introduced the EPA's 'equal value' provisions.[60] There was apparently no enthusiasm for the amendments in Government: the Regulations are said to have been introduced by 'a drunk and derisive Alan Clark (then Under-Secretary of State for Employment)'.[61] **4.12**

The Equal Treatment Directive complemented the Equal Pay Directive and was enacted a year later. Its purpose is expressly described as follows: **4.13**

> The purpose of this Directive is to put into effect in the Member States the principle of equal treatment for men and women as regards access to employment, including promotion, and to vocational training and as regards working conditions and, on the

---

55 Council Directive 79/7/EEC of 19 December 1978 on the progressive implementation of the principle of equal treatment for men and women in matters of social security (OJ L 006, 10 Feb 1979, 24–25).

56 Council Directive 86/378/EEC of 24 July 1986 on the implementation of the principle of equal treatment for men and women in occupational social security schemes (OJ L 225, 12 Aug 1986, 40–2).

57 OJ C 340, 10 Nov 1997.

58 *Commission of the European Communities v United Kingdom of Great Britain and Northern Ireland* Case 61/81 [1982] ECR 2601; [1982] ICR 578; [1982] IRLR 333.

59 SI 1983/1794.

60 See Chap 6.

61 A McColgan, *Discrimination Law, Text, Cases and Materials* (2nd edn 2005, Hart), 421.

> conditions referred to in paragraph 2, social security. This principle is hereinafter referred to as 'the principle of equal treatment'.[62]

It defines the principle of equal treatment so that: '[f]or the purposes of the following provisions, the principle of equal treatment shall mean that there shall be no discrimination whatsoever on grounds of sex either directly or indirectly by reference in particular to marital or family status.'[63] It requires Member States to abolish 'any laws, regulations and administrative provisions contrary to the principle of equal treatment' and amend or declare null and void 'any provisions contrary to the principle of equal treatment which are included in collective agreements, individual contracts of employment, internal rules of undertakings or in rules governing the independent occupations and professions'.[64] As mentioned in Chapter 2, its protection against sex discrimination also protects against discrimination connected with gender reassignment.[65] The original provisions of the Equal Treatment Directive were 'without prejudice to provisions concerning the protection of women, particularly as regards pregnancy and maternity'.[66] The amended Equal Treatment Directive now reads that:

> This Directive shall be without prejudice to provisions concerning the protection of women, particularly as regards pregnancy and maternity.
>
> A woman on maternity leave shall be entitled, after the end of her period of maternity leave, to return to her job or to an equivalent post on terms and conditions which are no less favourable to her and to benefit from any improvement in working conditions to which she would be entitled during her absence.
>
> Less favourable treatment of a woman related to pregnancy or maternity leave within the meaning of Directive 92/85/EEC shall constitute discrimination within the meaning of this Directive.

---

62 Art 1.

63 Art 2. This is without prejudice to provisions concerning the protection of women, particularly as regards pregnancy and maternity, Art 2. This does not provide any separate protection against marriage discrimination as such. It appears that it therefore does not guarantee any greater protection than that afforded by the Sex Discrimination Act 1975 (SDA) which at least provides for some marriage-based discrimination (albeit in limited fields and albeit not extending to discrimination based on unmarried status): *D and Kingdom of Sweden v Council of the European Union* joined cases C-122/99P and C-125/99P.

64 Art 3. This has been revised in consequence of the amendments made by Directive 2002/73 discussed below. Art 3 now requires (as is material) that, 'any laws, regulations and administrative provisions contrary to the principle of equal treatment are abolished; any provisions contrary to the principle of equal treatment which are included in contracts or collective agreements, internal rules of undertakings or rules governing the independent occupations and professions and workers' and employers' organisations shall be, or may be declared, null and void or are amended.'

65 *P v S and Cornwall County Council* Case C-13/94 1996] ICR 795; [1996] ECR I-2143, ECJ; [1996] IRLR 347; In *KB v National Health Service Pensions Agency and A'or* Case C-117/01 [2004] ICR 781; [2004] IRLR 240.

66 Art 2(3).

> This Directive shall also be without prejudice to the provisions of Council Directive 96/34/EC of 3 June 1996 on the framework agreement on parental leave concluded by UNICE, CEEP and the ETUC and of Council Directive 92/85/EEC of 19 October 1992 on the introduction of measures to encourage improvements in the safety and health at work of pregnant workers and workers who have recently given birth or are breastfeeding (tenth individual Directive within the meaning of Article 16(1) of Directive 89/391/EEC). It is also without prejudice to the right of Member States to recognise distinct rights to paternity and/or adoption leave. Those Member States which recognise such rights shall take the necessary measures to protect working men and women against dismissal due to exercising those rights and ensure that, at the end of such leave, they shall be entitled to return to their jobs or to equivalent posts on terms and conditions which are no less favourable to them, and to benefit from any improvement in working conditions to which they would have been entitled during their absence.[67]

This reflects, *inter alia*, case law from the ECJ holding that discrimination against a pregnant woman is sex discrimination *per se* without the need to compare her treatment to that afforded a non-pregnant person and, in particular, a man.[68] It also appears to expressly provide that a failure to afford the guarantees provided for in the Pregnant Workers Directive (as to which see below) itself constitutes discrimination ('less favourable treatment of a woman related to pregnancy or maternity leave within the meaning of Directive 92/85/EEC shall constitute discrimination within the meaning of this Directive').

The Equal Treatment Directive has led to significant changes to the Sex Discrimination Act 1975 (SDA), some of which will be addressed in the following chapters. The Burden of Proof Directive[69] has effected change to the burden of proof in sex discrimination cases and this is addressed in Chapter 14. The Equal Treatment Directive has now been amended by the Equal Treatment Amendment Directive[70] which was enacted in 2002 and the terms of which were required to be transposed into domestic law by 5 October 2005. The Equal Treatment **4.14**

---

67 Art 2(7), as amended by the Equal Treatment Amendment Directive 2002/73/EC, discussed below.

68 *Handels- og Kontorfunktionoerernes Forbund i Danmark*, C-179/88 [1992] ICR 332; [1991] IRLR 31; *Habermann-Beltermann*, C-421/92 [1994] IRLR 364; *Webb v Emo Air Cargo (UK) Ltd* Case C-32/93 [1994] ICR 770; [1994] IRLR 482; *Hoffmann v Barmer Ersatzkasse*, 184/83 [1984] ECR 3047.

69 Council Directive 97/80/EC of 15 Dec 1997 on the burden of proof in cases of discrimination based on sex, extended to the UK by Council Directive 98/52/EC (of 13 July 1998 on the extension of Directive 97/80/EC on the burden of proof in cases of discrimination based on sex to the United Kingdom of Great Britain and Northern Ireland). See SDA, ss 63A and 66A for its domestic implementation. Directive 97/80/EC also made changes to the meaning of indirect discrimination but these have since been superseded by the definitions in the Equal Treatment Amendment Directive.

70 Council Directive 2002/73/EC amending Council Directive 76/207/EEC on the implementation of the principle of equal treatment for men and women as regards access to employment, vocational training and promotion, and working conditions.

Amendment Directive introduced new concepts of discrimination, in particular a more liberal meaning of indirect discrimination and express provision addressing harassment and sexual harassment[71] and, as referred to above, provision addressing pregnancy and maternity.[72] Its context, as described in the Recitals to it, included the new Article 13 of the EC Treaty and the Directives enacted under it, which are addressed below.[73] Importantly too, the Equal Treatment Amendment Directive amended the scope of the Equal Treatment Directive so as to include 'pay'. Recital 16 to the Equal Treatment Amendment Directive provides that:

> The principle of equal pay for men and women is already firmly established by Article 141 of the Treaty and Council Directive 75/117/EEC of 10 February 1975 on the approximation of the laws of the Member States relating to the application of the principle of equal pay for men and women and is consistently upheld by the case-law of the Court of Justice; the principle constitutes an essential and indispensable part of the *acquis communautaire* concerning sex discrimination.

4.15 Article 3 of the Equal Treatment Directive as replaced by the Equal Treatment Amendment Directive now provides at (1)(c): 'Application of the principle of equal treatment means that there shall be no direct or indirect discrimination on the grounds of sex in the public or private sectors, including public bodies, in relation to: employment and working conditions, including dismissals, as well as pay as provided for in Directive 75/117/EEC.' This has very significant consequences for domestic law. It means that to the extent that there was any doubt as to the need to make provision for hypothetical comparators in direct discrimination pay claims this has been dispelled. The Equal Treatment Directive as amended by the Amended Equal Treatment Directive requires Member States to outlaw direct discrimination in pay. Direct discrimination is defined by the new Article 2 as occurring 'where one person is treated less favourably on grounds of sex than another is, has been or would be treated in a comparable situation' so allowing for hypothetical comparisons (*would be treated*). The EPA requires an actual comparator in all cases of direct discrimination, namely (where the complainant is a woman) a man employed in the same employment on like work with the woman, a man employed in the same employment on work rated as equivalent with that of a woman, or a man employed in the same employment on work which is, in terms of the demands

---

71 See amended Art 2.

72 See para 4.13 above.

73 Recital 6. The relevant context, according to the Recitals, also include International agreements addressing equality, in particular the 'Universal Declaration of Human Rights, the United Nations Convention on the Elimination of all forms of Discrimination Against Women, the International Convention on the Elimination of all Forms of Racial Discrimination and the United Nations Covenants on Civil and Political Rights and on Economic, Social and Cultural Rights and by the Convention for the Protection of Human Rights and Fundamental Freedoms, to which all Member States are signatories' (Recital 2). These are addressed below.

made (for instance under such headings as effort, skill, and decision), of equal value to that of a woman in the same employment.[74] This does not give proper effect to the amendments to the Equal Treatment Directive addressing pay.

In the context of pregnancy, domestic case law has had to give effect to Article 141 and the Equal Pay Directive which together require that in calculating earnings-related maternity pay a woman is entitled to have the benefit of a pay rise awarded between the beginning of the 'reference' period (ie the first day of any period used for calculating the maternity pay) and the end of the maternity leave.[75] In such cases, the ECJ has made it clear that there is no need to identify a comparator because a pregnant woman and a woman on maternity leave are not in a comparable position to a man or a non-pregnant woman. [76] As will be seen below, this has had a significant effect on the interpretation of the EPA. These rulings have also had the unfortunate effect of depriving women of full pay during maternity leave, notwithstanding that the reason for the failure to pay full pay in such circumstances is pregnancy and maternity, both of which are gender-specific conditions. The justification for these holdings (which in truth probably has much more to do with economic reality than law) is that such women are in 'a special position which requires them to be afforded special protection, but which is not comparable either with that of a man or with that of a woman actually at work'. Instead women on maternity leave are afforded the 'special protection' of the Pregnant Workers Directive, referred to below, which does not require full pay to be guaranteed during maternity leave.[77] **4.16**

The Equal Treatment Directive provides in its Recitals that 'the definition and progressive implementation of the principle of equal treatment in matters of social security should be ensured by means of subsequent instruments'. The Social Security Directive[78] was enacted shortly after the original Equal Treatment Directive. Later still, the Occupational Social Security Directive[79] was enacted.[80] **4.17**

---

[74] EPA, s 1(2). Specific provision is made addressing pregnancy and maternity pay at s1(2)(d)–(e).

[75] *Gillespie and o'rs v Northern Health and Social Services Board and o'rs*, Case C-342/93 [1996] ICR 498. This requirement is not limited to cases where the pay rise is backdated to the period covered by the reference pay: *Alabaster v Woolwich*, Case C-147/02 [2005] ICR 695.

[76] *Gillespie and o'rs v Northern Health and Social Services Board and o'rs*, ibid; *Alabaster v Woolwich*, ibid.

[77] *Gillespie and o'rs v Northern Health and Social Services Board and o'rs*, ibid, paras 16–18.

[78] Council Directive 79/7/EEC of 19 December 1978 on the progressive implementation of the principle of equal treatment for men and women in matters of social security (OJ L 006, 10 Feb 1979, 24–25).

[79] Council Directive 86/378/EEC of 24 July 1986 on the implementation of the principle of equal treatment for men and women in occupational social security schemes (OJ L 225, 12 Aug 1986, 40–42).

[80] In 1986.

The purpose of the Social Security Directive[81] is expressed in its Article 1, as follows:

> The purpose of this Directive is the progressive implementation, in the field of social security and other elements of social protection provided for in Article 3, of the principle of equal treatment for men and women in matters of social security, hereinafter referred to as 'the principle of equal treatment'.

Its scope is widely drafted and covers:

(a) statutory schemes which provide protection against the following risks:
- sickness
- invalidity
- old age
- accidents at work and occupational diseases
- unemployment;

(b) social assistance, in so far as it is intended to supplement or replace the schemes referred to in (a).[82]

4.18 The 'principle of equal treatment' is defined in materially the same way as in the original text of the Equal Treatment Directive as meaning 'that there shall be no discrimination whatsoever on ground of sex either directly, or indirectly by reference in particular to marital or family status'.[83] However, the Social Security Directive permitted exceptions relating to State retirement age for pension purposes,[84] subject to Member States periodically examining such 'matters excluded . . . in order to ascertain, in the light of social developments in the matter concerned, whether there is justification for maintaining the exclusions concerned'. This has meant that discriminatory retirement ages remain for State pension purposes, with women acquiring an entitlement to a State pension at 60 and men at 65.[85] It also permits Member States to use these different pensionable ages in relation to other benefits, but only where this is 'objectively necessary in

---

81 Council Directive 79/7/EEC of 19 December 1978 on the progressive implementation of the principle of equal treatment for men and women in matters of social security (OJ L 006, 10 Feb 1979, 24–25). It can be noted that the concept of 'pay' in Art 141 'cannot encompass social security schemes or benefits, in particular retirement pensions, directly governed by legislation without any element of agreement within the undertaking or the occupational branch concerned, which are compulsorily applicable to general categories of workers', *Barber v Guardian Royal Exchange Assurance Group*, n 44 above, para 22.

82 Art 3. For exceptions see Art 3(2) and see Art 7 for permitted exceptions.

83 Art 4. For examples of its impact see *Borrie Clarke v Chief Adjudication Officer* [1987] ECR 2865; *R (Taylor) v Secretary of State for Social Security* [1999] ECR I-8955; *Hockenjos v Secretary of State for Social Security (No 2)* [2004] EWCA Civ 1749. For the impact on transpersons, see *Richards v Secretary of State for Work and Pensions*, Case C-423/04 [2006].

84 Art 7.

85 From 6 April 2020, the State pension age for women will be 65, the same as for men. Women's State pension age will start moving gradually from 60 to 65 from 2010; Pensions Act 1995, s 126 and Sch 4.

order to avoid disrupting the financial equilibrium of the social security system or to ensure consistency between the retirement pension scheme and the other benefit scheme'.[86] This might be contrasted with the position under the Equal Treatment Directive which contains no such exception.[87] The Social Security Directive excluded occupational pensions but its Article 3(3) anticipated that separate provision was to be made by providing that:

> With a view to ensuring implementation of the principle of equal treatment in occupational schemes, the Council, acting on a proposal from the Commission, will adopt provisions defining its substance, its scope and the arrangements for its application.

Thereafter the Occupational Social Security Directive[88] was enacted and addressed gender discrimination in occupational schemes. It gives effect to a number of decisions of the ECJ, holding that occupational pensions and related benefits constitute 'pay' within the meaning of Article 141.[89] The Occupational Social Security Directive was amended in 1996[90] to give effect to later decisions of the ECJ on occupational pensions, in particular.[91] It does not permit discriminatory retirement ages.[92] The Occupational Social Security Directive along with decisions from the ECJ on 'pay' and 'pensions' have proved very important. In the UK they have caused the enactment of the Pensions Act 1995 and the Occupational Pension Schemes (Equal Treatment) Regulations 1995[93] made thereunder.[94] **4.19**

There have been other European Community measures which have been of significance to sex equality law, and which have compelled change in UK law, but which have been driven by other—non-discrimination—Treaty provisions. For example, the Pregnant Workers Directive[95] which, although it addresses the treatment of **4.20**

---

86 *R (Taylor) v Secretary of State for Social Security* [1999] ECR I-8955; *Hepple v Adjudication Officer; Adjudication Officer v Stec* [2000] ECR I-3701.

87 *Marshall v Southampton and South-West Hampshire Area Health Authority (Teaching)* C-152/84 [1986] ICR 335; [1986] IRLR 140. And see the Occupational Social Security Directive, discussed below, which does not allow for discriminatory retirement ages.

88 Council Directive 86/378/EEC of 24 July 1986 on the implementation of the principle of equal treatment for men and women in occupational social security schemes (OJ L 225, 12.8.1986, 40 – 0042).

89 Eg *Bilka-Kaufhaus GmbH v Weber Von Hartz*, n 42 above.

90 Amended by 96/97/EC.

91 *Bilka-Kaufhaus GmbH v Weber Von Hartz*, n 42 above; *Barber v Guardian Royal Exchange Assurance Group*, n 44 above.

92 Art 6(1)(f).

93 SI 1995/3183.

94 See Chap 6.

95 Council Directive 92/85/EEC of 19 Oct 1992 on the introduction of measures to encourage improvements in the safety and health at work of pregnant workers and workers who have recently given birth or are breastfeeding (tenth individual directive within the meaning of Art 16 (1) of Directive 89/391/EEC) (OJ L 348, 28 Nov 1992, 1). This has been given effect to in domestic law largely through provision made under the Employment Rights Act 1996 and also through the Management of Health and Safety at Work Regulations 1999, SI 1999/3242.

pregnant women at work (including provisions addressing maternity leave,[96] time off for ante-natal care,[97] risk assessments,[98] and prohibiting dismissal[99]) and is therefore very important to women's equality at work, it is primarily a health and safety measure enacted under EC health and safety law.[100] Its relationship to sex equality law has become formally closer since the enactment of the Equal Treatment Amendment Directive which makes specific reference to its terms, as noted above. In addition, the Parental Leave Directive[101] requires Member States to make provision for parental leave on birth or adoption and for time off for family emergencies.

4.21 A new consolidated—'Recast'—Directive has now been enacted merging the seven current Directives on equality between men and women in employment and occupation. Directive 2006/54/EC consolidates seven Directives and the ECJ's decisions interpreting these Directives into a single text. The seven Directives are: Directive 75/117/EC on the application of the principle of equal pay for men and women; Directive 76/207/EC on equal treatment for men and women as regards access to employment; Directive 2002/73/EC, amending Directive 76/207/EC, on equal treatment for men and women as regards employment, vocational training, and promotion and working conditions; Directive 86/378/EC on equal treatment for men and women in occupational social security schemes; Directive 96/97/EC, amending Directive 86/378/EC, on the implementation of the principle of equal treatment for men and women in occupational social security schemes; Directive 97/80/EC on the burden of proof in cases of discrimination based on sex; and Directive 98/52/EC on the extension of Directive 97/80/EC to the UK. The Recast Directive must be implemented by Member States by 15 August 2008 and the seven Directives that are being consolidated will be repealed from 15 August 2009.[102]

4.22 The new Gender Goods and Services Directive is addressed below at paragraph 4.47.

---

96 Art 8.

97 Art 9.

98 Arts 4 and 5.

99 Art 10.

100 Directive 89/391 and Art 118a of the EC Treaty (before consolidation) now Art 138.

101 Council Directive 96/34/EC of 3 June 1996 on the framework agreement on parental leave concluded by UNICE, CEEP, and the ETUC, extended to the UK by Council Directive 97/75/EC (of 15 December 1997 amending and extending, to the United Kingdom of Great Britain and Northern Ireland, Directive 96/34/EC on the framework agreement on parental leave concluded by UNICE, CEEP and the ETUC). This has been given effect to in domestic law largely through provision made the Employment Rights Act 1996.

102 Directive 2006/54/EC.

(3) Atypical workers

The Council Directive on the Protection of Young People at Work[103] makes provision requiring Member States to prohibit children from working and protecting young people at work.[104] There are a number of other Directives aimed at promoting equality between nationals of Member States or categories of workers. The former group includes the Posted Workers Directive,[105] protecting 'posted workers' (those being workers 'who, for a limited period, carr[y] out . . . work in the territory of a Member State other than the State in which [they] normally work.'[106]), and the Directive Safeguarding the Supplementary Pension Rights of Employed and Self Employed Persons moving within the Community.[107] Because of the disproportionate presence of women and certain minorities in atypical work, the latter group of Directives, addressing discrimination between categories of workers, are likely to impact significantly on the rights of women and some ethnic minorities at work. This group of Directives includes the Part-Time Workers Directive[108] and the Fixed-Term Workers Directive.[109] **4.23**

C. The Treaty of Amsterdam and the 'New' Directives

(1) Introduction

The amendments made to Article 141 by the Treaty of Amsterdam have been dealt with above. Prior to the Treaty of Amsterdam there was no competence in Europe to legislate against discrimination outside of those grounds originally **4.24**

[103] 94/33/EC of 22 June 1994.

[104] This has been given effect to in domestic law largely through provision made under the Working Time Regulations 1999, SI 1999/1833 and also through the Management of Health and Safety at Work Regulations 1999, SI 1999/3242.

[105] Directive 96/71/EC of the European Parliament and of the Council of 16 December 1996 concerning the posting of workers in the framework of the provision of services.

[106] Art 2(1).

[107] Council Directive 98/49/EC of 29 June 1998 on safeguarding the supplementary pension rights of employed and self-employed persons moving within the Community.

[108] Council Directive 97/81/EC of 15 December 1997 concerning the Framework Agreement on part-time work concluded by UNICE, CEEP and the ETUC - Annex: Framework agreement on part-time work, extended to the UK by Directive 98/23/EC (Council Directive 98/23/EC of 7 April 1998 on the extension of Directive 97/81/EC on the framework agreement on part-time work concluded by UNICE, CEEP and the ETUC to the United Kingdom of Great Britain and Northern Ireland). This has been given effect to in domestic law largely through provision made under the Employment Relations Act 1999 and through the Part-Time Workers (Prevention of Less Favourable Treatment) Regulations 2000, SI 2000/1551.

[109] Council Directive 1999/70/EC of 28 June 1999 concerning the framework agreement on fixed-term work concluded by ETUC, UNICE and CEEP. This has been given effect to in domestic law largely through provision made under the Employment Act 2002 and through the Fixed-Term Employees (Prevention of Less Favourable Treatment) Regulations 2002, SI 2002/2034.

protected by the Treaty of Rome, namely gender and nationality discrimination (as between nationals of Member States). Increasingly there were soft law measures addressing race,[110] disability,[111] and sexual orientation[112] for example, but no mandatory law outside the fields of gender and nationality. However, Article 13[113] of the EC Treaty, inserted by the Treaty of Amsterdam,[114] now importantly provides that:

> Without prejudice to the other provisions of this Treaty and within the limits of the powers conferred by it upon the Community, the Council, acting unanimously on a proposal from the Commission and after consulting the European Parliament, may take appropriate action to combat discrimination based on sex, racial or ethnic origin, religion or belief, disability, age or sexual orientation.

4.25 Pursuant to Article 13, three new Directives have been enacted: the Race Directive[115] which requires Member States to outlaw race discrimination in the employment and related fields and in the provision of education, goods, and services, housing, and in relation to 'social protections' and 'social advantages'; the Framework Directive[116] which requires Member States to outlaw discrimination connected to religion and belief, disability, sexual orientation, and age in the employment and related fields; and the Gender Goods and Services Directive[117]

---

110 See, for example, Resolution of the European Council and the Representatives of the Governments of the Member States, meeting within the Council of 29 May 1990, on the fight against racism and xenophobia, OJ C 157/1, 27 June 1990; European Council Consultative Commission on Racism and Xenophobia, Final Report, 12 April 1995, Doc SN2129/95; 1986 Joint Declaration against Racism and Xenophobia signed by European Parliament, European Commission, and European Council, OJ C 158/1, 25 June 1986; Report of the Committee of Inquiry on the Rise of Fascism and Fascism in Europe of the European Parliament, 25 Nov 1985.

111 For example, Council Recommendation (EEC) 86/379 of 27 July 1986 on the employment of disabled people in the Community OJ L 225/43.

112 Resolution of the European Parliament of 13 March 1984 on sexual discrimination at the workplace (OJ 1984 C 104, p 46); Commission recommendation of 27 Nov 1991 on the protection of the dignity of women and men at work (OJ L 49, p 1); resolution of the European Parliament of 8 Feb 1994 on equal rights for homosexuals and lesbians in the European Community (OJ C 61, p 40)).

113 Note too, Art 2 makes clear that social objectives and equality between men and women (though apparently not between other protected classes) are key objectives of the Community: 'The Community shall have as its task, by establishing a common market and an economic and monetary union and by implementing common policies or activities referred to in Articles 3 and 4, to promote throughout the Community a harmonious, balanced and sustainable development of economic activities, a high level of employment and of social protection, equality between men and women, sustainable and non-inflationary growth, a high degree of competitiveness and convergence of economic performance, a high level of protection and improvement of the quality of the environment, the raising of the standard of living and quality of life, and economic and social cohesion and solidarity among Member States.'

114 Art 6A: OJ C 340, 10 Nov 1997, 1.

115 Council Directive 2000/43/EC, of 29 June 2000 implementing the principle of equal treatment between persons irrespective of racial or ethnic origin (OJ L 180, 19 July 2000, 22).

116 Council Directive 2000/78/EC of 27 Nov 2000 establishing a general framework for equal treatment in employment and occupation (OJ L 303, 2 Dec 2000, 16).

117 Council Directive 2004/113/EC of 13 Dec 2004 implementing the principle of equal treatment between men and women in the access to and supply of goods and services (OJ L 373, 21 Dec 2004, 37–43).

which requires Member States to outlaw gender discrimination in the provision of goods and services, including insurance.

The context for Article 13 and these Directives is very important indeed. The driver for the enactment of Article 13 and then the Directives came, in particular, from the race lobby which became increasingly well organized following electoral gains made by the far right across Europe. The Race Directive and the Framework Directive were unanimously agreed in 'record time',[118] less than two years after the coming into force of the Treaty of Amsterdam 1997.[119] This speed was all the more extraordinary when placed against the context of a previously reluctant Council,[120] particularly resistant to legislative action on race. However, the 1980s, and particularly the 1990s, saw a significant increase in the lobbying by the European Parliament and the formation of an effective, organized pan-European lobby, galvanized around the issues of racial and religious discrimination, most notably in the form of the Starting Line Group. These two bodies 'propelled the European Union forward . . . [and] raised the profile of racism in Europe'.[121] The very important Starting Line Group was no doubt inspired in selecting its own name by the comment of the European Council on the Joint Declaration Against Racism and Xenophobia, signed by the European Parliament, Commission, and Council,[122] that this was not 'a starting point for concrete action'.[123] Unlike the European Council, the consciousness of the European Parliament was stirred in 1984 when the far right made 'unprecedented advances'[124] in the European elections—in particular 10 members of the French Front Nationale were elected attracting 11.2 per cent of the French vote.[125] This led the Parliament to establish 4.26

118 E Bleich and MC Feldmann, 'The Rise of Race? Europeanization and Antiracist Policymaking in the EU' [2004], Paper prepared for the conference 'The Impact of Europeanization on Politics and Policy in Europe: Trends and Trajectories,' held at the University of Toronto, 7–9 May 2004, available at: <http://individual.utoronto.ca/wittenbrinck/europeanization/BleichFeldmann.doc> citing (at n 20): 'EU agrees on measures to combat racial discrimination', *Deutsche Presse-Agentur*, 6 June 2000; 'EU to combat discrimination', *Financial Times*, 6 June 2000.

119 The Treaty of Amsterdam came into force on 1 May 1999.

120 M Bell, *Anti-Discrimination Law and the European Union* (2002, OUP), 61–63.

121 E Bleich and MC Feldmann, 'The Rise of Race? Europeanization and Antiracist Policymaking in the EU' [2004] Paper prepared for the conference 'The Impact of Europeanization on Politics and Policy in Europe: Trends and Trajectories,' held at the University of Toronto, 7–9 May 2004, available at: <http:// individual.utoronto.ca/wittenbrinck/europeanization/BleichFeldmann.doc>, 6.

122 [1986] OJ C 158/1.

123 Formigioni, *Debates of the European Parliament No 2-340/107*, 11 June 1986, cited in M Bell Anti-Discrimination Law and the European Union (2002, OUP), 61. See later for the Starting Point, being the chosen title for the Starting Line Group's call for an amendment to the EC Treaty.

124 M Bell and L Waddington, 'The 1996 Intergovernmental Conference and the Prospects of a Non-Discrimination Treaty Article' [1996], *Industrial Law Journal*, Vol 25, 320, 321.

125 G Ivaldi (2002) 'Overview of Extreme Right Parties in France' Overview Paper produced as part of the International Research Group on Extreme Right Electorates and Party Success, Johannes Gutenberg University Mainz (Germany), available at: <http://www.politik.uni-mainz.de/ereps/download/france_overview.pdf>.

a temporary committee of inquiry into the rise of fascism and racism in Europe. The resulting *Evrigenis Report*[126] found that xenophobia was rising with 'alarming intensity' and recommended action by the European Community to define Community powers more broadly by revision of the Treaties if necessary, so as to allow for Community action on race relations. In response, the Council, Commission, and Parliament issued the 'Joint Declaration against Racism and Xenophobia' referred to above on 11 June 1986,[127] important only for its symbolic status and characteristic of much of the subsequent activity in following a soft law route. It took several more years for any further measures to appear. The decade following the Joint Declaration was 'plagued by prevarication and symbolic politics',[128] illustrated by, for example, the 1990 Council Resolution on the fight against racism and xenophobia,[129] which identified policy measures useful in tackling such discrimination but which provided Member States with total discretion over which (if any) measures to adopt, and which was silent as to enforcement. The European Parliament continued to advocate the need for 'race competence' in the European Community, and commissioned Glyn Ford to produce a report on racism and xenophobia, presented in 1990.[130] The Parliament also passed a series of resolutions on racism (dated 21 April 1993, 3 December 1993, 27 October 1994, 27 April 1995, and 26 October 1995). In response, the Commission and the Council issued supportive statements, but took no significant or compelling action.[131] However, institutional attitudes began to shift in the 1990s. This shift coincided with the increase in cross-border racist activity, the perceived increase of violent racism, and again the electoral advances made by extreme right parties in Europe, in particular, in the 1994 European Parliament elections where the extreme right won more than eight million votes (claiming more than 10 per cent of the votes in France and Belgium, and with the German Republikaner Partei, a German neo-Nazi party, winning more than one million votes).[132]

4.27 As mentioned, of great significance was the establishment of an effective and organized anti-racism lobby, and in particular the formation of the Starting

126 European Parliament, Committee of Inquiry into the Rise of Fascism and Racism in Europe, (1985) Luxembourg, PE DOC A2-160/85.

127 [1986] OJ C 158/1.

128 M Bell and L Waddington, 'The 1996 Intergovernmental Conference and the Prospects of a Non-Discrimination Treaty Article' [1996] *Industrial Law Journal*, Vol 25, 320, 321.

129 [1990] OJ C 157/1.

130 *Report of the Committee of Inquiry on Racism and Xenophobia* (1991) Luxembourg, OOPEC, 1991; and published in a book in 1992: G Ford, *Fascist Europe: The Rise of Racism and Xenophobia* (1992, Pluto Press).

131 For a detailed account of the acts of the Council and the Parliament see further, I Chopin, 'The Starting Line Group: A Harmonised Approach to Fight Racism and to Promote Equal Treatment' (1999) *European Journal of Migration and Law* 117–20; and for activities of the Council, see M Bell, *Anti-Discrimination Law and the European Union* (2002, OUP), 69–72.

132 M Bell, *Anti-Discrimination Law and the European Union* (2002, OUP), 63–64.

Line Group. The Starting Line Group was formed in 1991 at the initiative of the Commission for Racial Equality, the Dutch National Bureau against Racism, and the Churches Commission for Migrants in Europe. They were joined by other national and European organizations so that by 1999 the Starting Line Group consisted of a 'network of nearly 400 non-governmental organisations, semi-official organisations, trade unions, churches, independent experts, and academics' based throughout the EU.[133] The Starting Line Group's strategy was law-based, calling for the adoption of legal measures and a harmonized approach to non-discrimination throughout the EU, resulting eventually in the publication of a draft Council Directive on the elimination of racial discrimination, known as the Starting Line.[134] The choice of a Directive was motivated in part by the prospect of EU enlargement, and the need to ensure that such a Directive would form part of the *acquis communautaire*, thereby being required to be incorporated into the national systems of acceding countries, which 'do not necessarily share the same tradition of human rights, protection of minorities or fighting racism'.[135] The Commission declined to act on the Starting Line proposals, asserting that there was no clear legal mandate to authorize such a measure.[136] Thereafter, the Starting Line Group revised its strategy to lobby for change to the EC Treaty so as to provide an authoritative basis for legal action against racial discrimination. The *Starting Point*, published in 1995, called for an amendment to Article 3 of the EC Treaty to include within the EC's objectives the elimination of discrimination based on race, colour, religion, or national, social, or ethnic origin, and the insertion of a new paragraph to provide competence to legislate on those matters.[137] In 1995, prior to the Intergovernmental Conference which resulted in the Amsterdam Treaty, the European Parliament called for an amendment to the Treaty to provide Community competence to address racial discrimination on at least two separate occasions.[138] In December 1995, the Commission finally endorsed the proposals for a general (rather than race-specific) non-discrimination clause to be inserted into the EC

[133] I Chopin 'The Starting Line Group: A Harmonised Approach to Fight Racism and to Promote Equal Treatment' (1999) *European Journal of Migration and Law* 1, 111.

[134] Ibid, 111–112.

[135] Ibid, 114.

[136] M Bell, *Anti-Discrimination Law and the European Union* (2002, OUP), 63.

[137] I Chopin 'The Starting Line Group: A Harmonised Approach to Fight Racism and to Promote Equal Treatment' (1999) *European Journal of Migration and Law* 1, 116.

[138] European Parliament resolution on racism, xenophobia, and anti-semitism, OJ C 126, 27 April 1995; the Parliament 'recommends that the Commission should introduce a proposal for an anti-discrimination directive ... [and] insists that, after the revision of the Treaties, the European Community should be entrusted with clear competencies which empower it to take action to combat racism, xenophobia and anti-semitism'. European Parliament resolution on racism, xenophobia, and anti-semitism, OJ C 308/140, 26 Oct 1995; the Parliament again called 'once more upon the Commission to submit a proposal for an anti-discrimination directive as a matter of urgency ... [and] [u]rge[d] the Consultative Commission to reiterate its demand for a Treaty change in 1996 to include unambiguously therein the fight against racism and xenophobia'.

Treaty.[139] Also in December 1995, the Council's Intergovernmental Conference 'Reflection Group' reported 'majority support' for the amendment of the EC Treaty to prohibit general discrimination and to provide competence to act in such matters.[140] As Mark Bell has observed, the UK was the main objector to such a move arguing that 'the problems of discrimination (particularly on such sensitive questions of race and religion) are best dealt with . . . through national legislation'.[141] However, the 1997 election of a new Labour Government in the UK, less than two months before the conclusion of the Amsterdam Treaty, 'removed the final obstacle'[142] and consensus was reached on the inclusion of Article 13.

4.28 There are significant differences between Article 13 and the *Starting Point* proposal.[143] Firstly, contrary to the recommendations of the Consultative Commission and the wishes of the Parliament, Article 13 is not directly effective; it is an enabling provision, not a compelling one.[144] Secondly, 'the European Parliament is assigned a very marginal role in the legislative process, with only the minimal right to consultation' which is particularly significant, given its central role in supporting legislative change.[145] Thirdly, the provision requires unanimity for the adoption of any legislative measure. And fourthly, contrary to the *Starting Point* proposal, Article 13 is general, rather than specifically referring to racial discrimination. Given these differences, and in particular the unanimity requirement, there were some doubts as to the likelihood of strong European legislation prohibiting racial discrimination.

4.29 The Commission's eventual draft Directive was part of a three-stranded package of proposals to implement the new Article 13, consisting of:

- a Directive to combat discrimination in the labour market on all grounds referred to in Article 13, with the exception of sex, to 'tackle the area in which discrimination on all grounds is most evident and where it is frequently most damaging to individuals' chances of success in society';

139 European Commission, *Communication on racism, xenophobia, and anti-semitism*, 13 December 1995, COM (95) 653, 18.

140 M Bell, *Anti-Discrimination Law and the European Union* (2002, OUP), 71–72.

141 Foreign and Commonwealth Office, *A Partnership of Nations* (1997, HMSO) para 57 cited in M Bell, *Anti-Discrimination Law and the European Union* (2002, OUP), 72.

142 Bell, ibid, 72.

143 For a full discussion, see I Chopin and J Niessen (ed), *The Starting Line and the Incorporation of the Racial Equality Directive into the National Laws of the EU Member States and Accession States* (2001) Commission for Racial Equality and Migration Policy Group.

144 And may be compared therefore to Art 141. As to direct effect, see below, para 4.64.

145 M Bell, 'The new Article 13 EC Treaty: a platform for a European policy against racism?' in G Moon and JUSTICE (eds), *Racial Discrimination: Developing and Using a New Legal Framework* (2000, Hart Publishing), 85.

- a Directive to combat discrimination on grounds of racial and ethnic origin beyond the labour market, taking 'account of the experience of the Community during the European Year against Racism and, in particular, of the strong political will which exists to take action to combat as many aspects as possible of racial discrimination';
- a programme of action addressing all grounds of discrimination covered by Article 13 except sex 'designed to complement the legislative proposals by supporting and supplementing the Member States' efforts to combat discrimination'.[146]

As mentioned, the Race Directive was negotiated and adopted by the Council in record time, only seven months after the Commission's proposals were published. This speed, however, was not indicative of any ease on the part of Member States towards the Commission's original proposal: 'In fact, though no Member State was opposed in principle to the idea of Community law on racial discrimination, a number of Governments had serious difficulties with particular points.'[147] **4.30**

The impetus for such speedy action when it came in the form of the Race Directive was, 'in part, . . . not surprising . . . After all, the Starting Line Group and the Parliament had been pressing specific proposals on the European Union since well before the Treaty amendments of 1997'.[148] However, also important was the raised profile of racism in Europe in late 1999 and early 2000, highlighted by the Commission's Communication references to the publication of the Stephen Lawrence Inquiry Report[149] in 1999, already referred to in Chapter 2, **4.31**

---

146 Communication from the Commission to the Council, the European Parliament, the Economic and Social Committee, and the Committee of the Regions on certain Community measures to combat discrimination, COM (1999) 564 final, 8 available at <http://ec.europa.eu/justice_home/doc_centre/rights/discrimination/doc_rights_discrim_en.htm>.

147 A Tyson 'The Negotiation of the European Community Directive on Racial Discrimination' [2001] *European Journal of Migration and Law* 3, 201. Adam Tyson, a member of the Commission, has identified a large number of areas which were the subject of particular negotiation, including: use of the term 'race' and possible links to theories supporting the existence of separate human races; the definition of indirect discrimination, including the use of ethnic statistical data, opposed by some countries (particularly against the context of the Holocaust) but supported by others, arguing for consistency with European gender standards; the formulation of incitement (changed to instructions) to discriminate and possible confusion with criminal standards; discussion over the scope of the concept of 'social advantages'; providing for positive action, without requiring such, amongst other things.

148 E Bleich and MC Feldmann, 'The Rise of Race? Europeanization and Antiracist Policymaking in the EU' (2004), paper prepared for the conference 'The Impact of Europeanization on Politics and Policy in Europe: Trends and Trajectories', held at the University of Toronto, 7–9 May 2004, available at: <http://individual.utoronto.ca/wittenbrinck/europeanization/BleichFeldmann.doc>.

149 *Report of an Inquiry by Sir William McPherson of Cluny* (1999 Cmnd 4262), para 6.34, available on the Home Office website at <http://www.archive.official-documents.co.uk/document/cm42/4262/4262.htm>.

and anti-immigrant riots in southern Spain in early 2000.[150] In addition, the Commission was concerned at the time over 'discrimination in parts of Central and Eastern Europe, especially as regards the Roma and persons with learning disabilities' and was keen 'to send out a signal about the importance of respect for fundamental rights to [those] countries . . . which were at the time seeking accession to the EU'.[151] Related to this was the concern of the Community institutions, like the Starting Line Group, to ensure that legislation based on Article 13 formed part of the *acquis communautaire* to which such acceding countries must commit.[152] One of the most significant reasons, however, for the speed of the Directive negotiations was the results of the October 1999 elections in Austria, which led to the inclusion of Jörg Haider's extreme right Freedom Party in the Austrian Government: 'the success of Jörg Haider's Freedom Party in joining the Austrian governing coalition changed the tempo of activity for the proposals.'[153] Nevertheless, there were concerns at the speed with which the Race Directive was adopted, and the UK House of Lords in particular criticized the lack of appropriate scrutiny of the final text.[154]

4.32 Paradoxically, and reflecting the history of the Race Relations Acts in the UK,[155] the Race Directive was also enacted against a backdrop of increasing intolerance towards immigration and a 'Fortress Europe'. This resulted in the galvanizing of 'national and European civil society into transnational action for anti-racism measures at EU level, so as to ameliorate the effects of immigration policies. Moreover, the EU institutions, in particular the Council, came under pressure to 'legitimise immigration policies through greater attention to promoting integration'.[156]

150 E Bleich and MC Feldmann, 'The Rise of Race? Europeanization and Antiracist Policymaking in the EU' (2004), Paper prepared for the conference 'The Impact of Europeanization on Politics and Policy in Europe: Trends and Trajectories', held at the University of Toronto, 7–9 May 2004, available at: <http://individual.utoronto.ca/wittenbrinck/europeanization/BleichFeldmann.doc>, reference 'Uneasy truce as Spain reels from racial unrest', *The Guardian*, 14 February 2000 and 'EU Parliament condemns racist violence in Spain', *Agence France Presse*, 17 February 2000.

151 E Ellis, *European Union Anti Discrimination Law* (2005, OUP), 29.

152 House of Lords Select Committee on the EU, *EU Proposals to Combat Discrimination*, HL Session 1999–2000, 9th Report, HL paper 68 (2000), para 7.

153 E Guild, 'The EC Directive on Race Discrimination: Surprises, Possibilities and Limitation' *Industrial Law Journal* [2000] Vol 29, 416. And see, A Tyson, 'The Negotiation of the European Community Directive on Racial Discrimination' [2001] *European Journal of Migration and Law* 3, 218, and J Niessen, 'The Amsterdam Treaty and NGO Responses', *European Journal of Migration and Law* [2000] 2, 203–14.

154 Housc of Lords Select Committee on the EU, *EU Proposals to Combat Discrimination*, HL Session 1999–2000, 9th Report, HL paper 68 (2000), para 7.

155 See Chap 2.

156 M Bell, *Anti-Discrimination Law and the European Union* (2002, OUP), 67, internal footnote removed.

(2) Race Directive

The Race Directive[157] provides that the 'principle of equal treatment shall mean that there shall be no direct or indirect discrimination based on racial or ethnic origin' within the scope protected by the terms of the Directive, namely employment and related areas, social protection and advantages, and access to goods and services including housing.[158] The Race Directive excludes nationality discrimination,[159] so does not interfere with immigration policy, and does not address 'colour' or 'national origins',[160] though the latter two concepts are plainly embraced by the concepts of 'race' and 'ethnicity'. This has had an impact domestically, as discussed below.[161] **4.33**

The Race Directive defines direct discrimination as occurring 'where one person is treated less favourably than another is, has been or would be treated in a comparable situation on grounds of racial or ethnic origin'.[162] Importantly, the Race Directive provides that: 'Indirect discrimination shall be taken to occur where an apparently neutral provision, criterion or practice would put persons of a racial or ethnic origin at a particular disadvantage compared with other persons, unless that provision, criterion or practice is objectively justified by a legitimate aim and the means of achieving that aim are appropriate and necessary.'[163] This provides for a much more liberal meaning of indirect discrimination than that contained in the original enactment of the Race Relations Act 1976 (RRA). In particular it does not require proof of the existence of a rule or condition constituting an absolute bar.[164] Further, and importantly, the new definition contains a test of 'disparate impact' which is far more liberal than that contained within domestic law even as amended, in the case of the SDA, in consequence of the Burden of Proof Directive.[165] The new meaning given to indirect discrimination does not require proof of statistical disadvantage in the same way that the old law did. There is no requirement to show *actual* group disadvantage ('would put persons under a particular disadvantage').[166] The explanation for **4.34**

157 2000/43/EC.

158 Arts 2 and 3. See Art 50 of EC Treaty for the meaning of 'services'.

159 Art 3(2).

160 Compare the RRA.

161 Para 4.40.

162 Race Directive, Art 2(2)(a) and Framework Directive, Art 2(2)(a).

163 Race Directive, Art 2.

164 Reflecting the approach to indirect discrimination found in the Burden of Proof Directive. Cf *Perera v The Civil Service Commission and the Department of Customs & Excise* [1983] IRLR 166 and *Meer v Tower Hamlets* [1988] IRLR 399.

165 Sex Discrimination (Indirect Discrimination and Burden of Proof) Regulations 2001 SI 2001/2660, since amended again to take account of the Amended Equal Treatment Directive as described above.

166 The new definition reflects the approach taken by the ECJ under Art 39 of the EC Treaty in *O'Flynn v Adjudication Officer* [1996] ECR 1-2617.

this,[167] alluded to above,[168] lies in the political traditions of certain European countries where the collection of statistics on racial origin in particular is prohibited for historic reasons. The effect of this change, which has been incorporated into domestic law, is likely to be very significant indeed.

4.35 Harassment is expressly defined and required to be prohibited:

> Harassment shall be deemed to be discrimination within the meaning of Paragraph 1, when an unwanted conduct related to racial or ethnic origin takes place with the purpose or effect of violating the dignity of a person and of creating an intimidating, hostile, degrading, humiliating or offensive environment. In this context, the concept of harassment may be defined in accordance with the national laws and practice of the Member States.[169]

4.36 As mentioned, the scope of the Directive is wide and extends to 'social protection' and 'advantages'. Such terms are not defined in the Directive. In the context of Regulation 1612/68/EEC on the free movement of workers within the Community the concept of 'social advantages'[170] has been given a wide meaning, as mentioned above. It is likely that the same meaning will be afforded the same expression in the Race Directive. Otherwise its scope is not clearly specified. Instead Article 3 identifies the scope of the Race Directive with the qualifying words 'Within the limits of the powers conferred upon the Community, this Directive shall apply to all persons, as regards both the public and private sectors, including public bodies, in relation to' the areas covered. This reflects the limitation in Article 13 but begs the question what relevant powers the Community confers. As seen above, the power to enact legislation under Article 13 is qualified by the words: 'Without prejudice to the other provisions of this Treaty and within the limits of the powers conferred by it upon the Community.'

4.37 The first phrase ('Without prejudice to the other provisions of this Treaty') might reflect the interpretative principle *generalibus specialia derogant*, that is that where there is a general enactment in an instrument which, if taken in its most comprehensive sense, would cover a situation for which specific provision is made by some other enactment within the instrument, it is presumed that the situation was intended to be covered by the specific provision.[171] Thus, in the case of Article 12 which contains the qualifying words 'without prejudice to any special provisions contained', the words refer to 'other provisions of the Treaty in which

---

167 Given by Mike O'Brien, the Parliamentary Under-Secretary of State at the Home Office, Minutes of Evidence 17 June 2000, HC 581, cited in (2000) EOR, No 93, 34–35.

168 N 147.

169 Race Directive, Art 2(3). Art 2(3) of the Framework Directive is in the same terms in respect of the grounds set down in Art 1 of the Framework Directive.

170 Regulation 7(2). See too, *Secretary of State for Defence v Elias* [2006] EWCA Civ 1293, para 56.

171 F Bennion, *Statutory Interpretation* (4th edn 2002, Butterworths), 998.

the application of the general principle set out in that Article is given concrete form in respect of specific situations. Examples of that are the provisions concerning free movement of workers, the right of establishment and the freedom to provide services'.[172] Such an approach to the qualifying words in Article 13 would suggest, therefore, that, for example, a case addressing obstacles to movement across Europe for reasons connected with national origins, where also connected to nationality, would fall to be considered under the 'free movement' provisions. Similarly, should an issue arise concerning race *and* gender, the gender aspect would require consideration under Article 141 and the gender Directives. In fact as can be seen, the first phrase would appear to qualify Article 13 rather more broadly than the analogous phrase in Article 12. Article 12 is subject only to *special provisions*; Article 13 is subject to *the other provisions*. However, if this were to have the effect that an Article 13 measure should not encroach upon the areas covered by other Treaty provisions, this would be of some concern. Firstly, there are a number of Treaty provisions which overlap with the areas protected by the Race Directive, for example Article 137(2) which provides competence to the European Council to enact measures directed at 'working conditions' and the 'social protection of workers', amongst other things (an area covered by the Directive); similarly Article 12 gives the European Council competence to enact legislation directed at prohibiting nationality discrimination (and though nationality discrimination is excluded from the Race Directive, discrimination connected to national origins is not and there is therefore obvious room for overlap). As has been observed, the importance of this potential for overlap and the need to define the boundaries lies in the fact that different decision-making procedures apply under the different Treaty Articles.[173] So, for example, whilst Article 13 requires unanimity by the Council and confers a less central role on Parliament, Article 137 allows for the adoption of Directives by qualified majority voting in Council and grants Parliament a more significant role through the co-decision power.[174] Mark Bell observes that:

> in Article 13, the phrase 'without prejudice to the other provisions of the Treaty' should be interpreted as referring to other Treaty articles where discrimination is dealt with in respect of a specific situation. In particular, Article 137(1) EC and Article 141 EC, both provide express powers to adopt measures for combating sexual discrimination in employment. Therefore, the proviso in Article 13 would suggest that measures concerning sexual equality in employment are to be dealt with under either of these more specific provisions. Indeed, the Commission's proposed amendments to the Equal Treatment Directive [by the Equal Treatment Amendment Directive] are based on Article 141(3).[175]

---

172 *Cowan v Tresor public*, Case 186/87 [1989] ECR 195, para 14.

173 M Bell, *Anti-Discrimination Law and the European Union* (2002, OUP), 129–130.

174 In Art 251.

175 M Bell, *Anti-Discrimination Law and the European Union* (2002, OUP), 129.

If Mark Bell is right, as is likely, there are few difficulties caused by the enactment of the Race Directive.[176] If the position is otherwise, there are obvious problems about the breadth of the Race Directive, to the extent that it overlaps with areas in respect of which competence is provided by other Articles, and in particular the question whether there was power under Article 13 to enact it.

4.38 In the second phrase in the qualifying clause in Article 13 ('within the limits of the powers conferred by it upon the Community'), the authority to make law under Article 13 depends, crucially, on the meaning to be given to the word 'powers'. This has caused much academic debate.[177] Again Article 13 may be contrasted with Article 12 which contains parallel provision but apparently different in reach so that its prohibition applies '[w]ithin the scope of application of [the] Treaty'. The ECJ has indicated that the situations covered by Article 12 therefore extend to areas over which the Treaty does not confer specific competence to the Community institutions.[178] It is difficult to deduce whether the reference to 'powers' gives Article 13 wider or narrower scope than Article 12. The limitation that any action be 'within the limits of the powers conferred by it upon the Community' may simply be there to delineate the boundaries between the powers assigned to the EC and the powers assigned to the EU.[179] More worryingly, the reference to 'powers' may be a reference to 'competence'[180] in which case Article 13 might only extend to enacting measures over which the Community already has competence. As has been observed, there appears to be no separate competence to legislate in certain of the areas covered by the Race Directive—in particular health care, the only analogue for which in the Treaty excludes harmonization laws[181] and excludes specific health care related issues.[182] The difficulty with a 'competence' condition, as Mark Bell has observed, is that it draws Article 13 back 'towards a market focus'[183] and this undermines the aspirations for the social

176 Save that such an approach 'essentializes' the experience of race, gender etc, see Chap 5.

177 As Mark Bell observes: M Bell, *Anti-Discrimination Law and the European Union* (2002, OUP), 131.

178 *Forcheri and A'or v Belgian State and A'or*, Case C-152/82 [1983] ECR 2323; *Bickel and Franz* Case C-274/96 [1998] ECR I-7637.

179 M Bell, *Anti-Discrimination Law and the European Union* (2002, OUP), 133, noting that the EU has power to take action against racism so that 'Without prejudice to the powers of the European Community, the Union's objective shall be to provide citizens with a high level of safety within an area of freedom, security and justice by developing common action among the Member States in the fields of police and judicial cooperation in criminal matters and by preventing and combating racism and xenophobia' (EU Treaty, Art 29). It seems unlikely, however, that Art 13 is intended to mark out this boundary when Art 29 of the EU Treaty is expressed as 'Without prejudice to the powers of the European Community'.

180 As certain other language versions suggests: M Bell, *Anti-Discrimination Law and the European Union* (2002, OUP), 134.

181 Art 152(4)(c).

182 Art 152(5) and these are probably covered by the Race Directive.

183 M Bell, *Anti-Discrimination Law and the European Union* (2002, OUP), 144.

impact of those who lobbied for it. It would obviously be absurd if the two qualifying phrases in Article 13 were taken to mean both that it permits legislation only where there is *no* specific competence elsewhere in the EC Treaty and that it permits legislation only where there *is* competence elsewhere in the EC Treaty, as such would render Article 13 substance-less. As to the first phrase, the proper interpretation is most likely to be as Mark Bell suggests—it restricts Article 13 to those situations not specifically covered by *anti-discrimination measures* contained in other parts of the EC Treaty.[184] As to the second phrase, this most likely refers to the broad limits of Community action—that is that it requires that the institutional legal requirements (institutional roles, voting etc) are complied with.

The Race Directive requires Member States to ensure that procedures are in place for the enforcement of the obligations under the Directives and that such procedures are available to all persons who consider themselves wronged by the failure to apply the principle of equal treatment.[185] It also requires Member States to abolish all laws contrary to the principle of equal treatment and render void any rules or provisions in collective agreements, rules of undertakings etc contrary to the principle of equal treatment,[186] and to introduce rules on sanctions applicable to infringements of any national provisions adopted pursuant to the Directives, and to take all measures necessary to ensure that they are applied. Such sanctions, which may include compensation to the victim,[187] must be 'effective, proportionate and dissuasive'.[188] Also importantly, the Race Directive requires that Member States 'designate a body or bodies for the promotion of equal treatment of all persons without discrimination on the grounds of racial or ethnic origin' with competence to provide 'independent assistance to victims of discrimination in pursuing their complaints of discrimination'; to conduct 'independent surveys' concerning discrimination; and to publish 'independent reports . . . making recommendations on any issue relating to such discrimination'.[189] Such provision was unique—neither the original gender Directives[190] nor the Framework Directive contained such provision. As will be mentioned below, the Gender Goods and Services Directive replicates this provision now for gender. 4.39

184 And as may be observed, in respect of all the activities identified under Art 3 of the EC Treaty, the EC must in any event 'aim to eliminate inequalities, and to promote equality, between men and women' (Art 3).

185 Art 7(1).

186 Art 14.

187 And such will be required where loss has been sustained: *Marshall v Southampton and South West Area Health Authority II*, Case C-271/91 [1993] ECR I-4367; [1993] ICR 893; [1993] IRLR 445.

188 Art 15. Equivalent provision is made in the other Directives and this has proved very important; see, eg, *Marshall v Southampton and South West Area Health Authority II*, Case C-271/91 [1993] ECR I-4367; [1993] ICR 893; [1993] IRLR 445.

189 Art 13.

190 The Equal Treatment Directive and the Equal Pay Directive.

4.40 As to its limitations, as observed above, Article 13 and therefore the Directive excludes nationality discrimination. In addition, the Race Directive creates permissive exemptions, allowing Member States to exempt discrimination based on 'genuine occupational requirements'[191] and in respect of 'positive action'.[192] These are explored as they arise later in the book. The Race Directive represents minimum standards and contains a non-regression clause, thus Member States must not use the Directive as an opportunity to reduce the protection already provided.[193] It required Member States to give effect to its terms by 19 July 2003.[194] The Race Directive has been given domestic effect by the Race Relations Act 1976 (Amendment) Regulations 2003[195] which, *inter alia*, enact a new meaning of indirect discrimination and harassment, but only affecting discrimination connected with race or ethnic or national origins (the latter on the assumption that it is embraced by one or other of the two preceding concepts).

(3) Framework Directive

4.41 The Framework Directive[196] was enacted only five months after the Race Directive and its enactment is often attributed to the momentum created by the passing of the Race Directive.[197] However, Article 13, as seen, provided authority for the enactment of legislation across a wide range of grounds—the Race Directive dealt with only one. Other campaigning groups had lobbied for the amendment of the EC Treaty to increase the EC's competence to legislate against discrimination across grounds,[198] and when the Commission proposed the Race Directive it did so as part of a package of measures which included a proposed Directive requiring Member States to prohibit discrimination connected with religion or belief, disability, age, and sexual orientation in the employment and related fields. The 'grouping of the four, seemingly somewhat disparate, grounds together was . . . part of the Commission's strategy: it believed that the Member States were more enthusiastic about some of the grounds than about others, and it wanted to exploit the political momentum', though, as has been observed, such shoe-horning risked creating a 'false consistency' and risked thereby failing to address any of the grounds adequately.[199] However, many of the key definitions

---

191 Art 4. See further Chap 8.

192 Art 5. See further Chap 13.

193 Art 6. Similar provision is made in the Framework Directive, the Amended Equal Treatment Directive, and the Gender Goods and Services Directive.

194 Art 16.

195 SI 2003/1626.

196 2000/78/EC.

197 M Bell, *Anti-Discrimination Law and the European Union* (2002, OUP), 113.

198 See, for discussion, M Bell and L Waddington, 'The 1996 Intergovernmental Conference and the Prospects of a Non-Discrimination Treaty Article' [1996] Vol. 25, *Industrial Law Journal*, 320.

199 E Ellis, *European Union Anti-Discrimination Law* (2005, OUP), 33.

and formulations contained in the Race Directive were simply transposed into the Framework Directive,[200] and it was well understood that whichever came first would inform the contents of the other.[201] Notwithstanding the similarity of many of their provisions, the House of Lords maintained that the contents of the proposed Framework Directive were far more controversial than the Race Directive,[202] in part because, unlike the Race Directive, the Framework Directive dealt with areas where there was little or no UK legislation. In fact, the speedily agreed Directive followed intense negotiations during which deals were done resulting in exemptions not found in the draft text,[203] many at the instigation of the UK Government. Despite this, the Framework Directive is an important measure.

The Framework Directive provides that the 'principle of equal treatment shall mean that there shall be no direct or indirect discrimination whatsoever on any of the grounds . . . [of] . . . religion or belief, disability, age or sexual orientation' within the scope protected by the terms of the Directive, namely employment and related areas.[204] Its scope is therefore much narrower than the Race Directive and the issues relating to competence do not arise.[205] **4.42**

The Framework Directive requires Member States to outlaw direct discrimination, indirect discrimination, and harassment, and these concepts are defined in materially the same way as under the Race Directive.[206] The concept of indirect discrimination provided for in the Framework Directive makes particular provision in relation to disabled persons. By Article 2(2)(b) indirect discrimination: **4.43**

> shall be taken to occur where an apparently neutral provision, criterion or practice would put persons having a particular religion or belief, a particular disability,

---

200 M Bell, *Anti-Discrimination Law and the European Union* (2002, OUP), 113.

201 Ibid, 113.

202 House of Lords Select Committee on the EU, 'EU Proposals to Combat Discrimination', HL Session 1999-2000, 9th Report, HL paper 68 (2000), para 8.

203 The House of Lords Select Committee Report notes that negotiations on the 17 October continued into the night, for an additional six hours, and the French Presidency's determination to finalize the Directive on that day worked to the UK's advantage, providing it with a great deal of 'bargaining power'. The Report (para 13) highlights several significant amendments made during the Council meeting, which secured the UK's approval, including an exemption for measures undertaken to protect public security, order, or health (Art 2(5)); an exemption from provisions on age and disability for the armed forces (Art 3(4)); a strengthening of the protection given to religious organisations (Art 4(2)); a reinforced exemption from age provisions for entitlement to pensions (Arts 3(3) and 6(2)); an extension of the implementation period for provisions on age and disability from three years to six (Art 18): House of Lords Select Committee on the EU, 'EU Proposals to Combat Discrimination', HL Session 1999-2000, 9th Report, HL paper 68 (2000). There was in consequence little substantive or meaningful consultation with the European Parliament on the final text as may be required by Art 13, raising the question (at least) whether the Directive is in consequence *ultra vires* Art 13 (see Art 5 of the EC Treaty identifying the limits of the Community's powers).

204 Arts 2 and 3.

205 There is plainly competence to enact labour market measures; see, for example, Art 137.

206 Art 2.

a particular age, or a particular sexual orientation at a particular disadvantage compared with other persons unless,

(i) that provision, criterion or practice is objectively justified by a legitimate aim and the means of achieving that aim are appropriate and necessary, or

(ii) as regards persons with a particular disability, the employer or any person or organisation to whom this Directive applies, is obliged, under national legislation, to take appropriate measures in line with the principles contained in Article 5 in order to eliminate disadvantages entailed by such provision, criterion or practice.

By Article 5 ('Reasonable Accommodation for Disabled Persons') it is provided that:

> in order to guarantee compliance with the principle of equal treatment in relation to persons with disabilities, reasonable accommodation shall be provided. This means that employers shall take appropriate measures, where needed in a particular case, to enable a person with a disability to have access to, participate in, or advance in employment, or to undergo training, unless such measures would impose a disproportionate burden on the employer. This burden shall not be disproportionate when it is sufficiently remedied by measures existing within the framework of the disability policy of the Member State concerned.

4.44 The Directive appears to allow Member States to choose either limb of Article 2(2)(b) as constituting a defence to indirect discrimination in the case of disability. The UK Government has purportedly followed the 'reasonable accommodation' limb so that an employer will be able to defend a claim of indirect disability discrimination by establishing that it has complied with any duty imposed to make reasonable adjustments. However, there is no express outlawing of indirect disability discrimination in the transposing regulations.[207] Instead, such is expected to be addressed fully by the 'reasonable adjustment' duties described in Chapter 6.

4.45 As mentioned above, the Framework Directive contains important exemptions, including, for example, that the:

> Directive shall be without prejudice to measures laid down by national law which, in a democratic society, are necessary for public security, for the maintenance of public order and the prevention of criminal offences, for the protection of health and for the protection of the rights and freedoms of others.[208]

Other permissive exemptions are provided for, allowing for Member States to opt to exclude, for example, the armed forces from the scope of any implementing measures[209] and to introduce certain exemptions relating to religious

---

[207] The Disability Discrimination Act 1995 (Amendment) Regulations SI 2003/1673.
[208] Art 2(5).
[209] Art 3(4).

organizations.[210] These and others of its relevant provisions are addressed in the following chapters.

Member States were required to give effect to the terms of the Framework Directive by 2 December 2003 (with an extended period allowed in the case of disability and age).[211] Its contents represent minimum standards and it contains a non-regression clause, thus Member States must not use the Directive as an opportunity to reduce the protection already provided.[212] The Framework Directive has been given domestic effect by the Employment Equality (Religion or Belief) Regulations 2003,[213] the Employment Equality (Sexual Orientation) Regulations 2003,[214] the Disability Discrimination Act 1995 (Amendment) Regulations 2003,[215] and lastly, exploiting the extended time allowed for transposition under the Directive insisted upon by the UK Government,[216] the Employment Equality (Age) Regulations 2006.[217] **4.46**

(4) Gender Goods and Services Directive

The Gender Goods and Services Directive[218] was the last of the three Article 13 Directives to be enacted. Member States must give effect to its terms by 21 December 2007.[219] It addresses some of those areas covered by the Race Directive, but for gender, which are not already covered by the Equal Treatment Directive and so provides that: **4.47**

> Within the limits of the powers conferred upon the Community, this Directive shall apply to all persons who provide goods and services, which are available to the public irrespective of the person concerned as regards both the public and private sectors, including public bodies, and which are offered outside the area of private and family life and the transactions carried out in this context.

The observations about competence made in relation to the Race Directive apply equally here. However, as can be seen, the Gender Goods and Services Directive does not extend so far as the Race Directive. Further, it contains important exemptions. It does not apply to 'the content of media and advertising'; **4.48**

---

210 Art 4(2). As mentioned, the Framework Directive also contains a non-regression clause: Art 8(2).

211 Art 18.

212 Art 8. Similar provision is made in the Framework Directive, the Amended Equal Treatment Directive, and the Gender Goods and Services Directive.

213 SI 2003/1660.

214 SI 2003/1661.

215 SI 2003/1673.

216 Art 18.

217 SI 2006/1031.

218 Council Directive 2004/113/EC of 13 December 2004 implementing the principle of equal treatment between men and women in the access to and supply of goods and services. See, R Allen and R Baker, 'Proposed Directive for wider age equality law' [2006] EOR 58 for a discussion on a proposed directive sponsored by 12 age-sector groups across Europe that would widen the law on age discrimination to cover the provision of goods, facilities, and services.

219 Though for its effect before then, see *Mangold v Helm*, Case C-144/04 [2006] IRLR 143. See Art 50 of EC Treaty for the meaning of 'services'.

'to education';[220] or to 'matters of employment and occupation [or] . . . to matters of self-employment, insofar as these matters are covered by other Community legislative acts'.[221] As with the Equal Treatment Directive, the Gender Goods and Services Directive is 'without prejudice to more favourable provisions concerning the protection of women as regards pregnancy and maternity'.[222] The Directive does not 'preclude differences in treatment, if the provision of the goods and services exclusively or primarily to members of one sex is justified by a legitimate aim and the means of achieving that aim are appropriate and necessary'.[223] The SDA goods and services provisions are discussed in Chapter 10.

4.49 The SDA and Equality Act 2006 cover most of the matters addressed by the Gender Goods and Services Directive. However, there are three issues which will require legislative action if the Directive is to be properly transposed. Firstly, the meaning of discrimination will need to be amended. This will be necessary to take account of the new meaning of indirect discrimination which reflects that contained in the Race Directive, the Framework Directive, and the Amended Equal Treatment Directive. The more formal meaning of indirect discrimination as contained in the original enactment of the SDA still applies outside the employment and related fields.[224] It will also be necessary to ensure that protection against harassment is afforded outside the employment field and in those areas covered by the Gender Goods and Services Directive.

4.50 Secondly, Article 5 of the Directive very importantly provides that Member States must ensure that in all new contracts concluded after 21 December 2007[225] at the latest, the use of sex as a factor in the calculation of premiums and benefits for the purposes of insurance and related financial services shall not result in differences in individuals' premiums and benefits, though they may decide before 21 December 2007 to permit proportionate differences in individuals' premiums and benefits where the use of sex is a determining factor in the assessment of risk based on relevant and accurate actuarial and statistical data (subject to reporting and review). In any event, costs related to pregnancy and maternity must not result in differences in individuals' premiums and benefits.

4.51 As will be seen, section 45 of the SDA[226] excludes from the scope of the SDA sex discrimination based on actuarial factors, both for the purposes of

220 Art 3(3).

221 Art 3(4).

222 Art 4(2).

223 Art 4(5). See s 29(3) for similar—though not so rigorous—provision in the SDA and see SDA, s 35 discussed in Chaps 10 and 13.

224 SDA, s 1(1)(b).

225 Though Member States may defer implementation of measures necessary to comply until two years after 21 December 2007 at the latest, in which case the Member State concerned must immediately inform the Commission.

226 Applicable to the employment and non-employment fields.

employment-related benefits and as regards access to financial services. In proposing the Gender Goods and Services Directive, the European Commission noted that it is common for insurance to be offered on different terms to women and to men (though sex is not in fact the main determining factor for life expectancy at least[227]). In the UK, this is said to be especially the case as regards critical illness insurance and car insurance. An amendment will need to be made to the SDA, therefore, to give effect to the Directive and its outlawing of what has become a convenient but sexually discriminatory approach to actuarial assessment in insurance.

Thirdly, because the concept of 'sex' within European sex equality law has been interpreted as protecting against gender reassignment,[228] and such law will now extend to goods and services, the SDA will need amendment so that those of its provisions addressing goods and services (including in respect of public authorities) apply to gender reassignment discrimination. As noted in Chapter 2, the SDA was amended to address gender reassignment discrimination but only in the employment and related fields,[229] that is, only to the extent required to match Community law obligations. These obligations now extend beyond employment and provision will have to be made to transpose them. **4.52**

D. EU Charter of Fundamental Rights and the Constitution

On 7 December 2000 the European Council, Parliament, and Commission solemnly proclaimed the Charter of Fundamental Rights of the European Union.[230] The Charter contains important provisions addressing discrimination and equality.[231] It provides, amongst other things, that:[232] **4.53**

- Human dignity is inviolable. It must be respected and protected.[233]

[227] As reported in M Rubenstein, 'Proposed Equal Treatment Directive Covers Insurance' (2004) EOR, No 125, 20.

[228] See Chap 2.

[229] See, for example (though apparently poorly reasoned), *Lalor and others v Gawthorpe and/or the Red Lion Public House* 14 August 2003; Case No NG211676 [2004] Equal Opportunities Review No 127, 23.

[230] [2000] OJ C 364, 18 Dec 2000 p 1. See too, the Community Charter of the Fundamental Social Rights of Workers (1989), Adopted on 10 Dec 1989, OJ COM 89/248, 9 Dec 89, which contains some equality provisions including in relation to men and women; disabled persons; children; and the elderly. The Charter was not signed by the UK until 1998, following the election of Tony Blair, when the UK changed its position on the signing of the Charter.

[231] Including under Chapter III, headed 'Equality'.

[232] Provision is made permitting the limitation of these rights in certain narrow circumstances: Art 52(1) provides: 'Any limitation on the exercise of the rights and freedoms recognised by this Charter must be provided for by law and respect the essence of those rights and freedoms. Subject to the principle of proportionality, limitations may be made only if they are necessary and genuinely meet objectives of general interest recognised by the Union or the need to protect the rights and freedoms of others.'

[233] Art 1.

- Everyone has the right to respect for his or her physical and mental integrity.[234]
- No one shall be subjected to torture or to inhuman or degrading treatment or punishment.[235]
- Everyone has the right to respect for his or her private and family life, home and communications.[236]
- Everyone is equal before the law.[237]
- Any discrimination based on any ground such as sex, race, colour, ethnic or social origin, genetic features, language, religion or belief, political or any other opinion, membership of a national minority, property, birth, disability, age or sexual orientation shall be prohibited.[238]
- The Union shall respect cultural, religious and linguistic diversity.[239]
- Children shall have the right to such protection and care as is necessary for their well-being. They may express their views freely. Such views shall be taken into consideration on matters which concern them in accordance with their age and maturity.[240]
- The Union recognises and respects the rights of the elderly to lead a life of dignity and independence and to participate in social and cultural life.
- The Union recognises and respects the right of persons with disabilities to benefit from measures designed to ensure their independence, social and occupational integration and participation in the life of the community.[241]
- Every worker has the right to working conditions which respect his or her health, safety and dignity.[242]

4.54 By Article 52: 'In so far as th[e] Charter contains rights which correspond to rights guaranteed by the Convention for the Protection of Human Rights and Fundamental Freedoms, the meaning and scope of those rights shall be the same as those laid down by the said Convention. This provision shall not prevent Union law providing more extensive protection.' The full impact of the Charter, however, is as yet unclear. Article 51 of the Charter provides that:

> The provisions of this Charter are addressed to the institutions and bodies of the Union with due regard for the principle of subsidiarity and to the Member States only when they are implementing Union law. They shall therefore respect the rights, observe the principles and promote the application thereof in accordance with their respective powers.[243]

---

234 Art 3(1).
235 Art 4.
236 Art 7.
237 Art 20.
238 Art 21.
239 Art 22.
240 Art 24.
241 Art 26.
242 Art 31(1).
243 Art 51.

The UK Government has stated that the Charter is not intended to be legally binding on Member States.[244] However, the European Commission has taken a different approach. It has stated: 4.55

> The institutions that will have proclaimed the Charter will have committed themselves to respecting it and the Court of Justice of the European Communities will refer to it in its case law. Considering the added value of the Charter, one can safely reckon that sooner or later, the Charter will be integrated into the Treaties.[245]

In addition, in a Commission memorandum of March 2001, the then President of the European Commission, Romano Prodi, and the then Commissioner responsible for Justice and Home Affairs, António Vitorino, 'declared that the Charter must become the touchstone of future action by the Commission'.[246] Since then, every new law or legislative instrument with any bearing at all on fundamental rights must contain the following formal statement: 'This act respects the fundamental rights and observes the principles recognized in particular by the Charter of Fundamental Rights of the European Union as general principles of Community.'[247] Further, the Charter has been referred to in the Court of First Instance and in several Advocate-Generals' opinions.[248] It is likely to be used increasingly as an aid to interpreting Community legal measures.

Importantly, the Constitution for the European Union adopted in June 2004[249] contains provisions addressing equality. Article I-2 describes the Union's values as follows: 4.56

> The Union is founded on the values of respect for human dignity, freedom, democracy, equality, the rule of law and respect for human rights, including the rights of persons belonging to minorities. These values are common to the Member States in

---

244 HC Debates col 354, 11 Dec 2000.

245 See, *Europa* website, <http://europa.eu.int/comm/justice_home/unit/charte/en/communications.html> and see, Commission Communication, COM (2000) 644, 11 Oct 2000, available at <http://ec.europa.eu/justice_home/unit/charte/en/communications.html>.

246 See <http://europa.eu/scadplus/leg/en/lvb/l33501.htm>.

247 *Europa* website at <http://europa.eu.int/scadplus/leg/en/lvb/l33501.htm>.

248 See, for example, *R v Secretary of State for Trade and Industry ex p Broadcasting, Entertainment, Cinematographic and Theatre Union*, Case C-173/99 [2001] IRLR 559 (Advocate-General Tizzano, paras 26–27); *Allonby v Accrington and Rossendale College and others*, Case C-256/01 [2004] ICR 1328; [2004] IRLR 224 (Advocate-General Geelhoed, para 53). The Charter has been repeatedly cited in the opinions of the Advocates-General and has on several occasions influenced the conclusions of the Court of Justice of the European Communities. The opinions of the Advocates-General are not binding on the Court, but suggest legal solutions that are likely to influence it. In some cases the reference to the Charter has been marginal, but in others the Advocates-General have used it to interpret fundamental rights, though noting that it is not legally binding. The Charter's lack of legal status does not mean, however, that it has no effect. Advocates-General Tizzano, Léger, and Mischo have stated that 'the Charter has undeniably placed the rights which form its subject-matter at the highest level of values common to the Member States,' *Europa* website, at <http://europa.eu.int/scadplus/leg/en/lvb/l33501.htm>.

249 Treaty Establishing a Constitution for Europe [2004] OJ C 310/1.

a society in which pluralism, non-discrimination, tolerance, justice, solidarity and equality between women and men prevail.

4.57 The Union's objectives are stated as including the combating of 'social exclusion and discrimination' and the promotion of 'social justice and protection, equality between women and men, solidarity between generations and protection of the rights of the child'.[250] The Constitution declares that the Union 'shall recognize the rights, freedoms and principles set out in the Charter of Fundamental Rights';[251] and that there is a duty placed on the Union to 'observe the principle of the equality of its citizens'.[252] Furthermore, the Charter of Fundamental Rights is incorporated in Chapter II and the equality chapter of the Charter is included in full.[253] The Constitution's list of competencies reproduces, with modifications, Article 13, described above[254] so that Article III-124 provides that:

> Without prejudice to the other provisions of the Constitution and within the limits of the powers assigned by it to the Union, a European law or framework law of the Council may establish the measures needed to combat discrimination based on sex, racial or ethnic origin, religion or belief, disability, age or sexual orientation. The Council shall act unanimously after obtaining the consent of the European Parliament.

The observations above about scope and competence apply equally. Article 141 of the EC Treaty is reflected in Article III-214 of the Constitution. Of greater interest is the impact of the Charter, with its additional protected classes (social origin, genetic features, language, political or any other opinion, membership of a national minority, property, and birth), in respect of which competence to legislate is not expressly provided for under the other enabling provisions of the EC Treaty or Constitution. According to the European Commission, in their Green Paper on Equality and Non-Discrimination, the integration of the Charter into the Constitution would 'not provide a new legal basis for further Community legislation in the field of non-discrimination' but the additional grounds protected by the Charter, such as genetic features, 'raise important and sensitive issues' and it will therefore be necessary 'to consider how to take the debate on such issues forward at EU level'.[255] This suggests a rather limited role for the 'constitutionalized' Charter. However, firstly, the Commission itself recognized that:

> In accordance with Article 51 of the Charter, the principles it sets out should guide the development of policy in the EU and the implementation of these policies by

250 Art I-3(3).

251 Art I-9.

252 Art I-45.

253 Art I-9, which declares both that the Union 'recognizes' the rights, freedoms, and principles set out in the Charter, and that the Charter shall constitute Part II of the Constitution.

254 For a discussion, see M Bell, 'Equality and the European Constitution' [2004] ILJ 33, 242.

255 Green Paper, *Equality and Non-Discrimination in an Enlarged European Union* (COM (2004) 379 Final, 28.05.2004), 11, available at <http://eur-lex.europa.eu/smartapi/cgi/sga_doc?smartapi!celexplus!prod!DocNumber&lg=en&type_doc=COMfinal&an_doc=2004&nu_doc=379>.

> national authorities. The European Court of Justice (ECJ) has consistently held that fundamental human rights, derived from the international instruments to which all the Member States are signatories, form part of the general principles of Community law, the observance of which it ensures.
>
> The Charter has already become an important reference document for the ECJ in its interpretation of Community law. The principle of non-discrimination on grounds of sex or nationality has been held on numerous occasions by the ECJ to be a fundamental right under Community law, any exceptions to which must be narrowly interpreted. This jurisprudence will, no doubt, influence the ECJ when it comes to examine the [Race and Framework] Directives for the first time.[256]

Secondly, and perhaps most importantly, at the time of publication of the Commission's Green Paper, the politically tricky Constitution had not been agreed and caution as to its impact may have been politically wise. It is perhaps the case that the full potential of the constitutionalized Charter has yet to be realized.

E. Implementing EU Law in the UK and Interpreting UK Anti-Discrimination Law

The UK has a 'dualist' system of law and, as with the European Convention on Human Rights described below, without more, the provisions of the EC Treaty and the Constitution would bind the UK as a matter of public international law but create no domestic legal rules. However, section 2 of the European Communities Act 1972 (ECA) gives domestic effect to the UK's obligations arising out of the EC and EU Treaties, as follows: **4.58**

> (1) All such rights, powers, liabilities, obligations and restrictions from time to time created or arising by or under the Treaties, and all such remedies and procedures from time to time provided for by or under the Treaties, as in accordance with the Treaties are without further enactment to be given legal effect or used in the United Kingdom shall be recognised and available in law, and be enforced, allowed and followed accordingly; and the expression 'enforceable Community right' and similar expressions shall be read as referring to one to which this subsection applies.
>
> (2) Subject to Schedule 2 to this Act, at any time after its passing Her Majesty may by Order in Council, and any designated Minister or department may by regulations, make provision—
>
> (a) for the purpose of implementing any Community obligation of the United Kingdom, or enabling any such obligation to be implemented, or of enabling any rights enjoyed or to be enjoyed by the United Kingdom under or by virtue of the Treaties to be exercised; or
>
> (b) for the purpose of dealing with matters arising out of or related to any such obligation or rights or the coming into force, or the operation from time to time, of subsection (1) above;

256 Ibid. Internal footnotes removed.

and in the exercise of any statutory power or duty, including any power to give directions or to legislate by means of orders, rules, regulations or other subordinate instrument, the person entrusted with the power or duty may have regard to the objects of the Communities and to any such obligation or rights as aforesaid.

4.59 The 'Treaties' referred to are listed under section 1 of the ECA and include the EC Treaty and the EU Treaty.[257] Thus the obligations arising under EC and EU law form part of our domestic legal system without further enactment. This creates significant consequences for interpreting domestic law. A full discussion of the impact of European law on domestic law is outside the scope of this book, but what follows are highlights which may be of particular use to equality lawyers. Importantly, European law and the principles of Community law interpretation have become increasingly important in the context of equality law. This is because, as discussed above, there is now specific Community and EU legislation addressing equality and non-discrimination across a wide range of grounds. There are a variety of possible remedies for any apparent failure by the UK to implement EU law. These are discussed below.

4.60 As seen, a designated Minister may make regulations under section 2 of the ECA 'for the purpose of implementing any Community obligation of the UK, or enabling any such obligation to be implemented'. The Community *obligation* underpinning the enactment of the Race Relations Act 1976 (Amendment) Regulations 2003[258] is that contained in Article 16 of the Race Directive which required Member States to give effect to its terms by 19 July 2003. The Community *obligations* underpinning the enactment of the Employment Equality (Religion or Belief) Regulations 2003,[259] the Employment Equality (Sexual Orientation) Regulations 2003,[260] the Disability Discrimination Act 1995 (Amendment) Regulations 2003,[261] and the Employment Equality (Age) Regulations 2006[262] are the obligations under Article 18 of the Directive[263] to adopt the laws, regulations, and administrative provisions necessary to comply with the terms of the Directive by 2 December 2003, or, if necessary, 2006 in the case of disability and age. The Community *obligations* purportedly underpinning the enactment of the Employment Equality (Sex Discrimination) Regulations 2005[264] are those contained in the Equal Treatment Amendment Directive,[265] though it is difficult

257 And all the amendments to the extent that are relevant to this work.

258 SI 2003/1626.

259 SI 2003/1660.

260 SI 2003/1661.

261 SI 2003/1673. The same is true of the Disability Discrimination Act 1995 (Pensions) Regulations 2003 SI 2003/2770.

262 SI 2006/1031.

263 2000/78/EC.

264 SI 2005/2467.

265 Art 2.

to see a legal basis for the exemptions to the SDA inserted thereby through the new section 6A. As will be seen, section 6A brings the scope of the SDA, in so far as it protects against pregnancy-related discrimination, in line with the Maternity and Parental Leave Regulations 1999[266] by creating certain new exemptions to section 6 of the SDA. However, prior to the enactment of this provision there were no such exemptions in the SDA and nor, more particularly, is there any obligation in EC law to enact them. As seen, the Equal Treatment and Equal Treatment Amendment Directives are without prejudice to provisions concerning the protection of women particularly as regards pregnancy and maternity, and the Equal Treatment Amendment Directive makes special provision addressing pregnancy but these provisions do not authorize the creation of *exemptions* where none existed before. In addition, not only do these provisions lack a legal basis but they and the new section 3A, inserted by the Employment Equality (Sex Discrimination) Regulations 2005, positively contradict Community law: Community law does not replicate national distinctions between different maternity leave periods (in the UK that being between Ordinary Maternity Leave and Additional Maternity Leave) but treats all maternity leave as similarly protected, unlike the new section 6A which creates distinctions between Ordinary Maternity Leave and Additional Maternity Leave.[267] Further, Community law does not require a comparator for a pregnancy-related discrimination case as seen in the new section 3A.[268] Other examples of provisions in the anti-discrimination enactments that are apparently inconsistent with Community law and the obligations arising under it are addressed in the following chapters as the issues arise.

Importantly, Directives have legal force from the date of their enactment, even if specific measures are not required until later.[269] As to the implementation of Community law, generally, there are a number of core relevant Treaty provisions and principles. Firstly, Article 249[270] provides that: 4.61

> In order to carry out their task and in accordance with the provisions of this Treaty, the European Parliament acting jointly with the Council, the Council and the Commission shall make regulations and issue Directives, take decisions, make recommendations or deliver opinions.

266 SI 1999/3312. Prior to this exemption a contractual right to, say, consultation over a change in jobs would fall outside the 1999 Regulations but inside the SDA. The same applies, eg to benefits determinant upon service (unless redundancy payments (s 6A(4)(c)(ii)). The two enactments were inconsistent but nevertheless the SDA provided more comprehensive coverage and so would always be relied upon. Such will now apparently fall outside the SDA.

267 *Land Brandenburg v Sass* [2005] IRLR 147 (when the objective and purpose of both periods of leave is the protection of women as regards pregnancy and maternity).

268 *Webb v EMO Air Cargo (UK) Ltd* [1994] QB 718; [1994] IRLR 482 ECJ. S 3A is addressed in Chap 6.

269 Though for its effect before then, see *Mangold v Helm*, Case C-144/04 [2006] IRLR 143 and discussion above, para 4.04.

270 Ex Art 189.

> A regulation shall have general application. It shall be binding in its entirety and directly applicable in all Member States.
>
> A Directive shall be binding, as to the result to be achieved, upon each Member State to which it is addressed, but shall leave to the national authorities the choice of form and methods.
>
> A decision shall be binding in its entirety upon those to whom it is addressed.
>
> Recommendations and opinions shall have no binding force.

Thus a Regulation needs no national implementing measures to give it legal force whilst a Directive binds Member States but leaves it to them to decide how to implement it domestically. As to Directives, and to give proper effect to Article 249:

> . . . Member States must define a specific legal framework in the sector concerned which ensures that the national legal system complies with the provisions of the Directive in question. The framework must be designed in such a way as to remove all doubt or ambiguity, not only as regards the content of the relevant national legislation and its compliance with the Directive, but also as regards the authority of that legislation and its suitability as a basis for regulation of the sector . . . Consequently, given that the Member State concerned is required to ensure the full and exact application of the provisions of any Directive, it falls short of its obligations so long as it has not completely complied with [the Directive], even if that [domestic] law has to a large extent already secured the objectives of the Directive.
>
> . . . Any rights conferred by [the] Directive must be guaranteed full protection . . . Regard must be had to the Court's consistent concern to ensure that the existing national legislation leaves no doubt as to the effects of the Directive upon the legal position of individuals. In the words of the Court, 'it is particularly important, in order to satisfy the requirement for legal certainty, that individuals should have the benefit of a clear and precise legal situation enabling them to ascertain the full extent of their rights and, where appropriate, to rely on them before the national courts'.[271]

4.62 Thus domestic law transposing Community law must conform to the principles of clarity and legal certainty[272] and be in the same 'sector', ensuring that 'the legal situation resulting from national implementing measures is sufficiently precise and clear to enable the individuals concerned to know the extent of their rights and obligations'.[273]

---

[271] *Commission v Netherlands*, C-144/99 [2001] ECR I-3541 at paras 15–17, per Advocate-General Tisane.

[272] This is more particularly so where the Community law measure is intended to confer rights on individuals (*Commission v Greece*, Case C-365/93 [1995] ECR I-499, para 9). These principles ensure that individuals know their rights and are in a position to rely upon them (*Commission v Germany*, Case 29/84 [1985] ECR 1661, para 28*)*. It is also to enable national courts to ensure that these rights and obligations are observed (*Commission v Italy*, Case C-306/91 [1993] ECR I 2133, para 14). In particular, any remedy must therefore be transparently available (*Commission of the European Communities v Federal Republic of Germany* [1985] ECR 1661 at 1666, cited by Lord Hoffman in *Consorzio del Prosciutto di Parma v Asda Stores Limited and Others* [2001] UKHL 7 at para 41.

[273] *Commission v France*, Case C-233/00, judgment of 26 June 2003; *Commission v Germany*, Case 29/84 [1985] ECR 1661, paras 22 and 23.

Secondly, in interpreting Community law (including Directives) and any domestic law purportedly giving effect to it, the following Community law principles apply: 4.63

- Domestic legislation which gives effect to Community law must be construed purposively, so as to give it a meaning consistent with Community law in so far as is possible.[274] This is so whether that legislation was passed before or after the coming into force of the relevant Community law. This means that the main anti-discrimination enactments must be interpreted consistently with the Directives described above, in so far as it is possible to do so.
- This interpretative obligation is a very compelling one and may require an interpretation which is inconsistent with the natural and ordinary meaning of the words being interpreted and may require the reading-in of words.[275]
- It is presumed that no provision of Community law is intended to infringe human rights and Community law is therefore to be interpreted and applied accordingly.[276] The importance of fundamental rights to the observance of Community law obligations cannot be overstated. The ECJ has repeatedly held that fundamental rights form part of the traditions of the European Community and will be taken into account in interpreting its laws.[277] In addition, Article 6 of the EU Treaty now provides in terms that the European Union is founded on the principles of liberty, democracy, respect for human rights and fundamental freedoms, and the rule of law. These are principles which, as Article 6 observes, are common to the Member States. The Community is also now, as a matter of Treaty obligation, to respect fundamental rights as guaranteed by the European Convention for the Protection of Human Rights and Fundamental Freedoms and as they result from the constitutional traditions common to the Member States, as general principles of Community law.[278] This means that the Directives and the main anti-discrimination enactments must be interpreted in a way which is compatible with fundamental rights including those contained in the European Convention on Human Rights.[279]
- It is presumed that Community law is intended to be effective to achieve its ends, and any court applying that law is required to act accordingly.[280]

---

274 *Litster v Forth Dry Dock and Engineering Co Ltd* [1990] 1 AC 546; *Marleasing SA v LA Comercial Internacional de Alimentacion* [1990] ECR I-4135).

275 *Litster v Forth Dry Dock and Engineering Co Ltd* [1990] 1 AC 546; *Marleasing SA v LA Comercial Internacional de Alimentacion* [1990] ECR I-4135). See too *Secretary of State for Defence v Elias* [2006] EWCA Civ 1293, para 70.

276 Bennion, n 171 above, section 400 and cases cited there under.

277 *Nold v Commission*, Case 4/73 [1974] I-ECR 491 at para 13; *Johnston v Chief Constable of the Royal Ulster Constabulary*, Case C-222/84 [1986] ECR 1651, para 18; *Elliniki Radiophonia Tiléorass-AE v Pliroforissis and Kouvelas ER*,T Case C-260/89 [1991] ECR 1-2925.

278 Ibid.

279 See further below.

280 Bennion, n 171 above, section 402 and cases cited there under.

This means that the Directives should be interpreted purposively so as to afford them proper effectiveness. Their purposes can be deduced from their recitals and the new Directives include express reference to the European Convention for the Protection of Human Rights and Fundamental Freedoms and to the United Nations Conventions referred to below.

- In giving effect to Community law which confers rights upon individuals, Member States are required to introduce the measures necessary to enable complainants to pursue their claims by judicial process and those measures must be effective in achieving the aim of the relevant Community law provision:

> the Member States must take measures which are sufficiently effective to achieve the aim of the Directive and . . . they must ensure that the rights thus conferred may be effectively relied upon before the national courts by the persons concerned.[281]

Thus procedural rules must not make it 'impossible in practice to exercise the rights which the national courts are obliged to protect' or 'render virtually impossible the exercise of rights conferred by Community law'.[282] Accordingly, '[a]lthough . . . full implementation of the directive does not require any specific form of sanction for unlawful discrimination, it does entail that that sanction be such as to guarantee real and effective judicial protection'.[283] The ECJ have held that the obligation to enable complainants to pursue their claims by judicial process: 'implies that the measures in question should be sufficiently effective to achieve the objective of the directive and should be capable of being effectively relied upon by the persons concerned before national courts . . . The objective is to arrive at real equality of opportunity and cannot therefore be attained in the absence of measures appropriate to restore such equality when it has not been observed . . . Those measures must be such as to guarantee real and effective judicial protection'.[284] Thus, by way of example only, a statutory limit on compensation has been held incompatible with the Community law requirement of effectiveness,[285] as has a defence of justification to a complaint of direct discrimination.[286]

---

281 *Johnston v Chief Constable of the Royal Ulster Constabulary*, Case 222/84 [1987] QB 129; [1987] ICR 83; [1986] IRLR 263, at para 17.

282 *Rewe-Zentralfinanz e.G. v Landwirtschaftskammer fur das Saarland* [1976] ECR 1989, 1997 and *Amministrazione delle Finanze dello Stato v SpA an Georgio* [1983] ECR 3595, 3612 both cited in *Biggs v Somerset CC* [1996] ICR 364. See too: *Preston & Others v Wolverhampton Healthcare NHS Trust & Others* and *Fletcher & Others v Midland Bank PLC* [2001] UKHL 5.

283 *Von Colson v Land Nordrhein-Westfalen* [1984] ECR 1891. In *Van Schijndel & Van Veen v Stichting Pensioenfonds voor Fysiotherapeuten* Cases C-430-431/93 [1995] ECR I-4705 the ECJ set out the steps which the court should follow in determining whether a national procedural provision rendered the application of Community law impossible or excessively difficult.

284 *Marshall v Southampton and South West Area Health Authority II*, Case C-271/91 [1993] ECR I-4367; [1993] ICR 893; [1993] IRLR 445, at paras 22–24.

285 Ibid.

286 *Dekker v Stichting voor Jong Volwassenen (VJV) Plus*, Case C-177/88 [1990] I-ECR 3941 (fault is not required to establish liability in direct discrimination).

These principles are self-evidently important in interpreting the equality Directives described above and the main anti-discrimination enactments.

Thirdly, and very importantly, much Community law has direct effect. This means that it has binding force in Member States whether or not action has been taken by a Member State to implement it. EC Treaty provisions may have direct effect where they are precise and unconditional (that is, their effect does not depend upon further action by the Community).[287] Articles 39 and 141 have been held to be directly effective[288] and Article 13 (which empowers the Community to take action only) is plainly not directly effective. Where it is not possible to interpret national legislation consistently with a directly effective Treaty provision, the incompatible domestic provisions must be disapplied in any proceedings.[289] As Article 249[290] makes plain, a Directive is *binding*, as to the result to be achieved, upon each Member State to which it is addressed. In consequence, as a matter of EC law, provisions of Directives which are 'sufficiently clear, precise and unconditional' may have direct effect and in such circumstances they may be relied upon against the State or an emanation of it (though not as against private persons).[291] Where it is not possible to interpret legislation consistently with a directly effective provision of a Directive, the incompatible domestic provisions must be disapplied in any proceedings involving the State or an emanation of it.[292] Illustrations of the disapplication of domestic law because of directly effective Community law can be seen in the equality law sphere.[293] In *Alabaster v Barclays* 4.64

---

287 Bennion, n 171 above, section 411 and cases cited thereunder. For examples in the discrimination law sphere, see *Defrenne (No 2)*, Case 43/75 [1976] ECR 455 and *Bilka-Kaufhaus GmbH v Weber von Hartz*, Case 170/84 [1986] ECR 1607 on the direct effect of Art 141 (ex Art 119); *Van Duyn v Home Office*, Case 41/74 [1974] ECR 1337 on the direct effect of Art 39 (ex Art 48). Importantly, not all courts and tribunals, and in particular employment tribunals, will have jurisdiction to hear free-standing complaints brought under the Treaty provisions; *Biggs v Somerset CC* [1996] ICR 364.

288 *Defrenne (No 2)*, Case 43/75 [1976] ECR 455 and *Bilka-Kaufhaus GmbH v Weber von Hartz*, Case 170/84 [1986] ECR 1607 on the direct effect of Art 141 (ex Art 119); *Van Duyn v Home Office*, Case 41/74 [1974] ECR 1337 on the direct effect of Art 39 (ex Art 48).

289 See, for example, *Bossa v Nordstress Ltd* [1998] ICR 694; [1998] IRLR 284; *Alabaster v Barclays Bank Plc (formerly Woolwich plc) and another and Secretary of State for Social Security (No.2)* [2005] EWCA Civ 508; [2005] ICR 1246; [2005] IRLR 576.

290 Ex Art 189.

291 The State being the party to whom the directive is addressed. See *Foster v British Gas Plc*, Case 188/89 [1990] ECR I-3313; [1990] IRLR 353. See, however, *Mangold v Helm* [2006] IRLR 143, for the impact of a directive on private persons, even before the transposition period has expired—the court being part of the State for these purposes.

292 *Marshall v Southampton and South West Area Health Authority II*, Case C-271/91 [1993] ECR I-4367; *Bossa v Nordstress Ltd* [1998] ICR 694; *Alabaster v Barclays Bank Plc (formerly Woolwich plc) and another and Secretary of State for Social Security (No.2)* [2005] EWCA Civ 508; [2005] ICR 1246; [2005] IRLR 576.

293 *Marshall v Southampton and South West Area Health Authority II*, Case C-271/91 [1993] ECR I-4367; *Bossa v Nordstress Ltd* [1998] ICR 694; *Alabaster v Barclays Bank Plc (formerly Woolwich plc) and Secretary of State for Social Security (No.2)* [2005] EWCA Civ 508; [2005] ICR 1246; [2005] IRLR 576.

Bank Plc (formerly Woolwich plc) and Secretary of State for Social Security (No 2),[294] for example, the Court of Appeal disapplied the very clear comparator provisions under section 1 of the EPA to give effect to the Community law requirement that a woman on maternity leave is entitled to the benefit of a pay rise awarded between the beginning of any reference period and the end of her maternity leave in the calculation of earnings related maternity pay.[295] Such a woman (as Community law makes clear) is not in a comparable position to a man and accordingly cannot compare herself to a man, as the EPA would otherwise require in pay-related discrimination cases.

4.65 Fourthly, where the State fails to give effect to Community law, a person suffering damage in consequence may have a remedy in compensation against the State if the breach is sufficiently serious: *Brasserie Du Pecheur SA v Federal Republic of Germany; R v Secretary of State for Transport, ex p Factortame Ltd and others (No 4)*.[296] In addition, a person may complain to the European Commission under Article 226 of the EC Treaty. Article 226[297] provides that:

> Where the Commission considers that a Member State has failed to fulfil an obligation under this Treaty, it shall deliver a reasoned opinion on the matter after giving the State concerned the opportunity to submit its observations.
>
> If the State concerned does not comply with the opinion within the period laid down by the Commission, the latter may bring the matter before the Court of Justice.

Accordingly, the Commission may itself take action against a Member State if it considers that it has not fulfilled any obligations arising under the Treaty or other law (including a Directive) directed at the Member State.[298]

4.66 Article 234[299] of the EC Treaty permits the ECJ to give preliminary rulings on the proper interpretation of Community law, following 'a reference' from a national court. This procedure is extremely important. Any national court may make such a reference where 'it considers it necessary to enable it to give judgment'.

---

294 [2005] EWCA Civ 508; [2005] ICR 1246; [2005] IRLR 576.

295 Even though the pay rise was not backdated to the relevant reference period for calculating her entitlement.

296 (Joined Cases C-46/93 and C-48/93) [1996] QB 404: 'That where, in a field governed by Community law in which national legislatures had a wide discretion, as in the present cases, there was a breach of Community law attributable to the national legislature, individuals suffering loss or injury thereby had a right flowing directly from Community law to reparation where (i) the rule of Community law breached was intended to confer rights on individuals, (ii) the breach of Community law was sufficiently serious, in that the member state had manifestly and gravely disregarded the limits on its discretion, and (iii) there was a direct causal link between the breach and the damage sustained', held. And see, *R v Secretary of State, Ex p Factortame Ltd (No 5)* [2000] 1 AC 524.

297 Ex Art 169.

298 An example of such action in the discrimination law field can be seen in *Commission v UK*, Case 61/81 [1982] ECR 2601; [1982] ICR 578.

299 Ex Art 177.

However, except where the legal provision concerned is *acte clair* (that is, sufficiently clear) the highest court (in the UK, the House of Lords) *must* ask for such a preliminary ruling.[300] There are many examples of such references being made by the UK courts in the discrimination law context[301] and these will be addressed throughout the following chapters as they arise.

F. The Human Rights Act and the European Convention on Human Rights

The European Convention for the Protection of Fundamental Rights and Freedoms (1950)[302] (ECHR) contains important provisions which form a significant context for the continuing development of equality law. The UK has signed and ratified the Convention and as a State is therefore bound by its terms. However, as mentioned above, the UK's system of law and its constitutional arrangements are such that international treaties do not become part of domestic law without further action.[303] The UK has given effect in large part to the Convention by the enactment of the Human Rights Act 1998 (HRA). In addition, the gravitational force of EC law, which must itself be construed consistently with the ECHR, gives some domestic effect to the ECHR in equality law.[304] **4.67**

The HRA obtained Royal Assent on 9 October 1998, and came fully into force on 2 October 2000. Scheduled to the Act are the 'Convention rights'.[305] All are important for equality law because all the rights guaranteed must be secured free from discrimination within the meaning of Article 14, described below. However, the most important of the rights for equality law are Articles 2, 3, 8, 9, 14, and 17. **4.68**

(1) Article 2

Article 2(1) provides that: **4.69**

> Everyone's right to life shall be protected by law. No one shall be deprived of his life intentionally save in the execution of a sentence of a court following his conviction of a crime for which this penalty is provided by law.

---

300 For a full discussion, see H Schermers and D Waelbroeck, *Judicial Protection in the European Union* (6th edn 1992, Kluwer), paras 572–81.

301 Including *Marshall v Southampton and South West Area Health Authority II*, Case C-271/91 [1993] ECR I-4367; *Webb v Emo Air Cargo (UK) Ltd* Case C-32/93 [1994] ICR 770; [1994] IRLR 482; *Alabaster v Woolwich and A'or*, Case C-147/02 [2005] ICR 695; [2004] IRLR 486.

302 CETS No 005. For an excellent and comprehensive review of human rights law.

303 For discussion on this 'dualist' system and the impact of the Convention pre-statutory incorporation, see R Clayton and H Tomlinson, *The Law of Human Rights* (2000, OUP) para 2.09 *et seq.*

304 See, for example, *Hauer v Land Rheinland-Pfalz*, Case 44/79 [1979] ECR 3727; *Elleniki Radiophonia Tileorassi (ERT) v Dimotiki Etatairia Pliroforissis (DEP)*, Case C-260/89 [1991] ECR I-2925, paras 43–5.

305 HRA, s 1.

There are exceptions provided for under Article 2(2), so that the deprivation of life shall not be regarded as inflicted in contravention of Article 2(1) when it results from the use of force which is no more than absolutely necessary; in defence of any person from unlawful violence; in order to effect a lawful arrest or to prevent the escape of a person lawfully detained; or in action lawfully taken for the purpose of quelling a riot or insurrection. These matters will rarely be relevant to equality law, though may arise in actions against the State where a death in custody has occurred in circumstances which are alleged to be discriminatory.[306] Otherwise the right conferred by Article 2 is absolute. Article 2 imposes on the State substantive obligations not to take life without justification and also to establish a framework of laws, precautions, procedures, and means of enforcement which will, to the greatest extent reasonably practicable, protect life. In addition, Article 2 imposes on Member States a procedural obligation to initiate an effective public investigation by an independent official body into any death occurring in circumstances in which it appears that one or other of the foregoing substantive obligations has been, or may have been, violated and it appears that agents of the State are, or may be, in some way implicated.[307] As Lord Bingham has remarked:

> Compliance with the substantive obligations referred to above must rank among the highest priorities of a modern democratic state governed by the rule of law. Any violation or potential violation must be treated with great seriousness.[308]

4.70 Article 2 issues have arisen in the context of disability[309] and in the context of deaths in custody, including where they have occurred in circumstances connected with gender or race.[310] Article 2 does not apply pre-natally.[311] It cannot be used, therefore, in support of an anti-abortion argument.[312]

---

306 In which context Art 5 should also be considered: *A and others v Secretary of State for the Home Department*; *X and another v Secretary of State for the Home Department* [2004] UKHL 56, [2005] 2 AC 68; *Regina (Middleton) v West Somerset Coroner and another* [2004] UKHL 10; [2004] 2 AC 182.

307 *Regina (Middleton) v West Somerset Coroner and another* [2004] UKHL 10; [2004] 2 AC 182, paras 2–3, *per* Lord Bingham and cases cited therein.

308 Ibid, para 5.

309 *Regina (Pretty) v Director of Public Prosecutions (Secretary of State for the Home Department intervening)* [2001] UKHL 61; [2002] 1 AC 800; *NHS Trust A v M; NHS Trust B v H* [2001] Fam 348. See too, *Airedale NHS Trust v Bland* [1993] AC 789; *R (on the application of Burke) v The GMC the Official Solicitor and others intervening* [2006] QB 273.

310 See, for example, the issues raised in the case of the death of Christopher Alder, *Report dated 27th February 2006, of the Review into the Events Leading up to and Following the Death of Christopher Alder on 1st April 1998* (2006) Independent Police Complaints Commission, HC 971-I and see, *Regina (Middleton) v West Somerset Coroner and another* [2004] UKHL 10; [2004] 2 AC 182.

311 *Paton v United Kingdom* (1980) 19 DR 244; *Vo v France* (2004) Applic No 53924/00, 8 July 2004.

312 Concerns have been expressed about the *discriminatory* nature of the Abortion Act 1967; s 1(1) provides that the legal abortion limit is 24 weeks save where the woman's life is put in danger by a continuation of the pregnancy or where she would be caused grave permanent injury or, at any

(2) Article 3

Article 3 of the ECHR provides that: 'No one shall be subjected to torture or to inhuman or degrading treatment.' Article 3 is unqualified—it absolutely prohibits inhuman and degrading treatment. 4.71

> Treatment is inhuman or degrading if, to a seriously detrimental extent, it denies the most basic needs of any human being. As in all Article 3 cases, the treatment, to be proscribed, must achieve a minimum standard of severity, and . . . in a context . . . not involving the deliberate infliction of pain or suffering, the threshold is a high one.[313]

It is possible to contemplate very serious incidents of discrimination that might meet that threshold of 'inhuman' or 'degrading' treatment (for example, seriously inadequate care in prisons and other State institutions).[314] Arrangements which deprived asylum seekers of any support in circumstances where they were also prohibited from working,[315] in certain circumstances, would put the State in breach of Article 3.[316] Such would occur, in particular, where an 'applicant with no means and no alternative sources of support, unable to support himself, is, by the deliberate action of the state, denied shelter, food or the most basic necessities of life. It is not necessary that treatment, to engage article 3, should merit the

time, where 'there is a substantial risk that if the child were born it would suffer from such physical or mental abnormalities as to be seriously handicapped'. Where the baby is likely to be 'seriously' disabled, therefore, there is no legal limit to the time at which an abortion may take place. The *discriminatory* nature of this measure (as opposed to abortion *per se* which raises different issues) is controversial. It gives rise to real concern that the life of a disabled person is legally viewed as less valuable or complete and that legislation and decisions are made with that unconscious prejudice in mind. So far, the cases under the Convention and the HRA have prioritized the right of human beings who have been born to personal autonomy, even where they conflict with views of others including medical practitioners. This approach is supported by the Disability Rights Commission. Nevertheless they wish to see the discriminatory measure in the Abortion Act 1967 repealed because of its obvious offensive connotations: 'In common with a wide range of disability and other organisations, the Disability Rights Commission believes the context in which parents choose whether to have a child should be one in which disability and non-disability are valued equally. In a positive manner the medical professions and others should ensure that parents receive comprehensive balanced information and guidance on disability, the rights of disabled people and on the support available': <http://www.drc-gb.org/library/policy/health_and_independent_living/drc_statement_on_section_11.aspx>.

313 *R v Secretary of State for the Home Department ex p Limbuela*; *R v Secretary of State for the Home Department ex p Tesema (Conjoined Appeals)* [2005] UKHL 66, para 7.

314 *Price v United Kingdom* (2002) 34 EHRR 1285. And for a discussion on Art 3 see R Clayton and H Tomlinson, *The Law of Human Rights* (2000, OUP), para 8.13 *et seq*. See *Chartier v Italy* (1982) 33DR 41, Ecomm HR; though no breach was found the Commission did suggest that the Italian authorities might take steps to mitigate the effects of or terminate the detention in circumstances where the applicant suffered from an hereditary illness causing obesity.

315 Nationality, Immigration and Asylum Act 2002, s 55(1) and Asylum and Immigration Act 1996, s 8 and the Immigration (Restrictions on Employment) Order 1996 (SI 1996/3225).

316 *R v Secretary of State for the Home Department ex p Adam; R v Secretary of State for the Home Department ex p Limbuela; R v Secretary of State for the Home Department ex p Tesema (Conjoined Appeals)* [2005] UKHL 66.

description used, in an immigration context, by Shakespeare and others in *Sir Thomas More* when they referred to 'your mountainish inhumanity'.[317] Importantly too, Article 3 imposes positive obligations on the State. In particular, 'vulnerable individuals . . . are entitled to State protection, in the form of effective deterrence, against . . . serious breaches of personal integrity'.[318]

4.72 Dignity interests are 'at the core of the rights protected by Article 3'.[319] Whether a particular set of circumstances constitutes 'inhuman or degrading treatment' is a matter of fact and degree but, as mentioned, to meet Article 3 standards the treatment complained of must reach a fairly high threshold. As the Court said in *Price v United Kingdom*:[320]

> The Court recalls that ill-treatment must attain a minimum level of severity if it is to fall within the scope of Article 3. The assessment of this minimum level of severity is relative; it depends on all the circumstances of the case, such as the duration of the treatment, its physical and mental effects and, in some cases, the sex, age and state of health of the victim. In considering whether treatment is 'degrading' within the meaning of Article 3, one of the factors which the Court will take into account is the question whether its object was to humiliate and debase the person concerned, although the absence of any such purpose cannot conclusively rule out a finding of violation of Article 3.

4.73 *Price* concerned a person who was four-limb-deficient (by reason of thalidomide) with numerous health problems including defective kidneys. She had been committed to prison for contempt of court in the course of civil proceedings. A breach of Article 3 was established in consequence of the conditions in which she was detained. The Court observed that:[321]

> There is no evidence in this case of any positive intention to humiliate or debase the applicant. However, the Court considers that to detain a severely disabled person in conditions where she is dangerously cold, risks developing sores because her bed is too hard or unreachable, and is unable to go to the toilet or keep clean without the greatest of difficulty, constitutes degrading treatment contrary to Article 3.

---

317 *R v Secretary of State for the Home Department ex p Adam; R v Secretary of State for the Home Department ex p Limbuela; R v Secretary of State for the Home Department ex p Tesema (Conjoined Appeals)* [2005] UKHL 66, para 7, *per* Lord Bingham.

318 *Lopes-Ostra v Spain* (1994) 20 EHRR 277 at 295, para 51. *R v Secretary of State for the Home Department ex p Adam; R v Secretary of State for the Home Department ex p Limbuela; R v Secretary of State for the Home Department ex p Tesema (Conjoined Appeals)* [2005] UKHL 66 ('The Article 3 jurisprudence is quite clear in recognising two situations in which the state can be held responsible for somebody's suffering. The first is when the state has itself subjected that person to such suffering. The second is when the state should have intervened to protect a person from suffering inflicted by others,' para 77, *per* Baroness Hale). Sec too, *N v Secretary of State for the Home Department (Terrence Higgins Trust intervening)* [2005] 2 AC 296.

319 *R (on the application of (1) A (2) B (by their litigation friend the Official Solicitor) (3) X (4) Y) v East Sussex County Council and The Disability Rights Commission* [2003] EWHC 167 (Admin).

320 *Price*, n 113 above, at 1292, para 24.

321 Ibid, at 1294, para 30.

And as was observed by Judge Greve (agreeing that there had been a violation of Article 3):

> It is obvious that restraining any non-disabled person to the applicant's level of ability to move and assist herself, for even a limited period of time, would amount to inhuman and degrading treatment—possibly torture. In a civilised country like the United Kingdom, society considers it not only appropriate but a basic humane concern to try to ameliorate and compensate for the disabilities faced by a person in the applicant's situation. In my opinion, these compensatory measures come to form part of the disabled person's bodily integrity. It follows that, for example, to prevent the applicant, who lacks both ordinary legs and arms, from bringing with her the battery charger to her wheelchair when she is sent to prison for one week, or to leave her in unsuitable sleeping conditions so that she has to endure pain and cold—the latter to the extent that eventually a doctor had to be called—is in my opinion a violation of the applicant's right to bodily integrity. Other episodes in the prison amount to the same.
>
> The applicant's disabilities are not hidden or easily overlooked. It requires no special qualification, only a minimum of ordinary human empathy, to appreciate her situation and to understand that to avoid unnecessary hardship—that is, hardship not implicit in the imprisonment of an able-bodied person—she has to be treated differently from other people because her situation is significantly different.

As can be seen, then, Article 3 is important in protecting disabled people and may require the different treatment of disabled people in certain situations to avoid a violation of Article 3. In addition, Article 3 will often be engaged in cases where decisions are made by disabled people and clinicians about appropriate treatment, particularly that which might prolong or end life and not just where the disabled person concerned is sentient and self-conscious. **4.74**

(3) Article 8

Article 8 provides that: **4.75**

> (1) Everyone has the right to respect for his private and family life, his home and his correspondence.
> (2) There shall be no interference by a public authority with the exercise of this right except such as is in the interests of national security, public safety, or the economic well-being of the country, for the prevention of disorder or crime, for the protection of health or morals, or for the rights and protections of others.

Article 8 then embraces four spheres: private life, family life, home, and correspondence. All of them concern intimate aspects of a person's life.

The protection afforded a person's 'home' will have obvious relevance in complaints of discrimination falling under the 'premises' provisions in the main anti-discrimination enactments.[322] Read with Article 14, Article 8 has also driven an **4.76**

[322] See Chap 10 and see *Ghaidan v Ghodin-Mendoza* [2004] UKHL 30, [2004] 2 AC 557; [2004] 3 WLR 113; *Council of the City of Manchester v (1) Romano (2) Samari (Disability Rights Commission intervening)* [2004] EWCA Civ 834 [2005] 1 WLR 2775.

interpretation of statutory tenancy rights which has protected the rights of same-sex partners.[323] Equality issues may arise too in the context of 'family' life. Much of the inequality surrounding 'family' life has arisen from a failure to recognize certain forms of family life. The concept has been underpinned by hetero-normative assumptions and a biological determinist approach to sex so that only opposite (biological) sex partnerships were recognized as forming 'families'. This approach was mitigated by the decision of the European Court of Human Rights (ECtHR) in *Goodwin v UK*.[324] In *Goodwin*, the ECtHR found that the UK's continuing failure to fully recognize a person's new gender following gender reassignment violated Article 8 and the right to private life. The recognition of a person's new gender thereafter (through the Gender Recognition Act 2004) necessarily had ramifications for transsexuals' 'family life' and the concept of family life embedded in Article 8, including by affording transsexuals a right to marry as the ECtHR required.[325] However, same-sex partnerships have still not been regarded unequivocally by the ECtHR as constituting 'family life' for the purposes of Article 8[326] and, so far, the House of Lords have not ruled clearly on the issue for present purposes.[327]

4.77 As to the concept of 'private life', this is the most nebulous concept found in Article 8 and indeed in the ECHR. It has been held to be wide enough to encompass personal identity and integrity; 'to a certain degree the right to establish and develop relationships with other human beings'[328] and personal autonomy while an individual is alive.[329] There may in some cases, therefore, be an overlap with Articles 2 and 3, as described above. According to the ECtHR in *Pretty v UK*:[330]

> [T]he concept of 'private life' is a broad term not susceptible to exhaustive definition. It covers the physical and psychological integrity of a person . . . It can

323 *Ghaidan v Ghodin-Mendoza*, ibid, though less important now because of the impact of the Civil Partnership Act 2004.

324 [2002] IRLR 664.

325 Ibid, para 97.

326 Though with increasing consensus on gay and lesbian rights among Member countries of the Council of Europe such is likely to happen very soon. See, for the progress of this issue in ECtHR case law, *Mata Estevez v Spain* (App No 00056501/00; 10 May 2001); *Karner v Austria* (2003) 14 BHRC 674.

327 *M v Secretary of State for Work and Pensions* [2006] UKHL 11 [2006] 2 AC 91 (Lord Nicholls (paras 26–7) and Lord Mance (paras 136 and 151) concluded that ECtHR case law presently holds that Art 8 does not accord to the relationship between same-sex couples the respect for family life guaranteed by Art 8 and that the same did not protect a same-sex relationship as a 'family' for Art 8 purposes during the relevant period ending in 2002. Lord Bingham did not expressly decide this issue (but agreed with Lord Walker); Lord Walker was prepared to accept that a same-sex couple with children do constitute family life (para 87) and Baroness Hale concluded that the relationship did constitute family life (para 112). See R Wintemute, 'Same-Sex Couples in *Secretary of State for Work and Pensions v M*; identical to *Karner* and *Godin-Mendoza*, Yet No Discrimination?' [2006] EHRLR 6, 722.

328 *Neimetz v Germany* (1992) 16 EHRR 97 para 29.

329 Though it does not confer a right to decide when or how to die; *Regina (Pretty) v Director of Public Prosecutions (Secretary of State for the Home Department intervening)* [2001] UKHL 61; [2002] 1 AC 800; (2002) 35 EHHR 1.

330 (2002) 35 EHHR 1 at paras 61 and 65, internal references removed.

> sometimes embrace aspects of an individual's physical and social identity . . . Elements such as, for example, gender identification, name and sexual orientation and sexual life fall within the personal sphere protected by Article 8 . . . Article 8 also protects a right to personal development, and the right to establish and develop relationships with other human beings and the outside world . . . Although no previous case has established as such any right to self-determination as being contained in Article 8 of the Convention, the Court considers that the notion of personal autonomy is an important principle underlying the interpretation of its guarantees . . .
>
> The very essence of the Convention is respect for human dignity and human freedom . . .

As with some of the other Convention guarantees, Article 8 imposes certain positive obligations on the State, '[I]n order to determine whether such obligations exist, regard must be had to the fair balance that has to be struck between the general interest and the interests of the individual'.[331]

The 'private life' guarantee therefore has obvious resonance for situations of inequality. The emphasis on personal integrity, identity, and autonomy found in the ECtHR case law would suggest that any State measures differentiating between people on grounds connected to personal status (gender, race, sexual orientation etc) or lifestyle choice would fall within the broad scope of 'private life' and therefore require the State to justify them. However, according to the House of Lords, not all incidents of adverse treatment touching upon a person's personality will engage Article 8 and less so impose a positive obligation on the State to remedy them. In the case of *M v Secretary of State for Work and Pensions*[332] the House of Lords considered that the penalty imposed on a mother in a same-sex relationship by reason of the then child support regulations (because of their failure to recognize her same-sex relationships as a single unit for calculation purposes as would have been the case were the relationship an opposite-sex relationship) was not sufficient to engage Article 8. According to Lord Bingham: **4.78**

> It is not difficult, when considering any provision of the Convention, including article 8 . . . , to identify the core values which the provision is intended to protect. But the further a situation is removed from one infringing those core values, the weaker the connection becomes, until a point is reached when there is no meaningful connection at all. At the inner extremity a situation may properly be said to be within the ambit or scope of the right, nebulous though those expressions necessarily are. At the outer extremity, it may not. There is no sharp line of demarcation between the two. An exercise of judgment is called for.[333]

331 *Botta v Italy* (1998) 26 EHRR 241, 257, para 33.

332 [2006] UKHL 11; [2006] 2 AC 91.

333 Para 4. See also Lord Nicholls, para 32, Lord Walker, para 88, Lord Mance, para 157.

This case has already been considered in Chapter 2[334] and the correctness of the judgment made in this case must be doubted, particularly given the repeated commands of the ECtHR that 'differences based on sexual orientation require particularly serious reasons by way of justification'.[335] However, other cases, particularly in the disability field, have taken a similar approach to the limits of Article 8 and the concept of 'private life'.

4.79 In *Botta v Italy*, the ECtHR were concerned with a complaint of a violation of Article 8 brought by a disabled person who was unable to visit a particular private beach because it was inaccessible. The Court rejected his complaint holding that:

> the right asserted by Mr Botta, namely the right to gain access to the beach and the sea at a place distant from his normal place of residence during his holidays, concerns interpersonal relations of such broad and indeterminate scope that there can be no conceivable direct link between the measures the State was urged to take in order to make good the omissions of the private bathing establishments and the applicant's private life.[336]

4.80 As can be seen above, Article 8 is qualified (Article 8(2)). Not all intrusions into the rights protected by Article 8 will violate Article 8. Interferences with private life are permitted only where they are 'in accordance with the law'; and 'necessary in a democratic society' in the interests of one of the values listed in Article 8(2) of the Convention. For an interference to be 'necessary in a democratic society' to achieve one of the legitimate aims listed in it, case law indicates that the following four elements must be satisfied:

(a) that there is a pressing social need for some restriction;
(b) that the restriction corresponds to (ie has a rational connection with) that need;
(c) that the restriction is a proportionate response to that need;
(d) that the reasons advanced by the authorities are 'relevant and sufficient'.[337]

Such requires a substantive assessment by a court.[338]

4.81 In addition, regard must be had to the hallmarks of a democratic society, namely 'pluralism, tolerance and broadmindedness'.[339] Ignorance, prejudice, and

334 Paras 2.08 and 2.10.

335 *Karner v Austria* (2003) 14 BHRC 674, para 37; *Smith and Grady v UK* (2000) 29 EHRR 493 at paras 89–90; *Lustig-Prean and A'or v UK* (2000) 29 EHRR 548 at para 83; *Dudgeon v the United Kingdom* (1982) 4 EHRR 149, paras 41. See R Wintemute, 'Same-Sex Couples in *Secretary of State for Work and Pensions v M*; identical to *Karner* and *Godin-Mendoza*, Yet No Discrimination?' [2006] EHRLR 6, 722.

336 *Botta v Italy*, n 330 above, para 35. See too: *Zehnalova v Czech Republic* (2002) (App No 38621/97).

337 *Handyside v United Kingdom* (1976) 1 EHRR 737; *Barthold v Germany* (1985) 7 EHRR 383.

338 *R (on the application of Begum, by her litigation friend, Rahman) v Headteacher and Governors of Denbigh High School* [2006] UKHL 15, para 30, *per* Lord Bingham.

339 *Handyside v United Kingdom* (1976) 1 EHRR 737 para 49.

intolerance should not therefore be regarded as good justificatory reasons under Article 8(2). The approach taken in *M v Secretary of State for Work and Pensions*,[340] discussed in Chapter 2,[341] in treating historical antipathy towards gay men and lesbians as justification for discrimination in a State scheme, can properly be regarded as inconsistent with the general thrust of the case law emanating from the ECtHR, not to say 'anachronistic'.[342]

(4) Article 9

Article 9 contains the important guarantees relating to religious freedom. Those guarantees fall into two parts. Firstly, Article 9(1) provides an absolute right to freedom of thought, conscience, and religion declaring that: **4.82**

> [e]veryone has the right to freedom of thought, conscience and religion; this right includes . . . freedom, either alone or in community with others and in public or private, to manifest his religion or belief, in worship, teaching, practice and observance.

Article 9(2), on the other hand, qualifies the right to manifest religion and belief by providing that '[f]reedom to manifest one's religion or beliefs shall be subject only to such limitations as are prescribed by law and are necessary in a democratic society in the interests of public safety, for the protection of public order, health or morals, or for the protection of the rights and freedoms of others'. As such, Article 9(2) allows for restrictions on the 'manifestation' of religion or belief.

Article 9 provides obviously important protections against religious discrimination. Its importance too is in its recognition that: **4.83**

> [r]eligious and other beliefs and convictions are part of the humanity of every individual. They are an integral part of his personality and individuality. In a civilized

---

340 [2006] UKHL 11; [2006] 2 AC 91.

341 Paras 2.08 and 2.10.

342 Cf, the observations of Lord Bingham, para 6: 'Ms M's complaint of discrimination is in my view anachronistic. By that I mean that she is applying the standards of today to criticize a regime which when it was established represented the accepted values of our society, which has now been brought to an end because it no longer does so but which could not, with the support of the public, have been brought to an end very much earlier. Historically, both the law and public opinion withheld their sanction from a relationship between a man and a woman which was not sanctified by marriage or at least regularized by civil ceremony, and homosexual relationships were criminalized or condemned. When extra-marital heterosexual relationships became more generally accepted by the law and public opinion, recognition of homosexual relationships (even of those no longer criminal) was still withheld. Even now there remain bodies of opinion in this country (and much larger bodies of opinion in some other countries) for whom such recognition is still a step too far. But a democratic majority, by enacting the Civil Partnerships Act 2004, has established a new consensus and removed the feature of the old social security and child support regimes of which Ms M. complains. If such a regime were to be established today, Ms M. could with good reason stigmatize the regime as unjustifiably discriminatory. But it is unrealistic to stigmatize as unjustifiably discriminatory a regime which, given the size of the overall task and the need to recruit the support of the public, could scarcely have been reformed sooner.'

society individuals respect each other's beliefs. This enables them to live in harmony. This is one of the hallmarks of a civilized society.[343]

4.84 As to the first limb of Article 9, a broad reach is given to it so that it protects adherents to mainstream religious faiths[344] and minority faiths, and those who adhere to belief systems which diverge from established religious thought.[345] The broad wording of Article 9(1) and the liberal approach taken by the ECtHR has made it unnecessary for the ECtHR to make a definitive ruling on what constitutes a 'religion' or protected thought,[346] but Article 9 has been held to protect, for example, believers in Druidism,[347] the Krishna consciousness movement,[348] and Jehovah's Witnesses.[349] A belief in a deity or other metaphysical element is not required so that certain ethical or philosophical convictions are protected, including pacifism[350] and veganism,[351] as are non-theistic beliefs, such as atheism and agnosticism.[352]

4.85 Whilst an individual must establish that she or he is an adherent to the religion being asserted to attract the protections of Article 9, and that the particular belief or practice that is being infringed is an element of that religion,[353] importantly the State has no role in marking out the parameters of protected religion or thought—such would otherwise obviously impair the protections granted by Article 9.[354] There are nevertheless some limits to the protections afforded by Article 9 so that a court may be 'concerned to ensure an assertion of religious belief is made in good faith: "neither fictitious, nor capricious, and that it is not an artifice", and make enquiries to that end.[355] Certain opinions or views, however strongly held, will fall

343 *R (Williamson) v Secretary of State for Education and Employment* [2005] UKHL 15, [2005] 2 AC 246, para 15, *per* Lord Nicholls.

344 *Ahmed v UK* (1981) 4 EHRR 126 (Islam); *Stedman v UK* (1997) 23 EHRR CD 168 (Christianity).

345 See the observation of Lord Nicholls in *R (Williamson) v Secretary of State for Education and Employment*, n 343 above, para 25.

346 See S Stavros, 'Freedom of Religion and Claims for Exemption from Generally Applicable Neutral Laws: Lessons from Across the Pond?' (1997) EHRLR Issue 6, 609, and P Edge, 'Religious rights and choice under the European Convention on Human Rights' (2000) 3 Web JCLI.

347 *Chappell v UK* (1987) 53 DR 241.

348 *Iskcon v UK* (1994) 76A DR 90.

349 *Kokkinakis v Greece* (1994) 17 EHRR 397.

350 *Arrowsmith v UK* (1978) 19 DR 5.

351 *X v UK (Commission)* Appl 18187/91 (10 Feb 1993); *H v United Kingdom* (1993) 16 EHRR CD 44.

352 *Kokkinakis v Greece* (1994) 17 EHRR 397.

353 See *X v UK* No 8160/78; *D v France* No 10180/82; *Chauhan v UK* No 1151/85.

354 *R (Williamson) v Secretary of State for Education and Employment*, n 343 above, para 12, *per* Lord Nicholls.

355 Ibid, para 22, per Lord Nicholls.

outside Article 9,[356] in particular those that can more properly be characterized as purely political beliefs.[357]

Article 9(1) affords protection against indoctrination of religion by the State[358] and may also require the State to protect an individual against improper influence to change her or his beliefs.[359] Paradoxically, as observed in Chapter 2, this right exists in the UK, a State with an established church with a primary and unique role in constitutional affairs. Article 9 has not forced any change in the constitutional position of the Church of England though such must be required if the promise of pluralism protected by Article 9 is to be constitutionally meaningful.[360] Certainly in a pluralistic and diverse community positive steps may need to be taken to allow people to freely choose the belief they hold, and if and how they may wish to manifest it, perhaps more so where the dominant religion has the unique sanction of the State. **4.86**

Article 9(2) embraces the right to manifest one's religion or belief. Such is in many respects a more important right—the right to hold a belief in secret, behind a veil, in a closet for many will lack real substance—and the distinction between holding a belief and manifesting it for some can be difficult to draw.[361] Article 9(2) only protects activities closely connected with religious belief so that it does not cover every act which is 'motivated or influenced by a religion or belief'[362] but instead is directed at protecting the area 'sometimes called the forum internum' and 'acts which are intimately linked to these attitudes such as acts of worship or devotion'.[363] The fact, therefore, that one might attribute a broad altruistic outlook to either religious or, as the case may be, atheistic commitment will not mean that campaigning for a socialist government will fall to be protected under Article 9(2).[364] **4.87**

Manifesting beliefs may necessarily interfere with others, particularly when that is done in public spaces. The guarantee in Article 9(2), as mentioned, therefore is more limited. This is so in two respects. Firstly, for any 'manifestation' to attract **4.88**

356 Though will usually be caught by the freedom of expression guarantees in Art 10.

357 See, for example, *McFeeley v UK* (1980) 20 DR 44; *Vereniging Rechtswinkels Utrecht v Netherlands* (1986) 46 DR 200; *Pretty v UK* (2002) 35 EHHR 1.

358 *Angelini v Sweden* (1988) 10 EHRR 123.

359 *Kokkinakis v Greece*, n 349 above.

360 See the discussion in *The Future of Multi-Ethnic Britain: The Parekh Report* (2000, Profile Books) Chap 17.

361 Particularly those for whom proselytizing is an inherent part of a belief system. See further discussion in Edge, n 346 above.

362 *Arrowsmith v UK*, n 350 above.

363 *C v UK* (1983) 37 DR 142.

364 See, for example, though not entirely internally logical *Arrowsmith v UK*, n 350 above (see, in particular, para 20). Art 10 (freedom of expression) is likely to be engaged in such circumstances.

the protection of Article 9(2), the belief manifested must 'satisfy some modest, objective minimum requirements . . . The belief must be consistent with basic standards of human dignity or integrity'.[365] Secondly, as can be seen, any manifestation may be restricted where the limitation is prescribed by law and necessary in a democratic society in the interests of public safety, for the protection of public order, health, or morals, or for the protection of the rights and freedoms of others. This has permitted a wide range of limitations in a variety of circumstances, most particularly where such does not prevent in absolute terms a manifestation of an important aspect of a person's religious belief, as where the person concerned is deemed able to choose to continue to enjoy such manifestation by, for example, changing job or school. The idea of 'choice' in this context is problematic,[366] but as has been noted the 'Strasbourg institutions have not been at all ready to find an interference with the right to manifest religious belief in practice or observance where a person has voluntarily accepted an employment or role which does not accommodate that practice or observance and there are other means open to the person to practise or observe his or her religion without undue hardship or inconvenience'.[367] The difficulty with this approach is compounded where the manifestation is sought to be enjoyed by a child who is likely to have even less choice as to schooling etc, than a worker as to employment.[368] Equally importantly, where the manifestation intrudes significantly on others' rights, a restriction is likely to be regarded as justified. In any case, as with justification under Article 8(2), a court is required to substantively scrutinize the reasons for any interference to determine whether it is lawful under Article 9(2), therefore going beyond the approach adopted traditionally in judicial review.[369] In so doing the rights and freedoms of others and the question whether any interference is proportionate will be key.[370] Dress codes (in particular pursuant to a State's desire to regulate dress in civic institutions so as to promote religious harmony);[371] contractual working hours;[372]

365 *R (Williamson) v Secretary of State for Education and Employment*, n 343 above, para 23, *per* Lord Nicholls.

366 Edge, n 346 above.

367 *R (on the application of Begum, by her litigation friend, Rahman) v Headteacher and Governors of Denbigh High School*, n 338 above, para 23, *per* Lord Bingham.

368 As in ibid, para 41, *per* Lord Nicholls (though not all their Lordships took the same view, see Lord Hoffman, para 50; Lord Scott, para 89).

369 Ibid, para 30, *per* Lord Bingham.

370 Ibid.

371 *R (on the application of Begum, by her litigation friend, Rahman) v Headteacher and Governors of Denbigh High School*, n 338 above; *Karaduman v Turkey* (1993) 74 DR 93; *Sahin v Turkey* (App No 44774/98, 10 Nov 2005, unreported), paras 14–111.

372 *Ahmad v United Kingdom* (1981) 4 EHRR 126; *Stedman v United Kingdom* (1997) 23 EHRR CD 168.

and military requirements[373] have been held to justifiably interfere with the manifestation of religious freedoms.[374]

4.89 Importantly too, the obligations inherent in Article 9(1), imposing as they do an obligation on the State to protect people against pressure to adopt particular religious beliefs, and, more particularly, the express limitations in Article 9(2), provide important protections for minorities *within* religious communities. For example, women and children, who may be particularly vulnerable to more powerful members of religious groups to which they belong, may gain valuable protection both from the freedoms inherent in Article 9 and the limitations imposed by it.[375] Article 9 therefore provides the opportunity for protecting those who regard religion as liberating and those who need liberating from it.

(5) Article 14

4.90 As mentioned in earlier chapters, Article 14 is the Convention's non-discrimination guarantee. It provides that:

> The enjoyment of the rights and freedoms set forth in this Convention shall be secured without discrimination on any ground such as sex, race, colour, language, religion, political or other opinion, national or social origin, association with a national minority, property birth or other status.

Article 14 complements the other substantive provisions of the Convention in that it has no independent existence since it has effect solely in relation to 'the enjoyment of the rights and freedoms' safeguarded elsewhere in the Convention. However, in order for Article 14 to be engaged, the complainant need not show that there has been a breach of a substantive provision, merely that the facts of his case fall within the ambit of one of the substantive provisions.[376] Broadly, five questions arise in an Article 14 inquiry,[377] namely:

(i) Do the facts fall within the ambit of one or more of the Convention rights?
(ii) Was there a difference in treatment in respect of that right between the complainant and others put forward for comparison?[378]

---

373 *Kalaç v Turkey* (1997) 27 EHRR 552, though see *Thlimmenos v Greece* [2000] 9 BHRC 12, discussed below.

374 *R (on the application of Begum, by her litigation friend, Rahman) v Headteacher and Governors of Denbigh High School*, n 338 above.

375 Ibid, paras 94–5 in particular and see, *R (Williamson) v Secretary of State for Education and Employment*, n 343 above.

376 *Abdulaziz Cabales and Balkandali v UK* (1985) 7 EHRR 471; *Ghaidan v Godin-Mendoza* [2004] UKHL 30, [2004] 2 AC 557, [2004] 3 WLR 113, *per* Lady Hale para 133.

377 *Ghaidan v Godin-Mendoza*, ibid, *per* Lady Hale para 133, based on the approach of Brooke LJ in *Wandsworth London Borough Council v Michalak* [2003] 1 WLR 617, 625, para 20, as amplified in *R (Carson) v Secretary of State for Work and Pensions* [2002] EWHC 978 (Admin), para 52 and [2003] EWCA Civ 797, [2003] 3 All ER 577.

378 And a de facto distinction may suffice: *Zarb Adami v Malta* (App No 17209/02).

(iii) Were those others in an analogous situation?
(iv) Was the difference in treatment objectively justifiable? ie did it have a legitimate aim and bear a reasonable relationship of proportionality to that aim?
(v) Was the difference in treatment based on one or more of the grounds proscribed—whether expressly or by inference—in Article 14?

4.91 As can be seen, these questions overlap and it will sometimes be appropriate to ask them in a different order. In *R (Carson) v Secretary of State for Work and Pensions*[379] the House of Lords found that the formulation described above was not without its difficulty[380] and preferred a less 'technical' or 'structured' approach. This approach is reflected in the observations of Lord Nicholls, as follows:

> Article 14 does not apply unless the alleged discrimination is in connection with a Convention right and on a ground stated in Article 14. If this prerequisite is satisfied, the essential question for the Court is whether the alleged discrimination, that is, the difference in treatment of which complaint is made, can withstand scrutiny. Sometimes the answer to this question will be plain. There may be such an obvious relevant difference between the Claimant and those with whom he seeks to compare himself that their situations cannot be regarded as analogous. Sometimes, where the position is not so clear, a different approach is called for. Then the court's scrutiny may be best directed at considering whether the differentiation has a legitimate aim and whether the means chosen to achieve the aim is appropriate and not disproportionate in its adverse impact.[381]

4.92 The reliance on a comparator present in both the more formulaic and 'less rigid' approaches adopted by the courts, as described above, creates the same dangers as are present in the analyses undertaken by the courts in assessing direct discrimination under the main anti-discrimination enactments. In particular, it allows a court to avoid the question whether any distinction requires justification by simply holding that the situations do not meet the threshold of comparability necessary to warrant justification.[382] Similarly, those differently situated because of the very characteristics Article 14 is directed at protecting (sex, race etc) may fall through its net because their situations are not regarded as 'analogous'. However, the blurring of the edges caused by the 'less rigid' approach advocated by, amongst others, Lord Nicholls perhaps makes this risk more real. The question whether 'the alleged discrimination . . . of which complaint is made, can withstand scrutiny' begs a number of questions and these may be lost in a broad

379 [2006] 1 AC 173; [2005] 2 WLR 1369.

380 [2006] 1 AC 173, *per* Lord Nicholls, 179, paras 2–3; *per* Lord Hoffman, 186–7, paras 28–33; *per* Lord Rodger, 188, para 43; *per* Lord Walker, 193–5, paras 61–70; *per* Lord Carswell, 203, para 97.

381 Ibid, 179, para 3.

382 See, eg, *R (on the application of Al-Rawi and O'rs) v Secretary of State for Foreign and Commonwealth Affairs and A'or* [2006] EWCA Civ 1279, para 78.

brush inquiry. Adopting the five-step inquiry set out above gives rise to a number of questions addressed below.

(a) Ambit

As to whether Article 14 is engaged at all, this depends on showing that the complaint made falls within the 'ambit' of one of the other Convention rights. 'Ambit' is a difficult concept and the reach of Article 14 has not been, and perhaps should not be, definitively prescribed. A number of formulations have been adopted to describe its scope so that Article 14 has been said to apply where the facts and circumstances of a case have a 'connection' with one of the substantive Convention rights,[383] where the subject matter of the disadvantage 'constitutes one of the modalities of the exercise of [a] right guaranteed',[384] where the measure in question is 'linked' to a guaranteed right,[385] and where the facts in issue fall 'within the ambit' of such a right.[386] The more remote the action or inaction complained of from the core values a particular Convention right is intended to protect, the less likely it will fall within its ambit:[387] **4.93**

> Plainly, expressions such as 'ambit', 'scope' and 'linked' used in the Strasbourg cases are not precise and exact in their meaning. They denote a situation in which a substantive Convention right is not violated, but in which a personal interest close to the core of such a right is infringed. This calls, as Lord Nicholls said in M,[388] at para 14, for a value judgment. The court is required to consider, in respect of the Convention right relied on, what value that substantive right exists to protect.[389]

Despite some early enthusiasm suggesting otherwise, it appears that a mere 'tenuous link' will not suffice, at least for domestic law purposes.[390] However, in the absence of any requirement that there be a breach of another Convention right, this 'represents a generous interpretation of Article 14, which extends the Convention's protection beyond the minimum treatment required by other Convention rights on their own, to treatment that a Member State has chosen voluntarily to provide, but has provided in a discriminatory manner. Voluntary treatment of this kind may violate Article 14 combined with another

383 *R (Carson) v Secretary of State for Work and Pensions* [2006] 1 AC 173, 179, para 3, *per* Lord Nicholls.

384 *Petrovic v Austria* (2001) 33 EHRR 14 at para 28; *National Union of Belgian Police v Belgium* (1979–80) 1 EHRR 578, at para 45.

385 *Schmidt and Another v Sweden* (1976) 1 EHRR 632 at para 39.

386 *Abdulaziz, Cabales and Balkandali v United Kingdom* (1985) 7 EHRR 471, at para 71.

387 *M v Secretary of State for Work and Pensions* [2006] UKHL 11; [2006] 2 AC 91, para 4, *per* Lord Bingham.

388 *M v Secretary of State for Work and Pensions* [2006] UKHL 11; [2006] 2 AC 91.

389 *R (on the application of Clift) v Secretary of State for the Home Department; R (on the application of Hindawi and another) v Secretary of State for the Home Department* [2006] UKHL 54, para 13.

390 Ibid, para 4, *per* Lord Bingham, para 60, *per* Lord Walker.

Convention right, even though it would not violate the other Convention rights on its own'.[391]

(b) Discrimination

4.94 Steps (ii) and (iii) above suggest that Article 14 is concerned with addressing 'differences' in treatment which would fit most comfortably into a direct discrimination model. Indeed, in the main, the cases under Article 14 have concerned direct discrimination.[392] However, the concept of discrimination under Article 14 (notwithstanding the formulation set out above) is broad enough to incorporate some forms of indirect discrimination. Depending on the factual circumstances, it may require accommodations to be made so as to secure substantive equality for persons otherwise disadvantaged by apparently neutral rules, so that:

> the right not to be discriminated against in the enjoyment of the rights guaranteed under the Convention is also violated when States without an objective and reasonable justification fail to treat differently persons whose situations are significantly different.[393]

4.95 As mentioned above, the comparator requirement introduced by the formulations identified above introduce the problems seen in the direct discrimination model found in the main anti-discrimination enactments, and this is discussed further in Chapter 6. According to the case law under the ECHR, in a direct discrimination case, Article 14 requires that the complainant be in an 'analogous situation'[394] to any person allegedly better treated. Some cases already decided under domestic law have avoided subjecting a *prima facie* discriminatory measure to close examination by simply holding that to the extent that it treats persons differently those persons are not similarly situated so any difference does not require objective justification.[395] This would seem to distort the Article's function and conflate the issues requiring scrutiny. If people are treated differently, justification may be readily proved if the explanation for that is that they are differently situated. By giving primacy to the question whether persons are 'similarly situated' the burden of proof does not shift to the State to establish the reason for the

391 R Wintemute, '"Within the Ambit": How Big is the "Gap" in Article 14 European Convention on Human Rights?' (2004) EHRLR, Issue 4, 370, and *Stec v UK* (2006) (App Nos 65731/01 and 65900/01).

392 And a *de facto* distinction may suffice: *Zarb Adami v Malta* (App No 17209/02).

393 *Thlimmenos v Greece* (2000) 31 EHRR 411 at para 44. *Stec v UK* (2006) (App Nos 65731/01 and 65900/01) ('Art 14 does not prohibit a Member State from treating groups differently in order to correct "factual inequalities" between them; indeed in certain circumstances a failure to attempt to correct inequality through different treatment may in itself give rise to a breach of the Art (see '*Case relating to certain aspects of the laws on the use of languages in education in Belgium' v Belgium (Merits)*, judgment of 23 July 1968, Series A no 6, § 10 and *Thlimmenos v Greece*, no 34369/97, § 44, ECHR 2000-IV)', para 51).

394 *Van der Mussele v Belgium* (1983) 6 EHRR 163, 179–180, para 46.

395 *R (Carson) v Secretary of State for Work and Pensions* [2006] 1 AC 173.

difference in treatment. In *R (Carson) v Secretary of State for Work and Pensions*,[396] for example, the House of Lords were required to determine two cases in which the identity of the comparator also determined the issue of justification. The first case concerned a British citizen who had spent most of her working life in England but at the date of her retirement was resident in South Africa. By reason of the relevant social security provisions, she remained entitled to her State pension but she was precluded from receiving the annual cost of living increase given to recipients of pensions who remained resident in the UK or other countries with which the UK had made a bilateral agreement allowing for reciprocal up-rating of benefits. She alleged discrimination under Article 14 and the House of Lords held that she was in a relevantly different position to those resident in the UK.[397] Accordingly the difference in treatment did not require justification. This gives the State a double bite at the cherry, encouraging in all cases an argument that differently treated classes are not comparable, leaving justification to the last resort. A progressive concept of equality would properly expect that differences are explained and justified to a greater or lesser degree depending upon the extent of the discriminatory treatment and the grounds for it. The justification test already allows for different levels of scrutiny, as discussed below, so that differences in treatment based on differences in status not connected to the 'suspect classes' (race, sex etc) will be more readily justifiable. Letting the State off the hook at an earlier stage undermines the significance of the Article 14 protections.

However, where the protected characteristic relied upon is one falling within a suspect class (race, gender etc), the existence of that characteristic will never itself be a reason to treat a person as being in a non-analogous situation. In such circumstances, justification will always be required for any differences in treatment, so that: **4.96**

> There are . . . some circumstances in which justification must be considered as a separate issue. The clearest case . . . is that of 'positive discrimination', in which a category of disadvantaged persons is accorded specially favourable treatment (and others are correspondingly worse treated) precisely because of some personal characteristic (such as race or gender) of the preferred group.[398] That personal characteristic obviously cannot be taken into account as a relevant difference negativing 'analogous circumstances'; positive discrimination must be justified, if at all, for reasons which focus on (and as it were make a virtue of) what would otherwise be a proscribed ground. That possibility has been recognised in the Strasbourg jurisprudence since the *Belgian* Linguistic Case (No 2) (1968) 1 EHRR 252, 284, para 10, in which the court observed that 'certain legal inequalities tend only to correct factual inequalities'.[399]

396 [2006] 1 AC 173.

397 Or in those countries with which the UK had bilateral agreements: *R (Carson) v Secretary of State for Work and Pensions* [2006] 1 AC 173, paras 8, 25, 33, 37, *per* Lord Hoffman; para 44, *per* Lord Rodger; para 79, *per* Lord Walker.

398 *A fortiori* if the discrimination is *negative*.

399 *R (Carson) v Secretary of State for Work and Pensions* [2006] 1 AC 173, para 70, *per* Lord Walker.

(c) Justification

4.97 Discrimination under Article 14 may be justified by an objective and reasonable justification. Importantly, it is the discrimination that must be justified, not any broader scheme of which it may form a part. Accordingly, anti-terrorist measures may be justified, but where such measures mark out for different treatment certain groups of non-UK nationals, *that* discrimination must be justified.[400] Any reliance upon justification must be carefully scrutinized and the burden of establishing the same rests with the respondent State in any case.[401] In determining whether any discriminatory treatment is justified, it is necessary to determine (a) whether the discriminatory treatment pursues a legitimate aim; and then, (b) whether there is a reasonable relationship of proportionality between the means employed and the aim sought to be realized.[402] Further, reflecting the approach taken in other jurisdictions, as mentioned, the level of scrutiny applied to any discriminatory measure will reflect the social and legal importance placed upon the distinguishing characteristic relied upon. Distinctions based on 'suspect classes', in particular sex,[403] race,[404] nationality,[405] religion,[406] and sexual orientation[407] will be subject to particularly rigorous scrutiny and will require 'very weighty reasons' if they are to be held justified.[408] Justification will not be made out for discrimination connected with such status on utilitarian grounds.[409] As to age, however, according to the House of Lords, 'discrimination on grounds of old age may be a contemporary example of a borderline case'.[410] 'Disability' has not yet been identified as a 'suspect' ground. Identifying suspect classes is a difficult task and depends upon social and historical circumstance. Discrimination on the grounds of sexual orientation, of course, was not always regarded as 'suspect'. Just as it was increasingly recognized that negative distinctions based on grounds connected with sexual orientation were morally repugnant, so, with increasing

---

400 *Ghaidan v Godin-Mendoza* [2004] UKHL 30, [2004] 2 AC 557, [2004] 3 WLR 113; *A v Secretary of State for the Home Department* [2005] 2 AC 68, para 54.

401 *Thlimmenos v Greece* (2000) 31 EHRR 411.

402 *Ghaidan v Godin-Mendoza* [2004] UKHL 30, [2004] 2 AC 557, [2004] 3 WLR 113; *A v Secretary of State for the Home Department* [2005] 2 AC 68, para 54.

403 *Balkandali v United Kingdom* (1985) 7 EHRR 471, 501, para 78; *Schmidt v Germany* (1994) 18 EHRR 513, 527, para 24; *Van Raalte v The Netherlands* (1997) 24 EHRR 503, 518–19, para 39; *Ghaidan v Godin-Mendoza* [2004] UKHL 30, [2004] 2 AC 557, [2004] 3 WLR 113, para 19.

404 *Ghaidan v Godin-Mendoza* [2004] UKHL 30, [2004] 2 AC 557, [2004] 3 WLR 113, para 19.

405 *Gaygusuz v Austria* (1996) 23 EHRR 364.

406 *Hoffmann v Austria* (1993) 17 EHRR 293, 316, para 36.

407 *Salgueiro da Silva Mouta v Portugal* (1999) 31 EHRR 1055, 1071, para 36; *Ghaidan v Godin-Mendoza* [2004] UKHL 30, [2004] 2 AC 557, [2004] 3 WLR 113.

408 *R (Carson) v Secretary of State for Work and Pensions* [2006] 1 AC 173, para 16–17, *per* Lord Hoffman; paras 57–8, *per* Lord Walker.

409 *R (Carson) v Secretary of State for Work and Pensions* [2006] 1 AC 173, para 16, *per* Lord Hoffman.

410 Ibid, para 17, *per* Lord Hoffman.

consensus internationally on the unacceptability of distinctions based on disability and age, it is likely that distinctions based upon age and disability will soon be regarded as 'suspect'. Lord Walker has observed that '[a]ge is a personal characteristic, but it is different in kind from other personal characteristics. Every human being starts life as a tiny infant, and none of us can do anything to stop the passage of the years . . . There is nothing intrinsically demeaning about age'.[411] It is true, there is nothing 'intrinsically demeaning about age' but nor is there anything intrinsically demeaning about being a woman, being black, or being gay, but making distinctions on those grounds certainly is. Age is different because all of us (if lucky) experience all ages but arbitrary treatment based on it can be demeaning as is increasingly recognized by law.[412]

'Positive' discrimination may be justified where it meets the requirements of legitimacy and proportionality.[413] Different treatment may also be justified where it has been introduced to address historic disadvantage even where the existence of that disadvantage has disappeared, for so long as is necessary to effect legislative change.[414] However, this assumes and depends upon there being some original justification for the rule which has since evaporated. A need for time to remedy a discriminatory scheme or a proposed and imminent change to a discriminatory scheme does not itself create justification.[415] Instead where a discriminatory measure has always lacked justification for it, a victim of it is entitled to a remedy.[416] **4.98**

411 Ibid, para 60, *per* Lord Walker.

412 Framework Directive 2000/78/EC; *Mangold v Helm*, Case C-144/04 [2006] IRLR 143.

413 *Belgian Linguistic Case (No 2)* (1968) 1 EHRR 252; *Lindsay v UK* (1986) 49 DR 181; *R (Wilkinson) v Inland Revenue Commissioners* [2005] 1 WLR 1718; *R (Wilkinson) v Inland Revenue Commissioners* [2005] 1 WLR 1718; *Stec v UK* (2006) (App Nos 65731/01 and 65900/01) ('Article 14 does not prohibit a Member State from treating groups differently in order to correct "factual inequalities" between them; indeed in certain circumstances a failure to attempt to correct inequality through different treatment may in itself give rise to a breach of the article (see "Case relating to certain aspects of the laws on the use of languages in education in Belgium" v. Belgium (Merits), judgment of 23 July 1968, Series A no. 6, § 10 and Thlimmenos v. Greece, no. 34369/97, § 44, ECHR 2000-IV)', para 51).

414 *R (Hooper) v Work and Pensions Secretary* [2005] 1 WLR 1681, paras 61–3 in particular.

415 Despite what was suggested by the decision in *Secretary of State for Work and Pensions v M* [2006] UKHL 11. See *R (Hooper) v Work and Pensions Secretary* [2005] 1 WLR 1681; *Bellinger v Bellinger (Lord Chancellor Intervening)* [2003] 2 AC 467.

416 ECHR Art 13; HRA, ss 6 and 7. Recent cases on justification include; *Esfandiari v Secretary of State for Work and Pensions* [2006] EWCA Civ 282 (decision not to make funeral payments to recent migrants for burials abroad would be justified (if recent migrants had an identifiable 'status')); *Francis v Secretary of State for Work and Pensions* [2006] 1 All ER 748 (Secretary of State had provided no rational justification for the refusal to make maternity grant to a person with personal responsibility); *R (Baiai) v Secretary of State for Home Department* [2006] 3 All ER 608 (requirement that a person subject to immigration control who wished to marry otherwise than in accordance with the rites of the Church of England should obtain a certificate of approval to marry pursuant to s 19 of the Asylum and Immigration (Treatment of Claimants etc) unjustified); *R (Morris) v Westminster City Council* [2006] 1 WLR 505 (statutory requirement that a child of a person eligible for housing assistance should be disregarded if they are subject to immigration control not justified).

(d) Ground

4.99 Article 14 protects against discrimination on those grounds it enumerates, namely sex, race, colour, language, religion, political or other opinion, national or social origin, association with a national minority, property, and birth. In addition, Article 14 protects against distinctions connected to 'other status'. 'Other status' has been held to cover a number of characteristics, including nationality[417] (as opposed to national origin which is expressly protected), immigration status,[418] sexual orientation,[419] and place of residence[420] and accordingly need not refer to intimate or immutable characteristics. As mentioned above, the degree of scrutiny applied to any distinctions will vary depending upon the ground upon which they are based.

4.100 As to identifying new protected—and suspect—classes, this is problematic. Our domestic courts have held that 'other status' must refer to some 'personal characteristic', analogous to the enumerated grounds in Article 14.[421] Such an approach has been criticized in other jurisdictions.[422] As will be considered in Chapter 5, some other jurisdictions use the existence of historic discrimination and present disadvantage as criteria for determining whether equality measures protect against distinctions on 'new' grounds.

4.101 However, the approach presently adopted domestically to the identification of 'other status' for Article 14 purposes requires that the alleged basis for any distinction relates to a characteristic intrinsic to the person concerned.[423] Accordingly, the following have been held not to constitute 'other status': being a rough sleeper (as opposed to a person in a hostel);[424] being a recent migrant who wished to bury

417 *Gaygusuz v Austria* (1996) 23 EHRR 364.

418 *A v Secretary of State for the Home Department* [2005] 2 AC 68.

419 *Salgueiro da Silva Mouta v Portugal* (1999) 31 EHRR 1055; *Ghaidan v Godin-Mendoza* [2004] UKHL 30, [2004] 2 AC 557, [2004] 3 WLR 113.

420 *R (Carson) v Secretary of State for Work and Pensions* [2006] 1 AC 173.

421 *R (Marper) v Chief Constable of South Yorkshire* [2004] 1 WLR 2196 ('other status' does not cover persons who have had to provide fingerprints to the police pursuant to a criminal investigation), see especially paras 50–1 (*per* Lord Steyn). And see *R (on the application of Clift) v Secretary of State for the Home Department; R (on the application of Hindawi and another) v Secretary of State for the Home Department* [2006] UKHL 54.

422 'An Intersectional approach to Discrimination: Addressing Multiple Grounds in Human Rights Claims, Discussion Paper' (2001), Ontario Human Rights Commission, p 8, available at, <http://www.ohrc.on.ca/english/consultations/intersectionality-discussion-paper.pdf>; D Kropp, '"Categorial" Failure: Canada's Equality Jurisprudence—Changing Notions of Identity and the Legal Subject' (1997) 23 Queen's LJ 201, online: QL. Para 1. See for a discussion on 'new' grounds, 'Promoting Equality: A New Vision' released 23 June 2000 and available from the Canadian Human Rights Act Review Panel (ISBN0-662-84622-2), Chap 17. See for a discussion of the 'analogous' grounds approach in the Canadian case law *Andrews v The Law Society of British Columbia* [1989] 1 SCR 143; *R v Turpin* [1989] 1 SCR 1296; *Corbiére v Canada* [1999] 2 SCR 203.

423 See, too, *R (on the application of Clift) v Secretary of State for the Home Department; R (on the application of Hindawi and another) v Secretary of State for the Home Department* [2006] UKHL 54.

424 *R (RJM) v Secretary of State for Work and Pensions* [2006] EWHC 1761 (Admin).

their loved ones in their country of origin;[425] being a potential (as opposed to an actual) claimant for compensation for asbestos-related disease.[426] On the other hand, being a person with parental responsibility for a child pursuant to a residence order (as compared with a person with parental responsibility for a child pursuant to an adoption order) is an 'other status' for the purpose of Article 14 (reflecting its close nexus to being a parent).[427]

(6) **Article 17**

Article 17 of the ECHR has been subject to very little attention indeed (perhaps less than any other of the Articles of the ECHR[428]). It is, however, an important provision. Article 17 limits the potential scope of the rights conferred by the Convention. It is headed 'Prohibition of Abuse of Rights' and provides that: **4.102**

> Nothing in this Convention may be interpreted as implying for any State, group or person any right to engage in any activity or perform any act aimed at the destruction of any of the rights and freedoms set forth herein or at their limitation to a greater extent than is provided for in the Convention.

Article 17 circumscribes the other Convention rights. It is one of the Articles scheduled to the HRA.[429] Its impact has been most significantly felt in the context of the exercising of the rights under Article 10 ('freedom of expression'), though its potential impact is much wider. The origins of Article 17 can be seen in Article 30 of the United Nations Universal Declaration of Human Rights[430] and finds reflection in Article 5 of the International Covenant on Civil and Political Rights (ICCPR),[431] in the latter case in materially identical terms to Article 17.[432] Article 30 provides: **4.103**

> Nothing in this Declaration may be interpreted as implying for any State, group or person any right to engage in any activity or to perform any act aimed at the destruction of any of the rights and freedoms set forth herein.

Accordingly in Article 30 the focus is on the destruction of rights whereas the focus in Articles 17 and 5 of the Convention and Covenant respectively is on both

---

425 *Esfandiari v Secretary of State for Work and Pensions* [2006] EWCA Civ 282.

426 *Re T & N Ltd* [2006] 3 All ER 697.

427 *Francis v Secretary of State for Work and Pensions* [2006] 1 All ER 748, para 27.

428 With the possible exception of ECHR Art 1.

429 Sch 1.

430 (1948). Adopted and proclaimed by General Assembly resolution 217 A (III) of 10 December 1948.

431 (1966). Adopted and opened for signature, ratification, and accession by General Assembly resolution 2200A (XXI) of 16 Dec 1966.

432 Art 55 of the Charter of Fundamental Rights of the European Union (2000/C364/01) is also in materially the same terms as ECHR Art 17.

the destruction and *limitation* of rights, and they therefore have a wider reach.[433] At first blush, '[t]he idea that a right, which is itself necessary in a democratic society (if it were not it would not be in the Convention in the first place) being restricted on the basis of an overriding and somehow deeper democratic necessity is contradictory only if the question is addressed solely as one of human rights'.[434] However:

> [I]f we see these fundamental freedoms as civil liberties, we are guided to look at them not as individual rights standing alone but rather as the building blocks of a democratic society; on this basis we can recognise them as political freedoms rather than personal entitlements. Once understood like this, it becomes clear that they may on occasion have to yield to the greater good of the political community as a whole.[435]

To this can be added the observation, in particular, that democratic rights where they are based on a majoritarian concept of democracy may not be adequate to protect minorities. If representative democracy is viewed as requiring a floor of guarantees allowing all to participate equally in society (as must be necessary for a true representative democracy to thrive) irrespective of the majority's will, then the Convention rights *and* limitations imposed upon them are indeed 'democratic' albeit potentially 'anti-majoritarian'.

4.104 In the case of Article 17 and the other limiting provisions described above, they are directed at abuses of power and so address the need to secure a proper balance between the rights of individuals. As has been noted, Article 17:

> makes possible fairly intrusive restrictions by public authorities on people's freedom to use rights where they conflict with the rights of others (a situation where the state must act as arbiter). At a collective level, it may also permit restrictions on people's freedom to advance political programmes which, if implemented, would undermine the political freedom or other human rights of others.[436]

Such restrictions may extend to otherwise highly protected political speech, though this is not always uncontroversial. Article 17 is also unusual in allowing both the State and individuals to rely upon it ('[n]othing in this Convention may be interpreted as implying for *any State, group or person*').

---

433 See too, Art 19 of the Universal Declaration of Human Rights which provides that 'Everyone has the right to freedom of opinion and expression'. It also provides that no right may be 'exercised contrary to the purposes and principles of the United Nations' (Art 29(3)). Art 1(3) of the United Nations Charter (1945) provides that a significant role of the UN is to promote and encourage respect for human rights and fundamental freedoms without distinction as to race or to sexual, linguistic, or religious orientation. Art 29(3), therefore, can reasonably be interpreted as limiting the protection for speech at least where it tends to promote racial, sexual, linguistic or religious discrimination: S Fredman (ed), *Discrimination in Human Rights, the Case of Racism* (2001, Oxford).

434 C Gearty, *Principles of Human Rights Adjudication* (2004, Oxford), 42.

435 Ibid.

436 D Feldman, *Civil Liberties and Human Rights in England and Wales* (2002, Oxford), 106.

Whilst most of the Convention rights (especially those where there may be important counter considerations) explicitly allow for other interests to be taken into account in determining their scope (in the qualifications contained within Articles 8(2) and 9(2), for example, as described above), where a person's reliance on a Convention right is 'aimed' at the destruction or excessive limitation[437] of the rights of others, then that balancing exercise is not required. Such a person is excluded from relying on the Convention right in its entirety. Article 17 does require that any activity be *aimed* at the destruction or excessive limitation of other Convention rights before it is engaged. Any incidental infringement will therefore fall to be considered under the ordinary express qualifications relevant to the specific Convention right (for example, Articles 8(2) and 9(2)). Further, although the State can invoke Article 17 against an individual, the fact that the individual aims to destroy or restrict the fundamental rights of others does not mean that he may be deprived of all his Convention rights. Article 17 only applies to the rights which are abused. In *Lawless v Ireland* the ECtHR decided that the State was not entitled to deprive the applicant of the right to liberty under Article 5 and fair trial rights under Article 6, merely because he was accused of being a member of a terrorist organization.[438] **4.105**

Article 17 should be regarded as the 'option of last resort'[439] and its application should be subject to 'strict scrutiny'.[440] Its application is closely linked to the application of a State's derogation powers in Article 15 and will only be applicable where the activity concerned poses a threat to democracy. Thus: **4.106**

> it applies only to persons who threaten the democratic system of the [parties to the Convention] and then to an extent strictly proportionate to the seriousness and duration of the threat.[441]

Much of the case law under Article 17 has centred on race hate activity—including Nazi or 'National Socialist' activity[442] and holocaust denial and 'revisionism' activity.[443] In *Glimmerveen and Hagenbeek v Netherlands*,[444] the European **4.107**

---

437 For a case in which it was argued (though unsuccessfully on the facts) that there had been a 'limitation to a greater extent than is provided for in the Convention', see *Ashingdane v UK* App No 8225/78.

438 *Lawless v Ireland (No 3)* (1961) 1 EHRR 15 para 22.

439 J Cooper and M Williams, 'Hate Speech, Holocaust Denial and International Human Rights Law' [1999] EHRLR 593, 605.

440 *Lehideux and Isorni v France* Reports 1998-VII, (1998) 5 EHRC 540, *per* Jambrek J.

441 *De Becker v Belgium*, Application No 214/56 B2 (1960) Com Rep, para 279.

442 *X v Germany*, Application No 12194/86; *BH, MW, HP and GK v Austria*, Application No 12774/87; *Kuhnen v Germany*, Application No 12194/86; *Ochensberger v Austria*, Application No 21318/93; and *Nachtmann v Austria*, Application No 36773/97.

443 See *Walendy v Germany*, Application No 21128/92 and see, too, J Cooper and M Williams, 'Hate Speech, Holocaust Denial and International Human Rights Law' [1999] EHRLR 593.

444 (1979) 18 DR 187, Ecomm HR.

Commission concluded that an individual with a conviction for distributing racist pamphlets could lawfully be excluded from participating in an election on a racist platform. In *Lehideux and Isorni v France*[445] the ECtHR (whilst holding that Article 17 did not apply on the facts of that case) observed that:

> [a]s such, it does not belong to the category of clearly established historical facts—such as the Holocaust—whose negation or revision would be removed from the protection of Article 10 [freedom of expression] by Article 17. In the present case, it does not appear that the applicants attempted to deny or revise what they themselves referred to in their publication as 'Nazi atrocities and persecutions' or 'German omnipotence and barbarism'.[446]

4.108 Generally political expression is closely guarded. The closer to true (however despicable) 'political' expression any particular activity is, the less likely it was to fall within Article 17 and be stripped of any protection under Article 10 (freedom of expression). As the ECtHR has observed:

> there can be no democracy without pluralism. It is for that reason that freedom of expression as enshrined in Article 10 is applicable, subject to paragraph 2, not only to 'information' or 'ideas' that are favourably received or regarded as inoffensive or as a matter of indifference, but also to those that offend, shock or disturb. The fact that their activities form part of a collective exercise of freedom of expression in itself entitles political parties to seek the protection of Articles 10 and 11 [freedom of assembly and association] of the Convention.[447]

4.109 Article 17 has an important and contemporary (as well as historical) relevance to race hate activity. Because of Article 17, mere race hate activity is unlikely to be protected by the Convention.[448] The restrictions on race hate activity are mandated by a number of other international instruments, as referred to above. In addition, the 'Joint Action of 15 July 1996, concerning action to combat racism and xenophobia'[449] (albeit a non-binding instrument[450]) requires that each Member State ensure effective judicial cooperation in respect of offences based on the following types of behaviour and, if necessary for the purposes of this cooperation, make such behaviour punishable as a criminal offence:

(i) public incitement to discrimination, violence, or racial hatred in respect of a group of persons or a member of such a group defined by reference to colour, race, religion or national or ethnic origin;

---

445 Application No 55/19997/839/1045, para 57.

446 See, too, *Witzsch v Germany* (1999) Application No 41448/98.

447 *ÖZDEP v Turkey*, Application No 23885/94, para 37. See too, *Rafeh Partisi (The Welfare Party) and O'rs v Turkey*, Application Nos 41340/98, 41342–4/98, dissenting joint opinions of Judges Fuhrmann, Loucaides, and Sir Nicholas Bratza.

448 *Garaudy v France*, Application No 65831/01.

449 96/443/JHA, OJ L 185, 24 July 1996, 5 adopted pursuant to Article K.3 of the Treaty on European Union, available at <http://europa.eu.int/eur-lex/lex/LexUriServ/LexUriServ.do?uri=celex:31996f0443:en:html>.

450 It is, however, referred to in Recital (11) to the Race Directive, see para 4.33 above.

(ii) public condoning, for a racist or xenophobic purpose, of crimes against humanity and human rights violations;
(iii) public denial of the crimes defined in Article 6 of the Charter of the International Military Tribunal appended to the London Agreement of 8 April 1945 insofar as it behaves behaviour which is contemptuous of, or degrading to, a group of persons defined by reference to colour, race, religion, or national ethnic origin;
(iv) public dissemination or distribution of tracks, pictures, or other material containing expressions of racism and xenophobia;
(v) participation in the activities of groups, organisations, or associations which involve discrimination, violence, or racial, ethnic, or religious hatred.

Other instruments, including the Convention on the Elimination of All Forms of Racial Discrimination,[451] address race hate activity.

As mentioned, Article 17 has typically been considered in 'expression' cases. However, its application extends to all those Convention Articles conferring rights and it has therefore a potentially wide scope. Apart from its impact on political and quasi-political activity, Article 17 has been relied upon to support a much broader range of issues, though usually unsuccessfully. For example, the Irish Government sought to rely upon Article 17 as justifying governmental interference in the Article 10 rights of the Open Door and Dublin Well Woman organizations. The organizations disseminated information about the availability of legal abortions abroad. The Government obtained injunctions to prevent them from doing so, and contended that the dissemination of such information limited, destroyed, or derogated from the right to life enjoyed by the unborn and accordingly ought not to be protected. This argument was unsuccessful before the ECtHR, but the court did not address the issue of principle, instead avoiding it by holding that the injunctions did not prevent women leaving Ireland for the purposes of having abortions abroad and that the information was in any event otherwise available.[452] **4.110**

(7) Protocol No 12

As seen above, Article 14 does not provide freestanding protection against discrimination. A new Protocol No 12 to the ECHR[453] has been drawn up within the Council of Europe by the Steering Committee for Human Rights. It was opened **4.111**

[451] Addressed at para 4.130 onwards below.

[452] *Open Door and Dublin Well Woman*, Application Nos 14234/88 and 14235/88, paras 78–9. See, too, *Lawless v Ireland (No 3)* (1961) 1 EHRR 15.

[453] <http://conventions.coe.int/Treaty/en/Treaties/Html/177.htm>.

for signature by the Member States of the Council of Europe on 4 November 2000. It provides that:

> Article 1—General prohibition of discrimination
> 1. The enjoyment of any right set forth by law shall be secured without discrimination on any ground such as sex, race, colour, language, religion, political or other opinion, national or social origin, association with a national minority, property, birth or other status.
> 2. No one shall be discriminated against by any public authority on any ground such as those mentioned in paragraph 1.

The Protocol therefore provides protection against discrimination in the enjoyment of rights already set down by law and in addition creates a prohibition against discrimination by public authorities. It will plainly provide greater protection against discrimination as compared to the rather weaker Article 14. It more closely matches the constitutional level guarantees seen in other jurisdictions, including as it does an equal protection guarantee, as well as a prohibition on discrimination by public authorities.[454]

4.112 The Protocol entered into force on 1 April 2005.[455] The UK Government has not signed or ratified Protocol No 12 and they have indicated that they do not presently intend to ratify it.[456] In the event that it is ratified by the UK, the UK will be bound by it as a matter of international law and individuals will be permitted to petition the ECtHR in reliance on it. However, it will not have any direct domestic force unless it is expressly incorporated, as many of the other Convention rights have been, through the HRA.

(8) Interpretation and the Human Rights Act 1998, section 3

4.113 Section 3 of the HRA provides the primary remedy for addressing any potential incompatibility between statutory law—including as contained in the main anti-discrimination legislation—and the Convention rights. Section 3 provides that:

> So far as it is possible to do so, primary legislation and subordinate legislation must be read and given effect in a way which is compatible with the Convention Rights.

It is Parliament's intention therefore that legislation must be read *and* given effect to in a way which is compatible with the Convention rights and the courts must give effect to that intention.[457] Section 3 does not depend on any existing

---

454 See Chap 2, para 2.02.

455 <http://conventions.coe.int/Treaty/Commun/ListeTraites.asp?CM=8&CL=ENG>.

456 Lord Bassam of Brighton (11 Oct 2000: Column WA37). For a critique of the reasons given by the Government for not ratifying Protocol No 12 see *Equal Opportunities Review* (2002) 105, 21–4.

457 *Ghaidan v Godin-Mendoza* [2004] UKHL 30, [2004] 2 AC 557, [2004] 3 WLR 113, including at para 59, *per* Lord Millett.

ambiguity, indeed the legislation may admit of *no* doubt, but section 3 may still require a different meaning.[458] The intention of Parliament in enacting section 3 was to an extent bound only by what is 'possible' and may therefore require the court to depart from the intention of the enacting Parliament.[459] It creates a very compelling and mandatory obligation and may require reading in words or reading them out. However, there is no necessity for an overemphasis on 'linguistic' features.[460] If the natural reading of a statute gives a meaning which is incompatible with a Convention right, then the court must strive to give it a compatible meaning. This is so whatever the actual words of the statute say so long as a completely opposite meaning to the purpose intended is not given to the statutory scheme—that is, as long as it is not 'as drastic as changing black into white' or 'remov[ing] the very core and essence, the "pith and substance" of the measure that Parliament had enacted'.[461]

Section 3 is the prime remedial measure and the linchpin of the scheme of the HRA which aimed to 'bring rights home'. Section 3, then, presents not merely a 'strong adjuration' but a command to construe compatibly wherever possible;[462] it is not an 'optional canon of construction'.[463] As such, section 3 alters the constitutional role to be played by judges in delineating the boundaries of a rights-based democracy[464]—it represents the very clear intention of Parliament to empower judges to modify the effect of other statutory provisions, no matter when they were enacted, if this is necessary in order to achieve Convention-compatibility, bounded only by what is possible. **4.114**

The proper approach to the use of section 3 is as follows: **4.115**

- The court must determine whether the legislation under scrutiny, in its ordinary and natural meaning, is incompatible with the Convention in a particular case.[465] This exercise requires the court to identify clearly the particular statutory provisions which are (or might be) incompatible.[466]
- If there is no Convention violation, it follows that there is no incompatibility and no need for recourse to section 3.[467]

---

458 Ibid, para 29–30, *per* Lord Nicholls.

459 Ibid, para 29–30, *per* Lord Nicholls.

460 Ibid, paras 38–52, *per* Lord Steyn; paras 111 and 121, *per* Lord Rodger).

461 Ibid, para 111, *per* Lord Rodger.

462 Ibid, including at para 59, *per* Lord Millett.

463 *Re S (Minors) (Care Order: Implementation of Care Plan)* [2002] 2 AC 291, para 37, *per* Lord Nicholls.

464 J Jowell, 'Judicial Deference: servility, civility or institutional capacity' [2003] PL 592 at 597.

465 *Ghaidan v Godin-Mendoza* [2004] UKHL 30, [2004] 2 AC 557, [2004] 3 WLR 113, para 60, *per* Lord Millett; *R v A (No 2)* [2002] 1 AC 45, para 106, *per* Lord Hope.

466 *Re S (Minors) (Care Order: Implementation of Care Plan)* [2002] 2 AC 291, para 41, *per* Lord Nicholls; *X v Y* [2004] EWCA Civ 662; [2004] IRLR 625.

467 *Ghaidan v Godin-Mendoza* [2004] UKHL 30, [2004] 2 AC 557, [2004] 3 WLR 113, para 60, *per* Lord Millett.

- If, however, there are violations of Convention rights, the obligation to read and give effect, if possible, to the relevant legislative provisions so as to render them compatible arises, as discussed above.

As stated, the only limitation placed upon the section 3 obligation is the limit of 'possibility' and this sole limitation, which applies equally to both primary and secondary legislation, has been considered on several occasions by the House of Lords. A review of the case law demonstrates that Convention-compatible interpretations are only impossible, in truth, in one circumstance which can be made manifest in a number of ways. That circumstance is where a court would thereby transgress the constitutional boundary sought to be preserved by the scheme of the HRA; that is the boundary between permissible judicial interpretation (which extends to modification, qualification, and rectification) and legislation. Such a constitutional transgression can occur where compatible constructions require the court to contradict a fundamental feature of the statutory provision in question[468] or require the court to make decisions for which it is not equipped[469] and which should therefore remain the constitutional province of another organ of the State. In *Bellinger v Bellinger (Lord Chancellor Intervening)*,[470] therefore, the House of Lords declined to read section 11(c) of the Matrimonial Causes Act 1973 in a way which did not invalidate the marriage of a transsexual female to a male. Section 11(c) requires that for a marriage to be valid the parties must be respectively male and female. The case concerned the recognition of the reassigned sex of a transgendered person—an issue raising questions of perceived moral, theological, and social complexity (liberating gender from biological determinism and liberating marriage from its heterosexual roots) which other organs of government (the elected legislature or the executive, for example) were, in the House of Lords' view, in a better position to address.

4.116 Where, unusually, it is not possible to construe the legislative measure compatibly, then, where the legislative measure is contained in primary legislation (or where primary legislation prevents removal of the incompatibility) a 'declaration of incompatibility' must be made pursuant to section 4 of the HRA. Such a declaration may only be made by the High Court and above.[471] A declaration of

468 *Ghaidan v Godin-Mendoza* [2004] UKHL 30, [2004] 2 AC 557, [2004] 3 WLR 113, para 33, *per* Lord Nicholls; *Re S (Minors) (Care Order: Implementation of Care Plan)* [2002] 2 AC 291, para 40, *per* Lord Nicholls; *R (Wilkinson) v Inland Revenue Commissioners* [2005] 1 WLR 1718 at para 17, *per* Lord Hoffman (in which it was the very point of the relevant provisions of the Income and Corporation Tax Act (ICTA) 1988, the 'grain', to create a tax-break for widows who were, at a particular juncture in the socio-economic history of this country, perceived to be in need of such relief by reason of their economic inactivity as part of the formal economic sector and thus reading the relevant provision as addressing widowers would contradict a fundamental feature).

469 *Bellinger v Bellinger (Lord Chancellor Intervening)* [2003] 2 AC 467.

470 Ibid.

471 HRA, s 4(5).

incompatibility does not affect the validity of any legislation and may be ignored by Parliament. However, a Minister who 'considers that there are compelling reasons for [so] proceeding . . . may by order make such amendments to the legislation as he considers necessary to remove the incompatibility'.[472] No such declaration may be made in the case of subordinate legislation, where primary legislation does not prevent the removal of the incompatibility. Instead the section 3 obligation may affect the 'validity, continuing operation or enforcement' of that subordinate provision.[473] Such subordinate legislation is not 'inevitably' incompatible and the court's obligation pursuant to section 3(1) of the HRA continues to apply to it.

There are a number of enactments which may have to be 'read down' to make them compatible with those Convention rights described above and therefore and to that extent equality compliant. Some of these have been described above.[474] In addition, the main anti-discrimination enactments must be read compatibly and this certainly leaves room for argument as to their proper meaning. Article 6 (guaranteeing access to a court and a fair trial in the determination of civil rights) and Article 14, for example, were relied upon in *Alabaster v Barclays Bank Plc (formerly Woolwich plc) and Secretary of State for Social Security (No 2)*,[475] described above,[476] for the purpose of arguing that the requirement in the EPA for a comparator should be disapplied in a case where the discrimination in issue related to maternity pay. **4.117**

Section 6 of the HRA makes it unlawful for a public authority,[477] including a court and a 'hybrid' authority,[478] to act incompatibly with a Convention right. **4.118**

G. International Instruments

Apart from the statutory obligation under section 3 of the HRA in relation to the Convention rights, courts will also have regard to the UK's international **4.119**

---

472 Ibid, s 10(2).

473 See A Bradley, 'The Impact of the Human Rights Act 1998 upon subordinate legislation promulgated before October 2, 2000' [2000] PL 358 at 358.

474 *Ghaidan v Godin-Mendoza* [2004] UKHL 30, [2004] 2 AC 557, [2004] 3 WLR 113, for example.

475 [2005] EWCA Civ 508; [2005] ICR 1246; [2005] IRLR 576.

476 Para 4.64.

477 Defined by HRA, s 6(3). See *Aston Cantlow and Wilmcote with Billesley Parochial Church Council v Wallbank and another* [2003] UKHL 37; [2004] 1 AC 546; *Poplar Housing and Regeneration Community Association Ltd v Donoghue* (2002) QB 48; *R (Beer) v Hampshire Farmer's Markets Ltd* (2004) 1 WLR 233.

478 Namely, a private body whilst carrying out functions of a public nature: HRA, s 6(3)(b)) and (5).

obligations in interpreting domestic law.[479] This is so as a matter of domestic law but in addition, because much EU law is now informed by international human rights instruments, the obligation to construe domestic law consistently with any EU law to which it gives effect, brings to the interpretation of much UK law the international human rights context. The three new Directives described above (Race, Framework, and Gender Goods and Services Directives[480]), in particular, refer to the ECHR, the Universal Declaration of Human Rights, the International Convention on the Elimination of All Forms of Racial Discrimination, the International Convention on the Elimination of all Forms of Discrimination Against Women, the International Covenant on Civil and Political Rights, and the International Covenant on Economic, Social and Cultural Rights.[481] These are some of the many international instruments to which the UK is a party, which bind the UK as a matter of international law and which might be used to inform a proper interpretation of domestic law and which are relevant to equality and non-discrimination. The important international instruments, for equality and non-discrimination rights in the UK, are described below.

H. United Nations

4.120 As to the United Nations, one of the four principles on which the UN was founded is that of non-discrimination. The UN Charter of 1945 proclaims that the UN's purposes include '. . . promoting and encouraging respect for human rights and for fundamental freedoms for all without distinction as to race, sex,

---

479 *R v Chief Immigration Officer, Heathrow Airport ex p Bibi* [1976] 1 WLR 979, 984; *Garland v British Rail Engineering Ltd* [1983] 2 AC 751, 771; *Regina (European Roma Rights Centre and others) v Immigration Officer at Prague Airport and another (United Nations High Commissioner for Refugees intervening)* [2004] UKHL 55; [2005] 2 AC 1; *A v Secretary of State for the Home Department* [2005] 2 AC 68. For a full discussion see, R Clayton and H Tomlinson, *The Law of Human Rights* (2000, OUP), particularly para 2.09 *et seq.*

480 Paras 4.33–4.52.

481 Recital 3 of the Race Directive 2000/43/EC refers to the ECHR, the Universal Declaration of Human Rights, the International Convention on the Elimination of All Forms of Racial Discrimination, the International Convention on the Elimination of all Forms of Discrimination Against Women, the International Covenant on Civil and Political Rights, and the International Covenant on Economic, Social and Cultural Rights; Recital 4 of the Framework Directive 2000/78/EC refers to the ECHR, the Universal Declaration of Human Rights, the International Convention on the Elimination of all Forms of Discrimination Against Women, the International Covenant on Civil and Political Rights, and the International Covenant on Economic, Social and Cultural Rights (and also International Labour Organisation Convention No 111); and Recital 2 of the Gender Goods and Services Directive refers to the ECHR, the Universal Declaration of Human Rights, the International Convention on the Elimination of All Forms of Racial Discrimination, the International Convention on the Elimination of all Forms of Discrimination Against Women, the International Covenant on Civil and Political Rights, and the International Covenant on Economic, Social and Cultural Rights.

language, or religion' (Article 1). The specific content of those rights has been codified and clarified in a number of human rights instruments since. In 1948 the General Assembly adopted the Universal Declaration of Human Rights (UDHR). This was intended not as a legally binding document as such but, as its preamble suggests, 'a common standard of achievement for all peoples and nations'. The document covers a wide range of rights with some of its key provisions relating to discrimination. The Declaration is underpinned by the concept of equality as a fundamental right with its preamble recognizing the inherent dignity and 'the equal and inalienable rights of all members of the human family' as the 'foundation of freedom, justice and peace in the world'.

The Declaration begins in Article 1 with the pronouncement that all human beings are 'born free and equal in dignity and rights'. Article 2 provides that: **4.121**

> Everyone is entitled to all the rights and freedoms set forth in this Declaration, without any distinction of any kind, such as race, colour, sex, religion, political or other opinion, national or social origin, property, birth or other status . . .

Article 7 of the Declaration declares the principle of 'equality before the law', as follows:

> All are equal before the law and are entitled without any discrimination to equal protection of the law. All are entitled to equal protection against any discrimination in violation of this Declaration and against any incitement to such discrimination.

Article 16 provides that '[m]en and women of full age, without any limitations due to race, nationality or religion, have the right to marry and to found a family' and Article 18 provides that 'everyone has the right to freedom of thought, conscience and religion'. The Declaration is not itself a legally enforceable document but the principle of non-discrimination that it enunciated has emerged as a core standard of international human rights law.[482]

In 1966 two Covenants were adopted by the UN to give legal force to the UDHR. **4.122** These are the International Covenant on Civil and Political Rights (ICCPR) and the International Covenant on Economic, Social and Cultural Rights (ICESCR). The ICCPR was adopted by the General Assembly in 1966 and came into force in 1976. The UK is a State party to the ICCPR.[483] As its name suggests, the ICCPR deals with civil and political rights, the so-called 'first generation' human rights. Article 2 of the ICCPR obliges States to 'ensure to all individuals . . . the rights recognised in the Covenant'. There are a number of provisions in the ICCPR addressing equality and non-discrimination. The prohibition on non-discrimination is accorded special weight in the ICCPR. Evidence of this is that

---

482 See, for example, *Barcelona Traction Case (Second Phase)*, ICJ Reports (1970) at 514–17. And see, *Namibia (South West Africa) Case* (1970), ICJ Reports, (1971) at 57.

483 Having ratified it on 20 May 1976.

even when the life of the nation is threatened by public emergency, although the State parties may take steps derogating from certain obligations under the Covenant, such measures may 'not involve discrimination solely on the ground of race, colour, sex, language, religion or social origin'.[484] Article 26 provides that:

> All persons are equal before the law and are entitled without any discrimination to the equal protection of the law. In this respect, the law shall prohibit any discrimination and guarantee to all persons equal and effective protection against discrimination on any ground such as race, colour, sex, language, religion, political or other opinion, national or social origin, property, birth or other status.

4.123 In their General Comments[485] the Human Rights Committee has provided guidance as to the meaning of 'discrimination' for the purposes of the ICCPR:

> [T]he Committee believes that the term 'discrimination' as used in the Covenant should be understood to imply any distinction, exclusion, restriction or preference which is based on any ground such as race, colour, sex, language, religion, political or other opinion, national or social origin, property, birth or other status, and which has the purpose or effect of nullifying or impairing the recognition, enjoyment or exercise by all persons, on an equal footing, of all rights and freedoms.

However, the enjoyment of rights and freedoms on an equal footing 'does not mean identical treatment in every instance'; 'not every differentiation of treatment will constitute discrimination, if the criteria for such differentiation are reasonable and objective and if the aim is to achieve a purpose which is legitimate under the Covenant'.[486] This right provides for more than mere formal equality under the law. As the Committee has stated, Article 26:

> does not merely duplicate the guarantee already provided for in article 2. Significantly, it is not limited to those rights which are provided for in the Covenant, but provides in itself an autonomous and free-standing right. It prohibits discrimination in law or in fact in any field regulated and protected by public authorities.[487]

4.124 The Committee has observed that 'the Covenant sometimes expressly requires [States parties] to take measures to guarantee the equality of rights of the persons concerned'. Thus in respect of certain of the obligations under the ICCPR, States are under a *positive duty*, not a mere negative obligation, to secure them and this

---

484 Art 4(1).

485 General Comment 18, Human Rights Committee, 37th session, 1989.

486 Thus, for example, the distinction between State subsidies for students at private and public schools has been found to be reasonable under the Covenant: 'the State Party cannot be deemed to be under an obligation to provide the same benefits to private schools; indeed, the preferential treatment given to public sector schooling is reasonable and based on objective criteria' (*Lindgren v Sweden* (298-99/1988) para 10.3).

487 General Comment 18, Human Rights Committee, 37th session, 1989.

might obligate a State to introduce positive action measures.[488] State parties are obliged to ensure that their legislators, courts, and public authorities (including the police, prison officers, and customs and immigration officials) perform their functions in a non-discriminatory way.[489]

As for specific protection for children, the ICCPR provides that each child 'shall have without any discrimination as to race, colour, sex, language, religion, national or social origin, property or birth, the right to such measures of protection as required by his status as a minor'.[490] **4.125**

Under the ICCPR, the factors mentioned in Article 2 (race, religion, national or social origin etc) may not bar persons from participating in public affairs.[491] In addition, the ICCPR prohibits any advocacy of national, racial, or religious hatred that constitutes incitement to discrimination, hostility, or violence.[492] Article 18 provides for the right to freedom of thought, conscience, and religion. Article 27 of the ICCPR provides protection for ethnic, religious, or linguistic minorities so that persons belonging to such minorities 'shall not be denied the right, in community with the other members of their group, to enjoy their own culture, to profess and practise their own religion, or to use their own language'.[493] **4.126**

[488] See for example, para 3, General Comment No 28: Equality of rights between men and women (Art 3): 29/03/2000CCPR/C/21/Rev.1/Add.10 including: 'The right to participate in the conduct of public affairs is not fully implemented everywhere on an equal basis. States parties must ensure that the law guarantees to women the rights contained in article 25 on equal terms with men and take effective and positive measures to promote and ensure women's participation in the conduct of public affairs and in public office, including appropriate affirmative action.' See further, General Comment 18, Human Rights Committee, 37th session, 1989.

[489] See, for the UK, Human Rights Committee: United Kingdom of Great Britain and Northern Ireland. 06/12/2001 CCPR/CO/73/UK;CCPR/CO/73/UKOT. (Concluding Observations/ Comments). And see, Concluding Observations of the Committee on Economic, Social and Cultural Rights: United Kingdom of Great Britain and Northern Ireland, United Kingdom of Great Britain and Northern Ireland—Dependent Territories. 05/06/2002. *E/C.12/1/*Add.79. (Concluding Observations/Comments).

[490] Art 24(1).

[491] Art 25(1).

[492] Art 20(2).

[493] Art 27 does not confer any rights to self-determination. Such a right is proclaimed in Art 1 of the ICCPR. But the ICCPR draws a distinction between the right to self-determination and the rights protected under Art 27. The former is expressed to be a right belonging to *peoples* and is not a right given legal force under the right to individual petition. Art 27, on the other hand, relates to rights conferred on *individuals* as such and is included in those rights that are justiciable under the right to individual petition (General Comment 23, Human Rights Committee, 50th session, 1994). See too, Declaration on the Rights of Persons Belonging to National or Ethnic, Religious and Linguistic Minorities (A/RES/47/135, 92nd plenary meeting, 18 December 1992). The UK has not introduced legislative measures explicitly protecting minorities to the extent that is apparently required by Art 27. To the extent that such protection exists, it is limited to (certain) linguistic minorities (eg Welsh language Act 1993). See further, *Chapman v UK* [2001] ECtHR (App No 27238/95). See S Wheatley, *Democracy, Minorities and International Law* (2005, CSIL) for a full discussion on minority rights and international law.

4.127 The principle of equality enshrined within the ICCPR 'requires States Parties to take affirmative action in order to diminish or eliminate conditions which cause or help to perpetuate discrimination prohibited by the Covenant'.[494] For example, it may be necessary under the Covenant for States to take affirmative action by 'granting for a time to the part of the population concerned certain preferential treatment in specific matters as compared with the rest of the population'.[495]

4.128 The International Covenant on Economic, Social and Cultural Rights 1966 (ICESCR) is the counterpart to the ICCPR and protects so-called 'second generation' economic, social, and cultural rights. The ICESCR entered into force in 1976 and the UK is a party to it.[496] Under the ICESCR State parties undertake to 'take steps . . . to achieve progressively the full realisation of the rights recognised in the present Covenant by all appropriate means, including particularly the adoption of legislative measures'.[497] Those rights include the right to work; the right to social security; the right to an adequate standard of living; and the right to education.

4.129 Article 2(2) provides that in relation to the socio-economic and cultural rights recognized in the ICESCR, the Covenant requires State parties to:

> undertake to guarantee that the rights enunciated . . . [are] . . . exercised without discrimination of any kind as to race, colour, sex, language, religion, political or other opinion, national or social origin, property, birth or other status (Article 2(2)).[498]

The Committee on Economic, Social and Cultural Rights, a body specifically created under the ICESCR to ensure compliance with the Covenant, has given little guidance on the meaning of 'discrimination' under the ICESCR. However, the Committee has indicated that positive discrimination will not violate the ICESCR:

> . . . special measures taken for the sole purpose of securing adequate advancement of certain groups or individuals requiring protection in order to ensure the equal enjoyment of economic, social and cultural rights are not considered discrimination, provided that such measures do not lead to the maintenance of separate rights for different groups and are not continued after their objectives have been achieved. This applies, for example, to affirmative-action program[s].[499]

---

494 See para 10 of General Comment 18 of the Human Rights Committee, and Harris and Joseph, *The International Covenant on Civil and Political Rights and United Kingdom Law* (1995), at 578.

495 See General Comment 18 of the Human Rights Committee, paragraph 10; General Comment 23, Human Rights Committee, 50th session, 1994.

496 Having ratified it on 20 May 1976.

497 Art 2(1).

498 A limited exception is made for developing countries and non-nationals: Art 2(3).

499 Fact Sheet No 16 (Rev 1), the Committee on Economic, Social and Cultural Rights, at <http://www.unhchr.ch/html/menu6/2/fs16.htm>.

The Committee has made it clear that the ICESCR's non-discrimination guarantee does more than impose negative obligations upon States parties. In particular the Committee has stated:

> This provision not only obliges Governments to desist from discriminatory behaviour and to alter laws and practices which allow discrimination, it also applies to the duty of State Parties to prohibit private persons and bodies (third parties) from practicing discrimination in any field of public life.[500]

The Committee has also strongly recommended that:

> [the UK] enact comprehensive legislation on equality and non-discrimination in United Kingdom law, in conformity with articles 2(2) and 3 of the Covenant.[501]

The International Convention on the Elimination of All Forms of Racial Discrimination (CERD) was signed in 1965 and entered into force in 1969. It is the oldest and one of the most widely ratified UN human rights conventions.[502] The UK is a State party to CERD.[503] Article 2(1) declares that: **4.130**

> States Parties condemn racial discrimination and undertake to pursue by all appropriate means and without delay a policy of eliminating racial discrimination in all its forms and promoting understanding among all races, and, to this end:
> (a) Each State Party undertakes to engage in no act or practice of racial discrimination against persons, groups of persons or institutions and to ensure that all public authorities and public institutions, national and local, shall act in conformity with this obligation;
> (b) Each State Party undertakes not to sponsor, defend or support racial discrimination by any persons or organizations;

---

500 Ibid. See too, for example, Art 7 (a) of the Covenant requires States parties to recognize the right of everyone to enjoy just and favourable conditions of work and to ensure, among other things, fair wages and equal pay for work of equal value. Art 3, in relation to Art 7 requires, *inter alia*, that the State party identify and eliminate the underlying causes of pay differentials, such as gender-biased job evaluation or the perception that productivity differences between men and women exist. Furthermore, the State party should monitor compliance by the private sector with national legislation on working conditions through an effectively functioning labour inspectorate. The State party should adopt legislation that prescribes equal consideration in promotion, non-wage compensation and equal opportunity and support for vocational or professional development in the workplace. Finally, the State party should reduce the constraints faced by men and women in reconciling professional and family responsibilities by promoting adequate policies for childcare and care of dependent family members (General comment No 16 (2005) 'The equal right of men and women to the enjoyment of all economic, social and cultural rights' (Art 3 of the International Covenant on Economic, Social and Cultural Rights), available at <http://www.unhchr.ch/tbs/doc.nsf/898586b1dc7b4043c1256a450044f331/7c6dc1dee6268e32c125708f0050dbf6/$FILE/G0543539.DOC>).

501 Concluding Observations of the Committee on Economic, Social and Cultural Rights: United Kingdom of Great Britain and Northern Ireland, United Kingdom of Great Britain and Northern Ireland—Dependent Territories, 5 June 2002. E/C.12/1/Add.79. (Concluding Observations/Comments).

502 <http://www.unhchr.ch/html/menu6/2/fs12.htm>.

503 Having ratified it on 7 March 1969.

(c) Each State Party shall take effective measures to review governmental, national and local policies, and to amend, rescind or nullify any laws and regulations which have the effect of creating or perpetuating racial discrimination wherever it exists;
(d) Each State Party shall prohibit and bring to an end, by all appropriate means, including legislation as required by circumstances, racial discrimination by any persons, group or organization;
(e) Each State Party undertakes to encourage, where appropriate, integrationist multiracial organizations and movements and other means of eliminating barriers between races, and to discourage anything which tends to strengthen racial division.

Further, CERD requires States parties to give a broad undertaking to secure equality before the law and in particular to guarantee the right to 'security of person and protection by the State against violence or bodily harm, whether inflicted by government officials or by any individual group or institution'.[504]

4.131 'Racial discrimination' is defined in CERD as:

> any distinction, exclusion, restriction or preference based on race, colour, descent or national or ethnic origin which has the purpose or effect of nullifying or impairing the recognition, enjoyment or exercise, on an equal footing, of human rights and fundamental freedoms in the political, economic, social, cultural or any other field of public life.[505]

CERD expressly permits 'positive' discrimination 'taken for the sole purpose of securing adequate advancement of certain racial or ethnic groups or individuals requiring such protection as may be necessary in order to ensure such groups or individuals equal enjoyment or exercise of human rights and fundamental freedoms'.[506] Such 'positive' action is not discrimination for the purposes of CERD 'provided . . . such measures do not as a consequence lead to the maintenance of separate rights for different racial groups and that they shall not be continued after the objectives for which they were taken have been achieved'.[507]

4.132 CERD, like the ICCPR, requires State parties to condemn racist and race hate propaganda and organizations. Article 4 of the Convention requires that States adopt measures to eradicate such propaganda and organizations; the 'dissemination of ideas based on racial superiority or hatred', and the provision of 'any assistance to racist activities, including financing thereof'.

4.133 As with the ICCPR and ICESCR, CERD imposes positive obligations upon States parties. A special feature of CERD is that it aims to secure substantive equality.

---

[504] Art 5.
[505] Art 1.
[506] Art 1(3).
[507] Art 1(3).

Article 1(4) permits States to take special measures, 'for the sole purpose of securing adequate advancement of certain racial or ethnic groups or individuals requiring such protection'. Furthermore, positive measures are *required* in certain circumstances, so that:

> State Parties *shall*, when the circumstances so warrant, take, in the social, economic, cultural and other fields, special and concrete measures to ensure the adequate development and protection of certain racial groups or individuals belonging to them, for the purpose of guaranteeing them the full and equal enjoyment of human rights and fundamental freedoms. These measures shall in no case entail as a consequence the maintenance of unequal or separate rights for different racial groups after the objectives for which they were taken have been achieved.[508]

The Convention provides that such 'special measures' shall 'not be deemed racial discrimination' simply because they do not apply to all races.[509] Accordingly, appropriate affirmative action will not constitute discrimination under CERD.

The scope of the prohibition of racial discrimination is not limited to racist State policies and practices (such as apartheid) but extends to all acts of discrimination based on motivations of a racial nature, including acts of individuals and groups, and calls the State to account whenever such activities (currently or potentially) impinge on the enjoyment of fundamental human rights.[510] In addition to the State's positive obligations to secure substantive equality by the exercising of its own functions, CERD requires States parties to prohibit and act against 'racial discrimination' by *any* person, group or organization.[511] This obligation requires States to prohibit racial discrimination by private bodies including, for example, private sector employers, private clubs etc.[512] In *Yilmaz-Dogan v Netherlands*,[513] for example, the Committee on the Elimination of Racial Discrimination decided that a State party had not sufficiently protected the complainant's right to work under CERD in circumstances where an employment tribunal had not properly taken into account discrimination against the complainant by her private employer. **4.134**

CERD guarantees remedies to victims of racial discrimination. Article 6 of CERD requires States parties 'to assure to everyone within their jurisdiction effective protection and remedies' through national tribunals and other State **4.135**

508 Art 2(2), emphasis added.

509 Art 1(4).

510 K Boyle and A Baldaccini, 'International Human Rights Approaches to Racism' in Sandra Fredman (ed.), *Discrimination and Human Rights: The Case of Racism* (2001, Oxford) 151.

511 Art 2(1)(d).

512 K Boyle and A Baldaccini, 'International Human Rights Approaches to Racism' in S Fredman (ed), *Discrimination and Human Rights: The Case of Racism* (2001, Oxford), 159.

513 CERD Communication 1/1984, para 9.3.

institutions and the right to seek 'just and adequate reparation or satisfaction' for any damage suffered through such tribunals.[514]

4.136 The International Convention on the Elimination of all Forms of Discrimination Against Women (CEDAW) was adopted by the UN General Assembly in 1979, entered into force in 1981, and is the most significant and comprehensive international instrument addressing women's rights and the elimination of gender-based discrimination. The UK became a party in 1986.[515] CEDAW is concerned with achieving equality between women and men and therefore requires States parties to prohibit sexual discrimination by embodying 'the principle of equality of men and women in their national constitutions or other appropriate legislation'.[516] Under CEDAW States are also obliged to eliminate all discrimination against women, and to adopt laws or other measures 'including sanctions where appropriate, prohibiting all discrimination against women'.[517]

4.137 CEDAW establishes the Committee on the Elimination of Discrimination against Women,[518] and in common with the other major UN human rights treaties, provides for a system of State reporting to monitor compliance.[519] As with CERD, the Committee has recommended that the UK Government give consideration to the introduction of legislation covering all aspects of the Convention, in particular introducing comprehensive legislation against discrimination including indirect discrimination.[520]

4.138 CEDAW acknowledges that women are a disadvantaged group and that their vulnerability to discrimination is increased when they belong to a racial or

514 For comments on the UK see <http://www.unhchr.ch/tbs/doc.nsf/(Symbol)/CERD.C.63.CO.11.En?Opendocument>. See too, *Secretary of State for Defence v Elias* [2006] EWCA Civ 1293, para 68.

515 Having ratified it on 7 April 1986.

516 Art 2(a).

517 Art 2(b).

518 Art 17.

519 Art 18. On 15 July 2004 the Lord Chancellor announced the completion of the Interdepartmental Review of International Human Rights Instruments. As part of this review the UK decided to accept the Optional Protocol to the Convention on the Elimination of all forms of Discrimination Against Women allowing individuals to petition the committee (reflecting the UK's position in relation to the other main UN Conventions): see <http://www.dca.gov.uk/peoples-rights/human-rights/pdf/report.pdf>. The Foreign Secretary signed the Optional Protocol in December 2004 and a three-month ratification period followed. As to the State, the UK has submitted its fifth periodic report in 2003, United Nations Convention on the Elimination of All Forms of Discrimination Against Women (CEDAW): 5th Periodic Report of the United Kingdom of Great Britain and Northern Ireland (June 2003), Available at <http://www.womenandequalityunit. gov.uk/eu_int/CEDAW5.doc>.

520 Concluding Observations of the Committee on the Elimination of Discrimination Against Women: United Kingdom of Great Britain and Northern Ireland, 1 July 1999, A/54/38, paras 278–318 (Concluding Observations/Comments).

ethnic minority group,[521] recognizing therefore 'intersectional' or 'multiple' discrimination.[522] Importantly, the Committee has expressed concern at the disadvantaged situation of women belonging to ethnic minorities in the UK, particularly in the context of unemployment, lower levels of education and training, lower wages and salaries, and fewer benefits as compared to white women. It has recommended that steps be taken to ensure the elimination of direct and indirect discrimination against ethnic minority women, including through positive action in recruitment, awareness campaigns, and targeted training, education, employment, and health-care strategies. It has also expressed concern about the 'high number of ethnic minority women in prison and the fact that many women have been imprisoned for drug-related offences or because of the criminalisation of minor infringements, which in some instances seem indicative of women's poverty'.[523]

Other relevant Treaties (containing equality guarantees) include the Convention on the Rights of the Child (CRC). The CRC was adopted by the UN General Assembly in 1989 and the Convention came into force a year later in 1990; the UK is a State party.[524] Under the Convention a broad range of children's rights are recognized including the right to life,[525] the right to education,[526] the right to protection from economic exploitation,[527] the right to survival and protection, and the right to be free from torture or other cruel, inhuman, or degrading treatment or punishment.[528] Further, Article 2(1) provides that States parties have a duty to respect and ensure the rights in the Convention to each child within their jurisdiction 'without discrimination of any kind, irrespective of the child's or his or her parent's or legal guardian's race, colour, sex, language, religion, political or other opinion, national, ethnic or social origin, property, disability, birth or other status'. In addition, Article 2(2) provides that States parties shall take all appropriate measures to ensure that children are protected 'against all forms of discrimination or punishment on the basis of the status, activities, expressed opinions, or beliefs of the child's parents, legal guardians, or family members'. Article 14 provides that 'States Parties shall respect the right of the child to freedom of thought, conscience and religion'[529] and 'respect the rights and duties of the parents and, when **4.139**

[521] See for, example, ibid, paras 278–318 (Concluding Observations/Comments).

[522] Discussed further in Chap 5.

[523] Concluding Comments of the Committee on the Elimination of Discrimination against Women: United Kingdom of Great Britain and Northern Ireland, 1 July 1999, A/54/38, paras 278–318 (Concluding Observations/Comments).

[524] Having ratified it on 16 December 1991.

[525] Art 6.

[526] Art 28.

[527] Art 32.

[528] Art 37.

[529] Typically, the freedom 'to manifest one's religion or beliefs may be subject . . . to such limitations as are prescribed by law and are necessary to protect public safety, order, health or morals, or the fundamental rights and freedoms of others' (Art 14(3)).

applicable, legal guardians, to provide direction to the child in the exercise of his or her right in a manner consistent with the evolving capacities of the child'. Article 30 provides protection for members of minority groups by requiring that:

> in those States in which ethnic, religious or linguistic minorities or persons of indigenous origin exist, a child belonging to such a minority or who is indigenous shall not be denied the right, in community with other members of his or her group, to enjoy his or her own culture, to profess and practise his or her own religion, or to use his or her own language.

4.140 The Convention establishes the 'Committee on the Rights of the Child'[530] which monitors the implementation of the Convention. The Convention puts in place a reporting system typical of the UN monitoring bodies.[531] Under that system State parties submit reports in which they detail the measures they have taken to comply with their Convention obligations. As to the UK, the Committee have expressed concern about the position of children belonging to certain minority groups. In particular, it has recently expressed the view that:

> the principle of non-discrimination is not fully implemented for all children in all parts of the State party and that there is unequal enjoyment of economic, social, cultural, civil and political rights, in particular for children with disabilities, children from poor families, Irish and Roma travellers' children, asylum-seeker and refugee children, children belonging to minority groups, children in care, detained children and children aged between 16 and 18 years old.[532]

The Committee has made a number of recommendations regarding the UK, including that it monitor the situation of such children, that it develop comprehensive strategies containing specific and well-targeted actions aimed at eliminating all forms of discrimination, and that it amend nationality law to allow transmission of nationality through unmarried as well as married fathers.

4.141 As to disability, the UN has developed and adopted[533] 'Standard Rules on the Equalization of Opportunities for Persons with Disabilities' (1993). Although not a legally binding instrument, the Standard Rules represent a strong moral and political commitment by States to take action to attain equalization of opportunities for persons with disabilities. The rules serve as an instrument for policy making and as a basis for technical and economic cooperation.[534] They include, for example, the requirement that 'States should take action to raise awareness in society about persons with disabilities, their rights, their needs, their potential and

---

530 Art 43.

531 Art 44.

532 Concluding observations: United Kingdom of Great Britain and Northern Ireland: CRC/C/15/Add.188, 9 Oct 2002.

533 Adopted by the United Nations General Assembly, 48th session, resolution 48/96, annex, of 20 Dec 1993.

534 <http://www.un.org/esa/socdev/enable/dissre00.htm>.

their contribution'; that 'States should ensure that responsible authorities distribute up-to-date information on available programmes and services to persons with disabilities, their families, professionals in the field and the general public. Information to persons with disabilities should be presented in accessible form'; that States should ensure that public education programmes reflect in all their aspects the principle of full participation and equality; and that 'States should invite persons with disabilities and their families and organizations to participate in public education programmes concerning disability matters'.[535]

Further, and very importantly, the UN General Assembly[536] has finally agreed the text of a Convention on disability.[537] The purpose of the Convention is to 'promote, protect and ensure the full and equal enjoyment of all human rights and fundamental freedoms by all persons with disabilities, and to promote respect for their inherent dignity'.[538] The general principles underpinning the Convention are described as 'respect for inherent dignity, individual autonomy including the freedom to make one's own choices, and independence of persons' and the 'full and effective participation and inclusion in society' and 'respect for difference and acceptance of disability as part of human diversity and humanity'.[539] The Convention requires States parties to 'prohibit all discrimination on the basis of disability and guarantee to persons with disabilities equal and effective legal protection against discrimination on all grounds' and to 'take all appropriate steps to ensure that reasonable accommodation is provided'.[540] The Convention addresses women and children with disabilities in particular.[541] It guarantees the right to life.[542] The Convention promotes autonomy through its provisions.[543] It requires, *inter alia*, States to 'take appropriate measures to ensure to persons **4.142**

535 Rule 1.

536 After many years of negotiation by an *ad-hoc* committee. For the resolution establishing an *ad hoc* committee to consider proposals for a 'comprehensive and integral international convention to promote and protect the rights and dignity of persons with disabilities, based on the holistic approach in the work done in the fields of social development, human rights and non-discrimination', see 56/168. Resolution adopted by the General Assembly [on the report of the Third Committee (A/56/583/Add.2)].

537 The text was agreed on 27 Aug 2006 and the draft Convention is expected to come before the UN General Assembly for final adoption later in 2006. The Convention will then be open for signing and ratification by all UN member countries, with 20 ratifications needed for it to enter into force. See 'Draft Convention on the rights of persons with disabilities and the Draft Optional Protocol to the International Convention on the Rights of Persons with Disabilities to be adopted simultaneously with the Convention', see <http://www.un.org/esa/socdev/enable/index.html>.

538 Art 1.

539 Art 3.

540 Art 5.

541 Arts 6 and 7.

542 Art 10. See para 4.70 above for the relationship between the right to life and disability under the ECHR.

543 See, for example, 'living independently and being included in the community' (Art 19).

with disabilities access, on an equal basis with others, to the physical environment, to transportation, to information and communications, including information and communications technologies and systems, and to other facilities and services open or provided to the public, both in urban and in rural areas. These measures . . . .include the identification and elimination of obstacles and barriers to accessibility.'[544]

I. The International Labour Organization

4.143 The International Labour Organization (ILO) has adopted a number of Conventions important for equality law. The ILO was created in 1919[545] primarily for the purpose of adopting international standards to cope with the problem of labour conditions involving 'injustice, hardship and privation'. The ILO is part of the UN system for the protection of human rights and its mandate has now been extended to include more general, but related, social policy, human, and civil rights matters. International labour standards are essentially expressions of international tripartite agreement on these matters involving States, workers' organizations, and employers' organizations. The ILO's standards take the form of international labour Conventions and Recommendations. The ILO's Conventions are international treaties, subject to ratification by ILO Member States.

4.144 ILO Convention 111, Discrimination (Employment and Occupation) Convention [1958],[546] is the most relevant. Article 2 of Convention 111 provides that:

> each member for which this Convention is in force undertakes to declare and pursue a national policy designed to promote, by methods appropriate to national conditions and practice, equality of opportunity and treatment in respect of employment and occupation, with a view to eliminating any discrimination in respect thereof.

The UK has (fairly recently) ratified Convention 111.[547] Article 1 of Convention 111 defines 'discrimination' for the purposes of the Convention. It provides that:

> 1. For the purpose of this Convention the term discrimination includes—
>   (a) any distinction, exclusion or preference made on the basis of race, colour, sex, religion, political opinion, national extraction or social origin, which has the

---

544 Art 9.

545 And is the only surviving major body of the Treaty of Versailles which brought the League of Nations into being. The ILO became the first specialized agency of the UN in 1946.

546 Ratified by the UK in 1999: <http://webfusion.ilo.org/public/db/standards/normes/appl/index.cfm?>. On 18 June 1998 the ILO adopted the ILO Declaration on Fundamental Principles and Rights at Work and its Follow-up in Geneva, identifying 'core' standards Member States are bound to respect whether or not they have ratified the Conventions in which they are contained, including the prohibition of discrimination as set out in Convention 111.

547 June 1999, <http://www.ilo.org/ilolex/english/convdisp1.htm>.

effect of nullifying or impairing equality of opportunity or treatment in employment or occupation;

(b) such other distinction, exclusion or preference which has the effect of nullifying or impairing equality of opportunity or treatment in employment or occupation as may be determined by the member concerned after consultation with representative employers and workers' organisations, where such exist, and with other appropriate bodies.

2. Any distinction, exclusion or preference in respect of a particular job based on the inherent requirements thereof shall not be deemed to be discrimination.
3. For the purpose of this Convention the terms employment and occupation include access to vocational training, access to employment and to particular occupations, and terms and conditions of employment.

The definition of discrimination under Convention 111 is sufficiently wide to include direct and indirect discrimination. Furthermore, a wide definition has been given to indirect discrimination so that it: **4.145**

> refers to apparently neutral situations, regulations or practices which in fact result in unequal treatment of persons with certain characteristics. It occurs when the same condition, treatment or criterion is applied to everyone, but results in a disproportionately harsh impact on some persons on the basis of characteristics such as race, colour, sex or religion, and is not closely related to the inherent requirements of the job.[548]

Positive action is specifically required by the Convention, the Committee having stated that: **4.146**

> In order to apply the Convention it is not sufficient to prohibit all kinds of discrimination, either by national legislation or by any other means; specific action must also be taken at the national level to help promote the essential conditions for all workers to benefit in practice from equality in employment and occupation. The national policy must be clearly expressed, which means that programmes must be established for this purpose; it must also be applied, which means that the State concerned must take appropriate measures. These measures must encompass both the public and private sectors.[549]

Convention 100 (Equal Remuneration Convention) addresses equal pay,[550] and requires that Member States 'shall, by means appropriate to the methods in operation for determining rates of remuneration, promote and, in so far as is consistent with such methods, ensure the application to all workers of the principle of equal remuneration for men and women workers for work of equal value'.[551] **4.147**

---

548 General Survey by the Committee of Experts on the Application of Conventions and Recommendations, ILO Conference, 83rd Session, Geneva, 1996, para 26.

549 Ibid. And see: 'Discrimination (Employment and Occupation) Recommendation, 1958' (R111), General Conference of the ILO.

550 Ratified by the UK in 1971.

551 Art 2.

J. Council of Europe

4.148 As to the Council of Europe, the UK is a party to the Council of Europe's counterpart to the ECHR, the European Social Charter (1965).[552] This addresses economic and social rights, much like the ICESCR. The Charter recognizes a wide range of social and economic rights, including the right to just conditions of work; the right to safe and healthy working conditions; and the right to fair remuneration sufficient for a decent standard of living for workers and their families.

4.149 The Charter does not contain a specific non-discrimination guarantee. However, it does address discrimination both in its preamble and in the substantive provisions. Its preamble provides that 'the enjoyment of social rights should be secured without discrimination on grounds of race, colour, sex, religion, political opinion, national extraction or social origin'.

4.150 In addition, the Charter makes provision relevant to equality law, including that:

> Children and young persons have the right to a special protection against the physical and moral hazards to which they are exposed.
>
> Employed women, in case of maternity, and other employed women as appropriate, have the right to a special protection in their work.
>
> Disabled persons have the right to vocational training, rehabilitation and resettlement, whatever the origin and nature of their disability.
>
> The family as a fundamental unit of society has the right to appropriate social, legal and economic protection to ensure its full development.
>
> Mothers and children, irrespective of marital status and family relations, have the right to appropriate social and economic protection.

Further, the Charter provides that 'the nationals of any one of the Contracting Parties have the right to engage in any gainful occupation in the territory of any one of the others on a footing of equality with the nationals of the latter, subject to restrictions based on cogent economic or social reasons' and 'migrant workers who are nationals of a Contracting Party and their families have the right to protection and assistance in the territory of any other Contracting Party'.[553] The Charter makes further specific provision for migrant workers including

---

552 See Preamble, ETS No 035. Signed by the UK on 18 October 1961 and ratified on 11 July 1962. The Charter came into force in 1965: <http://conventions.coe.int>. The UK has not ratified the Revised Social Charter.

553 Art 1.

guaranteeing equality in relation to pay and working conditions, membership of trades unions, and accommodation.[554]

The Revised Social Charter[555] is intended to replace the Social Charter. Importantly, the UK has not ratified the Charter,[556] and therefore it does not bind the UK. Unlike the original Charter, the Revised Charter does contain an explicit non-discrimination guarantee. Part V, Article E provides that: **4.151**

> The enjoyment of the rights set forth in this Charter shall be secured without discrimination on any ground such as race, colour, sex, language, religion, political or other opinion, national extraction or social origin, health, association with a national minority, birth or other status.

This provision is materially the same as that contained in Article 14 of the ECHR and it is therefore likely to be interpreted in much the same way.

The most important Council of Europe instrument concerning minorities is the Framework Convention for the Protection of National Minorities (1995).[557] The UK is a party to it.[558] It provides that 'every person belonging to a national minority shall have the right freely to choose to be treated or not to be treated as such and no disadvantage shall result from this choice or from the exercise of the rights which are connected to that choice'.[559] Such rights as are provided for by the Convention might be enjoyed 'individually as well as in community with others'.[560] The Convention contains an explicit non-discrimination provision, guaranteeing 'to persons belonging to national minorities the right of equality before the law and of equal protection of the law. In this respect, any discrimination based on belonging to a national minority shall be prohibited'.[561] The Framework Convention is plainly important in the protection and promotion of minority rights. **4.152**

---

554 Arts 18 and 19. In their most recent report the European Committee of Social Rights concluded that the UK was not in conformity with Art 18(3) ('liberalising individually or collectively regulations governing the employment of foreign workers' because it considered the UK's requirements in relation to work permits too excessive: Conclusions XV-2 Vol 2, European Committee of Social Rights.

555 CETS No 163.

556 The UK signed the Revised Social Charter on 7 Nov 1997.

557 CETS No 159. See S Wheatley, *Democracy, Minorities and International Law* (2005, CSIL) for a full discussion on minority rights and international law.

558 Having signed and ratified it on 1 Feb 1995 and 15 Jan 1998 respectively; <http://conventions.coe.int>. As for the procedures these can be found on the Council of Europe's website <http://www.coe.int/torcalT.asp>.

559 Art 3.

560 Art 3.

561 Art 4(1).

4.153 The UK Government has also signed and ratified[562] the European Charter for Regional or Minority Languages (1992).[563] This addresses languages that are:

> traditionally used within a given territory of a State by nationals of that State who form a group numerically smaller than the rest of the State's population; and different from the official language(s) of that State; it does not include either dialects of the official language(s) of the State or the languages of migrants.

The Charter contains a number of objectives and principles (and a framework for achieving them) in the fields of, amongst others, education, judicial proceedings, public services relating to minority language use, and protection. Its adoption followed increasing concern over the situation of regional or minority languages within Europe and the recognition that Article 14 of the ECHR, whilst laying down the principle of non-discrimination, did not create a system of positive protection for minority languages and the communities using them.[564] Again the Charter is self-evidently important for the treatment of minority groups.

562 2 March 2000 and 27 March 2001 respectively; <http://conventions.coe.int>.

563 CETS No 148.

564 European Charter for Regional or Minority Languages [1992]. Explanatory Report, <http://conventions.coe.int/Treaty/en/Reports/Html/148.htm>.

Part II

THE PROTECTED CLASSES AND DISCRIMINATION

5

THE PROTECTED CLASSES

A democratic, universalistic, caring and aspirationally egalitarian society embraces everyone and accepts people for who they are. To penalise people for being who and what they are is profoundly disrespectful of the human personality and violatory of equality. Equality means equal concern and respect across difference. It does not presuppose the elimination or suppression of difference. Respect for human rights requires the affirmation of self, not the denial of self. Equality therefore does not imply a levelling or homogenisation of behaviour or extolling one form as supreme, and another as inferior, but an acknowledgement and acceptance of difference. At the very least, it affirms that difference should not be the basis for exclusion, marginalisation and stigma. At best, it celebrates the vitality that difference brings to any society.[1]

[1] *Minister of Home Affairs and O'rs v Fourie & Bonthuys; Lesbian and Gay Equality Project and O'rs v Minister of Home Affairs and ors* (2005), Cases CCT 60/04, 10/05, *per* Sachs J, para 60.

A. Introduction

5.01 Each of the main anti-discrimination enactments prescribes the classes protected under them.[2] As mentioned in Chapter 2, there is no general prohibition against discrimination on open-ended grounds, though Article 14 of the European Convention on Human Rights (ECHR) (now given effect through the Human Rights Act 1998) is the closest approximation of such a measure in domestic law. Article 14 protects against discrimination within the ambit of the other Convention rights on a number of enumerated grounds (described inclusively as exemplars) including on the ground of 'other status'.[3]

5.02 By contrast with Article 14 and other universally applicable equality provisions, the main anti-discrimination enactments each define the classes protected under them exclusively but with more or less precision depending upon the ground in question. In short, the main anti-discrimination enactments protect against discrimination connected with sex, gender reassignment, married or civil partnership (but not unmarried or non-civil partnership) status, race, colour, ethnicity, national origins, nationality (though not usually immigration status), disability, sexual orientation, religion, belief, and age.[4]

5.03 Each of the above grounds on which discrimination is proscribed is addressed below. The specific definitions are considered and, where instructive, the genesis of the particular protected 'ground' is described. One of the important general observations which may be made of the approach adopted by the main anti-discrimination enactments is that it is not uncontroversial. The way in which the protected classes are defined assumes persons and groups covered thereby might best be described mono-characteristically. This assumes homogeneity within groups and can often obscure 'multiple' discrimination or 'intersectional' discrimination. This makes addressing the real experiences of certain minority groups problematic, particularly where the discrimination is experienced by reason of multiple characteristics. The main anti-discrimination enactments compel complainants to choose their ground or grounds, sometimes in the alternative or in

[2] The position is the same in Northern Ireland, though the grounds protected are wider so as to include the Irish Traveller community (Race Relations (Northern Ireland) Order 1997) and political opinion (Fair Employment and Treatment (Northern Ireland) Order 1998).

[3] The grounds protected by Article 14 are fully addressed in Chap 4.

[4] And in Northern Ireland the Irish Traveller community and political opinion; Race Relations (Northern Ireland) Order 1997 and Fair Employment and Treatment (Northern Ireland) Order 1998.

addition,[5] not always reflecting the experience of discrimination suffered.[6] 'Intersectional' discrimination claims have been brought in domestic law under the main anti-discrimination enactments, though usually by ignoring one characteristic or another, so that claims by black women as *black women* are often brought

[5] For a similar situation in the US, see *DeGraffenreid v General Motors Assembly Division* 413 F Supp 142 (Ed Mo 1976), cited in S Hannett, 'Equality at the Intersections: The Legislative and Judicial Failure to Tackle Multiple Discrimination' [2003] Oxford Journal of Legal Studies, Vol 23, No 1, 65–86, 75. This case concerned a claim under Title VII of the US Civil Rights Act 1964 brought by black women as black women in relation to a 'last-hired, first-fired' policy. Title VII of the Civil Rights Act 1964 adopts an atomized approach to the grounds protected and the court rejected their claim that 'black women are a special class to be protected from discrimination' (at 143) and stated that the combining of statutory remedies to create a 'new super-remedy' which would give the claimants relief beyond what the drafters of the relevant statutes intended was not permissible (ibid). In *Jefferies v Harris County Community Action Association* 615 F2d 1025 (5th Cir 1980) the court responded to a multi-discrimination claim by a black woman by applying a 'sex-plus' analysis so that the claimant was entitled to plead discrimination on the basis of sex plus one other discriminatory factor linked to sex. This approach was more progressive but was circumscribed in *Judge v Marsh* 649 F Supp 770 (DDC 1986) in which the court held that the 'sex-plus' approach was limited to the addition of one factor only so as to avoid turning discrimination law into 'a many headed hydra' with 'sub-groups... exist[ing] for every possible combination of race, colour, sex, national origin and religion' (ibid at 780). See discussion in S Hannett, 'Equality at the Intersections: The Legislative and Judicial Failure to Tackle Multiple Discrimination' [2003] Oxford Journal of Legal Studies, Vol 23, No 1, 65–86 and see K Crenshaw, 'Demarginalizing the Intersection of Race and Sex: A Black Feminist Critique of Anti discrimination Doctrine, Feminist Theory and Antiracist Politics', in C McCrudden (ed), *Anti-Discrimination Law* (2004, Ashgate) 479–507.

[6] Taking one practical example from the UK, whilst the increase in rights for part-time workers has without doubt positively impacted on women's experiences in the labour market, it is white women who have largely benefited, with black women more likely than white women to work full-time (*Black and Minority Ethnic Women in the UK* (2005, The Fawcett Society); see too the Equal Opportunities Commission's investigation into the participation, pay, and progression of ethnic minority women in the UK labour market, launch documents at <http://www.eoc.org.uk/Default.aspx?page=17696&lang=en>; A Hibbett, *Ethnic Minority Women in the UK* (2002, Women and Equality Unit), available at <http://www.womenandequalityunit.gov.uk/research/factsheets/ethnic_m_oct02.doc.>). This may be for many reasons (including economic reasons, ibid) but a gender agenda which focuses on prioritizing short working hours, though very important, is less likely to benefit black women whose experiences in work are likely to be qualitatively different. Being a black woman in the UK is not simply to experience being a white woman with an added 'problem' as the main anti-discrimination legislation would suppose. This approach does little to assist black women and can hinder a white woman's claim to non-discrimination. In deciding whether a measure is indirectly discriminatory (as to indirect discrimination, see Chap 6 below) a court will be required to look at all persons possessing the particular protected characteristic in issue to determine whether members of that group are collectively disadvantaged—whether or not the possession of other characteristics makes them inappropriate for inclusion in the group. Using the same example, a white woman seeking to argue that a requirement to work full time is disadvantageous to women and thus indirectly sexually discriminatory will find black women, who are more likely to work full time, counted for the purposes of determining whether 'women' are disadvantaged by the requirement, though their experiences are relevantly and tangibly different. This analysis helps neither the white woman, who may be obstructed in her claim to substantive equality, by the accommodating of a need to work part time, and renders black women's experiences irrelevant to 'women's' (that being white women's) experience and their claim to gender equality invisible.

as claims of race discrimination.[7] Whilst there have been cases brought which have rested on claims of multiple discrimination (by black women in particular) these have been rare and have been difficult to pursue within the mono-characteristic based framework that the main anti-discrimination enactments present.[8]

5.04 In addition, the classes protected under the main anti-discrimination enactments are closed and so difficult to adapt to changing social contexts. The classes are also described by reference to characteristics we all possess—that is, irrespective of disadvantage, marginalization, or other indicators of discrimination or inequality. Many legal and political theorists argue that in treating 'discrimination as atomized, involving different treatment of someone seen as having a specific characteristic (e.g. black, Muslim, female, with a disability, homosexual, etc.)' the UK's anti-discrimination legislation[9] adopts the wrong approach and that a 'generalized' approach, as seen in open-ended protections—like Article 14—would be preferable.

5.05 However, the UK does adopt an 'atomized approach' in all its anti-discrimination law and that approach is reflected elsewhere. Article 13 of the EC Treaty,[10] the Australian and New Zealand anti-discrimination legislation,[11] and the Caribbean Community in its 'model' legislation on equality of opportunity[12] all adopt a similar approach, that is one which offers protection on exclusively defined grounds. By contrast, Article 14 and other 'constitutional' level guarantees adopt the 'generalized approach'. Some of these are considered at paragraph 5.08 onwards below.

5.06 Importantly, the actual classes protected by the UK's main anti-discrimination legislation are, in some contexts, rather wider than might appear at first glance because certain of the enactments—though not all—protect persons who are not themselves the subject of the discriminatory animus complained of. In particular

[7] See, for example, the very striking illustration of this trend in *Burton and Rhule v De Vere Hotels* [1997] ICR 1 and see *Coker and Osamor v The Lord Chancellor and Lord Chancellor's Department* [2002] IRLR 80 for the difficulties in trying to establish the necessary disadvantage to show disparate impact for the indirect discrimination provisions where the existence of multiple characteristics are relied upon.

[8] See, eg, *Nwoke v Government Legal Service and Civil Service Commissioners* [1996] 28 EOR 6.

[9] B Hepple, M Coussey, and T Choudhury, *Equality: A New Framework, Report of the Independent Review of the Enforcement of UK Anti-Discrimination Legislation* (2000, Hart), at para 2.61.

[10] See Chap 4.

[11] There is no constitutional right to equality in Australia and New Zealand. Rather, under Australian law, it is unlawful to discriminate against a person on the basis of several grounds, each enumerated in individual ground-specific legalisation; and in New Zealand the Human Rights Act 1993 outlaws discrimination on enumerated grounds, exclusively defined (s 21).

[12] The Commonwealth Secretariat has collaborated with the Caribbean Community Secretariat (CARICOM) (for further information see <http://www.caricom.org/>) to develop model legislation in a number of areas for the Caribbean Commonwealth.

the Race Relations Act 1976 (RRA), the Sexual Orientation Regulations, and the Religion and Belief Regulations, protect against less favourable treatment *on the grounds of* race, sexual orientation, and religion or belief, so protecting a person against treatment on grounds of his or her own status or on the grounds of another's status. This is explained below in Chapter 6.

There is much to be learned from other jurisdictions in defining the grounds to be protected by any anti-discrimination scheme. The approaches adopted in South Africa and Canada, in particular, are instructive and these are considered below. **5.07**

B. South Africa

At Article 9(3) in its Bill of Rights[13] the South African Constitution provides that: **5.08**

> The state may not unfairly discriminate directly or indirectly against anyone on one or more grounds, including race, gender, sex, pregnancy, marital status, ethnic or social origin, colour, sexual orientation, age, disability, religion, conscience, belief, culture, language and birth.

This provides for enumerated, but inclusive,[14] grounds whilst providing expressly for the possibility of addressing discrimination on multiple grounds and by providing at least sufficient flexibility for addressing intersectional discrimination.

The South African Constitutional Court adopts a substantive approach to addressing inequality. This means that in deciding whether a breach of Article 9(3) has occurred, regard is given to the context of any difference in treatment and its impact (whether it promotes or ameliorates disadvantage). This approach is also used to determine whether Article 9(3) protects the 'ground' for any distinction and as such South African equality law is able to accommodate 'intersecting' and 'multiple' discrimination. The Constitutional Court has made some observations on intersectional or multiple discrimination indicating that this is so.[15] In *Harksen v Lane*[16] Goldstone J, in addressing the relationship between the enumerated **5.09**

---

[13] At Chap 2 of the Constitution.

[14] See the 'analogous grounds' protected under Art 9, eg, *Larbi-Odam v Member of the Executive Council for Education (North West Province) and Anr* [1998] (1) SA 745 (CC) (differentiation on the basis of citizenship under an employment statute held to constitute unfair discrimination under Art 9) and *Hoffmann v South African Airways* (2000) 21 ILJ 2357 (CC) (discriminating against employees on the ground of HIV status held to constitute discrimination; HIV status being an analogous ground of discrimination and discrimination on the basis of such deemed an affront to human dignity).

[15] *Brink v Kitshoff* [1996] (4) SA 197 (CC) at para 44, *per* O'Regan J; *National Coalition for Gay and Lesbian Equality and An'r v Minister of Justice and Others* (1998) (12) BCLR 1517, para 113, *per* Sachs J.

[16] [1997 (110) BCLR 1489 (CC)] CCT 9/97.

grounds protected by the Interim Constitution, identified the need for an equality analysis not restricted by over-rigidity:

> There is often a complex relationship between these grounds. In some cases they relate to immutable biological attributes or characteristics, in some to the associational life of humans, in some to the intellectual, expressive and religious dimensions of humanity and in some cases to a combination of one or more of these features. The temptation to force them into neatly self-contained categories should be resisted. Section 8(2)[17] seeks to prevent the unequal treatment of people based on such criteria which may, amongst other things, result in the construction of patterns of disadvantage such as has occurred only too visibly in our history.[18]

5.10 South Africa's Promotion of Equality and Prevention of Unfair Discrimination Act 2000[19]—one of the most important statutes enacted under Article 9 of the Constitution and described as 'a pivotal tool for facilitating South Africa's transition from a history of legislated discrimination to a future where equality is actively promoted through legislative measures'[20]—prohibits discrimination on the constitutionally listed grounds, but also on any other ground that causes or perpetuates systemic disadvantage. Its section 1(1) (xxii) defines the 'prohibited grounds' as '(a) race, gender, sex, pregnancy, marital status, ethnic or social origin, colour, sexual orientation, age, disability, religion, conscience, belief, culture, language and birth; or (b) any other ground where discrimination based on that other ground— (i) causes or perpetuates systemic disadvantage; (ii) undermines human dignity; or (iii) adversely affects the equal enjoyment of a person's rights and freedoms in a serious manner that is comparable to discrimination on a ground in paragraph (a)'.[21] This focus on substantive equality, the breadth of the grounds protected, and the quasi-generalized approach reflects the approach of the Constitutional Court in its case law under Article 9(3) and makes tackling multiple and intersectional discrimination more likely.

---

17 Of the Interim Constitution which defined the grounds protected as 'one or more' of a fewer number of enumerated grounds than those found in Art 9 of the final Constitution but again described inclusively.

18 Para 49.

19 The Act is intended to prevent and prohibit unfair discrimination, harassment, and hate speech and to promote equality, and refers to South Africa's historical patterns of discrimination, and has a particularly important role in addressing past disadvantage and promoting equality.

20 P Lane 'South Africa's Equality Courts: An Early Assessment' [2005] Centre for the Study of Violence and Conciliation, <http://www.csvr.org.za/papers/paprctp5.htm>.

21 The content of some of the prohibited grounds is also expanded upon; ss 7–8. There is some controversy over the grounds included in the Act. During the drafting phase, many grounds were the subject of lobbying, including nationality, HIV status or perceived status, and socio-economic status. Whilst these grounds were rejected by Parliament, the Equality Review Committee (established under Chap 7 of the Act) were tasked with reporting on whether HIV/Aids, nationality, socio-economic status, and family responsibility and status should be added to the prohibited grounds in s 1(xxii). The Committee reported back in the affirmative, but the government has yet to amend the legislation.

C. Canada

As to Canada, the Canadian Charter of Rights and Freedoms[22] contains an express equality guarantee in its section 15[23] which provides that: 5.11

(1) Every individual is equal before and under the law and has the right to the equal protection and equal benefit of the law without discrimination and, in particular, without discrimination based on race, national or ethnic origin, colour, religion, sex, age or mental or physical disability.
(2) Subsection (1) does not preclude any law, program or activity that has as its object the amelioration of conditions of disadvantaged individuals or groups including those that are disadvantaged because of race, national or ethnic origin, colour, religion, sex, age or mental or physical disability.

Typically for a constitutional instrument, section 15 again adopts a generalized approach with inclusively drafted enumerated grounds. In determining whether any non-enumerated ground is protected, the court will ask whether the ground sought to be protected is an 'analogous ground'[24] to those enumerated in section 15. The Supreme Court has adopted a wide approach to the grounds protected by section 15 so that:

> [b]oth the enumerated grounds themselves and other possible grounds of discrimination recognized under s. 15(1) must be interpreted in a broad and generous manner, reflecting the fact that they are constitutional provisions not easily repealed or amended but intended to provide a 'continuing framework for the legitimate exercise of governmental power' and, at the same time, for 'the unremitting protection' of equality rights.[25]

This recognizes the value in a framework that has sufficient flexibility as to accommodate societal changes, something not readily available in the UK's anti-discrimination enactments.

The Canadian Supreme Court has, like South Africa, taken an explicitly contextual approach to developing the law under section 15, including in the identification of the grounds protected. In *R v Turpin*[26] the court reiterated the importance of determining what constitutes an analogous ground by examining not only the 5.12

[22] Adopted in 1982 as a constitutionally entrenched 'Bill of Rights' forming part of the Constitution of Canada; Part 1 of the Constitution Act 1982.

[23] Other provisions relevant to equality include ss 27 and 28.

[24] *R v Swain* [1991] 1 SCR 933.

[25] *Andrews v The Law Society of British Columbia* [1989] 1 SCR 143, 175. The decision on discrimination was not unanimous, with McIntyre J being in the minority with Lamer J. However, the opinion on the approach to s 15 was unanimous (see too quoted citations therein, from *Hunter v Southam Inc* [1984] 2 SCR 145, 155). See too, Wilson J in *Andrews*, ibid, 152.

[26] [1989] 1 SCR 1296.

context of the law subject to the claim but also the 'context of the place of the group in the entire social, political and legal fabric of our society'.[27] If the larger context is not examined, the section 15 analysis 'may become a mechanical and sterile categorization process conducted entirely within the four corners of the impugned legislation'.[28] In addition, the court noted that:

> it is only by examining the larger context that a court can determine whether differential treatment results in inequality or whether, contrariwise, it would be identical treatment which would in the particular context result in inequality or foster disadvantage. A finding that there is discrimination will . . . in most . . . cases, necessarily entail a search for disadvantage that exists apart from and independent of the particular legal distinction being challenged.[29]

5.13 The case law under section 15 has recognized several 'analogous' grounds, including non-citizenship[30] and sexual orientation.[31] The courts have also rejected as analogous grounds certain characteristics, including marijuana usage.[32]

5.14 Notwithstanding the broad approach taken by the Canadian Supreme Court in identifying 'analogous grounds', its approach is not without its critics.[33] The Ontario Human Rights Commission[34] has identified at least two reasons for criticizing the Charter's focus on enumerated and analogous grounds. Firstly, 'a limited view of identity ensures that those persons who are unable to categorize or caricaturize themselves according to one of the enumerated categories find themselves "falling through the cracks" of Canadian equality and anti-discrimination law'.[35]

---

27 *Andrews v The Law Society of British Columbia* [1989] 1 SCR 143, 152.

28 *R v Turpin* 1989] 1 SCR 1296, 1332, *per* Wilson J.

29 Ibid at 1331–2. It has been noted that the 'criterion of general disadvantage in addition to the particular prejudicial distinction under challenge has not gone uncriticized, but has generally remained a key consideration for section 15 claims.' MC Hurley, 'Charter Equality Rights: Interpretation of Section 15 in the Supreme Court of Canada Decisions' [2004] Parliamentary Research Branch, Library of Parliament: Canada, 3. See too discussion in, G Garton (ed), *The Canadian Charter of Rights Decisions Digest* (2004, Canadian Legal Information Institute: Montreal) available at: <www.canlii.org/ca/com/chart/s-15-1.html>.

30 *Andrews v The Law Society of British Columbia* [1989] 1 SCR 143.

31 *Egan v Canada* [1995] 2 SCR 513 in which the exclusion of homosexual couples as 'spouses' under the Old Age Security Act was challenged as discriminatory—appeal dismissed.

32 *R v Malmo-Levin* [2003] 3 SCR 571.

33 P Hughes, 'Recognising Substantive Equality as a Foundational Constitutional Principle' [1999] Dalhousie Law Journal 5, 43 cited in E Grabham, 'Law v Canada: A New Direction for Equality Under the Canadian Charter?' [2002] Oxford Journal of Legal Studies, Vol 22 (40), 641 cited at 649. D Majury, 'The Charter, Equality Rights, and Women: Equivocation and Celebration' [2002] Osgoode Hall Law Journal Vol 40 (3&4), 297, 310.

34 *An Intersectional Approach to Discrimination: Addressing Multiple Grounds in Human Rights Claims* (2001), Ontario Human Rights Commission, Discussion Paper, 8, available at: <http://www.ohrc.on.ca/english/consultations/intersectionality-discussion-paper.pdf>.

35 Citing D Kropp, "'Categorial' Failure: Canada's Equality Jurisprudence—Changing Notions of Identity and the Legal Subject' [1997] 23 Queen's LJ 201, online: QL, para 1.

Secondly, there may be cases where there is evidence to support discrimination on one ground, but 'to focus solely on that ground would do an injustice to the lived realities of those facing discrimination'. However, whilst the Canadian Supreme Court has not yet issued authoritative guidance on intersectional discrimination, the dissenting judgments of some members of the Supreme Court evince a growing recognition of this form of discrimination. Most notably L'Heureux-Dubé J has observed that:

> It is increasingly recognized that categories of discrimination may overlap, and that individuals may suffer historical exclusion on the basis of both race and gender, age and physical handicap, or some other combination. The situation of individuals who confront multiple grounds of disadvantage is particularly complex . . . Categorizing such discrimination as primarily racially oriented, or primarily gender-oriented, misconceives the reality of discrimination as it is experienced by individuals. Discrimination may be experienced on many grounds, and where this is the case, it is not really meaningful to assert that it is one or the other. It may be more realistic to recognize that both forms of discrimination may be present and intersect.[36]

In *Corbiére v Canada*,[37] then, the Supreme Court upheld the identification of a new 'analogous' ground—that being non-reserve Aboriginals (a multifaceted identity). The court was, however, divided on the application of section 15(1) and the reasons for its finding. As has been noted,[38] McLaughlin J held as distinct the inquiry into the identification of analogous grounds and the contextual analysis of whether the distinction was discriminatory. On the other hand, L'Heureux-Dubé J's judgment placed the question of intersectionality at the heart of the analysis whether discrimination had occurred.[39] She also recognized the particular impact the measure in issue had on Aboriginal women 'who can be said to be doubly disadvantaged on the basis of both sex and race . . . because of their history and circumstances in Canadian and Aboriginal society'.[40] Despite the difference in approach, the decision in *Corbiére* 'stands as the preliminary affirmation of the multidimensional possibilities of section 15'.[41] 5.15

36 *Canada (Attorney General) v Mossop* [1993] 1 SCR 554, 645–6. And see Ibachicio J, speaking for the court in *Law v Canada (Minister of Employment and Immigration)* [1999] 1 SCR 497: there 'is no reason in principle, therefore, why a discrimination claim positing an intersection of grounds cannot be understood as analogous to, or as a synthesis of, the grounds listed in s. 15 (1)' (para 94).

37 [1999] 2 SCR 203.

38 E Grabham, 'Law v Canada: A New Direction for Equality Under the Canadian Charter?' [2002] Oxford Journal of Legal Studies, Vol 22 (40), 641, 651–3.

39 Para 61.

40 Para 72.

41 E Grabham, 'Law v Canada: A New Direction for Equality Under the Canadian Charter?' [2002] Oxford Journal of Legal Studies, Vol 22 (40), 641, 661.

D. The UK

5.16 The UK schemes would not permit of the approaches seen in South Africa and Canada. As stated, the main anti-discrimination enactments adopt an 'essentialist'[42] or 'atomized' approach to addressing inequality; they lack the flexibility to address intersectional discrimination and, often, multiple discrimination and they do not focus on disadvantage. They do, however, have the virtue of certainty. The grounds protected are defined with more or less precision but in all cases with enough clarity that one can be generally sure whether any particular differentiation will be caught by one or other of the enactments. Each of the grounds—distinctly protected—by the main anti-discrimination enactments is addressed below.

E. Sex and Gender: The Sex Discrimination Act 1975 and the Equal Pay Act 1970

5.17 The Sex Discrimination Act 1975 (SDA) protects against 'sex' discrimination and, in certain contexts, discrimination on the ground of marital and civil partnership status,[43] gender reassignment,[44] and pregnancy and maternity.[45] Each of these expressions is considered below.

5.18 The Equal Pay Act 1970 (EPA) protects 'women' and 'men'[46] from gender-based inequality in pay by the statutory implication of an 'equality clause' into contracts of employment.[47] The EPA materially replicates the provision made in the interpretation section of the SDA[48] by providing at section 11(2) that 'in this Act the expression "man" and "woman" shall be read as applying to persons of whatever age' but without further guidance as to the meaning to be afforded those expressions. The observations made below about the meaning of those expressions in the SDA apply equally to the EPA. The meaning given to 'discrimination' connected to these classes or 'grounds' is addressed in Chapter 6.

---

42 S Hannett, 'Equality at the Intersections: The Legislative and Judicial Failure to Tackle Multiple Discrimination' [2003] Oxford Journal of Legal Studies, Vol 23, No 1, 65–86, 75.

43 SDA, s 3.

44 Ibid, s 2A.

45 SDA, s 3A.

46 EPA, s 1(1) and (13).

47 EPA, s 1(1).

48 SDA, s 82(1).

(1) Sex

'Sex' is not defined by the SDA. However, section 2 provides: 5.19

> (1) Section 1 [which defines discrimination for the purposes of the SDA], and the provisions of Parts II and III[49] relating to sex discrimination against women, are to be read as applying equally to the treatment of men, and for that purpose shall have effect with such modifications as are requisite.
>
> (2) In the application of sub-section (1) no account shall be taken of special treatment afforded to women in connection with pregnancy or childbirth.

Thus the SDA assumes that 'sex' is to be determined by reference to certain biological characteristics which make individuals 'male' or 'female' and which require no further definition or explication. It is recognized, however, that special treatment may be afforded to women in connection with pregnancy or childbirth which might not be extended to men. Further, a 'man' or 'woman' includes a 'male' or a 'female' 'of any age'.[50] Discrimination is defined in terms which protect 'women' but, by reason of section 2, the legislation is intended to protect men as well.

As to the saving clause in respect of pregnancy and childbirth, this has become increasingly important having regard to recent changes to the SDA made to give effect to the Equal Treatment Amendment Directive.[51] This is discussed further below and in Chapter 6. 5.20

There is very little case law on the meaning of 'sex'. Such case law as there has been has focused, firstly, on the issue of gender reassignment and its relationship to the concept of 'sex', and, secondly, on the impact of pregnancy. The expressions 'women' and 'men' are treated as self-explanatory. Much of the other case law relevant to the interpretation of 'sex' has concentrated on the question of the proper comparator (as to which see Chapter 6). Many of the judicial attempts to identify the 'proper' comparator have treated concepts or definitions of 'female' and 'male' as entirely unproblematic. The case law so produced has tended to entrench commonly held but socially created understandings both of the terms themselves and the conduct to be expected of gendered individuals. Some of the older cases were most explicit in so doing.[52] More recently this phenomenon has been seen in the 'dress code' cases and the sexual orientation cases brought under the SDA which are discussed below (paragraph 5.24). 5.21

---

49 Which create the unlawful acts under the SDA, see Chap 7 onwards.

50 SDA, s 82(1).

51 Council Directive 2002/73/EC amending Council Directive 76/207/EEC on the implementation of the principle of equal treatment for men and women as regards access to employment, vocational training and promotion, and working conditions.

52 And Lord Denning's notorious judgments have already been referred to in Chap 1.

5.22 Far from tackling gender inequality, an assumption that sex, in the sense of gender, is only biologically determined can reinforce gender stereotyping. The ignoring of the socially imposed aspects of what it means to be a 'man' or a 'woman' forces both genders to conform to norms of behaviour perceived to be 'natural' but with which they may be less than comfortable. The fact that the SDA, and judicial interpretations of its provisions, have tended to reinforce these forms of biological determinism has made it less effective at challenging historical gender inequality.

5.23 The definition of direct discrimination contained in the SDA demonstrates some of the difficulties identified. The definition of direct discrimination is largely predicated on the assumption that women aspire to be like men.[53] Thus in considering whether a woman has been discriminated against, her treatment will be compared to that afforded a man. If the treatment in question is the same, or not materially different, she cannot be said in law to have been discriminated against.[54] If her sex, as biologically determined, puts her apart from a man—makes her non-comparable—then she cannot have been treated in a relevantly discriminatory way. She is therefore stuck between the social paradigm of gender with the assumption that it is biologically rooted and the law's paradigm of discrimination with its assumption that women aspire to be like men. This has proved particularly difficult in developing protection against pregnancy discrimination, as is discussed below and in Chapter 6.

5.24 The dress code and sexual orientation cases under the SDA have caused the courts to consider the 'social' aspects of gender norms but have, notably, not challenged them. As to dress codes, as has been observed by David Pannick '[p]art of the difficulty in achieving equal treatment for the sexes is to overcome traditional attitudes which are built on differences in gender between men and women'[55] and '[o]ne of the more pervasive and important types of gender distinction is that concerned with the dress of men and women'.[56] Dress codes have changed, of course, over time, but because the law treats 'sex' as an immutable biological characteristic, it pays little regard to this at least insofar as the one constant in dress norms is a differentiation between the sexes.[57] In ignoring the social aspects of gender, far from challenging sexual stereotypes, the courts have paradoxically, through the device of the SDA, entrenched them:

> The . . . [court's] decision, validating a [policy of refusing to allow women to wear trousers to work] if analogous, albeit different, restrictions are imposed on men, is

---

53 See Chap 6.

54 SDA, s 1(1) and (2)(a).

55 'Gender' in this context referring to the socially constructive differences between the sexes.

56 D Pannick, *Sex Discrimination Law* (1985, Oxford), 183.

57 See, for example, *Schmidt v Austicks Bookshops Limited* [1978] ICR 85 and discussion in Chap 6.

> not convincing. That an employer is requiring men to do what they normally do—wear trousers—and asking women to do what they normally do—wear skirts—cannot, of itself, amount to a non-discriminatory policy. Otherwise employers would always have a defence if their practices mirrored social behaviour. This would clearly conflict with the major objective of the 1975 Act, which was introduced precisely because aspects of social behaviour were unfair to women.[58]

Nevertheless the courts remain resolutely unwilling to address socially constructed notions of difference as between the sexes where to do so would challenge deeply entrenched social norms. Dress codes are one example,[59] but 'gender' identity, as it manifests itself more broadly and specifically by sexual orientation, has largely fallen outside the protection of the SDA because of the narrow reading of 'sex'.

The courts do not regard sexual orientation (or presumably, therefore, any sexual expression) as 'gendered' or attributable to socially constructed gender roles, but rather it is viewed as something biologically or psychologically determined; something that specifically situates us. This means that the courts regard gay men and lesbians as differently situated compared with people who choose opposite-sex partners. As Robert Wintemute has observed in his writing, what causes discrimination against lesbians and gay men is not actually the sex of their partners but their own sex. In the case of a gay man, the relevant characteristic when considering the unfavourable treatment of him is his preference for male sexual partners. The relevant comparator, therefore, is a woman who has a preference for male sexual partners. This acknowledges that those who treat gay men and lesbians less favourably than they treat heterosexuals do so because of their sex; not because they love men (or women) but because they are men who love men (or women who love women). It is *their own* sex, rather than the sex of their partners, which is the problem.[60] Nevertheless in addressing sexual orientation discrimination, the courts have assumed that men and women will conform to their gender roles and women will be sexually orientated towards men and men towards women. **5.25**

58 D Pannick, *Sex Discrimination Law* (1985, Oxford), 187.

59 See *Department for Work and Pensions v Thompson* [2004] IRLR 348 for a more recent example of a gendered dress code—according to the EAT the question whether it was lawful or not turned on whether, 'applying contemporary standards of conventional dress wear, the level of smartness which [the employer] required of all its staff could only be achieved for men by requiring them to wear a collar and tie. . . The issue is not resolved by asking whether the requirement on men to wear a collar and tie meant that a higher level of smartness was being required of men rather than women. It is resolved by asking whether an equivalent level of smartness to that required of the female members of staff can only be achieved in the case of men, by requiring them to wear a collar and tie' (at para 30), thus reinforcing gender stereotyping.

60 Dr R Wintemute, 'Recognising new kinds of direct sex discrimination: transsexualism, sexual orientation and dress codes' (1997) 60 MLR 334 and 'Lesbian and gay inequality 2000: The Potential of the Human Rights Act 1998 and the need for an Equality Act 2002' [2000] EHRLR 603 and see too, Hale LJ in *Pearce v Governing Body of Mayfield Secondary School* [2002] ICR 198 at para 7.

Any departure from this—and into homosexuality—must be reflected in the identity of any comparator for the purposes of determining whether discrimination has occurred. So a lesbian must compare her treatment to that which was or ought to have been afforded a gay male and, assuming the treatment is equally bad, no discrimination will therefore be shown. That the treatment reflects the fact that she has departed from her socially constructed gender role, by preferring a female partner, and thus is discrimination against her as a woman and a woman who has not conformed to her gender stereotype, is not sufficient to afford her the protection of the SDA. In *Pearce v Governing Body of Mayfield Secondary School*,[61] the House of Lords distinguished 'sexual orientation' from sex in deciding that harassment of a lesbian teacher, because she was a lesbian, was not sex discrimination for the purposes of the SDA. The appropriate comparator,[62] according to the House of Lords, was a gay male who would have been treated equally poorly.[63]

5.26 The assumption was, then, in *Pearce* and in other cases adopting the same approach,[64] that sexual orientation is not gendered and indeed gender neutral, as certain of their Lordships held in terms.[65] Queer theorists and many feminists would argue otherwise. Indeed many commentators recognize that sexual orientation is socially or culturally constructed and consequentially very much gendered. However, that is not so far reflected in our own case law.

5.27 European sex discrimination law has provided no compulsion for our courts to read sex discrimination law as addressing sexual orientation discrimination. In *Grant v South-West Trains Ltd*,[66] the European Court of Justice (ECJ) considered whether a woman, who applied for travel concessions for her female partner and who was refused on the ground that concessions would only be granted for a partner of the opposite sex, could properly complain of discrimination under Article 141 and the Equal Pay Directive.[67] These protected against sex discrimination connected with pay and related benefits. According to the ECJ, since the condition imposed by the employer applied in the same way to female and male workers, it could not be regarded as constituting discrimination directly based on sex.[68] Further, the ECJ considered 'in the present state of the law within the Community,

---

61 Heard with *Macdonald v Ministry of Defence* [2003] ICR 937.

62 For further discussion on comparators see Chap 6.

63 See Lord Nicholls at paras 3 to 9; *per* Lord Hope at para 66; *per* Lord Hobhouse at para 109; *per* Lord Scott para 114; *per* Lord Rodger paras 153–8 and 176–7.

64 See *Smith v Gardner Merchant Limited* [1999] ICR 134 and *R v Ministry of Defence ex p Smith and Others* [1996] ICR 740.

65 See Lord Hope at para 61 and Lord Scott at para 114.

66 Case C-249/96 [1998] ICR 449.

67 As to which see Chap 4.

68 Para 28.

stable relationships between two persons of the same sex are not regarded as equivalent to marriages or stable relationships outside marriage between persons of opposite sex. Consequently, an employer is not required by Community law to treat the situation of a person who has a stable relationship with a partner of the same sex as equivalent to that of a person who is married to or has a stable relationship outside marriage with a partner of the opposite sex'.[69] The position has now changed in Europe, as described in Chapter 4, and domestically, as described in Chapters 1 and 2, because of the enactment of legislation addressing sexual orientation discrimination. The case law remains significant, however, for its insight into the way in which the courts have failed to understand, and have therefore failed to properly circumscribe, the wide reach of gender-based discrimination.

Whilst transgenderism, transvestitism, and cross-dressing challenge the presumptive relationship between sex and gender identity, the phenomenon of gender reassignment has wholesale challenged the assumptions made about sex and gender. In an obvious sense the law cannot regard sex—and therefore gender—as immutable when it is changeable. It has historically addressed this dilemma by pathologizing transpersons. But with the increasing pervasiveness of human rights values and respect for human dignity, gender reassignment has been recognized and protected. Many commentators now recognize that 'gender'—that is the social aspects of an assigned sex—can be and are usually far more determinative of a person's identity than physiology. However, as mentioned, the SDA treats 'sex' and 'gender' as immutable and biologically determined. When forced, as will be seen below, by the ECJ to protect transpersons against discrimination, the UK did so not by adopting a socially determinative concept of 'sex' under the SDA, but by amending the SDA so as to make specific—and separate—provision addressing gender reassignment.[70] **5.28**

(2) Pregnancy

As to pregnancy, there has been much debate about the extent to which the concept of 'sex' protects against pregnancy-related discrimination. As was observed early on in the history of the SDA: **5.29**

> [i]t is one of the many paradoxes of sex discrimination law that while women have been systematically denied employment and other opportunities because they are, or might become, pregnant, industrial tribunals and the Employment Appeal Tribunal have yet to accept adverse treatment on grounds connected with pregnancy can constitute a violation of the Sex Discrimination Act 1975.[71]

69 Para 35.

70 See para 5.34 below.

71 D Pannick, *Sex Discrimination Law* (1985, Oxford), 145.

In *Turley v Allders Department Stores Ltd*,[72] for example, in rejecting a claim under the SDA from a woman alleged to have been dismissed on grounds of pregnancy, the Employment Appeal Tribunal concluded that:

> Suppose to dismiss her for pregnancy is to dismiss her on the grounds of her sex. In order to see if she has been treated less favourably than a man the sense of the section is that you must compare like with like, and you cannot. When she is pregnant a woman is no longer just a woman. She is a woman, as the Authorized Version of the Bible accurately puts it, with child, and there is no masculine equivalent.[73]

5.30 Later cases adopted a different approach (without reliance on the Bible), holding that a woman could claim sex discrimination arising out of adverse treatment connected with pregnancy but by comparing herself to a man in 'analogous circumstances (such as sickness)'.[74] If a sick man would have been treated in like manner then no sex discrimination was proved. This obviously provided limited protection—an employer could often readily prove that a man absent in fact, or expected to be so, for some weeks due to sickness would be dismissed. Both approaches faithfully reflect the scheme of the legislation which, as mentioned in Chapter 2, focuses on affording the *same* treatment to women as that afforded men. If a woman's actual condition could not be compared to a man, then either a comparable gender-neutral (or male) condition must be found to attribute to her male comparator or the claim could not be proved. However, such an approach necessarily deprived women of significant protection against discrimination connected to their gender and many strived to find a way around it.

5.31 In fact the courts were compelled to accept that discrimination connected with pregnancy was discrimination on the grounds of sex automatically, going further than the sick, or otherwise analogous, male comparator. The imperative for this came, again, from the ECJ, though the result is difficult to fit within the scheme of the SDA as originally enacted. In *Webb v Emo Air Cargo (UK) Limited*[75] the complainant was dismissed after having informed her employer that she was pregnant. She argued that pregnancy discrimination was automatic sex discrimination under the SDA because, although a comparison was required as between a woman complainant and a notional man, it was only possible to reach a result which accorded with the intention of the SDA if the phrase 'relevant circumstances' in section 5(3) of the SDA[76]—which requires that in undertaking any comparison 'the relevant circumstances in the one case' must be 'the same, or not materially

---

[72] [1980] ICR 66.

[73] At 70.

[74] *Hayes v Malleable Working Men's Club and Institute and O'rs* [1985] IRLR 367, having regard to SDA, s 5(3), see Chap 6.

[75] [1990] IRLR 124.

[76] See Chap 6.

different, in the other'—ignored the factor of sex (and so disregarded pregnancy). Where treatment was 'solely by reason of the physiological function of a woman in her pregnancy, which is unique and which is incapable of comparison with a male condition, then it must follow that the adverse treatment because of pregnancy is direct discrimination'.[77] This would be consistent with what would appear to be the thrust of the legislation and would ensure that gendered factors were disregarded in undertaking any comparison.[78] However, the 'automatic' sex discrimination approach to pregnancy contended for in *Webb* did not attract the support of either the Employment Appeal Tribunal or the Court of Appeal.[79] The House of Lords referred the question to the ECJ[80] asking for a preliminary ruling on the question whether dismissing a female employee because of pregnancy was discrimination on the grounds of sex contrary to the Equal Treatment Directive.[81] The *Webb* case was particularly challenging because Ms Webb had been employed as a replacement for a member of staff who was due to be absent herself on maternity leave. It was envisaged that she would remain in employment but nevertheless at the outset she was to function as a maternity replacement. Nevertheless the ECJ[82] concluded that dismissal in such circumstances because of pregnancy was direct discrimination on grounds of sex,[83] holding that:

> contrary to the submission of the United Kingdom, dismissal of a pregnant woman recruited for an indefinite period cannot be justified on grounds relating to her inability to fulfil a fundamental condition of her employment contract. The availability of an employee is necessarily, for the employer, a precondition for the proper performance of the employment contract. However, the protection afforded by Community law to a woman during pregnancy and after childbirth cannot be dependent on whether her presence at work during maternity is essential to the proper functioning of the undertaking in which she is employed. Any contrary interpretation would render ineffective the provisions of the Directive.[84]

---

77 See EAT, *Webb v Emo Air Cargo (UK) Limited* [1990] ICR 442, 447–8.

78 And would be consistent with the guidance, eg, from the House of Lords in *James v Eastleigh Borough Council* [1990] 751, see 763–4, *per* Lord Bridge and see too *Peake v Automotive Products Limited* [1977] ICR 480, 488 ('in deciding whether the circumstances of the two cases are the same, and not materially different, one must put out of the picture any circumstances which necessarily follow from the fact that one is comparing the case of a man and of a woman'). This decision was reversed by the Court of Appeal (CA) on other grounds: [1977] ICR 968, but the CA decision was itself disapproved of by a different division of the CA in *Ministry of Defence v Jeremiah* [1980] ICR 13 with Lord Denning sitting on both cases.

79 [1992] ICR 445; [1992] IRLR 116.

80 [1993] ICR 175; [1993] IRLR 27.

81 As to which see Chap 4.

82 *Webb v Emo Air Cargo (UK) Limited*, Case C-32/93 [1994] ICR 770; [1994] IRLR 482.

83 Following its earlier decision in *Handels-OG Kontorfunktionaerernes Forbund i Danmark v Dansk Arbejdsgiverforening*, Case 179/88 [1992] ICR 332.

84 Para 26.

5.32 The House of Lords[85] were, therefore, bound to give effect to the judgment of the ECJ, notwithstanding the difficulties of fitting an 'automatic' sex discrimination paradigm within the SDA. As Lord Keith observed:

> Sections 1(1)(a) and 5(3) of the Act of 1975 set out a . . . precise test of unlawful discrimination, and the problem is how to fit the terms of that test into the ruling [of the ECJ]. It seems to me that the only way of doing so is to hold that, in a case where a woman is engaged for an indefinite period, the fact that the reason why she will be temporarily unavailable for work at a time when to her knowledge her services will be particularly required is pregnancy is a circumstance relevant to her case, being a circumstance which could not be present in the case of the hypothetical man. It does not necessarily follow that pregnancy would be a relevant circumstance in a situation where the woman is denied employment for a fixed period in the future during the whole of which her pregnancy would make her unavailable for work, nor in a situation where after engagement for such a period the discovery of her pregnancy leads to cancellation of the engagement.[86]

This suggests that pregnancy itself, as a gender-specific condition, should usually be disregarded in determining the 'relevant circumstances', but that a complete inability to perform the only task required of the job, even if attributable to pregnancy, might nevertheless remain relevant. However, in *Tele Danmark A/S v Handels-Og Kontorfunktionoerernes Forbund i Danmark*[87] the ECJ held that the Equal Treatment Directive protects a woman against dismissal on grounds of pregnancy throughout her pregnancy and during her maternity leave and such protection was afforded equally to women employed under fixed term contracts as those employed under indefinite contracts. Indeed the approach taken by the ECJ is that the impact of pregnancy, as well as pregnancy itself, is protected by the principle of equal treatment, and this protection embraces not only absence attributable to pregnancy but also sickness attributable to pregnancy.[88] Accordingly, adverse treatment connected to pregnancy will always be automatic sex discrimination and to that extent the concept of 'sex' embraces pregnancy and its effects in the SDA, albeit that the same does not fit comfortably within its original scheme.

5.33 Amendments have now been made to the SDA to give effect to the Equal Treatment Amendment Directive,[89] and pregnancy discrimination is specifically

85 *Webb v Emo Air Cargo (UK) Limited (No 2)* [1995] ICR 1021; [1995] IRLR 645.

86 [1995] ICR 1021, 1027; [1995] IRLR 645, 647.

87 [2001] IRLR 853.

88 *Brown v Rentokil Ltd*, Case C-394/96, [1998] ECR I-04185 (pregnancy related illness); *Caisse Nationale D'Assurance Travailleurs Salaries (CNAVTS) v Thibault*, Case C-136/95 [1998] ECR I-2011; [1998] IRLR 399 (deprival of the right to an annual assessment of performance and, therefore, of the opportunity of qualifying for promotion to a higher pay grade as a result of absence on account of maternity leave); *Land Brandenburg v Sass*, Case C-284/02 [2005] IRLR 147 (failure to have regard—for seniority purposes—to periods whilst absent on maternity leave).

89 Council Directive 2002/73/EC amending Council Directive 76/207/EEC on the implementation of the principle of equal treatment for men and women as regards access to employment, vocational training and promotion, and working conditions. See Chap 4.

addressed.[90] Now section 3A of the SDA defines discrimination for certain purposes as including less favourable treatment on the ground of a woman's pregnancy, where such treatment occurs 'at a time in a protected period' or on the ground that a woman is exercising or seeking to exercise, or has exercised or sought to exercise, her statutory right to maternity leave. The protected period is defined[91] and the scope of the protection afforded against this form of pregnancy discrimination is limited.[92] However, the provision made is likely to be seen as regressive and incompatible with EU sex discrimination law.[93] This is because the Employment Equality (Sex Discrimination) Regulations 2005[94] which amend the SDA purportedly to give effect to the Equal Treatment Amendment Directive and which are discussed in Chapters 4 and 6 narrow the circumstances in which pregnancy discrimination will constitute 'automatic' discrimination and in which pregnancy discrimination is outlawed.[95] Firstly, pregnancy-related discrimination is only outlawed where 'at a time in a protected period [namely between the beginning of pregnancy and the end of maternity leave], and on the ground of the woman's pregnancy, the person treats her less favourably than he would treat her had she not become pregnant'.[96] No such comparison is required by EU law.[97] Secondly, when treated as automatic sex discrimination the courts, including the House of Lords in *Webb*, made no distinction between the different unlawful acts created by the SDA. Pregnancy discrimination was automatic sex discrimination apparently whatever the circumstance, at least in so far as there were no other 'relevant' circumstances[98] because it was the definitional section in Part I that was interpreted in a way as to protect against pregnancy discrimination. This meant that pregnancy discrimination was outlawed across all activities within the scope

[90] The only reference to pregnancy in the context of discrimination had been in SDA, s 2(2) which provided that in the application of the provision requiring that s 1 should be read as applying equally to the treatment of men (so that discrimination as defined is made out where a man is treated less favourably as where a woman is treated less favourably etc) 'no account shall be taken of special treatment afforded to women in connection with pregnancy or childbirth', thus apparently allowing for, though not requiring more favourable treatment to be afforded women on account of their pregnancy.

[91] See s 3A(3), discussed at Chap 6.

[92] See SDA, s 3A(5), discussed at Chap 6.

[93] See Chap 4.

[94] SI 2005/2467.

[95] SDA, ss 3A and 6A.

[96] S 3A. See s 3A(2) for protection in relation to maternity leave and, therefore, a form of pregnancy-related victimization, discussed in Chap 6.

[97] *Gillespie v Northern Health and Social Services Board*, Case C-342/93 [1996] ICR 498 ('women taking maternity leave. . . are in a special position which requires them to be afforded special protection, but which is not comparable either with that of a man or with that of a woman actually at work', para 17).

[98] As in the case of *Webb* where it was suggested that, as seen above, an absence from work for the entirety or bulk of the contract in the case of a fixed term contract may be a relevant circumstance.

of the SDA, without exception. As discussed in Chapter 8, section 6A has modified this position. For the consequences of any regressive impact of the new Regulations and the new protection against pregnancy discrimination, see Chapter 4. It is certainly arguable that to the extent that any pregnancy discrimination does not fall within the new section 3A, it must be regarded as falling within the unamended direct discrimination provisions because the House of Lords in *Webb* have so held and it would be contrary to EU law to hold that any amended provision reduces the extended protection hitherto provided.[99]

(3) Gender reassignment

5.34 As to the impact of a change in sex or assigned sex, the courts have addressed this issue in a series of cases which have resulted in domestic legislative change, driven principally by EU and ECHR law.

5.35 In *P v S and Cornwall County Council*[100] the ECJ considered the question whether discrimination connected to gender reassignment fell within the scope of the Equal Treatment Directive.[101] The case concerned a male employee who proposed to undergo gender reassignment. On informing her employer of the same she was dismissed. She complained of discrimination on the grounds of sex. On a reference to the ECJ, it was held that the Equal Treatment Directive provided protection against discrimination in such circumstances. According to the ECJ '[t]he scope of the Directive cannot be confined simply to discrimination based on the fact that a person is of one or other sex'. In the view of the ECJ, the purpose of the Equal Treatment Directive is also such as to apply to discrimination arising from the gender reassignment of the person concerned because '[t]o tolerate such discrimination would be tantamount, as regards such a person, to a failure to respect the dignity and freedom to which he or she is entitled, and which the court has a duty to safeguard'.[102]

5.36 In consequence the UK Government made amendments to the SDA so as to make specific provision under a new section 2A[103] that outlawed direct discrimination in the employment field on the ground that a person intended to undergo, was undergoing, or had undergone gender reassignment.[104] The UK Government therefore gave minimum effect to the judgment of the ECJ outlawing only that discrimination which the ECJ found in the particular case. The amendments

---

99 See Chap 6.

100 Case C-13/94 [1996] ICR 795; [1996] IRLR 347.

101 As to which, see Chap 4.

102 Paras 20–2. See too the instructive views of Advocate-General Tesauro, paras 9 and 17.

103 Inserted by regulations made under the European Communities Act 1972 (Sex Discrimination (Gender Reassignment) Regulations 1999 SI 1999/1102.

104 S 2A(1).

made did not extend to indirect discrimination or discrimination outside the employment and related fields. It is difficult to see how the absence of protection against indirect discrimination can be consistent with the judgment in *P v S* which made no distinction between 'sex' for the purposes of the direct discrimination provisions of the Equal Treatment Directive and for the purposes of the indirect discrimination provisions. In *KB v National Health Service Pensions Agency and A'or*,[105] the ECJ concluded that a rule which restricted a survivor's pension to married couples, excluding unmarried couples, was contrary to Article 141 where domestic law prohibited transpersons from marrying contrary to ECHR law. Such was plainly a form of indirect discrimination because 'there is inequality of treatment which, although it does not directly undermine enjoyment of a right protected by Community law, affects one of the conditions for the grant of that right'.[106] Any doubts that may have remained after *P v S* as to whether the EU law outlaws indirect discrimination against transpersons must be regarded as extinguished by the judgment in *KB*. The SDA has not been further amended, so only direct discrimination against transpersons is expressly outlawed, but a court or tribunal would be bound to construe the indirect sex discrimination provisions[107] as protecting against indirect gender reassignment discrimination post *KB* in the employment sphere at least.[108]

The decision in *KB* followed the decision of the ECtHR in *Goodwin v UK*.[109] In *Goodwin* the ECtHR held that the UK's continuing failure to recognize the chosen sexual identity of a gender-reassigned transperson constituted a breach of Articles 8 and 12 of the ECHR. Thereafter, in *Bellinger v Bellinger*[110] the House of Lords concluded that the requirement that the parties to a marriage be 'male' and 'female' under 11(c) of the Matrimonial Causes Act 1973 was such as to exclude a gender-reassigned person marrying in their reassigned sex. The expressions 'male' and 'female', according to the House of Lords, were to be given their ordinary meaning and they referred to a person's biological gender as **5.37**

---

105 Case C-117/01 [2004] IRLR 240.

106 Para 30.

107 SDA, s 1(1)(b) and (2)(b).

108 That is the sphere covered by the Equal Treatment Directive (see Article 3). See too, *Richards v Secretary of State for Work and Pensions*, Case C-423/04 [2006] for the impact of gender reassignment on sex discriminatory retirement ages. Once the UK is required to give effect to Council Directive 2004/113/EC of 13 December 2004 (implementing the principle of equal treatment between men and women in the access to and supply of goods and services) (see Chap 4), it will be bound to extend the protection afforded against gender reassignment discrimination further.

109 (2002) 35 EHRR 447. See, too, *Grant v United Kingdom* (App No 32570/03) BLD 2505061689; [2006] All ER (D) 337 (May).

110 [2003] 2 AC 467.

determined at birth.[111] However, the House of Lords declared as incompatible[112] section 11(c) of the Matrimonial Causes Act 1973 with Articles 8 and 12 of the ECHR. The effect of *Bellinger v Bellinger* on the meanings to be given the expressions 'sex', 'male', and 'female', however, is limited.[113] 'Sex' and 'gender' are still to be regarded as principally biologically determined with a limited 'blurring' in the case of transpersons.[114] This is acknowledged by the Gender Recognition Act 2004 which now provides a framework for recognizing a person's reassigned gender and gives effect to the decisions of the ECtHR and responds to the declaration of incompatibility in the House of Lords in relation to the same. It provides by its section 1 that a person of either gender may make an application for a 'Gender Recognition Certificate' on the basis of living in the other gender or having changed gender under the law of a country or territory outside the UK and that such application is to be determined by a Gender Recognition Panel.[115] The Panel must grant the application if satisfied that the applicant has or has had gender dysphoria, has lived in the acquired gender throughout the period of two years ending with the date on which the application is made, intends to continue to live in the acquired gender until death, and complies with certain evidential requirements imposed by section 3.[116] Where an application is made in respect of a person who has had a change in gender approved by an 'approved country or territory', again the Panel must grant the application so long as the evidential requirements imposed by section 3 are complied with. Section 3 imposes certain evidential requirements, so that there must be evidence from certain medical practitioners and the like. Such applications are determined by a Panel in private, notwithstanding calls by the religious right wing Evangelical Alliance for the Panels to hear applications for registration in public and for objections to be permitted by amongst others the applicant's relations and employers.[117]

---

[111] See paras 36–49, 56–8, 62–5, 71, 77, 80–3. The House of Lords was significantly influenced by the ramifications of any decision the other way and the significance of a change in the law in relation to the recognition of those who had undergone gender reassignment. As Lord Nicholls observed: 'this would represent a major change in the law, having far-reaching ramifications. It raises issues whose solution calls for extensive enquiry and the widest public consultation and discussions. Questions of social policy and administrative feasibility arise at several points, and their interaction has to be evaluated and balanced. The issues are altogether ill-suited for determination by Courts and Court procedures. They are pre-eminently a matter for Parliament, the more especially when Government, in unequivocal terms, has already announced its intention to introduce comprehensive primary legislation on this difficult and sensitive subject' (para 37).

[112] Under HRA, s 4.

[113] For Lord Nicholls' observations on sex and gender, see *Bellinger v Bellinger* [2003] 2 AC 467 at paras 28–31.

[114] Such has nothing much to say about intersex persons: *Bellinger v Bellinger* [2003] 2 AC 467 para 75, *per* Lord Hobhouse.

[115] S 1(1).

[116] S 2(1).

[117] See discussion in A McColgan, *Discrimination Law, Text, Cases and Materials* (2nd edn 2005, Hart), 720.

There are restrictions in relation to the granting of a full Certificate, so that one may not be granted to a married applicant, though in respect of such a person an interim Certificate may be granted and the issue of an interim Certificate amounts to a ground for divorce which, if granted, must then be followed by a full Gender Recognition Certificate. Again the reassigned person who has been issued with a full Certificate by the Panel is entitled to marry in his or her acquired gender but a conscience clause is provided for ministers from the Church of England and the Church of Wales who might otherwise be required (as ministers of established churches) to solemnize marriages where one or both parties to which are gender reassigned.[118]

The Gender Recognition Act goes further than the decision in *Goodwin* in that it does not require that a person has completed gender reassignment by, in particular, undergoing surgery for a Gender Recognition Certificate to be granted. Though surgery may be taken into account as evidence of transition it is not a necessary requirement for a Gender Recognition Certificate. The Act is not without its critics, however. It does not by itself provide for a non-discrimination or equality guarantee[119] and it requires that a person who is married must divorce prior to the issuing of a full Certificate which may create a friction as between the right to full legal recognition of the transperson's acquired sex and his or her right to a private life. The Equal Opportunities Commission, in particular, expressed concern about the position of spouses who may have provided significant support to a person who has undergone gender reassignment and whose financial position, together with those of their spouses, might be seriously jeopardized by divorce.[120] 'Press for Change'[121] and the Joint Committee on Human Rights were also critical about the requirement for divorce as a precondition for a full Certificate, but the Government did not give way, holding instead that 'marriage is of course an institution for opposite sex couples'.[122] **5.38**

The absence of protection against discrimination for transpersons outside the employment field is now difficult to sustain. The enactment of legislation addressing 'sex' discrimination outside the employment field by the European Council in the form of the Gender Goods and Services Directive[123] will inevitably impact on the Government's obligations to legislate in the field of gender reassignment **5.39**

---

118 S 11 and Sch 4.

119 Though a person in their reassigned sex might have the protection of the SDA in certain circumstances.

120 See A McColgan, *Discrimination Law, Text, Cases and Materials* (2nd edn 2005, Hart), 721.

121 A campaigning organisation for transpersons, <http://www.pfc.org.uk/>.

122 HC Debs 23 Feb 2004 col 53, *per* David Lammy for the Government, cited in A McColgan, *Discrimination Law, Text, Cases and Materials* (2nd edn 2005, Hart), 721.

123 Discussed in Chap 4. For its impact before the date upon which Member States must implement specific measures, see *Mangold v Helm*, Case C-144/04 [2006] IRLR 143.

discrimination. By Article 1 of that Directive, its purpose is defined as laying 'down a framework for combating discrimination based on sex in access to and supply of goods and services, with a view to putting into effect in the Member States the principle of equal treatment between men and women'. Given the judgment of the ECJ in *P v S*, the UK will be driven to make provision prohibiting discrimination against transpersons outside the employment field, if for no other reason but to give effect to their obligations in EU law.

5.40 As is discussed above (and further below), the progressive and expansive approach to the concept of gender discrimination seen reflected in the decision in *P v S* did not find reflection in either the domestic or EU cases on sexual orientation. Instead separate statutory provision was required.

(4) Married and civil partnership status

(a) Marital status

5.41 Apart from 'sex' discrimination, the SDA in its original enactment outlawed discrimination against 'married persons' in certain fields.[124] To this protection has been added protection for 'civil partners', discussed below. The married persons protected may be of 'either sex'[125] but otherwise no further guidance as to the meaning of the expression 'married persons' is given by the SDA. However, 'marriage' is regulated by the common law and statute, in secular society, and by religious law. It is, as is well-known, a hetero-normative institution and historically one which was patriarchal in nature.[126]

5.42 Both the common law and statutory definition of marriage, with which the courts in our jurisdiction would be most concerned, restrict marriage to opposite-sex partners. Section 11(c) of the Matrimonial Causes Act 1973 provides that a marriage shall be void if the parties are not respectively male and female. This reflects the common law definition of marriage.[127] In so far as this poses an obstacle to marriage for those who have undergone gender reassignment, then it is incompatible with Articles 8 and 12 of the ECHR, as scheduled to the Human Rights

---

124 SDA, s 3.

125 Ibid, s 3(1), now see s 3(3).

126 Indeed under the common law doctrine of 'coverture', 'marriage constituted of a legal obliteration of women's identity' (S Fredman, *Discrimination Law* (2002, OUP), 27), such that '[t]he very being or legal existence of the wife is suspended during the marriage or at least incorporated and consolidated into that of the husband under whose wing, protection and cover she performs everything' (W Blackstone, *Commentaries on the Law of England* (15th edn, T Cadell and W Davies, 1809), Book 1, Chapter XV p 430, cited in S Fredman, *Discrimination Law* (2002, OUP), 27).

127 *Hyde v Hyde* (1866) LR 1 P&D 130.

Act 1998, as addressed above.[128] Section 3 of the SDA, however, protects only 'married persons' (civil partners are addressed below) and not, therefore, those who have chosen not to marry or who, by reason of some legal impediment, cannot marry.

Adverse treatment connected with unmarried status, even where this arises because of an absence of an entitlement to marry in law, cannot therefore found a claim under the SDA unless it constitutes indirect sex discrimination.[129] This means that less favourable treatment of a gay man or lesbian on grounds of unmarried status, because legally unable to marry, will not found a claim under the SDA.[130] As to sexual orientation and marriage discrimination, EU law would not appear to provide any basis for contending that discrimination based on unmarried status, where the complainant is gay or lesbian so cannot marry, constitutes sex discrimination.[131] Instead EU law regards the situation of gay men and lesbians as relevantly different to opposite-sex partners for the purposes of marriage and so unable to claim discrimination in relation to benefits associated with marriage.[132] As mentioned above, adverse treatment based on non-married status may constitute indirect gender reassignment discrimination, at least for the period prior to the coming into force of the Gender Recognition Act 2004.[133] **5.43**

In addition, discrimination based on non-married status may be sex discrimination where a man in a comparable situation would not have been so treated. In *O'Neill v Governors of St Thomas More RCVA Upper School and Another*,[134] the Employment Appeal Tribunal concluded that a teacher of religious education at a **5.44**

128 See Chap 4 and para 5.37, and *Bellinger v Bellinger* [2003] 2 AC 467. S 11(c) was also the subject of an unsuccessful legal challenge by two women married to each other in Canada. They unsuccessfully alleged that the bar on the recognition of same-sex marriage was in violation of their Convention rights; *Wilkinson v Kitzinger (Lord Chancellor and Attorney-General Intervening)*, Case No FD005D04600 [2006] EWHC 835 (Fam).

129 As it probably would in the case of transpersons at least for the period prior to the Gender Recognition Act 2004, discussed above.

130 The Sexual Orientation Regulations SI 2003/1661, Regulation 25 excludes from its reach 'anything which prevents or restricts access to a benefit by reference to marital status where the right to the benefit accrued or the benefit is payable in respect of periods of service prior to the coming into force of the Civil Partnership Act 2004' and permits 'the conferring of a benefit on married persons and civil partners to the exclusion of all other persons'.

131 See discussion above, para 5.27.

132 *Grant v South-West Trains*, Case C-249/96 [1998] ICR 449 and *D and Kingdom of Sweden v Council of the European Union*, joined Cases C-122/99P and C-125/99P.

133 See, for example, *KB v National Health Service Pensions Agency and A'or*, Case C-117/01 [2004] IRLR 240. The Act came into force, in the main, on 4 April 2005: Gender Recognition Act 2004 (Commencement) Order 2005 SI 2005/54.

134 [1997] ICR 33; [1996] IRLR 372. See too, *Percy v Church of Scotland Board of National Mission* [2006] IRLR 195; [2005] UKHL 73, in which, although not involving pregnancy, similar issues arose.

Roman Catholic school had been discriminated against on the grounds of her sex when she was dismissed having become pregnant following a relationship with a locally known Roman Catholic priest. The employment tribunal concluded that she had not been discriminated against on the grounds of her sex because an important motive for the dismissal was not her pregnancy *per se* but the fact that the pregnancy was by a Roman Catholic priest. The Employment Appeal Tribunal concluded that this was sex discrimination, noting that a distinction between pregnancy *per se* and pregnancy in the circumstances of the case was legally erroneous, the concept of pregnancy *per se* being misleading because it suggests that mere pregnancy is likely to be the sole ground for adverse treatment. Instead pregnancy always has surrounding circumstances, some arising prior to pregnancy, some accompanying it, and some consequential upon it. Although the case did not turn on the absence of marriage, the same result would have followed had the school dismissed the teacher because she was pregnant and unmarried.[135]

5.45 As can be seen, there may be a close relationship between sex discrimination and marital discrimination. Marital discrimination is sometimes used as a proxy for sex discrimination, as where an employer will not employ a married woman because of an expectation that she will get pregnant.[136] Similarly, some forms of sex discrimination will constitute indirect marital discrimination (for example, a refusal to employ any persons who have children, thus apparently applying a gender-neutral condition). In particular, there has historically been a close relationship between sex discrimination and marital discrimination with women being refused employment when married because of prejudice about married women working and, importantly, concern about them getting pregnant and thereafter assuming childcare responsibilities. Marital discrimination is probably less common now, no doubt reflecting in part the increase in the number of families not connected by marital partnership (either because the parents have never married, are divorced, or comprise single parent households).[137]

(b) Civil partnered status

5.46 Recent amendments have extended the protection afforded under section 3 of the SDA to 'civil partners'.[138] A 'civil partner' is not defined by the SDA but like

135 An issue apparently alluded to in the case. See reference to the same at [1997] ICR 39 and [1996] IRLR, para 29 and 58 (and ICR p 48).

136 See the arguments in *Hurley v Mustoe* [1981] ICR 490; [1981] IRLR 208.

137 See discussion in T Modood and R Berthoud, *The Fourth National Survey of Ethnic Minorities, Ethnic Minorities in Britain, Diversity and Disadvantage* (1997, Policy Studies Institute), 23 *et seq.*

138 S 3, as substituted by the Civil Partnership Act 2004, s 251(1), (2).

marriage has a well-recognized meaning in law. Section 1 of the Civil Partnership Act 2004 defines a civil partnership as is set out in Chapter 2.[139]

As is well-known, civil partnerships may only be entered into, as section 1(1) makes clear, by same-sex partners. Opposite-sex partners may not enter into civil partnerships and same-sex partners are still prohibited from marrying in the UK. Much of the disadvantage attributable to a bar on same-sex marriage has been remedied by the Civil Partnership Act which affords civil partners most of the benefits afforded married partners, but the device adopted to remedy that disadvantage—different and segregated status—is not uncontroversial. There are some who consider that marriage is not an appropriate institution for recognizing same-sex relationships either because, for reasons of faith, tradition, or otherwise, they consider that marriage is a uniquely heterosexual institution, or because they consider that given its oppressive, patriarchal, and hetero-normative origins gay men and lesbians should achieve recognition of their unions by more progressive devices. However, the 'separate but equal' philosophy underpinning civil partnerships—which, as stated, are not available to opposite-sex partners—sits uncomfortably with an equality agenda.[140] In ruling that the common law and statutory bar on same-sex marriage in South Africa was unconstitutional, the Constitutional Court identified certain principles which were to govern remedial action by Parliament, as follows: **5.47**

> Parliament [must] be sensitive to the need to avoid a remedy that on the face of it would provide equal protection, but would do so in a manner that in its context and application would be calculated to reproduce new forms of marginalisation. Historically the concept of 'separate but equal' served as a threadbare cloak for covering distaste for or repudiation by those in power of the group subjected to segregation. The very notion that integration would lead to miscegenation, mongrolisation or contamination, was offensive in concept and wounding in practice. Yet, just as is frequently the case when proposals are made for recognising same-sex unions in desiccated and marginalised forms, proponents of segregation would vehemently deny any intention to cause insult. On the contrary, they would justify the apartness as being a reflection of a natural or divinely ordained state of affairs. Alternatively they would assert that the separation was neutral if the facilities provided by the law were the substantially the same for both groups . . . Our equality jurisprudence . . . emphasises the importance of the impact that an apparently neutral distinction could have on the dignity and sense of self-worth of the persons affected . . . In a context of patterns of deep past discrimination and continuing homophobia,

139 Se 1(1)(b) refers to Chap 2 of Part 5 which deems certain overseas relationships, between same-sex partners, to be civil partnerships whether the parties to that relationship desire it or not. This was the subject of an unsuccessful legal challenge, based on the Convention rights, heard in the Family Division in the summer of 2006; *Wilkinson v Kitzinger (Lord Chancellor and Attorney-General Intervening)*, Case No FD005D04600 [2006] EWHC 835 (Fam).

140 *Brown v Board of Education* (1954) 347 US 483.

appropriate sensitivity must be shown to providing a remedy that is truly and manifestly respectful of the dignity of same-sex couples.[141]

5.48 The difficulty with the Civil Partnership Act 2004 is that it aims to secure the same relevant benefits to gay men and lesbians whilst maintaining the present and continual exclusion of gay men and lesbians from the important social institution of marriage. It is therefore an exclusionary device and thus problematic in equality terms. Nevertheless, as mentioned in Chapter 2, the Civil Partnership Act 2004 provides many benefits for gay and lesbian people, and the SDA provides comparable protection to gay men and lesbians who are in civil partnerships as it does married partners, that is that they may not be discriminated against as such in certain spheres.[142]

F. Race

(1) Introduction

5.49 The Race Relations Act 1976 (RRA) outlaws 'race' discrimination. Like gender, much, probably most, of the underpinning of the concept of race is socially constructed. The assumption that there are significant biological differences between communities has long since been discredited. 'Race' is in reality much to do with the creation of an 'other', sometimes for the purposes of perpetuating economic exploitation.[143] It is sometimes defined as a cultural phenomenon, making '"race" into a synonym for ethnicity and a sign for the sense of separateness which endows groups with an exclusive, collective identity'.[144] 'Race' is now widely recognized as a social and political construct with a long history, originating in economic and expansionist imperatives and directed at legitimizing domination.

---

141 *Minister of Home Affairs and O'rs v Fourie and O'rs* (2005) Case CCT 60/04, *per* Sachs J, paras 150–1.

142 SDA, s 3. Paradoxically, it now means that the SDA does not protect gay men and lesbians as such against discrimination (*Pearce v Governing Body of Mayfield Secondary School* [2002] ICR 198) or for being unmarried, albeit that the law prevents them from entering into marriage (Matrimonial Causes Act 1973, s 11(c) and see para 5.42 above and SDA, s 3) but nor will the Sexual Orientation Regulations protect gay men and lesbians in respect of any discrimination against them caused by the fact that they are not married (Regulation 25). The law will only protect them under the SDA if they enter the institution established by Parliament to afford separate, discrete recognition (ie a civil partnership) so maintaining their status as 'other'. There is no protection afforded gay men and lesbians under the SDA for failing to conform to a gender (sex) norm through their choice of sexual partner or the through their inability (or failure to) marry. The SDA might therefore be seen to be a conservative measure in as gay men and lesbians are concerned.

143 As in the context of slavery.

144 P Gilroy, *There Ain't no Black in the Union Jack* (1992, Routledge), 3, citing E Lawrence 'In the abundance of water the full is thirsty: Sociology and Black Pathology' in Centre for Contemporary Cultural Studies, *The Empire Strikes Back* (1982, Hutchinson), 95.

As has been observed, '[r]acism is, therefore, not about objective characteristics, but about relationships of domination and subordination, about hatred of the "Other" in defence of "Self", perpetrated and apparently legitimated through images of the "Other" as inferior, abhorrent, even sub-human'.[145] So: **5.50**

> the differences between individuals which come to be seen as 'racial' [do not] have an objective basis. These differences do not bear with them a unique or constant order of determinate effects which applies regardless of the conditions in which they have to exist. 'Race' has to be socially and politically constructed and elaborate ideological work is done to secure and maintain the different forms of 'racialisation' which have characterised capitalist development. Recognising this makes it all the more important to compare and evaluate the different historical situations in which 'race' has become politically pertinent.[146]

However, to a large extent the RRA views 'race' and the characteristics that are usually ascribed to it as immutable and inherent in each of us. Also, like its sister Act the SDA, it is 'essentialist' in its approach so that diversity within communities is not recognized. In this respect it carries the danger of bolstering racism rather than challenging it.[147]

As mentioned in Chapter 1 and above,[148] it is not possible to speak of ethnic minority communities as experiencing racism, discrimination, or disadvantage in the same way and nor is it possible to speak of all people *within* ethnic minority communities as experiencing racism, discrimination, or disadvantage in the same way. They do not. (That is not to say that minority communities do not share the experience of racism—that is the common experience.[149]) The RRA does not recognize this, but like the SDA requires a complainant to assume a fixed and singular identity. Like the SDA, it guarantees equal treatment in the main[150] as measured against a comparator of a 'different' racial group (the preferred or 'in' group). As the SDA assumes that women aspire to the male norm, so the RRA largely assumes that black and people from minority communities aspire to conform to a 'White' or 'In' norm. **5.51**

Apart from its older historical roots, the concept of 'blackness', in more recent decades, has also been self-consciously politically constructed by those who regard themselves as 'other' and proudly adopt the mantle of blackness as part of political struggle. However, with increasing diversity within minority communities[151] **5.52**

---

145 S Fredman, *Discrimination Law* (2002, OUP), 53.

146 P Gilroy, *There Ain't no Black in the Union Jack* (1992, Routledge), 35.

147 S Fredman, *Discrimination Law* (2002, OUP), 53–4.

148 Para 5.03.

149 T Modood and R Berthoud, *The Fourth National Survey of Ethnic Minorities, Ethnic Minorities in Britain, Diversity and Disadvantage* (1997, Policy Studies Institute), 342 *et seq* and 353 in particular.

150 Indirect discrimination being a limited exception to this paradigm.

151 Some of whom now, of course, are white in colour having arrived from Eastern Europe.

and a greater conscious alignment with religion and other cultural indicators, upon which in turn prejudice and oppression is often now based, the concept of 'blackness' and colour-based racism is less easy to see as the most prominent identifier of a socially constructed concept of race. Nevertheless colour remains a key indicator of disadvantage[152] and 'blackness' a political badge with which many are familiar and can identify. The expressions 'black' and 'ethnic minority' are used below to describe those 'other' who by reason of the social constructions of race have historically and presently suffer disadvantage, albeit differently, and without the assumption of homogeneity which is often associated with such expressions.

(2) Racial groups and the Race Relations Acts

(a) The 1965 and 1968 Race Relations Acts

5.53 The first RRA in 1965 regulated discrimination in limited circumstances where it was on the ground of 'colour, race, or ethnic or national origins'.[153] As discussed in Chapter 2, the RRA 1965 was enacted to address discrimination against black people (or 'coloured people' as then described) and in particular recent black immigrants from the new Commonwealth.[154] The 1965 Act did not define colour, race, or ethnic or national origins, and there was some concern expressed early in its life about the extent to which it might cover certain vulnerable ethnic minority communities who did not appear to fall plainly within the expressions used in the Act. The Race Relations Board,[155] in its first report in 1967,[156] stated that:

> The limitation of the Act to discrimination on the ground of 'colour, race or ethnic or national origins' may exclude certain groups such as the Jews, Sikhs and the gypsies, which may not be primarily ethnic or racial, but which are so regarded by those who discriminate against them. The position of such groups should be clarified.[157]

It seems plain that the Government intended and anticipated that the expression 'ethnic origins' would be wide enough to embrace all disadvantaged minority groups. According to the Home Secretary promoting the Bill, the word 'ethnic' was included 'to try to ensure that we include every possible minority group in the country'.[158]

---

152 T Modood and R Berthoud, *The Fourth National Survey of Ethnic Minorities, Ethnic Minorities in Britain, Diversity and Disadvantage* (1997) Policy Studies Institute, 352.

153 RRA 1965, s 1(1).

154 See discussion in *Report of the Race Relations Board for 1966–67* (1967, HMSO) and the White Paper preceding the RRA 1976, 'Racial Discrimination' (1975) Home Office, Cmnd 6234, especially paras 3–23.

155 The predecessor of the Commission for Racial Equality, established under the RRA 1965 'for the purposes of securing compliance with the provisions of. . . [the RRA] and the resolution of difficulties arising out of those provisions', RRA 1965, s 2(1).

156 *Report of the Race Relations Board for 1966–67* (1967, HMSO).

157 Ibid, para 38(V).

158 711 HC Deb 3 May 1965 Cols 932–3.

Notwithstanding the concerns expressed by the Race Relations Board about the scope of the expressions used in the 1965 Act, the 1968 Act contained the same formulation.[159] However, it appears that Parliament's intention was not to limit the scope of protection but rather it considered the formulation already provided for was sufficiently expansive. Thus in promoting the 1965 Bill, Sir Frank Soskice, then Home Secretary, stated

> It is an objective which is of prime importance in the Bill that no grouping of citizens of whom one could, in ordinary parlance, predicate that they have, or are thought to have, or are merely represented to have, some common features or characteristics or origins that, broadly speaking, one relates to the stem from which they proceed . . . should be excluded.[160]

Prior to the White Paper preceding the RRA 1976[161] the House of Lords considered the meanings to be given to the classes protected under the RRA 1968 in *London Borough of Ealing v Race Relations Board*.[162] The case concerned the meaning of 'national origins' and a challenge to the conditions of acceptance on to a local authority housing waiting list. It was a condition of access to the list that any applicant 'be a British subject within the meaning of the British Nationality Act 1948'. A Polish national who was otherwise qualified by residence for housing accommodation was not accepted on the waiting list by reason of this rule. The Race Relations Board considered that the Council had unlawfully discriminated and brought proceedings pursuant to its power so to do.[163] The House of Lords were concerned with the question whether a rule relating to nationality was unlawful by reason of the prohibition in relation to discrimination on the grounds of 'national origins'. The House of Lords concluded that it was not. According to the House of Lords 'national origins' indicated a person's connection by birth with a group of people who could be described as a 'nation' and did not mean the same as 'nationality' in the sense of citizenship of a particular State. According to Lord Dilhorne: **5.54**

> 'Nationality' in the sense of citizenship of a certain State, must not be confused with 'nationality' as meaning membership of a certain nation in the sense of race. Thus, according to international law, Englishmen and Scotsmen are, despite their different nationality as regards race, all of British nationality as regards their citizenship. Thus further, although all Polish individuals are of Polish nationality qua race, for many generations there were no Poles qua citizenship. (Oppenheim's International Law, 8th ed. (1955), Vol. 1, page 645) . . . Just as 'nationality' can be used in these two senses, so can the word 'national'. Bearing in mind the racial objects of the Acts of

159 RRA 1968, s 1(1).

160 716 HC Deb 16 July 1965 Cols 970–1.

161 See Chap 2.

162 [1972] AC 342.

163 Under the 1968 Act. There were issues regarding the jurisdiction of the High Court to entertain proceedings for a declaration by the Council that the rule was lawful but these are of no contemporary relevance.

> 1965 and 1968, and that the words 'national origins' with the other words with which it appears explain what is meant by the word 'racial' in the long title, I think that the word 'national' in 'national origins' means national in the sense of race and not citizenship.[164]

The House of Lords decided therefore that 'national origins' was not a broad enough concept to embrace 'nationality'. This was so notwithstanding that the Act contained express exemptions addressing nationality. As was argued before their Lordships, it would be surprising if Parliament considered it necessary to exclude from the scope of the RRA discrimination on the grounds of 'nationality' if the grounds protected by the Act did not extend to it.[165] In any event this case is of very great contemporary importance because of the exclusion of 'nationality' from the classes protected by the new provisions introduced by the Race Relations Act 1976 (Amendment) Regulations 2003,[166] described above and further below.[167]

(b) The Race Relations Act 1976

5.55 The White Paper preceding the RRA 1976 drew attention to the 'anomaly' caused by the majority decision of the House of Lords in the *Ealing* case, discussed above, observing that:

> [t]he resulting gap in the legislation has created some anomalies and difficulties. For example, it is not unlawful to discriminate against someone because he is an Indian national but it is unlawful to discriminate against him because he is of Indian national origin (i.e. of Indian descent). It is contrary to the Treaty of Rome to discriminate against an EEC worker or his family on the basis of nationality. It is unclear to what extent the Courts would regard a person's place of birth as constituting his national origins. Moreover, the distinction between nationality and national origins creates an obvious pretext for discriminating on racial grounds.[168]

Accordingly the White Paper indicated that the Government had decided to widen the definition of unlawful discrimination to include nationality and citizenship,

---

164 At 358. See too, Lord Donovan at 354 and Lord Simon, at 363–4. At 365 Lord Kilbrandon alone dissented noting that the practical consequences of removing nationality from the protection of the Act were 'striking'. As he observed 'if "national origins" is not wide enough to include "nationality" then exclusion of persons by a notice which read, for example, "no Poles admitted" would have been of debatable legality according as the discrimination were interpreted as being against Polish Nationals or against persons of Polish origin' (at 368). Having regard to the practicalities, Lord Kilbrandon concluded that the result contended for by the Board 'leads to a result less capricious and more consistent with reality' (at 369).

165 See RRA 1969 ss 8(11) and 27(9) that made specific exception in relation to nationality in particular contexts. These provisions, according to their Lordships, did not shed 'crucial light' on the interpretation of 'national origins' (see Lord Donovan at 355) and were for the avoidance of 'doubt' (ibid), the references being made 'ex abundanti cautela' (*per* Viscount Dilhorne at 359 and Lord Simon at 363).

166 SI 2003/1626.

167 Chaps 2 and 4.

168 *Racial Discrimination* (1975) Cmnd 6234, para 56.

making appropriate exceptions where nationality or citizenship were justifiable grounds for distinction.[169] The RRA 1976, then, was more expansive in its protection, though not every community of persons, though a self-described group with a collective identity, commitment to a set of beliefs, way of life, or to a particular region, will constitute a racial group for the purposes of the RRA, as is considered further below.

Section 3(1) of the RRA 1976 defines 'racial grounds' and 'racial group', both of which are used as the foundation for the definition of 'racial discrimination' which is outlawed by the RRA 1976, as follows: **5.56**

> In this Act, unless the context otherwise requires—
>
> 'Racial grounds' means any of the following grounds, namely colour, race, nationality or ethnic or national origins;
>
> 'Racial group' means a group of persons defined by reference to colour, race, nationality or ethnic or national origins,
>
> and references to a person's racial group refer to any racial group into which he falls.

No other guidance is given by the RRA 1976 save that the fact 'that a racial group comprises two or more distinct racial groups does not prevent it from constituting a particular racial group for the purposes' of the RRA 1976.[170] Further, as is implicit in section 3(1) set out above, a person might be a member of more than one racial group (for example, White/UK) and references to a person's racial group include any racial group into which they fall.[171]

For the avoidance of doubt, the interpretation provision of the RRA 1976 provides that 'racial grounds' and 'racial group' have the meaning given by section 3(1) as just set out[172] and 'nationality' includes citizenship.[173] The RRA 1976 therefore uses in its title and in its main provisions 'race' as the benchmark for affording protection. This recognizes that which we all understand—nebulous though the concept is—namely, what 'race' means. For a racist it means superiority or inferiority depending on which group one is a member of and for others, at least, it means difference which, even if not capable of biological determination, can be recognized by all of us socially. **5.57**

---

169 Ibid.

170 RRA 1976 s 3(1) and (2).

171 See, too *Orphanos v Queen Mary College* [1985] IRLR 349 in which the claim was pursued, successfully, on the basis that the claimant fell into three racial groups. The Commission for Racial Equality provides guidance on 'Ethnic monitoring categories for England and Wales' available at <http://www.cre.gov.uk/gdpract/em_cat_ew.html>.

172 RRA, s 78(1).

173 Ibid.

5.58 According to the *Street Report*[174] protection against discrimination 'on the ground of colour, race, or ethnic or national origins' prevented discrimination:

> on the ground that a person is a Negro or a national of a particular country. The terms 'race' and 'ethnic' origins plainly overlap, but they are not to be treated as synonymous. We know that discrimination against Jews was intended to be proscribed by Parliament which apparently took the view that even if it could be argued that Jewish people are not a race they must be treated as having separate ethnic origins. At the same time, the Act deliberately did not interfere with discrimination on religious grounds.[175]

5.59 Each of the expressions used in section 3(1) is considered below. Importantly, because of amendments made to the Race Relations Act 1976 (RRA) to give effect to the Race Directive,[176] certain of its provisions do not apply to certain 'racial groups' as defined. The amendments made by the Race Relations Act 1976 (Amendment) Regulations 2003[177] only address discrimination connected with race or ethnic or national origins (the latter on the assumption that it is embraced by one or other of the two preceding concepts, both of which are covered by the Race Directive). These differences are addressed fully in Chapter 6. The exclusion of 'nationality' discrimination from the new provisions introduced by the Regulations is likely to be very significant, as discussed above and further below.

(c) *Colour/race/ethnic origins*

5.60 As mentioned, there is an obvious overlap between the concepts of colour and race and the latter is often used as a proxy for the first. Differences in treatment based on 'colour' are plainly within the scope of the RRA.[178] 'Colour' is self-explanatory as a matter of fact and given the origins of the RRA and its aspirations to protect 'coloured' communities against discrimination, its presence in the RRA is unsurprising. The concept of 'colour', however, is not merely to describe physical characteristics, and the comparing of skin complexion, as one tribunal recently did,[179] is neither required by the RRA nor is it appropriate. 'Blackness', and correspondingly

---

174 See Chap 2.

175 H Street, G Howe, and G Bindman, *Street Report on Anti-Discrimination Legislation* (1967, Political and Economic Planning) (the *Street Report*), para 1.1.

176 Council Directive 2000/43/EC, of 29 June 2000 implementing the principle of equal treatment between persons irrespective of racial or ethnic origin (those terms not being defined in the directive). See Chap 4.

177 SI 2003/1626, which, *inter alia*, enact a new meaning of indirect discrimination and harassment: see Chap 6.

178 See, by way of example only *(1) Armitage, (2) Marsden and (3) H M Prison Service v Johnson* [1997] IRLR 162 (prolonged racial harassment of black prison officer) and *Lambeth LBC v Commission for Racial Equality* [1990] IRLR 231 (advertisements for certain vacancies required that applicants be from the 'black community').

179 Tribunal sitting at Stratford (Chairman Mr S M Duncan): *X H Diem (known as Anita Ho) v Crystal Services Plc* [2005] UKEAT/0398/05, available at <http://www.employmentappeals.gov.uk/Public/Upload/UKEAT03980511112005.doc>.

'non-whiteness', have come to describe a collection of characteristics which are politically or socially constructed, as discussed above, and so sometimes, depending on context, such 'blackness' will be addressed by protection against 'colour'-based discrimination and sometimes not.

As to the concepts of 'race' and 'ethnic origins', these are not defined. They are best dealt with together because the uncertainty in their meaning is such that there tends to be an overlap in their use. 'Race' is said to denote the possession of particular biological characteristics, and is predicated on the discredited assumption that there are groups possessing significantly different biological characteristics to other groups.[180] In fact, as discussed above, there is no such thing as 'race' if the word is said to suggest 'that there exists an indissoluble association between mental and physical characteristics which make individual members of certain "races" either inferior or superior to members of certain other "races".[181] For this reason and to avoid the pejorative associations that might be said to exist with use of the term 'race', 'ethnic origins' is usually used. As has been observed: **5.61**

> 'Ethnic' is preferred to 'racial' as a descriptive term (though both are found in the legislation) because it stresses that groups to which it refers are the product of social organization and behaviour rather than a biological description of innate human differences.[182]

However, the concept of 'race' has been relied upon but usually where no other epithet seems appropriate. In *R v White*[183] it was argued that the word 'African' was too imprecise to describe a racial group because of the breadth of colours, religions, cultures, and traditions in that continent and the geographical breadth covered by it. Notwithstanding this, Pill LJ concluded that the court was not tied to the precise definition in any dictionary. Instead it was intended that the statutory language be given a broad, non-technical, meaning:

> Moreover words are to be construed as generally used in the jurisdiction of England and Wales. In our judgment, the word 'African' does describe a 'racial group' defined by reference to race. In ordinary speech, the word 'African' denotes a limited group of people regarded as of common stock and regarded as one of the major divisions of humankind having in common distinct physical features. It denotes a person characteristic of the blacks of Africa, to adopt a part of the definition in the dictionary.[184]

Certainly, what is clear is that whatever other reasons there may have been, the inclusion of the concept of 'ethnicity' was intended to give the RRA a wide ambit, **5.62**

---

180 See discussion in *Mandla (Sewa Singh) v Dowell Lee* [1983] 2 AC 548, 561.

181 A Montagu (ed), *The Concept of Race* (1964, Free Press), cited in A Lester and G Bindman, *Race and Law* (1972, Penguin), 154.

182 A Lester and G Bindman, *Race and Law* (1972, Penguin), 155.

183 [2001] 1 WLR 1352.

184 Para 17.

as discussed above.[185] Case law, however, has set parameters around it. In *Mandla v Dowell Lee*[186] the House of Lords addressed the proper meaning to be given to the expression 'ethnicity' for the purposes of the RRA by identifying what it considered were the core characteristics of an 'ethnic group'. According to Lord Fraser, for a group to constitute an ethnic group, it must regard 'itself, and be regarded by others, as a distinct community by virtue of certain characteristics'. Some of these characteristics are essential whilst others are not, but one or more of them will commonly be found and the existence of these will help to distinguish the group from the surrounding community. The 'essential' conditions are:

(1) a long shared history, of which the group is conscious as distinguishing it from other groups, and the memory of which it keeps alive;
(2) a cultural tradition of its own, including family and social customs and manners, often but not necessarily associated with religious observance.

In addition to those two essential characteristics the following characteristics were regarded as relevant, namely:

(3) either a common geographical origin, or descent from a small number of common ancestors;
(4) a common language, not necessarily peculiar to the group;
(5) a common literature peculiar to the group;
(6) a common religion different from that of neighbouring groups or from the general community surrounding it;
(7) being a minority or being an oppressed or a dominant group within a larger community, for example a conquered people or their conquerors.[187]

5.63 In consequence of the wide meaning given to the concept of 'ethnicity', Jews,[188] Sikhs,[189] Romany Gypsies,[190] European Roma,[191] and Irish Travellers[192] have all been held to constitute distinct ethnic groups for the purposes of the RRA. As to 'Gypsies', the Court of Appeal have held that they constitute an ethnic group for the purposes of the RRA when defined in the narrow sense of Romany Gypsies

185 See para 5.53 above and 711 HC Deb 3 May 1965 cols 932–3.

186 [1983] 2 AC 548.

187 *Per* Lord Fraser 562–5.

188 *Seide v Gillette Industries Limited* [1980] IRLR 427.

189 *Mandla (Sewa Singh) v Dowell Lee* [1983] 2 AC 548.

190 *Commission for Racial Equality v Dutton* [1989] IRLR 8, CA.

191 *Regina (European Roma Rights Centre and others) v Immigration Officer at Prague Airport and another (United Nations High Commissioner for Refugees intervening)* [2004] UKHL 55; [2005] 2 AC 1.

192 *O'Leary v Allied Domecq Inns Limited*, CL 950275, July 2000, Central London County Court (unreported, available from the author). Indeed Irish travellers are expressly recognized as a racial group (when defined as 'the Irish traveller community') within the Race Relations (Northern Ireland) Order 1997 SI No.869, NI6 which implements the RRA in Northern Ireland.

because of their shared history, geographical origin, distinct customs, and language.[193] Importantly, as the House of Lords in *Mandla* expressly recognized, the wide meaning given to the concept of 'ethnicity' means that 'ethnic' characteristics need not be 'immutable' or even born into. So, for example, a group defined by reference to 'ethnic origins' would 'be capable of including converts, for example, persons who marry into the group, and of excluding apostates. Provided a person who joins the group feels himself or herself to be a member of it, and is accepted by other members, then he is, for the purposes of the Act, a member'.[194]

Rastafarians and Muslims, on the other hand, though very much subject to prejudice and disadvantage, have not been held to comprise distinct ethnic groups for the purposes of the RRA. In *Dawkins v Department of the Environment*[195] the Court of Appeal decided that although Rastafarians as a group possessed certain identifiable characteristics, they did not meet the definition of an ethnic group, in part at least because their shared history (then around 60 years) was not sufficiently long to satisfy the tests set down in *Mandla*. Similarly, though for different reasons, Muslims have been held not to comprise a distinct ethnic group because of the wide geographical spread of adherents to Islam.[196] In both cases adverse treatment may constitute direct or indirect discrimination on other grounds. For example, in *Samuels v Capitol Security Services Limited*[197] discrimination against a black man of Caribbean origin for wearing his hair in locks was found to be discrimination on grounds of colour because the style was 'peculiar to black people'. In *JH Walker Limited v Hussain*,[198] discrimination against Muslim workers taking time off to observe Eid amounted to indirect discrimination against Asian workers. **5.64**

Efforts have been made in the past to include religion expressly within the RRA. **5.65** These proved unsuccessful, the Government arguing that a separate Act would be required to deal with all the issues peculiar to religion and that the RRA would anyway cover many cases of religious discrimination.[199] However, the effect of the decision in *Mandla* in particular was the morally and logically indefensible position that some religious groups, but not others, were protected against

193 *Commission for Racial Equality v Dutton* [1989] IRLR 8.

194 *Per* Lord Fraser, 562.

195 [1993] IRLR 284.

196 *Nyazi v Rymans Limited*, EAT/6/8 (unreported) (Race Discrimination Law Reports, Commission for Racial Equality, 85).

197 [1997] DCLD 31, 3.

198 [1996] ICR 291.

199 See HC Standing Committee A, 29 April 1976 and 4 May 1976, Cols 84–118.

discrimination under the RRA on the basis that they were also 'ethnic' groups. The Commission for Racial Equality took this issue up some time ago. In their first review of the RRA,[200] the Commission for Racial Equality drew attention to the House of Lords decision in *Mandla* and in particular its recognition of the often close connection between religion and ethnicity indicating that the RRA offered 'considerable assistance where the religious practice is a cultural norm associated with the ethnic group as in the case of Muslims, Sikhs and Jews'.[201] The Commission made no specific recommendations at this time beyond recommending that 'the question whether religious discrimination should be made unlawful and, if so, in what circumstances needs to be considered but in the wider context than that of an amendment to the Race Relations Act'.[202] In their second review, however, the Commission for Racial Equality had become bolder. They remarked that:

> [f]or many members of the ethnic minorities, their faith and their personal identity through their faith, and the reaction of the rest of society to that faith and to them as belonging to it are of the utmost importance. Indeed, for many, identity through their faith will be more important from day to day than identity through national origins.[203]

In their second review the CRE concluded that religious identity needed protection in law in a similar way to racial identity. The RRA was not, of course, amended to include religion in terms but instead, in consequence of EU law, separate provision was made addressing discrimination on the grounds of religion and this is addressed below.

5.66 The Scots and the English are not distinct racial groups defined by reference to ethnicity for the purposes of the RRA, according to case law.[204] In *Boyce and Others v British Airways Plc*[205] the Scots were held not to comprise a racial group by reference to ethnic origins, though the Scots, English, and Welsh comprise distinct racial groups as defined by national origins, as to which see below.

5.67 It appears that language alone will not be sufficient to define an 'ethnic' group. In *Gwynedd CC v Jones*[206] the Employment Appeal Tribunal rejected an argument

---

200 *Review of the Race Relations Act 1976: Proposals for change* (1985) Commission for Racial Equality, submitted to the Right Honourable Leon Britton QC MP on 13 June 1985.

201 Ibid, para 2.6.2.

202 Proposal 3.

203 *Reform of the RRA: Proposals for Change* (1998) Commission for Racial Equality, 7. Submitted by the Commission for Racial Equality to the Right Honourable Jack Straw MP, Secretary of State for the Home Department, on 30 April 1998.

204 *Northern Joint Police Board v Power* [1997] IRLR 610; *BBC Scotland v Souster* [2001] IRLR 150.

205 [1997] EAT 385/97. See too, for references to the same, *British Airways Plc v Boyce* [2001] IRLR 157.

206 [1986] ICR 833.

that the Welsh could be sub-divided as Welsh-speaking and non-Welsh-speaking ethnic groups.

In cases where there is any doubt about the extent to which a particular group constitutes a racial group for the purposes of the RRA, expert evidence will invariably be required and the issues are likely to be complex and, save in the most straightforward of cases or where there is already decided authority, problematic to resolve.[207] However, there may be fewer controversies now because those areas of particular dispute have generally engaged the overlap between religion and race. With increasing protection against religious discrimination[208] some of the old arguments about the scope of the RRA are likely to be of no more than historical interest. **5.68**

(4) Nationality/national origins

As has been seen above, the courts have drawn a distinction between 'nationality' and 'national origins',[209] though plainly the expressions may overlap. The distinction, however, is increasingly important as protection against 'nationality discrimination' is differently provided for under the RRA.[210] **5.69**

As to national origins, in *Northern Joint Police Board v Power*[211] the Employment Appeal Tribunal held that a claim based on being English could relevantly be brought as a matter of law 'under the umbrella of the phrase "national origins"'.[212] Reflecting the approach taken in the *Ealing* case, the Employment Appeal Tribunal considered that: **5.70**

> [n]ationality . . . has a juridical basis pointing to citizenship, which, in turn, points to the existence of a recognized State at the material time. Within the context of England, Scotland, Northern Ireland or Wales the proper approach to nationality is to categorize all of them as falling under the umbrella of British, and to regard the population as citizens of the United Kingdom.[213]

'National' origins, conversely, refers to 'identifiable elements, both historically and geographically, which at least at some point in time reveals the existence of

---

207 Examples can be seen in the case of *Mandla (Sewa Singh) v Dowell Lee* [1983] 2 AC 548 and *O'Leary v Allied Domecq Inns Limited*, CL 950275, July 2000, Central London County Court (unreported, available from the author), in the latter case involving disputed expert evidence; live evidence from expert witnesses and a 5-day trial before a judge sitting with assessors.

208 See para 5.142 below.

209 See para 5.54 above.

210 As mentioned above, see Race Relations Act 1976 (Amendment) Regulations 2003 SI 2003/1626.

211 [1997] IRLR 610 in which the Employment Appeal Tribunal were concerned with a claim by an Englishman that he was discriminated against on racial grounds when he was not short listed for the post of Chief Constable of the Northern Constabulary.

212 Ibid, para 5.

213 Ibid, para 9.

a nation'.[214] Thus discrimination against Scottish people and English people as such is discrimination on the grounds of national origins.[215] The same reasoning would apply equally to discrimination against Welsh people and, with at least equal force, against Irish people.

5.71 In *Tejani v Superintendent Registrar for the District of Peterborough*[216] the Court of Appeal concluded that 'national origins' referred to a particular place or country of origin. They concluded, therefore, that where a person was treated less favourably on the grounds that he was born abroad, without reference to any particular place or country, there was no discrimination on grounds of national origin. This was so, according to the Court of Appeal, even where a person born in the UK would have been treated differently. This judgment has been strongly criticized and would appear inconsistent with the general trend of the RRA and the other case law under it. It would seem to sanction discrimination against those from 'abroad' provided a discriminator had the good sense (or indeed profound ignorance) not to identify a particular country and would seem inconsistent with a purposive construction.[217] It is also inconsistent with case law suggesting that membership of a racial group may be defined negatively so that a condition of 'not being of UK origin' would suffice to mark out a 'racial group'. In *Orphanos v Queen Mary College*[218] (which was not cited to the Court of Appeal in *Tejani*[219]) the House of Lords was asked to determine a claim of indirect discrimination on grounds of nationality. Mr Orphanos alleged that a policy of charging 'overseas' students higher fees than 'home' students[220] amounted to indirect discrimination on grounds of nationality. Their Lordships accepted that a person could be a member of a number of racial groups at the same time and that racial groups could be defined negatively as, for example, non-British or non-EEC citizens.[221] Similarly, 'immigrants' and 'foreigners' will constitute racial groups[222] within the

---

214 Ibid.

215 Though not discrimination on the grounds of nationality and the occupants of the constituent states of the UK cannot be described as discrete 'ethnic' groups, see above.

216 [1986] IRLR 502.

217 As is usual with an Act with some social end and the RRA in particular, see Chap 3.

218 [1985] IRLR 349.

219 And as such the decision in *Tejani* 'was plainly per incuriam': *Attorney General's Reference (No 4 of 2004)* [2005] EWCA Crim 889 [2005] 1 WLR 2810, para 18.

220 In the case of 'home' students that being a reference to those ordinarily resident in the UK or other EEC country for at least 3 years before 1982.

221 The observations of the House of Lords on this point are arguably *obiter* but will be persuasive and they have been successfully relied upon since, see, eg, *Attorney General's Reference (No 4 of 2004)* [2005] EWCA Crim 889 [2005] 1 WLR 2810; *Jadhav v Secretary of State and others* (2003) Case Nos 2304705/01 and others (2004) EOR No 130, 19. And see too, *Dhatt v MacDonalds Hamburgers Ltd* [1991] ICR 238; [1991] IRLR 130.

222 *Attorney General's Reference (No 4 of 2004)* [2005] EWCA Crim 889 [2005] 1 WLR 2810, see too, *Director of Public Prosecutions v McFarlane* [2002] EWHC 485 (Admin).

broad concepts under section 3(1) of the RRA. However, the holding in *Tejani* has recently been upheld by the Court of Appeal in *Secretary of State for Defence v Elias*,[223] which had *Orphanos* cited to it[224] though it does not address it in this context. In *Elias* the Court of Appeal concluded that 'less favourable treatment on the ground that you were not born in a particular country is different from less favourable treatment on the ground of "national origins" . . . . . . [P]lace of birth is not a racial ground'[225] (though it may found a claim in indirect national origins discrimination[226]). This appears inconsistent with the broad reach given to the concept of national origins in the case law more generally and with the broad and purposive approach that the courts have urged upon the interpretation of the main anti-discrimination enactments.[227]

G. Disability

(1) Introduction

The Disability Discrimination Act 1995 (DDA) affords protection against discrimination[228] to 'disabled persons', or persons who have had a disability in the past, only. The DDA defines a 'disabled person' and 'disability' for the purposes of its provisions. The concept of disability does not have an autonomous meaning in law or otherwise. As with other protected classes the concept of 'disability' may be regarded as socially or environmentally constructed. As has been observed in Chapter 2, much 'disability' arises from social, including attitudinal, and environmental barriers. 5.72

The meaning given to 'disability' and 'disabled person' under the DDA applies only for the purposes of the DDA and is quite distinct from the meaning afforded to the concept of disability in other contexts. The fact, therefore, that a person might be 'disabled' for the purposes of some other set of provisions will not afford them the protection of the DDA unless they can also demonstrate that they fall within the meaning of a 'disabled person' as defined by the DDA itself.[229] The meaning of 'disability' provided for by the DDA, as will be seen below, is based very much on medical diagnosis and functional ability, with limited exceptions.[230] 5.73

223 [2006] EWCA Civ 1293, paras 91–7 and 122.
224 See, eg, para 162.
225 Para 122.
226 But this may, of course, be justified, see Chap 6.
227 See Chap 3.
228 Except in the case of victimization, see Chap 6.
229 Though for persons who have been registered disabled see below para 5.127.
230 Severe disfigurements, past disabilities, and other deemed disabilities, as to which see below.

The DDA principally concerned with diagnosis and the functional ability of persons who wish to be classified as 'disabled' under its terms, and therefore largely does not adopt a social model of disability and this is one of its weaknesses. It does not protect against discrimination on the basis of perceived disability.[231] Nor does it protect persons who are treated less favourably by reason of their association with a disabled person (for example, because they have a parent with a disability arising out of a genetic predisposition or because they have a disabled child).[232] This issue has been referred to the ECJ[233] and is discussed further in Chapter 6.

5.74 Other jurisdictions adopt more progressive concepts of disability in their anti-discrimination legislation. The Canadian Human Rights Act 1977, for example, defines 'disability' widely to mean 'any previous or existing mental or physical disability and includes disfigurement and previous or existing dependence on alcohol or a drug'.[234] It is more widely defined still in the Canadian Employment Equity Act 1995 which defines 'persons with disabilities' as:

> persons who have a long-term or recurring physical, mental, sensory, psychiatric or learning impairment and who (a) consider themselves to be disadvantaged in employment by reason of that impairment, or (b) believe that a employer or potential employer is likely to consider them to be disadvantaged in employment by reason of that impairment, and includes persons whose functional limitations owing to their impairment have been accommodated in their current job or workplace.[235]

This is a wide definition of disability, introducing a subjective element acknowledging the social aspects of disability.

5.75 Ireland also addresses the concept of 'disability' widely. Its Employment Equality Acts 1998 and 2004 describe the protection afforded on the 'disability ground' as extending to a situation where a disability exists, existed, may exist in the future, or is imputed to the person concerned.[236] In addition, the Acts protect against discrimination by reason of association with a disabled person.[237] The Ireland model,

---

231 This is likely to be inconsistent with EU law in the context of employment and related fields. See para 5.130.

232 This is also likely to be inconsistent with EU law in the context of employment and related fields. See Chap 4.

233 By the London South employment tribunal in the case of *Coleman v Attridge Law*, see *Equal Opportunities Review* (2006) No 155, 27.

234 Human Rights Act 1977, s 25. See too, Canada includes mental or physical disability in its constitutional equality guarantee in s 15 of the Charter. The inclusion of disability followed a specific campaign for its inclusion. See, <http://www.ccdonline.ca/FAQs/history.htm>, for history. Section 15 reads: '(1) Every individual is equal before and under the law and has the right to the equal protection and equal benefit of the law without discrimination and, in particular, without discrimination based on race, national or ethnic origin, colour, religion, sex, age or mental or physical disability.'

235 Canadian Employment Equity Act 1995, s 3.

236 S 6(1)(a).

237 S 6(1)(b).

again, therefore reflects the social manifestations of disability, reflecting the actual experience of impairment but also its imputation that may also cause prejudice and disadvantage.[238] The Ireland Equal Status Acts 2000 and 2004 define disability in the same way as the Employment Equality Acts.[239] The focus then is less on medical diagnosis and functional ability and more on the barriers, including attitudinal, facing people with actual or perceived impairments.

A medical model, as is largely adopted by the DDA, on the other hand, can act as an expensive distraction. Disability cases in the UK often become focused on whether a person has an impairment and then whether that impairment satisfies the rigid and medically based formulation provided for by the DDA (a study of the law reports illustrates this clearly[240]). This provides no support for those who are discriminated against because of perceptions around 'disability' or because of the prejudice associated with the presence of certain characteristics which might not, on closer examination, constitute a 'disability' in the sense required by the DDA but which amount to identifiable impairments. Though the issue is controversial some might argue, as is reflected in the comparative law described above, that an effective anti-disability discrimination scheme would focus on removing environmental and social barriers to full participation, rather than on the expensive (often in terms of time, monetary cost, and personal energy) exercise of determining whether a particular person has a relevant 'impairment'.[241] This is a matter upon which the Disability Rights Commission are presently consulting.[242] **5.76**

As mentioned in Chapter 4, the United Nations (UN) General Assembly have adopted the text of a Convention on the Rights of Persons with Disabilities.[243] It defines persons with disabilities as *including* 'those who have long-term physical, mental, intellectual, or sensory impairments which in interaction with various barriers may hinder their full and effective participation in society on an equal basis with others'.[244] This expressly recognizes the relationship between the **5.77**

238 See too Equal Status Acts 2000 and 2004 and Guidance issued by the Equality Authority on the same: *The Equal Status Acts 2000–2004*, Equality Authority available at <http://www.equality.ie/index.asp?locID=106&docID=226>.

239 Section 3(1).

240 For a full review, see K Monaghan *The Disability Discrimination Legislation* (2005, OUP).

241 See Chap 2 for a discussion on the Disability Rights Commission's consultation on the meaning of 'disability' Definition of disability: Consultation Document (2006) Disability Rights Commission.

242 See Chap 2 for a discussion on the Disability Rights Commission's consultation on the meaning of 'disability' Definition of disability: Consultation Document (2006) Disability Rights Commission.

243 International Convention on the Rights of Persons with Disabilities, <http://www.un.org/esa/socdev/enable/rights/ahc8adart.htm#art1>.

244 Article 1.

social and environmental barriers to equality faced by persons with impairments and the concept of disability.[245] The UK's approach is explained below.

(2) 'Disability' and the Disability Discrimination Act 1995

5.78 The meanings of 'disability' and 'disabled person' are defined in the first place by section 1 of the DDA, which provides that:

> (1) Subject to the provisions of Schedule 1, a person has a disability for the purposes of this Act[246] if he has a physical or mental impairment which has a substantial and long-term adverse effect on his ability to carry out normal day to day activities.
> (2) In this Act[247] 'disabled person' means a person who has a disability.

Each of these elements is further defined by Schedule 1, so that the effect of an impairment is a long-term effect if it has lasted at least 12 months; the period for which it lasts is likely to be at least 12 months; or it is likely to last for the rest of the life of the person affected.[248] Where an impairment ceases to have a substantial adverse effect on a person's ability to carry out normal day-to-day activities, it is treated as continuing to have that effect if that effect is likely to recur.[249] Further, an impairment is to be taken to affect the ability of the person concerned to carry out normal day-to-day activities only if it affects one of the following:

(a) mobility;
(b) manual dexterity;
(c) physical coordination;
(d) continence;
(e) ability to lift, carry, or otherwise move everyday objects;
(f) speech, hearing, or eyesight;
(g) memory or ability to concentrate, learn, or understand; or
(h) perception of the risk of physical danger.[250]

---

245 Though the ad-hoc committee chair at the penultimate session on negotiations on the text, suggested a definition of disability which reflected a more social model by describing 'disability' as resulting 'from the interaction between persons with impairments, conditions or illnesses and the environmental and attitudinal barriers they face. Such impairments, conditions or illnesses may be permanent, temporary, intermittent or imputed, and include those that are physical, sensory, psychosocial, neurological, medical or intellectual.' (*Working Text International Convention on the Rights of Persons with Disabilities* at the seventh session of the Ad-hoc Committee (16 January/3 February 2006)).

246 And for the purposes of Part III of the Special Educational Needs and Disability (Northern Ireland) Order 2005, SI 2005/1117, Articles 2(3), 48(1), (2).

247 And Part III of the Special Educational Needs and Disability (Northern Ireland) Order 2005, SI 2005/1117, Articles 2(3), 48(1), (2).

248 DDA, Sch 1, para 2(1).

249 DDA, Sch 1, para 2(2).

250 DDA, Sch 1, para 4(1).

Each element of the definition of 'disability' must be satisfied, so that the existence of an impairment, whilst necessary, is inadequate by itself to establish disability.

(a) The Guidance

The DDA now gives the Secretary of State power to issue guidance about matters to be taken into account in determining whether a person is a disabled person.[251] In its original enactment the DDA provided the Secretary of State with power to issue guidance about more limited matters, namely whether any impairment had a substantial adverse effect on a person's ability to carry out normal day-to-day activities and whether such impairment had a long-term effect.[252] The Secretary of State issued such Guidance early on,[253] and that Guidance remains material in respect of any complaints about acts occurring before 1 May 2006.[254] In respect of acts occurring after that date, the new Guidance applies.[255] The new Guidance takes account of the changes made by the DDA 2005. In either case, a court, tribunal, or other adjudicating body[256] must 'take into account any guidance which appears to it to be relevant' when it is determining whether a person is disabled.[257] An adjudicating body is not legally bound to follow the Guidance. However, the Guidance was formulated only after consultation[258] and was subject to Parliamentary approval (under the negative resolution procedure).[259] It is therefore regarded as important and authoritative[260] and explicit reference should always be made to any relevant provision of the Guidance which has been taken into account.[261] The Guidance, however, is just that—it does not impose a series of threshold tests and accordingly 'it would be wrong to search the guide and use what it says as some kind of extra hurdle over which the claimant must jump'.[262] As the Guidance itself makes clear: 'In the vast majority of cases there is unlikely 5.79

251 DDA, s 3(A1), as amended by the DDA 2005.

252 DDA, s 3(1).

253 *Guidance on Matters to be taken into Account in Determining Questions Relating to the Definition of Disability*, and this Guidance came into force on 31 July 1996: SI 1996/1996.

254 Disability Discrimination (Guidance on the Definition of Disability) Appointed Day Order 2006 SI 2006/1005; Disability Discrimination (Guidance on the Definition of Disability) Revocation Order 2006 SI 2006/1007.

255 Ibid.

256 Part 4 being the education provisions. See DDA, s 3(3A) for the meaning of an 'adjudicating body'.

257 DDA, s 3(3). Before the amendments made to the DDA 1995 by the DDA 2005, the more limited guidance was only *required* to be taken into account in deciding 'whether an impairment has a substantial and long-term adverse effect on a person's ability to carry out normal day to day activities' (unamended DDA, s 3(3)).

258 DDA, s 3(4) and (5).

259 DDA, s 3(6) to (12).

260 DDA, s 3(6) to (8).

261 *Goodwin v The Patent Office* [1999] IRLR 4; [1999] ICR 302.

262 Ibid.

to be any doubt whether or not a person has or has had a disability, but this guidance should prove helpful in cases where the matter is not entirely clear'.[263]

5.80 Unless otherwise stated the new Guidance is referred to below.

(b) *Impairment*

5.81 As has been observed above, the definition of 'disability' provided for by the DDA requires that the person concerned has a 'physical or mental impairment'. In the original enactment, the DDA required that in the latter case, where the impairment comprised a 'mental illness', it had to be 'clinically well recognized'[264] but that problematic requirement was repealed by the DDA 2005.[265] The DDA does not now define either 'physical impairment' or 'mental impairment'. The Guidance provides only that:

> [t]he definition requires that the effects which a person may experience must arise from a physical or mental impairment. The term mental or physical impairment should be given its ordinary meaning. In many cases, there will be no dispute whether a person has an impairment. Any disagreement is more likely to be about whether the effects of the impairment are sufficient to fall within the definition. Even so, it may sometimes be necessary to decide whether a person has an impairment so as to be able to deal with the issues about its effects.[266]

It has been held that 'impairment' for the purposes of the DDA may:

> include medical 'conditions' of various kinds; . . . the expression may include some damage or defect not itself a clinically treatable medical condition such as a disfigurement.[267]

'Impairment', therefore, has been taken to mean:

> some damage, defect, disorder or disease compared with a person having a full set of physical or mental equipment in normal condition. The phrase 'physical or mental impairment' refers to a person having (in everyday language) something wrong with them physically, or something wrong with them mentally.[268]

'Impairment' in the DDA 'bears its ordinary and natural meaning . . . [it] may result from illness or it may consist of an illness'.[269] Of course, not all impairments for these purposes are visible.[270] A non-exhaustive list of illustrative impairments

263 *Guidance on Matters to be Taken into Account in Determining Questions Relating to the Definition of Disability* (2006), para 3.

264 DDA, Sch 1(1).

265 DDA 2005, s 18(2).

266 Para A3.

267 *Rugamer v Sony Music Entertainment UK Ltd; McNicol v Balfour Beatty Rail Maintenance Ltd* [2002] ICR 381; [2001] IRLR 644, para 29.

268 Ibid, para 34.

269 *McNicol v Balfour Beatty Rail Maintenance Limited* [2002] EWCA Civ 1074, [2002] ICR 1498, [2002] IRLR 711, para 17, *per* Mummery LJ.

270 Para A5.

is given in the Guidance.[271] Importantly, it will not 'always be possible, nor is it necessary, to categorize a condition as either a physical or a mental impairment'.[272] In the end it is a matter of fact whether a person has either a physical or a mental impairment—the underlying cause of any impairment may be hard to establish and it is not necessary to identify causation.[273]

The issue of causation may be particularly difficult to resolve in cases of *functional overlay* and *somatoform disorder*. In such cases, physical symptoms will have originated in psychiatric illness or psychological conflicts and will have become translated into physical problems or complaints. This is discussed further below. Further, as the Guidance makes clear, '[t]here may be adverse effects which are both physical and mental in nature. Furthermore, effects of a mainly physical nature may stem from an underlying mental impairment, and vice versa'.[274] The DDA does not require, notwithstanding the suggestion in some of the case law discussed further below, that the cause of any impairment be identified. **5.82**

Certain impairments are expressly excluded and these are discussed further below. **5.83**
However, the fact that it is not necessary to consider how an impairment was caused means that even if the cause is in consequence of a condition which is excluded (for example an illness caused by alcohol dependency[275]) it will still count as an impairment for the purposes of the DDA,[276] so '[t]hat the *identification* of an "impairment" for the purposes of the Act is a different thing from the *causes* that give rise to its being present, and also from its *effects* in terms of the limitations it places on a person's functions and ability to carry out activities, is apparent . . . from the structure of the legislation'.[277] Thus:

> [t]he Act contemplates (certainly in relation to mental impairment) that an impairment can be something that results from an illness as opposed to itself being the illness—Schedule 1 paragraph 1(1). It can thus be cause or effect. No rigid distinction seems to be insisted on and the blurring which occurs in ordinary usage would seem to be something the Act is prepared to tolerate.[278]

---

271 Para A6.

272 Para A7.

273 *Millar v Inland Revenue Commissioners* [2006] IRLR 112, which concerned the position before the amendments made by the DDA 2005, but the broad observations about causation and physical impairments (see para 23) can be taken to apply equally to mental and physical impairments now that the 'mental illness' criterion in DDA, Sch 1, para 1(1) has been repealed.

274 Para A7.

275 See para 5.93 below.

276 Guidance, para A14. And see *Power v Panasonic UK Ltd* [2003] IRLR 151.

277 *Rugamer v Sony Music Entertainment UK Ltd; McNicol v Balfour Beatty Rail Maintenance Ltd* [2002] ICR 381; [2001] IRLR 644, para 32.

278 *College of Ripon and York St John v Hobbs* [2002] IRLR 185 at para 32, approved by Mummery LJ in *McNicol v Balfour Beatty Rail Maintenance Limited* [2002] EWCA Civ 1074, [2002] ICR 1498, [2002] IRLR 711, paras 17, 18.

However, as is discussed further below, for the purposes of making out any claim in discrimination under the DDA, the *cause* of any discrimination, as opposed to the cause of any impairment, must be established and if the *cause* is an excluded condition, then any claim under the DDA will fail.

5.84 The identification of an impairment as 'mental' or 'physical' was important before the amendments made to the DDA 1995 by the DDA 2005. As mentioned, in its original enactment the DDA 1995 required that 'mental impairment' for its purposes included impairments resulting from or consisting of a mental illness only if the illness was 'clinically well-recognised'.[279] This meant that any mental illness relied upon to found a claim in disability discrimination had to be recognized by a respected body of medical opinion.[280] In consequence it was sometimes important for a court or tribunal to establish the origins of a particular impairment so as to determine whether it was necessary to go on and find whether such impairment was clinically well-recognized. The requirement to establish whether a mental illness was clinically well-recognized was controversial. The requirement imposed a threshold which operated as a time-consuming distraction often inundating the courts with medical reports and lengthy argument. This is not now required in cases arising after 5 December 2005.[281]

(c) Physical impairments

5.85 As has been mentioned above, the DDA does not define 'physical impairment' and it is not possible to provide a comprehensive list of all the physical impairments that might be covered by the DDA. The concept will include common conditions, such as epilepsy, asthma, damage to limbs or bones, muscle damage, cancer, diabetes, and physical injury. Sensory impairments are caught and thus deafness, other hearing impairments, blindness, and sight impairments are covered. There is no requirement that the physical impairment be 'clinically well recognized'.[282] The concept of 'physical impairment' is apparently wide enough to cover any physical impairment even if it has not been conclusively diagnosed.[283] The following have been held by the courts to constitute physical impairments: myalgic

279 DDA, Sch 1, para 1(1).

280 Guidance Part 1, para 14. See too, *Morgan v Staffordshire University* [2002] ICR 475, [2002] IRLR 190 at para 9.

281 DDA 2005, s 18(2) and SI 2005/2774, Art 3(1).

282 As was the position in relation to mental illness before the DDA 2005.

283 *Millar v Inland Revenue Commissioners* [2006] IRLR 112, paras 22–3. See too, *Howden v Capital Copiers (Edinburgh) Ltd*, ET Case No S/400005/97, cited in 'Disability Discrimination' (2002) IDS, 35 in which the claimant experienced sharp, griping pains which forced him to lie down as well as having other adverse effects on his well-being. Though no satisfactory cause was found for his pain, the tribunal accepted that his condition amounted to a physical impairment even in the absence of an exact diagnosis.

encephalomyelitis (ME);[284] soft tissue injury to the back;[285] epilepsy;[286] photosensitive epilepsy;[287] cerebral palsy;[288] multiple sclerosis;[289] and migrainous neuralgia (migraine).[290]

Difficulties have arisen in relation to 'functional overlay' cases, as mentioned above. These are cases where the claimant has physical symptoms but these are unexplained by any organic or physical cause but are the manifestation of the claimant's psychological state. This phenomenon is described as 'functional or physical overlay' or, sometimes, somatoform disorder. Such a condition has been held not to amount to a physical impairment for the purposes of the DDA. This was important because of the distinction in the original DDA between mental and physical impairments. In the former case, as seen above, it was necessary to show that where such comprised a mental illness, it was clinically well recognized. In *McNicol v Balfour Beatty Rail Maintenance Limited*[291] the Court of Appeal considered the question of disability in circumstances where the claimant contended that he had a physical impairment resulting from a compression injury to his spine but about which there was no evidence before the employment tribunal of any organic physical pathology. The medical evidence before the employment tribunal suggested that the explanation for the claimant's symptoms might lie in some psychological or psychiatric impairment, or that they were fabricated. The employment tribunal concluded that the claimant was not disabled. The Court of Appeal rejected an appeal by the claimant principally on the basis that there was no error of law disclosed by the decision of the employment tribunal. In so doing the Court of Appeal observed that the claim had been advanced as one of physical impairment and that the case highlighted the importance of (a) claimants making clear the nature of the impairment on which the claim of discrimination was advanced, and (b) of both parties obtaining relevant medical evidence on the issue of impairment.[292] It was made clear by the Court of Appeal that it was for the tribunal to make a decision in each case on whether the available evidence established that the claimant had a physical or mental impairment with the stated effects.[293] This approach did create real complexities; it did not appear to reflect the approach of the Guidance or indeed earlier authority expressly endorsed by 5.86

284 *O'Neill v Symm & Co Ltd* [1998] ICR 481.

285 *Clark v TDG Ltd, t/a Novacold* [1999] ICR 951 [1999] IRLR 318.

286 *British Gas Services Ltd v McCaull* [2001] IRLR 60.

287 *Ridout v TC Group* [1998] IRLR 628.

288 *Kenny v Hampshire Constabulary* [1999] ICR 27.

289 *Buxton v Equinox Design Ltd* [1999] ICR 269.

290 *London Clubs Management Ltd v Hood* [2001] IRLR 719.

291 *McNicol v Balfour Beatty Rail Maintenance Limited* [2002] EWCA Civ 1074, [2002] ICR 1498, [2002] IRLR 711.

292 Ibid, para 16, *per* Mummery LJ.

293 Ibid, para 19, *per* Mummery LJ.

Mummery LJ in *McNicol*.[294] However, as has been observed, *McNicol* 'was a singularly inauspicious case in which to elaborate sophisticated rules for the interpretation and application of the 1995 Act'.[295] Permission to appeal had been granted because it raised an issue of importance, but the fact is that the employment tribunal did not appear to accept that the claimant gave credible evidence as to those matters which founded his claim of disability making it a difficult case for establishing principle.

5.87 As is apparent from the above discussion, the focus of the DDA and the Guidance suggests that no fine distinctions are made between the origins of the effects founding the basis of the claim in disability but that the focus is on the impact of that upon the person's ordinary life. However, the facts of *College of Ripon and York St John v Hobbs*, expressly endorsed by Mummery LJ in *McNicol*,[296] are somewhat difficult to reconcile with the judgment of Mummery LJ in *McNicol*. In *College of Ripon and York St John v Hobbs* a joint medical expert found that the claimant had symptoms of muscle fasciculation consisting of twitching, and muscle weakness which created difficulty in mobility, amongst other things. The expert reported that the claimant required help in a number of day-to-day tasks and had mobility difficulties. However, he concluded that there was 'no evidence to indicate presence of a disease affecting the central or . . . nervous system to account for [the claimant's] described disability'. He concluded that there was 'no organic disease process causing the symptoms described by [the claimant] and that her disability [was] not therefore organic' and he was unable to provide an opinion on psychological aspects. Notwithstanding this report, the employment tribunal concluded that the claimant was a disabled person within the meaning of the DDA. They concluded that she had a 'physical impairment' on the basis that in the DDA the same meant that 'there is something wrong with the body as opposed to the mind'. They noted the extent of the claimant's muscle twitching which they said suggested that 'this symptom or manifestation is a product of a physical impairment'. They therefore concluded that the claimant had a 'physical impairment' and that it was not necessary for them to know what underlying disease or trauma had caused the physical impairment. This decision was upheld by the Employment Appeal Tribunal. The Employment Appeal Tribunal, in particular, noted that the claimant had not 'nailed . . . her colours to one of only . . . two possible masts', namely a physical or alternatively a mental impairment, and that it was correct for the tribunal to ask itself whether there was evidence before it on which it could hold directly or by ordinary reasonable inference that there was

---

[294] Namely *College of Ripon and York St John v Hobbs* [2002] IRLR 185, para 32; see *McNicol v Balfour Beatty Rail Maintenance Limited*, para 18, *per* Mummery LJ.

[295] *Millar v Inland Revenue Commissioners* [2006] IRLR 112, para 20.

[296] *McNicol v Balfour Beatty Rail Maintenance Limited*, para 18, *per* Mummery LJ.

something wrong with 'the claimant' physically, something wrong with her body.[297] The catalogue of symptoms and effects of symptoms described were sufficient to allow the tribunal to conclude that there was a physical impairment within the meaning of the DDA.[298] The medical evidence by itself concluded that there was nothing 'organic' to explain the symptoms but, the Employment Appeal Tribunal concluded, that was not sufficient necessarily to point to a conclusion that there was no 'physical impairment'.[299] Accordingly the tribunal's decision was permissible. This case sits uncomfortably with *McNicol* but, as mentioned, *McNicol* was a difficult case not least because the claimant may not have been believed. In any event *McNicol* may now be regarded as less significant given the unimportance now to be attached to the distinction between a physical and mental impairment, the requirement to show that any mental illness is clinically well recognized having been repealed.[300] As such, physical symptoms, whatever their cause, may be regarded as physical impairments, whatever, and without the need now, to identify their cause.

(d) Mental impairments

Section 68 of the DDA[301] provides that: **5.88**

> 'Mental impairment' does not have the same meaning as in the Mental Health Act 1983 . . . but the fact that an impairment would be a mental impairment for the purposes of that Act does not prevent it from being a mental impairment for the purposes of this Act.[302]

The Mental Health Act 1983 defines 'mental impairment' as:

> a state of arrested or incomplete development of mind (not amounting to severe mental impairment)[303] which includes significant impairment of intelligence and social functioning and is associated with abnormally aggressive or seriously irresponsible conduct on the part of the person concerned and 'mentally impaired' should be construed accordingly.[304]

'Mental impairment', within the meaning of the DDA, embraces a much wider range of conditions than those provided by the Mental Health Act 1983.

---

297 Para 33.

298 Para 34.

299 Para 35.

300 See para 5.84 above.

301 The interpretation section.

302 Prior to the DDA 2005 the provision read that 'mental impairment' was also not to have the same meaning as 'in the Mental Health Act 1983 or the Mental Health (Scotland) Act 1984', which was repealed, in material respects, subject to savings, by the Mental Health (Care and Treatment)(Scotland) Act 2003.

303 Which is also defined under the Mental Health Act 1983, s 1.

304 Mental Health Act 1983, s 1(2).

5.89 As mentioned above, the DDA 1995 provided that a 'mental impairment', for the purposes of its provisions, 'includes an impairment resulting from or consisting of a mental illness only if the illness is a clinically well-recognised illness'.[305] That requirement was repealed by the DDA 2005.[306] It is still necessary to consider the impact of this requirement because it applies to claims arising before the coming into force of the repeals under the DDA 2005.[307] The 1996 Guidance[308] advised that '[i]t is very likely that [a clinically well recognized illness] would include those specifically mentioned in publications such as the World Health Organization's International Classification of Diseases [WHOICD]'.[309] Chapter V(F) of ICD-10 classifies a whole series of conditions which might be described as mental illnesses including Alzheimer's disease; schizophrenia; mood (affective) disorders, including bipolar affective disorder (manic depression); and panic disorders.[310] Similarly, the Diagnosis and Statistical Manual of Mental Disorders (DSM-IV)[311] classifies Alzheimer's, schizophrenia, manic depression, major depressive disorder, psychotic disorder, Asperger's disorder, and many others. A mental illness that falls within either of these classification systems will be regarded as 'clinically well recognized'.[312] It follows that if an impairment is recognized within one classification system but not another it may nevertheless be 'clinically well recognized' for the purposes of the DDA—the DDA does not require that it be universally well recognized. The WHOICD and DSM-IV manuals, for example, are not identical and they may contain different diagnostic criteria for the same condition. This means that the application of certain criteria can produce different outcomes according to which classification system is relied upon. In *Blackledge v London General Transport Services Ltd*[313] the claimant claimed that he suffered from post-traumatic stress disorder arising out of experiences whilst serving in the Coldstream Guards when he saw a friend being killed and witnessed shootings and deaths. In consequence he suffered flashbacks and intrusive memories of the

---

305 DDA, Sch 1, para 1(1).

306 DDA 2005, s 18(2).

307 In the case of this repeal, 5 December 2005: Disability Discrimination Act 2005 (Commencement No 2) Order 2005 SI 2005/2774.

308 *Guidance on Matters to be taken into Account in Determining Questions Relating to the Definition of Disability* (the Guidance), and this guidance came into force on 31 July 1996: SI 1996/1996.

309 Ibid, para 14. See, International Statistical Classification of Diseases and Related Health Problems, 10th Revision, Version for 2006, available at http://www3.who.int/icd/currentversion/fr-icd.htm.

310 Ibid. Also see *Morgan v Staffordshire University* [2002] ICR 475, [2002] IRLR 190 at para 9.

311 Published by the American Psychiatric Association, this provides another classification system for the identification of mental impairments.

312 Guidance Part 1, para 14. Also *Morgan v Staffordshire University* [2002] ICR 475; [2002] IRLR 190.

313 EAT 1073/00; 2003 WL 21491959.

violence he had witnessed. He was seen by a clinician and diagnosed with post-traumatic stress disorder with a co-morbid alcohol and drug dependent syndrome. The diagnosis was made in accordance with the diagnostic criteria set out in ICD-10. Thereafter he was seen by a consultant psychiatrist instructed on behalf of the respondents who concluded that whilst the claimant had experienced post-traumatic stress symptoms his condition did not warrant a diagnosis of post-traumatic stress disorder according to the diagnostic criteria set out in DSM-IV. The tribunal found that his symptoms did not warrant a diagnosis of post-traumatic stress disorder, having regard to DSM-IV. The Employment Appeal Tribunal allowed an appeal on the basis that the tribunal at first instance had applied different aspects of both classification systems. They noted that ICD-10 was the classification system recognized by the National Health Service (NHS) and it was therefore difficult to see why that was not used by the tribunal.[314] Reliance should therefore be placed on one or other classification system and the conflation of more than one may impose a threshold upon the claimant which is unfair. It seems there is some indication that ICD-10 should be used in preference, at least where it does not disadvantage a claimant.

In *Morgan v Staffordshire University*[315] Lindsay J for the Employment Appeal Tribunal identified four possible routes to establishing the existence of a mental impairment for the purposes of the DDA, namely proof of a *mental illness* specifically mentioned as such in the World Health Organization's International Classification of Diseases (WHOICD), proof of a *mental illness* specifically mentioned in a publication 'such as' that classification (presumably therefore referring to some other classification of very wide professional acceptance), and proof by other means of a *mental illness* recognized by a respected body of medical opinion. A fourth route derives from the use of the word 'includes' in paragraph 1(1), Schedule 1 of the DDA: **5.90**

> If, as a matter of medical opinion and possibility, there may exist a state recognizable as mental impairment yet which neither results from nor consists of a mental illness, then such state could be accepted as a mental impairment within the Act because the statutory definition is inclusive only, rather than purporting to exclude anything not expressly described by it. This fourth category is likely to be rarely if ever invoked and could be expected to require substantial and very specific medical evidence to support its existence.

The first three routes are uncontroversial and of decreasing importance given the amendments made by the DDA 2005. The fourth route should also be

314 In addition, the extra requirement in DSM-IV imposed was more relevant to deciding the effect on function which a mental impairment has rather than deciding whether a mental impairment existed, paras 18–20.

315 [2002] ICR 475; [2002] IRLR 190, para 9.

uncontroversial but for the comments of Lindsay J. Cases where a person has a 'mental impairment' which does not arise from a mental illness are unlikely to be rare; they might include mental impairments arising from congenital conditions as with some forms of learning disabilities. Though Lindsay J assumes such impairments will be 'rare' there is no reason to suppose this is so.[316] The 1996 Guidance makes it clear that the concept of 'mental impairment' includes a wide range of impairments, including those which are often known as learning disabilities, relating to mental functioning.[317] Such impairments did not and do not need to be 'clinically well recognized' in the same way as impairments arising from mental illnesses. However, they will require specific proof usually by some expert evidence.[318] It is unlikely to be sufficient to put a case on the basis that the claimant had difficulties at school or was 'not very bright'.[319]

5.91 Many mental impairments have been found to constitute mental impairments for the purpose of the DDA, including schizophrenia,[320] depression,[321] dyslexia,[322] Asperger's syndrome,[323] and borderline moderate generalized learning difficulties.[324]

5.92 Guidance on establishing a mental impairment given by the courts before the amendments made by the DDA 2005[325] should be treated with a degree of circumspection because such guidance was principally concerned with establishing whether any alleged impairment amounted to a 'mental illness' and then whether it was 'clinically well recognized'. In view of the amendments described above, these matters are much less important and in the usual case will now be irrelevant.

(e) Excluded conditions

5.93 A number of 'impairments' are excluded from the scope of the DDA. Paragraph 1(2)(b) of Schedule 1 to the DDA provides that Regulations may make provision 'for conditions of a prescribed description to be treated as not amounting to impairments'. The Disability Discrimination (Meaning of Disability) Regulations

316 *Dunham v Ashford Windows* [2005] IRLR 608, para 32.

317 Para 13.

318 *Dunham v Ashford Windows* [2005] IRLR 608, paras 37–38, which might include an appropriately qualified psychologist.

319 *Dunham v Ashford Windows* [2005] IRLR 608, para 37.

320 *Goodwin v The Patent Office* [1999] IRLR 4; [1999] ICR 302.

321 *Kapadia v The London Borough of Lambeth* [2000] IRLR 699 (reactive depression).

322 *Holmes v Bolton Metropolitan Borough Council*; ET case No. 2403516/98, cited in 'Disability Discrimination' (2002) IDS 49. And *Hewett v Motorola Ltd* [2004] IRLR 545 (Asperger's syndrome).

323 *Hewett v Motorola Ltd* [2004] IRLR 545.

324 *Dunham v Ashford Windows* [2005] IRLR 608.

325 See, for example, *Morgan v Staffordshire University* [2002] ICR 475; [2002] IRLR 190.

1996,[326] made pursuant *inter alia* to paragraph 1(2)(b), whilst not defining 'conditions' for these purposes as such, expressly provide that addiction to alcohol, nicotine, or any other substance is to be treated as not amounting to an impairment for the purposes of the DDA.[327] 'Addiction' for these purposes includes 'a dependency'.[328] In addition, the following conditions are to be treated as not amounting to impairments: a tendency to set fires; a tendency to steal; a tendency to physical or sexual abuse of other persons; exhibitionism; voyeurism;[329] and seasonal allergic rhinitis (commonly known as hay fever).[330]

However, these exceptions are more limited than at first glance might appear. **5.94** Firstly, as to the exempted addictions, this exemption does not apply to addiction which was originally the result of the administration of medically prescribed drugs or other medical treatment.[331] Secondly, and as to all the excluded conditions, these exceptions are material only where the *reason* for any treatment complained of is related to an excluded condition,[332] an issue which is discussed further below. Thirdly, and as to hay fever, this exception does not prevent that condition from being taken into account where it aggravates the effect of another condition.[333] Fourthly, and as observed above, an impairment *caused* by an excluded condition is not itself excluded. In *Power v Panasonic UK Ltd*,[334] the claimant was absent from work and was both depressed and drinking heavily. Expert evidence was called by either side and both experts tried to identify which came first, the depression or the alcohol abuse. The employment tribunal ruled that the claimant failed to show that she was a disabled person for the purposes of the DDA having regard to the 'addiction' exemption. The Employment Appeal Tribunal concluded that it was not material to a decision whether a person has a disability within the meaning of the DDA to consider how the particular impairment was caused.[335] It was material only to ascertain whether the impairment was a disability within the meaning of the DDA or whether, where relevant, it was an impairment which was excluded by reason of the Regulations from being treated as such. The claimant suffered from depression and it was for the tribunal therefore to judge whether this had a substantial long-term adverse effect on her ability to carry out normal day-to-day activities, regardless of its cause.

326 SI 1996/1455.

327 Disability Discrimination (Meaning of Disability) Regulations 1996, Regulation 3(1).

328 Ibid, Regulation 2.

329 Ibid, Regulation 4(1).

330 Ibid, Regulation 4(2).

331 Ibid, Regulation 3(2).

332 *Nuttall Edmund Ltd v Butterfield* [2006] ICR 77.

333 Disability Discrimination (Meaning of Disability) Regulations 1996, Regulation 4(3)—this might be relevant, for example, to conditions such as asthma.

334 [2003] IRLR 151.

335 See too discussion above.

5.95 The relationship between any excluded condition and an alleged act of discrimination is important. As noted above, these exceptions are material only where the *reason* for any treatment complained of is related to an excluded condition.[336] There is authority suggesting otherwise. In *Murray v Citizens Advice Bureau Ltd*,[337] the claimant complained of disability discrimination when his application to undertake voluntary[338] work with the respondents was not progressed following their discovery that he had been convicted of a violent crime as a result of paranoid schizophrenia. The respondents had no concerns about the claimant's illness as such but were concerned about the violent incident in which he had been involved.[339] The employment tribunal concluded that the claimant had a disability, namely paranoid schizophrenia, but concluded that because the respondents' concern was the possibility of a manifestation of the claimant's schizophrenia through violence and since that was excluded, as amounting to a tendency to physical abuse, the claimant's claim failed.[340] The Employment Appeal Tribunal allowed the claimant's appeal holding that 'conditions' within the meaning of paragraph 1(2)(b) of Schedule 1 to the DDA, under which the 1996 Regulations described above were made, refer to 'free standing' conditions 'and not to those conditions that are the direct consequences of a physical or mental impairment within the meaning of section 1(1)'[341] of the DDA. This is a broad approach but problematic. It is difficult to see how discrimination grounded in an excluded condition was really intended by Parliament to be covered by the DDA, in view of the terms of paragraph 1(2)(b) of Schedule 1 to the 1996 Regulations. It is especially difficult to see how the 1996 Regulations would be meaningful if the approach in *Power* were correct. Most tendencies to violence, exhibitionism etc are not 'free standing', as the law reports illustrate. In the main such tendencies arise from, or are manifestations or symptoms of, psychological or psychiatric disorder, like schizophrenia or depression. As was observed in *Nuttall Edmund Ltd v Butterfield*,[342] the real question in determining whether a particular impairment is excluded is not what caused the impairment[343] but what caused the discrimination complained of. Where a discriminatory act was *by reason*[344] of an excluded condition, then any claim will fail. However, if any discrimination was by reason of a non-excluded condition, then the fact that a person also has an excluded condition will be nothing to the point. Where the excluded

---

336 *Nuttall Edmund Ltd v Butterfield* [2006] ICR 77.

337 [2003] ICR 643 [2003] IRLR 340 EAT.

338 See Chap 8 for volunteers.

339 Para 5.

340 The employment tribunal found that such would have been justified in the alternative. For justification, see Chap 6.

341 Para 14.

342 [2005] IRLR 751; [2006] ICR 77.

343 As suggested in *Power v Panasonic UK Ltd* [2003] IRLR 151.

344 See Chap 6 for the meaning of discrimination under the DDA.

condition and the non-excluded condition form part of the reason for the treatment complained of then a claimant will have to show, not that the non-excluded condition was the *sole* reason for the treatment complained of, but that the non-excluded condition was an effective cause of the discrimination.[345]

(f) 'Normal day-to-day activities'

As seen above, the definition of 'disability' in the DDA requires that any physical or mental impairment covered must have an adverse effect on the disabled person's 'ability to carry out normal day-to-day activities'. The DDA thereby adopts a 'functional' model; that is, it focuses on how a person's functions are actually affected. As set out above, Schedule 1[346] provides that an impairment is to be taken to affect the ability of the person concerned to carry out normal day-to-day activities only if it affects one of the 'abilities, capacities or capabilities'[347] listed. This is an exhaustive list. It excludes certain functions that might be regarded as constituting 'normal day-to-day activities', for example, the ability to care for oneself, the ability to communicate and interact with others, and the perception of reality (though the concept of 'understanding' may include understanding normal social interaction among people, and/or the subtleties of human non-factual communication).[348] Such capacities are not to be regarded as relevant to determining whether a person has a disability unless they also fall within one of the enumerated capacities in Schedule 1 as set out above. **5.96**

In determining whether or not an activity is a 'normal day-to-day activity', regard should be had to the fact that this expression is not intended to include activities that are normal only for a particular person or group of people. In this respect in deciding whether an activity is a 'normal day-to-day activity' account should be taken of how far it is normal for most people and carried out by most people on a daily or frequent basis.[349] Thus the expression does not, for example, include work of any particular form because no particular form of work is 'normal' for most people.[350] The same is true of playing a particular game, taking part in a particular hobby, playing a musical instrument, playing sport, or performing a highly skilled task.[351] Impairments which affect only such an activity and have no effect on 'normal day-to-day activities' are not covered. **5.97**

---

345 *Nuttall Edmund Ltd v Butterfield* [2005] IRLR 751; [2006] ICR 77, para 29.

346 DDA, Sch 1, para 4.

347 *Ekpe v The Commissioner of Police of the Metropolis* [2001] ICR 1084 [2001] IRLR 605 at para 30.

348 Joint Committee on the Draft Disability Discrimination Bill, First Report (May 2004), para 88. See, *Hewett v Motorola Ltd* [2004] IRLR 545.

349 Guidance, para D5.

350 Guidance, para D7.

351 Guidance, para D8.

5.98 However, though work of any particular form is not to be regarded as 'normal' for most people, the boundary between particular work and 'normal day-to-day activity' cannot be regarded as precisely drawn. So, for example, where a person's work includes normal day-to-day activities, evidence of that work and the way that person performs it can be relevant.[352] For example, the making of beds, housework and minor DIY tasks, sewing, travelling by underground or plane, putting in hair rollers, or applying make-up have all been held to be illustrations of 'normal day-to-day activities',[353] and each of these might be material to both work and otherwise, depending on the nature of one's work. Further, evidence of a person's ability to carry out normal day-to-day activities at work could have a bearing upon their credibility and the extent to which they are able to carry out normal day-to-day activities outside of work.

5.99 In addition, in *Cruickshank v VAW Motorcast Ltd*[354] the claimant's asthma was triggered by his work environment and the Employment Appeal Tribunal held that in a case where the effect of an impairment on the ability to carry out normal day-to-day activities fluctuates and may be exacerbated by conditions at work, consideration should be given to whether the impairment has a substantial and long-term adverse effect on the employee's ability to perform normal day-to-day activities both while actually at work and while not at work. 'Normal day-to-day activities' are only a yardstick for deciding whether an impairment is serious enough to qualify for protection under the DDA. In assessing whether a disability has a substantial and long-term effect on the ability to do everyday tasks, it is not appropriate to confine the evaluation to the extent to which the claimant is disabled only in a normal day-to-day environment. If, while at work, a claimant's symptoms are such as to have an effect on his ability to perform day-to-day tasks, such symptoms are not to be ignored simply because the work itself may be specialized and unusual, so long as the disability and its consequences can be measured in terms of the ability of a claimant to undertake day-to-day tasks. *Cruickshank v VAW Motorcast Ltd* suggests that a person might be 'disabled' for some jobs but not others. The Employment Appeal Tribunal, which decided the issue, was obviously concerned that to conclude otherwise in that case 'would risk turning the Act on its head'.[355] If an employer were able to avoid liability to make

---

352 Guidance D9; *Law Hospital NHS Trust v Rush* [2001] IRLR 611; the claimant was a nurse and the employment tribunal erred in so far as it intended to imply that the extent to which the claimant was able to perform her nursing duties was not a relevant factor for deciding whether or not she was disabled.

353 *Vicary v British Telecommunications Plc* [1999] IRLR 680; *Abadeh v British Telecommunications Plc* [2001] ICR 156; [2001] IRLR 23; and *Ekpe v Metropolitan Police Commissioner* [2001] ICR 1084, [2001] IRLR 605.

354 [2002] ICR 729; [2002] IRLR 24.

355 Para 21.

reasonable adjustments[356] at work by dismissing the employee, resulting in an improvement in any condition and especially where the working environment contributed to the condition, this would be inconsistent with the purpose of the DDA. This does appear difficult to reconcile with the Guidance and the concept of 'normal' day-to-day activities. However, it does suggest that a person who is adversely affected by the conditions in which he is placed by reason of a relevant relationship[357] is entitled to have those effects taken into account.

In determining whether an activity is a *normal* day-to-day activity, no regard should be had to the question whether it is normal for the particular claimant. Thus where travelling by underground might be regarded as a normal day-to-day activity, the fact that the particular claimant does not live or work in London is immaterial (save that it may mean that the effect of the impairment is not substantial).[358] Transport should be viewed overall. Travelling by car or public transport can be regarded as normal day-to-day activities for most people and an inability to use these forms of transport marks an adverse effect on day-to-day activities.[359] However, what is to be regarded as 'normal' 'can not sensibly depend on asking the question whether the majority of people do it. The antithesis for the purposes of the Act is between that which is "normal" and that which is "abnormal" or "unusual" as a regular activity, judged by an objective population standard'.[360] **5.100**

(g) Adverse effects

In determining whether or not an impairment has an adverse effect on a person's ability to carry out normal day-to-day activities, the focus of the DDA is on what a person *cannot* do and what a person can only do with difficulty,[361] removing the need to concentrate on what a person *can do* and so to do will be an error:[362] **5.101**

> The determination of whether there is a substantial adverse impact must depend upon what a person cannot do, rather than what he can still do. It is not a question of balancing individual losses of function directly against retained abilities . . . [I]f . . . the focus should be upon whether or not the *ability referred to in paragraph 4(1) of the Schedule* has been affected, there is little room for drawing up such a balance sheet to answer the question whether there has been any adverse impact; the question

---

356 See Chap 6 for the meaning of 'reasonable adjustments'.

357 Employment; tenant/landlord; recipient of goods and services; student etc. See the unlawful acts in Chap 7 onwards.

358 *Abadeh v British Telecommunications Plc* [2001] ICR 156; [2001] IRLR 23, paras 35–7 and 42.

359 Ibid.

360 *Ekpe v Metropolitan Police Commissioner* [2001] ICR 1084, [2001] IRLR 605, para 32.

361 Guidance, para B8; *Vicary v British Telecommunications Plc* [1999] IRLR 680, para 5; *Ekpe v Metropolitan Police Commissioner* [2001] ICR 1084, [2001] IRLR 605, para 28.

362 *Goodwin v The Patent Office* [1999] IRLR 4; [1999] ICR 302, para 34 and *Leonard v Southern Derbyshire Chamber of Commerce* [2001] IRLR 19.

> 'Has manual dexterity been affected?' in circumstances where a person manipulates buttons only with difficulty cannot sensibly be answered by the riposte: 'Well she can still write a letter without difficulty . . .[363]

5.102 Regard must also be had to the fact that disabled people may 'play down' the effect that their disabilities have on their daily lives. The fact that a disabled person can manage his day-to-day activities does not mean that there is no adverse effect upon him or that 'his ability to carry them out ha[s] not been impaired'.[364] Disabled people may change the way in which they perform normal day-to-day activities or indeed refrain from certain of them entirely, consistent with medical advice or otherwise. That must be taken to evidence an indirect effect rather than suggest the absence of an effect.[365] In addition, the fact that a person is able to perform certain activities but they cause pain or fatigue is to be regarded as a relevant effect.[366] Further, disabled people may develop coping strategies or play down the effects of an impairment—this will not obviate the existence of the effect.

(h) Babies and young children

5.103 The effect of an impairment in babies and young children may not be apparent or so apparent because they are too young to have developed the ability to act in the respects contemplated by Schedule 1, paragraph 4, as described above. The Disability Discrimination (Meaning of Disability) Regulations 1996[367] make provision for this. Regulation 6 provides that:

> where a child under six years of age has an impairment which does not have an effect falling within paragraph 4(1) of Schedule 1 to the Act that impairment is to be taken to have a substantial and long-term adverse effect on the ability of that child to carry out normal day-to-day activities where it would normally have a substantial and long-term adverse effect on the ability of a person aged 6 years or over to carry out normal day-to-day activities.

Accordingly, the impairment upon which the disability is founded will have to be hypothetically transposed into an adult to determine the likely effect.

(i) When the effect of an impairment is to be measured

5.104 The effect of an impairment is to be determined at the time of the alleged discrimination.[368]

---

363 *Ekpe v The Commissioner of Police of the Metropolis* [2001] ICR 1084, [2001] IRLR 605, para 28.

364 *Goodwin v The Patent Office* [1999] IRLR 4; [1999] ICR 302, para 34.

365 Guidance, para D11.

366 Ibid.

367 SI 1996/1455.

368 *Cruickshank v Vaw Motorcast Ltd* [2002] ICR 729; [2002] IRLR 24, para 28.

(j) 'Substantial' adverse effects

Section 1 of the DDA requires that the effects of an impairment on a person's normal day-to-day activities must be *adverse* and *substantial*.[369] 'Substantial' is not defined by the DDA. The Guidance provides that 'a substantial' effect is one which is more than 'minor' or 'trivial',[370] and gives illustrations of 'substantial effects'.[371] Whether or not the effect of an impairment is substantial is not a medical question. It is a question of fact to be determined on the evidence of the claimant and any of his witnesses who can give evidence as to the severity of the effect of any impairment.[372] **5.105**

In determining whether the effects of any impairment are substantial, regard should be had to the time taken by a person to carry out a normal day-to-day activity compared with the time that might be expected to be taken if the person did not have the impairment.[373] In addition, the way in which a person carries out a normal day-to-day activity should be considered when assessing whether the effect of an impairment is substantial.[374] The comparison should be with the way in which the person would be expected to carry out the activity if he or she did not have the impairment.[375] **5.106**

The Guidance gives a series of examples of what it would, and what it would not, be reasonable to regard as substantial adverse effects.[376] However, these are indicators and not qualifying tests. Their effect is not that if a person can do an activity listed then he or she does not experience any substantial adverse effects; the person may be inhibited in other activities, and this instead may indicate a substantial effect.[377] **5.107**

In determining whether a person has a 'disability', care must be taken not to rely on stereotypical assumptions about disability. As has been pointed out: **5.108**

> a relatively small proportion of the disabled community are what one might describe as visibly disabled, that is people in wheel chairs or carrying white sticks or other aids. It is important therefore, that when [courts and tribunals] are approaching the question as to whether someone suffers from a disability, they should not have in their minds a stereotypical image of a person in a wheelchair or moving around with considerable difficulty. Such persons may well have a physical impairment within the

369 DDA, s 1(1).

370 Guidance, para B1.

371 Ibid.

372 *Vicary v British Telecommunications Plc* [1999] IRLR 680, para 16 and *Abadeh v British Telecommunications Plc* [2001] ICR 156; [2001] IRLR 23, para 9.

373 Guidance, para B2.

374 Guidance, para B3.

375 Ibid.

376 Guidance, para D16 *et seq.*

377 Guidance, paras D16 and 17.

meaning of the Act and of course be treated as disabled, but it does not follow that other persons who are not in such a condition are inherently less likely to have a physical or mental impairment of a sort which satisfies the terms of the legislation.[378]

(k) Effects of behaviour—coping

5.109 Disabled people may have the inclination to 'play down' the effects of an impairment. On the other hand, in determining whether the effects of an impairment are 'substantial' for the purposes of the DDA the Guidance provides that '[a]ccount should be taken of how far a person can reasonably be expected to modify his or her behaviour to prevent or reduce the effects of an impairment on normal day-to-day activities'.[379] If a person can behave in such a way that an impairment ceases to have a substantial adverse effect on his or her ability to carry out normal day-to-day activities, the person no longer satisfies the definition of disability.[380]

5.110 Where a person has 'coping' strategies which cease to work in certain circumstances (for example, when under stress), regard should be had to the possibility that their ability to manage the effects of an impairment will break down so that effects will still sometimes occur, and this should be taken into account when assessing the effects of an impairment.[381] This must be contrasted, however, with a situation where a person is receiving advice by a medical practitioner to behave in a certain way in order to reduce the impact of a disability when such behaviour might count as 'treatment' and therefore be disregarded.[382] The question as to where the line is drawn between mere coping strategies and treatment, particularly given that such treatment need not be medical, is not always clear. The impact of 'treatment' is discussed below.

(l) Cumulative effects

5.111 In determining whether an impairment has a substantial adverse effect, the cumulative impact of the impairment on one or more of the eight capacities should be considered.[383] Accordingly, a person with mild cerebral palsy may experience minor effects in a number of the respects listed in Schedule 1 which together could create substantial adverse effects on a range of normal day-to-day activities: fatigue may hinder walking, visual perception may be poor, coordination and balance may cause some difficulties. In addition, a person may have more than one impairment, any one of which alone would not have a substantial effect.

---

378 *Vicary v British Telecommunications Plc* [1999] IRLR 680, para 20.
379 Guidance, para B7.
380 Ibid.
381 Guidance, para B9.
382 See Guidance, paras B11 to B15 and see below.
383 Guidance, paras B4 to B6.

Again, account should be taken of whether the impairments together have a substantial effect overall on a person's ability to carry out normal day-to-day activities.

(m) *Effects of environment*

The question whether adverse effects are substantial may depend on environmental conditions which might vary, for example temperature, humidity, time of day or night, and how tired the person is or how much stress he or she is under.[384] In determining whether adverse effects are substantial, the extent to which such environmental factors are likely to have an impact should be considered.[385] **5.112**

(n) *'Long-term' impairment*

The substantial and adverse effects of a person's impairment must be 'long-term' for the protection of the DDA to apply. An effect of an impairment is long-term if it has lasted at least 12 months, or it is likely to last for at least 12 months, or it is likely to last for the rest of the affected person's life.[386] In the case of a past disability, the effect of an impairment is a long-term one if it lasted for at least 12 months.[387] **5.113**

As the Guidance makes clear, it is not necessary for the effect to be the same throughout the relevant period. An effect may change, as where activities which are initially very difficult become possible to a much greater extent. Indeed the main adverse effect might even disappear temporarily or permanently whilst another effect continues or develops. So long as the impairment continues to have, or is likely to have, such an effect throughout the period, there is a long-term effect.[388] **5.114**

'Likely', for the purposes of determining whether the effects of an impairment are likely to last for at least 12 months or for the rest of the person's life, simply means 'more probable than not'.[389] **5.115**

(o) *When is 'long-term' to be measured?*

As to when the likelihood of an effect lasting for any period should be tested, the Guidance confirms that the total period over which the effect exists should be taken into account.[390] This therefore includes any time before the point when the **5.116**

384 Guidance, para B10.

385 Ibid.

386 DDA, Sch 1, para 2 (1).

387 Ibid, Sch 2, para 5. The other provisions of the DDA are to be read as addressing persons who have had a disability in the past, with such modifications as are necessary being made to ensure the same: DDA, Sch 2, DDA, see below para 5.128.

388 Guidance, para C6.

389 Guidance, para C2.

390 Guidance, para C3.

discriminatory behaviour occurred as well as any time afterwards,[391] including any period up until the hearing of any claim.[392]

(p) Recurrent effects

5.117 If an impairment has had a substantial adverse effect on a person's ability to carry out normal day-to-day activities but that effect ceases, the substantial effect is treated as continuing if it is likely to recur; that is, it is more likely than not that the effect will recur.[393] In the case of a past disability, the question is whether a substantial adverse effect has in fact recurred.[394] Such applies equally to conditions which recur only sporadically or for short periods (for example, epilepsy).[395]

5.118 The following questions should be asked in determining whether the 'recurrent effects' provisions apply:

> Firstly, was there at some stage an impairment which had a substantial adverse effect on the applicant's ability to carry out normal day-to-day activities? . . . Secondly, did the impairment cease to have a substantial adverse effect on the applicant's ability to carry out normal day-to-day activities, and if so when? . . . Thirdly, what was the substantial adverse effect? . . . Fourthly, is *that* substantial adverse effect likely to recur? . . . The tribunal must be satisfied that the same effect is likely to recur and that it will again amount to a substantial adverse effect on the applicant's ability to carry out normal day-to-day activities.[396]

A substantial adverse effect is 'likely to recur' if it is more probable than not that the effect will recur.[397] Importantly it is not necessary for any underlying illness causing the impairment to recur. What is critical is whether the substantial effect of the impairment on day-to-day activities is likely to recur, and not whether the illness itself is likely to recur.[398] Likelihood of recurrence should be considered taking all the circumstances of the case into account. This should include what the person could reasonably be expected to do to prevent the recurrence.[399] As to the effect of continuing medical treatment on the likelihood of recurrence, see below.[400]

5.119 It is not then necessary for the effect to be the same throughout the period which is being considered in determining whether the effect of any impairment is

391 This may be contrasted with the question of substantial and adverse effect, which is to be tested at the time of the alleged discrimination, see para 5.104 above.

392 *Greenwood v British Airways Plc* [1999] ICR 969, [1999] IRLR 600.

393 DDA, Sch 1, para 2(2).

394 Ibid, Sch 2, para 5. See para 5.128 below for past disabilities.

395 Guidance, para C4.

396 *Swift v Chief Constable of Wiltshire Constabulary* [2004] ICR 909 [2004] IRLR 540, paras 20–6.

397 Ibid, para 28.

398 Ibid, para 34.

399 Guidance, para C8. This is subject, of course, to the discussion regarding coping strategies, medical treatment, environmental effects, and effect of treatment.

400 Para 5.121.

'long-term'. A person may still satisfy the long-term element of the definition even if the effect is not the same throughout the period. It may change; for example activities which are initially very difficult may become possible to a much greater extent. The effect might even disappear temporarily.[401]

(q) Deemed effect and deemed disability

The DDA and Regulations made thereunder deem certain impairments and conditions in certain circumstances to have a 'substantial adverse effect' even where that is not the present experience of the disabled person concerned. In addition, certain people are deemed disabled whatever the nature or experience of their impairment. **5.120**

Firstly, an impairment which would be likely to have a substantial adverse effect on the ability of the person concerned to carry out normal day-to-day activities, but for the fact that measures are being taken to treat or correct it, is to be treated as having that effect.[402] In other words the effect of treatment is to be ignored. 'Measures' *include*, in particular, medical treatment and the use of a prosthesis or other aid.[403] Although medical treatment is not defined in the DDA, the Court of Appeal has confirmed that counselling with a consultant clinical psychologist falls within the meaning of medical treatment.[404] It appears that such 'measures' may involve non-medical treatment or aids ('measures' being non-exhaustively defined). This provision may, for example, therefore apply to regulating sleep (where irregular sleep may result in, for example, epileptic seizures) or diet. This provision applies even where the measures result in the effects being completely under control or not at all apparent.[405] **5.121**

This provision does not apply in relation to the impairment of a person's sight to the extent that the impairment is correctable by spectacles or contact lenses.[406] In relation to sight corrections, the only effects that are to be considered are those that remain when the spectacles or contact lenses are used.[407] This provision does not include the use of devices to correct sight which are not spectacles or contact lenses.[408] **5.122**

401 Guidance, para C6.

402 DDA, Sch 1, para 6(1).

403 Ibid, Sch 1, Para 6(2). In *Vicary v British Telecommunications Plc* [1999] IRLR 680 the Employment Appeal Tribunal indicated that it thought the use of an automatic can opener was probably not an 'aid' but that 'aid' referred, for example, to Zimmer frames, sticks, and wheelchairs and not to household objects, though the point was not necessary for decision and was not decided.

404 *Kapadia v Lambeth LBC* [2000] IRLR 699, paras 9, 18, and 23; see too, *Carden v Pickerings Europe Ltd* [2005] IRLR 720; Guidance, para B13.

405 Guidance, para B12.

406 DDA, Sch 1, para 6(3).

407 Ibid, Sch 1, para 6(3).

408 Ibid, Sch 1, para 6(3). Guidance, para B4.

5.123 Where treatment cures an impairment, rather than merely masks it or controls it, then, of course, a person is no longer disabled (though they may, depending on the circumstances, qualify for protection as a person who has had a disability in the past[409]). However, where the outcome of any treatment cannot be known or where it is known that removal of the medical treatment will 'result in either a relapse or a worsened condition, it would be reasonable to disregard the medical treatment in accordance with paragraph 6 of Schedule 1'.[410] The impact of treatment should also be disregarded (assuming it has not cured the person of any impairment) in determining whether the effect of an impairment is likely to recur.[411]

5.124 Secondly, where a person has a progressive condition (for example muscular dystrophy) and as a result of that condition he has an impairment which has (or had) an effect on his ability to carry out normal day-to-day activities but the effect is not (or was not) a substantial adverse effect, he is nevertheless to be taken to have an impairment which has a substantial adverse effect if the condition is likely to result in him having such an impairment.[412] This does not protect a person by reason only of a diagnosis of a progressive condition where the condition has always been asymptomatic.[413] The DDA 2005 has amended the DDA so that, in addition to 'progressive' conditions described above, and overlapping with them, a person who has cancer, HIV infection,[414] or multiple sclerosis is to be deemed to have a disability, and therefore to be a disabled person, asymptomatic or not.[415] Regulations may provide that this deeming provision does not apply to certain cancers of a prescribed description, including prescribed by reference to consequences for a person of his having it.[416] However, no such regulations have yet been made. This means that persons with cancer, HIV infection, or multiple sclerosis will always be treated as disabled for the purposes of the DDA. Persons with other progressive conditions, such as systemic lupus erythematosis (SLE), various types of dementia, rheumatoid arthritis, and motor neurone disease[417] will be treated as disabled where as a result of their condition they have some impairment

---

409 See para 5.128.

410 Guidance, para B12.

411 Guidance, para C9. See 'recurrent effects' above, para 5.117 *et seq*.

412 DDA, Sch 1, para 8(1).

413 Guidance, para A15. See too *Mowat-Brown v University of Surrey* [2002] IRLR 235: it is not enough simply for an applicant to establish that he has a progressive condition and that it has or has had an effect on his ability to carry out normal day-to-day activities. The claimant must go on and show that it is more likely than not that at some stage in the future he will have an impairment, which will have a substantial adverse effect on his ability to carry out normal day-to-day activities.

414 As to the meaning of which, namely infection by a virus capable of causing the Acquired Immune Deficiency Syndrome, see DDA, Sch 1, para 9.

415 DDA, Sch 1, para 6A(1).

416 Ibid, Sch 1, para 6A(2).

417 Guidance, para B18.

which has (or had) an effect on their ability to carry out normal day-to-day activities if the condition is likely to result in their having an impairment which has such a substantial adverse effect.

Thirdly, an impairment which consists of a severe disfigurement is to be treated as having a substantial adverse effect on the ability of the person concerned to carry out normal day-to-day activities, whatever its actual effect.[418] Examples of disfigurements include scars, birthmarks, limb or postural deformation, or diseases of the skin.[419] Assessing severity will be mainly a matter of the degree of the disfigurement. It may be necessary to take account of where the feature in question is, for example, on the back as opposed to on the face.[420] **5.125**

A disfigurement which consists of a tattoo (which has not been removed) is not to be treated as a severe disfigurement. Also excluded is a piercing of the body for decorative purposes including anything attached through the piercing.[421] **5.126**

Fourthly, persons who were registered as disabled persons under section 6 of the Disabled Persons (Employment) Act 1944 both on 12 January 1995 *and* on 2 December 1996[422] are deemed to have a disability for a period of three years beginning on 2 December 1996 and thereafter to have had a disability and hence to have been a disabled person during that period[423] (and have had a disability in the past if such disability does not remain present). A person is also deemed to have a disability,[424] and hence to be a disabled person, where he is certified as blind or partially sighted by a consultant ophthalmologist in accordance with the relevant guidance *or* he is registered as blind or partially sighted in the relevant registers.[425] The 'relevant guidance' is, in relation to a consultant ophthalmologist in England and Wales, the Department of Health Circular LASSL(90)1 entitled 'Certification of Blind and Partially Sighted People: Revised form BD8 and the Procedures' and, in relation to a consultant ophthalmologist in Scotland, the Social Work Services Group Circular SWSG8/86, NHS 1998 (PCS) entitled 'Registration of Blind and Partially Sighted People'.[426] **5.127**

---

418 DDA, Sch 1, para 3(1).

419 Guidance, para B21.

420 Guidance, paras B21.

421 Disability Discrimination (Meaning of Disability) Regulations 1996, SI 1996/1455, Regulation 5 and Guidance, para B20.

422 When this provision came into force: SI 1996/1474, Art 2(3), Part III of the Schedule.

423 DDA, Sch 1, para 7(1), (2), and (7).

424 Disability Discrimination (Blind and Partially Sighted Persons) Regulations 2003, SI 2003/712.

425 In England and Wales, in the register maintained by or on behalf of the local authority under s 29 of the National Assistance Act 1948 or in Scotland, in a register maintained by or on behalf of a local authority.

426 Disability Discrimination (Blind and Partially Sighted Persons) Regulations 2003, SI 2003/712. Provision is made for the provision of 'conclusive evidence' of the matters identified by the Regulations under Regulation 4 thereof.

(r) Past disabilities

5.128 As mentioned above, the DDA applies in relation to a person who has had a disability in the past as they apply in relation to a person who has that disability.[427] Further guidance is provided by Schedule 2 of the DDA. By Schedule 2, paragraph 2 'References in Part II [to 4][428] [and 5A][429] to a disabled person are to be read as references to a person who has had a disability'. By paragraph 2A, references in the education provisions to a disabled pupil are to be read equally as references to a pupil who has had a disability. By paragraph 2B, references to a disabled student are to be read as references to a student who has had a disability, and similar and consequential changes are made. Consequential amendments are made so that the other provisions of the DDA, including those defining disability, are to be read as addressing past disabilities in the same way.[430] As mentioned above, in deciding whether a past condition constituted a disability, its effects are considered long-term if they lasted 12 months or more after the first occurrence, or if a recurrence happened or continued until more than 12 months after the first occurrence.[431] In *Greenwood v British Airways Plc*[432] the claimant was off work between October 1993 and March 1994 due to 'nervous tension'. He was thereafter absent on three occasions on dates between December 1996 and February 1997 which, along with his earlier absence, triggered the sickness absence procedure. He was refused a promotion shortly afterwards on the basis, among others, that he was viewed as unreliable due to his previous sickness record. He went sick with depression in August 1997 and when he was refused promotion brought a complaint under the DDA on the basis that he had been discriminated against for a reason relating to his disability. Overturning the decision of the employment tribunal, the Employment Appeal Tribunal concluded that the claimant had had a disability in the past which was covered by section 2; the tribunal had failed to have regard to the fact that the adverse effect of the claimant's depression recurred and he was therefore to be regarded as having had a past disability by virtue of paragraph 5(2) of Schedule 2.

(s) Future disabilities

5.129 The DDA does not protect persons who have some disposition to become disabled in the future by reason of some genetic condition or otherwise. This is by reason of the functional nature of the test for disability and the fact that, outside

---

427 DDA, s 2.

428 See Chap 9.

429 See Chap 11. This applies also to 'Part III of the 2005 Order', namely, the Special Educational Needs and Disability (Northern Ireland) Order 2005, SI 2005/1117, art 48(1), (9).

430 DDA, Sch 2. Guidance, para A15.

431 Ibid, s 2, Sch 2, para 5. Guidance, para C10.

432 [1999] ICR 969, [1999] IRLR 600.

specific conditions, including progressive conditions, a person who is and remains symptom-free will not be caught by the test provided for in the DDA.

(3) Framework Directive

As seen in Chapter 4, the Framework Directive addresses disability discrimination, amongst other things. It does not define 'disability' for the purposes of its provisions. In *Chacón Navas v Eurest Colectividades SA*[433] the claimant was dismissed on grounds of sickness. Spanish law outlawed discriminatory dismissals on the grounds, amongst others, of disability and treated them as void. The Spanish court hearing the claimant's case considered that a causal link existed between sickness and disability, and that therefore a worker in the situation of the claimant was protected by the prohibition on disability discrimination. The court, however, referred to the ECJ the question whether the Framework Directive covered a worker dismissed by her employer solely because she was sick. According to the ECJ, the concept of 'disability' under the Framework Directive required an autonomous and uniform interpretation throughout the EU, and, given its context in the Directive: 5.130

> the concept of 'disability' must be understood as referring to a limitation which results in particular from physical, mental or psychological impairments and which hinders the participation of the person concerned in professional life [and] [i]n order for the limitation to fall within the concept of 'disability', it must therefore be probable that it will last for a long time.[434]

This meant something other than mere 'sickness'.

The ECJ, then, appears to amalgamate the issue of status as it is protected under the Framework Directive (disability) and the protected activities (employment and related areas[435]) so that 'disability' for the purposes of the Framework Directive arises only where the impairment interferes with professional life. This is difficult to fit within the domestic scheme, because the DDA defines disability in the same way for the purposes of all its provisions (employment and non-employment) and its meaning does not depend upon a *specific* activity being hindered. Nevertheless, it might be said that in certain respects the test set by the ECJ in *Chacón Navas* imposes a somewhat lower threshold than that set by the DDA. The ECJ requires that a person has a limitation which results in particular from a physical, mental, or psychological impairment which '*hinders*' over '*a long period of time*' a person's participation in professional life. It is not necessary, for the Directive, to show that there has been an adverse *and substantial* effect on a 5.131

433 Case C-13/05 (2006).
434 Ibid, paras 43 and 45.
435 See Chap 4.

person's normal day-to-day activities.[436] However, where a person's disability does not affect their participation in professional life, as opposed to other aspects of their life or not at all,[437] then it is not clear that the Directive protects them, at least unless they are *perceived* to be disabled within the meaning of that concept as explained by the ECJ in *Chacón Navas*, as to which see below. For the purposes of the DDA, the judgment in *Chacón Navas* will not *reduce* the protection afforded by it because the Directive sets *minimum* standards.[438] Indeed where the effect of an impairment at work is relied upon to establish a disability, it will only be necessary now to show that the impairment 'hinders' over 'a long period of time' a person's participation in professional life, not that the effect is *substantial.*

5.132 Further, whilst as will be seen[439] the meaning given to 'direct' discrimination under the DDA (in consequence of Regulations introduced to give effect to the Framework Directive) protects only a *disabled person*,[440] the Framework Directive appears to have wider reach. The Directive defines direct discrimination as occurring where 'one person is treated less favourably than another is, has been or would be treated in a comparable situation, on . . . [the] grounds' of disability.[441] The Directive meaning would therefore protect a person who is not disabled but perceived to be so; or is treated less favourably because of their association with a disabled person—'disability' and 'disabled person' having the meanings given to them by the ECJ in *Chacón Navas*. A person, therefore, who is perceived by his employer to have a limitation which results from a physical, mental, or psychological impairment which is perceived to 'hinder' over 'a long period of time' his or her participation in professional life should be regarded as disabled for the purposes of the Framework Directive. As will be seen,[442] this is not the approach taken by the DDA and it is therefore doubtful whether it is fully compliant with EC law.

H. Sexual Orientation

5.133 The Employment Equality (Sexual Orientation) Regulations 2003 (Sexual Orientation Regulations)[443] protect against sexual orientation discrimination in

436 S 1(1), see para 5.105.

437 For example, where they are asymptomatic but deemed disabled under the provisions discussed above at para 5.120.

438 By Art 8 the directive sets *minimum* standards. Further, a reduction in provision already made by a Member State on the ground of implementation of the directive is precluded by the non-regression provision also in Art 8, see Chap 6.

439 See Chap 6.

440 DDA, s 3A(5).

441 Article 2(2).

442 Chap 6.

443 SI 2003/1661.

certain fields (employment and related fields). The Regulations give effect to the Framework Directive.[444] The Framework Directive, as mentioned in Chapter 4, lays down 'a general framework for combating discrimination on the grounds of [*inter alia*] . . . sexual orientation . . . with a view to putting into effect in the Member States the principle of equal treatment'.[445] Sexual orientation is not defined. Understanding the concept of 'sexual orientation' is not unproblematical. Thus Eric Heinze observes:

> 'Studies' (and Courts) have sometimes confused homosexuals, bisexuals, trans-sexuals, and trans-genderists,[446] drawing no distinction between these various groups' behaviours, desires and identities. (The concept of pederasty, adult sexual preference for youths or children, although entirely distinct—it may, for example, be heterosexual or homosexual—is also commonly thrown into this view, equated frequently, and erroneously, with male homosexuality, as is suggested, for example, by the traditional pejorative French word pédé, used to designate all homosexual men).[447]

As for defining sexual orientation, for the purposes of discrimination law, a concept adopted for the purposes of human rights law can readily be applied. Eric Heinze describes it as follows: **5.134**

> Sexual orientation, for the purposes of human rights law, can be understood as encompassing sexual acts or preferences either sufficiently conforming to the normative-heterosexual paradigm to avoid discrimination, or sufficiently derogating from the normative-heterosexual paradigm to prompt discrimination . . . [t]hus . . . , the term 'sexual orientation', should be understood to correspond to 'being' as well as 'doing'; that is, to any possible source of discrimination. Finally, discrimination on the basis of sexual orientation can be defined, in general terms, as invidious treatment made, in law or practice, on the basis of actual or imputed derogation from the normative-heterosexual paradigm.[448]

Eric Heinze therefore includes in the concept of sexual orientation heterosexuality, homosexuality, bisexuality, asexuality, trans-sexualism, trans-genderism, intersexualism, and hermaphrodism.[449]

The Sexual Orientation Regulations do define sexual orientation but rather more narrowly. By Regulation 2(1): **5.135**

> 'sexual orientation' means a sexual orientation towards—
> (a) persons of the same sex;
> (b) persons of the opposite sex; or
> (c) persons of the same sex and of the opposite sex.

---

444 2000/78/EC, discussed in Chap 4.

445 Article 1.

446 That is those individuals who feel and wish to express strong psychological or social identification with the opposite sex including, for example, transvestites and cross-dressers.

447 E Heinze, *Sexual Orientation: A Human Right* (1995, Martinus Nijhoff/Kluwer), 49, internal references removed.

448 Ibid, 59–60.

449 Ibid, at 60.

'Same sex' and 'opposite sex' are not further defined. The concept of 'sex' under the Sexual Orientation Regulations is assumed to be self-explanatory. As with the SDA, it is likely that the concept of 'sex' under the Sexual Orientation Regulations will be regarded as biologically rooted.

5.136 Prior to the making of the Regulations, the Government consulted on their contents.[450] In their consultation paper, the Government indicated their preference to define 'sexual orientation' so as to outlaw discrimination only on the grounds of 'heterosexual, homosexual or bisexual orientation'.[451] According to the Government this would provide clarity and address the concerns which were apparently voiced by some during negotiations on the text of the Framework Directive that in addition to outlawing discrimination against people based on their heterosexual, homosexual, or bisexual orientation, protection against sexual orientation discrimination might also protect 'paedophiles'.[452] As the Government made clear in their consultation paper, the obligations contained in the Framework Directive were expressly without prejudice to the right of Member States to 'take measures . . . which, in a democratic society, are necessary for public security, for the maintenance of public order and for the prevention of criminal offences, for the protection of health and for the protection of the rights and freedoms of others'. The Government's approach probably reflects entrenched homophobic attitudes rather than legitimate practical concerns, as Eric Heinze observes in the extract above. It is extremely unlikely that the expression 'sexual orientation' which is widely understood, both domestically and internationally, would be interpreted to include paedophilia or other unlawful or dangerous sexual acts, particularly in the context of a human rights instrument and in light of the saving clause in the Directive just described. Certainly, Convention rights would provide no further guarantees, the ECtHR long since having differentiated sexual orientation, that is as pertaining to the sex of one's sexual partner, and other, particularly harmful, sexual activity, such as sadomasochism.[453]

5.137 As seen, then, the Sexual Orientation Regulations confine the protection afforded to heterosexuality, homosexuality, and bisexuality only. Asexuality is apparently not recognized and certainly not protected. Instead, all of us are assumed to have a sexuality and a sexual drive towards persons of one sex or another, or both. The Regulations do give a broad meaning to direct sexual orientation discrimination,[454] and this does mean that less favourable treatment connected with the manifestations

---

[450] *Towards Equality and Diversity, Implementing the Employment and Race Directives: Consultation Documents* (2001) Department of Trade and Industry and Cabinet Office.

[451] Ibid, para 12.5.

[452] Ibid, para 12.6.

[453] *Laskey, Jaggard and Brown v UK* (1997) 24 EHRR 39.

[454] See Chap 6.

of sexual orientation or perceived sexual orientation, within the meaning of the Regulations, will be protected by the prohibition on direct discrimination. This is discussed below.[455]

The Regulations do not protect other queer activity. Transsexualism is dealt with through the SDA by the amendments made in respect of gender reassignment (and otherwise through the Convention rights[456]). Trans-genderism, intersexualism, and hermaphrodism are not distinctly protected by the main anti-discrimination enactments. Only if adverse treatment connected with such status were also to comprise 'sex' discrimination, or discrimination connected with gender reassignment, or sexual orientation discrimination would protection be afforded. Otherwise any protection will arise only under the Convention rights. In particular, the Regulations only protect against discrimination connected with a narrow range of sexual expression. The Regulations have nothing to say about discrimination connected with sexual expression which, apart from the choice of one's sexual partner, does not conform to socially accepted sexual norms. It will not therefore fill the gaps identified above in the SDA. Firstly, as mentioned, it would have nothing to say about a person discriminated against because they were asexual, such persons, so far as the Regulations are concerned, having no sexuality at all (or none justifying protection). Secondly, it would have nothing to say about persons who engage in conduct which challenges gender norms but which is, for example, heterosexual and therefore within the range of 'acceptable' sexual expression. A woman, for example, who dresses as a man, wears a prosthetic phallus, and has sex with men, would be regarded under the Regulations as 'heterosexual'. If she were to be treated less favourably as compared to other heterosexual people, because she dresses as a man and wears a prosthetic phallus, and has, perhaps penetrative, sex with a man she would probably not be protected. Such a woman might well not be protected under the SDA either. This is because, as described above and in Chapter 6, she would have to compare herself to a man similarly situated and, as the case law makes clear, these characteristics would probably have to be imputed into her male comparator. Assuming a man who dresses as a woman and allows himself to be buggered by women would be treated in the same way, there would neither be, so far as the law is concerned, sex discrimination in play, and nor would there be sexual orientation discrimination in play. There is, then, a significant lacuna in the protection against gender discrimination, as described above, and this is not addressed by the Sexual Orientation Regulations. **5.138**

As mentioned above, the wide meaning given to direct discrimination would protect against discrimination based on activities which are manifestations of sexual orientation, like entering a marriage or a civil partnership, or bringing **5.139**

455 See Chap 6.

456 And now, too, through the Gender Recognition Act 2004. See Chap 2.

along a same-sex, or an opposite-sex, partner to a party, for example.[457] In addition, the indirect discrimination provisions would protect gay men and lesbians against disadvantageous treatment associated with other conduct closely connected to their sexual orientation or expression of their sexual orientation.

5.140 As mentioned above,[458] much indirect discrimination against gay men and lesbians has arisen because of the historical and present bar on same-sex marriage. The Civil Partnership Act 2004 has remedied almost all of the tangible disadvantages associated with the absence of a right to marry,[459] but any remaining disadvantages, because of discrimination in the accrual of benefits before its coming into force, would not found a claim, even in indirect discrimination, under the Employment Equality (Sexual Orientation) Regulations 2003. This is because Regulation 25 provides that:

> [n]othing in Part II or III shall render unlawful—
> (a) anything which prevents or restricts access to a benefit by reference to marital status where the right to the benefit accrued or the benefit is payable in respect of periods of service prior to the coming into force of the Civil Partnership Act 2004.[460]

This is apparently intended to reflect Recital 22 to the Framework Directive which states that: 'This Directive is without prejudice to national laws on marital status and the benefits dependent thereon'.[461]

5.141 The Equality Act 2006 provides the Secretary of State with power to make regulations addressing discrimination and harassment on grounds of sexual orientation.[462] 'Sexual orientation' is to have the meaning given to it by section 35 of the Equality Act.[463] Section 35 (an interpretation provision) provides that:

> '*Sexual orientation*' means an individual's sexual orientation towards—
> (a) persons of the same sex as him or her,
> (b) persons of the opposite sex, or
> (c) both.

---

457 *R (on the application of Amicus-MSF section and others) v Secretary of State for Trade and Industry and Christian Action Research Education and others (Interveners)* [2004] EWHC 860 (Admin); [2004] IRLR 430.

458 See Chap 2.

459 There are some remaining disadvantages, in relation to pensions in particular which are discussed further below.

460 Otherwise benefits conferred on married persons and civil partners to the exclusion of all other persons are exempted, so not providing any further rights to unmarried same-sex partners, unless they are civil partners, or indeed unmarried opposite-sex partners (Regulation 25(b)).

461 See *R (On the Application of Amicus-MSF section and others) v Secretary of State for Trade and Industry and Christian Action Research Education and Others* [2004] IRLR 430 and *Towards Equality and Diversity, Implementing the Employment and Race Directives: Consultation Documents* (2001) Department of Trade and Industry and Cabinet Office., para 12.8.

462 Equality Act 2006, s 81, see Chap 2.

463 Ibid, s 81(2).

Therefore, 'sexual orientation' is defined in materially the same way under the Sexual Orientation Regulations as the Equality Act and the observations above apply.

I. Religion and Belief

The Employment Equality (Religion or Belief) Regulations 2003[464] (Religion or Belief Regulations) protect against discrimination connected with religion and belief in certain fields (employment and related fields). As with the Sexual Orientation Regulations, they give effect to the Framework Directive[465] which, as discussed above,[466] requires Member States to regulate discrimination in certain fields where that is connected to 'religion or belief'. 'Religion' and 'belief', like sexual orientation and the other strands addressed by the Directive, are not defined. However, as has been observed,[467] the Directive refers in its recitals to the ECHR and it was intended by the Government[468] that the expressions 'religion' and 'belief' contained in the Religion or Belief Regulations would be afforded the same meaning as the expressions set out in Article 9 of the ECHR,[469] as is likely to be the case. Article 9 of the ECHR confers the right to 'freedom of thought, conscience and religion' and these concepts have been held to embrace a wide range of beliefs, encompassing mainstream religious faiths and minority faiths and belief systems which diverge from established religious thought.[470] 5.142

There is some learning from other jurisdictions which might be helpful in understanding the broader concepts of 'religion' and 'belief', particularly in light of Article 9. 5.143

464 SI 2003/1660.

465 2000/78/EC, discussed in Chap 4.

466 Chap 4.

467 See Chap 4.

468 Explanation of the provisions of the Employment Equality (Sexual Orientation) Regulations 2003 and Employment Equality (Religion or Belief) Regulations 2003, DTI, available at <http://www.dti.gov.uk/employment/discrimination/emp-equality-regs-2003/page21856.html>, paras 10 *et seq.*

469 See Chap 4 for a full discussion on the protection afforded fundamental rights in EC law.

470 As to the concept of 'religion', in the context of Racial and Religious Hatred Bill (which became the Racial and Religious Hatred Act 2006), in the second reading in the House of Lords, Lord Falconer, promoting the Bill, made the following observations about the meaning of 'religious belief' for its purposes, as follows: 'It will . . . be for the courts, as they have already done, to decide what constitutes a religious belief for the purposes of this legislation. In doing so, they will take into account existing case law on the issue; for example, the case of *Campbell & Cosans v The United Kingdom* suggests that any religious belief will need to attain a certain level of cogency, seriousness, cohesion and importance . . . [T]he beliefs must also be worthy of respect in a democratic society and not incompatible with human dignity. We expect, therefore, that religious beliefs that advocate child abuse or violence would not be protected by the Bill. As for groups such as Scientologists or the Moonies, it may be that the courts will decide that their beliefs equate to religious beliefs. However, we need to be clear that what we are talking about is stirring-up of hatred against people, not their beliefs, and that, just because people might have beliefs which seem objectionable, it would be wrong for the law to state that it was ok for hatred to be stirred up against them' (Hansard HL 11 Oct 2005, Col 161).

In the Canadian Supreme Court case of *R v Morgentaler & Others*,[471] Wilson J considered the same expressions as in Article 9, under section 2(a) of the Canadian Charter of Rights and Freedoms and observed as follows:

> [I]n a free and democratic society 'freedom of conscience and religion' should be broadly construed to extend to conscientiously-held beliefs, whether grounded in religion or in a secular morality. Indeed, as a matter of statutory interpretation, 'conscience' and 'religion' should not be treated as tautologous if capable of independent, although related, meaning.[472]

5.144 The concept of 'conscience' has been described as 'self-judgment on the moral quality of one's conduct or the lack of it'.[473] As discussed in Chapter 4, the case law from the ECtHR also suggests that 'conscience' requires some philosophical basis.[474] As to 'religion' and 'belief', the UN Human Rights Committee has recommended that the concepts be interpreted broadly to include theistic, non-theistic, and atheistic beliefs.[475] The US Supreme Court has indicated that the terms should include moral, ethical, or religious beliefs about what is right and wrong where they are held with the strength of traditional religious convictions.[476] As to freedom of 'conscience' the US Supreme Court has held that freedom of conscience 'implies respect for an innate conviction of paramount duty'.[477] The UN Human Rights Committee have indicated that a right to conscientious objection to military service can be derived from the right under Article 18 of the International Covenant on Civil and Political Rights (ICCPR) (which protects the right to freedom of thought, conscience, and religion).[478]

5.145 Before the making of the Religion or Belief Regulations, the Government made it clear in the Consultation Paper[479] that they did not intend to cover 'political belief' in the Regulations. However, they also considered it inappropriate to

471 [1988] 1 SCR 30.

472 At 179.

473 *Re MacKay v Government of Manitoba*, 24 DLR (4th) 587, 594 (in which the Supreme Court upheld the decision of the Manitoba Court of Appeal that a person's right to hold or express any position or belief by the provisions of the Election's Finances Act which provided for the provinces paying a portion of the campaign expenses of candidates and parties receiving a fixed proportion of the votes in the provincial election. The Manitoban Court of Appeal, in addition, found the provision did not restrict the applicant's freedom of conscience, though tax payers contributed to the funds so distributed). Supreme Court reference [1989] 2 SCR357 (quote in text from Appeal Court).

474 *Arrowsmith v United Kingdom* (1980) 19 DR 5.

475 UN General Comments 22–2.

476 *Welsh v US*, 398 US 333 (1970) 335–44.

477 Dissenting judgment of Hughes CJ in *United States v MacIntosh*, 283 US 605 cited in *US v Seeger*, 380 US 163, 176.

478 Human Rights Committee, general comment 22, para 11.

479 *Towards Equality and Diversity, Implementing the Employment and Race Directives: Consultation Documents* (2001) Department of Trade and Industry and Cabinet Office.

define 'religion or belief', 'given the wide variety of different faiths and beliefs in this country' and accordingly considered that it was appropriate to leave it to the courts to resolve the definitional issues as they arose.[480] It was their view that 'belief' 'extends only to religious beliefs and profound philosophical convictions similar to religious belief which deserve society's respect'.[481] The apparent requirement to 'deserve' society's respect may be a little worrying because it assumes it is appropriate for there to be some assessment of the worthiness or otherwise of a particular belief. As the authorities make clear under the ECHR,[482] this is not the role of the courts or indeed Government in regulating rights relating to freedom of religion and belief. However, in the final enactment, the Religion or Belief Regulations defined religion and belief rather widely as follows:

> any religion, religious belief, or similar philosophical belief.[483]

There has been some uncertainty around the expression 'similar philosophical beliefs'. It appears that the expression is intended to cover not only theistic beliefs but also the absence of belief and the belief in the absence of a God, as well as 'persons who might describe themselves as "unconcerned" by religious beliefs, or "unsure" of them'.[484] 5.146

Thus in the House of Lords debate during which the Regulations were approved, the Government Minister moving the motion approving the Regulations in the Lords, Lord Sainsbury of Turville, said as follows: 5.147

> Members of Muslim, Christian and other communities have been dismissed, victimised and turned down for work unfairly simply because of their faith. Of those who are not religious, atheists and humanists, for example, have also experienced discrimination at work because of their beliefs or absence of them. These regulations will make this kind of unacceptable treatment unlawful.[485]

During the debate that followed, Lord Lester of Herne Hill QC suggested that the Minister should make clear that it was Government's intention to protect against discrimination connected with the lack of religious belief so as to cover humanist,

---

480 Ibid, para 13.4–13.5.

481 Ibid, para 13.5.

482 See Chap 4.

483 Regulation 2(1), Religion and Belief Regulations. Guidance issued by ACAS contains an Appendix providing some explanation of all the main religions and beliefs in Britain together with their main customs, needs and festivals; *Religion or Belief in the Workplace: a Guide for Employers and Employees* (2003, ACAS) (available at <http://www.acas.org.uk/media/pdf/f/l/religion_1.pdf>), though the Regulations will cover both the major and smaller religions. See para s 5.152–3 for amendments not yet in force at the time of writing.

484 Explanation of the provisions of the Employment Equality (Sexual Orientation) Regulations 2003 and Employment Equality (Religion or Belief) Regulations 2003, DTI, available at <http://www.dti.gov.uk/employment/discrimination/emp-equality-regs-2003/page21856.html>, para 14.

485 Hansard, HL Vol 649, Col 786 (17 June 2003).

agnostic, atheist, 'or any other godless person or person without faith'. The Minister replied:

> It is clearly the intention that where people have strongly held views, which include humanism, or atheism or agnosticism, they would be covered under the phrase 'or similar philosophical belief'.[486]

5.148 Political belief is not expressly excluded though, as mentioned, it is plain that it was not the Government's intention to include protection against discrimination connected with political belief. This might be contrasted with the position in Northern Ireland to which the Religion or Belief Regulations do not extend.[487] It has been suggested, however, that notwithstanding the Government's intention to exclude political belief from the scope of the Regulations, some political ideology might be protected under the expression 'religious belief, or similar philosophical belief'. According to Nicholas de Marco,

> [a] person may hold a political ideology as strongly as any religion or other similar philosophical belief, such as humanism, the ideology may have a similar coherent system of beliefs, or world-view, but it may not have the question of the existence of God as its focus. For instance, a communist may argue that his political belief is that 'similar philosophical belief' in the sense of the Regulations; he has an ideology, or belief system, that could be described as a philosophy. The same may be true for a libertarian. However the expression of a particular political idea, for instance opposition to a European Single Currency, or belief in the repatriation of immigrants, cannot be protected by the Regulations.[488]

A recent first instance decision of the employment tribunal concluded—almost certainly correctly having regard to the Article 9 case law—that membership of the British National Party did not constitute a 'similar philosophical belief' to religious belief.[489] This is obviously not binding but in any event perhaps more challenging will be those convictions which are intimately connected to religious belief or form part of religious ideology. They might include, in the case of Roman Catholics, opposition to abortion[490] or the liberation theology adopted by certain parts of the Catholic Church (particularly in Latin America) and the Dutch Reform Church, embracing both the left and the right ends of the political spectrum.

5.149 Because of the meaning given to direct discrimination, as with the Sexual Orientation Regulations, the class of persons likely to be protected by the Religion

---

486 Ibid, Col 792.

487 The Sexual Orientation and Religion or Belief Regulations extend only to Great Britain; Regulations 1(2). See Fair Employment and Treatment Order (Amendment) Regulations (Northern Ireland) 2003 SR 2003/520 and Employment Equality (Sexual Orientation) Regulations (Northern Ireland) 2003 SR 2003/497.

488 N de Marco, *Blackstone's Guide to the Employment Equality Regulations 2003* (2004, OUP) 13–14.

489 *Baggs v Fudge* (2005) Case No 1400114/05.

490 For the opposite position, see the Canadian case of *R v Morgentaler & Others* [1988] 1 SCR 30.

or Belief Regulations is wide. However, unlike the Sexual Orientation Regulations,[491] there is an express limitation. As will be seen in Chapter 6, a person less favourably treated on the grounds of the discriminator's religion or belief will not be protected by the Religion or Belief Regulations.[492] Interesting issues are nevertheless likely to arise as to the precise extent of the protection afforded. As with the Sexual Orientation Regulations, the Religion or Belief Regulations contain a wide concept of direct discrimination. It prohibits less favourable treatment 'on grounds of religion or belief'.[493] As with the protection against sexual orientation discrimination, this is likely to embrace certain manifestations of the complainant's religious belief (prayer, dress etc).[494] This is controversial. It is apparently not what Government expected[495] but apparently this is its effect.[496] Drawing the lines around religion and belief and *conduct* connected to it will be difficult, and therefore drawing the lines around direct and indirect discrimination (discussed further in Chapter 6) may be problematic. It might be argued that treating a Sikh man less favourably because he wears a turban is to treat him less favourably on grounds of religion because the wearing of a turban is inextricably linked to his religion and belief. These forms of discrimination have traditionally been addressed by the guarantees against indirect discrimination.[497] The extent to which the scope of protection afforded under the direct discrimination provisions will be informed by the limitations under the ECHR on manifestations of religious belief (under Article 9(2), see Chapter 4) has not been the subject of any discussion yet in the case law. There is no general defence of justification to direct discrimination under the Religion or Belief Regulations and there is no reason therefore to suppose that

491 And indeed the Race Relations Act 1976, see Chap 6.

492 Regulation 3(1)(a) and (2).

493 Regulation 3(1).

494 See *R (On the Application of Amicus-MSF Section and Others) v Secretary of State for Trade and Industry and Christian Action Research Education and Others* [2004] IRLR 430 which addresses materially the same provision in the Sexual Orientation Regulations.

495 Explanation of the provisions of the Employment Equality (Sexual Orientation) Regulations 2003 and Employment Equality (Religion or Belief) Regulations 2003, DTI, available at <http://www.dti.gov.uk/employment/discrimination/emp-equality-regs-2003/page21856.html>, paras 15: 'The definition of "religion or belief" does not include the "manifestation" of, or conduct based on or expressing a religion or belief (see also the distinction made in ECHR Art 9). For example, a person might wear certain clothing, or pray at certain times in accordance with the tenets of her religion, or she may express views, and say or do other things reflecting her beliefs. In such a case it would not in itself constitute direct discrimination on grounds of religion or belief under the Regulations (see below) if a person suffers a disadvantage because she has done or said something in this way. It would only be direct discrimination if a person with different beliefs (or no beliefs) was treated more favourably in similar circumstances. However, if an employer does set down requirements about (for example) clothing or breaks for prayers, these may constitute indirect discrimination (see below) under the Regulations unless they are justified.'

496 *R (On the Application of Amicus-MSF Section and Others) v Secretary of State for Trade and Industry and Christian Action Research Education and Others* [2004] IRLR 430.

497 *Mandla v Dowell Lee* [1983] 2 AC 548.

because a prohibition on the manifestation of religion or belief is justified in ECHR law, that should restrict the protection under the Religion or Belief Regulations. This is important, and increasingly so as the scope of protection against discrimination connected with religion and belief is extended through statutory measures.

5.150 The Equality Act 2006 (EA),[498] when in force, will outlaw discrimination connected with religion and belief outside the employment fields, as discussed in Chapter 2. For its purposes it defines religion and belief as follows:

> 'religion' means any religion,
> 'belief' means any religious or philosophical belief,
> a reference to religion includes a reference to lack of religion, and
> a reference to belief includes a reference to lack of belief.[499]

As with the Religion or Belief Regulations, the Government intends that Article 9 will define the parameters of 'religion' for these purposes, so that:[500]

> *Section 44(a)* defines 'religion' as 'any religion', a broad definition in line with the freedom of religion guaranteed by Article 9 of the ECHR. It includes those religions widely recognized in this country such as Christianity, Islam, Hinduism, Judaism, Buddhism, Sikhism, Rastafarianism, Baha'is, Zoroastrians and Jains. Equally, denominations or sects within a religion can be considered as a religion or religious belief, such as Catholics or Protestants within Christianity. The main limitation on what constitutes a 'religion' for the purposes of Article 9 of the ECHR is that it must have a clear structure and belief system.

5.151 However, importantly, the EA introduces some material changes as compared to the definition provided for under Regulation 2(1) of the Religion or Belief Regulations. Firstly, the EA expressly makes non-belief equivalent to belief for the purposes of the EA (and, as seen below, in due course for the purposes of the Religion or Belief Regulations too). Secondly, it does not contain any express requirement that any protected 'belief' be '*similar*' to a religious belief. The explanation for this was given by Baroness Scotland when promoting the Equality Bill in the House of Lords:

> [T]here is no sinister motive in that. The intention behind the wording . . . is identical to that in the employment regulations. However, in drafting . . . it was felt that the word 'similar' added nothing and was, therefore, redundant. This is because the term 'philosophical belief' will take its meaning from the context in which it appears; that is, as part of the legislation relating to discrimination on the grounds of religion or belief. Given that context, philosophical beliefs must therefore always be of a similar nature to religious beliefs. It will be for the courts to decide what constitutes

498 Expected to be brought into force in April 2007.
499 EA, s 44.
500 See Explanatory Notes to EA.

> a belief . . . , but case law suggests that any philosophical belief must attain a certain level of cogency, seriousness, cohesion and importance, must be worthy of respect in a democratic society and must not be incompatible with human dignity. Therefore an example of a belief that might meet this description is humanism, and examples of something that might not—I hope I do not give any offence to anyone present in the Chamber—would be support of a political party or a belief in the supreme nature of the Jedi Knights.[501]

Whether or not Baroness Scotland's view is accurate will have to await consideration by the courts. However, the fact that the 'similarity' requirement has been removed may make arguments that some political convictions are protected by the concept of 'belief' more likely to succeed. In this regard it can be noted that the Framework Directive does not impose any requirement of 'similarity' with religious beliefs on the protection afforded beliefs.[502]

The Religion or Belief Regulations will be amended by the EA so that its definitional provisions on religion and belief[503] will match those in the EA when it is in force. **5.152**

The EA defines discrimination in a way which provides expressly that a person may be directly discriminated against on grounds of a person's religion or belief whether or not it is also the discriminator's religion or belief, and that a reference to a person's religion or belief includes a reference to a religion or belief to which he is thought to belong or subscribe.[504] Because of the wide 'grounds of' formulation in the direct discrimination provisions of the Regulations both instances of discrimination are already covered by the Regulations and this is discussed further in Chapter 6. However, in the context of the EA, this position is explicit. As with the Religion or Belief Regulations, the religion or beliefs of the discriminator are not material, thus direct discrimination occurs where: **5.153**

> a person ('A') discriminates against another ('B') for the purposes of this Part if on grounds of the religion or belief of B or of any other person except A (whether or not it is also A's religion or belief) A treats B less favourably than he treats or would treat others (in cases where there is no material difference in the relevant circumstances).[505]

This makes materially the same provision as Regulation 3(2) of the Religion or Belief Regulations which will be repealed and replaced by new provision in the EA when the EA is in force. Section 77(2) and (3) of the EA will replace Regulation 3(1) and repeal Regulation 3(2)of the Religion or Belief Regulations with the

501 Hansard HL Vol 673 Col 1109-10 (13 July 2005).
502 Article 1.
503 EA, s 77.
504 Ibid, s 45(1) and (2).
505 Ibid, s 45(1).

following formulation to the same effect, so that direct discrimination will occur where:

> on the grounds of the religion or belief of B or of any other person except A (whether or not it is also A's religion or belief) A treats B less favourably than he treats or would treat other persons.[506]

The observations made above in relation to direct discrimination apply equally and this is discussed further in Chapter 6.

J. Age

5.154 As mentioned in Chapter 2, there is much stereotyping and prejudice around those who are both young and old. There are also many socially constructed ideas about what is age-appropriate conduct and dress. However, the meaning to be afforded the concept of 'age' and the determination of a person's 'age' is usually not difficult. 'Age' has a well-understood meaning and will refer to the number of days, weeks, and years, as appropriate, that a person has been alive. Accordingly, the case law under Article 14 addressing age discrimination does not reveal any difficulties in identifying age or understanding its meaning.[507]

5.155 It is unsurprising, therefore, that the Framework Directive does not define 'age' and nor do the Employment Equality (Age) Regulations 2006[508] (the Age Regulations) which give effect to its terms in respect of age.[509] It is unlikely that the meaning given to the concept of 'age' will arise as an issue in any proceedings under the Age Regulations, particularly given the fact that, as will be seen below, 'apparent age' is addressed by the Regulations.

5.156 However, the Age Regulations contain a rather narrower formulation of direct discrimination than that contained in certain of the other anti-discrimination enactments as is discussed further in Chapter 6. They do not in consequence address discrimination against a person by reason of their association with persons of a particular age (for example, that a person is the mother of small children or the carer of elderly relatives etc).[510] Nevertheless, because of explicit provision, as with the other main anti-discrimination enactments, less favourable treatment based on the perception of the complainant's age will be unlawful. Regulation 3(3)(b)

---

506 Ibid, s 77(2).

507 *R (Carson) v Secretary of State for Work and Pensions* [2006] 1 AC 173.

508 SI 2006/1031.

509 See, in particular, Regulation 2, the Interpretation Provision, which contains no reference to age at all.

510 Regulation 3(1)(a).

expressly provides that reference to the complainant's age includes the Complainant's 'apparent' age.[511] Accordingly, a person may bring a claim under the Regulations even if any discrimination is based on an inaccurate assumption about her or his age and without disclosing her or his actual age.

The Age Regulations, then, protect against discrimination connected with a person's actual age and discrimination connected with a person's presumed age.[512] In this way the Regulations have the facility to address prejudice and stereotyping around non-compliance with age norms. For example, a person who is treated less favourably because she or he appears too old or too young to be dressing as she or he does should be protected under the Age Regulations whether she or he was dressing 'age appropriately', in social terms, and even if she or he was not. Either situation would be covered by the direct discrimination provisions.[513] **5.157**

The Age Regulations define 'age group' for the purposes of the indirect discrimination provisions, in particular, as meaning a group of persons defined by reference to age, whether by reference to a particular age or a range of ages.[514] This means that the pool for comparison for the purposes of indirect discrimination need not be persons of the *same* age.[515] Indirect discrimination is considered in Chapter 6. **5.158**

K. Human Rights Act 1998

The classes protected by Articles 9 and 14 and the other Convention rights are addressed in Chapter 4. **5.159**

511 Age Regulations, Regulation 3(3)(b).
512 Regulation 3(3)(b).
513 See further Chap 6.
514 Regulation 3(3)(a).
515 Cf the indirect discrimination provisions of the other main anti-discrimination enactments: Chap 6.

6

'DISCRIMINATION'

> Democracy is founded on the principle that each individual has equal value. Treating some as automatically having less value than others not only causes pain and distress to that person but also violates his or her dignity as a human being. The essence of the Convention, as has often been said, is respect for human dignity and human freedom . . . Second, such treatment is damaging to society as a whole. Wrongly to assume that some people have talents and others do not is a huge waste of human resources. It also damages social cohesion, creating not only an under class, but an under class with a rational grievance. Third, it is the reverse of the rational behaviour we now expect of Government and the State. Power must not be exercised arbitrarily. If distinctions are to be drawn, particularly upon a group basis, it is an important discipline to look for a rational basis for those distinctions. Finally, it is a purpose of all human rights instruments to secure the protection of the essential rights of members of minority groups, even when they are unpopular with the majority. Democracy values everyone equally even if the majority does not.[1]

A. Introduction

6.01 Unlike the position in some other jurisdictions, the main anti-discrimination enactments define 'discrimination' for the purposes of their provisions closely and regulate it only within defined parameters. This chapter explains the concepts of discrimination under the main anti-discrimination enactments. The unlawful acts and other regulating provisions of the main anti-discrimination enactments are addressed in Chapters 7 onwards.

6.02 The main anti-discrimination enactments, except the Equal Pay Act 1970 (EPA), largely define discrimination in the same way, although there are important differences in some of the definitions and the Disability Discrimination Act 1995 (DDA), in particular, adopts a rather different approach to defining the concept of discrimination than that taken by the other main anti-discrimination enactments. In general, the approach taken by the main anti-discrimination enactments, the DDA aside, is to address individual instances of formal inequality. As mentioned in Chapter 2, the indirect discrimination provisions, which are discussed in full below, aspire to a more substantive realization of equality but these provisions have proved complex in practice. The direct discrimination provisions are most commonly relied upon and they are concerned only with formal distinctions in treatment, with protection afforded symmetrically. This approach means that positive discrimination and most positive action is made unlawful by all of the main anti-discrimination enactments (except the DDA) outside such narrow circumstances as to make the exceptions almost irrelevant.[2] The EPA

---

1 *Per* Baroness Hale, *Ghaidan v Godin-Mendoza* [2004] AC 605, para 132 (internal reference removed).

2 See Chap 13 for discussion on the positive action provisions.

addresses sex discrimination in pay and related benefits quite differently and this is addressed in paragraphs 6.270 onwards below.

In short summary, all the main anti-discrimination enactments (except the EPA) define and proscribe direct discrimination, harassment, and victimization in certain circumstances. The Race Relations Act 1976 (RRA), the Sex Discrimination Act 1975 (SDA), the Religion or Belief Regulations, the Sexual Orientation Regulations, and the Age Regulations (but not the DDA) all define indirect discrimination and proscribe it in certain circumstances. The DDA also defines disability-related discrimination and makes a failure to comply with a duty to make reasonable adjustments a form of discrimination for its purposes, and proscribes these two forms of discrimination in certain circumstances. In its original enactment the DDA did not use the expression 'direct discrimination' and though its prohibitions on disability-related discrimination covered direct discrimination, this was subject to a justification defence. However, in consequence of the obligations contained within the Framework Directive, the DDA has been amended to expressly prohibit direct discrimination[3] in the employment and related fields,[4] such direct discrimination not being subject to a justification defence. **6.03**

As mentioned in Chapter 1, all the main anti-discrimination enactments except the DDA adopt a similar structure. They all define discrimination and harassment in Part 1 and, in the original enactments, discrimination was defined in the same way for the purposes of all the provisions in the following parts of the Acts. However, because of amendments made for the purposes of compliance with EU law,[5] the meanings given to certain forms of discrimination in the RRA and SDA now depend upon the particular activity concerned. The differences will be fully explained below. As to the DDA, its structure has always been different. It defines discrimination differently and proscribes it discretely, depending on the particular activity concerned. Again, each form of discrimination provided for under the DDA and the circumstances in which they are applicable is described fully below. **6.04**

B. Other Jurisdictions

Like the UK, some jurisdictions adopt a formalistic approach to addressing inequality through law, adopting concepts similar to those contained in UK law. **6.05**

---

[3] DDA, s 3A(5) inserted by the Disability Discrimination Act 1995 (Amendment) Regulations 2003 SI 2003/1673 which came into effect on 1 Oct 2004. DDA, s 3A(5) applies only to the unlawful acts created by Part II of the DDA (employment and related activities): see Chap 8.

[4] In DDA, Parts 2 and 3, by providers of employment services (s 21A) and by General Qualifications Bodies (s 31AA) (although the latter provision is not in force at the time of writing).

[5] Though some provisions are not, arguably, compliant with EU law as will be discussed below.

EU anti-discrimination law matches UK law closely, largely because of the UK's role both in developing it[6] and in enacting domestic legislation to give effect to it.[7] Other jurisdictions adopting a similar approach include New Zealand (see, in particular, the New Zealand Human Rights Act 1993) and Australia (see, in particular, the Australian Sex Discrimination Act 1984 and Disability Discrimination Act 1993[8]).

6.06 Some jurisdictions, however, adopt more substantive concepts of equality and discrimination—that is, concepts which are concerned with securing particular equality outcomes. The promotion of substantive equality through law is sometimes achieved by adopting a 'human dignity' threshold, closely reflecting the values protected in most human rights instruments. If it is accepted that *everyone* has an inherent dignity arising from their humanity and an entitlement to respect for it, as most modern human rights instruments do, then measures which are disrespectful of individuals or groups because of human characteristics they possess (sex, race etc), or because of historic disadvantage associated with those characteristics, will necessarily violate dignity. A 'dignity' model acknowledges prejudice and stereotyping but also recognizes an entitlement to 'personal development', forging a link between dignity and autonomy,[9] so that 'the idea that we should ask whether [a measure] affects membership in society in a basic way or denies participation in important social institutions suggests that these forms of participation are crucial in their own right to a life with dignity'.[10] The close relationship

[6] See Chap 4.

[7] Though not always properly, as is discussed below.

[8] The Australian Racial Discrimination Act 1975 at least (uniquely amongst Australian federal anti-discrimination legislation) provides for a general right of equality before the law (s 10(1): 'If, by reason of, or of a provision of, a law of the Commonwealth or of a State or Territory, persons of a particular race, colour or national or ethnic origin do not enjoy a right that is enjoyed by persons of another race, colour or national or ethnic origin, or enjoy a right to a more limited extent than persons of another race, colour or national or ethnic origin, then, notwithstanding anything in that law, persons of the first-mentioned race, colour or national or ethnic origin shall, by force of this section, enjoy that right to the same extent as persons of that other race, colour or national or ethnic origin.'). The Australian Age Discrimination Act 2004 adopts a similar approach to the Sex Discrimination Act 1984 and Disability Discrimination Act 1993.

[9] See discussion in D Reaume, 'Discrimination and Dignity' (2003) Louisiana Law Review 63, 645–95, 673, reprinted in C McCrudden, *Anti-discrimination Law* (2nd edn 2003, International Library of Essays in Law and Legal Theory, Second series), 248–97, 275.

[10] Ibid, 645–95, 674. Economic inequality and its effects may be relevant to a 'dignity' analysis: *Egan v Canada* [1995] 2 SCR 513, *per* L'Heureux-Dube J ('The *Charter* is a document of civil, political and legal rights. It is not a charter of economic rights. This is not to say, however, that economic prejudices or benefits are irrelevant to determinations under s. 15 of the *Charter*. Quite the contrary. Economic benefits or prejudices are relevant to s. 15, but are more accurately regarded as symptomatic of the types of distinctions that are at the heart of s. 15: those that offend inherent human dignity', 544).

between equality and respect for human dignity has been acknowledged in the case law from Canada and South Africa, in particular.[11]

At the constitutional level in South Africa, for example, the test of 'unfair discrimination' under Article 9 of the Constitution[12] depends upon an analysis of past patterns of discrimination and disadvantage, the purpose of any discriminatory measure complained of (and whether it is intended to achieve a worthwhile societal goal, like furthering the right to equality), the extent to which the discrimination has affected the complainant's rights or interests, and whether the discrimination has led to an impairment of the complainant's fundamental human dignity or to an impairment of a comparably serious nature.[13] 6.07

In Canada a dignity model was developed under section 15 of the Canadian Charter of Rights and Freedoms.[14] Prior to the Charter, case law under the equality provision in the Canadian Bill of Rights (1960) produced a very formalistic test of discrimination,[15] and the formulation of the Charter equality guarantee was in part a response to this.[16] The Charter adopts a substantive approach to equality. By this is meant that it 'pays attention to the actual conditions of life of members of disadvantaged groups [so that] rules creating, or exacerbating, or 6.08

[11] For a full discussion on 'dignity' and its role in equality law, see, G Moon and R Allen, 'Dignity Discourse in Discrimination Law: A Better Route to Equality' (2006) EHRLR 610.

[12] '(1) Everyone is equal before the law and has the right to equal protection and benefit of the law; (2) Equality includes the full and equal enjoyment of all rights and freedoms. To promote the achievement of equality, legislative and other measures designed to protect or advance persons, or categories of persons, disadvantaged by unfair discrimination may be taken; (3) The state may not *unfairly* discriminate directly or indirectly against anyone on one or more grounds, including race, gender, sex, pregnancy, marital status, ethnic or social origin, colour, sexual orientation, age, disability, religion, conscience, belief, culture, language and birth; (4) No person may unfairly discriminate directly or indirectly against anyone on one or more grounds in terms of subsection (3). National legislation must be enacted to prevent or prohibit unfair discrimination; (5) Discrimination on one or more of the grounds listed in subsection (3) is unfair unless it is established that the discrimination is fair' (emphasis added).

[13] *President of South Africa and Anr v Hugo* (1997) 4 SA 1 (CC).

[14] (1982); Constitution Act 1982, enacted as Schedule B to the Canada Act 1982 (UK) ('(1) Every individual is equal before and under the law and has the right to the equal protection and equal benefit of the law without discrimination and, in particular, without discrimination based on race, national or ethnic origin, colour, religion, sex, age or mental or physical disability; (2) Subsection (1) does not preclude any law, program or activity that has as its object the amelioration of conditions of disadvantaged individuals or groups including those that are disadvantaged because of race, national or ethnic origin, colour, religion, sex, age or mental or physical disability.')

[15] See *AG of Canada v Lavell* [1974] SCR 1349 (provision of the Indian Act 1876 which deprived Indian women (but not men) of their status as Indian under the Act upon marriage to a non-Indian did not violate Bill of Rights because applied equally to all those to whom it was directed ie Indian women); *Bliss v AG of Canada* [1979] 1 SCR 183 (provision of Unemployment Insurance Act (1971, 1970-71-72) which excluded absences caused by pregnancy from qualifying for sickness benefits and which provided more restrictive benefits to pregnant women did not deny equality because it treated all 'pregnant persons' alike).

[16] A McColgan, *Women Under the Law, the False Promise of Human Rights* (2000, Longman) 40.

perhaps simply not correcting background inequalities should be changed, even if they distribute some benefit equally within their own four corners'.[17] Section 15(1) of the Charter must be understood, according to the case law, as 'protecting and promoting human dignity [and that] infuses all elements of the discrimination analysis'.[18] Four factors may indicate a violation of human dignity and indicate discrimination for the purposes of section 15(1) of the Charter, namely:

(i) pre-existing disadvantage;
(ii) correlation (or lack of it) between the grounds of the claim and the actual needs, capacities, and circumstances of the complainant (legislation which takes into account the actual needs, capacities, or circumstances of the claimant and others with similar traits in a manner that respects their value as human beings and members of society will be less likely to have a negative effect on human dignity);
(iii) the ameliorative purpose or effect of the law on historically disadvantaged groups; and
(iv) the nature and scope of any interest affected.[19]

6.09 The 'dignity' and 'disadvantage' models adopted by the constitutional courts of South Africa and Canada accommodate and may require positive measures. Affirmative action is a 'composite part' of the equality guarantee in the South African Constitution,[20] and in Canada ameliorative measures are embraced by the equality guarantee.[21] In Canada, section 15 may require accommodations to be made,[22] and in South African equality law, too, a duty to make accommodations or adjustments arises across all grounds protected.[23]

6.10 Recognizing the 'dignity' inherent in all of us by virtue of our status as human beings, then, can ensure that everybody is treated as having value or worth,

---

17 D Reaume, 'Discrimination and Dignity' (2003) Louisiana Law Review 63, 645–95, 648, reprinted in C McCrudden, *Anti-discrimination Law* (2nd edn 2003, International library of Essays in Law and Legal Theory, Second series), 247–97, 250, internal reference removed.

18 *Law v Canada (Minister of Employment and Immigration)* [1999] 1 SCR 497, para 54, *per* Iacobucci J.

19 *Law v Canada (Minister of Employment and Immigration)* [1999] 1 SCR 497, para 62–75, *per* Iacobucci J. The statutory measures in South Africa and Canada reflect the 'dignity' and 'disadvantage' models seen in the jurisprudence of their constitutional courts. In determining the 'unfairness' of any alleged discrimination, South Africa's Promotion of Equality and Prevention of Unfair Discrimination Act 2000 requires that the following, amongst other, features are taken into account; 'whether the discrimination impairs or is likely to impair human dignity; and 'the position of the complainant in society and whether he or she suffers from patterns of disadvantage or belongs to a group that suffers from such patterns of disadvantage' (s 14(3)).

20 *Minister of Finance and Another v Frederik Jacobus Van Heerden* (1994) CCT 63/03.

21 *Lovelace v Ontario* [2000] SCC 37.

22 *Andrews v Law Society of British Columbia* [1989] 1 SCR 143, 169, 'for the accommodation of differences, which is the essence of true equality, it will frequently be necessary to make distinctions. See too, Canadian Human Rights Act 1977, s 16.

23 The case law emerging under the Constitutional equality guarantee is plainly wide enough to incorporate a duty to make accommodations or adjustments. As mentioned, Art 9(1) is concerned,

whoever they are, and embraces, respects, and promotes diversity whilst eschewing arbitrary distinctions. The 'dignity/equality' models also provide a principled mechanism for managing 'conflicts' between rights. Any pluralistic democracy will have to address the friction that may arise between the interests of different classes of persons. In a legislative context, this may be achieved by providing for specific statutory exceptions;[24] 'justification' defences and/or 'reasonableness' limitations tested case by case by balancing competing interests;[25] or by creating a 'hierarchy' of grounds such that some interests are valued above others.[26] The 'dignity' models, however, have the capacity to address 'conflicts' in a more nuanced way. [27]

according to the case law, with promoting substantive equality. This may require formal differences in treatment to reflect differences in respective situations. The Promotion of Equality and Prevention of Unfair Discrimination Act 2000 makes express provision requiring the extent to which an alleged discriminator has 'taken such steps as being reasonable in the circumstances to (i) address the disadvantage which arises from or is related to one or more of the prohibited grounds; or (ii) accommodate diversity to be taken into account' (s 14(1)–(3)).

[24] For example, exempting the appointment of clergy from sex discrimination law, as the SDA does in s 19.

[25] As in the indirect discrimination provisions in the UK's anti-discrimination legislation; SDA, s 1(1)(b)(ii) and (2)(b)(iii); RRA, s 1(1)(b)(ii) and (1A)(c); Religion or Belief Regulations, regulation 3(1)(b)(iii); Sexual Orientation Regulations, regulation 3(1)(b)(iii); and Age Regulations, regulation 3(1)(b).

[26] See, for example, the US Supreme Court jurisprudence which subjects distinctions based on race to strict scrutiny (*Loving v Virginia* (1967) 388 US 1, Court unanimously stated 'At the very least, the Equal Protection Clause demands that racial classifications, especially suspect in criminal statutes, be subjected to the "most rigid scrutiny"' (p 13) and declared unconstitutional Virginia's Racial Integrity Act 1924—an anti-miscegenation statute—thus ending all race-based legal restrictions on marriage)—but distinctions based on sexual orientation and sex to only 'rational' or intermediate scrutiny, respectively (*Romer v Evans* 517 US 620 (1996); *Craig v Boren* (1976) 429 US 190, declared, by a majority, that statutory or administrative sex-based classifications were subject to an intermediate level of judicial review in examining whether the enactment of different drinking ages for men and women violated the equal protection clause). It should be noted, however, that since *Craig* the court has not been 'altogether consistent in its articulation of the appropriate standard of review in gender discrimination cases'. Stone et al, *Constitutional Law* (4th edn 2001, Aspen), 607. The same observations may be made about the application of the 'rational' scrutiny test to sexual orientation discrimination, see discussion in *Romer v Evans* 517 US 620 (1996) ('laws of the kind now before us raise the inevitable inference that the disadvantage imposed is born of animosity toward the class of persons affected. "[I]f the constitutional conception of 'equal protection of the laws' means anything, it must at the very least mean that a bare . . . desire to harm a politically unpopular group cannot constitute a legitimate governmental interest." *Department of Agriculture v Moreno*, 413 US 528, 534 (1973). Even laws enacted for broad and ambitious purposes often can be explained by reference to legitimate public policies which justify the incidental disadvantages they impose on certain persons. Amendment 2, however, in making a general announcement that gays and lesbians shall not have any particular protections from the law, inflicts on them immediate, continuing, and real injuries that outrun and belie any legitimate justifications that may be claimed for it. We conclude that, in addition to the far-reaching deficiencies of Amendment 2 that we have noted, the principles it offends, in another sense, are conventional and venerable; a law must bear a rational relationship to a legitimate governmental purpose, *Kadrmas v Dickinson Public Schools*, 487 US 450, 462 (1988), and Amendment 2 does not', *per* Kennedy J for the majority of the court).

[27] See discussion in, S Fredman, 'The Future of Equality in Britain', Working Paper Series No 5 (2002, Equal Opportunities Commission), 30–1.

6.11 Despite these advantages, the invocation of 'dignity' in equality discourse has not been uncontroversial. Indeed, using 'dignity' as a threshold or measure in the equality context has come in for a good deal of criticism.[28] It is said to be 'vague to the point of vacuous and, therefore, too easily usable to dress up decisions based on nothing more than conservative gut reaction or excessive deference to Parliament'.[29] It is also said that the concept 'has no coherent internal dynamic: it is analogous to the "empty" concept of equality . . . being fundamentally a "shell concept" open to diverse, but usually majoritarian interpretations that do not challenge the status quo'.[30] However, it might be said that such criticisms could be more forcefully made about the formalistic approach taken by the UK's comparative based anti-discrimination laws, as will be seen below.[31]

6.12 The 'dignity' model has also been criticized for its individualistic focus,[32] but this ignores the importance in a modern democracy of valuing each individual for their own worth—a scheme otherwise is unlikely to attract broad community respect (that is, from all individuals and groups, whether forming part of the majority or minority) and meet the standards of modern human rights values. A model which recognizes disadvantage in determining what distinctions are objectionable and unlawful satisfies the need to respect individuals, accommodate diversity, and address disadvantage. In any case, 'dignity' is not 'an individualistic or abstract notion but is firmly grounded in the notion of community and social participation', as seen from the discussion above.[33]

6.13 The formal and more precise approach taken by UK anti-discrimination law has at least the virtue of certainty.[34] Though the meanings given to the concepts of discrimination under the main anti-discrimination enactments are complex and

---

28 See D Reaume, 'Discrimination and Dignity' (2003) Louisiana Law Review 63, 645–95, 646, reprinted in C McCrudden, *Anti-discrimination Law* (2nd edn 2003, International Library of Essays in Law and Legal Theory, Second series), 247–297, 248.

29 Ibid.

30 E Grabham, 'Law v Canada: New Directions for Equality under the Canadian Charter?' (2002) Oxford Journal of Legal Studies, Vol 22, No 4, 641–61, 654, internal references removed.

31 See eg, some of Lord Denning's notorious early judgments (*Peake v Automotive Products Limited* [1978] QB 233 at 238, in particular); the dress code cases (*Department for Work and Pensions v Thompson* [2004] IRLR 348).

32 E Grabham, 'Law v Canada: New Directions for Equality under the Canadian Charter?' (2002) Oxford Journal of Legal Studies, Vol 22, No 4, 641–61, 654.

33 S Fredman and S Spencer, *Age is an Equality Issue, Legal and Policy Perspective* (2003, Hart), 3.

34 It should be noted that the protection of human dignity is not completely alien to UK anti-discrimination law. The concept of dignity expressly informs (albeit a small) part of the UK's existing anti-discrimination scheme, emerging both from the case law (see, eg, *Burton & Rhule v De Vere Hotels* [1996] IRLR 596, *Insitu Cleaning Co v Heads* [1995] IRLR 4, amongst others, citing with approval the EC Recommendation on European Commission Recommendation No 92/131/EEC entitled 'On the protection of the dignity of women and men at work') and the statutory protections (see the harassment provisions in the main anti-discrimination enactments described below); however, its reach and focus (harassment) is narrow.

have increased in number with the impact of EU law in particular, their parameters can be fairly easily discerned. Each form of discrimination defined and proscribed by the main anti-discrimination enactments is described in detail below.

C. Direct Discrimination

(1) Introduction and EU law

'Direct' discrimination is regulated under all the main anti-discrimination enactments and, in the main,[35] is outlawed across all the activities covered by them,[36] except in the case of the DDA. In one sense the concept of direct discrimination is easy to understand—it addresses those instances where people are treated differently because of their race, sex etc and, conversely, a prohibition against it requires that people are treated in the same way, irrespective of race, sex etc. The RRA provides, for example, that: **6.14**

> A person discriminates against another in any circumstances relevant for the purposes of any provision of this Act if—on racial grounds he treats that other less favourably than he treats or would treat other persons.[37]

In practice, understanding and applying the legal meaning of direct discrimination has proved very complicated indeed. The meanings (because there are more than one) given to direct discrimination by the main anti-discrimination enactments, though shortly phrased, are highly technical. There are subtle but very important distinctions between the meanings given to direct discrimination by some of the main anti-discrimination enactments as compared to others, and unravelling all this has led to a very great deal of case law, as is discussed below.

In its original enactment, the DDA did not outlaw direct discrimination in terms.[38] Provision is now made in the DDA to address direct discrimination. In particular, section 3A(5) was inserted by the Disability Discrimination Act 1995 (Amendment) Regulations 2003,[39] which came into effect on **6.15**

[35] Direct discrimination connected to gender reassignment, marital and civil partnership status, and in respect of the express provision addressing pregnancy, applies only to the employment and related fields: SDA, ss 2A, 3, and 3A.

[36] SDA, s 1(1)(a) and (2)(a); RRA, s 1(1)(a); DDA, s 3A(5); Sexual Orientation Regulations, regulation 3(1)(a); Religion or Belief Regulations, regulation 3(1)(a); Age Regulations, regulation 3(1)(a).

[37] RRA, s 1(1)(a).

[38] Unless it also constituted disability-related discrimination, as is described below.

[39] SI 2003/1673. It applies only to the unlawful acts created by Part II of the DDA (employment and related activities): see Chap 8.

1 October 2004 and which were made[40] to give effect to the requirement in the Framework Directive[41] that Member States outlaw disability discrimination (including direct disability discrimination) in the employment and related fields.[42] Section 3A(5) accordingly applies only to the employment and related fields. Provision is now also made addressing direct disability discrimination by those providing employment services,[43] in further and higher education,[44] and by general qualifications bodies.[45]

6.16 As discussed in Chapter 5, express provision is now made addressing direct pregnancy- and maternity-related discrimination in the SDA, following the making of the Employment Equality (Sex Discrimination) Regulations 2005.[46] Importantly, however, direct pregnancy and maternity discrimination is also likely to constitute direct sex discrimination.[47] This is discussed further below.[48]

6.17 'Direct' discrimination is now regulated in all the main anti-discrimination enactments, principally through two models.[49] The RRA and the Sexual Orientation Regulations protect against less favourable treatment on 'racial grounds'[50] and 'on grounds of sexual orientation',[51] respectively. The SDA, the DDA, and the Age Regulations regulate less favourable treatment 'on the ground of [the complainant's] sex',[52] 'on the ground of [the complainant's] disability',[53] and 'on the ground of [the complainant's] age',[54] respectively. There is an important difference between the two formulations. The RRA and the Sexual Orientation Regulations do not require that the treatment complained of be connected to or grounded in the complainant's race or sexual orientation. The RRA and Sexual Orientation Regulations, therefore, are wide enough to cover less favourable treatment connected with another person's race or sexual orientation—for example, a partner's or friend's—and to less favourable treatment connected to a refusal to comply with an instruction or practice which is

---

40 Under s 2(2) of the European Communities Act 1972, see Chap 4.

41 2000/78/EC.

42 Article 2(2)(a).

43 DDA, s 21A(5).

44 Ibid, s 28S(10), as inserted by the Disability Discrimination Act 1995 (Amendment) (Further and Higher Education) Regulations 2006 SI 2006/1721.

45 DDA, s 31AB(8), though this provision is not in force at the date of writing.

46 SI 2005/2467. See, new s 3A, the lawfulness of which must be doubted, see Chap 5.

47 S 1(1)(a) and s 1(2)(a), SDA.

48 Para 6.51 onwards.

49 The meaning given to direct discrimination in the Religion or Belief Regulations is addressed below at para 6.24.

50 RRA, s 1(1)(a).

51 Sexual Orientation Regulations, regulation 3(1)(a).

52 SDA, s 1(1)(a) and (2)(a).

53 DDA, s 3A(5).

54 Age Regulations, regulation 3(1)(a).

grounded in race or sexual orientation.[55] Such a formulation also allows for claims to be brought based on perceived race or sexual orientation. Less favourable treatment on the grounds that an employer believes a person to be gay would be outlawed by the direct discrimination provisions, even if as matters transpired she or he was straight.[56]

The SDA and DDA, on the other hand, require that the treatment complained of be on the ground of the *complainant's* sex or disability (in the latter case, requiring too that the complainant be *disabled*, within the meaning of the DDA). This limitation applies equally to the protection afforded against direct discrimination connected to gender reassignment, marital or civil partnership status, and the express protection afforded against direct pregnancy- and maternity-related discrimination.[57] This means that the discrimination must be grounded in the *complainant's actual* status. It may be that in relation to protection against discrimination connected to *perceived* sex, this is a limited constraint within the context of the SDA overall. This is because sex (in the sense covered by the SDA[58]) would usually be obvious save in cases of gender reassignment which attracts separate protection discussed already in Chapter 5 and further below, and because the SDA does not protect against a social model of gender.[59] However, the issue may be very relevant in disability cases, where a person may be apparently disabled but, according to the very rigid formulation in the DDA for determining 'disability',[60] is not as a matter of law disabled (for example, a person who has regular epileptic seizures but, on enquiry, not sufficiently severe or regular to meet the definition of 'disability' in the DDA). Importantly, too, the direct discrimination provisions in the SDA and DDA do not protect against less favourable treatment connected to another person's sex (for example, the sex of one's partner or the disability status of a partner or child) or a refusal to comply with instructions to discriminate.[61] **6.18**

55 *Race Relations Board v Applin* [1973] 1 QB 815; *Zarcynska v Levy* [1978] IRLR 532; *Weathersfield Ltd (t/a Van & Truck Rentals) v Sargent* [1999] ICR 425; IRLR 94; *Redfearn v SERCO LTD t/a West Yorkshire Transport Service* [2006] EWCA Civ 659; [2006] IRLR 623.

56 See *Sexual Orientation and the Work Place: Putting the Employment Equality (Sexual Orientation) Regulations 2003 into Practice, for Employers and their Staff*, ACAS Guidance, available at <http://www.acas.org.uk/index.aspx?articleid=337>.

57 SDA, ss 2A, 3, and 3A require that the less favourable treatment be 'on the ground that B intends to undergo, is undergoing or has undergone gender reassignment'; 'on the ground of the fulfilment of the condition', namely that he is married or a civil partner and 'on the ground of the woman's pregnancy' or 'on the ground that the woman is exercising or seeking to exercise, or has exercised or sought to exercise, a statutory right to maternity leave' or 'on the ground that section 72(1) of the Employment Rights Act 1996 (compulsory maternity leave) has to be complied with in respect of the woman', respectively.

58 See Chap 5.

59 See Chap 5.

60 See Chap 5.

61 See, however, Chap 15 for other protection in relation to 'instructions'.

6.19 The Age Regulations have the same limitation in their formulation of direct discrimination, except that in relation to *perceived* age and *instructions* to discriminate, express provision is made. Thus Regulation 3(2)(b) provides that the reference in the direct discrimination provision 'to B's age includes B's apparent age'[62] and Regulation 5 treats less favourable treatment connected to instructions to discriminate as discrimination. The Age Regulations, therefore, would not protect a person against less favourable treatment associated with another person's age (the age of their children or persons for whom they have caring responsibilities, for example), but would protect against some of the more obvious forms of stereotyping around age by protecting a person who is perceived to be too old or too young, for example, against less favourable treatment, as well as providing protection in respect of instructions to discriminate.

6.20 The narrower formulations in the SDA, DDA, and the Age Regulations are probably not compliant with EU law. The Equal Treatment Directive,[63] as amended by the Equal Treatment Amendment Directive,[64] requires Member States to outlaw direct sex discrimination in certain circumstances. The Equal Treatment Amendment Directive defines direct sex discrimination as occurring:

> Where one person is treated less favourably on grounds of sex than another is, has been or would be treated in a comparable situation.[65]

The Framework Directive[66] requires Member States to outlaw direct discrimination connected with the grounds it protects, and defines direct discrimination as follows:

> Direct discrimination shall be taken to occur where one person is treated less favourably than another is, has been or would be treated in a comparable situation, on any of the grounds referred to in Article 1 [namely, religion or belief, disability, age or sexual orientation].

6.21 The two Directives, therefore, would seem clear in obliging Member States to outlaw direct sex, disability, and age discrimination (at least in the activities covered by the Directives[67]) more broadly than the definitions presently provided for under the SDA, the DDA, and the Age Regulations, in particular by outlawing less favourable treatment *on the grounds* of sex, disability, age etc. As discussed, such a formulation is wide enough to cover less favourable treatment on the grounds of another's sex, disability status, or age, as well as discrimination based on perceived sex, disability, and age, and less favourable treatment connected to

62 As discussed in Chap 5.

63 See Chap 4.

64 See Chap 4.

65 Art 2(2), as amended by the Equal Treatment Amendment Directive. The Equal Treatment Directive in its unamended form also prohibited direct discrimination 'on grounds of sex'.

66 See Chap 4.

67 The employment and related fields, see Chap 4.

discriminatory instructions. Further, the Equal Treatment Amendment Directive and the Framework Directive make express provision addressing discriminatory instructions and provide that 'an instruction to discriminate' on one of the protected grounds 'shall be deemed to be discrimination'.[68] Whilst limited protection is provided for under the DDA and SDA against instructions to discriminate,[69] these are not treated as forms of discrimination and are therefore not actionable by persons treated less favourably in consequence, in breach of the Directives.[70]

It is easy to see why an unrestricted meaning of direct discrimination, consistent with that given in the Directives described above, could have the effect of protecting against discrimination rooted in experiences that the particular enactment is not intended to address. Thus, for example, as just alluded to, if direct age discrimination were defined in the same way as in the Framework Directive, a person might properly complain under the Age Regulations that she was discriminated against because she had young children.[71] It might be argued, convincingly, that the Age Regulations were not designed to address gender discrimination and any remedy for such discrimination lies under the SDA rather than the Age Regulations. However, the Directives are clear and consistent in their requirement that less favourable treatment 'on grounds of' the strands covered be outlawed by Member States, and this does give a wide reach to the concepts of direct discrimination. Importantly, too, it recognizes the very close connection between each of the grounds that often exist and that social experiences of gender, age, and sometimes race cannot always be easily disentangled.[72] Women as older women, women with young children or disabled children, and women otherwise at different 'ages', do experience particular patterns of disadvantage.[73] The same may be said, in certain circumstances, of men.[74] Recital (3) of the Framework Directive acknowledges this by its direction that: **6.22**

> [i]n implementing the principle of equal treatment [under the Framework Directive, addressing religion or belief, disability, age, and sexual orientation], the Community should, in accordance with Article 3(2) of the EC Treaty, aim to eliminate inequalities, and to promote equality between men and women, especially since women are often the victims of multiple discrimination.

---

68 Art 2(4), as amended by the Equal Treatment Amendment Directive; Art 2(4), Framework Directive.

69 See Chap 15.

70 Both of which require that individuals have access to proper judicial process in respect of any violation of the Directives; Equal Treatment Amendment Directive, Art 6; Framework Directive, Art 9. See Chap 4.

71 See the example in *Hurley v Mustoe* [1981] ICR 490.

72 See discussion in Chap 5.

73 See, for example, discussion in C Wolff, 'Retired Women—The Disadvantaged Majority' (2006) EOR 149, 16.

74 See *Secretary of State for Trade and Industry v Rutherford & Others* [2006] UKHL 19; [2006] IRLR 551.

In addition, the Equal Treatment Directive, as amended by the Equal Treatment Amendment Directive,[75] requires Member States to 'actively take into account the objective of equality between men and women when formulating law . . . policies [etc]' in the areas covered by the Equal Treatment Directive. This obliges Member States to promote gender equality through any laws, including discrimination laws, falling within the scope of the Directive (employment and related fields) whether or not explicitly directed at gender.

6.23 The question whether the DDA formulation of direct discrimination is compliant with the Framework Directive has been referred to the European Court of Justice (ECJ) in *Coleman v Attridge Law*,[76] a case which illustrates clearly the connection between the strands protected. The complainant, Ms Coleman, is the mother of a disabled child and she claimed direct disability discrimination under the DDA,[77] contending that she was discriminated against because she is the primary carer for her disabled child. A London South Employment Tribunal has referred a number of questions to the ECJ, in particular whether the Framework Directive protects from direct discrimination[78] only persons who are themselves disabled and, if not, whether it also protects employees who are not themselves disabled but who are treated less favourably on the ground of their association with a disabled person. The ECJ's decision is awaited.

6.24 The Religion or Belief Regulations, regulate direct discrimination in the same way as the RRA and Sexual Orientation Regulations by prohibiting discrimination, in certain circumstances, as follows:

> For the purposes of these regulations, a person ('A') discriminates against another person ('B') if—(a) on the grounds of religion or belief, A treats B less favourably than he treats or would treat other persons.[79]

As with the observations above, this would appear to give a wide reach to the protection against direct discrimination under the Religion or Belief Regulations. However, by Regulation 3(2), it is provided that 'the reference in paragraph (1)(a) to religion or belief does not include A's religion or belief'. This limits the reach of the Regulations. It means, for example, that a woman not given employment or allowed access to a meeting or other public place because the employer or the persons convening the meeting held particular religious views which, according to the tenets of their faith, justified the exclusion of women, would not have a remedy under the Religion or Belief Regulations. She would, of course, have a

75 See Chap 4.

76 Referred by a London South Employment Tribunal (Chair: M Stacey), EOR (2006) No 155, 27.

77 DDA, s 3A(5).

78 And harassment, see further below.

79 Regulation 3(1)(a).

remedy[80] under the SDA. It is not at all clear that this is what motivated the Government to include the limitation in Regulation 3(2). It certainly, however, recognizes the close relationship between religion and gender.[81] It has been suggested that the qualification in Regulation 3(2) is designed to ensure that motive is not had regard to in determining whether direct discrimination is made out, so that if the treatment is based on actual or perceived religion, it matters not what the discriminator's religion or belief is.[82] It is unlikely that this is the explanation, particularly when one has regard to the fact that there was already a good deal of case law, including from the House of Lords, indicating that motive is irrelevant to the determination of a direct discrimination complaint.[83] The most likely explanation, as I have described, is that the Government wished to limit the scope of the Regulations so as to ensure that there was no overlap between the Religion or Belief Regulations and, for example, the SDA and Sexual Orientation Regulations. Such an overlap would have the important effect of allowing claims rooted in gender and sexual orientation to be brought under the Religion or Belief Regulations and affect the exemptions which would then apply.[84]

The Equality Act 2006 (EA) makes materially the same provision in relation to direct religion and belief discrimination in the context of the unlawful acts it creates.[85] In addition, when in force it will amend the meaning of direct religion and belief discrimination in the Religion or Belief Regulations, but in both cases its meaning of direct discrimination is materially identical to that presently found in the Religion or Belief Regulations.[86] **6.25**

Direct discrimination under all the main anti-discrimination enactments requires that the treatment complained of be both on the prohibited grounds (race, sex etc) and be less favourable than the treatment that was or would have been afforded other persons. This requires a comparative analysis, which has not always proved easy in practice. Each of the elements of the direct discrimination provisions is discussed below. **6.26**

---

[80] Assuming the activity concerned fell within one of the unlawful acts provided for under the SDA, and was not subject to any specific exclusion, as to which see Chap 13.

[81] As illustrated, eg, in the case of *R (on the application of Begum, by her litigation friend, Rahman) v Headteacher and Governors of Denbigh High School* [2006] UKHL 15.

[82] N de Marco, *Blackstone Guide to the Employment Equality Regulations* (2004, OUP), 17.

[83] See below, para 6.73.

[84] See Chap 13.

[85] See Chaps 9–12. They are not in force at the time of writing.

[86] EA, ss 45(1) and 77 ('on the grounds of the religion or belief of B or of any other person except A (whether or not it is also A's religion or belief) A treats B less favourably than he treats or would treat other persons'). The new meaning puts beyond doubt that the provisions cover religious discrimination even where the less favourable treatment is directed at a person who is of the same religion as the discriminator so long as it is the victim's religion, rather than the discriminator's, which is material. If a Catholic employer refused to employ a Catholic in an abortion clinic because he thought abortion contrary to Catholic belief, he would be directly discriminating against any potential Catholic employee in refusing them work for that reason.

(2) Less favourable treatment

6.27 The direct discrimination provisions in each of the main anti-discrimination enactments regulate *less favourable treatment*. 'To 'treat' for these purposes means simply to 'deal with' or 'behave towards' and this is therefore an expansive expression.[87] *Less favourable treatment* is a concept wide enough to cover any 'disadvantage'.[88] It is not necessary for there to be any tangible loss.[89] Indeed a favourable financial outcome might conceal unlawful discrimination—one cannot buy a right to discriminate or set off one discriminatory act against another (so, for example, permitting women to leave work five minutes earlier than men is not saved by a rule that all men are paid more money than women).[90] Nor is it necessary to know of any disadvantage for it to cause actionable less favourable treatment.[91] A mere deprivation of choice will be sufficient to found a claim of less favourable treatment.[92] Words or acts of discouragement can amount to less favourable treatment of a person thereby discouraged.[93]

6.28 Many of the unlawful acts created by the main anti-discrimination enactments outlaw discrimination, as defined, where such causes a 'detriment'[94] to the complainant. In considering the meaning to be given to 'less favourable treatment' the courts have generally adopted the same test as that applied to determining whether a 'detriment' has occurred and have set a low threshold. The meanings given to 'less favourable treatment' and to 'detriment' therefore now coincide. The test for less favourable treatment has become largely (though not wholly) subjective, as with the concept of 'detriment'. A striking illustration can be seen in the case of *Chief Constable of West Yorkshire Police v Khan*.[95] Detective Sergeant Khan complained that he was subject to less favourable treatment[96] when he was refused a reference by the force to which he was attached in respect of a position with a different force. The force argued that Detective Sergeant Khan had suffered no less favourable treatment because, had they provided the reference, the reference would have been poor and he would not have been

87 *Alder v Crown Prosecution Service* [2006] EWCA Civ 1741, para 16.

88 *Jeremiah v Ministry of Defence* [1980] ICR 13; [1980] QB 87; [1979] IRLR 436.

89 *Chief Constable of West Yorkshire Police v Khan* [2001] UKHL 48; [2001] 1WLR 1947, paras 52–3; *Gill v El Vino Co Ltd* [1983] QB 425.

90 *Ministry of Defence v Jeremiah* [1980] QB 87.

91 *Garry v London Borough of Ealing* [2001] IRLR 681.

92 *Gill v El Vino Co Ltd* [1983] QB 425 and *R v Birmingham City Council ex p Equal Opportunities Commission* [1989] AC 1155, [1989] IRLR 173.

93 *Simon v Brimham Associates* [1987] ICR 596; [1987] IRLR 307—though the result in this case is somewhat unfathomable; see, 'Highlights' [1987] IRLR 305–06.

94 See Chap 7 onwards.

95 [2001] UKHL 48; [2001] 1 WLR 1947; [2001] ICR 1065; [2001] IRLR 830.

96 The case in fact concerned victimization, as to which see below, but both direct discrimination and victimization set a threshold requirement of 'less favourable treatment' and the meaning to be given to the concept under both will be the same.

interviewed. As it was, because no reference was provided, Detective Sergeant Khan was granted an interview by the second force. He did not, in the event, succeed in his application but it was contended that he gained the benefit of an interview of which he otherwise would have been deprived, and therefore enjoyed a greater chance of obtaining the posting he sought than if the reference had been provided. The House of Lords concluded that, notwithstanding the absence of any tangible disadvantage, Detective Sergeant Khan had suffered less favourable treatment for the purposes of the discrimination provisions.[97]

The legal meaning given to the concept of 'detriment' in the anti-discrimination enactments is discussed further in Chapter 8 and the observations made there apply equally to the expression 'less favourable treatment'. **6.29**

(3) Segregation

Uniquely, the RRA makes provision in relation to segregation. As discussed in Chapter 2,[98] this provision recognized the US's experience of segregation and is found in the first place in the RRA 1968. That provision was re-enacted in section 1(2) of the 1976 RRA which now provides that: **6.30**

> it is hereby declared that, for the purposes of this Act, segregating a person from other persons on racial grounds is treating him less favourably than they are treated.

As was observed in the seminal case of *Brown v Board of Education*,[99] in relation to racial segregation in public education:

> to separate [children] from others of a similar age and qualification solely because of their race generates a feeling of inferiority as to their status in the community that may affect their hearts and minds in a way unlikely ever to be undone . . . in the field of public education the doctrine of "separate but equal" has no place. Separate educational facilities are inherently unequal.[100]

The same observations can usually be made in respect of other areas of private[101] and public life. Separating people along racial lines will usually reflect ideas of superiority and inferiority as between racial groups and will be inherently less favourable. The only exception to this may be where special provision is made for particular racial groups for the purposes of assisting them in overcoming disadvantage or meeting special needs; these issues are discussed under 'positive action' in Chapter 13.

---

97 Paras 52–3.

98 Para 2.29.

99 *Brown v Board of Education of Topeka and Others* (1954) 347 US 483.

100 Ibid, 494.

101 Outside the intimate.

6.31 There has been very little consideration of section 1(2) of the RRA. In *Furniture, Timber and Allied Trades Union v Modgill: Pell Limited v Modgill*,[102] a fairly early case under the RRA 1976, a factory paint shop had a workforce comprised entirely of Asian employees. White employees had been employed in the past, but as vacancies had arisen they had been filled entirely by Asian employees, largely because employment was by 'word of mouth', and so vacancies had been filled by Asian workers alerting other Asian potential workers to those vacancies. A complaint of segregation contrary to the RRA was made by some of the Asian paint shop workers but dismissed. According to Slynn J:

> had there been evidence of a policy to segregate, and of the fact of segregation arising as a result of the company's acts, that might well have constituted a breach of the legislation; but it does not seem . . . that there was evidence to support that position. We do not consider that the failure of the company to intervene and to insist on white or non-Asian workers going into the shop, contrary to the wishes of the men to introduce their friends, itself constituted the act of segregating persons on racial grounds within the meaning of section 1(2).[103]

For a claim of direct discrimination based on 'segregation' under section 1(2) of the RRA, it would seem that 'accidental' segregation is insufficient—a deliberate policy of segregation must exist. I am not aware of a single case having succeeded under the segregation provisions of the RRA 1976. This is notwithstanding some *de facto* segregation.[104]

6.32 Segregation on other grounds is not automatically deemed *less favourable treatment* under the main anti-discrimination legislation. However, the SDA anticipates that certain forms of segregation will constitute less favourable treatment because it makes express provision exempting certain single-sex services and separately provided services where they are provided along gender lines,[105] presuming therefore that they may otherwise be unlawful.

(4) Identifying the proper comparator, their relevant characteristics, and the relevant circumstances

6.33 Direct discrimination requires that a comparison be undertaken between the treatment afforded the complainant and the treatment which was or would have been afforded another person.[106] All the main anti-discrimination enactments

102 [1980] IRLR 142.
103 Ibid, 166.
104 See Chap 1.
105 See Chap 13.
106 For a critique of the comparator requirement, see A McColgan, 'Cracking the Comparator Problem: Discrimination, "Equal" Treatment and the role of Comparisons' [2006] EHRLR 650.

require that the discriminator treats the complainant less favourably than *he treats or would treat* other persons. This requires consideration of the identity of 'the "others", or the comparators or control group, as they are usually known'.[107] The characteristics of the relevant comparator in any particular case are prescribed by the enactments themselves, with more or less precision.

(a) *The parameters of the proper comparator*

The core characteristics of any comparator in a direct discrimination case are set out in the first place by the formulation of direct discrimination in each of the enactments: **6.34**

(a) For direct sex discrimination, the SDA requires that any treatment be less favourable than that which was or would have been afforded '*a man*' or '*a woman*', as the case may be (that is, a person of a different sex to the complainant).[108]

(b) For direct gender reassignment discrimination, the SDA requires that any treatment be less favourable than that which was or would have been afforded '*other persons*'[109] save that, where the less favourable treatment concerns absence, the treatment must be compared to that which would have been afforded *her* or *him* (*that is, the complainant*) 'if the absence was due to sickness or injury' or 'if the absence was due to some other cause and, having regard to the circumstances of the case, it is reasonable for him to be treated no less favourably'.[110]

(c) For direct marital or civil partnership discrimination, the SDA requires that any treatment be less favourable than that which was or would have been afforded a person '*who does not fulfil the condition*', that is, a person who is not 'married or a civil partner'.[111]

---

107 *Chief Constable of West Yorkshire Police v Khan* [2001] UKHL 48; [2001] 1 WLR 1947; [2001] ICR 1065; [2001] IRLR 830, *per* Lord Nicholls, para 25.

108 SDA, s 1(1)(a) and (2)(a). And see s 2: 'Section 1, and the provisions of Parts II and III relating to sex discrimination against women, are to be read as applying equally to the treatment of men, and for that purpose shall have effect with such modifications as are requisite'. SDA, s 1(1)(4) did read 'If a person treats or would treat a man differently according to the man's marital status, his treatment of a woman is for the purposes of subsection (1)(a) or (2)(a) to be compared to his treatment of a man having the like marital status', following an amendment made by the Sex Discrimination (Indirect Discrimination and Burden of Proof) Regulations 2001 SI 2001/2660. This requirement has been repealed by the Employment Equality (Sex Discrimination) Regulations 2005 SI 2005/2467; but if marriage is material, then this may be a relevant circumstance (and the claim might properly be brought under the marital discrimination provisions under SDA, s 3); and if non marriage is material a claim based on direct discrimination may be appropriate if the discrimination arises out of gender stereotyping or gender prejudice (*O'Neill v Governors of St Thomas More RCVA Upper School and Another* 1997] ICR 33; [1996] IRLR 372).

109 SDA, s 2A(1).

110 Ibid, s 2A(2) and (3).

111 Ibid, s 3(1)(a) and (2).

(d) For a case brought under the provisions expressly[112] addressing direct pregnancy- and maternity-related discrimination, the SDA requires that any treatment be less favourable than that which was or would have been afforded *the complainant herself* 'had she not become pregnant' or 'if she were neither exercising nor seeking to exercise, and had neither exercised nor sought to exercise, [a statutory right to maternity leave]' or 'if [section 72(1) of the Employment Rights Act 1996 (compulsory maternity leave)] . . . did not have to be complied with in respect of her', as the case may be.[113]

(e) For direct race discrimination, the RRA requires that any treatment be less favourable than that which was or would have been afforded '*other persons*'.[114]

(f) For direct disability discrimination, the DDA requires that any treatment be less favourable than that which was or would have been afforded '*a person not having that particular disability whose relevant circumstances, including his abilities, are the same as, or not materially different from, those of the disabled person*'.[115]

(g) For direct religion or belief discrimination, the Religion or Belief Regulations and the EA require that any treatment be less favourable than that which was or would have been afforded '*other persons*' or '*others*', respectively.[116]

(h) For direct sexual orientation discrimination, the Sexual Orientation Regulations require that any treatment be less favourable than that which was or would have been afforded '*other persons*'.[117]

(i) For a case of direct age discrimination, the Age Regulations require that any treatment be less favourable than that which was or would have been afforded '*other persons*'.[118]

6.35 This means that in a case of direct sex discrimination, *prima facie*, a woman complainant is never entitled to compare the treatment afforded her with that which was afforded another woman. The position in fact is rather different where a pregnancy discrimination claim is brought as one of direct sex discrimination, because of the case law described below (paragraph 6.51 onwards). In addition, in cases of direct marital or civil partnership discrimination and direct disability discrimination, a complainant is not entitled to compare the treatment afforded them with that afforded another married person or civil partner or a person with

---

112 As discussed below, direct pregnancy and maternity discrimination is likely to constitute direct sex discrimination and therefore be unlawful under the direct sex discrimination provisions of the SDA, see below, para 6.51 onwards.

113 SDA, s 3A(1)(a) and (b) and (2).

114 RRA, s 1(1)(a).

115 DDA, s 3A(5).

116 Religion or Belief Regulations, regulation 3(1)(a) (the amendments which will be made by EA, s 77 will not affect this) and EA, s 45(1).

117 Sexual Orientation Regulations, regulation 3(1)(a).

118 Age Regulations, regulation 3(1)(a).

the same disability, respectively. The situation may be otherwise in claims of direct race discrimination where the comparator is not so closely prescribed. Where a person is dismissed, for example, for failing to comply with a racially discriminatory instruction, she or he can compare herself or himself with a person of the same racial group who has complied.[119] The same applies to direct religion or belief, sexual orientation, or age discrimination but not, as mentioned, in relation to the other protected grounds. This means that in a case of sex discrimination based on gender stereotyping (for example that all women with children are inherently likely to be unreliable, or that a mother should conduct herself in a particular way) a woman cannot compare herself to a woman without a child[120] for the purposes of establishing the legal requirements of direct sex discrimination (though in both cases such may be evidentially relevant).

(b) The relevant circumstances

The characteristics of any comparator are further prescribed by the requirement in all the enactments that the comparisons 'must be such that the relevant circumstances in the one case are the same, or not materially different, in the other'.[121] Further, section 3A(5) of the DDA provides that the chosen comparator's 'abilities' must 'be the same as, or not materially different from, those of the disabled person',[122] and Regulation 3(3) of the Sexual Orientation Regulations provides that in undertaking any comparison 'the fact that one of the persons (whether or not [the complainant]) is a civil partner while the other is married shall not be treated as a material difference between their respective circumstances'. **6.36**

Identifying the *relevant* circumstances for the purposes of undertaking any comparison is absolutely critical. There is some case law suggesting that discriminatory and exculpatory[123] circumstances may be material to the comparison to be undertaken, but the weight of authority indicates otherwise. Ignoring the discriminatory circumstances for the purposes of the comparison exercise is important to ensure that discrimination is not condoned (or 'justified') in the process, as discussed below. Distinguishing the relevant circumstances from the explanation provided for discriminatory treatment is also crucial to ensuring that the burden of proof on particular issues is properly applied, as to which see paragraph 6.92 onwards below. **6.37**

---

119 *Weathersfield Ltd (t/a Van & Truck Rentals) v Sargent* [1999] ICR 425; [1999] IRLR 94; see further para 6.69 below.

120 *Hurley v Mustoe* [1981] ICR 490.

121 SDA, s 5(3); RRA, s 3(4) (though this appears to assume that the comparison will be between persons of different racial groups which, as described above, is not necessary); DDA, s 3A(5); Religion or Belief Regulations, regulation 3(3); Sexual Orientation Regulations, regulation 3(2).

122 DDA, s 3A(5).

123 *Dhatt v McDonald Hamburgers Ltd* [1991] ICR 238; [1991] IRLR 130; *Shamoon v Chief Constable of the Royal Ulster Constabulary* [2003] ICR 337, discussed below.

6.38 As to the general requirement that comparisons 'must be such that the relevant circumstances in the one case are the same, or not materially different, in the other',[124] this does not mean that all the circumstances must be identical as between them. It is only necessary that the *relevant* circumstances are not materially different. For example, if an employer is recruiting for qualified lawyers, without regard to where the legal qualification was obtained, then the fact that a complainant obtained their legal qualification from a different institution to the comparator will be *irrelevant.*

6.39 Discriminatory circumstances are not 'relevant circumstances' for these purposes. In *James v Eastleigh BC*,[125] therefore, the House of Lords concluded that, in determining whether Mr James, a 61-year-old, had been directly discriminated against by his local authority which offered free swimming for pensioners (those being men over 65 and women over 60), the proper comparator was a woman aged 61. Being a pensioner, itself a discriminatory criterion because of the differing State retirement ages, was not a relevant circumstance:

> It is only by wrongly treating pensionable age as a relevant circumstance . . . that it is possible to arrive at the conclusion that the provision of facilities on favourable terms to persons of pensionable age does not involve direct discrimination under section 1(1)(*a*) but may involve indirect discrimination under section 1(1)(*b*). On a proper application of section 5(3)[126] the relevant circumstance which was the same here for the purpose of comparing the treatment of the plaintiff and his wife was that they were both aged 61.'[127]

Further, in *Showboat Entertainment Centre Ltd v Owens*,[128] the respondents had sought to argue that in dismissing a white manager for failing to carry out an instruction to exclude black customers from the amusement centre they were treating him no differently than they would have treated any other member of management who refused to carry out discriminatory instructions, whatever his racial origins. Browne-Wilkinson J[129] rejected that argument:

> Although one has to compare like with like, in judging whether there has been discrimination you have to compare the treatment actually meted out with the treatment which would have been afforded to a man having all the same characteristics

124 SDA, s 5(3); RRA, s 3(4) (though this appears to assume that the comparison will be between persons of different racial groups which, as described above, is not necessary); DDA, s 3A(5); Religion or Belief Regulations, regulation 3(3); Sexual Orientation Regulations, regulation 3(2). EA, s 45(1) provides that there must be 'no material difference in the relevant circumstances' and so is to the same effect.

125 [1990] 2 AC 751; [1990] IRLR 288.

126 Of the SDA.

127 [1990] 2 AC 751, 766; [1990] IRLR 288, para 13.

128 [1984] ICR 65; [1984] IRLR 7.

129 As he then was.

> as the complainant except his race or his attitude to race. Only by excluding matters of race can you discover whether the differential treatment was on racial grounds. Thus, the correct comparison in this case would be between the applicant and another manager who did not refuse to obey the unlawful racialist instructions.[130]

A similar argument was unsuccessful in *Smyth v Croft Inns Limited*,[131] a case brought under the direct religious discrimination provisions of the Fair Employment (Northern Ireland) Act 1976[132] which contained the same requirement as that found in the main anti-discrimination enactments that any comparison must be such that the relevant circumstances in the one case are the same, or not materially different, in the other.[133] In *Smyth*, the complainant was a Roman Catholic barman employed in a pub with Protestant customers in a 'loyalist' area of Belfast. He left his employment when threats were received advising him 'not to be in the bar' the following week and the bar manager took no action at all. The pub's owners sought to argue that there was no discrimination because they would not have treated a Protestant working in a Catholic area and subject to such threats any differently. The Northern Ireland Court of Appeal dismissed that argument as 'fallacious'. In such circumstances the employer would be guilty of religious discrimination against both the barman working in the Protestant area and the barman working in the Catholic area: 'His conduct cannot cease to be unlawful discrimination if, instead of owning only the one bar patronized by Protestants, he also owns a second bar in a Roman Catholic neighbourhood, patronized by Roman Catholics, in which he dismisses a Protestant barman.'[134] **6.40**

There is some case law suggesting that discriminatory circumstances may sometimes be relevant, but this case law must be regarded as inconsistent with the clear and authoritative case law described above. In *Dhatt v McDonalds Hamburgers Ltd*,[135] the complainant was of Indian nationality and, under the Immigration Act 1971, was entitled to live and work in the UK without restriction. He applied to the respondents for work and completed an application form, answering 'yes' to the question did he have a work permit. He was employed but then dismissed for failing to provide evidence of his right to work. The Court of Appeal concluded that the respondents did not racially discriminate against Mr Dhatt in asking questions relating to entitlement to work only of non-EEC nationals. According to the Court of Appeal, the proper comparison was between **6.41**

---

130 [1984] ICR 65, 74; [1984] IRLR 7, para 20.

131 [1996] IRLR 84.

132 Since repealed and replaced by the Fair Employment and Treatment (Northern Ireland) Order 1998 SI/3162.

133 Fair Employment (Northern Ireland) Act 1976, s 16(4A): 'A comparison of the cases of persons of different religious belief or political opinion under subsection (2) must be such that the relevant circumstances in the one case are the same, or not materially different, in the other.'

134 90, para 28.

135 [1991] ICR 238; [1991] IRLR 130.

British citizens and EEC nationals on the one hand and other applicants on the other hand, because in the case of someone seeking work his nationality is a relevant circumstance 'because Parliament itself recognizes and seeks to enforce by reference to nationality a general division between those who by reason of their nationality are free to work and those who require permission'.[136] It is extremely difficult to square this case with *James v Eastleigh*, in particular, a decision of the House of Lords in which, as described above, discriminatory pensionable ages (prescribed by statute) were to be disregarded in determining the relevant circumstances. The Court of Appeal in *Dhatt* purported to distinguish *James* but the distinction drawn is unconvincing. According to Neill LJ in *Dhatt*, the position in *James*:

> would have been different if Parliament itself had enacted that concessions granted by local authorities on the ground of age should depend on the attainment of pensionable age. In that event the discrimination against the plaintiff could properly be regarded as being based not on his sex but on his lack of pensionable status. The qualifying criterion would have been laid down by Parliament and the question whether someone had or lacked pensionable status would have been a relevant circumstance within section 5(3) of the Act of 1975.[137]

This is not persuasive. Firstly, as will be seen in Chapter 13, the SDA, like the RRA, contains exceptional provisions addressing circumstances where acts are done pursuant to statutory authority—these provisions did not apply in either *James* or *Dhatt*. Secondly, pensionable ages, just like immigration status, were established by statute but statutory law did not (then) require that an employer ensure that applicants for work were free to do so, any more than it required local authorities to provide free swimming for persons of pensionable age. Any true distinction is therefore difficult to draw and *Dhatt* should be regarded as inconsistent with *James* and against the weight of authority otherwise. It is also inconsistent with the thrust of the direct discrimination provisions which do not permit of a general defence of justification and are not concerned with motive. Allowing discriminatory circumstances to infect the comparison exercise risks allowing for the justification of direct discrimination. As in *Dhatt*, immigration status may explain a difference in treatment but, importantly, it does not legally permit it.[138]

6.42 However, the Court of Appeal recently adopted the same approach, in circumstances which are equally problematical having regard to the scheme of the

---

136 Ibid, para 31.

137 Ibid, para 26.

138 Unless it falls within one of the exceptions, in particular s 41, see Chap 13.

legislation and case law. In *R (on the Application of Al Rawi & Others) v Secretary of State for Foreign and Commonwealth Affairs & Anor*[139] the Court of Appeal were concerned with an application in judicial review brought by certain detainees held in Guantanamo Bay by US forces and by their family members. The detainees were all British residents but none were British nationals. They argued that the British Government's response to their detention was racially discriminatory because the Government had failed, despite requests, to make certain representations to the US administration, in particular calling for their release. The claimants argued, *inter alia*, that such representations would have been made had they been British citizens, and accordingly the Government's failure to do so in their case was unlawfully racially discriminatory.[140] The Government argued that the circumstances of nationals and non-nationals were materially and relevantly different because non-British people were not entitled to diplomatic protection under international law by means of State-to-State claims made by the British Government. The Court of Appeal accepted the Government's argument. According to the Court of Appeal:[141]

> A person who is not a British national is not entitled to the protection of a State to State claim made by the first respondent. That is not an *attribute* of the non-British national. It is not a function of how he is likely to behave. It is . . . simply a legal fact. There is no question of the non-British national being, by virtue of that characteristic, more likely to do or not do this, that, or anything. Contrast the Roma who, by virtue of being Roma,[142] was or was believed to be more likely to make a false asylum claim. The national and the non-national are in truth in materially different cases one from the other for the purpose of the exercise of the right of diplomatic protection by means of State-to-State claims. On the learning such a difference ought only to be disregarded if it assumes or implies a process of racial stereotyping. But it does not. The difference is therefore a proper and legitimate basis of distinction for the purposes of the RRA. The non-nationals have been treated differently from the nationals not because of their race (nationality) but because one group is entitled to diplomatic protection and the other is not. Their respective relevant circumstances are not the same. On the contrary they are materially different (s.3(4)). Accordingly there is no violation of s.1(1)(a).[143]

However, this analysis does not bear scrutiny. The Court of Appeal assumes that the fact that the distinguishing feature, though grounded in nationality, was not a personal characteristic but was extraneous, deferring as it did to a legal fact, was relevant. However, as described above, the distinction in *James*, a decision of the

---

139 [2006] EWCA Civ 1279.

140 Under RRA, s 19B, see Chap 11.

141 Laws LJ giving the judgment for the court.

142 Referring to the *R (on the application of European Roma Rights Centre) v Immigration Officer at Prague Airport* [2003] EWCA Civ 666 [2004] QB 811, see para 6.88 below.

143 Ibid, para 78.

House of Lords, was analytically indistinguishable. In *James*, the distinction turned on the age at which men and women were entitled to a pension—an extraneous, legal fact. The fact that a particular effect of nationality may place a person in a legally different position as compared to another of a different nationality is recognized not by section 3(4) but by the exemptions which exclude nationality discrimination found, in particular, in section 41 of the RRA, as is discussed in Chapter 13.[144] In considering *why* the detainees were treated as they were, that is, the explanation for their treatment, the Court of Appeal allows the distinction based on the impugned ground (nationality) to be justified. The RRA, like the other enactments, does not allow for that. Instead it adopts specific exemptions relating to particular factual situations[145] and either they applied or (as it seems) they did not. The fact that specific exemptions apply in relation to nationality discrimination makes it clear that Parliament intended for nationality not to constitute a material or relevant difference where the claim is one of direct discrimination based on that very ground. The decision in *Al Rawi*, then, like *Dhatt* is contrary to *James* and Parliament's apparent intention.

6.43 In relation to disability, as seen above at paragraph 6.34, the DDA provides that the chosen comparator's 'abilities' must 'be the same as, or not materially different from, those of the disabled person'.[146] This means that the disabled person with their actual abilities must be considered as they are in fact and, so far as relevant to the complaint, imputed to any comparator. In some cases, there will be particular reasonable adjustments which an employer was required by the DDA to make,[147] but in fact failed to make. It may be that those adjustments would have had an effect on the disabled person's abilities to do a job, for example. However, in making the comparison for direct discrimination purposes, the disabled person's abilities should be considered as they in fact were, and not as they would or might have been had adjustments been made. By the same token, however, if adjustments have in fact been made which have had the effect of enhancing the disabled person's abilities, then it is those enhanced abilities that should be considered. In all cases the disabled person's abilities must be considered as they in fact were at the material time (and not as they might have been if the adjustments had been made in the former case or had they not been made in the latter case).[148]

144 See too RRA, s 19D.

145 See Chap 13.

146 DDA, s 3A(5).

147 See para 6.193 onwards.

148 Code of Practice on Employment and Occupation (2004) DRC, para 4.22 (ISBN 0 11 703419 3; Disability Discrimination Codes of Practice (Employment and Occupation, and Trade Organisations and Qualifications Bodies) Appointed Day Order 2004, SI 2004/2302. See Chap 15 for the impact of the statutory Codes of Practice).

In addition, the relevant circumstances may include the risk posed to others by reason of the particular disability.[149]

In relation to sexual orientation, it is made explicit, as seen above (paragraph 6.36), that the fact that one person is a civil partner and another married is not a relevant circumstance for the purpose of undertaking the comparison exercise. Such circumstances are discriminatory, just as pension ages were in *James*—only opposite-sex partners can marry under existing law and only same-sex couples can enter civil partnerships.[150] This makes clear the intention that the discriminatory context must be ignored in the comparison exercise. **6.44**

Comparators are considered in the context of stereotyping at paragraph 6.82 onwards below. **6.45**

(c) Hypothetical comparators

As the wording indicates, it is not necessary that there be an actual comparator to prove direct discrimination—a hypothetical comparator will suffice. In either case the chosen comparator's relevant circumstances must be the same as, or not materially different from, those of the complainant, as described above. **6.46**

Identifying the relevant characteristics of a hypothetical comparator and undertaking the necessary comparison exercise has not always proved easy in practice. Where the treatment is explicitly based on a protected ground—race, sex etc, as the case may be—then it will be easy to see that a person of a different status would not have been afforded the same treatment. But however overt the treatment, a comparison must always be undertaken and discrimination is not to be presumed.[151] Where no real comparator exists, a court or tribunal is bound to consider whether a hypothetical comparator of different status would have been treated in the same way.[152] This is important because in some cases there will be no actual comparator or, as the evidence emerges, the chosen comparator might prove to be in materially different circumstances. **6.47**

Constructing a hypothetical comparator is conceptually difficult. However, it is permissible to rely on persons who do not prove to be actual comparators **6.48**

149 *High Quality Lifestyles Ltd v Watts* (2006) UKEAT/0671/05/ZT.

150 See Chap 2.

151 *McDonald v Advocate General for Scotland* [2003] UKHL 34, [2003] ICR 937; *Pearce v Governing Body of Mayfield Secondary School* [2001] EWCA Civ 1347, [2002] ICR 198; [2003] IRLR 512 in which the House of Lords overruled a line of cases which indicated that where treatment was race- or gender-specific no comparison exercise was required but that of itself constituted less favourable treatment on the protected ground.

152 *Balamoody v UK Central Council for Nursing, Midwifery and Health Visiting* [2001] EWCA Civ 2097, [2002] ICR 646; [2002] IRLR 288.

but whose circumstances, though not identical, are not wholly dissimilar.[153] But where there are no, even non-identical, comparators determining whether an alleged discriminator would have treated a comparable person of a different class differently is analytically and forensically difficult. The exercise is undertaken in the usual case by scrutinizing the explanation for any adverse treatment. If the explanation is shown to be a sham, or otherwise unsustainable, a court can be invited to infer that any less favourable treatment was on the protected ground (race, sex etc).[154] However, as discussed below it is important to treat the issues which arise in determining direct discrimination discretely, if the burden of proof provisions discussed in paragraph 6.92 are to be properly respected.

(d) Hypothetical circumstances

6.49 The case law on direct discrimination under the SDA and RRA indicates that the characteristics of a *reasonable* person in the position of the discriminator (*a hypothetical discriminator*) are immaterial. The only question is how the particular discriminator would have treated the comparator. If a person treats all people—irrespective of status—equally poorly, direct discrimination is not made out.[155]

6.50 In addition, the only relevant *circumstances* are the actual circumstances of the particular case. Regard should not be had to hypothetical circumstances or alternative possible circumstances for determining whether or not there has been comparatively less favourable treatment.[156]

(5) Pregnancy discrimination, direct sex discrimination, and comparators

6.51 The difficulties consequent upon a test of discrimination which depends upon the identification of a comparator whose circumstances are relevantly the same, or not materially different, are most clearly illuminated by the pregnancy cases. Section 2(2) of the SDA provides that, in applying the direct (and indirect) discrimination provisions of the SDA, no account shall be taken of the special treatment afforded to women in connection with pregnancy or childbirth, so allowing for limited positive action measures associated with pregnancy. However, until recently, no other special provision was made addressing direct pregnancy or maternity discrimination. There was an obvious difficulty in comparing a woman in a

---

153 *Chief Constable of West Yorkshire Police v Vento* [2001] IRLR 124 at 125, cited approvingly in *Shamoon v Chief Constable of the Royal Ulster Constabulary* [2003] UKHL 11; [2003] ICR 337; [2003] IRLR 285, paras 81–2.

154 See para 6.92 for proving discrimination and *Shamoon v Chief Constable of the Royal Ulster Constabulary* [2003] UKHL 11; [2003] ICR 337; [2003] IRLR 285.

155 *Zafar v Glasgow CC* [1998] ICR 120; [1998] IRLR 36; *Shamoon v Chief Constable of the Royal Ulster Constabulary* [2003] UKHL 11; [2003] ICR 337; [2003] IRLR 285, though unreasonable treatment may be relevant in proving discrimination, see para 6.92, below.

156 See, *Smyth v Croft Inns Ltd* [1996] IRLR 84 and see the position in relation to disability and reasonable adjustments, both discussed above, para 6.193.

condition to which a man could never find himself to a man. Logically this might mean that a woman treated less favourably because she was pregnant should have no claim in direct discrimination, notwithstanding that pregnancy is a gender-based condition—exposing the flaws in a comparator-based model. The earlier case law then struggled with a test of direct discrimination which was nigh on impossible to apply to pregnancy- and maternity-related discrimination.[157] Excluding pregnancy- and maternity-based discrimination from the protection of the SDA would, of course, have excluded a key form of gender-based discrimination. However, earlier cases under the SDA did just that, holding that the purpose of the direct discrimination provisions of the SDA was to compare a man with a woman and to see that they were not treated unequally because they were a man or a woman, and that a pregnant woman was 'no longer just a woman . . . [but] a woman . . . with child, and there is no masculine equivalent' and that, accordingly, to dismiss a woman because she was pregnant did not fall within the direct discrimination provisions.[158] Later cases adopted a more inclusive approach, though still not without difficulties. In *Hayes v Malleable Men's Club*[159] it was held that there was no principle of law preventing the application of the SDA to a woman who claimed direct discrimination on grounds connected with her pregnancy, and that there could be circumstances—for example, in the case of a sick male employee—which could be properly regarded as comparable.[160] This provided limited protection for women who because of pregnancy are uniquely likely to be absent from work for long periods for reasons other than ill-health, and are therefore uniquely vulnerable to adverse treatment because of their sex.

The impetus for a different approach came from the EU law, as discussed in Chapter 4. In a series of cases, the ECJ made it clear that the Equal Treatment Directive required Member States to protect against some forms of direct pregnancy-related discrimination.[161] According to the ECJ in *Dekker v Stichting Vormingscentrum voor Jong Volwassenen (VJV-Centrum) Plus*,[162] the question whether a refusal to employ a pregnant woman was to be regarded as direct discrimination within the meaning of the Equal Treatment Directive depended on whether 'the fundamental reason for the refusal of employment [was] one which applie[d] without distinction to workers of either sex or, conversely, whether it applies exclusively to one sex'.[163] As only women could be refused 6.52

157 See Chap 5, para 5.29 onwards.

158 *Turley v Allders Department Stores Ltd* [1980] ICR 66, 70.

159 [1985] ICR 703.

160 Ibid, 709.

161 *Dekker v Stichting Vormingscentrum voor Jong Volwassenen (VJV- Centrum) Plus* (Case 179/88) [1992] ICR 325 and *Handels-Og Kontorfunktionaerernes Forbund I Danmark v Dansk Arbejdsgiverforening* [1992] ICR 332.

162 (Case 179/88) [1992] ICR 325.

163 Ibid, 328, para 10.

employment on the ground of pregnancy, such amounted to direct discrimination on the ground of sex, according to the ECJ.[164] The view of the ECJ, therefore, was diametrically opposed to that taken by the UK courts in the early days of the SDA, as discussed above. The ECJ took the view that because *only* women could get pregnant, less favourable treatment connected to pregnancy was necessarily sex discrimination. This approach has the virtue of providing some substance to the protection afforded under the Equal Treatment Directive and the SDA, which soon after, as will be seen below, was interpreted consistently with the ECJ's reasoning.

6.53 The decision of the ECJ in *Dekker*, that less favourable treatment based on the gender-specific condition of pregnancy was direct (as opposed to indirect) discrimination, was important. It reflected the reality that to discriminate against a woman because of her pregnancy was to discriminate against her as a woman and meant that such discrimination could not be justified (as would be the case were it to constitute indirect discrimination only).[165] Arguments, therefore, about the costs of employing pregnant women and perceptions about the unreliability or difficulties otherwise of employing pregnant women were made irrelevant. The only question, so far as the ECJ was concerned, was whether or not the refusal to employ a woman was her pregnancy—if so, direct sex discrimination was made out.

6.54 Following *Dekker*, a pregnancy as sex discrimination case arrived at the House of Lords. In *Webb v EMO Air Cargo (UK) Limited*,[166] the House of Lords considered a complaint by a woman that she had been directly discriminated against on the ground of her sex when, having been engaged by the respondent employers with a view to replacing a pregnant employee during her maternity leave, she herself discovered that she was pregnant, at which point her employers dismissed her. The House of Lords considered that such was not direct discrimination and that the proper comparison to be made under section 5(3) of the SDA was with a hypothetical man who would also have been unavailable for work at the material time, the precise reason for the unavailability being irrelevant.[167] However, in light of *Dekker*,[168] the House of Lords referred the issue to the ECJ. The ECJ, predictably in the light of its earlier decision, determined that dismissal by reason of pregnancy of a woman employed for an indefinite period constituted direct discrimination and accordingly breached the Equal Treatment Directive.

164 Ibid, 329, para 12.

165 See para 6.123 below.

166 [1993] ICR 175.

167 Ibid, 182, *per* Lord Keith.

168 And the decision of the ECJ in *Handels-Og Kontorfunktionaerernes Forbund I Danmark v Dansk Arbejdsgiverforening* [1992] ICR 332, decided on the same day as *Dekker* and to the same effect.

When the case was remitted back to the House of Lords, in a short decision in which Lord Keith gave the only reasoned judgment, the SDA was interpreted to give it a meaning consistent with the judgment of the ECJ by holding that 'in a case where a woman is engaged for an indefinite period, the fact that the reason why she will be temporarily unavailable for work at a time when to her knowledge her services will be particularly required is pregnancy is a circumstance relevant to her case, being a circumstance which could not be present in the case of the hypothetical man' and accordingly no comparison is required and direct discrimination is made out automatically.[169] The House of Lords indicated that their judgment was not to be taken as meaning necessarily that pregnancy would always be a relevant circumstance and in particular that it would be a relevant circumstance where a woman was refused employment for a fixed period in the future during the whole of which her pregnancy would make her unavailable for work.[170]

6.55 Since the decision in *Webb* the ECJ, in a series of cases, has put to bed any suggestion that the length or type of employment is relevant to the question whether pregnancy discrimination constitutes direct sex discrimination. They are not. In *Tele Danmark* and *Jeméz Melgar*[171] the ECJ considered two separate cases. The first case concerned a woman employed on a six-month contract starting in July, whilst pregnant and due to give birth in November of the same year, who was dismissed during her pregnancy on the ground that she had not informed her employer of her pregnancy at the time of recruitment. The second case concerned a woman employed on successive short fixed-term contracts who was refused a renewal on the grounds of her pregnancy. In both cases the ECJ concluded that direct discrimination contrary to the Equal Treatment Directive had been established and confirmed that the principle of equal treatment contained therein applied irrespective of the duration of the employment and whether or not it was for a fixed or indefinite period. In *Mahlburg v Land Mecklenburg-Vorpommern*[172] the ECJ went further by holding that the refusal to employ a woman in a post for an indefinite period on the grounds of her pregnancy where the employer was prohibited as a matter of law from employing pregnant women in such work was direct sex discrimination and contrary to the Equal Treatment Directive.

6.56 Just as the motives for any less favourable treatment of a pregnant woman are irrelevant to the question whether direct sex discrimination and a violation of the Equal Treatment Directive has occurred, so the conduct of the woman less

---

169 *Webb v EMO Air Cargo (UK) Limited (No 2)* [1995] ICR 1021, 1027, *per* Lord Keith.

170 Ibid, 1027, *per* Lord Keith.

171 *Tele Danmark A/S v Handels-og Kontorfunktionurernes Forbund i Danmark (HK) (acting on behalf of Brandt-Nielsen)* (Case-109/00) [2001] IRLR 853; *Jeméz Melgar v Ayuntamiento de los Barrios* (Case C-438/99) [2004] ICR 610.

172 (Case C-207/98) [2001] ICR 1032.

favourably treated is irrelevant. Once it is established that pregnancy is the cause of her less favourable treatment, then that is automatic sex discrimination.[173]

6.57 The approach of the ECJ that less favourable treatment on the grounds of pregnancy is automatic sex discrimination without the need for a comparator, to which the House of Lords was required to give effect in *Webb (No 2)*, has extended beyond cases involving the recruitment and dismissal of pregnant women. Any less favourable treatment of a woman on the grounds of her pregnancy will constitute automatic sex discrimination under the Equal Treatment Directive and, therefore, because of the obligation on Member States to give effect to its provisions, domestically.[174] Thus all the following constitute automatic sex discrimination: dismissal of a worker during pregnancy for absences due to incapacity for work resulting from her pregnancy;[175] denial to a woman of the opportunity to defend herself at a disciplinary hearing because she is on maternity leave;[176] denial of access to a performance assessment where that assessment informs subsequent pay reviews because a woman is on maternity leave;[177] denial of a loyalty bonus because a woman is absent on maternity leave throughout the whole of the relevant period due to pregnancy-related sickness and maternity leave.[178]

6.58 The ECJ has not, however, been wholly consistent in its approach to addressing less favourable treatment connected with pregnancy and maternity leave. The Pregnant Workers Directive[179] provides a framework for protecting the health and safety of pregnant women workers and women on maternity leave.[180] It does so by, amongst other things, providing that during maternity leave there should be an entitlement to a payment of '*an adequate allowance*', that being sufficient to guarantee income at least equivalent to that which a woman would receive in the event of absence on sick leave.[181] Such payment may be conditional upon fulfilling conditions of eligibility, including minimum service requirements.[182] The ECJ has held that in light of that, the Equal Treatment Directive does not require full pay to be continued during maternity leave, even where any reduction

173 In *Tele Danmark*, above, the ECJ considered it irrelevant that the complainant had not informed her employer of her pregnancy. See too *Busch CH v Klinikum Neustadt* [2003] ECR I-02041.

174 See Chap 4.

175 *Brown v Rentokil Limited* (Case C-394/96) [1998] ECR 1-04185. See also *New Southern Railways Ltd v Quinn* [2006] IRLR 266.

176 *Abbey National v Formosa* [1999] IRLR 222.

177 *Caisse Nationale D'assurance Jemenénez Vieillesse des Travailleurs Salariés (CNAVTS) v Thibault* (Case C-136/95) [1999] ICR 160.

178 *Gus Home Shopping Limited v Green & McLaughlin* [2001] IRLR 75. And see *Sarkatzis Herreoro v Instituto Madrileno de la Salud* [2006] IRLR 296.

179 92/85/EC, see Chap 4.

180 See Chap 4.

181 Article 11(2)(b) and (3).

182 *Boyle and others v Equal Opportunities Commission* (Case C-411/96) [1998] IRLR 717.

in pay is plainly attributable to pregnancy and/or maternity leave.[183] It is difficult to reconcile this with those cases which hold that any adverse treatment connected to pregnancy and maternity leave is automatic sex discrimination. According to the ECJ, 'women taking maternity leave provided for by national legislation . . . are in a special position which requires them to be afforded special protection, but which is not comparable either with that of a man or with that of a woman actually at work',[184] precisely the rationale adopted by the English courts under the SDA in its early years as a basis for depriving women of the protection of the direct discrimination provisions in such circumstances, and rejected as a proper basis for so doing by the ECJ in *Dekker* and other cases. There is, then, a paradox for women in the non-comparability of pregnancy and maternity.

The difference in approach taken by the ECJ in relation to full pay during maternity leave might, perhaps, be legally resolved by regarding pure maternity pay as falling outside the Equal Treatment Directive because special provision is made for it inside the Pregnant Workers Directive. However, more difficult is the decision in *North Western Health Board v McKenna*.[185] In *McKenna*, the ECJ was required to consider whether a sick pay scheme, which conferred an entitlement to full pay for a period, and thereafter reduced sick pay to half pay, was unlawfully discriminatory where it treated pregnancy-related illness in the same way as other illnesses so as to reduce the amount of sick pay to half pay where pregnancy-related illness was the cause of the sick absence. The ECJ, in a decision which is not easy to understand, concluded that the scheme did not violate a pregnant woman's rights under Article 141 because Community law did not require the maintenance of full pay for a female worker who was absent during her pregnancy by reason of an illness related to that pregnancy. According to the ECJ, during an absence resulting from such an illness, a female worker may thus suffer a reduction in her pay, provided that she is treated in the same way as a male worker who is absent on grounds of illness, and provided that the amount of payment made is not so low as to undermine the objective of protecting pregnant workers.[186] The ECJ held that pay within the terms of Article 141 EC and Directive 75/117 cannot also come within the scope of Directive 76/207[187] and in so holding appeared to entrench a distinction between the Equal Treatment **6.59**

[183] *Gillespie v Northern Health and Social Services Board* (Case C-342/93) [1996] ICR 499; [1996] IRLR 214 whatever or whenever the reference period is for calculating maternity pay; *Alabaster v Woolwich* (Case C-147/02) [2005] ICR 695; *Boyle v Equal Opportunities Commission* (Case C-411/96) [1998] IRLR 717.

[184] *Gillespie v Northern Health and Social Services Board* (Case C-342/93) [1996] ICR 499; [1996] IRLR 214, para 17.

[185] (Case C-191/03) [2005] IRLR 895.

[186] Ibid, paras 61–2.

[187] Para 30.

Directive and the Equal Pay Directive.[188] This is a difficult distinction to draw. Discrimination is defined in the same way materially for both the Equal Pay Directive and the Equal Treatment Directive, and the ECJ has determined certain pay-related claims under Article 141 in a way which has guaranteed the rights of workers absent on maternity leave.[189] Since *McKenna*, the deadline for compliance with the Equal Treatment Amendment Directive, which expressly includes pay[190] and treats a violation of the Pregnant Workers Directive as discrimination,[191] has expired and such a distinction would now seem impossible to draw. Pragmatically, the difference in approach taken by the ECJ in relation to full pay during maternity leave and during pregnancy-related sickness probably reflects real social and economic policy considerations—a requirement to pay full pay in all cases would impose a considerable economic burden on States.

6.60 As to the exemption in relation to full pay during maternity leave, this is limited. It does not extend to other pay benefits earned whilst at work or before maternity leave, or referable to a period whilst at work, in the past or in the future,[192] even if due in a period whilst a woman is on maternity leave, or to pay increases falling due during maternity leave where maternity pay is earnings related.[193] This means that any pay increase paid or back-dated into a period whilst a woman is pregnant or on maternity leave must be taken into account in calculating any earnings-related maternity pay.[194]

6.61 In short summary, therefore, less favourable treatment on the grounds of pregnancy, pregnancy-related sickness, or absence resulting from pregnancy or pregnancy-related illness which occurs during pregnancy, or maternity leave constitutes automatic sex discrimination without the need to compare the treatment afforded with that which was or might have been afforded a person who was not at material times pregnant or on maternity leave. The only exception to this is in relation to maternity pay which is not required to be paid at the rate of full pay because maternity pay is regulated by the Pregnant Workers Directive (and not the Equal Treatment Directive). However, where maternity pay is earnings related, a woman is entitled to the benefit of any pay increases referable to any period before the end of maternity leave. The *McKenna* exemption is more

---

188 Discussed in Chap 4.

189 Eg, *Alabaster v Woolwich* (Case C-147/02) [2005] ICR 695.

190 See Art 3 of the Equal Treatment Directive 76/207/EEC, as amended by Directive 2002/73/EC.

191 See Chap 4.

192 *Lewen v Denda* (Case C-333/97) [2000] ICR 648; *GUS Home Shopping Limited v Green and A'er* [2001] IRLR 75; *Handels-og Kontorfunktionaerernes Forbund I Danmark, acting on behalf of Berit Hoj Pedersen v Faellesforeningen for Danmarks Brugsforeninger and others* (Case C-C66/96) [1999] IRLR 55); *North Western Health Board v McKenna* (Case C-191/03) [2005] IRLR 895.

193 *Gillespie v Northern Health and Social Services Board* (Case C-342/93) [1996] ICR 499; [1996] IRLR 214, para 22; *Alabaster v Woolwich* (Case C-147/02) [2005] ICR 695.

194 *Alabaster v Woolwich*, ibid.

difficult to reconcile with the general approach of the ECJ to addressing pregnancy- and maternity-related discrimination, but might be regarded now as distinguishable since pay has been brought expressly within the Equal Treatment Directive by the Equal Treatment Amendment Directive.[195]

In the context of the SDA, therefore, and as discussed, no comparator is required to make out a claim of direct discrimination based on maternity or pregnancy leave. Instead a simple causation test is applied.[196] Because of an exclusion under the SDA relating to 'benefits consisting of the payment of money when the provision of those benefits is regulated by the woman's contract of employment'[197] many such claims must be brought under the EPA which is addressed below.[198] However, the EPA is constructed around the legal assumption that a comparator must exist for any claim of discrimination and this has made addressing pregnancy and maternity pay claims difficult, and has led to some amendments to the Act, though these do not wholly address the problem.[199] This is considered further at paragraph 6.316 onwards. **6.62**

Further, as discussed below, express provision is now made for pregnancy and maternity discrimination and provision is made in relation to a comparator under section 3A of the SDA. However, *Webb* and the cases described above remain good law in relation to pregnancy and maternity leave and direct sex discrimination. The later amendments described below do not operate to reduce the protection already provided, as a matter of statutory construction and EU law.[200] This means that a woman may still choose to bring a claim of pregnancy- and maternity-related discrimination under the direct sex discrimination provisions of the SDA, in particular where the new provisions do not apply. **6.63**

(6) New protection against pregnancy/maternity discrimination: the comparative approach revisited

New provision has now been made by the Employment Equality (Sex Discrimination) Regulations 2005[201] made under the European Communities **6.64**

[195] See Chap 4. If the *McKenna* exemption remains good law, then it should anyway be subject to comparable limitations as those applied in the case of the full pay during maternity leave exemption, so that if earnings related, sick pay must take account of pay increases and all the benefits earned whilst actually at work, see para 6.60.

[196] *O'Neill v Governors of St. Thomas More RCVA Upper School and Another* [1997] ICR 33; [1996] IRLR 372; *P&O Ferries v Iverson* [1999] ICR 1088.

[197] As to which see, *Hoyland v ASDA Stores Ltd* [2006] IRLR 468.

[198] Along with the Pensions Act 1995 which makes materially similar provision in relation to occupational pensions, see para 6.277.

[199] *Gillespie v Northern Health and Social Services Board* (Case C-342/93) [1996] ICR 499; [1996] IRLR 214; *Alabaster v Woolwich* (Case C-147/02) [2005] ICR 695 and see EPA, s 1(2)(d)–(f), (5A), and (5B).

[200] Because of the non-regression clause in the Equal Treatment Amendment Directive described in Chap 8.

[201] SI 2005/2467, Regulation 4.

Act 1972 as referred to in Chapter 4, which inserts a new section 3A into the SDA. This section expressly addresses pregnancy- and maternity-related direct discrimination, providing that:

> (1) In any circumstances relevant for the purposes of a provision to which this subsection applies, a person discriminates against a woman if—
> (a) at a time in a protected period, and on the ground of the woman's pregnancy, the person treats her less favourably than he would treat her had she not become pregnant; or
> (b) on the ground that the woman is exercising or seeking to exercise, or has exercised or sought to exercise, a statutory right to maternity leave, the person treats her less favourably than he would treat her if she were neither exercising nor seeking to exercise, and had neither exercised nor sought to exercise, such a right.
>
> (2) In any circumstances relevant for the purposes of a provision to which this subsection applies, a person discriminates against a woman if, on the ground that section 72(1) of the Employment Rights Act 1996 (compulsory maternity leave) has to be complied with in respect of the woman, he treats her less favourably than he would treat her if that provision did not have to be complied with in respect of her.

The 'protected period' is defined by section 3A(3) as beginning each time a woman becomes pregnant and ends where she is only entitled to ordinary maternity leave, at the end of her ordinary maternity leave, or, if earlier, when she returns to work after the end of her pregnancy. Where a woman is entitled to both ordinary and additional maternity leave the protected period ends at the end of her period of additional maternity leave or, if earlier, when she returns to work after the end of her pregnancy. And where a woman is not entitled to ordinary maternity leave, the protected period ends at the end of the two weeks beginning with the end of the pregnancy (that being the period of compulsory maternity leave provided for under section 72(1) of the Employment Rights Act 1996).[202] In addition, where a person's treatment of a woman is on grounds of illness suffered by the woman as a consequence of her pregnancy, that treatment is to be taken to be on the ground of the pregnancy.[203]

6.65 This new concept of pregnancy discrimination applies only to the employment and related fields of the SDA.[204] Modifications are also made to certain unlawful acts as they apply to this form of pregnancy- and maternity-related discrimination, as is discussed in Chapter 8.

6.66 As can be seen, and as referred to above at paragraph 6.34, the new meaning of pregnancy- and maternity-related direct discrimination requires that a

---

202 'Ordinary maternity leave' and 'additional maternity leave' are to be construed in accordance with ss 71 and 73 of the Employment Rights Act 1996: SDA, s 3A(4).

203 SDA, s 3A(3)(b).

204 Ibid, Part 2, ss 35A and 35B; any other provision of Part 3, so far as it applies to vocational training.

comparison be undertaken between the treatment afforded the complainant and that to which she was or would have been subjected 'had she not become pregnant', 'if she were neither exercising nor seeking to exercise, and had neither exercised nor sought to exercise, [a statutory right to maternity leave]', or 'if [section 72(1) of the Employment Rights Act 1996 (compulsory maternity leave)] . . . did not have to be complied with in respect of her', as the case may be.[205] This appears in stark contradistinction to the case law of the ECJ above which (outside full pay during material times[206]) does not require a comparator in a claim of direct discrimination. As referred to in Chapter 4, the lawfulness of these new provisions must be doubted.

The fact that the new provisions require that the comparator be the complainant herself in a non-pregnant/maternity condition might at first sight seem benign, and it can be evidentially helpful in determining a claim of pregnancy- or maternity-related discrimination to consider the treatment afforded the woman concerned before she became pregnant. However, the legal requirement that she compare herself to her pre-pregnant/maternity condition imposes just the burden that the ECJ lifted in *Webb* and the other cases described above for the good reasons described there. Simple examples illuminate the difficulties. A woman who is refused permission to have a toilet break once in a morning both before and during pregnancy, so that there is no difference in treatment, will nevertheless be less favourably treated for a reason relating to pregnancy when she is denied the use of the toilet for a second time in a morning when she needs to use it more because of her pregnancy. Such less favourable treatment is 'related' to pregnancy and accordingly, under the Directive, is unlawful. Similarly, it is not clear whether a woman who is refused an appraisal or is not consulted on a redundancy process when absent due to pregnancy-related sickness should have her treatment compared to that which she would have been afforded had she not become pregnant, all other circumstances being materially the same (that is that she had been absent because of a non-pregnancy-related illness). If so, this would be contrary to the decision of the ECJ in *Brown v Rentokil*, referred to above. As mentioned in paragraph 6.63, the direct discrimination provisions would still apply in such circumstances. **6.67**

(7) The characteristics of the discriminator

The characteristics of the discriminator are not relevant. Hypothetical characteristics, in particular, are not to be imputed to the alleged discriminator, as mentioned above.[207] **6.68**

205 SDA, s 3A(1)(a) and (b) and (2).
206 See paras 6.58–6.60 above.
207 Para 6.49.

(8) 'Grounds of'

6.69 As described above, the direct discrimination provisions in the main anti-discrimination enactments all require that the less favourable treatment complained of be on protected 'grounds'. The formulations vary, as described above, so that in the case of race and sexual orientation discrimination, the less favourable treatment need only be on *racial grounds* or *grounds of sexual orientation* respectively, covering a wide range of discriminatory acts, including instructions to discriminate and discrimination based on perception and association. In the case of sex, disability, and age discrimination, by contrast the less favourable treatment must be based on the *complainant's* sex, disability, or age, as the case may be, save that the Age Regulations expressly cover less favourable treatment connected with perceived age. The Religion or Belief Regulations adopt a wide formulation, but because of the exclusionary provision made under Regulation 3(2) (excluding the discriminator's religion or belief as a material ground), its reach is somewhat narrower than that provided for by the formulation under the RRA and the Sexual Orientation Regulations. This is discussed further above at paragraphs 6.17–6.20.

6.70 The RRA and the Sexual Orientation Regulations have the widest reach. However, in all cases, in determining their scope, regard must be had to the purpose of the main anti-discrimination enactments. The fact that less favourable treatment occurs in a context which is influenced by considerations of race or sexual orientation will not always be enough to make out direct discrimination. This is so, in particular, where finding racial or sexual orientation discrimination in such circumstances would be antithetical to the purposes of the enactments. In *Redfearn v Serco Limited t/a West Yorkshire Transport Service*[208] the complainant, a white male member of the British National Party and a candidate for election to Bradford City Council at material times, complained of race discrimination when he was dismissed by his employers 'on the grounds of health and safety' when his political activities became known. The complainant was employed by the respondent employers as a bus driver escorting children and adults with special needs; 70 to 80 per cent of his employers' passengers were of Asian origin as were 35 per cent of the workforce, and his employers took the view that continuing to employ Mr Redfearn would cause problems. Mr Redfearn then brought a claim of direct race discrimination alleging that his dismissal was 'on racial grounds'. An employment tribunal dismissed his complaint. The Employment Appeal Tribunal, however, allowed Mr Redfearn's appeal, relying on the wide construction given to the expression 'on racial grounds', as described above.[209] The Court of Appeal overturned the decision of the Employment Appeal Tribunal.

208 [2006] EWCA Civ 659; [2006] IRLR 623.

209 Para 6.17.

The Court of Appeal confirmed the wide breadth of the expression '*on racial grounds*' and that direct race discrimination is not limited to occasions where less favourable treatment is based on the race of the complainant him or herself, but extends to treatment based on the racial characteristics of another person; discriminatory instructions; and association with a person of a particular racial group.[210] However, according to the Court of Appeal the 'on racial grounds' formulation is not wide enough to cover any case in which the less favourable treatment in issue was significantly influenced by considerations of race. Such a proposition, according to the Court of Appeal, was far too wide, wrong in principle, and unsupported by authority.[211] As the Court of Appeal observed, if that proposition were right, it would mean that it would be an act of direct race discrimination for an employer to dismiss an employee whom he discovered had committed an act of race discrimination, such as racially abusing a fellow employee or a customer.[212] That would be inconsistent with the purpose of the legislation and not a case for which it was designed.[213] The position of an employee dismissed for failing to comply with a racially discriminatory policy may be contrasted with the situation in *Redfearn*. In the case of an employee dismissed for failing to comply with a racially discriminatory policy, the '*racial grounds*' operate directly in the less favourable treatment of the employee, whether the race or colour in question be that of the employee or that of a third party.[214] Such a situation concerns a policy contrary to the purpose of the RRA, rather than a policy consistent with it.[215] 'Racial considerations' alone, therefore, are not sufficient to make out 'racial grounds', and the same point can logically be made about direct sexual orientation and religion or belief discrimination.

Identifying whether the treatment complained of was on a protected ground is very important and not always easy. In *James v Eastleigh BC* discussed above, the differential charges as between Mr and Mrs James were found to have been on the grounds of sex. The claim could have been formulated as one of indirect discrimination by contending that the treatment was done on the grounds of pensionable age—described as a sex-neutral condition—which had the effect of disadvantaging men. This would carry the risk, from the claimant's perspective, that the treatment might be justified. The distinction, then, between direct and indirect discrimination is not always clear, particularly where the condition resulting in the less favourable treatment is race or gender specific (as with **6.71**

210 *Redfearn v Serco Limited t/a West Yorkshire Transport Service* [2006] EWCA Civ 659; [2006] IRLR 623, para 36.

211 Ibid, para 43, *per* Mummery LJ.

212 Para 43.

213 Ibid.

214 Ibid, para 44.

215 Ibid, para 44.

pensionable ages). However, 'the particular *form* of discrimination matters, even if there are present in the circumstances of the case a discriminatory purpose and discriminatory effects. The [legislation] makes an important broad distinction between two different forms of discrimination. This distinction is consistent with the Directive and [the] court[s] must observe it'.[216]

6.72 In determining whether any treatment was on one of the protected grounds, a simple causation test is to be applied: 'but for' the protected ground would she or he have been treated as she or he was?[217] It is not necessary that the protected characteristic (race, sex etc) be the sole ground for any treatment.[218] Case law holds that the protected ground must have had 'a significant influence on the outcome',[219] that is an influence which is more than trivial.[220] The Burden of Proof Directive[221] and the Framework Directive are 'emphatic in [their] definition in [their] Article 2(1) of the principle of equal treatment as meaning that there shall be no discrimination whatsoever . . . , and in requiring . . . that once the burden shifts for the second stage it is for the respondent to prove that there has been no breach of that principle'.[222] The Race Directive does not adopt the same injunction 'but it would be idle to suggest that that omission entails a meaning different from that of the other Directives. The language of the definitions in the French texts of the three Directives is in effect the same'.[223] In cases where race, sex etc has had *no* significant (that is, no more than a trivial[224]) influence on the act complained of, then this may be insufficient to found a claim in direct discrimination. However, care must be taken to respect the very clear words of the Directives so that where the protected grounds have had a material influence (even if not the only influence) on the outcome, such is outlawed.[225]

6.73 Motive and intention are not material (though a hostile motivation may be relevant to the drawing of inferences, see below). A person may have a very benign motive for treating a person less favourably on a protected ground (for example,

216 *Secretary of State for Defence v Elias* [2006] EWCA Civ 1293, para 114.

217 *James v Eastleigh Borough Council* [1990] 2 AC 751; [1990] IRLR 288; *R v Birmingham City Council ex p Equal Opportunities Commission* [1989] AC 1155, [1989] IRLR 173.

218 *Owen and Briggs v James* [1982] ICR 618; [1982] IRLR 502.

219 *Nagarajan v London Regional Transport* [2000] 1 AC 501; [1999] ICR 877; [1999] IRLR 572, *per* Lord Nicholls.

220 *Igen Ltd (formerly Leeds Careers Guidance) and others v Wong; Chamberlin and another v Emokpae; Webster v Brunel University* [2005] EWCA Civ 142 [2005] ICR 931; [2005] IRLR 258, para 37, *per* Peter Gibson LJ giving judgment for the court.

221 97/80/EC.

222 *Igen Ltd (formerly Leeds Careers Guidance) and others v Wong; Chamberlin and another v Emokpae; Webster v Brunel University* [2005] EWCA Civ 142 [2005] ICR 931; [2005] IRLR 258, para 36, *per* Peter Gibson LJ giving judgment for the court.

223 Ibid, para 36, *per* Peter Gibson LJ giving judgment for the court.

224 Ibid, para 37.

225 Ibid.

to protect them from hostility from others[226]) but, as is referred to below,[227] there is no general defence of justification to direct discrimination[228] and accordingly, once direct discrimination is made out, the explanation for it is irrelevant.[229]

Unintentional, accidental, and thoughtless acts of less favourable treatment are all covered by the direct discrimination provisions where they are done on the protected grounds. Discrimination may be unconscious as well as conscious. People hold prejudices that they do not admit even to themselves, and people are entitled to be, and are, as a matter of law, protected against unintentional discrimination as well as intentional discrimination.[230] **6.74**

(9) Justification

There is no general defence of justification available to direct discrimination in any of the main anti-discrimination enactments except the Age Regulations. There are some limited exceptions applicable to certain of the unlawful acts and these are discussed in Chapter 13. **6.75**

Direct age discrimination, however, may be justified. This is in addition to the wide-reaching exemptions which apply to age discrimination, described in Chapter 8. Regulation 3 of the Age Regulations provides that indirect *and direct* discrimination is made out only where 'A [the discriminator] cannot show the treatment or, as the case may be, provision, criterion or practice to be a proportionate means of achieving a legitimate aim'. This makes the Age Regulations unique in the anti-discrimination legislation. All the other anti-discrimination enactments outlaw direct discrimination without permitting any general defence of justification.[231] **6.76**

The Framework Directive allows Member States to permit 'differences of treatment on grounds of age' where 'within the context of national law, they are objectively and reasonably justified by a legitimate aim, including legitimate employment policy, labour market and vocational training objectives, and if the means of achieving that aim are appropriate and necessary'.[232] The Directive gives **6.77**

---

226 See *Smyth v Croft Inns Ltd* [1996] IRLR 84.

227 Para 6.75.

228 There are some limited exemptions operating in specific fields, described in Chap 13.

229 *Nagarajan v London Regional Transport* [2000] 1 AC 501; [1999] ICR 877; [1999] IRLR 572, *per* Lord Nicholls at para 13–14; *R v Commission for Racial Equality ex p Westminster City Council* [1985] ICR 827; [1984] IRLR 230 (concerning the withdrawal of an offer of employment to a black road sweeper by a manager who feared industrial action in consequence, such was held to be racially discriminatory).

230 *Nagarajan v London Regional Transport* [2000] 1 AC 501; [1999] ICR 877; [1999] IRLR 572; *King v Great Britain-China Centre* [1992] ICR 516; [1991] IRLR 513.

231 Although the upshot of the DDA approach outside the employment and related fields (where direct discrimination is not expressly outlawed and is only proscribed through the prohibitions on disability-related discrimination, which is justifiable) is that direct discrimination in the context of some activities is justifiable under the DDA.

232 Framework Directive, Art 6(1).

three (non-exhaustive) examples of circumstances where differences of treatment might be justified: 'the setting of special conditions on access to employment and vocational training, employment and occupation, including dismissal and remuneration conditions, for young people, older workers and persons with caring responsibilities in order to promote their vocational integration or ensure their protection'; 'the fixing of minimum conditions of age, professional experience or seniority in service for access to employment or to certain advantages linked to employment'; and 'the fixing of a maximum age for retirement which is based on the training requirements of the post in question or the need for a reasonable period of employment before retirement'.[233]

6.78 There is, then, a limited power to provide for justification in the case of direct age discrimination contained within the Framework Directive itself. However, the breadth of the justification defence in the Age Regulations is highly controversial. It is not restricted to exemptions in national law based on objectively and reasonably justified legitimate aims, but instead leaves the issue of justification wide open in any case. The drafting history of the Age Regulations is instructive. The Government originally proposed to have a restricted list of legitimate aims that could justify direct discrimination. The draft Regulations provided for three situations in which less favourable treatment on grounds of age might be considered to be a proportionate means of achieving a legitimate aim, and these were taken directly from the examples set out in the Directive. But in the final consultation on the draft Regulations this list was removed, with the Government explaining that 'an exhaustive list of legitimate aims for direct discrimination would be too restrictive and prescriptive'.[234] This means the question as to what constitutes a 'legitimate aim' for the purposes of the Regulations will, ultimately, be left to the courts and tribunals to determine.

6.79 The Government's Consultation document suggested some objectives which might constitute legitimate aims for the purposes of the wide justification defence in the Age Regulations, namely: health, welfare, and safety (including protection of young people or older people); facilitation of employment planning; particular training requirements; encouraging and rewarding loyalty; the need for a reasonable period of employment before retirement; and recruiting or retaining older people. These are not set down in law,[235] however, and two particularly contentious areas have been identified by commentators,[236] namely whether cost

---

233 Ibid, Art 6(1)(a)–(c).

234 'Equality and Diversity: Coming of Age, Consultation on the draft Employment Equality (Age) Regulations 2006' (2006) Department of Trade and Industry, 33.

235 Though see regulation 32 for an exemption in relation to benefits based on length of service and regulation 7(4) for an exemption in relation to applicant employees who have reached or who are near to retirement age (within 6 months of).

236 M Rubenstein, 'Age Regulations 2006' (2006) EOR 152, 14.

might ever constitute a legitimate aim (or more particularly, the saving of it) and whether customer preference may constitute a legitimate aim and, if so, in what circumstances. The Government Consultation document indicated that, for any aim to be legitimate, it must 'correspond with the real need on the part of the employer . . . economic factors such as business needs and considerations for efficiency may also be legitimate aims. However, discrimination will not be justified merely because it may be more expensive not to discriminate'.[237] As discussed below (paragraph 6.123), the Employment Appeal Tribunal in *Cross v British Airways*[238] suggested that in the context of justification for indirect sex discrimination, cost may be a relevant factor in determining justification 'if combined with other reasons'[239] so that '[a]lbeit that, in the weighing exercise, cost justifications may often be valued less, particularly if the discrimination is substantial, obvious and even deliberate, economic justification such as the saving, or the non-expenditure, of costs (which must, for example, include the avoidance of loss) must be considered'.[240]

In addition to identifying a legitimate aim, any employer seeking to justify age discrimination will need to satisfy the requirement that it is a proportionate means of achieving that legitimate aim. There is a good deal of case law on the meaning of proportionality, both in the context of discrimination in EU law and more broadly, as discussed at paragraph 6.123 onwards. In very broad terms the concept of proportionality requires a balancing exercise to be undertaken, measuring the value of the aim and its importance against the impact of the discriminatory measure. The more severe the impact of the discriminatory measure on the protected group, the more weighty the aim would need to be to satisfy the requirement of proportionality. This is a significant obligation and requires 'every derogation from an individual right to reconcile, so far as is possible, the requirements of the principle of equal treatment with those of the aim pursued'.[241] Blanket rules in relation to age will therefore be very difficult to justify.[242] In particular, where " device, the discriminatory measure is unlikely to be regarded as proportionate. Reliance on stereotyping, cost alone, assumptions about customer preference and prejudice, and intolerance will not be good justificatory reasons. An early challenge to the general defence of justification to direct discrimination in the Age Regulations is expected. 6.80

[237] 'Equality and Diversity: Coming of Age, Consultation on the draft Employment Equality (Age) Regulations 2006' (2006) DTI, 33.

[238] [2005] IRLR 423.

[239] Ibid, para 60.

[240] Ibid, para 63.

[241] *Mangold v Helm* [2006] IRLR 143.

[242] Ibid.

6.81 The absence of a defence of justification to direct discrimination, though not entirely uncontroversial, is critical to its strength.[243] To ensure that the position is properly respected, care must be taken to ensure that 'justification' for direct discrimination is not allowed through the construction of the comparator and the relevant circumstances, as discussed above.[244]

(10) Stereotyping/social norms, less favourable treatment, and the proper comparator

6.82 Notwithstanding the broad meaning given to the concept of *less favourable treatment*, as described above, not every difference in treatment will be regarded by the courts as less favourable. This is particularly so where the difference in treatment reflects entrenched social norms.

6.83 As mentioned in earlier chapters,[245] some older cases under the SDA had the effect of reinforcing gender stereotypes through holdings of no less favourable treatment in circumstances where the differences in treatment afforded men and women reflected normal social habits.[246] Whilst these cases have been replaced by more modern case law recognizing gender stereotyping as antithetical to equality law,[247] some gender-based norms continue to be reinforced through the court's approach to the identification of less favourable treatment and often, too, in the identification of the appropriate comparator. This can be seen most particularly in the 'dress code' cases.[248] A long line of cases have indicated that the courts will not regard sex distinct dress codes[249] as constituting less favourable treatment by reason only that they are sex distinct.[250]

---

243 See J Bowers and E Moran, 'Justification in Direct Sex Discrimination Law: Breaking the Taboo' (2003) 31 ILJ 307; T Gill and K Monaghan, 'Justification in Direct Discrimination: Taboo Upheld' (2003) 32 ILJ 115. The authors of a recent important study sought views on whether direct discrimination should be capable of justification and only two respondents answered positively. They said it would provide a safety valve in extreme cases and gave an example of dress codes. All other respondents thought a general defence would create uncertainty and confusion in an area where the present law works well and would undermine the principle of equality: B Hepple, M Coussey, and T Choudhury, *Equality: a New Framework* (2000, University of Cambridge), para 2.43.

244 Para 6.37–6.42.

245 Chaps 1 and 5.

246 See Chap 5.

247 See, for example, *Hurley v Mustoe* [1981] ICR 490 at 496 and *Moyhing v Barts and London NHS Trust* [2006] IRLR 860.

248 It is difficult to see how a difference in treatment based on racial group would be anything but less favourable. However examples might, as with gender, include differences in dress codes so that exceptions to dress codes which permit Sikhs to wear turbans or Muslims to wear hijabs might constitute differences in treatment which do not amount to less favourable treatment of non-Sikhs or non-Muslims (and indeed a blanket dress rule may sometimes be indirectly racially discriminatory, see below).

249 L. Flynn, 'Gender Equality Laws and Employers Dress Codes' (1995) 24 ILJ 255; R. Wintemute, 'Recognising New Kinds of Direct Sex Discrimination: Transexualism, Sexual Orientation and Dress Codes' (1997) 60 MLR 343.

250 *Schmidt v Austicks Bookshops Limited* [1977] IRLR 360 (no trouser rule for women); *Burrett v West Birmingham Health Authority* (1994) IRLR 7 (requirement that female nurses wear a cap); and see, for examples of first instance decisions, footnote 89 in R Wintemute, 'Recognising New Kinds of Direct Sex Discrimination: Transexualism, Sexual Orientation and Dress Codes' (1997) 60 MLR 343.

In *Smith v Safeways Plc*,[251] Mr Smith complained that a rule requiring male delicatessen staff to keep their hair at no longer than 'short collar length' was directly discriminatory against men because women delicatessen staff were required only to have 'tidy hair . . . shoulder length hair must be clipped back. No unconventional hair styles or colouring'. The Employment Appeal Tribunal by a majority (with the judicial member Pill J dissenting) held that the rule was 'self evidently less favourable and sex discriminatory'.[252] The majority of the Employment Appeal Tribunal were particularly impressed by the fact that there was no relevant physiological difference between men and women, and the restriction on hair length had an effect on male employees not only during their working hours but at all times.[253] Notwithstanding this, the Court of Appeal allowed an appeal by Safeways, holding that 'a code which applies conventional standards is one which, so far as the criterion of appearance is concerned, applies an even-handed approach between men and women, and not one which is discriminatory'.[254] The Court of Appeal recognized that 'one of the objects of the prohibition of sex discrimination was to relieve the sexes from unequal treatment resulting from conventional attitudes'[255] but nevertheless such did not 'render . . . discriminatory an appearance code which applies as standard what is convention'.[256] In deciding whether the approach taken to a dress code was 'even-handed', according to the Court of Appeal, a 'package approach to the effect of an appearance code'[257] should be taken. This means that the effect of any particular requirement in a dress code must be considered in the overall context to determine whether differential rules on dress, as between men and women, constitute less favourable treatment. The decision in *Smith* and the earlier cases adopting a similar approach to differential dress codes as between men and women[258] have been heavily criticized since.[259] According to Phillips LJ:

> [a] code which made identical provisions for men and women, but which resulted in one or other having an unconventional appearance, would have an unfavourable impact on that sex being compelled to appear in an unconventional mode. Can there be any doubt that a code which required all employees to have 18-inch hair, earrings and lipstick would treat men unfavourably by requiring them to adopt an appearance at odds with the conventional standards?[260]

That analysis is too simplistic and ignores the impact of mandatory dress code requirements which are different for men and women and which reinforce **6.84**

[251] [1996] IRLR 456.

[252] Ibid, para 18.

[253] Ibid, paras 19–20.

[254] Ibid, para 16, *per* Phillips LJ.

[255] Ibid.

[256] Ibid.

[257] Ibid, para 13, *per* Phillips LJ.

[258] See, in particular, *Turley v Allders Department Stores Limited* [1980] ICR 66 and *Schmidt v Austicks Bookshops Limited* [1978] ICR 85.

[259] D Pannick, *Sex Discrimination Law* (1985, Clarendon Press), 204.

[260] *Smith v Safeways Plc* [1996] IRLR 456, para 16.

gender stereotyping. Requiring a woman or a man to dress in a way which conforms to their sex stereotype is disadvantageous to both of them. That disadvantage is not saved by applying the discriminatory rule to both, and nor is it excused by the fact that another discriminatory rule (that both sexes dress in accordance with the sexual stereotype applicable to one sex only, thereby disadvantaging the other sex) might impose more significant disadvantage on one or other sex. The answer instead must be that dress codes respect choice and do not require that choice to be exercisable only within the constraints set by gender-specific social rules on dress.

6.85 After *Smith*, there were some decisions suggesting that, at least at first instance, the courts might take a more progressive view about clothing rules.[261] However, these were followed by the decision of the Employment Appeal Tribunal in *Department for Work and Pensions v Thompson*[262] in which the Employment Appeal Tribunal overturned a finding of the employment tribunal that a requirement that men wear a collar and tie to work whereas women were required only to 'dress appropriately and to a similar standard' was sex discriminatory. The Employment Appeal Tribunal adopted the same approach as that taken in *Smith v Safeways*, observing that:

> in the context of the overarching requirement for its staff to dress in a professional and businesslike way, the question [is] whether, applying contemporary standards of conventional dress wear, the level of smartness . . . required of all . . . staff could only be achieved for men by requiring them to wear a collar and tie . . . [T]he issue is not resolved by asking whether the requirement of men to wear a collar and tie meant that a higher level of smartness was being required of men rather than women. It is resolved by asking whether an equivalent level of smartness to that required of the female members of staff could only be achieved, in the case of men, by requiring them to wear a collar and tie . . .[263]

As Robert Wintemute has observed:

> 'conventional standards' of appropriate dress and appearance for men and women are not sex-neutral and are clearly defined by reference to sex. One cannot decide whether 'conventional standards' permit a person to wear trousers or a skirt without knowing their sex. Indeed, 'conventional' in this context really means 'sex-appropriate' [citing David Pannick,[264] 'Grooming codes . . . define the

261 See, for example, *Owen v Professional Golf Association* (2000) Unreported, Case No 1303043/99 in which case the employment tribunal found that a dress code which prohibited the woman complainant wearing trousers was unlawful sex discrimination; and *Thompson v Department for Work and Pensions*, reported in the Employment Appeal Tribunal at [2004] IRLR 348, in which at first instance the employment tribunal concluded that a requirement that men employed in 'job centre plus' wear a collar and tie was unlawful discrimination.

262 [2004] IRLR 348.

263 Ibid, para 30, *per* Keith J.

264 D Pannick, *Sex Discrimination Law* (1985, Clarendon Press), 189.

treatment of individuals according to social expectations of what is appropriate for each sex'].[265]

The rationale for permitting such dress codes, according to some of the case law, is that a conventional image is necessary for commercial reasons,[266] thus apparently deferring to the prejudices of customers, a ground which would not in other contexts justify differences in treatment. In *Thompson*, the justification for the dress code was said to be the need to set an example to those using Job Centre Plus services, amongst other things, in the hope of encouraging job applicants to dress appropriately,[267] so perpetuating gendered dress stereotypes. **6.86**

As mentioned above, the court's approach to the identification of the proper comparator in a direct discrimination case has also been used to reinforce gender stereotyping and social norms. As mentioned[268] and discussed further below, the courts have interpreted the comparator requirement under the SDA so that it does not protect women who choose female sexual partners and men who choose male sexual partners and who are discriminated against because of that choice. This is because, according to the courts, being gay is a relevant circumstance so that less favourable treatment of a woman because she chooses female sexual partners must be compared to that afforded a man who chooses male sexual partners.[269] If the discriminator treats all gay people (women and men) equally badly, there is no direct sex discrimination. This despite the fact that the treatment occurs because the lesbian woman does not conform to her social stereotype in the choice of her partner (which social norms would have as a man) and similarly so in the case of the gay man. **6.87**

Apart from the case law on gender stereotyping, recent judicial dicta indicate that reliance on racial stereotyping or 'profiling' may not always constitute less favourable treatment on racial grounds. In *R (on the application of European Roma Rights Centre) v Immigration Officer at Prague Airport*,[270] (*Roma Rights*) the Court of Appeal was concerned with a pre-clearance scheme operated by UK immigration officers at Prague Airport and whether or not the scheme operated to discriminate on racial grounds against Roma applicants for leave to enter the UK.[271] The claimants contended that there was a practice in existence of questioning Roma applicants for longer and more intensively than non-Roma **6.88**

265 R Wintemute, 'Recognising New Kinds of Direct Sex Discrimination: Transexualism, Sexual Orientation and Dress Codes' (1997) 60 MLR 343.

266 *Smith v Safeways Plc* [1996] IRLR 456.

267 *Department for Work and Pensions v Thompson* [2004] IRLR 348, para 4.

268 Chap 5.

269 *Pearce v Governing Body of Mayfield Secondary School* [2001] EWCA Civ 1347, [2002] ICR 198; [2003] IRLR 512.

270 [2003] EWCA Civ 666 [2004] QB 811.

271 The case is considered further in Chap 11.

applicants, and that such was discriminatory and unlawful under section 19B(1) of the RRA,[272] which makes it unlawful for a public authority to discriminate in carrying out its functions. The object of the pre-clearance scheme was to stem the flow of asylum seekers from the Czech Republic, the vast majority of whom were of Romani ethnic origin (Roma). The question was posed by Simon Brown LJ:

> [w]hat is the position in law if, as seems to the court wholly inevitable, immigration officers, aware of the fact that the overwhelming majority of those seeking asylum from the Czech Republic are Roma (it may be doubted, indeed, whether any such are non-Roma) bring a greater degree of scepticism to bear on a Roma's application for leave to enter for some permitted purpose than upon an apparently comparable application by Czech non-Roma?[273]

According to the Court of Appeal:

> [B]ecause of the greater degree of scepticism with which Roma applicants will inevitably be treated, they are more likely to be refused leave to enter than non-Roma applicants. But this is because they are less well placed to persuade the immigration officer that they are not lying in order to seek asylum. That is not to say, however, that they are being stereotyped. Rather it is to acknowledge the undoubtedly disadvantaged position of many Roma in the Czech Republic. Of course it would be wrong in any individual case to assume that the Roma applicant is lying, but I decline to hold that the immigration officer cannot properly be warier of that possibility in a Roma's case than in the case of a non-Roma applicant. If a terrorist outrage were committed on our streets today, would the police not be entitled to question more suspiciously those in the vicinity appearing to come from an Islamic background? Similarly in the case of sectarian violence in Northern Ireland. These seem to me to be the relevant analogies here, not the now defunct practice of repeatedly stopping and searching black youths, clearly an unjustifiable interference with their liberty unless reasonable grounds exist for suspecting those actually stopped.[274]

The reasoning of Simon Brown LJ is self-evidently flawed. Subjecting Roma passengers to more intense questioning because they are Roma is to stereotype them as members of a particular class, in just the same way that young black men were stereotyped and thus harassed by regular and repeated stops under the old 'suss' laws, in accordance with the perception of the activities of young black men (true or not). Laws LJ disagreed in a compelling dissent[275] acknowledging that where an officer at Prague Airport stopped a Roma person and subjected him or her to more intrusive inquiry 'the officer has applied a stereotype; though one which may very likely be true. That is not permissible'.

---

272 As to which see Chap 11.

273 *R (on the application of European Roma Rights Centre) v Immigration Officer at Prague Airport* [2003] EWCA Civ 666 [2004] QB 811, para 86 *Centre* [2003] EWCA Civ 666 [2004] QB 811, para 66.

274 *R (on the application of European Roma Rights Centre) v Immigration Officer at Prague Airport* [2003] EWCA Civ 666 [2004] QB 811, para 86.

275 See para 109 in particular.

6.89 The decision of the Court of Appeal in *Roma Rights* has been heavily criticized.[276] The decision was overturned by the House of Lords.[277] According to Baroness Hale:

> The underlying concept in both Race and Sex Discrimination laws is that individuals of each sex and all races are entitled to be treated equally. Thus it is just as discriminatory to treat men less favourably than women as it is to treat women less favourably than men; and it is just as discriminatory to treat whites less favourably than blacks as it is to treat blacks less favourably than whites . . . if direct discrimination . . . is shown, that is that. Save for some very limited exceptions, there is no defence of objective justification. The whole point of the law is to require suppliers to treat each person as an individual, not as a member of a group. The individual should not be assumed to hold the characteristics which the supplier associates with the group, whether or not most members of the group do indeed have such characteristics, a process sometimes referred to as stereotyping. Even if, for example, most women are less strong than most men, it must not be assumed that the individual woman who has applied for the job does not have the strength to do it. Nor, for that matter, should it be assumed that an individual man does have that strength. If strength is a qualification, all applicants should be required to demonstrate that they qualify.[278]

6.90 The issue was revisited in *R (on the application of Gillan and Another) v Commissioner of Police for the Metropolis and Another*[279] in a case which did not directly concern the issue of race at all. The case concerned the powers granted under sections 44 to 47 of the Terrorism Act 2000 which allows the police in certain circumstances to stop and search persons in a specified area for articles of a kind which could be used in connection with terrorism, and that power could be exercised whether or not the police officer concerned had grounds for suspecting the presence of such articles.[280] The House of Lords were concerned with the parameters of the power, holding that the European Convention on Human Rights (ECHR) imposes a lawfulness requirement in respect of any interferences material to the issues in that case (Articles 5, 8, 10, and 11[281]) and that arbitrary interferences or those predicated on malice would not meet that requirement—'arbitrariness' being 'the antithesis of legality'.[282] In that context arguments were made as to the impact of a racially discriminatory stop. What if the police, after a terrorist incident on the public transport system, stopped only Asian travellers? Such would seem to fall squarely within the principle (not new) in the *Roma*

276 See R Singh, 'Equality: The Neglected Virtue' (2004) EHRLR 2004, 2, 141–157; 'Highlights: September 2003' [2003] IRLR 549.

277 [2005] 2 AC 1; [2005] IRLR 115.

278 Ibid, paras 73–4.

279 [2006] UKHL 12.

280 The circumstances in which the powers arose are prescribed in the Terrorism Act 2000, s 44 onwards.

281 For the Convention rights, see Chap 4.

282 *R (on the application of Gillan and Another) v Commissioner of Police for the Metropolis and Another* [2006] UKHL 12, para 34 *per* Lord Bingham.

Rights case and would be plainly unlawful. However, according to Lord Hope 'an appearance which suggests that the person is of Asian origin may attract the constable's attention in the first place. But a further selection process will have to be undertaken, perhaps on the spur of the moment otherwise the opportunity will be lost, before the power is exercised. It is a further selection process that makes the difference between what is inherently discriminatory and what is not'.[283] Thus, according to Lord Hope, the pool from which selection is determined can be constructed along racial lines without causing offence to the principle of legality or, apparently, to the RRA. This is contrary to the clear dicta in the *Roma Rights* case. It sanctions the closer scrutiny of members of a particular racial group, because they are members of that group and because of stereotypes assumed to apply to them (rightly or wrongly), it is also contrary to the principle established by the RRA, and the other anti-discrimination legislation, that persons are entitled to be treated as individuals and not stereotyped by reference to their membership of a racial, gender etc group. Lord Scott seemed to recognize that stopping persons of Asian origin more frequently than others would, *prima facie*, constitute discrimination, but to the extent that the Terrorism Act powers 'might require some degree of stereotyping in the selection of the persons to be stopped and searched and arguably, therefore, some discrimination' such would not be unlawful under the RRA because they were mandated under the Terrorism Act 2000.[284] Lord Brown (that being Simon Brown LJ, who had by now been appointed to the House of Lords) took the opportunity to revisit the decision in the *Roma Rights* case, noting that he did not find it 'altogether easy to distinguish between on the one hand the greater scepticism logically felt by immigration officers towards Roma than non-Roma applicants (held in the *Roma Rights* case to have been unlawfully discriminatory) and on the other hand the greater preparedness which police officers understandably have to stop and search those of Asian appearance . . . given the perceived source of the main terrorist threat today'.[285] He resolved the two by drawing a distinction which he did 'not pretend to find . . . entirely satisfactory'[286] namely that in the *Roma Rights* case the immigration officers had not sufficiently had regard to each Roma applicant as an individual but rather merely as a stereotypical member of the group and treated them identically. As Lord Simon Brown said:

> it would, of course have been wrong for immigration officers to have treated every Roma applicant identically irrespective of how his answers to questions put to

[283] Ibid, para 46.

[284] Lord Scott referred to ss 41 and 42 of the RRA, discussed in Chap 13, though, as he observes, this was not a matter addressed in argument by counsel, and it appears he assumes that ss 41 and 42 have a rather broader effect than they do, as to which see Chap 13.

[285] *R (on the application of Gillan and Another) v Commissioner of Police for the Metropolis and Another* [2006] UKHL 12, para 89.

[286] Ibid, para 90.

> him affected the interviewing officer's view as to the genuineness of his particular application. But that surely, so far from according with commonsense, would have been not merely wrong but also silly. Nevertheless the House appears to have concluded that this was indeed the immigration officer's approach.[287]

That is a mischaracterization of the judgments of the House of Lords. As was made quite clear in the *Roma Rights* case, the motive for treating the Roma passengers in a particular way was immaterial. Stereotyping them as members of a particular group and subjecting them to more intensive scrutiny in consequence was unlawful racial discrimination. In any event, Lord Brown, as with Lord Hope, regarded it as legitimate to identify the pool of persons for whom selection was to be made along racial lines, and that the powers in issue could not be 'impugned as either arbitrary or as "inherently systematically discriminatory" (Lord Steyn's characterisation of the Prague operation) simply because they are used selectively to target those regarded by the police as most likely to be carrying terrorist connected articles, even if this leads, as usually it will, to the deployment of this power against a higher proportion of people from one ethnic group than another'.[288] These judgments run counter to the principles underpinning the RRA and they are profoundly disrespectful to those who a police officer may judge as having the 'appearance of being Asian', to whom the application of an offensive stereotype might then, according to certain of their Lordships, be lawfully applied.

In other areas, as has been observed above, the law has been more astute to the dangers posed by stereotyping.[289] In the context of disability the Employment Code of Practice issued by the Disability Rights Commission gives the following guidance: **6.91**

> [If] the less favourable treatment occurs because of the employer's generalized, or stereotypical, assumptions about the disability or its effects, it is likely to be direct discrimination. This is because an employer would not normally make such assumptions about a non-disabled person, but would instead consider his individual abilities.[290] [For Example:]
> A blind woman is not short-listed for a job involving computers because the employer wrongly assumes that blind people cannot use them. The employer makes no attempt to look at the individual circumstances. The employer has treated the woman less favourably than other people by not short-listing her for the job. The treatment was on the ground of the woman's disability (because assumptions would not have been made about a non-disabled person).[291]

287 Ibid.

288 Ibid, para 92.

289 *Hurley v Mustoe* [1981] ICR 490; *Coleman v Sky Rail Oceanic Limited* [1981] ICR 864 [1981] IRLR 398; *Horsey v Dyfed County Council* [1982] ICR 755, [1982] IRLR 395.

290 Code of Practice on Employment and Occupation (2004) DRC, ISBN 0 11 703 419 3; Disability Discrimination Codes of Practice (Employment and Occupation, and Trade Organisations and Qualifications Bodies) Appointed Day Order 2004 SI 2004/2302.

291 Ibid, both at para 4.8.

(11) Proving direct discrimination

6.92 There is specific provision made in all the main anti-discrimination enactments addressing the incidence of the burden of proof in direct discrimination and the shifting of it in certain circumstances. This requires that, where a complainant proves facts from which a court or tribunal *could* conclude, in the absence of an adequate explanation, that the alleged discriminator has committed an act of discrimination or harassment, then the court or tribunal must uphold the complaint unless the alleged discriminator proves that he did not. The burden of proof provisions are described and explained at Chapter 14 below.

6.93 However, in the context of direct discrimination there has been much relevant guidance from the courts on proving direct discrimination, most particularly in cases where the ground for the treatment is not overt. In short summary, a court or tribunal may infer that direct discrimination has occurred (and indeed may be bound to do so[292]) on proof of a difference in treatment and a difference in status, where there is no non-discriminatory explanation for the treatment complained of shown by the alleged discriminator. The guidance given by the courts was summarized in an extremely helpful judgment of Sedley LJ in *Anya v University of Oxford and another*,[293] as follows:

> Deciding such questions is not easy. The problem was classically addressed in this court by Neill LJ in *King v Great Britain-China Centre* [1992] ICR 516. In a well known passage, at pp 528-529, which the industrial tribunal clearly had in mind, he summarized the relevant principles in this way:
>
> 'From [the] several authorities it is possible, I think, to extract the following principles and guidance. (1) It is for the applicant who complains of . . . discrimination to make out his or her case. Thus if the applicant does not prove the case on the balance of probabilities he or she will fail. [this is now to be treated as qualified by the burden of proof changes[294]] (2) It is important to bear in mind that it is unusual to find direct evidence of . . . discrimination [on a proscribed ground]. Few employers will be prepared to admit such discrimination even to themselves. In some cases the discrimination will not be ill-intentioned but merely based on an assumption that "he or she would not have fitted in." (3) The outcome of the case will therefore usually depend on what inferences it is proper to draw from the primary facts found by the tribunal. These inferences can include, in appropriate cases, any inferences that it is just and equitable to draw . . . from an evasive or equivocal reply to a questionnaire.[295] (4) Though there will be some cases where, for example, the non-selection of the applicant for a post or for promotion is clearly not on [proscribed] . . . grounds, a finding of discrimination and a finding of a difference in

---

292 See the burden of proof provisions, discussed in Chap 14.

293 [2001] EWCA Civ 405; [2001] ICR 847, 851–5, *per* Sedley LJ. See too, *Qureshi v Victoria University of Manchester* now reported at [2001] ICR 863 for the very helpful guidance of Mummery LJ.

294 Author's notes in square brackets.

295 For the questionnaire procedure, see Chap 14.

> [protected status] will often point to the possibility of . . . discrimination. In such circumstances the tribunal will look to the employer for an explanation. If no explanation is then put forward or if the tribunal considers the explanation to be inadequate or unsatisfactory it will be legitimate for the tribunal to infer that the discrimination was on [proscribed] . . . grounds. This is not a matter of law but, as May LJ put it in North West Thames Regional Health Authority v Noone [1988] ICR 813, 822, "almost common sense". (5) . . . At the conclusion of all the evidence the tribunal should make findings as to the primary facts and draw such inferences as they consider proper from those facts. They should then reach a conclusion on the balance of probabilities, bearing in mind both the difficulties which face a person who complains of unlawful discrimination and the fact that it is for the complainant to prove his or her case.'
>
> It should be made clear that, when Neill LJ refers under head (4) to discrimination, he means it in its literal, not its objectionable, sense: that is to say, he is referring simply to a choice or a process of selection such as occurred here. It is not unduly onerous, as has sometimes been suggested, to proceed from the simple fact of such a choice, if it is accompanied by difference in [status], to a request for an explanation. In the allocation of jobs by any sensibly-run institution, the explanation will be straightforward: the candidates were interviewed by an unbiased panel on an equal footing, using common criteria which contained no obvious or latent elements capable of favouring one . . . group over another; and the best one was chosen. By parity of reasoning, evidence that one or more members of the panel were not unbiased, or that equal opportunities procedures were not used when they should have been, may point to the possibility of conscious or unconscious . . . bias having entered into the process.

It is important in all cases to have regard to the circumstantial evidence where such evidence might indicate one way or another whether objectionable discrimination has occurred. Such evidence might include evidence relating to an alleged discriminator's compliance with good equal opportunities practice[296] and compliance with the relevant provisions of the Codes of Practice, discussed in Chapter 15. Statistical evidence may be relevant where it suggests a discernible pattern of treatment by the alleged discriminator towards a particular group.[297] In addition, the questionnaire procedure is a very important tool for the drawing of inferences. The questionnaire procedure is explained in Chapter 15. Surrounding circumstances may be relevant even when not themselves tainted by discrimination, but a court or tribunal is required to make primary findings of fact on all the circumstantial evidence relied upon and then decide, having regard to those primary findings, whether or not the proper inference to draw from all those facts is an inference of unlawful discrimination in respect of the particular complaint of direct discrimination made. 6.94

296 See the observations of Sedley LJ, para 6.93.
297 *West Midlands PTE v Singh* [1988] ICR 614.

6.95 Unreasonable treatment without more is not objectionable discrimination. However, 'hostility *may* justify an inference' of discrimination 'if there is nothing else to explain it: whether there is such an explanation . . . will depend not on a theoretical possibility that the employer behaves equally badly to employees . . . but on evidence that he does'.[298] Such an inference may also be rebutted by the employer leading evidence of a genuine non-discriminatory reason for the hostility.[299]

(12) Direct discrimination: the importance of isolating the questions

6.96 As described above, each of the elements of direct discrimination must be established, but establishing them discretely can sometimes be problematic. This is particularly so in cases where a hypothetical comparator is relied upon, as discussed above. In many cases, the question whether any treatment was comparatively less favourable and the question whether or not the treatment was on a protected ground are closely related. The case law indicates that in such circumstances a single enquiry might be more appropriate—that is 'did the claimant, on the proscribed ground, receive less favourable treatment than others?'[300] This might be most simply analysed by asking the question 'Why' a person was treated as they were. If it was on a protected ground then that person has been subject to less favourable treatment as compared to a person not possessing the relevant characteristics. If not, then not:[301]

> Thus, on this footing also, the less favourable treatment issue is incapable of being decided without deciding the reason-why issue. And the decision on the reason-why issue will also provide the answer to the less-favourable-treatment issue. This analysis seems . . . to point to the conclusion that . . . tribunals may sometimes be able to avoid arid and confusing disputes about the identification of the appropriate comparator by concentrating primarily on why the claimant was treated as she was. Was it on the proscribed ground which is the foundation of the application? . . . If [so] . . . ,there will be usually no difficulty in deciding whether the treatment, afforded to the claimant on the proscribed ground, was less favourable than was or would have been afforded to others.[302]

6.97 Whilst the 'reason why' question must be distinguished from any question of intent or motivation, there are two real difficulties with this 'compendious question'[303] approach.

---

298 *Anya v University of Oxford and another* [2001] EWCA Civ 405; [2001] ICR 847, 857A, *per* Sedley LJ.

299 *Bahl v (1) Law Society (2) Robert Sayer (3) Jane Betts* [2004] EWCA Civ 1070; [2004] IRLR 799.

300 *Shamoon v Chief Constable of the Royal Ulster Constabulary* [2003] ICR 337, *per* Lord Nicholls at para 8.

301 Ibid, at para 10.

302 Ibid, at paras 10 and 11.

303 *R (Carson and Another) v Secretary of State for Work and Pensions* [2003] 3 All ER 577, 604, para 61, *per* Laws LJ, in the context of Article 14, see Chap 4.

Firstly, it poses the risk of permitting the justification of direct discrimination by the infection of the comparator analysis. Such was seen, for example, in *Dhatt*, described above. An approach to direct discrimination which identifies a person as non-comparable because there is a good reason for treating them differently (for example, that they have a different immigration status or pension age, or that they will not get pregnant, with the associated costs) risks the implication of a justification defence which Parliament plainly did not intend. Its focus, too, on the reason *why*, makes the compendious enquiry approach particularly vulnerable to justificatory reasons, excusing objectionable direct discrimination. In *James v Eastleigh BC*,[304] discussed above, the requirement to be a pensioner explained *why* Mr James was treated as he was, but motive is irrelevant as discussed above, and the fact that the motive was benign (offering subsidies to persons presumed to be living on pension income) was immaterial—the benevolent discriminator is as culpable in law as the malevolent discriminator. **6.98**

Secondly, it makes the imposition of the burden of proof complicated. Without rigorous analysis throughout the process of answering the compendious question, it is likely to be difficult to discern where the burden of proof lies at various stages, and there is a risk of imposing too high a burden on a complainant. If treatment is less favourable than that afforded a legal comparator, the reason why is immaterial at the first stage of the enquiry.[305] Instead the burden should shift to the alleged discriminator to show the absence of objectionable discrimination. **6.99**

If the absence of a justification defence and the burden of proof provisions are to be properly respected, then very great care must be taken in applying a compendious question to the enquiries required by the direct discrimination provisions. **6.100**

D. Indirect Discrimination

(1) Introduction and EU law

Indirect discrimination is concerned with neutral patterns of treatment, that is, treatment which does not differentiate between relevant persons of different protected classes, but which disadvantages disproportionately members of a particular protected class. Its origins in UK anti-discrimination law are described in Chapter 2. One of the most common examples of indirect discrimination is seen in working hours.[306] A rule imposed on a whole workforce that they work **6.101**

[304] [1990] 2 AC 751; [1990] IRLR 288.

[305] Unless it is inadequate; *Igen Ltd (formerly Leeds Careers Guidance) and others v Wong; Chamberlin and another v Emokpae; Webster v Brunel University* [2005] EWCA Civ 142 [2005] ICR 931; [2005] IRLR 258.

[306] See, eg, *London Underground Limited v Edwards (No 2)* [1998] IRLR 364.

9.00 am to 5.00 pm from Monday to Friday, whilst not differentiating between groups, may disadvantage women (who are still, in the main, the primary child carers) and certain ethnic groups (where they comprise or are dominated by a particular religious faith, the requirements of which necessitate absence from work on certain days).

6.102 All the main anti-discrimination enactments, except the DDA, regulate indirect discrimination. The DDA instead adopts a reasonable adjustments model which is described below. In their original enactments the SDA and the RRA defined indirect discrimination in materially the same way, and that definition applied for the purposes of all their provisions. The meaning given to indirect sex discrimination was then amended, for the purposes of the employment and related fields only, to comply with new EU law.[307] The meaning given to indirect sex and race discrimination was then amended again to comply with EU law, and again for the purposes of limited activities only. This new meaning of indirect discrimination is also the meaning adopted for the purposes of the Religion or Belief, Sexual Orientation, and Age Regulations.

6.103 Unfortunately, applying the concepts of indirect discrimination is complex. As recently observed:

> The available arguments have become more convoluted, while continuing to multiply. Separating the wheat from the chaff takes more and more time. The short snappy decisions of the early days of the industrial tribunals have long since disappeared. They have been replaced by what truly are 'extended reasons' which have to grapple with factual situations of escalating complexity and with thicker seams of domestic and EC law, as interpreted in cascades of case law from the House of Lords and the European Court of Justice.[308]

Each of the meanings given to the concept of indirect discrimination and the scope of their application are described below.

(2) The first meaning of indirect discrimination

6.104 The first meaning of indirect discrimination was the only form of indirect discrimination outlawed in the SDA and RRA in their original enactments. It applies only to race and sex discrimination. It has been given a restricted meaning by the courts which has limited its impact, as is discussed below. In the SDA this form of indirect discrimination is defined as follows:[309]

---

307 Sex Discrimination (Indirect Discrimination and Burden of Proof) Regulations 2001 SI 2001/2660, made to give effect to the Burden of Proof Directive 97/80/EC.

308 *Rutherford and Another v Secretary of State for Trade and Industry (No 2)* [2004] EWCA; Civ 1186 [2004] IRLR 892. This case subsequently went to the House of Lords, at [2006] UKHL 19; [2006] IRLR 551.

309 SDA, s 1(1)(b).

a person discriminates against a woman if he applies to her a requirement or condition which he applies or would apply equally to a man but

(i) which is such that the proportion of women who can comply with it is considerably smaller than the proportion of men who can comply with it, and
(ii) which he cannot show to be justifiable irrespective of the sex of the person to whom it is applied, and
(iii) which is to her detriment because she cannot comply with it.

The first meaning of indirect race discrimination is in materially the same terms.[310] The comparison under (i) in the case of indirect race discrimination is between persons of the same racial group and persons not of that racial group.

In the case of sex discrimination, this meaning of indirect discrimination applies to any provision under the SDA except any provision of Part 2 (employment and related fields), sections 35A and 35B (barristers and advocates), and any other provision of Part 3 (discrimination in other fields), so far as it applies to vocational training.[311] This is because, in consequence of EU law as described below, separate provision addressing indirect discrimination is made in respect of these activities. **6.105**

The position is more complicated under the RRA. The first meaning of indirect discrimination is restricted to all the provisions of the RRA except those mentioned in section 1(1B),[312] when the new and more generous provision addressing indirect discrimination (the 'third' meaning described below) applies. The new meaning, importantly, however, does not apply to nationality discrimination because the Race Directive to which it gives effect excludes nationality discrimination, as is explained in Chapter 4. In addition, it applies expressly only to discrimination connected to race, ethnicity, and national origins (again closely matching the scope of the Directive) but, given the overlap between the concept of race and colour,[313] indirect colour discrimination will be covered by the new meaning. **6.106**

As seen, this first meaning of indirect discrimination requires that the discriminator has applied a 'requirement or condition'. The courts have construed this element strictly, requiring that any requirement or condition be mandatory if the provision is to apply.[314] Discretionary rules fall outside the scope of this form of indirect discrimination and this might be contrasted with the position otherwise under the new forms of indirect discrimination described below. However, the **6.107**

310 RRA, s 1(1)(b).

311 See SDA, s 1(1) and (2). For the unlawful acts, see Chaps 7 onwards.

312 RRA, s 1(1A) and (1C).

313 See Chap 5.

314 *Perera v The Civil Service Commission and the Department of Customs & Excise (No 2)* [1983] ICR 428; [1983] IRLR 166 and *Meer v Tower Hamlets* [1988] IRLR 399. This was probably not compatible with EU law, see *Falkirk Council v Whyte and Others* [1997] IRLR 560. The introduction of a new meaning of indirect discrimination in those areas covered by EU law remedies this deficiency, see below.

inclusion of both the words 'requirement' and 'condition' is such as to include anything which fairly falls within the ordinary meaning of either word. The concept of 'requirement' for these purposes is not limited in the sense of meaning 'qualification' and the concept of 'condition' is not limited to a qualification for holding a position but instead extends to a qualification for immunity from a disadvantage. Accordingly a redundancy procedure which provided that part-time workers would be selected before full-time workers thereby applied a requirement or condition within the meaning of section 1(1)(b) of the SDA in that, in order to qualify for selection on the basis of last in first out, an employee had to be employed full time.[315]

6.108 The test for determining whether the proportion of the protected class who can comply with the requirement or condition is considerably smaller than the proportion not of that class who can comply with it ('disparate impact') is complicated. The impact of any requirement or condition must be such that the proportion of persons from one protected group (women/men or particular racial group) who can comply with it is considerably smaller than the proportion of persons from another (men/women, a different racial group from the first).[316] In summary, this means determining the pool of persons to whom the condition or requirement is applied and then determining the proportion of persons of the one protected group who can comply ('the advantaged group') and conversely who cannot comply ('the disadvantaged group'), and the proportion of persons of the comparator group who can comply and conversely who cannot comply. The whole group to whom the condition or requirement is applied must be considered[317] and that pool should not be limited in scope by any criterion which has no relevance to the impact of the requirement or condition in question.[318] For example, in a case where a complaint was made by a woman who graduated as a mature student that an upper age bar for appointment to a post discriminated against women, the pool for comparison was all people otherwise qualified for the post, and it was wrong to narrow the pool to people who had graduated as mature students.[319] The fact that the reason why the age bar may have discriminated

[315] *Clarke v Eley Kynoch Ltd* [1982] IRLR 482; [1983] ICR 165. See too, *Home Office v Holmes* [1984] IRLR 299; [1984] ICR 678.

[316] SDA, s 1(b)(i); RRA, s 1(b)(i).

[317] *R v Secretary of State for Employment ex parte Seymour-Smith and Perez* (Case C-167/97) [1999] 2 AC 554; [1999] IRLR 253, paras 58–9; *Allonby v Accrington and Rossendale College and Others* (Case C-256/01) [2004] IRLR 224; *Rutherford and Another v Secretary of State for Trade and Industry (No 2)* [2006] UKHL 19; [2006] IRLR 551.

[318] *Rutherford and Another v Secretary of State for Trade and Industry (No 2)* [2006] UKHL 19; [2006] IRLR 551, paras 77 and 82, *per* Baroness Hale.

[319] *University of Manchester v Jones* [1993] IRLR 218; see too, *Perera v Civil Service Commission (No 2)* [1982] IRLR 147 (proportion of older immigrants irrelevant; upheld by the Court of Appeal [1983] IRLR 166 without mention of this point); *London Underground v Edwards (No 2)* [1998] IRLR 364, 370

against women was because they are more likely to graduate at an older age explains the disparity in impact but does not determine whether it actually has disparate impact. Instead, in determining whether there is disparate impact it is best to take 'the unvarnished statistics' as they are found, in most cases looking both at the advantaged and disadvantaged groups.[320] In some cases looking at the disadvantaged group will not be necessary, especially where the disparity is obvious from the advantaged group[321] (for example where the composition of the whole pool comprises half men and half women and 90 per cent of the men can comply but only 10 per cent of the women can comply). Importantly, the numbers of people from the particular protected group affected is much less significant than the proportion of such persons. A rule may apply to a very large pool of people, perhaps comprising many hundreds of thousands of people, but it is not enough that many people from a protected group are disadvantaged by it. It must be shown that a *considerably smaller proportion* of them can comply as compared to the comparator group. The critical question is whether a protected group has suffered some disadvantage.[322]

Problems may arise where the pool affected, or the group said to be affected within a group, is very small because of historic discrimination or otherwise. In such circumstances, it may be necessary to look at a wider pool to test the disadvantage against. The indirect discrimination provisions are concerned with discrimination and disadvantage. If any disparate impact is minimal it may still disclose discrimination, but to ensure any such impact reveals something inherently discriminatory about the requirement or condition, rather than a mere fortuitous distinction in numbers, it may be appropriate to scrutinize the requirement or condition, examine whether it is likely to be discriminatory, and look at broader demographic evidence.[323] For example, a requirement that workers be clean shaven may indirectly discriminate against Sikh workers.[324] A single Sikh worker in a workforce of 2,000 non-Sikhs and 20 Sikhs,[325] all of whom can comply except him, would not be deprived of challenging such a rule simply because the numbers who cannot comply are small. In such a situation one out of 20 Sikhs cannot comply (5 per cent against 95 per cent who can comply) and all of the non-Sikhs **6.109**

(proportion of single parents irrelevant); and *Barry v Midland Bank plc* in the Court of Appeal [1998] IRLR 138, 144 and in House of Lords [1999] IRLR 581, 586 (pool incorrectly limited to one specialized department).

320 *Rutherford and Another v Secretary of State for Trade and Industry (No 2)* [2006] UKHL 19; [2006] IRLR 551, para 66–7, *per* Lord Walker, though this decision is difficult to understand on its facts unless explained by the very small differential in impact caused by the allegedly discriminatory rule.

321 Ibid, para 67, *per* Lord Walker.

322 See ibid, para 82, *per* Baroness Hale.

323 *London Underground v Edwards (No 2)* [1998] IRLR 364.

324 For example in *Mandla v Dowell Lee* [1983] 2 AC 548 a requirement to wear a school cap appears to have been presumed to be discriminatory against a Sikh schoolboy.

325 *London Underground v Edwards (No 2)* [1998] IRLR 364.

can comply (100 per cent). Though the number who cannot comply is small and the percentage differential is small, disparate impact and discrimination may be proved by looking at the impact of such a rule more broadly. Plainly a rule which requires that workers be clean shaven is liable to discriminate against Sikh workers, and the absence of a significant numerical disadvantage in any pool will not save an employer from the need to show justificatory reasons for it. The purpose of the disparate impact requirement must, then, be had regard to:

> [T]here is a dual statutory purpose underlying the provisions . . . and in particular the necessity . . . to show that the proportion of women who can comply with a given requirement or condition is 'considerably smaller' than the proportion of men who can comply with it. The first is to prescribe as the threshold for intervention a situation in which there exists a substantial and not merely marginal discriminatory effect (disparate impact) as between men and women, so that it can be clearly demonstrated that a prima facie case of (indirect) discrimination exists, sufficient to require . . . justification of] the application of the condition or requirement in question . . . The second is to ensure that a tribunal charged with deciding whether or not the requirement is discriminatory may be confident that its disparate impact is inherent in the application of the requirement or condition and is not simply the product of unreliable statistics or fortuitous circumstance. Since the disparate impact question will require to be resolved in an infinite number of different . . . situations, . . . an area of flexibility (or margin of appreciation), is necessarily applicable to the question of whether a particular percentage is to be regarded as 'substantially smaller' in any given case.[326]

As to whether the complainant can 'comply' and whether it is to her detriment,[327] this requires that the complainant cannot comply with the requirement or condition in practice, or 'consistently with the custom and cultural conditions'[328] of her group. It is not necessary to show that she cannot physically comply. 'Detriment' means no more than disadvantage for these purposes.[329]

6.110 If disparate impact is proved, 'justification' will be required if the application of the requirement or condition is to be lawful.[330] The burden of proving justification rests on the discriminator. This requires that the discriminator show '(1) that the allegedly discriminatory rule reflects a legitimate aim of its . . . policy, (2) that this aim is unrelated to any discrimination based on [the protected grounds], and (3) that the . . . [discriminator] could reasonably consider that the means chosen were suitable for attaining that aim'.[331] Generalized assumptions will not suffice.[332]

---

326 Ibid, para 23.

327 SDA and RRA, s 1(b)(iii).

328 *Mandla v Dowell Lee* [1983] 2 AC 548, 565H–566B, 568A–D, 570A.

329 Ibid, and see Chap 8.

330 SDA and RRA, s 1(b)(ii).

331 *R v Secretary of State for Employment ex p Seymour-Smith and Perez (No 2)* [2000] ICR 244, 260, *per* Lord Nicholls; *Hampson v Department of Education and Science* [1989] ICR 179, 191 (this case went to the House of Lords but on a different point and the observations on justification were undisturbed, [1991] 1 AC 171); *Bilka-Kaufhaus GmbH v Weber von Hartz* (Case 170/84) [1987] ICR 110.

332 *R v Secretary of State for Employment ex parte Seymour-Smith and Perez (No 2)* [2000] ICR 244, 261, *per* Lord Nicholls; *Rinner-Kuhn v FWWSpezial-Gebaudereinigung GmbH & Co KG* (Case 171/88) [1989] ECR 2743.

(3) The second meaning of indirect discrimination

6.111 The second meaning of indirect discrimination is found only in the SDA and has been repealed and substituted by the third meaning described below, but still applies in respect of any claim arising between 12 October 2001[333] and 1 October 2005.[334] For the purposes of that period, section 1(2)(b) of the SDA provided that indirect discrimination occurs where a discriminator:

> applies to [a women] a provision, criterion or practice which he applies or would apply equally to a man, but—
>
> (i) which is such that it would be to the detriment of a considerably larger proportion of women than of men, and
> (ii) which he cannot show to be justifiable irrespective of the sex of the person to whom it is applied, and
> (iii) which is to her detriment.

This meaning of indirect discrimination applied to Part 2 (employment and related fields), sections 35A and 35B (barristers and advocates), and any other provision of Part 3 (discrimination in other fields) of the SDA, so far as it applies to vocational training.[335] Materially the same provision was made in respect of indirect marital discrimination.[336]

6.112 This form of indirect discrimination was introduced into the SDA to give effect to the Burden of Proof Directive[337] which defines indirect discrimination as occurring:

> where an apparently neutral provision, criterion or practice disadvantages a substantially higher proportion of the members of one sex unless that provision, criterion or practice is appropriate and necessary and can be justified by objective factors unrelated to sex.

This definition is 'largely declaratory of the case law of the Court of Justice'.[338] It differs from the first meaning in two respects. Firstly, it does not require proof of a requirement or condition but instead addresses provisions, criteria, and practices.

---

333 The commencement date of the Sex Discrimination (Indirect Discrimination and Burden of Proof) Regulations 2001 SI 2001/2660 which introduced the second meaning of indirect discrimination (Regulation 2).

334 The commencement date of the Employment Equality (Sex Discrimination) Regulations 2005 SI 2005/2467 which repealed this second meaning of indirect discrimination and introduced the third meaning described below (Regulation 1).

335 SDA, s 1(3).

336 Ibid, s 3(1)(b).

337 97/80/EC, see Chap 4.

338 See Recital (18) of the Directive and also the Opinion of the Economic and Social Committee, Official Journal C113 p 34, paras 3.1.1–3.1.3; also the judgment of the Court of Justice in *Nikoloudi v Organismos Tilepikoinonion Ellados AE* [2005] ECR I-01789, para 69, and see *Rutherford and Another v Secretary of State for Trade and Industry (No 2)* [2006] UKHL 19; [2006] IRLR 551, para 46, *per* Lord Walker.

This difference is discussed below (paragraph 6.120). Secondly, it does not require that a complainant 'cannot comply' with the measure under challenge, merely that it is to her disadvantage. Given the liberal meaning given to the 'cannot comply requirement', as discussed above (paragraph 6.109), this change was of no material significance.

6.113 As to disparate impact, this meaning of indirect discrimination still required that any measure under challenge 'be to the detriment of a considerably larger proportion of women than of men', and therefore the observations as to disparate impact made under the first meaning above (paragraph 6.108) apply equally.[339]

(4) The third meaning of indirect discrimination

6.114 The third meaning of indirect discrimination is the (only) meaning given to indirect discrimination under the Religion or Belief Regulations,[340] the Sexual Orientation Regulations,[341] and the Age Regulations,[342] reflecting the meaning given to 'indirect discrimination' in the Framework Directive (see Chapter 4). It also now applies to indirect sex discrimination falling within Part 2 (employment and related fields), sections 35A and 35B (barristers and advocates), and any other provision of Part 3 (discrimination in other fields), so far as it applies to vocational training, of the SDA,[343] having been introduced by the Employment Equality (Sex Discrimination) Regulations 2005[344] made to give effect to the Equal Treatment Amendment Directive[345] (see Chapter 4).

6.115 Further, it applies to indirect race discrimination falling within the following provisions of the RRA:

- Part 2 (employment and related fields);
- sections 17 to 18D (education);
- section 19B (public functions), so far as relating to
  - (i) any form of social security,
  - (ii) health care,
  - (iii) any other form of social protection, and
  - (iv) any form of social advantage, which does not fall within section 20;
- sections 20 to 24 (goods, facilities and services, and premises);
- sections 26A and 26B (barristers and advocates);
- sections 76 and 76ZA (government appointments and office holders); and
- Part IV, in its application to the areas just referred to,

339 *Rutherford and Another v Secretary of State for Trade and Industry (No 2)* [2006] UKHL 19; [2006] IRLR 551.

340 Regulation 3(1)(b).

341 Regulation 3(1)(b).

342 Regulation 3(1)(b).

343 SDA, s 1(3).

344 SI 2005/2467.

345 2002/73/EC.

having been introduced by the Race Relations Act 1976 (Amendment) Regulations 2003,[346] made to give effect to the Race Directive (see Chapter 4). The expressions 'social protection' and 'social advantage' are not defined but given their origin in the Regulations which give effect to the Race Directive, they will be interpreted consistently with EU law.[347]

Section 1(2)(b) of the SDA now reads that indirect discrimination occurs where a discriminator: **6.116**

> applies to [a women] a provision, criterion or practice which he applies or would apply equally to a man, but—
>
> (i) which puts or would put women at a particular disadvantage when compared with men,
> (ii) which puts her at that disadvantage, and
> (iii) which he cannot show to be a proportionate means of achieving a legitimate aim.[348]

Section (1A) of the RRA makes materially the same provision in respect of disadvantage connected to race, ethnicity, and national origins (matching the scope of the Race Directive) but, given the overlap between the concept of race and colour,[349] indirect colour discrimination will be covered by the new meaning. However, as mentioned above, disadvantage associated with nationality (unless it is associated with race, colour, ethnicity, and national origins) is not covered by the new meaning.[350] This is intended to and does reflect the limitation in the Race Directive which itself excludes nationality.[351] **6.117**

Section 3(1)(b) of the SDA makes similar provision in relation to indirect discrimination connected to marriage and civil partnership, in each case the control group for comparison comprising unmarried people or non-civil partners.[352] **6.118**

The Religion or Belief Regulations,[353] the Sexual Orientation Regulations,[354] and the Age Regulations[355] also make materially the same provision in relation to indirect discrimination. As described above (paragraph 6.36), Regulation 3(3) of the Sexual Orientation Regulations provides that, in undertaking any comparison, 'the fact that one of the persons (whether or not [the complainant]) is a civil partner while the other is married shall not be treated as a material difference between their respective circumstances' and accordingly marriage and civil **6.119**

346 SI 2003/1626, see Chaps 2 and 4.
347 As to which, see Chap 4.
348 SDA, s 1(2)(b).
349 See Chap 5.
350 See Chap 5.
351 Article 3(2).
352 SDA, s 3(1)(b).
353 Regulation 3(1)(b).
354 Regulation 3(1)(b).
355 Regulation 3(1)(b).

partnership status are to be equated and any comparator control group must not distinguish between them. 'Age group', for the purposes of the indirect age discrimination provisions, is defined as meaning a group of persons defined by reference to age, whether by reference to a particular age or a range of ages.[356] This means that the pool for comparison need not be persons of the *same* age.

6.120 This third meaning of indirect discrimination is much less rigid than the first meaning found in the earlier enactments. The need only for a 'provision, criterion or practice' gives the definition 'broad scope'.[357] The measure concerned may be 'formal and general or informal and particular, ranging from national legislation applicable to all employment in a Member State to an administrative change in a single employer's shift system'.[358] The measure need not be mandatory (as with a 'requirement or condition', see paragraph 6.107 above). Common examples of indirect discrimination to which the new provisions (as well as the old) will apply include differential terms for part-time workers as compared to full-time workers (the former category more likely to be dominated by women), and requirements for a minimum qualifying period of service before an employee acquires statutory rights (because women's family responsibilities make it more difficult for them to achieve stable long-term employment).[359] Outside the employment field, examples include school uniform requirements (to wear a school cap,[360] for example); residence requirements as a condition of access to certain social benefits (which may disadvantage people of non-UK ethnic or national origin);[361] and 'anti-terrorist' policies which target people who have visited certain countries overseas (which may again disadvantage people of non-UK ethnic or national origin).

6.121 In *British Airways plc v Starmer*,[362] the Employment Appeal Tribunal considered whether a 'policy' which was discretionary, such that the particular decision in any case applied only to the specific employee concerned, could constitute a 'provision, criterion or practice'. In this case British Airways had a policy of allowing certain of its workers to work either 50 per cent or 75 per cent of normal full-time working, to accommodate personal circumstances, such as child care. The complainant applied to work 50 per cent of her normal full-time working hours but was refused and instead offered the opportunity to work 75 per cent of full-time working hours. An employment tribunal upheld her complaint of

---

356 Regulation 3(3)(a).

357 *Rutherford and Another v Secretary of State for Trade and Industry (No 2)* [2006] UKHL 19; [2006] IRLR 551, para 47, *per* Lord Walker, in relation to the meaning in the Burden of Proof Directive which addresses provisions, criteria, or practices.

358 Ibid.

359 Ibid.

360 *Mandla v Dowell Lee* [1983] 2 AC 548.

361 Though such would not be caught if it concerned nationality only.

362 [2005] IRLR 862.

indirect sex discrimination and found that the employer's decision, in her specific case, amounted to the application of a 'provision, criterion or practice' that the complainant had to work full time or 75 per cent of full time and that this was to the detriment of a considerably larger proportion of women than of men. The Employment Appeal Tribunal upheld this decision, confirming that a provision did not have to operate as an absolute bar but could allow for exceptions. The Employment Appeal Tribunal also confirmed that there was no necessity for a provision actually to apply to others, but what was required in order to determine whether such a provision was discriminatory was to extrapolate it to others (*would* apply equally to a man).

As to disparate impact, it is not now necessary to show that 'a considerably' smaller **6.122** proportion of the protected group can comply with the measure in issue. It is only necessary to show that the particular provision, criterion, or practice is such that it 'puts or *would* put' persons belonging to the particular protected group at a 'particular disadvantage' when compared with others. This allows for 'hypothetical' comparisons and does not depend upon actual relative disadvantage being established in the particular pool affected by the provision, criterion, or practice. So, for example, if because of the particular composition of the pool in question (that being, perhaps, that most of the women within the pool choose to and want to work full time), an obligation to work full time is not actually disadvantageous to the women as compared to the men in the relevant pool, a claim may still succeed. Broader evidence of disadvantage is likely to be relevant and admissible in cases of indirect discrimination. This might be expert evidence of women's general working and career patterns, for example. This is likely to be important in establishing indirectly discriminatory patterns in the future. It is only necessary too that a complainant show that the provision, criterion, or practice under challenge *would* be applied to a person not of their protected group—if they were present in the particular pool affected—and thus there is no requirement for persons not of the relevant protected group to be present in the pool affected. Both the advantaged and disadvantaged groups may be hypothetically constructed. As stated, this allows for demographic, sociological, and other evidence (of community habits, for example) to be had regard to. Certainly, proof of statistical disadvantage will not be necessary, as is usually the case under the first meaning.[363] The explanation for this approach[364] lies in the political traditions of certain European countries where the collection of statistics on racial origin in particular is prohibited for historic reasons.

[363] See para 6.108 above.

[364] Given by Mike O'Brien, the Parliamentary Under-Secretary of State at the Home Office, Minutes of Evidence 17th June 2000, HC 581, cited in EOR, No 93, [2000] pp 34–35.

6.123 The meaning given to justification codifies the meaning given to it by the case law emanating from the ECJ. The case law required that any discriminatory practice correspond to a legitimate aim or objective, and that the means chosen for achieving that objective served a real need on the part of the business, were appropriate with a view to achieving the objective in question, and necessary to that end.[365] Regard must be had to the fact that what is sought to be justified is the limiting of a fundamental right, and accordingly it is not an easy burden to discharge.[366] As to whether cost may ever constitute justification by itself, in *Cross and Others v British Airways plc*[367] a group of women employed by British Airways as cabin crew challenged the contractual retirement age applicable to them of 55. For various historical reasons, the requirement to retire at 55 applied only to staff employed after November 1971. Staff employed before that date were allowed to retire at 60, and that group comprised many more men than women, whereas British Airways generally employed more women than men. The employment tribunal dismissed complaints of indirect discrimination in relation to the retirement age on the grounds that, whilst there was a provision, criterion, or practice applied to cabin crew employed after November 1971 in that they had to retire at age 55, and that there were significantly more women than men not entitled to that privilege, and significantly more men than women entitled to that privilege, the policy was justified. Set against the fact, according to the tribunal, that the discriminatory impact weighed lightly, the tribunal took into account the cost implications of altering the retirement age and concluded that cost might justify the discrimination 'if combined with other reasons'. The Employment Appeal Tribunal dismissed the appeal and, on analysis of the detailed language of the authorities from the ECJ, held that an employer was entitled to rely on cost in seeking to justify a discriminatory practice, though it cannot do so where cost is the sole consideration so that:

> An employer seeking to justify a discriminatory [provision, criterion, or practice] cannot rely *solely* on considerations of cost. He can however put cost into the balance, together with other justifications, if there are any.[368]

6.124 The correctness of this holding must be doubted. As has been observed, there are no cases where the ECJ has said in terms that cost may justify indirect discrimination and 'if cost is to be accepted as even a partial justification for indirect discrimination, it should rest on a firmer foundation than a semantic analysis of an ECJ translation'.[369] There is no other case law indicating that cost will be

---

365 *Bilka-Kaufhaus GmbH v Weber von Hartz* (Case 170/84) [1987] ICR 110; [1986] ECR 1607; [1986] IRLR 317; *Secretary of State for Defence v Elias* [2006] EWCA Civ 1293, paras 164–181.

366 *Secretary of State for Defence v Elias* [2006] EWCA Civ 1293, para 165.

367 [2005] IRLR 423. This case went to the Court of Appeal, but not on this point ([2006] IRLR 804).

368 Ibid, para 72.

369 See Observations in 'Highlights' (2005) IRLR 409, 411.

material to justification, and some care needs to be taken in relying upon cost as a justificatory reason because, as has been observed, cost will often be a consideration in addressing entrenched discriminatory patterns, and it will very often be cheaper to maintain them: 'The cost of not discriminating is often one of the main reasons why employers continue to discriminate.'[370] If cost, perhaps with administrative inconvenience, were sufficient to justify discrimination, much of the force of the anti-discrimination provisions would be lost.

In *Hardys and Hansons plc v Lax*,[371] the Court of Appeal was more rigorous in its analysis of the test of justification in indirect discrimination. The case concerned a woman who sought a change in her working conditions after she became pregnant so as to be allowed to work part time or to job share on her return from maternity leave. Her request was rejected. While on maternity leave her post became redundant and she refused an offer of employment in a new full-time post. Her employers informed her that there was no part-time role available for her and she was then dismissed on the grounds of redundancy. Her complaint of sex discrimination was upheld, and on appeal the Court of Appeal upheld that decision, holding that the test of justification under the indirect discrimination provisions in the SDA did not afford an employer a margin of discretion in deciding whether to permit a job share. Instead the principle of proportionality required the tribunal to take into account the reasonable needs of the business, but it was required to make its own judgment, upon a fair and detailed analysis of the working practices and business considerations involved, as to whether the decision was reasonably necessary. The fact that 'necessary' was qualified by 'reasonably' in the case law from the ECJ[372] did not permit any margin of discretion to be afforded an employer, or any 'range of reasonable responses' test to be applied.[373] This case was decided under the second meaning of indirect sex discrimination described above (paragraph 6.111) but the meaning given to justification is not affected by what is, as mentioned above, a codification of the ECJ case law.[374] An objective assessment of justification is required and the reasons given by an alleged discriminator for any measure under review must not be uncritically accepted.[375] Further, where there is a close intended or factual nexus between the discriminatory provision, criterion, or practice and the protected 6.125

[370] Ibid.

[371] [2005] EWCA Civ 846; [2005] IRLR 726.

[372] *Bilka-Kaufhaus GmbH v Weber von Hartz* (Case 170/84) [1987] ICR 110; [1986] ECR 1607; [1986] IRLR 317.

[373] *Hardys and Hansons plc v Lax* [2005] EWCA Civ 846; [2005] IRLR 726, para 32.

[374] Para 6.123. The meaning given to justification certainly will not be more generous to a discriminator post the amendments, not least because such would violate the non-regression provisions of the Directives, see Chap 4.

[375] *British Airways plc v Starmer* [2005] IRLR 862, para 33 and references therein. See too, *Secretary of State for Defence v Elias* [2006] EWCA Civ 1293, paras 164–181.

ground (sex, race, etc) a particularly rigorous standard of scrutiny will be applied in determining whether the reasons advanced for it amount to legal justification:[376] 'A stringent standard of scrutiny of the claimed justification is appropriate because the discrimination, though indirect in form, is so closely related in substance to the direct form of discrimination, which can never be justified.' [377] As a general proposition, it is possible to justify an indirectly discriminatory measure *ex post facto*. However, such a case will be unusual indeed because it necessarily indicates that no judgment at all was made as to whether the measure was proportionate or otherwise justified at the time the decision was made to introduce it.[378] In respect of indirect discrimination by public authorities, compliance with the statutory duties, discussed in Chapter 15, will be significant. Where the public authority has, in a material way, failed to comply with a statutory equality duty imposed upon it, this will add difficulty to any attempts to justify the imposition of an indirectly discriminatory criterion. In such circumstances the public authority will be endeavouring to justify an act of discrimination:

> committed in the carrying out [its] functions when, in breach of an express duty, [it] failed even to have due regard to the elimination of that form of unlawful race discrimination. [It] has to justify something which [it] did not even consider required any justification. In these circumstances the court should consider with great care the ex post facto justifications advanced at the hearing.[379]

(5) The fourth meaning of indirect discrimination

6.126 The EA introduces a further meaning of indirect discrimination. Section 45(3) (not in force at the date of writing) provides that:

> A person ('A') discriminates against another ('B') for the purposes of this Part if A applies to B a provision, criterion or practice—
>
> (a) which he applies or would apply equally to persons not of B's religion or belief,
> (b) which puts persons of B's religion or belief at a disadvantage compared to some or all others (where there is no material difference in the relevant circumstances),
> (c) which puts B at a disadvantage compared to some or all persons who are not of his religion or belief (where there is no material difference in the relevant circumstances), and
> (d) which A cannot reasonably justify by reference to matters other than B's religion or belief.

This new meaning adopts part of the formulation of indirect discrimination in the other enactments. It applies to provisions, criteria, or practices, and the

---

376 *Secretary of State for Defence v Elias* [2006] EWCA Civ 1293, paras 159–162.
377 Ibid, para 161.
378 Ibid, para 129.
379 Ibid, para 133 and see para 175.

observations made above in relation to those expressions apply equally. The comparator group are some persons or all persons not of the same religion or belief as the complainant. This means that a complainant can choose which part of the whole group to whom the provision, criterion, or practice would apply that she wishes to compare herself against. For example, an atheist may compare herself to Christians *or* Muslims in the whole group for the purposes of identifying disadvantage. The circumstances otherwise between the complainant's group and the comparator group must be materially the same, and the observations above (at paragraph 6.36 onwards) apply equally. The relevant pool in any case must be persons to whom the provision, criterion, or practice *would* apply, and the observations made at paragraph 6.122 above apply.

As to disparate impact it is only necessary that the complainant and other members of her group are disadvantaged and the observations above (at paragraph 6.122) apply. **6.127**

As to justification, a different formulation has been used. As can be seen, any discriminatory measure under EA, section 45(3) will be saved if the discriminator can *reasonably* justify it by reference to matters other than the complainant's religion or belief. It is not clear whether this is intended to impose a less rigorous test of justification than that found in the other main anti-discrimination enactments, but this seems unlikely because 'reasonableness' is used in the context of the formulation of justification found in EU case law from which the test of justification found in the other main anti-discrimination enactments is derived (paragraph 6.125 above). The Explanatory Notes give little assistance. They state that: **6.128**

> [i]t would not be unlawful . . . if the action causing disadvantage to person B could be reasonably justified by reference to matters other than B's religion or belief: for example, if it was performed to meet security or health and safety concerns, or if the efficiency of a business would be seriously jeopardized by failure to take the action complained about.[380]

The probability is that the test of justification will develop to match that found under the other main anti-discrimination enactments.

(6) Intention and motive

Intention and motive are irrelevant to a claim in indirect discrimination, save that a hostile and discriminatory motive will not, of course, justify any discriminatory impact. Intention may be relevant, however, to remedies. In particular, in claims of indirect sex and race discrimination falling within the first definition described in paragraph 6.104 above, and indirect religion and belief discrimination falling under Part 2 of the EA (goods, facilities, services, premises, education, and **6.129**

380 Para 174.

public functions), an award of compensation in respect of indirect discrimination will not be made where the discriminator proves that the requirement, condition, provision, criterion, or practice in question was not applied with the intention of treating the claimant unfavourably on the ground of his sex, racial group, or religion as the case may be.[381] The same applies to indirect religion or belief, sexual orientation, and age discrimination under the Religion or Belief Regulations, the Sexual Orientation Regulations, and the Age Regulations, except that if the discriminator establishes the relevant lack of intention an award of compensation might still be made if, having regard to the other orders available, it is just and equitable to do so.[382]

6.130 In determining 'intentionality' for these purposes, intention to apply the requirement or condition under challenge, together with knowledge of its impact on the complainant as a member of the particular group disadvantaged, is sufficient.[383] In *Walker Ltd v Hussain & Ors*[384] the Employment Appeal Tribunal rejected an appeal against an award of compensation made to a number of Muslims who were disciplined for taking time off during Eid. Mummery J ruled that:

> As a matter of ordinary English, 'intention' in this context signifies the state of mind of a person who, at the time when he does the relevant act (i.e. the application of the requirement or condition resulting in indirect discrimination),
>
> (a) Wants to bring about the state of affairs which constitutes the prohibited result of unfavourable treatment on racial grounds; and
> (b) Knows that that prohibited result will follow from his acts . . .
>
> Depending on the circumstances, the Tribunal may infer that a person wants to produce certain consequences from the fact that he acted knowing what those consequences would be . . . [385]

Intention might, accordingly, be inferred from knowledge of the consequences which in most cases will not be difficult to establish.

---

[381] SDA, s 66(3) and (3A); RRA, s 57(3), EA, s 68(3). This limitation had applied across the board in the original enactment but was amended first in relation to sex (following a number of employment tribunal decisions holding that the limitation in the SDA was inconsistent with the requirements of the Equal Treatment Directive 76/207/EEC and a decision of the Employment Appeal Tribunal in *McMillan v Edinburgh Voluntary Organisations Council* (unreported, EAT/1995/536) that the SDA's 'unambiguous' provisions could not be interpreted so as to permit an award in respect of unintentional indirect discrimination, whereafter the Sex Discrimination and Equal Pay (Miscellaneous Amendments) Regulations 1996 were made removing the limitation in relation to discrimination in the employment and related fields, matching the scope of the Directive) then race (effectively by the enactment of RRA, s 1(1A) by the making of the Race Relations Act 1976 (Amendment) Regulations 2003 SI 2003/1626, which give effect to the Race Directive, see s 57(3)).

[382] Religion or Belief Regulations and Sexual Orientation Regulations, regulations 30(2), and Age Regulations, regulation 38(2).

[383] *London Underground v Edwards* [1995] IRLR 355.

[384] [1996] ICR 291; [1996] IRLR 11.

[385] Ibid, para 39.

(7) Relevant, discriminatory, and hypothetical circumstances

As described above under 'direct discrimination', any comparison undertaken 'must be such that the relevant circumstances in the one case are the same, or not materially different, in the other'.[386] This means, at least, that the pool must only comprise those to whom the requirement, condition, provision, criterion, or practice was, is, or would be applied, because only they comprise the relevant control groups.[387] Proving the composition of the pool and disparate impact is, however, a question of evidence, and, as mentioned, if statistics are not relied upon or available, evidence about the impact on the broader community may be relied upon to substantiate a claim that the requirement, condition, provision, criterion, or practice does or would have disparate impact.[388] In either case, the relevant circumstances must be the same for each group.[389] **6.131**

However, as with 'direct discrimination', the comparison exercise must not itself be tainted with discrimination. The pool for comparison, therefore, must not be constructed in a way which itself is discriminatory. Any discriminatory infiltration into the 'relevant circumstances' will flaw the comparsion exercise.[390] **6.132**

E. Harassment

All the main anti-discrimination enactments now define and proscribe harassment in certain circumstances. In addition, harassment on the protected (and indeed other) grounds may infringe the Human Rights Act 1998 where it is committed by a public authority[391] and may, depending on the circumstances, amount to a common law tort and may contravene the Protection from Harassment Act 1997.[392] Section 1 of the Protection from Harassment Act 1997 prohibits harassment by providing that: **6.133**

> [a] person must not pursue a course of conduct (a) which amounts to harassment of another, and (b) which he knows or ought to know amounts to harassment of the other

[386] SDA, s 5(3); RRA, s 3(4) (though this appears to assume that the comparison will be between persons of different racial groups which, as described above, is not necessary); Religion or Belief Regulations, regulation 3(3); Sexual Orientation Regulations, regulation 3(2).

[387] *Price v Civil Service Commission* [1978] ICR 27; [1977] IRLR 291.

[388] *London Underground v Edwards (No 2)* [1998] IRLR 364.

[389] *Rutherford and Another v Secretary of State for Trade and Industry (No 2)* [2006] UKHL 19; [2006] IRLR 551.

[390] *Kidd v DRG (UK) Ltd* [1985] IRLR 190; *R v Secretary of State for Education ex p Schaffter* [1987] IRLR 53.

[391] *Smith and Grady v UK* (2000) 29 EHRR 493; *Lustig-Prean and A'or v UK* (2000) 29 EHRR 548 and see Chap 4.

[392] *Majrowski v Guy's and St Thomas' NHS Trust* [2006] UKHL 34. And in respect of each of these statutory provisions against harassment, like the common law torts, an employer might be vicariously liable for the harassment of his employees, ibid.

or

> pursue a course of conduct (a) which involves harassment of two or more persons, and (b) which he knows or ought to know involves harassment of those persons, and (c) by which he intends to persuade any person (whether or not one of those mentioned . . .), (i) not to do something that he is entitled or required to do, or (ii) to do something that he is not under any obligation to do.[393]

For these purposes, 'the person whose course of conduct is in question ought to know that it amounts to or involves harassment of another if a reasonable person in possession of the same information would think the course of conduct amounted to harassment of the other'.[394] Sections 2 and 3 of the Act provide for criminal sanctions and civil remedies in respect of harassment as just defined.

6.134 Express provision against harassment in the main anti-discrimination enactments has come rather recently and in consequence of EU law. In particular the Race Directive, the Framework Directive, and the Equal Treatment Amendment Directive[395] all define harassment and require Member States to outlaw it; this is discussed below.

6.135 In addition to the new meanings of harassment, harassment on the protected grounds will amount to less favourable treatment and may therefore amount to direct discrimination or disability-related discrimination.[396] The protection afforded against harassment through the prohibitions on direct discrimination, however, is limited by the requirement contained therein for a comparator. If the harassment is, for example, sex or race specific (for example, sexual and racial abuse), it will usually follow that a person of a different sex or race would not have been so treated and direct discrimination will be made out,[397] but this cannot be presumed. In all cases, the comparison exercise must be undertaken.[398] This means, for example, that treatment which is 'offensive and humiliating' to a woman, as a woman, is not caught by the direct discrimination provisions for that reason alone. If the woman concerned has not been exposed to the offensive treatment *because of her sex*, but instead because, like others of both sexes, she has been placed in the particular environment in which it took place, it cannot be said that, 'but for her sex', she would not have suffered the treatment complained of or would have been treated any differently. Accordingly direct discrimination is not made out.[399]

---

393 Protection from Harassment Act 1997, s 1(1) and (1A).

394 Ibid, s 1(2).

395 See Chap 4.

396 Case law has held that directly discriminatory harassment constitutes a 'detriment' and therefore will usually be unlawful in the areas covered by the main anti-discrimination enactments: *Wadman v Carpenter Ferrer Partnership* [1993] IRLR 374; *Insitu Cleaning Co Ltd v Heads* [1995] IRLR 4; *Driskel v Peninsula Business Services Ltd and Others* [2000] IRLR 151.

397 Though see the exclusionary provisions, described below in relation to 'detriment'.

398 *McDonald v Advocate General for Scotland* [2003] UKHL 34, [2003] ICR 937; *Pearce v Governing Body of Mayfield Secondary School* [2001] EWCA Civ 1347, [2002] ICR 198; [2003] IRLR 512.

399 *Brumfitt v Ministry of Defence and another* [2005] IRLR 4.

The absurdity and inadequacy of this approach (which faithfully reflects the comparator model) is illustrated by the case of *Stewart v Guest (Engineering) Ltd*[400] in which the Employment Appeal Tribunal upheld a decision of the employment tribunal that the display of calendars and other pictures of nude and partially nude women, by her male co-workers, did not amount to discrimination against Ms Stewart on the ground of her sex. This was so notwithstanding that, as the employment tribunal found, she was genuinely and reasonably offended by them and indeed complained about them. According to the employment tribunal, a 'hypothetical' male might have been equally offended by the display, and the pictures were not 'aimed at women or a woman' and so there was no less favourable treatment. The Employment Appeal Tribunal held that the employment tribunal's conclusion that the display of pictures was gender-'neutral' because a man might find them equally offensive was one which they were entitled to reach. This ignores what underpins sexual and other forms of harassment and what usually makes it so uniquely offensive—that is, a lack of respect for the dignity of a person *as* a woman, *as* a black person, *as* a disabled person, *as* a gay person, or *as* a Muslim, as the case may be. The nude pictures genuinely and reasonably undermined Ms Stewart's dignity *as a woman* in the workplace. Though such pictures may have offended men, they plainly would not have undermined their dignity *as men*, and so the effect is qualitatively different. However, such highlights the problems with a comparator model. **6.136**

Nonetheless case law has established that harassment on the protected grounds, where comparatively less favourable, will constitute a 'detriment'[401] and be unlawful under those provisions of the main anti-discrimination enactments which outlaw discriminatory treatment resulting in a 'detriment'.[402] The test for determining whether 'less favourable treatment' and a 'detriment' had been caused by any harassment had become principally subjective, as described above[403] (paragraph 6.28), such that any conduct capable of being regarded as offensive, or conduct which had been rejected and repeated notwithstanding that **6.137**

[400] [1994] IRLR 444.

[401] *Wadman v Carpenter Ferrer Partnership* [1993] IRLR 374; *Insitu Cleaning Co Ltd v Heads* [1995] IRLR 4; *Driskel v Peninsula Business Services Ltd and Others* [2000] IRLR 151.

[402] See Chaps 8 and 10.

[403] And see *Reed & Bull Information Systems Ltd v Stedman* [1999] IRLR 299, at paras 27–28 and 30 ('The essential characteristic of sexual harassment is that it is words or conduct which are unwelcome to the recipient and it is for the recipient to decide for themselves what is acceptable to them and what they regard as offensive. A characteristic of sexual harassment is that it undermines the victim's dignity at work. It creates an "offensive" or "hostile" environment for the victim and an arbitrary barrier to sexual equality in the workplace. Because it is for each individual to determine what they find unwelcome or offensive, there may be cases where there is a gap between what a tribunal would regard as acceptable and what the individual in question was prepared to tolerate. It does not follow that because the tribunal would not have regarded the acts as unacceptable, the complaint must be dismissed.')

objection had been taken to it, was regarded as *less favourable* and a *detriment.*[404] The guidance relied upon by the courts for determining whether any particular acts constituted objectionable harassment and therefore a 'detriment' was that found in the European Commission's Code of Practice on Sexual Harassment[405] which defined sexual harassment as follows:

> Unwanted conduct of a sexual nature, or other conduct based on sex affecting the dignity of women and men at work. This can include unwelcome physical, verbal or non-verbal conduct.[406]

6.138 The European Commission's Code of Practice and, in the main, the case law on harassment under the detriment provisions have been directed at employment-related sexual harassment. However, the meaning given to harassment can be applied to non-employment-related harassment and harassment on other of the protected grounds, in those areas where discriminatory 'detriments' are outlawed by the main anti-discrimination enactments.[407] Importantly, however, as is discussed below (paragraph 6.144), the new provisions exclude from the concept of 'detriment' certain instances of harassment where they fall within the new meanings of harassment. The old law on harassment remains relevant, however, to those cases where the new harassment provisions do not apply, and to identify the minimum protection afforded under the new harassment provisions, which, having regard to their origins in the Directives, must not reduce the protection afforded prior to their enactment.[408]

6.139 Article 2(3) of the Race Directive[409] states that:

> Harassment shall be deemed to be discrimination . . . when an unwanted conduct related to racial or ethnic origin takes place with the purpose or effect of violating the dignity of a person and of creating an intimidating, hostile, degrading, humiliating or offensive environment.[410]

The Framework Directive[411] makes materially the same provision in relation to the grounds it protects.[412] The definitions in the Directives are in fact somewhat narrower than that developed under the direct discrimination provisions, in

---

404 *Insitu Cleaning Co Ltd v Heads* [1995] IRLR 4; *Driskel v Peninsula Business Services Ltd and Others* [2000] IRLR 151.

405 Annexed to the European Commission's Recommendation on the Protection of Dignity of Women and Men at Work: 91/131/EEC; *Wadman v Carpenter Ferrer Partnership* [1993] IRLR 374. The Commission for Racial Equality in their Guidance states that this definition 'can usefully be extended to racial harassment', 'Racial Harassment at Work: What Employers Can Do About It' (1995, CRE) 9.

406 European Commission's Code of Practice on Sexual Harassment, para 2.

407 See Chaps 8 and 10.

408 Because of the non-regression provisions contained therein, see Chap 4.

409 See Chap 4.

410 Race Directive, Art 2(3).

411 Framework Directive, Art 2(3).

412 Chap 4.

particular, by requiring both that the conduct was intended to violate the dignity of the victim, or that it actually had that effect *and* that the conduct intended to create an intimidating, hostile, degrading, humiliating, or offensive environment for the victim, or that it actually had that effect. That dual requirement was not imposed by the domestic concept of harassment which had developed under the direct discrimination and *detriment* provisions, as described above. As discussed in Chapter 4, the Directives contain non-regression clauses[413] and, accordingly, the new definitions of harassment go wider in some respects than the Directives formulation. The meaning given to harassment by section 3A of the RRA is as follows:

> A person subjects another to harassment in any circumstances . . . where, on grounds of race or ethnic or national origins, he engages in unwanted conduct which has the purpose or effect of—
> (a) violating that other person's dignity, or
> (b) creating an intimidating, hostile, degrading, humiliating or offensive environment for him.

Materially the same provision is made in the DDA,[414] the Religion or Belief Regulations,[415] the Sexual Orientation Regulations,[416] and the Age Regulations.[417]

The Equal Treatment Amendment Directive defines harassment and sexual harassment as follows: **6.140**

> harassment: where an unwanted conduct related to the sex of a person occurs with the purpose or effect of violating the dignity of a person, and of creating an intimidating, hostile, degrading, humiliating or offensive environment,
>
> sexual harassment: where any form of unwanted verbal, non-verbal or physical conduct of a sexual nature occurs, with the purpose or effect of violating the dignity of a person, in particular when creating an intimidating, hostile, degrading, humiliating or offensive environment.[418]

The SDA now expressly provides for three forms of harassment, reflecting the approach of the Equal Treatment Amendment Directive, as follows:

> . . . a person subjects a woman to harassment if—
> (a) on the ground of her sex, he engages in unwanted conduct that has the purpose or effect—
> (i) of violating dignity, or
> (ii) of creating an intimidating, hostile, degrading, humiliating or offensive environment for her,

---

413 Race Directive, Art 6; Framework Directive, Art 8; and Equal Treatment Amendment Directive, Art 8(e).

414 DDA, s 3B. No equivalent provision is made in the EA.

415 Religion or Belief Regulations, regulation 5.

416 Sexual Orientation Regulations, regulation 5.

417 Age Regulations, regulation 6.

418 Equal Treatment Amendment Directive, Art 2(2).

(b) he engages in any form of unwanted verbal, non-verbal or physical conduct of a sexual nature that has the purpose or effect—
  (i) of violating her dignity, or
  (ii) of creating an intimidating, hostile, degrading, humiliating or offensive environment for her, or

(c) on the ground of her rejection of or submission to unwanted conduct of a kind mentioned in paragraph (a) or (b), he treats her less favourably than he would treat her had she not rejected, or submitted to, the conduct.[419]

The SDA, therefore, expressly outlaws sexual harassment in addition to the ordinary form of harassment seen in the other enactments. Sexual harassment, unlike the other forms, does not require that the conduct be 'on the grounds of sex', so that sexual conduct (sexually explicit words, sexual abuse etc) is caught whether or not it was done 'on the ground' of the complainant's sex. This removes the requirement for comparative less favourable treatment so that nude pictures of women exhibited in a workplace may found a claim in sexual harassment, even if not directed at the women workers. Similarly, touching a woman's bottom would be caught even if the particular harasser does the same to men.

6.141 The SDA makes provision for harassment connected to gender reassignment and defines it in materially the same way as the RRA[420] save that, as with harassment connected to sex, harassment connected to gender reassignment is defined as including treatment on the ground of a person's rejection of or submission to unwanted conduct of a kind mentioned in the gender reassignment harassment provisions.[421]

6.142 As with the meaning of harassment that had developed under the case law described above, the conduct must be 'unwanted' if it is to found a cause of action under the new provisions. However, this does not mean that express objection must be made to the conduct before it qualifies as unwanted. Some forms of conduct are self-evidently unwanted or likely to be so and such will be caught by the provisions.[422]

6.143 All the enactments provide that:

> [c]onduct shall be regarded as having the effect mentioned . . . only if, having regard to all the circumstances, including in particular the perception of the [victim], it should reasonably be considered as having that effect.[423]

This is discussed further below.[424]

---

419 SDA, s 4A(1).

420 RRA, s 4A(3)(a).

421 SDA, s 4A(3)(b). Comparable provision is not made under the RRA.

422 *Insitu Cleaning Co Ltd v Heads* [1995] IRLR 4.

423 SDA, s 4A(2) and (4); RRA, s 3A(2); DDA, s 3B(2); Religion or Belief and Sexual Orientation Regulations, regulations 5(2); Age Regulations, regulation 6(2).

424 Para 6.145.

The new harassment provisions apply only within defined parameters. In the SDA, harassment is expressly outlawed, in summary, in the employment and related fields;[425] in the exercising of public functions (except in the case of gender reassignment harassment);[426] in further and higher education;[427] in relation to barristers and advocates;[428] and after such relationships have ended where closely connected to them,[429] matching closely the scope of the Equal Treatment Amendment Directive. In the RRA, the new meaning of harassment applies for the purposes of any provision identified in section 1(1B) (and express provision is made outlawing harassment as described in those areas[430]) as described in paragraph 6.115. As with the new meaning of indirect discrimination, the new meaning of harassment does not apply to nationality-based discrimination for the same reasons that the new meaning of indirect discrimination does not apply to the same (see paragraph 6.117 above). In the DDA, the new form of harassment is outlawed in the employment and related fields (including in employment services, further and higher education, and by general qualifications bodies).[431] In the Religion or Belief Regulations, the Sexual Orientation Regulations, and the Age Regulations, the new form of harassment is outlawed across all the activities provided for in the Regulations (namely in the employment and related fields).[432] The unlawful acts regulating the new forms of harassment create exclusive wrongs by which it is meant that they do not overlap with the provisions outlawing 'detriments'. This is because the main anti-discrimination enactments provide that 'detriment' 'does not include harassment' within the new meanings provided for.[433] Where the new meaning does not apply at all, this does not exclude reliance on the detriment provisions.[434] 6.144

The new harassment provisions are not entirely uncontroversial. There is some concern that they may be regressive, given the condition that any conduct shall only be regarded as having the prescribed effect mentioned where 'having regard 6.145

425 Under SDA, Part 2, (SDA, ss 6(2A), 9(2A), 10B(4), 11(2A), 12(3A), 13(1A), 14(1A), 15(1A), 16(1) and (1A), 20A(4).

426 SDA, s 21A(1)(b).

427 SDA, s 22(3).

428 SDA, s 35(2A) and 35B(A).

429 SDA, ss 20A and 35C.

430 RRA, ss 4(2A), 7(3A), 10(1B), 11(4), 12(1A), 13(3), 14(1A), 15(1), 17(2), 18(1) and (2), 18A, 18BA, 18D, 19B(1A), 20(3), 21(2A), 26A and B, 27A(2).

431 Under Part 2 DDA, ss 4(3), 4B(2), 4D(4), 4G(3), 6A(2), 7A(3), 7C(3), 13(3), 14A(2), 14C(2), 15B(2), 16A(3), 21A(2), 28R(3B) with 28SA, 31AA(2) with 31AC.

432 Including further and higher education, See chaps 8 and 9.

433 SDA, s 82(1); RRA, s 78(1); DDA, s 18D(2) (except in the case of instructions under s 16C(2)(b)); Religion or Belief Regulations, regulation 2(3); Sexual Orientation Regulations, regulation 2(3); Age Regulations, regulation 2(2).

434 Nor would any other construction be consistent with the non-regression provisions of the Directives, see Chap 4.

to all the circumstances, including in particular the perception of the [victim], it should reasonably be considered as having that effect',[435] not seen in the case law under the direct discrimination and detriment provisions described above. Some objective requirement might be implicit in the case law formulation[436] (not least for reasons of legal certainty), but if the non-regression provisions are to be respected care will need to be taken to ensure that the threshold set is no higher than under the old case law. In addition, the meaning given to harassment under the SDA is problematic. As seen, the new meaning requires, for the ordinary form of harassment, that any unwanted conduct be 'on the ground of [the complainant's] sex'. The Equal Treatment Amendment Directive, however, requires that protection be afforded against unwanted conduct 'related to' the sex of a person. This is clearly a broader meaning, addressing not only conduct which is engaged in *because of* a woman's sex, but any conduct that has any connection with her sex. This would include gender-specific conduct or abuse which might not be engaged in *because of* the sex of the victim, in that different but equally hurtful gender-specific conduct might be used in relation to employees of the opposite sex,[437] but which is clearly *related to* the sex of the victim because its precise form is dictated by and targeted at her sex. Some such conduct would be caught by the prohibition against 'sexual harassment', when it is 'of a sexual nature'. However, this may not always be the case. Conduct or abuse may be gender-specific and thus related to a person's sex without being 'of a sexual nature'.[438] The likelihood is that a wide interpretation will be given to the harassment provisions under the SDA so that the 'ground of' expression accords with the 'related to' expression in the Equal Treatment Amendment Directive.[439] This might be done by holding that any gender-specific conduct shall be treated as 'on the ground of sex' (if not of a sexual nature, when it will be caught by the sexual harassment provisions). Such would ensure compliance with the obligations in the Equal Treatment Amendment Directive.

6.146 In addition, the new forms of harassment do not expressly outlaw harassment by third parties in the context of the activities covered by the enactments. This means, for example, that an employer will not be liable for the harassment of an

---

435 SDA, s 4A(2) and (4); RRA, s 3A(2); DDA, ss 3B(2), 28SA(2), 31AC(2); Religion or Belief and Sexual Orientation Regulations, regulations 5(2); Age Regulations, regulation 6(2).

436 *Driskel v Peninsula Business Services Ltd and Others* [2000] IRLR 151 and see, eg, *Smith v Vodafone UK Ltd* [2001] EAT 0054/01.

437 *McDonald v Advocate General for Scotland*; *Pearce v Governing Body of Mayfield Secondary School* [2003] UKHL 34, [2003] ICR 937; [2003] IRLR 512.

438 See illustrations in *Pearce v Governing Body of Mayfield Secondary School* [2003] UKHL 34, [2003] ICR 937; [2003] IRLR 512, such as 'lez', 'lesbian shit', and 'dyke', words which are not clearly of a sexual nature. Others might include, 'dollybird', 'the skirt', 'floozy', or 'dumb blonde'. See too, *Brumfitt v Ministry of Defence and another* [2005] IRLR 4.

439 See Chap 4 for the interpretative obligations arising in respect of EU law.

employee by a customer.[440] Nor is such outlawed by the direct discrimination and detriment provisions of the main anti-discrimination enactments unless the employer, in the example just given, in failing to take action to stop the harassment, treated the employee comparatively less favourably on one of the protected grounds. It appears, however, that the Directives require that such harassment be outlawed, at least where a person caught by the terms of the Directives (employers and related bodies in the case of the Framework Directive and the Equal Treatment Amendment Directive, and a wider range of bodies under the Race Directive[441]) might have prevented it. Recital 9 of the Equal Treatment Amendment Directive provides that 'employers and those responsible for vocational training should be encouraged to take measures to combat all forms of sexual discrimination and, in particular, to take preventative measures against harassment and sexual harassment in the workplace, in accordance with national legislation and practice'.

Whilst the EC institutions declined to set out a precise obligation on Member **6.147** States to require employers to introduce procedures to prevent sexual harassment, it appears that this was on the grounds that this might properly be regarded as too detailed and specific, and addressed to employers rather than Member States.[442] However, it appears from the language of the Equal Treatment Amendment Directive that some third party harassment at least should be outlawed. The Equal Treatment Amendment Directive addresses harassment where unwanted conduct with the prohibited purpose or effect *occurs*,[443] and that such is a form of discrimination.[444] The principle of equal treatment requires that there be no discrimination in relation to, amongst other things, working conditions,[445] and Member States must ensure that judicial and/or administrative procedures are available for the enforcement of obligations under the Directive for persons who consider themselves wronged by the failure to apply the principle of equal treatment to them.[446] Where harassment 'occurs', therefore, in the context of the activities

440 See example in *Burton & Rhule v De Vere Hotels Ltd* [1997] ICR 1; [1996] IRLR 596.

441 See Chap 4.

442 Explanatory Notes to the Common Position (Common Position (EC) No 32/2001) of 23 July 2001, para 3.6: OJ C 307/5, 31 Oct 2001 ('The Council did not wish to incorporate a provision on setting up a system of confidential counsellors at the workplace, or other measures intended to prevent sexual harassment at the workplace, as it considered that this measure was far too detailed and was in fact addressed to employers rather than to the Member States or even the social partners. Furthermore, in this area as well, the Council was concerned to ensure parallelism with Directives 2000/43/EC and 2000/78/EC. As sexual harassment was a form of harassment, rather than a completely separate phenomenon, the Council did not think it appropriate to set up this kind of specific mechanism)', available at <http://eur-lex.europa.eu/LexUriServ/site/en/oj/2001/c_307/c_30720011031en00050015.pdf>.

443 Equal Treatment Amendment Directive, Art 2(2).

444 Ibid, Art 2(3).

445 Ibid, Art 3.

446 Ibid, Art 6.

covered by the Equal Treatment Amendment Directive, a breach of the principle of equal treatment has occurred. Importantly, this does not appear to be conditional upon any formal relationship between the discriminator, or harasser, and the complainant[447]—where discrimination and harassment pertains to working conditions, and in the other areas covered by the Directive, it is apparently outlawed by the Equal Treatment Amendment Directive.[448] The European Commission's Code of Practice on Sexual Harassment[449] makes it clear that employers are under a proactive obligation to minimize the risk of harassment occurring, and focuses on prevention in particular. In determining whether liability should arise as against an employer, or other person caught by the provisions of the Directive, for sexual harassment by a third party, the European Commission's Code of Practice on Sexual Harassment[450] provides a framework for assessing responsibility. The same observations might be made equally about both the Race Directive and the Framework Directive which address harassment which 'takes place' within the protected spheres.[451]

6.148 As to proving harassment, the burden shifts in precisely the same circumstances as described under the direct discrimination provisions above (paragraph 6.92). Importantly, in determining whether any conduct, objectively, violates dignity or creates an intimidating, hostile, degrading, humiliating, or offensive environment, care must be taken to focus on the complainant's perspective (see paragraph 6.145 above), and the context needs to be sensitively considered. Acts may by themselves appear petty, but the context may produce a different picture, particularly where acts are repeated or a power dynamic is involved.[452] As with direct

---

447 And EU equality law does not defer to domestic concepts, thus a 'contract of employment' that lacks any mutuality of obligation nevertheless falls within the scope of the Equal Treatment Amendment Directive (*Wippel v Peek & Cloppenburg GmbH & Co KG* (Case C-313/02) [2005] IRLR 211, paras 30-31). Instead the focus of the Equal Treatment Amendment Directive is on the conditions at work or affecting work rather than the presence of any formal or particular relationships. (And see too, *Coote v Granada Hospitality Limited* [1998] ECR 1-5199 where the Directive was held to protect an employee against victimization in circumstances where there was no contract of employment at all, it having been terminated). Thus EC law contemplates conditions of work which might be affected by something other than the formal terms of an employment contract.

448 This interpretation of the Directive is supported by the European Commission's Code of Practice on Sexual Harassment, annexed to the European Commission's Recommendation on the Protection of Dignity of Women and Men at Work: 91/131/EEC referred to above which, as observed, treats sexual harassment as capable of constituting a breach of the principle of equal treatment and it does so without imposing any pre-conditions as to the identity of the harasser, but focuses on conduct based on sex affecting the dignity of women and men *at work* (Article 1). Indeed the Recommendation provides that it addresses conduct '*including* conduct of superiors and colleagues', thus anticipating that the conduct might come from elsewhere (Article 1) (emphasis added).

449 Referred to above and annexed to the European Commission's Recommendation on the Protection of Dignity of Women and Men at Work: 91/131/EEC.

450 Ibid.

451 Articles 2(3).

452 *Driskel v Peninsula Business Services Ltd and Others* [2000] IRLR 151; *Reed and Bull Information Systems Ltd v Stedman* [1999] IRLR 299.

discrimination, intention is irrelevant,[453] save that a hostile intent may disclose that the treatment is *on grounds* of sex.

F. Disability-Related Discrimination

The DDA, uniquely, outlaws discrimination 'related to' disability. This form of discrimination is outlawed across all the activities covered by the DDA, although its precise meaning, specifically as concerns justification, varies, as is described below. Section 3A(1) of the DDA defines disability-related discrimination for the purposes of Part 2 of the DDA (employment and related fields[454]) as follows: **6.149**

> A person discriminates against a disabled person if—
> (a) for a reason which relates to the disabled person's disability, he treats him less favourably than he treats or would treat others to whom that reason does not or would not apply, and
> (b) he cannot show that the treatment in question is justified.

Disability-related discrimination is also defined and proscribed in materially the same way for the purposes of the other unlawful acts provided for under the DDA.[455] Justification, however, is defined differently depending on the activity concerned and this is addressed discretely below.

(1) Less favourable treatment

For disability-related discrimination, *less favourable treatment* must be shown, and, appearing as it does in the same enactment, this expression has the same meaning as in the context of direct discrimination, as described above (paragraph 6.27). However, unlike direct discrimination, it is not necessary that the treatment be on the *ground* of disability. Instead the less favourable treatment must be 'for a reason which relates to the disabled person's disability' and as such the treatment must be less favourable than that which was or would have been afforded to a person *to whom that reason does not or would not apply*. It only requires, therefore, that there is *a* relationship between the disabled person's disability and the reason for the treatment.[456] This is a wider concept of discrimination **6.150**

---

453 *Driskel v Peninsular Business Services Ltd and Others* [2000] IRLR 151.

454 Employment, contract workers, office holders, partners, barristers and advocates, trade organizations, qualifications bodies, practical work experience, and, from 4 December 2006, local council members.

455 DDA, s 20(1) (note the exemption in relation to transport services in s 21ZA and the limitations on that exemption introduced by the Disability Discrimination (Transport Vehicles) Regulations 2005 SI 2005/3190, see Chap 10); DDA, ss 21D(1), 21G(1), 24(1), 28B(1), 28S(1), 31AB(1) (though not all in force at the date of writing).

456 *Clark v TDG Limited t/a Novacold* [1999] ICR 951; [1999] IRLR 318; *Manchester City Council v Romano (Disability Rights Commission Intervening) and Another* [2004] EWCA Civ 834; [2005] 1 WLR 2775, para 93 in particular.

than that afforded by direct discrimination.[457] As discussed below, it is wide enough to embrace some acts of indirect discrimination.[458]

(2) 'Related to'

6.151 As mentioned, there must be *a* relationship between the disabled person's disability and the reason for the treatment, for disability-related discrimination to be made out.[459] Treatment which is on the ground of disability, that is, directly connected to it, is plainly covered. However, importantly, the 'related to' formulation does not require that the treatment be directly caused by disability or (subject to what is said below, paragraph 6.153) that disability operates on the mind of the discriminator at the material time.[460] Treatment, for example, caused by absence from work—for instance, a dismissal or a cut in pay—where that absence is attributable to disability, is treatment *related to* disability.[461]

(3) The proper comparator

6.152 For disability-related discrimination the proper comparator is not restricted to a non-disabled (or differently disabled) person to whom all the material circumstances would otherwise be the same, but instead is a person to whom the reason for the treatment does not apply. In a case where a person is less favourably treated due to absence from work where that absence is attributable to disability, the reason for his treatment is absence, and accordingly the proper comparator is a person who has not been absent.[462] Similarly, a sight-impaired person who is refused access to a restaurant with an assistance dog, because the restaurant has a 'no dogs' policy, is treated less favourably because he has a dog, namely a reason related to his disability. The proper comparator therefore is a customer to whom that reason (the presence of the dog) does not apply, namely a customer who does not have a dog.[463] In this way many incidences of indirect disability discrimination are caught by the DDA, though indirect discrimination is not in terms proscribed under the DDA. A 'no dogs' rule is a *prima facie* disability-neutral criterion, but one which would disproportionately impact on sight-impaired people, and as such is a form of indirect discrimination. It is caught by the concept of disability-related discrimination, just as a status-neutral policy impacting adversely on the

---

457 See para 6.69 above and see *Clark v TDG Limited t/a Novacold* [1999] ICR 951; [1999] IRLR 318.

458 *Clark v TDG Limited t/a Novacold* [1999] ICR 951; [1999] IRLR 318.

459 *Manchester City Council v Romano (Disability Rights Commission Intervening) and Another* [2004] EWCA Civ 834; [2005] 1 WLR 2775.

460 *Clark v TDG Limited t/a Novacold* [1999] ICR 951; [1999] IRLR 318.

461 Ibid.

462 Ibid.

463 Ibid; Mc Aully Catholic High School v (1) CC (2) PC and Special Educational Needs and Disability Tribunal [2003] EWHC 3045 (Admin) [2004] 2 ALL ER 436, para 58; *VK v Norfolk CC* [2005] ELR 342.

other protected classes might be caught by the indirect discrimination provisions of the other main anti-discrimination enactments.[464]

(4) Knowledge

Until recently it seemed tolerably clear that knowledge of the disabled person's disability was not required for disability-related discrimination to occur, outside of very limited fields, where express provision is made requiring knowledge.[465] As has been observed, there is nothing in the statutory language that requires that the relationship between the disability and the treatment be judged subjectively through the eyes of the discriminator. The correct test is an objective one of whether the relationship between the less favourable treatment and disability exists, not whether the discriminator knew of it.[466] If the test were not objective, difficulties would arise 'with credible and honest yet ignorant or obtuse employers who fail to recognize or acknowledge the obvious'.[467] In this way, dismissing an employee due to absence, where that absence is attributable to disability, has been regarded as disability-related discrimination, whether or not the employer knew disability was the cause of the absence, or, more particularly, whether or not disability was the reason for dismissal in the employer's mind at the time of dismissal.[468] **6.153**

A recent decision of the Court of Appeal has confusingly thrown some doubt upon the proper approach to disability-related discrimination. In *Taylor v OCS Group Limited*,[469] the Court of Appeal held instead that for disability-related discrimination the discriminator must know about the disability, apparently in the sense of knowing of the impairment and its impact (though not necessarily that it meets the requirements of the legal test of disability)[470] and that 'the [discriminator] should have a certain state of mind'. According to the Court of Appeal, in the context of the DDA, disability-related discrimination does not occur 'unless [the discriminator] treats the disabled [person] differently for a **6.154**

464 See para 6.101 above.

465 See para 6.193 below.

466 *H J Heinz Co Limited v Kenrick* [2000] IRLR 144; *London Borough of Hammersmith & Fulham v Farnsworth* [2000] IRLR 691; and *Royal Liverpool Children's NHS Trust v Dunsby* [2006] IRLR 351.

467 *H J Heinz Co Limited v Kenrick* [2000] IRLR 144, para 26. See too *Collins v Royal National Theatre Board Limited* [2004] EWCA Civ 144; [2004] IRLR 395, para 32, *per* Sedley LJ.

468 Ibid. And see Code of Practice on 'Rights of Access, Goods Facilities, Services and Premises' ISBN 0117028606 (Disability Discrimination Code of Practice (Goods, Facilities, Services and Premises) (Appointed Day) Order 2002 SI 2002/720) para 3.11: 'A service provider may have treated a disabled person less favourably for a reason related to their disability even if it did not know the person was disabled. The test which has generally been adopted by the courts is whether, as a matter of fact, this was the reason why the disabled person was less favourably treated'. For the effect of the codes, see Chap 15.

469 [2006] EWCA Civ 702; [2006] IRLR 613.

470 Ibid, para 70.

reason [present in his, the [discriminator's] mind] which is related to the [complainant's] disability', though this need not be the only reason or be consciously influential, so long as the disability-related reason consciously or sub-consciously had a significant influence on the discriminator's decision. Mr Taylor had complained of disability-related discrimination in relation to his dismissal. According to the Court of Appeal, even if Mr Taylor's 'inability (on account of his deafness) to explain his conduct, contributed to his dismissal . . . as a matter of causation [so that] if Mr Taylor had not been deaf or had had an interpreter present at the first disciplinary hearing, he might not have been dismissed . . .' that would not be sufficient. Instead 'the issue is whether the employer had a disability-related reason in his mind when he dismissed the employee',[471] and there was no evidence of that in Mr Taylor's case. This is a surprising decision and the correctness of its legal analysis must be doubted. It conflates the test of direct discrimination with that of disability-related discrimination, requiring that the less favourable treatment be, at least in part, on the 'grounds of' disability. Earlier decisions suggesting that the test was objective were distinguished on the basis that the fact of the impairment and its effect, in those particular cases, was known about by the discriminators concerned,[472] but this is unconvincing, particularly when one scrutinizes the reasoning in those cases.[473] It also sits uncomfortably with the other provisions of the DDA. Firstly, disability-related discrimination[474] and certain of the reasonable adjustment duties (described below at paragraph 6.193) expressly require that an alleged discriminator know of a person's disability for liability to be triggered, suggesting that the omission of knowledge in the definition of disability-related discrimination was deliberate. Secondly, certain of the provisions outlawing disability discrimination concern transient relationships, like restaurateurs and customers, when knowledge of disability may be extraordinarily unlikely to occur in the mind of a discriminator (save in the case of visible disability). Thirdly, certain of the provisions outlawing disability-related discrimination do not allow for justification where a duty to make adjustments arises and has not been discharged, save where it would have been justified had the discriminator complied with the duty. Since a duty only arises where the discriminator has knowledge of the disability,[475] this leaves a residual defence of justification available where no duty arises at all, including because of an absence of relevant knowledge. This indicates that Parliament anticipated that disability-related discrimination might occur (and might still be justified) where a discriminator

[471] Ibid, para 73.

[472] *Taylor v OCS Group Limited* [2006] EWCA Civ 702; [2006] IRLR 613, paras 69–70.

[473] *H J Heinz Co Limited v Kenrick* [2000] IRLR 144; *Clark v TDG Limited t/a Novacold* [1999] ICR 951; [1999] IRLR 318.

[474] See DDA, s 28(B)(4).

[475] DDA, ss 3A(6), 4A(3), 31AB(5) (in the latter case not in force at the time of writing).

does not have knowledge of the disability. Fourthly, the Framework Directive requires Member States to outlaw indirect disability discrimination and this is achieved domestically through the prohibition on disability-related discrimination and the reasonable adjustments duties in the fields covered by the Directive. Indirect discrimination most certainly does not require knowledge of the impact on the protected group or knowledge of that status of the affected group. In addition, and finally, the fact that disability-related discrimination can be justified at all suggests that a broad interpretation should be given to the concept of disability-related discrimination, mindful that in all cases such might be legally justified. For all these reasons, as well as its inconsistency with earlier authorities, *Taylor* should be regarded as wrongly decided.

(5) Justification

As mentioned, disability-related discrimination may be justified. The defence of justification is differently constructed, and has different effect, depending on the activity concerned. **6.155**

(a) Employment and related fields

Disability-related discrimination in the employment and related fields[476] may be justified 'if, but only if, the reason for [the treatment] . . . is both material to the circumstances of the particular case and substantial'.[477] There are two significant limitations to the justification defence. Firstly, it does not apply to disability-related treatment which also constitutes direct discrimination[478] (and there is a clear and obvious overlap between the concepts), and secondly, it does not apply where the employer is under a duty to make reasonable adjustments in relation to a disabled person but fails to comply with that duty, unless it would have been justified even if he had complied with that duty.[479] Otherwise, the justification test sets a 'very low'[480] threshold, so that it is only necessary that the reasons 'relate to the individual circumstances in question' and are not 'trivial or minor'.[481] **6.156**

Controversially,[482] in *Jones v Post Office*[483] the Court of Appeal ruled that the function of an employment tribunal in determining whether justification is made out is 'not very different from the task which they have to perform in cases of **6.157**

476 DDA, Part 2 (Employment, contract workers, office holders, partners, barristers and advocates, trade organizations, qualifications bodies, practical work experience, and, from 4 December 2006, local council members).

477 DDA, s 3A(3).

478 Ibid, s 3A(4).

479 Ibid, s 3A(6).

480 *H J Heinz Co Limited v Kenrick* [2000] IRLR 144, para 16.

481 Ibid, para 20.

482 'Briefings' Discrimination Law Association, Vol 13, 212; 'Highlights' [2001] IRLR 321.

483 [2001] EWCA Civ 558, [2001] ICR 805; [2001] IRLR 384.

unfair dismissal'. In an unfair dismissal case, a tribunal's role is to determine whether a dismissal was within 'a range of reasonable responses', and in 'justification', its role is to consider the materiality and substantiality of the employer's reason:

> [i]n both cases, the members of the tribunal might themselves have come to a different conclusion on the evidence, but they must respect the opinion of the employer, in the one case if it is within the range of reasonable responses and in the other if the reason given is material and substantial.[484]

This means that the justification test under the DDA requires a much less rigorous scrutiny of an employer's action as compared to that required in indirect discrimination.[485] In *Jones* itself, therefore, the Court of Appeal allowed an appeal against an employment tribunal's decision that Mr Jones, who was employed as a mail delivery driver, was unlawfully discriminated against when he was removed from driving duties. Mr Jones had non-insulin dependent diabetes but was eventually diagnosed with insulin dependent diabetes and was then removed from his driving duties in accordance with the Post Office's medical fitness standards. It was conceded by the employers that, by removing Mr Jones from all driving duties, they had discriminated against him. An employment tribunal concluded that the 'decision in this case as to what is justified must be ours'. It concluded that a correct appraisal of Mr Jones' medical condition would have led to the conclusion that he should have been allowed to drive throughout his shift. The tribunal heard expert evidence that the deterioration in Mr Jones' condition signalled by his reliance on insulin made no material difference to the existing risk that he would experience a hypoglycaemic episode while driving a Post Office van. Since it considered that the employers' conclusion was wrong, the tribunal held that the reason for the treatment could not be either 'material' or 'substantial' and therefore was not justified. The Court of Appeal concluded that the tribunal's approach was wrong and remitted the case back for a fresh hearing.

6.158 Given many cases of disability-related discrimination will be instances of indirect discrimination it is difficult to see how *Jones* can survive the Framework Directive. As has been seen, the Directive requires Member States to outlaw indirect discrimination save where such discrimination is 'justified by a legitimate aim and the means of achieving that aim are appropriate and necessary' or 'as regards persons with a particular disability, the employer or any person or organisation to whom [the Framework Directive] applies is obliged, under national legislation', to make reasonable adjustments 'to eliminate disadvantages entailed by such provision, criterion or practice'.[486] Consistent with the Directive,

484 Ibid, *per* Pill LJ, at para 28.

485 See above, para 6.110.

486 Framework Directive, Arts 2(2)(b) and (5).

disability-related discrimination cannot be justified where the employer is under a duty to make reasonable adjustments in relation to a disabled person but fails to comply with that duty, unless it would have been justified even if he had complied with that duty.[487] However, the justification defence provided for in *Jones* is a long way from that required by the Framework Directive and EU law.[488] Where a duty does not arise, but indirect discrimination occurs (as where an employer requires all its workers to work full time and does not appreciate that a particular affected worker is disabled), it is difficult to see why the more rigorous defence of justification in the Directive should not apply. Having regard, then, to the UK's obligations under the Directive,[489] it is unlikely that *Jones* could withstand a challenge now.

Specific provision is made in relation to justification and 'qualifications bodies', where the discrimination arises because of the application of a 'competence standard',[490] namely an academic, medical, or other standard applied by or on behalf of a qualifications body for the purpose of determining whether or not a person has a particular level of competence or ability.[491] In such a case disability-related discrimination may be justified where the qualifications body can show that the standard is, or would be, applied equally to persons who do not have the disabled person's particular disability, and its application is a proportionate means of achieving a legitimate aim.[492] This imposes an objective test and therefore is quite distinct from the general defence of justification provided for in relation to disability-related discrimination. Instead it is reminiscent of the defence of justification provided for in EU law and the Convention rights, discussed in paragraph 6.123 and seen in other fields addressed by the DDA. Importantly, too, the modified test of justification only applies to the actual application of a competence standard. If a qualifications body applies a competence standard incorrectly, then it is not applying the standard and the special exemption does not apply. In such circumstances the ordinary test of justification applies, unless the application of the standard is directly discriminatory, in which case no defence of justification is available. **6.159**

(b) Goods, facilities, and services

In the context of Part 3 of the DDA, disability-related discrimination[493] in the provision of goods, facilities, and services may be justified, but the test for **6.160**

487 DDA, s 3A(6).
488 See Chap 4 for the impact of EC law and domestic law and remedies for a breach of EC law.
489 See Chap 4.
490 DDA, s 14A(3).
491 Ibid, s 14A(5).
492 Ibid, s 14A(3)(a) and (b).
493 Ibid, s 20(1).

justification is rather different from that seen in the context of employment and related fields. Section 20(3) of the DDA provides that:

> . . . treatment is justified only if—
>
> (a) in the opinion of the provider of services, one or more of the conditions mentioned in sub-section (4) are satisfied; and
>
> (b) it is reasonable, in all the circumstances of the case, for him to hold that opinion.

The conditions mentioned in sub-section (4) are that:

- in any case, the treatment was necessary in order not to endanger the health or safety of any person (including that of the disabled person);
- in any case, the disabled person was incapable of entering into an enforceable agreement, or of giving an informed consent, and for that reason the treatment was reasonable in that case;
- in a case of a refusal to provide or a deliberate failure to provide services, the treatment was necessary because the provider of the services would otherwise have been unable to provide the service to members of the public;
- in a case of discrimination in the standard of service, or the manner of service, or in the terms of service, the treatment was necessary in order for the provider of services to be able to provide the service to the disabled person or to other members of the public;
- in a case of discrimination in the terms on which a service is provided, the difference in the terms on which the service was provided to the disabled person and those on which it was provided to other persons reflects the greater cost to the provider of the services in providing the service to the disabled person.[494]

The justification defence, then, imposes a mixed subjective and objective test with the subjective and objective elements being conjunctive. For justification, a service provider must believe that one or more of the relevant conditions are satisfied *and* it must be reasonable in all the circumstances of the case for the service provider to hold that opinion. Opinions or beliefs based on generalizations and the stereotyping of disabled people, however firmly held or benign, would not therefore be adequate.[495]

6.161 A number of further observations might be made. Firstly, the discriminator must genuinely believe *at the time of the discrimination* that one of the conditions set out under sub-section (4) is in fact met[496] and accordingly the circumstances under sub-section (4) cannot be used *ex-post facto* to excuse mere prejudice or hostility. Secondly, the question whether a service provider has established justification will

494 Ibid, s 20(4).

495 Code of Practice on 'Rights of Access, Goods, Facilities, Services and Premises' (2002) DRC, para 7.12.

496 *Rose v Bouchet* [1999] IRLR 463.

depend on the opinion held by the service provider at that time and whether, *at that time*, it was reasonable in all the circumstances of the case for him to hold that opinion.[497] Thirdly, the list of conditions is exhaustive. Fourthly, certain of the conditions apply only to certain of the discriminatory acts and reliance cannot be placed on a condition which does not apply to the particular discriminatory act. A refusal to supply services to a disabled person based only on the fact that there will be a greater cost to the provider of the services in providing the service to the disabled person cannot be justified on that ground. Any difference in the terms, as to cost, upon which a service is provided may be justified. However, where any increase in the costs of providing a service to a disabled person results from compliance with a duty to make reasonable adjustments under section 21 of the DDA, discussed below (at paragraph 6.220), that cost must be disregarded in determining whether there is any greater cost to the provider of the services in providing the service to the disabled person.[498]

During the committee stages of what became the DDA 2005, concern was expressed about the mixed subjective/objective test which is replicated (with modifications as to the conditions) in the public function provisions enacted under the DDA 2005 and discussed below (paragraph 6.246). In particular, the joint committee on the draft Disability Discrimination Bill[499] observed that they had heard evidence that in applying the dual test, 'the courts have not always applied the reasonable opinion test in an objective way'.[500] In particular, it appeared that opinion might be based on generalized assumptions or stereotyping, and such might justify discrimination, even if not apt in a particular case, so long as the opinion was 'a reasonable one for [the discriminator] to reach' based on the information the discriminator had available, even if the information was inaccurate or incomplete.[501] In determining reasonableness, some case law suggests that it is not always necessary for a discriminator to check the position or make enquiries to determine whether their assumption or opinion is factually sound; instead 'the need for further inquiry will depend very much on the facts and circumstances of a particular case'.[502] Evidence before the joint committee indicated concern that 'the reason for discrimination can be based on wrongly held prejudices and stereotypes of disabled people and as long as there are those prejudices and they are viewed by a judge or a tribunal as being reasonably held **6.162**

[497] *Rose v Bouchet* [1999] IRLR 463; *Manchester City Council v Romano (Disability Rights Commission Intervening) and Another* [2005] 1 WLR 2775.

[498] DDA, s 20(5) and (4); *Ross v Ryanair Limited* [2005] 1 WLR 2447.

[499] Joint Committee on the draft Disability Discrimination Bill—First Report (April 2002), HL 82-I/HC 352-I.

[500] Citing evidence from various sources and citing, in particular, *Rose v Bouchet* [1999] IRLR 463.

[501] *Rose v Bouchet* [1999] IRLR 463, para 36.

[502] Ibid, para 37.

then that can be used to justify discrimination'.[503] However, such an approach would be contrary to the objects of the DDA and, to the extent that case law suggests that such an approach is mandated by the DDA, its correctness must be doubted. Addressing stereotyping and prejudice towards disabled people is a key purpose of the DDA, and to ensure that proper effect is given to the Act, the objective element of the test of justification must be applied rigorously so as to impose a proper check on the discriminator's opinion. Where a discriminator's opinion is based on an assumption, it will only meet the reasonableness threshold if it is supported by proper inquiry. If a discriminator forms the opinion that a disabled person who uses a wheelchair, for example, cannot access premises entered by stairs only, the discriminator should check with the disabled person to ensure that that opinion is not ill-founded. In that way, the objective element is met. Otherwise the justification defence would deprive the unlawful acts[504] and the rights conferred thereby of any meaningful effect.

6.163 Some broad observations can be made about the breadth of the conditions. As to *health or safety*, this condition might relate to the health or safety of the disabled person themselves or the health or safety of another. 'Health' for these purposes might be interpreted in accordance with the World Health Organization definition of the word 'health': 'health is a state of complete physical, mental and social well-being and not merely the absence of disease and infirmity'.[505] Health is endangered if it is 'put at risk'.[506] 'Trivial risks' to a person's health should be disregarded.[507] Any action taken in relation to health or safety must be proportionate to the risk and in this respect there must be a balance between protecting against the risk and restricting disabled people from using the service provider's services. All people are entitled to make the same choices and to take the same risks within the same limits.[508]

6.164 As to *capacity to contract*, if a disabled person is genuinely unable to understand a particular transaction, a service provider may refuse to enter into it with him. However, to avoid stereotyping, service providers should assume that a disabled person is able to enter into a contract, not the converse. In particular, simple transactions must not be assumed to be beyond the capacity of a person with a learning disability, for example. In addition, the condition in relation to capacity does not apply where a disabled person is acting through another person by virtue

503 Joint Committee on the draft Disability Discrimination Bill—First Report (April 2002), HL 82-I/HC 352-I, para 192.

504 Chap 7 onwards.

505 *Manchester City Council v Romano (Disability Rights Commission Intervening) and Another* [2005] 1 WLR 2775, para 69.

506 Ibid, para 70.

507 Ibid, para 75.

508 Code of Practice on 'Rights of Access, Goods, Facilities, Services and Premises' (2002) DRC, para 7.12; *White v Clitheroe Grammar School* (2002) Preston CC (Ashton DJ) Case No BB002640 (unrep).

of a power of attorney or similar.[509] Where another person is legally acting on behalf of the disabled person, a service provider cannot discriminate in the provision of services by reliance on the capacity condition.

As to whether any discrimination is justified because *a service provider would otherwise be unable to provide the service to members of the public*, as the language of the condition makes clear, this will apply only where other people would be effectively prevented from using the service at all unless the service provider treated the disabled person less favourably than other people. Inconvenience or delay would not suffice. The interests of disabled people in fair and equal participation are, thereby, equated in the DDA with the interests of non-disabled people, and are not relegated for the convenience of others. **6.165**

As to whether any discrimination is justified so as *to enable the service provider to provide the service to a disabled person and other members of the public* this will apply only where the discrimination is necessary in order to provide the service to the disabled person or other members of the public. This is a narrow condition but one which may apply where the difference in service is the only means by which the service might be provided at all to the disabled person or others.[510] **6.166**

As to *greater cost*, where a service provider charges more for services provided to a disabled person because the service is individually tailored to the requirements of that disabled person, it might justify the higher charge. For example, where a pedicurist charges clients a flat rate for certain foot treatments which generally take 30 minutes she may be justified in charging double the usual rate to a disabled customer who has a treatment which, due to arthritis in his feet, takes one hour.[511] Importantly, however, as mentioned above, this condition cannot be relied upon to justify discriminatory charging where the extra costs are attributable to the service provider discharging its duty to make reasonable adjustments. Instead it is concerned with individually tailored services. **6.167**

[509] Disability Discrimination (Services and Premises) Regulations 1996 SI 1996/1836, Regulation 8 ('Section 20(4)(b) of the [DDA] (treatment justified where disabled person is incapable of entering into an enforceable agreement or giving informed consent) shall not apply where a disabled person is acting through another person by virtue of, (a) a power of attorney; or (b) functions conferred by or under Part 7 of the Mental Health Act 1983; or (c) powers exercisable in relation to the disabled person's property or affairs in consequence of the appointment, under the law of Scotland, of a guardian, tutor or judicial factor') and from 4 December 2006, Disability Discrimination (Service Providers and Public Authorities Carrying Out Functions) Regulations 2005 SI 2005 2901, Regulation 3 which is to the same effect.

[510] Code of Practice on 'Rights of Access, Goods, Facilities, Services and Premises' (2002) DRC, para 7.21 and see 7.22.

[511] Code of Practice on 'Rights of Access, Goods, Facilities, Services and Premises' (2002) DRC, para 7.24.

6.168 Special provision is made in relation to insurance, guarantees, and deposits, in addition to the general justification defence.[512] In summary, disability-related discrimination in the context of the provision of goods, facilities, or services is taken to be justified where the less favourable treatment is, in connection with insurance business carried on by the provider of services, based upon information (for example, actuarial or statistical data or a medical report) which is relevant to the assessment of the risk to be insured, is from a source on which it is reasonable to rely, and is reasonable having regard to the information relied upon and any other relevant factors.[513] Reliance upon untested assumptions, stereotyping or generalizations in respect of a disabled person, and the risk to be attributed to any particular characteristic would not be sufficient. Accordingly, an insurer is not permitted to adopt a general policy or practice of refusing to provide insurance to disabled people or people with particular disabilities unless this can be justified by reference to all the conditions above, and nor should an insurer adopt a general policy or practice of insuring disabled people or people with particular disabilities on different terms.[514]

6.169 Specific provision is also made in relation to guarantees and deposits. A service provider who provides a guarantee (whether legally binding or not) that the purchase price of services will be refunded or goods replaced, repaired, or their price refunded if not of satisfactory quality will be justified in refusing to replace, repair, or refund where damage, or excessive damage,[515] has occurred for a reason which relates to the disabled person's disability, and it is reasonable in all the circumstances of the case for him to so refuse.[516] A refusal to return a deposit, or a refusal to return the deposit in full, where the deposit was refundable if the goods or facilities were undamaged and damage to the goods or facilities has occurred for a reason related to disability, is also treated as justified where the damage is above the level at which the provider would normally refund the deposit in full, and it is reasonable in all the circumstances of the case for the provider to refuse to refund

---

512 DDA, s 20(8) provides that 'regulations may make provision, for the purposes of this section, as to circumstances (other than those mentioned in sub-section (4)) in which treatment is to be taken to be justified'. Regulations have been made pursuant to that power and, as described below, make special provision in relation to insurance, guarantees, and deposits. The special provision as to justification under the regulations described below do not appear, then, to substitute the justification defence under s 20(1)(b) and (2)(b) but rather supplement it.

513 Disability Discrimination (Services and Premises) Regulations 1996 SI 1996/1836, Regulation 2 and as of 4 Dec 2006, Disability Discrimination (Service Providers and Public Authorities Carrying Out Functions) Regulations 2005 SI 2005/2901, which makes materially identical provision in Regulation 4.

514 Code of Practice on 'Rights of Access, Goods, Facilities, Services and Premises' (2002) DRC, para 8.5.

515 That is, above the level at which the provider would normally refund the deposit in full.

516 Disability Discrimination (Services and Premises) Regulations 1996 SI 1996/1836, Regulation 5, revoked from 4 Dec 2006 and replaced by materially identical provision in Disability Discrimination (Service Providers and Public Authorities Carrying Out Functions) Regulations 2005 SI 2005/2901, Regulation 7.

the deposit in full.[517] This special provision does not permit a service provider to charge a disabled person a higher deposit than it would normally charge other people or to pay a deposit at all in circumstances where the service provider would not ordinarily expect a deposit to be paid.

(c) *Employment services*

Specific provision is made in relation to employment services under Part 3 of the DDA by the modification of the provision made in relation to goods, facilities, and services.[518] In particular, as with the employment and related fields, disability-related discrimination which amounts to direct discrimination within the meaning of section 3A(5)[519] cannot be justified.[520] **6.170**

(d) *Public authorities*

Disability-related discrimination by a public authority in the carrying out of its functions is outlawed from 4 December 2006.[521] The new provisions provide for two categories of justification. The first matches closely that seen in the goods, facilities, and services provisions in form. The second matches the approach seen in the employment and related fields in form. **6.171**

As to the first form of justification, disability-related discrimination will be justified where in the opinion of the public authority one or more of the conditions mentioned in section 21D(4) are satisfied and it is reasonable, in all the circumstances of the case, for him to hold that opinion. Accordingly it adopts the same approach as that seen in the goods, facilities, and services provisions, described above.[522] The particular conditions differ. The conditions mentioned in section 21D(4) are: **6.172**

- that the treatment is necessary in order not to endanger the health or safety of any person (including that of the disabled person);
- that the disabled person is incapable of entering into an enforceable agreement, or of giving an informed consent, and for that reason the treatment is reasonable in that case;[523]

---

517 Disability Discrimination (Services and Premises) Regulations 1996 SI 1996/1836, Regulation 6, revoked from 4 Dec 2006 and replaced by materially identical provision in Disability Discrimination (Service Providers and Public Authorities Carrying Out Functions) Regulations 2005 SI 2005/2901, Regulation 8.

518 See paras 1.160 above.

519 See para 6.17 above.

520 DDA, s 21A(5), inserting sub-s (3A) after s 20(3).

521 S 21B as inserted by the DDA 2005.

522 DDA, s 21D(3).

523 This condition will not apply where another person is acting for the disabled person by virtue of a power of attorney; functions under Part 7 of the Mental Health Act 1983 or powers exercisable in relation to the disabled person's property or affairs in consequence of the appointment, under the law of Scotland, of a guardian, tutor, or judicial factor (Disability Discrimination (Service Providers and Public Authorities Carrying Out Functions) Regulations 2005 SI 2005/2901, Regulation 3).

- that treating the disabled person equally in the particular case would involve substantial extra costs and, having regard to resources, the extra costs in that particular case would be too great; and
- that the treatment is necessary for the protection of the rights and freedoms of others.

6.173 As with justification under the goods, facilities, and services provisions, for this form of justification a mixed subjective and objective test applies. At the time of the discriminatory treatment, a public authority must believe that one or more of the relevant conditions, which are exhaustive, is satisfied, *and* it must be reasonable in all the circumstances of the case for it to hold that opinion. The observations made above (paragraph 6.160) apply equally.

6.174 As to the second form of justification, '[t]reatment . . . is justified under this sub-section if the acts of the public authority which give rise to the treatment . . . are a proportionate means of achieving a legitimate aim'.[524] This does not limit justification to particular circumstances, and to this extent replicates the provision made in the employment and related fields. However, this form of justification imposes a wholly objective test. If one of the conditions under sub-section (4) is not met, this defence will be available only where, on objective scrutiny, the treatment meets a legitimate aim and is proportionate. This form of justification adopts an approach reminiscent of the approach to the qualifications found in the Convention rights[525] and to the justification defences seen in EU law, both of which require rigorous scrutiny of any discriminatory measure, as is discussed in Chapter 4. Stereotyping and generalizations will not found this form of justification, as the case law emanating from the ECHR makes clear.[526] The requirement for a legitimate aim calls for the identification of a non-discriminatory aim and the requirement to show that the discrimination was a 'proportionate' means of achieving *that* aim will require consideration as to whether there were other, non-discriminatory, means of achieving that aim.

(e) Premises

6.175 Disability-related discrimination in the disposal and management of premises[527] may be justified where, in the opinion of the discriminator, one or more of the conditions mentioned in section 24(3) of the DDA is satisfied, and it is reasonable, in all the circumstances of the case, for him to hold that opinion.[528] Accordingly the same approach is taken to justification here as seen in the goods,

524 SDA, s 21D(5).
525 Articles 8(2) and 9(2), for example, see Chap 4.
526 Chap 4.
527 DDA, s 22.
528 Ibid, s 22(2) and see para 6.160.

facilities, and services provisions described above. The particular conditions differ.

The conditions mentioned in section 24(3) are: 6.176

- that the treatment is necessary in order not to endanger the health or safety of any person (including the disabled person);
- that the disabled person is incapable of entering into an enforceable agreement, or of giving an informed consent, and for that reason the treatment is reasonable in that case;[529]
- in relation to the way in which a discriminator permits a disabled person to use any benefits or facilities, that the treatment is necessary in order for the disabled person or the other occupiers of other premises forming part of the building to make use of the benefit or facility;
- in relation to a refusal by a discriminator to allow a disabled person to use any benefits or facilities, that the treatment is necessary in order for the occupiers of other premises forming part of the building to make use of the benefit or facility;
- in relation to a letting or sale of premises to a disabled person on terms which are less favourable, that the treatment is in order to recover costs which, as a result of the disabled person having a disability, are incurred in connection with the disposal of premises, save where the costs are attributable to compliance with a duty to make adjustments;[530] and, finally,
- in relation to treatment of a disabled person amounting to a detriment (other than eviction), that the detriment is in order to recover costs which as a result of the disabled person having a disability are incurred in connection with the management of premises, save where the costs are attributable to compliance with the duty to make adjustments.[531]

As with justification under the goods, facilities, and services provisions, for this form of justification a mixed subjective and objective test applies. At the time of the discriminatory treatment, a landlord or another person disposing of premises[532] must believe that one or more of the relevant conditions, which are exhaustive, is satisfied *and* it must be reasonable in all the circumstances of the case for him to hold that opinion. The observations above (paragraph 6.160) apply equally. 6.177

---

529 This condition will not apply where another person is acting for the disabled person by virtue of a power of attorney; functions under Part 7 of the Mental Health Act 1983 or powers exercisable in relation to the disabled persons property or affairs in consequence of the appointment, under the law of Scotland, of a guardian, tutor or judicial factor (Disability Discrimination (Premises) Regulations 2006, SI 2006/887, Regulation 2, in force from 4 Dec 2006).

530 As to which see para 6.234 below.

531 See DDA, s 24(3)(3A), (3B), and (3C) and see para 6.234 below for the duties to make adjustments.

532 Defined materially under DDA ss 24A(3) and (4) and 24G(3) and (4).

6.178 As seen, the health and safety condition is concerned with the health or safety of the disabled person themselves or the health and safety of others.[533] 'Health' for these purposes has a wide meaning, as discussed in paragraph 6.163 above and, where engaged, regard must be had to the Convention rights.[534] In the context of housing this may be particularly important having regard to the breadth of Article 8.[535] It is difficult to conceive of a case arising under section 22 where Article 8 will not be engaged.

6.179 Where a belief, therefore, is reasonably held that a person (being the disabled person or another) might have their health, very broadly construed, 'put at risk' in the absence of the treatment complained of, the conditions in section 24(2) read with section 24(3) are likely to be satisfied. Such a situation may arise where anti-social behaviour by the disabled person, even where attributable to disability, puts the well-being of neighbours at risk.[536]

6.180 Special provision is made in relation to deposits on premises, in addition to the general justification defence.[537] In summary, where a disabled person has provided a deposit in respect of a right to occupy premises, which is refundable at the end of the occupation provided that the premises and contents are not damaged and the deposit in full or part is not returned on the basis that the premises or contents have been damaged for a reason which relates to the disabled person's disability and the damage is above the level at which the provider would normally refund the deposit in full, so long as it is reasonable in all the circumstances of the case to refuse to refund the deposit in full, such will be justified.[538]

(f) Commonholds

6.181 New provision is made under the DDA addressing discrimination in the context of commonholds.[539] Disability-related discrimination is outlawed with the defence

---

533 *Manchester City Council v Romano (Disability Rights Commission Intervening) and Another* [2005] 1 WLR 2775.

534 See Chap 4 above.

535 See, eg, *Hatton v United Kingdom* [2003] 37 EHRR 28 which held that environmental pollution might prevent individuals from enjoying their homes in such a way as to affect their private and family life adversely, without however seriously endangering their health, para 96. See too, the observations in *Manchester City Council v Romano (Disability Rights Commission Intervening) and Another* [2005] 1 WLR 2775, para 74.

536 *Manchester City Council v Romano (Disability Rights Commission Intervening) and Another* [2005] 1 WLR 2775.

537 Disability Discrimination (Services and Premises) Regulations 1996 SI 1996/1836, Regulation 7, and, as of 4 Dec 2006, (which revoke the 1996 Regulations, as is material and substitute provision) the Disability Discrimination (Premises) Regulations 2006 SI 2006/887, regulation 3, both of which were made under s 24(5) of the DDA, amongst other provisions.

538 Ibid.

539 Defined in DDA, s 22A. See too, Disability Discrimination (Premises) Regulations 2006 SI 2006/887. These provisions are in force from 4 Dec 2006.

of justification being the same as that applicable in relation to the 'premises' provisions, and the observations above apply equally.[540]

(g) Clubs

Disability-related discrimination by clubs is regulated in a similar way to discrimination in the provision of goods, facilities, and services. Such treatment might be justified, and the model adopted reflects closely that adopted under the goods, facilities, and services provisions. Disability-related discrimination by clubs[541] will be justified where, in the opinion of the club, one or more of the enumerated conditions is met, so long as it is reasonable, in all the circumstances, for it to hold that opinion.[542] The conditions are: **6.182**

- that the treatment is necessary in order not to endanger the health or safety of any person (including the disabled person);
- that the disabled person is incapable of entering into an enforceable agreement, or giving an informed consent, and for that reason the treatment is reasonable in that case;[543]
- in a case relating to the terms upon which membership is granted, including a variation of any such terms, or the way in which access to benefits, facilities, or services is afforded, or in relation to any other detriment, that the treatment is necessary in order for the club to be able to afford members, associates, or guests of the club, or the disabled person, access to a benefit, facility, or service;
- in a case relating to a refusal to admit a disabled person as a member or to afford him access to any benefit, facility, or service or by depriving him of membership,[544] that the treatment is necessary because the association would otherwise be unable to afford members, associates, or guests of the association access to a benefit, facility, or service;
- in a case concerning a difference between the terms upon which a disabled person is granted membership, including any variation of those terms, or access to any benefits, facilities, or services, that the difference reflects the greater cost to the club of affording the disabled person access to those benefits, facilities, or services,[545] save that any cost attributable to complying with a duty to make reasonable adjustments must be disregarded.[546]

540 DDA, s 24(1) read with s 22A. These provisions are in force from 4 Dec 2006.

541 As to which see Chap 10.

542 DDA, s 21G(2).

543 The condition will not apply where another person is acting for the disabled person by virtue of a power of attorney; functions under Part 7 of the Mental Health Act 1983 or powers exercisable in relation to the disabled person's property or affairs in consequence of the appointment, under the law of Scotland, or a guardian, tutor, or judicial factor; Disability Discrimination (Private Clubs etc) Regulations 2005 SI 2005/3258, Regulation 3.

544 Or his right as an associate or guest which are also protected.

545 And parallel provision is made in relation to associates and guests.

546 DDA, s 21G(3).

The model adopted, therefore, reflects closely that made in relation to the provision of goods, facilities, and services, and the observations above apply equally (paragraph 6.160).

6.183 Special provision is made in relation to guarantees and deposits which matches that provided for under the goods, facilities, and services provisions (paragraph 6.168).[547]

(h) Schools

6.184 As mentioned above, disability-related discrimination is somewhat differently defined in the schools provisions of the DDA. In relation to schools, where a responsible body[548] does not know that a pupil, or prospective pupil, is disabled and could not reasonably have been expected to know, then the taking of any particular step will not amount to less favourable treatment.[549] In most cases a school will have the requisite knowledge because of the arrangements in place for the assessment of special educational needs through the special educational needs framework.[550] Information given to a member of staff will be imputed to the responsible body and it is therefore unlikely that a responsible body would be able to rely on an absence of knowledge of which its staff ought to have been aware.[551] In addition, because of the special relationship between pupils and schools and the pastoral role implicit in that relationship, as well as the expertise of those involved in teaching more generally, establishing a lack of knowledge where under-achievement or challenging behaviour has been exhibited is likely to be difficult.[552]

6.185 Disability-related discrimination by schools may be justified on two bases, namely where it is the result of a 'permitted form of selection'[553] or 'where the reason for it is both material to the circumstances of the particular case and substantial'.[554]

6.186 'Permitted forms of selection' are defined by the DDA but essentially allow for selective admission arrangements operated by grammar schools, maintained schools,

547 Disability Discrimination (Private Clubs etc) Regulations 2005 SI 2005/3258 Regulations 4 and 5.

548 As to the meaning of which, see Chap 9.

549 DDA, s 28B(4).

550 'Disability Discrimination Act 1995 Part IV, Code of Practice for Schools' (2002), DRC, Disability Discrimination Codes of Practice (Education) (Appointed Day) Order 2002, SI 2002/2216, para 7.7.

551 'Disability Discrimination Act 1995 Part IV, Code of Practice for Schools' (2002) DRC, para 7.11; 'Disability Discrimination Act 1995 Part IV, Code of Practice for Providers of Post Sixteen Education and Related Services' (2002), DRC, para 4.20.

552 Ibid, para 7.8 and see 'Disability Discrimination Act 1995 Part IV, Code of Practice for Providers of Post 16 Education and Related Services' (2002), DRC (Disability Discrimination Codes of Practice (Education) Appointed Day) Order 2002, SI 2002/2216, para 4.17–4.18.

553 DDA, s 28B(6).

554 Ibid, s 28B(7).

and independent schools.[555] There are statutory limits on the extent to which a maintained school might make provision for selection by ability, and only where allowed will such arrangements constitute a 'permitted form of selection' for the purposes of justifying disability-related discrimination.[556]

As to the second form of justification, this matches the provision made in the context of employment and related fields, and the observations above apply equally (paragraph 6.156). Importantly, where a duty to make reasonable adjustments arises and a school fails without justification to comply with it, disability-related discrimination will only be justified if that treatment would have been justified even if the duty had been complied with.[557] Justification for a failure to comply with a duty to make reasonable adjustments is discussed below (paragraph 6.250). **6.187**

(i) Post-sixteen education

The provisions made addressing disability-related discrimination in the fields of further and higher education have been recently amended to give effect to the Framework Directive.[558] These amendments address justification for disability-related discrimination as well as the duties to make reasonable adjustments, described below.[559] The amendments are significant, and therefore the Disability Rights Commission has issued a new code of practice[560] explaining the new provisions.[561] **6.188**

The new provisions provide for two forms of justification.[562] The first form of justification relates to the application of a 'competence standard'. Where less favourable treatment arises because of the application of a competence standard to a disabled person, such is justified 'if, but only if, the [responsible] body[[563]] can show that (a) the standard is, or would be, applied equally to persons who do not have his particular disability, and (b) its application is a proportionate means of achieving a legitimate aim'.[564] It is expressly provided that treatment cannot **6.189**

555 Ibid, ss 28B(6) and 28Q(9), (10).

556 DDA, s 28Q(9)(a) and Schools Standards and Framework Act 1998, ss 100–2.

557 DDA, s 28B(8).

558 Disability Discrimination Act (Amendment) (Further and Higher Education) Regulations 2006 SI 2006/1721.

559 Para 6.259.

560 As to the effects of the Code of Practice, see Chap 15.

561 'Code of Practice: Post-16 Education' (2006) DRC, in force from 1 Sept 2006.

562 The unamended provisions also provided for two discrete defences of justification but the new provisions impose more rigorous tests.

563 As to the meaning of which see Chap 9.

564 DDA, s 28S(6), as amended by the Disability Discrimination Act 1995 (Amendment) (Further and Higher Education) Regulations 2006 SI 2006/1721.

be justified, under this form of justification or otherwise, if the treatment amounts to direct discrimination.[565]

6.190 The application of the competence standard must be *a proportionate means of achieving a legitimate aim*, so the application of the competence standard is subject itself to an objective test. As discussed at paragraph 6.159 above, the test adopted is reminiscent of the approach seen in the Convention rights and in EU law, and this requires a rigorous assessment of the aim and impact of the standard in question. A 'competence standard' for these purposes means an academic, medical, or other standard applied by or on behalf of a responsible body[566] for the purpose of determining whether or not a person has a particular level of competence or ability.[567] It is therefore necessary to show that the standard in issue is genuinely an academic, medical, or other standard applied for the purpose of determining whether or not a person has a particular level of competence or ability, and it is then necessary to determine that that meets some legitimate aim and it is a proportionate means of so doing. As mentioned above,[568] the proportionality analysis will require consideration as to whether there were other, non-discriminatory, means of achieving the aim in question.

6.191 As to the second form of justification, '[t]reatment . . . is justified . . . if, but only if, the reason for it is both material to the circumstances of the particular case and substantial'.[569] This matches the justification defence found under the employment and related provisions of the DDA,[570] and the observations above apply equally. There are two limitations to this defence. Firstly, as with the first form of justification, this justification defence does not apply to disability-related discrimination, which also constitutes direct discrimination;[571] and secondly, where a responsible body[572] is under a duty to make reasonable adjustments in relation to a disabled person but fails to comply with that duty, less favourable treatment cannot be justified unless the treatment would have been justified even if it had complied with that duty.[573] The second form of justification does not apply where a

565 DDA, s 28S(9), read with 28S(10) (as inserted by the Disability Discrimination Act 1995 Amendment) (Further and Higher Education) Regulations 2006 SI 2006/1721.

566 As to the meaning of which, see Chap 9.

567 DDA, s 28S(11) (as inserted by the Disability Discrimination Act 1995 Amendment) (Further and Higher Education) Regulations 2006 SI 2006/1721).

568 Para 6.125

569 DDA, s 28S(5) (as inserted by the Disability Discrimination Act 1995 Amendment) (Further and Higher Education) Regulations 2006 SI 2006/1721).

570 Discussed at para 6.156 above.

571 DDA, s 28S(9) (again as inserted by the 2006 regulations).

572 As to the meaning of which, see Chap 9.

573 The observations as to the impact of this limitation are discussed at para 6.156 above.

competence standard is in issue, in which case the first form of justification exclusively applies.[574]

(j) General qualifications bodies

The DDA 2005 amended the DDA 1995 to insert new provisions addressing discrimination by general qualifications bodies (being, broadly, examination bodies[575]). These provisions are not yet in force. However, when in force they will outlaw disability-related discrimination by general qualifications bodies, and adopt an approach to justification which matches closely that found in the provisions addressing discrimination in further and higher education.[576] Two forms of justification are therefore provided for, one applying to 'competence standards' and one general defence applicable where the treatment 'is both material to the circumstances of the particular case and substantial'.[577] The 'competence standard' justification defence makes exclusive provision in relation to competence standards, and a 'competence standard' is defined in the same way as under the further and higher education provisions discussed above (paragraph 6.190).[578] As with disability-related discrimination in other fields, such cannot be lawfully justified where it amounts to direct discrimination,[579] and can only be justified where there has been a failure to comply with a duty to make reasonable adjustments, where it would have been justified had that duty been complied with.[580] **6.192**

G. The Duties to Make Reasonable Adjustments

The DDA, alone amongst the main anti-discrimination enactments, imposes duties on those caught by its provisions to make reasonable adjustments to accommodate disabled people. These duties impose positive obligations on employers, service providers, public authorities, and others to take action to modify tangible and intangible barriers to equal participation for disabled people in those areas of life covered by the DDA. The reasonable adjustments duties reflect a more social model of disability,[581] recognizing that 'disability' often has less to do with individual impairment and more to do with attitudinal, environmental, and **6.193**

574 DDA, s 28S(5), (6) and (7) (as inserted by the Disability Discrimination Act 1995 Amendment) (Further and Higher Education) Regulations 2006 SI 2006/1721).

575 See Chap 9.

576 Para 6.189 above.

577 DDA, s 31AB(3) and (4).

578 Ibid, s 31AB(3), (4), and (9).

579 Ibid, s 31AB(7).

580 Ibid, s 31AB(5).

581 Though this is undermined by the far from 'social' model adopted for the definition of 'disability, see Chap 5.

social barriers. As mentioned above, other jurisdictions which adopt more substantive concepts of equality for the purposes of their anti-discrimination law use a reasonable accommodation or adjustments model across grounds.[582] However, in the UK, the reasonable adjustments model, as said, is seen only in the DDA, and the reasonable adjustments duties arising under the DDA apply only in respect of 'disabled'[583] people.

6.194 The DDA does not make provision in relation to indirect discrimination but the duties to make reasonable adjustments impose obligations on those caught by their terms to remove or modify many indirectly discriminatory barriers. In broad terms, the reasonable adjustments duties under the DDA fall into two groups. The first group, applicable in the employment and related fields, amongst others, are *reactive*. That is, the duties are only triggered where a provision, criterion, practice, or a physical feature of premises disadvantages a particular disabled person. The second group are *anticipatory*. That is, they impose duties on service providers, amongst others,where the existence of a practice, policy, or procedure, or physical feature of premises makes it impossible or unreasonably difficult for disabled people to make use of a service provided.[584] The second group do not require the identification of a particular disabled person before they are triggered. Instead they require service providers, and others, to anticipate the use by disabled people of their services and to take proactive action to make their services accessible. The anticipatory duties are of very real importance. As the Disability Rights Commission's Code of Practice explains:

> the policy of the act is not a minimalist policy of simply ensuring that some access is available to disabled people; it is, so far as is reasonably practicable, to approximate the access enjoyed by disabled people to that enjoyed by the rest of the public. Accordingly, the purpose of the duty to make reasonable adjustments is to provide access to a service as close as it is reasonably possible to get to the standard normally offered to the public at large.[585]

6.195 The obligations the reasonable adjustments duties impose are compelling and may extend to making changes to the physical features of buildings. However, there may be legal obstacles to discharging any duty to make adjustments. The DDA, as with the other main anti-discrimination enactments, does not override other mandatory statutory provisions.[586] Particular provision is made

582 See para 6.09 above.

583 See Chap 5.

584 See para 6.220 below.

585 'Code of Practice—Rights of Access: Services to Public, Public Authority Functions, Private Clubs and Premises' (2006) DRC (Disability Discrimination Code of Practice (Services, Public Functions, Private Clubs and Premises) (Appointed Day) Order 2006 SI 2006/1967, bringing the code into force on 4 Dec 2006).

586 DDA, s 59, discussed in Chap 13.

addressing new builds, and alterations to existing buildings, which is directed at securing access for disabled people,[587] but meeting these requirements does not always affect whether a duty to make reasonable adjustments arises in respect of the building's physical features.[588] The Building Regulations are concerned with providing a minimum standard of accessibility and do not address the specific, idiosyncratic needs of individuals (and certain of the duties, as mentioned and as will be seen below, are very individually focused).

The DDA does, however, make provision addressing legally binding contractual terms and other legally binding obligations (for example, mortgages, charges, and restrictive covenants) which prohibit a person from altering premises to give effect to a duty to make adjustments without another's consent. In such a case, the DDA enacts certain statutory presumptions, so that it is deemed always reasonable for a person subject to such an obligation to have to request consent before making the alteration in question,[589] and it is never reasonable for such a person to have to make the alteration in question before having obtained that consent.[590] In this way, any binding agreement or obligation is given precedence over the duty to make adjustments.[591] Provision is also made modifying the terms of any lease which prevents a relevant alteration to the premises. A lease is deemed to allow for consent, on reasonable conditions, not to be withheld unreasonably, where alterations are necessary to discharge a duty to make adjustments.[592] **6.196**

---

587 The Building Regulations 2000 SI 2000/2531, Schedule 1, M; Building (Scotland) Regulations 2004. See too, 'Design of Buildings and their Approaches to meet the needs of Disabled People—Code of Practice' British Standard 8300:2001, referred to in 'Code of Practice: Employment and Occupation' (2004) DRC, para 12.9. However, as has been noted, 'The 2004 edition Approved Document M when implemented in May 2004 has adopted many of the DS8300 standards and in some cases the standards contained in Approved Document M are higher than those contained within the British Standard. It would seem that for those standards that are higher, these are additional standards that should be applied to physical adaptations to work towards meeting design requirements under the DDA' ('Access to the Build Environment: Disability Discrimination Act 1995: British Standard 8300:2001, Design of Buildings and their Approaches to meet the needs of Disable People—Code of Practice; etc.', presentation by Paul Day, 12 March 2004, Centre for Disability Studies, School of Sociology and Social Policy, University of Leeds) (see too, 'Access to the Built Environment: Is it Improving?: British Standard 8300-001, Design of Buildings and Approaches to meet the needs of Disabled People—Code of Practice; etc.', presentation by Paul Day, 11 March 2005, Leeds University, Dept of Sociology and Social Policy).

588 The partial exemption from the duty to make adjustments to physical features in relation to service providers is referred to in para 6.196 below.

589 DDA, s 18B(3).

590 Ibid.

591 It should be noted that whilst it is always reasonable for a person to have to seek consent, that does not include taking steps to apply to a court or tribunal: DDA, s 18B(4). The obligation is therefore not onerous.

592 DDA, s 18A(2). Where a lessee fails to apply to the lessor in writing for consent to the making of the alteration, he cannot rely on any constraints attributable to the fact that he occupies the premises under a lease (on a provision prohibiting him making the alteration, for example) in defending any claim that he has failed to comply with his duty to make reasonable adjustments; DDA, Sch 4, Part 1, para 1.

Further, in relation to providers of goods, facilities, and services only, regulations provide that it is not reasonable for a provider of services to have to remove or alter a physical feature where the feature concerned was specifically for the purpose of assisting people to have access to the building, the feature satisfies the 'relevant design standard',[593] and less than 10 years has elapsed since it was constructed or installed. The relevant design standards are defined and in relation to a building in England or Wales, a physical feature satisfies the relevant design standard where it accords with the relevant objectives, design considerations and provisions in approved document M,[594] and in Scotland, the 'Technical Standards'.[595] This ensures that a service provider who has taken steps to comply with good design standards, aimed at achieving accessibility, is not required to modify those physical features for a period of 10 years.[596]

6.197 The duties to make reasonable adjustments vary in their content and application according to the activity covered. They are, therefore, considered discretely below in the context of the activity to which they respectively apply. Importantly, the duties do not create any cause of action in their own right but define discrimination for the purposes of the unlawful acts.[597]

Where the lessor himself is a superior lessor, such that he is prevented from consenting to the alteration without the consent of his landlord, the superior lease is deemed modified so as to require the lessee of that lease to apply in writing to its lessor where it wishes to consent to the alteration. Again, such consent may not be withheld unreasonably but reasonable conditions may be attached to it; Regulation 9 Disability Discrimination (Employment Field) (Leasehold Premises) Regulations 2004 SI 2004/153. Provision for the obtaining of consent and the effect of a refusal to grant this consent. The Disability Discrimination (Employment Field) (Leasehold Premises) Regulations 2004 makes further provision. For similar provision outside the employment fields, see further, K Monaghan, *Blackstone's Guide to the Disability Discrimination Legislation* (2005, OUP), 156–158.

593 Disability Discrimination (Service Providers and Public Authorities carrying out Functions) Regulations 2005 SI 2005/2901, regulation 11 and Disability Discrimination (Private Clubs etc) Regulations 2005 SI 2005/3258, regulation 12.

594 The Disability Discrimination (Service Providers and Public Authorities carrying out Functions) Regulations 2005 SI 2005/2901, Schedule 1, para 1(1), this being the 1992 edition of the document of that title approved by the Secretary of State as practical guidance on meeting the requirements of part M of Schedule 1 to the Building Regulations 1991, first published for the Department of the Environment by Her Majesty's Stationery Office in 1991 (ISBN 0117524476) or the 1999 (ISBN 0117534692) or 2004 (ISBN 0117539015) editions of the same document in respect of the Building Regulations 1991 or the Building Regulations 2002, as the case may be, para 2(1); Disability Discrimination (Private Clubs etc) Regulations 2005 SI 2005/3258, Regulation 12 and Schedule 1 which makes materially the same provision.

595 Defined in the Disability Discrimination (Service Providers and Public Authorities carrying out Functions) Regulations 2005 SI 2005/2901, Schedule 1, para 3 and Disability Discrimination (Private Clubs etc) Regulations 2005 SI 2005/3258, Schedule, para 3 which makes materially the same provision.

596 For a full discussion see K Monaghan, *Blackstone's Guide to the Disability Discrimination Legislation* (2005, OUP), 175–81.

597 As is plain from the wording of the relevant provisions, but see too DDA, ss 21E(10), 28C(8), and 28G(4), 31AD(7).

(1) Employment and related fields

By section 3A(2) of the DDA, 'a person . . . discriminates against a disabled person if he fails to comply with a duty to make reasonable adjustments imposed on him in relation to the disabled person'. The duties to make reasonable adjustments are described in the first place by section 4A(1)[598] which provides that: 6.198

> (1) where—(a) a provision, criterion or practice applied by or on behalf of an employer, or (b) any physical feature of premises occupied by the employer, places the disabled person concerned at a substantial disadvantage in comparison with persons who are not disabled, it is the duty of the employer to take such steps as it is reasonable, in all the circumstances of the case, for him to have to take in order to prevent the provision, criterion or practice, or feature, having that affect'.

The 'disabled person concerned' is, in relation to a provision, criterion, or practice for determining to whom employment should be offered, any disabled person who is, or has notified the employer that he may be, an applicant for that employment, and in any other case, a disabled person who is an applicant for the employment concerned or an employee of the employer concerned.[599]

As can be seen, the duties are only triggered in relation to a particular disabled person ('the disabled person concerned') and, as is discussed below, knowledge of both the particular disabled person and that she has a disability, amongst other things, are required for the duty to be triggered. 6.199

The duties have changed in consequence of amendments made to the DDA to give effect to the Framework Directive.[600] The introduction of a requirement that reasonable adjustments be made in respect of 'a provision, criterion or practice' is meant to reflect the obligation in the Framework Directive that Member States outlaw indirect disability discrimination in the employment and related fields.[601] Indirect discrimination in the Framework Directive is defined so as to address indirectly discriminatory provisions, criteria, and practices.[602] It is not clear, however, that the modifications to the duties to make reasonable adjustments go far enough. Whilst the obligations go some way to addressing indirect discrimination, they are not anticipatory in nature, and this might be contrasted with the meaning given to indirect discrimination in the 6.200

598 It can be noted that the duty to make reasonable adjustments in the employment and related fields has been significantly modified by the Disability Discrimination Act 1995 (Amendment) Regulations 2003 SI 2003/1673, made to give effect to the Framework Directive, see Chap 4.

599 DDA, s 4A(2).

600 See n 594 above.

601 See, 'Towards Equality and Diversity, Implementing the Employment and Race Directives' (2001), the Cabinet Office, 46.

602 As is reflected in the meaning given to indirect discrimination in the main anti-discrimination enactments now for certain of their purposes, see para 6.114 above.

Framework Directive.[603] In addition, the duties to make reasonable adjustments require that an employer know of the disabled person's disability or could reasonably be expected to know, and no such obligation is imposed by the Framework Directive.[604]

6.201 As to the scope of the duties, they arise in respect of all employment-related activities, namely recruitment, employment, dismissal, and other activities arising out of and closely connected with the employment relationship.[605] The duties extend, then, to all the unlawful acts created in the employment field.[606] Whilst the duties are owed at all stages of the employment relationship, it is likely that the steps necessary to discharge the duty in the case of an existing employee will be more substantial than, for example, those required to discharge any obligation to a person merely contemplating applying for employment, though each case will plainly turn on its own facts.[607]

(a) Knowledge

6.202 No duty is imposed upon an employer in relation to a disabled person if the employer does not know and could not reasonably be expected to know, in the case of an applicant or potential applicant for employment, that the disabled person concerned is, or may be, an applicant for the employment, and in any case that the disabled person concerned has a disability and is likely to be put to a substantial disadvantage by reason of a provision, criterion, or practice applied by, or any physical feature of premises occupied by, the employer.[608] Such knowledge, however, may be actual or imputed, as where an employer's agent or employee knows of the disability.[609] A transferee of an undertaking will be deemed to have relevant knowledge obtained by the transferor.[610] The burden of establishing an

---

603 See Chap 4 and paras 6.114–6.122 above. The Disability Rights Commission have recommended that the duty should be anticipatory so as to ensure institutional barriers are properly addressed: 'Disability Equality: Making it Happen, First Review of the Disability Discrimination Act 1995' (2003, DRC), 27.

604 For remedies in respect of the same see Chap 4.

605 DDA, ss 4 and 16A, discussed in Chap 8.

606 In its original enactment, the duty to make adjustment in the employment field did not unequivocally extend to 'dismissals' and 'detriments' or to private households (there being a small employer exemption). This position was modified by the Disability Discrimination Act 1995 (Amendment) Regulations 2003 SI 2003/1673.

607 'Code of Practice: Employment and Occupation' (2004) DRC ISBN 0117034193 (Disability Discrimination Codes of Practice (Employment and Occupation, and Trade Organisations and Qualifications Bodies) Appointed Day Order 2004, SI 2004/2302), para 5.6.

608 DDA, s 4A(3) read with s 4A(1).

609 'Code of Practice: Employment and Occupation' (2004) DRC, para 5.15. The position might be otherwise where an employer contracts with an agency to provide independent counselling or other services to its employees under contracts which provide the counsellors are not acting on the employer's behalf while acting in that role, 'Code of Practice: Employment and Occupation', ibid, para 5.16.

610 *Jolley v (1) Namdarkhan (2) Greene King Retail Services Limited* (EC Case No. 2602411/03) (2004) EOR 132, 21. This is a first instance decision but its holding is consistent with the purpose

absence of the requisite knowledge rests with an employer.[611] On any analysis, once the duty arises, the issue of knowledge becomes immaterial. The question whether the employer has discharged the duty upon him is to be determined by an objective test, regardless of knowledge (actual or imputed) as to the extent and effects of the disability.[612]

(b) Provisions, criteria, practices, and physical features

As seen, the duty is triggered by the application of provisions, criteria, and practices, and the presence of physical features. The words 'provision', 'criterion', and 'practice' are not exclusively defined by the DDA. However, they are words capable of attaching to a wide range of arrangements.[613] They are plainly intended to have the same meaning as those words in the indirect discrimination provisions found in the other main anti-discrimination enactments,[614] and the observations there apply. The expression 'physical feature' is also widely defined as including: **6.203**

> any of the following (whether permanent or temporary)—
> (a) any feature arising from the design or construction of a building of the premises,
> (b) any feature on the premises of any approach to, exit from or access to such a building,
> (c) any fixtures, fittings, furnishings, furniture, equipment or material in or on the premises,
> (d) any other physical element or quality of any land comprised in the premises.[615]

Physical features will include steps, stairways, kerbs, exterior surfaces and paving, parking areas, building entrances and exits (including emergency escape routes), internal and external doors, gates, toilets and washing facilities, lighting and ventilation, lifts and escalators, floor coverings, signs, furniture, and temporary or moveable items, amongst other things.[616]

The duty to make adjustments arises only where a provision, criterion, or practice applied by or on behalf of an employer, or any physical feature of premises **6.204**

of the Transfer of Undertakings (Protection of Employment) Regulations 2006 SI 2006/246. If a transferee were to evade the reach of the DDA by arguing that they did not have relevant knowledge, when such knowledge was available to the transferor, arguably regulation 4(2) (transferors' duties and liabilities shall be transferred to the transferee) would not be given full effect.

611 *Ridout v TC Group* [1998] IRLR 628 suggests this sets a low threshold for an employer but the accuracy of that must be doubted in the light of the more onerous obligations required by the Framework Directive, as discussed above.

612 *Wright v (1) The Governors of Bilton High School (2) Warwickshire County Council* [2002] ICR 1643 and see *British Gas Services Limited v McCaull* [2001] IRLR 60. The fact that it as an objective test means that a duty does not arise where someone is perceived to have a particular disability which they do not, as matters transpire, in fact have so that they are not actually placed at a substantial disadvantage: *Copal Castings v Hinton* [2005] UK EAT/0903/04.

613 DDA, s 18D(2) defines 'provision, criterion or practice' as *including* 'any arrangements'.

614 See para 6.120 above.

615 DDA, s 18D(2).

616 'Code of Practice, Employment and Occupation' (2004) DRC, para 5.10.

occupied by the employer, in fact places a particular disabled person at a substantial disadvantage compared with people who are not disabled. A 'substantial disadvantage' must, therefore, be shown in the particular case. 'Substantial' means more than 'minor' or 'trivial'.[617] It is not necessary for a disabled person to point to an actual non-disabled person who is not placed at a substantial disadvantage by reason of the particular provision, criterion, or practice, or physical feature of the premises, and indeed the fact that such would not substantially disadvantage another disabled person or, conversely, would substantially disadvantage other non-disabled persons is irrelevant.[618]

(c) Discharging the duty

6.205 Section 18B of the DDA sets out a number of non-exhaustive factors to be had regard to in determining whether it is reasonable for a person to have to take a particular step in order to comply with a duty to make reasonable adjustments.[619] These factors are:

- the extent to which taking the step would prevent the effect in relation to which the duty is imposed;
- the extent to which it is practicable for him to take the step;
- the financial and other costs which would be incurred by him in taking the step and the extent to which taking it would disrupt any of his activities;
- the extent of his financial and other resources;[620]
- the availability to him of financial or other assistance with respect to taking the step;
- the nature of his activities and the size of his undertaking;
- where the step would be taken in relation to a private household, the extent to which taking it would
  - (i) disrupt that household, or
  - (ii) disturb any person residing there.[621]

Section 18B also gives examples of the steps which a person might need to take in relation to a disabled person in order to comply with a duty to make reasonable

[617] 'Code of Practice: Employment and Occupation' (2004) DRC, para 5.11 and see *H J Heinz Co Limited v Kenrick* [2000] IRLR 144, para 20. (Note the concepts of 'arrangements' has been given a very wide meaning: *Archibald v Fife Council* [2004] UK HL 32; [2004] ICR 954; [2004] IRLR 651).

[618] *Smith v Churchills Stair Lifts PLC* [2006] IRLR 41.

[619] In determining whether or not an employer has discharged the duty upon him the proper approach to addressing the questions that arise was addressed in the case of *Morse v Wiltshire County Council* [1998] ICR 1023; [1998] IRLR 352.

[620] For this reason the identity of the true employer must be properly and carefully established: *Murphy v Slough Borough Council* [2005] ICR 721.

[621] DDA, s 18B(1). Importantly, the duties are imposed on the *employer*. The fact that an employee cannot identify a reasonable adjustment is not sufficient by itself to discharge the duty upon the employer: *Cosgrove v Caesar and Howie* [2001] IRLR 653, though the fact that a disabled person has in fact suggested an adjustment will be material to the question whether the employer has taken such steps as are reasonable.

adjustments. These include[622] making adjustments to premises, allocating some of the disabled person's duties to another person, transferring him to fill an existing vacancy, altering his hours of working or training, providing a reader or interpreter.

Many adjustments will involve little or no cost or disruption to an employer at all, and in such circumstances it is likely that it will be reasonable for an employer to have to make them.[623] However, the obligation to make reasonable adjustments goes further than that. The obligations are compelling and may require an employer to incur costs, make substantial changes to the work or workplace of an employee, make changes to job descriptions, recruitment arrangements, and disciplinary and dismissal arrangements,[624] and make adjustments to pay or pay schemes.[625] The duties may extend to transferring an employee to another post at a higher grade or level of pay without a competitive interview if that would remove the disadvantage the disabled person would otherwise face,[626] and, in appropriate cases, creating a new post in substitution for an existing post.[627] **6.206**

There is some case law indicating that the obligations concern only matters related to the job in which any disabled employee is, might be, or has been employed, so that it does not extend to extraneous matters such as the provision of carers to attend to personal needs, for example assistance in going to the toilet.[628] However, since the amendments made to give effect to the Framework Directive the position may be otherwise,[629] and, in any event, an employer might still be obliged to make adjustments to accommodate the presence of a personal carer provided by the disabled employee herself.[630] The cases suggesting that the duties extend only to 'job related' matters[631] were decided under the unamended DDA which contained more limited reasonable adjustment duties.[632] In particular the duties applied only to 'arrangements for determining to whom employment should be offered' and 'any term, condition or arrangements on which employment, promotion, a transfer, training or any other benefit is offered **6.207**

622 They are not set out in full here but are listed under DDA, s 18B(2).

623 'Code of Practice: Employment and Occupation' (2004), para 5.25.

624 *Cosgrove v Caesar and Howie* [2001] IRLR 653; *Fu v London Borough of Camden* [2001] IRLR 186; *Nottinghamshire County Council v Meikle* [2004] EWCA Civ 859, [2004] IRLR 703; *Beart v HM Prison Service* [2003] EWCA Civ 119, [2003] ICR 1068, [2003] IRLR 238.

625 *London Clubs Management v Hood* [2001] IRLR 719; *Nottinghamshire County Council v Meikle* [2004] EWCA Civ 859, [2004] IRLR 703.

626 *Archibald v Fife Council* [2004] UK HL 32; [2004] ICR 954; [2004] IRLR 651.

627 *Southampton City College v Randall* [2006] 18.

628 *Kenny v Hampshire Constabulary* [1999] ICR 27; [1999] IRLR 76.

629 Disability Discrimination Act 1995 (Amendment) Regulations 2003 SI 2003/1673.

630 *Kenny v Hampshire Constabulary* [1999] ICR 27; [1999] IRLR 76.

631 Ibid.

632 S 6(1) and (2) of the unamended DDA.

or afforded'. Having regard to the overall phraseology therein, the duties appeared to apply to matters closely connected to the performance of the job itself or benefits incidental to the job (for example, pay), and that appears to be the view taken by the courts in some cases.[633] Those limitations have now gone and the duty applies across all the unlawful acts provided for under the employment provisions of the DDA, which include a prohibition on subjecting an employee to a 'detriment'.[634] 'Detriment' in the context of the main anti-discrimination enactments has been given a very wide meaning indeed.[635] Accordingly, the question whether a reasonable adjustment duty might extend now to the provision of a carer is less clear, and it is certainly arguable that the same may be required where such constitutes a reasonable step in order to prevent any arrangement or otherwise substantially disadvantaging a disabled person.

6.208 The duties to make adjustments do not require that a particular step should prevent the effect in question. Instead, in determining whether it is reasonable to take the step, an employer is bound to consider the extent to which the step would prevent the effect in question. However, there will often be steps which, ahead of their being taken, cannot be guaranteed to succeed 'but that, of itself, is no reason to absolve the employer to take it or is such, without more, to deny the appellation "reasonable"'.[636]

6.209 The extent to which the duties to make adjustments may encompass a duty in all cases to make an assessment of what adjustments may be necessary is controversial. As mentioned, the test for determining whether a duty to take particular steps arises is an objective one.[637] This means that the question whether or not an employer has discharged the duty placed upon him by taking such steps as it is reasonable for him to have to take is a matter for the court or tribunal to determine on the particular facts. The fact that an employer may not have known that a particular step was reasonable, or indeed that it went towards discharging the duty placed upon him by the reasonable adjustments duty, is nothing to the point. An employer who fails to undertake an assessment but nevertheless takes such steps as are reasonable will have discharged the duty upon him. Conversely, an employer who undertakes an assessment but, because the assessment is flawed or fails to have regard to some material fact or another, fails to take such steps as are reasonable, does not discharge the duty merely because he has

633 *Kenny v Hampshire Constabulary* [1999] IRLR 76.

634 DDA, s 4(2)(d).

635 See Chaps 8 and 10.

636 *Beart v HM Prison Service* (2002) EAT/650/01, this case went to the Court of Appeal but the guidance of the Employment Appeal Tribunal was undisturbed: [2003] EWCA Civ 119; [2003] ICR 1068; [2003] IRLR 238.

637 *Smith v Churchills Stair Lifts PLC* [2006] IRLR 41; *British Gas Services Limited v McCaull* [2001] IRLR 60.

done the assessment. This has led the Employment Appeal Tribunal to doubt the correctness of those decisions which suggest that a duty to make an assessment is implicit in the reasonable adjustments duties.[638] In *Mid Staffordshire General Hospitals NHS Trust v Cambridge*[639] the Employment Appeal Tribunal concluded that a duty to undertake an assessment is implicit in the reasonable adjustment duties. Its reasoning, however, lends itself to criticism. According to the Employment Appeal Tribunal:

> [t]here must be many cases in which the disabled person has been placed at a substantial disadvantage in the workplace, but in which the employer does not know what it ought to do to ameliorate that disadvantage without making enquiries. To say that a failure to make those inquiries would not amount to a breach of the duty . . . would render [the duty] practicably unworkable in many cases. We do not believe that that could have been Parliament's intention . . . A proper assessment of what is required to eliminate the disabled persons disadvantage is therefore a necessary part of the duty imposed . . . since that duty cannot be complied with unless the employer makes a proper assessment of what needs to be done.[640]

This reveals a misunderstanding about the nature of the reasonable adjustment duties and, more particularly, how compliance is to be determined. As mentioned, compliance with a duty to make reasonable adjustments is determined objectively. An employer may have adequate information to discharge a duty but fail to do so and he may have inadequate information to discharge the duty but, fortuitously, he may discharge the duty nonetheless. In either case the question whether he had made an assessment and obtained the necessary information does not by itself answer the question whether he has discharged the duty. The *Mid Staffordshire* case can therefore be regarded as incorrect to the extent that it holds that as a matter of law a requirement to undertake an assessment is implicit in the reasonable adjustments duties. The Code of Practice: Employment and Occupation[641] also indicates that an assessment might be required as part of the duty to make adjustments itself.[642] However, as has been observed, the Code of Practice was issued after the judgment in the *Mid Staffordshire* case was handed down and the likelihood is that it was influenced by it.[643] More particularly, the Code of Practice, apparently unlike the decision in the *Mid Staffordshire* case, does not assert that in all cases, as a matter of law, an obligation to undertake an assessment is required by the duties to make reasonable adjustments. Nevertheless the proposition of law established in *Mid Staffordshire* presently remains undisturbed,

638 See discussion in *Tarbuck v Sainsbury Supermarkets Limited* [2006] UK EAT/0136/06/LA.
639 [2003] IRLR 566.
640 Ibid, para 17.
641 (2004) DRC.
642 Ibid, para 5.20.
643 *Tarbuck v Sainsbury Supermarkets Limited* [2006] UK EAT/0136/06, para 74.

though its correctness has been doubted in powerful *obiter dicta* from another division of the Employment Appeal Tribunal.[644]

(d) Other workers, trade organizations, and qualifications bodies

6.210 Part 2 of the DDA outlaws discrimination against contract workers, office holders, partnerships, barristers and advocates, disabled persons undergoing work experience, and council members,[645] and outlaws discrimination by trade organizations and qualifications bodies.[646] The duties to make reasonable adjustments are defined in materially the same way for the purposes of these provisions as in relation to employment (paragraph 6.198 above). There are some modifications.

6.211 The duty to make adjustments, in respect of contract workers, is imposed upon both principal and employer.[647] In the case of employers, the duty arises where 'by virtue of a provision, criterion or practice applied by or on behalf of all or most of the principals' to whom a disabled contract worker 'is or might be supplied, or a physical feature of premises occupied by such persons, he is likely, on each occasion when he is supplied to a principal to do contract work, to be placed at a substantial disadvantage in comparison with persons who are not disabled which is the same or similar in each case'.[648] In such circumstances, the employer is bound to take such steps as he would have to take if the provision, criterion, or practice were applied by him or on his behalf, or, as the case may be, if the premises were occupied by him.[649] In the case of principals, the duties arise in precisely the same circumstances as in the context of employment, and as if the principal and contract worker were employer and employee (or prospective employer and employee).[650] Given that the test is always reasonableness, the length of any contract and the notice before its commencement might be relevant to the extent of the steps required by a duty.[651] Exceptionally, a principal is not required to take a step in relation to a disabled contract worker if the disabled contract worker's employer is required to take the step in relation to him.[652]

6.212 As to office holders, again the duty to make adjustments is defined in materially the same way as under the employment provisions.[653] The 'disabled person concerned', that is the person to whom the duty is owed, is defined to materially the

644 Ibid, paras 65–74.
645 From 4 December 2006.
646 DDA, Part 2.
647 Ibid, ss 4A and 4B.
648 Ibid, s 4B(4).
649 Ibid, s 4B(5).
650 Ibid, s 4B(6).
651 'Code of Practice: Employment and Occupation' (2004) DRC, para 9.8–9.9.
652 DDA, s 4B(7).
653 Ibid, s 4E.

same effect with appropriate modifications.[654] In addition, the 'relevant person', that being the person owing the duty (normally the person with power to make the appointment), is defined.[655] A duty arises in respect of any physical feature of premises only where they are under the control of the relevant person, and the functions of an office or post are performed from those premises.[656]

In relation to firms, the duty to make adjustments is owed to disabled partners, or prospective partners, and again it is defined in materially the same way as under the employment provisions described above (paragraph 6.198).[657] As to the expenses incurred by a firm in making any adjustments, the cost of taking those steps is to be treated as being an expense of the firm,[658] and where the disabled person concerned is or becomes a partner, his contribution to that cost is not to exceed an amount that is reasonable having regard in particular to the proportion in which he is entitled to share in the firm's profits.[659] Accordingly the greater any disparity between the percentage profit share and contribution to costs (where they exceed the percentage profit share) the less likely that the contribution requirement will be reasonable. **6.213**

The duty to make reasonable adjustments also applies to barristers, barristers' clerks, and advocates (in Scotland).[660] Again the duty to make adjustments is defined in materially the same way as under the employment provisions, save that in Scotland the duty is not owed to advocates, reflecting the difference in practice arrangements.[661] **6.214**

Duties to make reasonable adjustments may arise in relation to disabled people seeking or undertaking a work placement.[662] The duties are again defined in materially the same way, and they are owed by the placement provider,[663] that is, the person providing the work placement.[664] As with contract workers, the length of any placement is likely to be relevant to the reasonableness of any particular step. However, in the context of work placements, special regard must be paid to the fact that some students undertaking work placements may be able to fund their own adjustments out of the Disabled Student's Allowance.[665] In addition, **6.215**

---

654 Ibid, s 4E(2).
655 Ibid, s 4E(1) read with s 4F(2).
656 Ibid, s 4E(1)(b).
657 Ibid, s 6B(1).
658 Ibid, s 6B(4).
659 Ibid, s 6B(4).
660 Ibid, ss 7B(1) and 7D(1). In this context, the person to whom the duty is owed may be a tenant, pupil, or an applicant for pupillage or tenancy; DDA, ss 7B(b) and 7D(2).
661 Ibid, ss 7B(1) and 7(d)(1).
662 Ibid, s 14D.
663 Ibid, s 14D(1).
664 Ibid, s 14C(4), that being a person who provides a work placement to a person whom he does not employ.
665 'Code of Practice: Employment and Occupation' (2004), para 9.48.

some disabled people may have their own equipment that they are prepared to use in the workplace, and in such cases the placement provider may have to make reasonable adjustments in order to facilitate the use of that equipment (for example, by ensuring that it is transported and stored safely and adequately, and insured whilst in the workplace).[666]

6.216 The DDA also imposes duties upon trade organizations and qualifications bodies.[667] The duties to make adjustments are expressed in the same way as under the employment provisions,[668] with a difference relating to qualifications bodies described below.

6.217 As with the duties to make reasonable adjustments imposed upon employers, there are no duties imposed on those others falling within the scope of Part 2, just described,[669] where the person owing the duty does not know and could not reasonably be expected to know, in the case of an applicant or potential applicant, that the disabled person concerned is or may be an applicant, or in any case that the disabled person has a disability and is likely to be affected in a way that would otherwise trigger the duty.[670] Similarly, a failure to comply with a duty to make reasonable adjustments cannot be justified by any of the persons owing the duty. Further as mentioned above, where a person is subject to a duty to make reasonable adjustments he cannot justify disability-related discrimination unless he can show that the treatment of the disabled person would have been justified even if he had complied with that duty.[671]

6.218 In relation to qualifications bodies, a discrete exception is made in relation to the duty to make adjustments. The duties do not arise in relation to a 'competence standard',[672] the meaning of which is given above (paragraph 6.159).[673] It is critical to identify whether a particular measure constitutes a 'competence standard', therefore, because it will determine whether a duty to make adjustments arises at all.[674] Competence standards concern those measures used for determining whether or not a person has a particular level of competence or ability, for example a certain standard of eyesight for a pilot's qualification.[675]

---

666 Ibid.

667 See Chap 8 for their meaning.

668 DDA, s 14(1). The duty was modified by the Disability Discrimination Act 1995 (Amendment) Regulations 2003 SI 2003/1673 which extended the duty so that it now covers 'physical features'.

669 Contract workers, partners, office holders etc, see para 6.210.

670 DDA, ss 4B(6), 4E(2), 6B(3), 7B(4), 7D(3), 14B(3), and 14D(3).

671 DDA, s 3(A)(6). This is discussed at para 6.156 above.

672 Ibid, s 14B(1) read with s 14A(5).

673 Ibid, s 14A(5).

674 As well as affecting the defence of justification that may arise in relation to disability-related discrimination, see para 6.159 above.

675 'Code of Practice: Trade Organisations and Qualifications Bodies' (2004) DRC ISBN 0117034185 (Disability Discrimination Codes of Practice (Employment and Occupation, and Trade Organisations and Qualifications Bodies) Appointed Day Order 2004, SI 2004/2302), para 8.72.

On the other hand, mere experience in particular work is unlikely to constitute a competence standard if it does not determine by itself a particular level of competence or ability.[676] In general terms, there is also a difference between a competence standard and the process by which attainment of that standard is determined. For example, the passing of an examination may not involve a competence standard or impose one, whilst the knowledge necessary to pass it may constitute a competence standard.[677] There will be occasions where the process of assessing whether a competence standard has been achieved is inextricably linked to the standard itself so that the ability to take the test may itself amount to a competence standard.[678]

(e) Justification

In relation to discrimination falling within the employment and related fields in the DDA there is no defence of justification available to a failure to comply with the duty to make reasonable adjustments. **6.219**

(2) **Goods, facilities, services, and clubs**

The duties to make reasonable adjustments in the context of goods, facilities, and services,[679] and clubs[680] reflect a substantive and proactive concept of equality. As mentioned, they are anticipatory in nature and so do not require that a specific disabled person is disadvantaged before they are triggered. Though the duties in the original enactment of the DDA were wide and progressive, they were not fully brought into force until 1 October 2004, the long lead-in time reflecting the expectation that their impact would be very significant indeed.[681] **6.220**

Section 21 of the DDA now provides that, firstly, where a provider of services has a practice, policy, or procedure which makes it impossible or unreasonably difficult for disabled people to make use of a service which he provides, or is prepared to provide to other members of the public, it is his duty to take such steps as it is reasonable, in all the circumstances of the case, for him to have to take in order to change that practice, policy, or procedure so that it no longer has that effect.[682] Secondly, where a physical feature[683] makes it impossible or unreasonably difficult for disabled people to make use of such a service, it is the duty of the **6.221**

676 Ibid, para 8.29.
677 Ibid, para 8.30.
678 Ibid, para 8.31.
679 DDA, ss 19(1)(b) and 21(1), (2), (4).
680 Ibid, s 21G(6) and Discrimination (Private Clubs etc) Regulations 2005 SI 2005/3258, regulations 6 to 9.
681 K Monaghan, *Blackstone's Guide to the Disability Discrimination Legislation* (2005) OUP, 159–60.
682 Ibid, s 21(1).
683 For example, one arising from the design or construction of a building or the approach or access to premises, DDA, s 21(2).

provider of that service to take such steps as it is reasonable, in all the circumstances of the case, for him to have to take in order to (a) remove the feature; (b) alter it so that it no longer has that effect; (c) provide a reasonable means of avoiding the feature; or (d) provide a reasonable alternative method of making the service in question available to disabled people.[684] Thirdly, where an auxiliary aid or service (for example, the provision of information on audio tape or of a sign language interpreter) would (a) enable disabled people to make use of a service which a provider of services provides, or is prepared to provide, to members of the public, or (b) facilitate the use by disabled people of such a service, it is the duty of the provider of that service to take such steps as it is reasonable, in all the circumstances of the case, for him to have to take in order to provide that auxiliary aid or service.[685] The duty to make adjustments therefore comprises a series of duties falling into three groups: modifying practices, policies, and procedures; addressing physical features; and providing auxiliary aids and services. Regulations made under section 21H of the DDA make broadly the same provision in relation to private members' clubs,[686] in respect of disabled members, associates, and guests (and benefits, facilities, or services provided and membership rights), and disabled people who might wish to become members or associates, or who are likely to become guests,[687] and the observations below in relation to services apply equally to clubs.

6.222 The duties do not generally extend to making alterations to or the removal of a physical feature of a vehicle used in providing a service; nor do they impose any obligation on a service provider to take steps which would affect whether vehicles are provided in the course of the service or what vehicles are provided, or, where a vehicle is provided in the course of the service, affect what happens in the vehicle while someone is travelling in it.[688] However, specific exemptions are made to this general exclusion so that certain of the duties will apply to prescribed modes of transport. The duties to change a practice, policy, or procedure and provide auxiliary aids[689] as described above will apply to those vehicles exempted from the exclusion, namely certain hire vehicles; private hire vehicles; public service vehicles; rail vehicles; taxis; and vehicles deployed by a breakdown

---

684 DDA, s 21(2).

685 Ibid, s 21(4).

686 The duties are in force from 4 Dec 2006.

687 DDA, s 21H and Discrimination (Private Clubs etc) Regulations 2005 SI 2005/3258, regulations 6 to 9.

688 DDA, s 21ZA.

689 By the Regulations, certain matters are treated as not being auxiliary aids for these purposes, namely, devices, structures, or equipment the installation, operation, or maintenance of which would necessitate making a permanent alteration to or which would have a permanent effect on either the internal or external physical fabric of a vehicle: Regulation 7, Disability Discrimination (Transport Vehicles) Regulations 2005 SI 2005/3190.

or recovery operator.[690] However, the duties to adjust physical features do not arise in relation to the provision or use of a vehicle, with two exceptions. In the case of certain rental vehicles, the full duties in respect of physical features described above apply. In the case of breakdown recovery vehicles, the duty applies only in part, in that the duty to overcome a physical feature extends only to providing a reasonable alternative method of making the service available, as described above.[691] In the case of certain rental vehicles, only certain features are to be treated as physical features, particularly any part of the vehicle that requires alteration in order to make provision for hand controls (except fixed seating and in-built electrical systems) to enable a disabled person to operate braking and accelerator systems for the vehicle, and facilities for stowing a wheelchair (except fixed seating), whether the alterations required are temporary or permanent.[692]

The reasonable adjustment duties applicable to service providers are owed to disabled people at large, unlike the individually owed duties arising in the employment and related fields. The duties arise where the mere existence of a practice, policy, or procedure, or physical feature makes it impossible or unreasonably difficult for disabled people to make use of the service provided by the service provider. Accordingly, they are duties owed to all disabled people, children and adults, and they do not require the existence or presence of a specific disabled person seeking to trigger their invocation. As mentioned, the duties are instead *anticipatory* in nature. The duties, then, require service providers to plan in advance to ensure that their services are reasonably accessible to disabled customers.[693] In addition, the duties create a continuing obligation so that adjustments made will not discharge them once and for all. Instead, compliance must be kept under continuing review.[694] **6.223**

In determining whether or not services are *unreasonably difficult* for disabled people to use so as to trigger the duties, service providers should take account of whether the difficulties would be considered unreasonable by other people if they had to endure them, having regard, in particular, to factors such as time, inconvenience, effort, discomfort, anxiety, or loss of dignity.[695] **6.224**

690 Disability Discrimination (Transport Vehicles) Regulations 2005 SI 2005/3190, regulation 3 (all these expressions are defined by regulation 2). See Chap 10.

691 Disability Discrimination (Transport Vehicles) Regulations 2005 SI 2005/3190, regulation 3 (all these expressions are defined by regulation 2). See Chap 10.

692 Disability Discrimination (Transport Vehicles) Regulations 2005 SI 2005/3190, regulation 8. See too, 'Code of Practice: Provision and Use of Transport Vehicles' (Disability Discrimination Code of Practice (Supplement to Part 3 Code of Practice) (Provision and Use of Transport Vehicles) (Appointed Day) Order 2006 No 1094), para 6.35.

693 'Code of Practice—Rights of Access: Services, Private Clubs and Premises' (2006) DRC (Disability Discrimination Code of Practice (Services, Public Functions, Private Clubs and Premises) (Appointed Day) Order 2006 SI 2006/1967, para 6.16.

694 Ibid, para 6.22–3.

695 Ibid, para 6.36.

(a) Practices, policies, procedure, physical features, and auxiliary aids

6.225 As can be seen, the duty to make reasonable adjustments extends to any *practice, policy, or procedure* which makes it impossible or unreasonably difficult for disabled persons to make use of a service provided to other members of the public.[696] These words are not further defined under the goods, facilities, and services provisions, but in other parts of the DDA the same words include any *provision or criterion*[697] and these include *any arrangements*.[698] It is likely therefore that these words will be given a wide reach. The expressions are apparently intended to cover what a service provider actually does (its practices), what a service provider intends to do (its policy), and how a service provider plans to go about it (its procedures).[699]

6.226 The duty to address the impact of *physical features* will apply to any feature arising from the design or construction of a building on the premises occupied by the provider of services; any feature on the premises occupied by the provider of services of any approach to, exit from, or access to such a building; any fixtures, fittings, furnishings, furniture, equipment, or materials in or on the premises occupied by the provider of services; any fixtures, fittings, furnishings, furniture, equipment, or materials brought onto premises (other than those occupied by the provider of services) by or on behalf of the provider of services in the course of providing services to the public or to a section of the public and for the purpose of providing such services; and any other physical element or quality of any land comprised in the premises occupied by the provider of services.[700] The observations made above apply equally (paragraph 6.203).[701] Physical features may include the sheer proportions (size or sizes) of premises. They may be inside or outside a service provider's building but, so long as they are within the boundaries of a service provider's premises, the duty to make adjustments (where such physical features make it impossible or unreasonably difficult for disabled people to use the service) will apply.

6.227 As to *auxiliary aids*, the DDA gives two examples of auxiliary aids or services, namely the provision of information on audio tape and the provision of sign language interpreters.[702] The expressions 'auxiliary aids' and 'services' extend to aids

---

696 DDA, s 21(1).

697 Ibid, s 21A(6).

698 Ibid, ss 4A and S 18D.

699 'Code of Practice—Rights of Access: Services, Private Clubs and Premises' (2006) DRC, para 7.7.

700 Disability Discrimination (Service Providers and Public Authorities Carrying Out Functions) Regulations 2005 SI 2005/2901, regulation 9; Discrimination (Private Clubs etc) Regulations 2005 SI 2005/3258, regulation 10.

701 See too, 'Code of Practice—Rights of Access: Services, Private Clubs and Premises' (2006) DRC, para 7.45.

702 DDA, s 21(4).

other than those relating to communication, for example to viewing platforms[703] or a temporary ramp, amongst other things. An auxiliary aid or service may be temporary or permanent and, accordingly, auxiliary aids might necessitate permanent alterations to the fabric of a building or its furnishings as with, for example, an induction loop. Whilst the expressions suggest equipment of one sort or another, they extend also to services, such as assistance to disabled customers.[704]

(b) Discharging the duty

The duties require service providers to take such steps as it is reasonable, in all the circumstances of the case, for them to have to take in order to achieve the result required by the three duties described above. No guidance in the DDA is given as to the steps which might be reasonable.[705] What is a *reasonable step* will depend on all the circumstances of the case and will vary according to the type of service being provided, the nature of the service provider and its size and resources, and the effect of the disability on the individual disabled person.[706] The factors are likely to include (amongst others): the extent to which it is practicable for the service provider to take the step; the financial and other costs of making the adjustment; the extent of any disruption which taking the step would cause; the amount of any resources already spent on making adjustments and the availability of financial or other assistance.[707] As discussed above, the policy of the DDA is one of inclusiveness. Any adjustment should strive to accommodate disabled people in the same way as non-disabled people. Differently provided services are unlikely to meet the requirements of the duties, unless achieving complete equivalence would not meet the needs of disabled people or would not be reasonable for other identifiable reasons. In addition, the purpose of taking a particular step is to ensure that the barrier in question no longer has the effect of making it impossible or unreasonably difficult for disabled people to use the service, and whether a step will be considered a *reasonable* step will be measured against that benchmark in the first instance. The same applies to an auxiliary aid. If any step taken to discharge the duty in relation to auxiliary aids would not enable disabled people to make use of any service or facilitate their use, it is unlikely to be reasonable. **6.228**

In relation to the *physical features* of premises, the DDA anticipates different ways of addressing accessibility, that is by the removing of the feature, altering it, **6.229**

703 *Baggley v Kingston upon Hull CC* [2002] (Case No KH101929), in which the court accepted that the provision of a viewing platform was capable of amounting to an auxiliary aid or service, although on the facts of the case no breach of the duty was made out.

704 'Code of Practice—Rights of Access: Services, Private Clubs and Premises' (2006) DRC, para 7.14.

705 Cf the position in the employment and related fields, see para 6.205 above. It is likely that some of those factors will be relevant outside the employment field.

706 'Code of Practice—Rights of Access: Services, Private Clubs and Premises' (2006) DRC, para 6.24.

707 Ibid, para 6.25.

providing a reasonable means of avoiding the feature, or by providing a reasonable alternative method of making the service in question available to disabled people.[708] The DDA does not explicitly create any hierarchy insofar as the alternatives described are concerned. The focus instead is on results: that is, on achieving the aim of ensuring that the services are accessible to disabled people, rather than how that aim is achieved. However, accommodating difference on approximate terms promotes equality and respect for the dignity of disabled customers. Given that the objective of the DDA is to secure equality and promote inclusiveness, as reflected in the reasonable adjustments duties, it is likely that in the first instance removing or altering a barrier will be regarded as a reasonable step, and only where such is unreasonable for identifiable reasons will it then be reasonable to consider alternative means of providing the service to disabled people.[709]

(c) *Justification*

6.230 Unlike the reasonable adjustments duties in the employment and related fields, a failure to comply with the duty to make adjustments can be legally justified. Justification is defined in broadly the same way as is applicable to disability-related discrimination.[710] However, where there has been a failure to comply with a duty to make reasonable adjustments, the only two conditions applicable are the first two, namely that the treatment is necessary in order not to endanger the health and safety of any person (which may include that of the disabled person), and that the disabled person is incapable of entering into an enforceable agreement, or of giving an informed consent, and for that reason the treatment is reasonable in that case.[711]

6.231 The cost of making a reasonable adjustment must not be passed on to disabled customers in particular. The costs of providing reasonable adjustments must be treated as part of the general expenses of any business, and any difference in charges or cost in the provision of services to disabled persons will not be justified by the making of a reasonable adjustment.[712]

(3) Employment services

6.232 Discrimination by those providing employment services[713] is regulated in Part 3 of the DDA, alongside provision addressing discrimination by providers of

---

708 DDA, s 21(2).

709 'Code of Practice—Rights of Access: Services, Private Clubs and Premises' (2006) DRC, paras 7.34–38.

710 Para 6.160.

711 DDA, s 20(4) read with s 19(1). As to the second condition this is limited as described in n 504 above. Note the limitation on the justification defence for reasonable adjustments is identical in relation to clubs, see DDA, s 21G(3)(a)–(b) read with s 21F.

712 DDA, ss 20(5) and 21G(4).

713 Defined by DDA, s 21A(1).

goods, facilities, and services. However, the concepts of discrimination adopted match closely those provided for in the employment field, and, in particular, the duties to make reasonable adjustments largely reflect those found in the employment provisions.[714] The duties cover practices, policies, and procedures, and they are triggered where disabled people are placed at a substantial disadvantage in comparison with people who are not disabled.[715] A 'practice, policy or procedure' includes a 'provision or criterion', so bringing the breadth of the duty expressly in line with the employment provisions.[716] Where a provider of such services fails to comply with the duty to make reasonable adjustments to a practice, policy, or procedure, this cannot be justified.[717]

Importantly, however, the duties to make reasonable adjustments are anticipatory in nature so that they are owed to disabled people at large. They do not require the identification of a specifically disadvantaged disabled person for the duties to be triggered, and in this respect they differ from the duties found in the employment field and instead reflect those found in the goods, facilities, and services provisions. Accordingly the observations at paragraph 6.220 above apply. **6.233**

(4) Premises

Until the enactment of the DDA 2005, there was no obligation arising under the DDA to make adjustments under the provisions addressing discrimination in the disposal and management of premises. However, the position has now changed. In relation to the disposal and management of premises,[718] a person who lets or manages premises[719] may now fall under a duty to make reasonable adjustments. **6.234**

The duties applicable to the disposal and management of premises are more limited than those found in the provisions addressing goods, facilities, services, and clubs. The duties comprise a series of obligations relating to the provision of auxiliary aids and services, the changing of practices, policies, and procedures, and the changing of a term of the letting.[720] Importantly, the duties do not require that any steps are taken which would consist of or include the removal or alteration of a physical feature.[721] 'Physical features' comprise any feature arising from the design or construction of the premises; any feature or any approach to, exit from, **6.235**

714 See para 6.198 above.

715 DDA, s 21A(4), inserting s 19(1)(aa), where the complaint relates to employment services, and DDA, s 21A(6).

716 DDA, s 21A(6). As to the meaning of these expressions, see para 6.200 above.

717 DDA, s 21A(5) read with ss 20(1) and (2) and 21. The same does not apply to physical features or auxiliary aids, DDA, s 21A(5).

718 The unlawful acts in respect of which are defined at Chap 10.

719 DDA, s 24A(3).

720 Ibid, ss 24C and 24D. In the latter case only in relation to premises that are let; DDA, s 24D(b).

721 Ibid, ss 24E(1), 24J(5).

or access to the premises; any fixtures in or on the premises; and any other physical element or quality of any land comprised in the premises. Any furniture, furnishings, materials, equipment, or other chattels in or on the premises are not to be treated as physical features.[722] The replacement or provision of any signs or notices, the replacement of any taps or door handles, the replacement, provision, or adaptation of any doorbell, or door entry system, or changes to the colour of any surface (such as, for example, a wall or door) are not to be treated as alterations to physical features for these purposes.[723]

6.236 There is a small dwellings exception so that the duties to make reasonable adjustments do not apply to small dwellings.[724] In addition, the reasonable adjustment duties do not apply if the premises are or have been the principal home or only home of the individual who is letting or seeks to let the premises (or is a near relative of such person) save where, since entering into the letting, a professional manager has been used to manage the premises, or, in the case of premises to let, an estate agent has been used to let the premises.[725]

6.237 In addition to the duties themselves, it is unlawful for a controller of let premises to discriminate against a person to whom the premises are let because of costs incurred in connection with taking steps to avoid liability under the reasonable adjustments duties, whether in respect of the tenant or a lawful occupier under the tenancy (a child or partner, for example).[726]

6.238 The duties to make adjustments are directed at specific disabled people, namely a person to whom the premises have been let or who is lawfully living with the person to whom the premises are let, such as a disabled child or partner,[727] or, in relation to premises to let, a person who is considering taking a letting of the premises.[728] The duties only arise at all if the person who lets or manages the premises is requested to make an adjustment by the person to whom the duty is owed, or a person on their behalf.[729]

6.239 The 'premises' provisions of the DDA do not define what constitutes a reasonable step for the purposes of discharging a duty to make adjustments, but the factors described above[730] are likely to be material.[731]

---

722 Disability Discrimination (Premises) Regulations 2006 SI 2006/887, Regulation 4.

723 Ibid.

724 Defined in DDA, s 23(2), see s 24B(3).

725 DDA, s 24B(1).

726 Ibid, s 24F.

727 Ibid, s 24E(3).

728 Ibid, s 24J(6).

729 Ibid, ss 24C(1), 24D(2)(b), 24J(1)(a)–(b), 24J(3)(c)–(d), and 24J(6).

730 Para 6.205.

731 Guidance is also given in the 'Code of Practice—Rights of Access: Services to the Public, Public Authority Functions, Private Clubs and Premises' (2006) DRC, para 15.46.

As to the provision of auxiliary aids or services, as mentioned above, the provision of certain aids or services is not to be regarded as alterations to physical features, and so will be regarded as auxiliary aids or services if requested.[732] The obligation to provide an auxiliary aid or service applies only where the auxiliary aid or service would enable, or make it easier for, a disabled person to enjoy the premises or make use of some of any benefit or facility which she is entitled to use, but would be of little or no practical use to her if she were neither the tenant of the premises nor occupying them, *and* it would be impossible or unreasonably difficult for her to enjoy the premises or make use of the benefit or facility if the auxiliary aid or service were not provided.[733] **6.240**

In relation to premises which are to let (the previous conditions applying where they are in fact let), the conditions are that the auxiliary aid or service will enable or make it easier for the disabled person to take a letting of the premises, but would be of little or no practical use to him or her if he or she were not considering taking a letting of the premises; and if the auxiliary aid or service were not provided, it would be impossible or unreasonably difficult for the disabled person to take a letting.[734] Such would apply, for example, to ramps, furnishings, and additional services.[735] **6.241**

The duty to modify practices, policies, and procedures arises where, in relation to let premises, a controller of premises has a practice, policy, or procedure which has the effect of making it impossible or unreasonably difficult for a disabled person to enjoy the premises or to make use of any benefit or facility which she is entitled to use;[736] in relation to premises to let, a controller of premises has a practice, policy, or procedure which makes it impossible or unreasonably difficult for a disabled person to take a letting of the premises;[737] and in either case the practice, policy, or procedure would not have the effect if the relevant disabled person did not have a disability. **6.242**

The duty to change terms applies where a term of a letting makes it impossible or unreasonably difficult for a disabled person to enjoy the premises, or to make use of any benefit or facility which she is entitled to use, and the term would not have that effect if the disabled person did not have a disability.[738] The modification of terms prohibiting the making of alterations or improvements to premises will be **6.243**

[732] Disability Discrimination (Premises) Regulations 2006, SI 2006/887, Regulation 5(1).

[733] DDA, s 24C(1)(c) which requires that either of two conditions are met, those conditions being described by DDA, s 24C(3).

[734] Ibid, s 24J(1)–(2).

[735] 'Code of Practice—Rights of Access: Services to the Public, Public Authority Functions, Private Clubs and Premises' (2006) DRC para 15.35.

[736] DDA, s 24D(1)(a), (2)–(3).

[737] Ibid, s 24J(3)–(4).

[738] Ibid, s 24D(1)(b)–(3).

a reasonable step, and therefore such modifications will have to be made for the purposes of complying with the reasonable adjustments duty, in certain prescribed circumstances.[739] Where the landlord or manager of premises is required herself to obtain the consent of another person to change a term of a letting, provision is made addressing that so that it is reasonable for her to request that consent, but it is not treated as reasonable for her to have to change the term pending consent being obtained.[740] Separate provision is made addressing circumstances where a tenant, in certain circumstances, is entitled under a lease to make improvements to the premises with the consent of the landlord and seeks consent.[741]

6.244 A failure to comply with a duty to make reasonable adjustments is justified only in limited circumstances, being those applicable to a failure to comply with a duty to make adjustments in the context of the provision of goods, facilities, and services.[742]

(5) Commonholds

6.245 Commonholds[743] are treated as premises that are let and a commonhold association is treated as a person who manages the premises. The terms of any commonhold community statement and other applicable terms are treated as terms of a letting. A benefit or facility which a disabled person is entitled to use under a commonhold community statement is treated as a benefit or facility which they are entitled to use under a letting, and a person lawfully occupying a commonhold unit, though not a unit holder or a person occupying the premises under a letting, is treated as a person lawfully occupying the premises under a letting. Accordingly the reasonable adjustments duties applicable in relation to premises apply in relation to commonhold premises in materially the same way.[744]

(6) Public authorities

6.246 As mentioned in Chapter 2, the DDA 2005 introduced provisions outlawing discrimination by public authorities, including by failing to comply with a duty to make adjustments. The duties prescribed are very close in content to those applying to providers of goods, facilities, and services.[745] In general terms,

739 Disability Discrimination (Premises) Regulations 2006 SI 2006/887, regulation 7.

740 Disability Discrimination (Premises) Regulations 2006 SI 2006/887.

741 DDA, s 49G, which applies to those tenants as to which the Housing Act 1980, ss 81–85 and the Housing Act 1985, ss 97–99 do not apply.

742 DDA, s 24K.

743 See Chap 10.

744 DDA, s 24A–F and the Disability Discrimination (Regulations) 2006 SI 2006/887, regulation 9.

745 DDA 2005, ss 21D and 21E. For the position in relation to providers of goods, facilities, and services, see para 6.220 above.

therefore, the observations made above (paragraph 6.220 onwards) apply equally. However, there are some differences.

The duties apply to public authorities in carrying out public functions and the disadvantage caused to disabled people by any practice, policy, or procedure, or physical feature must occur in the context of the carrying out of a function by a public authority.[746] The duties are again owed to disabled people at large,[747] and in broad terms they will be triggered in the same circumstances as described above,[748] and the factors that will be had regard to in determining whether a duty is discharged will apply equally. No specific provision is made prohibiting the passing on of any costs attributable to the making of a reasonable adjustment, but this reflects the fact that, in general, public authorities are prohibited from charging for carrying out their functions unless specifically statutorily authorized.[749] 6.247

The circumstances in which a duty is triggered[750] are differently expressed as compared to the provision made elsewhere in the DDA. This is because, in carrying out public functions, public authorities may be taking negative action in relation to a particular person as well as positive action, by the conferring of a benefit or the provision of a service or otherwise. Reflecting this, the duties to make adjustments are described as triggered where it is impossible or unreasonably difficult for disabled people to receive any benefit that is or may be conferred, or it is *unreasonably adverse* for disabled people to experience being subject to any detriment to which a person is or may be subject.[751] Similarly, the duty in respect of the provision of auxiliary aids or services is triggered where such would enable disabled people to receive, or facilitate the receiving by disabled people of, any benefit that is or may be conferred, or reduce the extent to which it is adverse for disabled people to experience being subjected to any detriment to which a person is or may be subject.[752] The threshold of disadvantage required by the expressions 'unreasonably difficult' and 'unreasonably adverse' are intended to be approximate, and accordingly the observations made under paragraph 6.224 above apply equally. 6.248

A failure to comply with a duty to make reasonable adjustments may be justified on the same grounds as those applicable to a failure by a provider of goods, 6.249

746 DDA, s 21E.

747 Ibid, s 21E.

748 Para 6.220 onwards.

749 'Code of Practice—Rights of Access: services to the public, public authority functions, private clubs and premises' (Revised, 2006) DRC, para 6.31.

750 And indeed liability arises.

751 DDA, s 21E(1), (3).

752 Ibid, s 21E(6).

facilities, and services.[753] In addition, the broader test of justification applicable to disability-related less favourable treatment, as explained in paragraphs 6.172 and 6.174 above, also applies, and the observations made above apply equally.[754] Further, the duty to make reasonable adjustments is not taken to mean that a public authority is required to take any steps which it has no power to make.[755] Otherwise, the provision made in respect of the provision of goods, facilities, and services, and the making of reasonable adjustments apply equally to public authorities in the exercising of public functions.[756]

(7) Schools

6.250 There are limited reasonable adjustment duties imposed on the responsible bodies[757] of schools. In particular, a school must take such steps as it is reasonable for it to take to ensure that, in relation to the *arrangements it makes for determining the admission* of pupils to the school, disabled people are not placed at a substantial disadvantage in comparison with people who are not disabled, and, in relation to *education and associated services* provided for, or offered to, pupils at the school by it, that disabled pupils are not placed at a substantial disadvantage in comparison with pupils who are not disabled.[758] The threshold for triggering the duties is 'substantial disadvantage', and that expression will be given the same meaning as in the reasonable adjustment duties arising in the employment and related fields.[759]

6.251 The duties arising under the schools provisions explicitly do not require a responsible body to remove or alter a physical feature of premises or provide auxiliary aids or services.[760] This is because the 'special educational needs' framework is designed to identify, assess, and make provision for children with special educational needs, and such provision will include, where necessary, educational aids and services.[761] As to what constitutes an auxiliary aid or service, this is

753 Namely, 'health and safety' and 'incapacity to contract': DDA, s 21D(4)(a)(b). See para 6.230 above.

754 Save that the condition 'that treating the disabled person equally would in the particular case involve substantial extra costs and, having regard to resources, the extra costs in that particular case would be too great' (DDA, s 21D(4)(c)) does not apply, but costs will, of course, be material in determining reasonableness for the purposes of discharging the duty.

755 DDA, s 21E(9).

756 Disability Discrimination (Service Providers and Public Authorities Carrying Out Functions) Regulations 2005 SI 2005/2901.

757 See Chap 9.

758 DDA, s 28C(1).

759 See para 6.204.

760 DDA, s 28C(2).

761 Disability Discrimination Act 1995 Part IV, Code of Practice for Schools' (2002), DRC, Disability Discrimination Codes of Practice (Education) (Appointed Day) Order 2002, SI 2002/2216, para 7.7; Part 4 of the Education Act 1996 as amended by the Special Educational Needs and Disability Act 2001.

not uncontroversial. In the context of the provision of goods, facilities, and services, the expressions 'auxiliary aids' and 'services' are given a wide meaning (paragraph 6.227 above). However, if a similar approach were taken to the exclusionary provision applicable to the duties to make reasonable adjustments imposed on schools, such might reduce the impact of the duties in a way which was not intended. It was anticipated that the expressions 'education' and 'associated services' would be given a broad reach so as to cover all aspects of school life.[762] A broad meaning of auxiliary aids and services would intrude upon a broad meaning of education and associated services. In *McAully Catholic High School v (1) CC (2) PC and Special Educational Needs and Disability Tribunal*,[763] consideration was given to the question whether pastoral support might constitute an auxiliary aid for the purposes of the exemption. The court upheld a finding of the Special Educational Needs and Disability Tribunal[764] that, in failing to make adjustments consisting of the provision of support for a child with autistic spectrum disorder during unstructured times and arrangements to assist him in his transition from one year to the next, the school was in breach of its duties to make reasonable adjustments. The tribunal concluded, in a decision upheld by the court, that the school had failed to take reasonable steps by failing to give the pupil the necessary personal guidance and support within the context of the school's pastoral system.[765] No argument appears to have been put that such support might have constituted an auxiliary service, and the court (which can be taken to have had the exemption in mind because it is annexed to its judgment) treated the provision of such support as an issue of 'planning and organization' (and not 'resourcing').[766] This gives a purposive interpretation to the duties and the exemptions, and ensures that the duties are meaningful in the context of education and associated services, and are engaged in relation to planning, management, and support for disabled pupils. Part 4 of the DDA aims to mainstream education provision so as to make it accessible for disabled pupils. Such an aspiration would be undermined if much provision could be characterized as an auxiliary service so as to fall outside the scope of the duties. The exemption is therefore probably best viewed as covering exceptional or unusual and additional aids or services, but not those that would ordinarily be provided as part of the ordinary school day or curriculum, even if differently provided according to the different needs of the particular child.[767]

---

762 'Disability Discrimination Act 1995 Part IV, Code of Practice for Schools' ibid, para 4.23.

763 [2003] EWHC 3045 (Admin) [2004] 2 ALL ER 436.

764 As to which see Chap 14.

765 *McAully Catholic High School v (1) CC (2) PC and Special Educational Needs and Disability Tribunal* [2003] EWHC 3045 (Admin) [2004] 2 ALL ER 436, para 58.

766 Ibid, para 59.

767 See, for an example of an auxiliary service which was peculiar to a particular child and beyond the school's usual services, *R v SENDIST and Governing Body of Slough Grammar School ex p K* (2006) EWHC 622.

6.252 In the case of independent schools, a school may make specialist tuition available and can charge parents for this. Where it does so, however, such charges must properly reflect the cost of such provision. Any attempt to deter a disabled pupil or treat him or her less favourably for a reason relating to disability would remain unlawful, as disability-related discrimination, notwithstanding that there is no duty to provide auxiliary aids and services.[768]

6.253 As mentioned, there is no duty on a school to remove or alter a physical feature (for example, one arising from the design or construction of the school premises or the location of resources).[769] However, the duties to make adjustments may require that other adjustments are made to mitigate the effects of a physical feature.[770]

6.254 The duties to make adjustments in the field of education are in some senses wider and in some senses narrower than those provided for in the context of the provision of goods, facilities, and services. Whilst the duties do not extend to making adjustments to physical features or to the provision of auxiliary aids and services, they are not limited to practices, policies, or procedures, but create anticipatory duties[771] across the board applying to the exercise of any function, both in relation to the admission of pupils and in relation to the provision of education and associated services.[772] There is, then, no need to identify a practice, policy, or procedure in place which makes the enjoyment of any benefit impossible or unreasonably difficult for disabled pupils. Instead the focus is on the impact of *any* arrangements for disabled pupils, and the management of those to ensure effective access and to eliminate disadvantage for such pupils. The duties are, then, very broad indeed.

6.255 As to discharging the duties, it is provided expressly that 'in considering whether it is reasonable for [a school] to have to take a particular step in order to comply with its duty, a responsible body must have regard to any relevant provisions of a code of practice issued under Section 53A'.[773] This imposes a mandatory duty to

768 'Disability Discrimination Act 1995 Part IV, Code of Practice for Schools' (2002) DRC, para 6.22.

769 DDA, s 28C(2)(a).

770 'Disability Discrimination Act 1995 Part IV, Code of Practice for Schools' (2002) DRC, para 6.23. In addition, in England and Wales and in Scotland, there are planning duties requiring schools to secure accessibility for disabled pupils that may require adjustments to physical features, though a failure to do so does not give rise to an individual cause of action under the school's provisions of the DDA; see DDA, s 28D ('Accessibility Strategies and Plans') and Education (Disability Strategies and Pupils Educational Records) (Scotland) Act 2002. In that way the physical environment of schools is addressed by the imposition of public law duties rather than individual statutory causes of action.

771 For the impact of which see, eg, *R (on the application of D) v Governing Body of Plymouth High School for Girls* [2004] EWHA 1923.

772 DDA, ss 28C. For circumstances where there has been a 'confidentiality request', see DDA, s 28(C)(6) and (7).

773 And thereafter s 14 of the Equality Act 2006, from a date yet to be appointed.

consider the provisions of the applicable statutory code, in this case the 'Disability Discrimination Act 1995 Part IV, Code of Practice for Schools'.[774] The statutory codes of practice, more generally, are considered in Chapter 15. The Code identifies a number of factors to be taken into consideration in determining what might constitute a reasonable step, including the need to maintain academic, musical, sporting, and other standards, and the financial resources available to the responsible body, amongst other matters.[775]

As with disability-related discrimination, a failure to comply with a duty to make reasonable adjustments may be justified if the reason for it is both material to the circumstances of the particular case and substantial.[776] As discussed in paragraph 6.156 above, this form of justification, as understood in the employment and related fields, sets a 'surprisingly low' threshold.[777] The case law deriving from the employment and related provisions applies equally to discrimination by schools, both as a matter of ordinary statutory construction and according to the case law.[778] There is, however, a tension in its application to the reasonable adjustments duties. In the context of the duties to make reasonable adjustments, it would appear to permit a person who has failed to act reasonably (which must be judged objectively),[779] to vindicate that failure by reliance on the undemanding test of justification, explained by *Jones*.[780] The relationship between justification and a failure to comply with the duties to make reasonable adjustments was not considered in *Jones*, though at that stage a failure to comply with the duty to make reasonable adjustments in the employment field could be justified by reference to the test considered in *Jones*.[781] It is difficult to see how Parliament could have intended that the test for determining whether a duty to make adjustments has been complied with should be objective, whilst a failure to comply with that duty should then be judged against a very low threshold which turns principally on the perception of the discriminator. In *Collins v Royal National Theatre Board Limited*[782] the Court of Appeal considered this form of justification and the meaning that should properly be afforded to it where the discrimination concerned a failure to make reasonable adjustments. Importantly, no challenge was made to the decision of the **6.256**

774 (2002) DRC.

775 Ibid, para 6.30.

776 DDA, s 28B(2) and (7). Unlike 'permitted forms of selection', which apply to disability-related discrimination only and not a failure to make reasonable adjustments, DDA, s 28B(6).

777 *Collins v Royal National Theatre Board Limited* [2004] EWCA Civ 144; [2004] IRLR 395, para 15.

778 *R v Governing Body of OL Primary School ex p T* [2005] ELR 522.

779 *Collins v Royal National Theatre Board Limited* [2004] EWCA Civ 144; [2004] IRLR 395, para 20.

780 Para 6.157 above.

781 That position has changed since the enactment of the Disability Discrimination Act 1995 (Amendment) Regulations 2003 SI 2003/1673.

782 [2004] EWCA Civ 144; [2004] IRLR 395.

Court of Appeal in *Jones* in *Collins*; instead it was argued that a different interpretation should be placed on the justification defence as it applied to a breach of the duty to make reasonable adjustments.[783] That argument was accepted so that the Court of Appeal in *Collins* concluded that 'the only workable construction of [this form of justification], in the context of the DDA and its manifest objects, is that it does not permit justification of a breach of [a duty to make reasonable adjustments] to be established by reference to factors properly relevant to the establishment of a duty . . .'.[784] The approach of the Court in *Collins* meant that the meaning of the materially identical defences in two adjacent sub-sections (as they were before amendment in the employment and related fields) was materially different. In the case of a failure to make reasonable adjustments, 'what is material and substantial for the purposes of justifying an established failure to take such steps as are reasonable to redress disadvantage cannot, consistently with the statutory scheme, include elements which have already been, or could already have been, evaluated in establishing that failure'.[785] As the Court of Appeal itself acknowledged, this departed significantly from the meaning and effect of the justification defence in a case of disability-related discrimination but this is 'fully explained by the fact that justification [under the provisions relating to disability-related discrimination] starts from a form of discrimination—*less favourable treatment*—which is established without the need of any evaluative judgment'.[786] It is difficult to see now how the justification defence could have any meaningful force in a case of a failure to make reasonable adjustments, having regard to the guidance in *Collins*. It would not permit matters to be relied upon which were relevant to the establishment of a duty, and it is difficult to see how any matters which might be 'material to the circumstances of the particular case' and 'substantial' would not also be relevant to the question whether a duty to take a particular step arises. Although *Collins* was decided in the context of Part 2 of the DDA in the employment field, given that the very same wording appears in the schools provisions, it is likely that it will apply equally to those provisions, and indeed it may justify a reconsideration of *Jones* altogether.

(8) Local education authorities

6.257 The DDA outlaws discrimination by education authorities when discharging their functions. Such provision applies only where the discrimination complained of does not fall within one of the other provisions of Part 4 as it applies

[783] *Jones* having been a case of disability-related discrimination.

[784] *Collins v Royal National Theatre Board Limited* [2004] EWCA Civ 144; [2004] IRLR 395, para 32, decided under s 5(3) and (4), of the unamended DDA which made materially the same provision as is found in the 'schools' provisions in the employment and related fields.

[785] Ibid, para 32.

[786] Ibid, para 32.

to schools.[787] A duty to make reasonable adjustments is imposed in such circumstances and this duty requires that:

> [e]ach authority . . . takes such steps as it is reasonable for it to have to take to ensure that, in discharging any function to which section 28F applies [the functions of a local education authority under the Education Acts and related functions], (a) disabled persons who may be admitted to a school as pupils are not placed at a substantial disadvantage in comparison with persons who are not disabled; and (b) disabled pupils are not placed at a substantial disadvantage in comparison with pupils who are not disabled.[788]

As with the duty arising in the context of schools, the duty is anticipatory in nature. The duty does not require authorities to remove or alter a physical feature or provide auxiliary aids or services[789] and the observations as made above apply equally (paragraph 6.251). A duty to make reasonable adjustments may arise in relation to all the functions of a local education authority, and such authorities are therefore required to consider proactively what adjustments ought to be made. The duties apply to the whole range of education provision, including nursery education, arrangements for home and hospital tuition, and pupil referral units (in England and Wales), as well as the school stages of education,[790] otherwise the observations made above apply equally. **6.258**

(9) Further and higher education

The duties to make adjustments imposed upon the responsible bodies[791] of further and higher education institutions have recently been amended to give effect to the Framework Directive. The duties now apply in respect of provisions, criteria, and practices, and the physical features of premises, in certain situations. **6.259**

The duties reflect some of the features seen in the duties applicable to the employment and related fields and some of the features seen in the duties applicable to the non-employment sphere. Certain parts of the duties are anticipatory in nature whilst other parts are individually focused. In particular, the reasonable adjustment duties apply to provisions, criteria, or practices applied by or on behalf of the institution relating to the *arrangements* it makes for determining admissions to the institution, or to *student services* provided for, or offered to, students by the institution, where those provisions, criteria, or practices place disabled people at a substantial disadvantage in comparison with people who are not disabled. These duties, therefore, are owed to disabled people at large, and are anticipatory **6.260**

[787] DDA, s 28F(4).
[788] Ibid, s 28G(2).
[789] Ibid, s 28G(3).
[790] 'Disability Discrimination Act 1995 Part IV, Code of Practice for Schools' (2002), para 10.4.
[791] See Chap 9.

in nature. However, there is a further duty applicable to provisions, criteria, or practices applied by or on behalf of the institution, for determining *on whom a qualification is to be conferred*, but only where any provision, criterion, or practice places a disabled person at a substantial disadvantage in comparison with people who are not disabled, and that disabled person has notified the institution that he may be an applicant for the conferment of that qualification.[792] In addition, where a provision, criterion, or practice of either sort just described is applied by or on behalf of an institution, and it places a disabled person who holds a qualification conferred by the institution or who has applied for a qualification which the institution confers, at a substantial disadvantage in comparison with persons who are not disabled, a duty to make reasonable adjustments arises. The duties in relation to provisions, criteria, and practices, therefore, are a mixture of the anticipatory and the idiosyncratic.

6.261 A further duty is applied in relation to the physical features of premises occupied by an institution where they place disabled people at a substantial disadvantage in comparison with people who are not disabled in relation to the arrangements which that institution makes for determining admissions to the institution, and in relation to student services provided for, or offered to, students by that institution. Similarly, where any physical feature of premises occupied by an institution places a particular disabled person who applies for a qualification which that institution confers, or who holds a qualification which was conferred by that institution, at a substantial disadvantage in comparison with persons who are not disabled, a duty arises. Again the duty in respect of the physical features of premises is a mixture of the anticipatory and idiosyncratic.[793]

6.262 Where a duty arises a responsible body is under an obligation to take such steps as it is reasonable, in all the circumstances of the case, for it to have to take in order to prevent the provision, criterion, or practice, or the physical feature, as the case may be, from having the effect specified.[794]

6.263 The duties to make reasonable adjustments in relation to provisions, criteria, and practices do not apply to 'competence standards',[795] the meaning given to which is described above (paragraph 6.190) and the observations there apply.

[792] S 28T(1) and (1A) as inserted by the Disability Discrimination Act 1995 (Amendment) (Further and Higher Education) Regulations 2006 SI 2006/1721.

[793] S 28T(1C) and (1D) as inserted by the Regulations just described. A new Code of Practice has been issued addressing discrimination in the context of further and higher education: 'Code of Practice: Post-16 Education' (2006) DRC, in force from 1 Sept 2006; The Disability Discrimination (Code of Practice) (Further and Higher Education) (Appointed Day) Order (Northern Ireland) 2006, Statutory Rule 2006 No. 17.

[794] DDA, s 28T.

[795] Ibid, ss 28T(1)(a), (1A)(a), (1B)(a).

A failure to comply with the duty to make adjustments by further and higher education institutions cannot be justified.[796]

Unlike the duties in other fields outside the employment and related areas, liability for a failure to make reasonable adjustments will not arise where a responsible body can show that at the time in question it did not know and could not reasonably have been expected to know that the disabled person concerned was disabled, and that its failure to take that step was attributable to that lack of knowledge.[797] However, where the duties are anticipatory in nature, unless there is something very unusual about the particular disabled person's needs, it will be difficult for a responsible body to show that any failure to make adjustments was attributable to a lack of knowledge. It is in the nature of the anticipatory duties, as described above, that a person caught by its terms must take proactive action to ensure that a disabled person is not disadvantaged in advance of any disabled person using or seeking to use the facilities concerned. **6.264**

(10) Youth and community services and adult education

The duties to make adjustments apply equally to local educational authorities providing community and adult education and other statutory youth services.[798] The duty is modified so that each responsible body: **6.265**

> must take such steps as it is reasonable for it to have to take to ensure that (a) in relation to its arrangements for enrolling persons on a course of further or higher education provided by it and (b) in relation to services provided, or offered by it, disabled persons are not placed at a substantial disadvantage in comparison with persons who are not disabled.[799]

There is no express provision made in relation to auxiliary aids, services, or physical features, but from 31 August 2003 and 31 August 2005, respectively, the obligations to make reasonable adjustments would apply in relation to them.[800]

(11) General qualifications bodies

General qualifications bodies (which might be distinguished from qualifications bodies[801]), being broadly speaking examination bodies, will be, when the provisions are in force, subject to duties to make reasonable adjustments.[802] The duties closely reflect those found in the employment and related provisions. **6.266**

796 Following the amendments made by the regulations just described.

797 DDA, s 28S(3).

798 Ibid, s 28U and Sch 4C as amended by the Amending Regulations.

799 Ibid, Sch 4C, para 2, substituting s 28T with provision therein.

800 Special Educational Needs and Disability Act 2001 (Commencement No 5) Order 2002, Art 6 and Sch 2.

801 Their meaning is described at paras 6.189–6.190.

802 The provisions addressing discrimination by general qualifications bodies are not in force at the time of writing.

They apply to provisions, criteria, and practices, other than competence standards (as defined above, paragraph 6.190), and the physical features of premises. However, for the duties to be triggered the provisions, criteria, and practices caught by their terms must place a particular disabled person at a substantial disadvantage in comparison with people who are not disabled.[803] The provisions, criteria, and practices caught are those for determining on whom a relevant qualification is to be conferred, in respect of a disabled person who is or who has notified the body that he may be an applicant for the conferment of that qualification, and provisions, criteria, and practices other than for determining on whom a relevant qualification is to be conferred, in respect of a disabled person who holds a relevant qualification conferred by the body or who has applied for a relevant qualification which the body confers.

6.267 The duty when triggered is to take such steps as it is reasonable in all the circumstances of the case for it to have to take in order to prevent the provision, criterion, or practice having the effect of placing the disabled person at a substantial disadvantage in comparison with persons who are not disabled.

6.268 As to the duty to make adjustments to the physical features of premises, the duty applies to a disabled person who holds a relevant qualification conferred by the body or has applied for a relevant qualification which the body confers and who is placed at a substantial disadvantage in comparison with persons who are not disabled.[804] However, matching the duty under the employment and related fields, no duty arises where the body does not know, and could not reasonably be expected to know, in the case of an applicant or potential applicant for the conferment of a relevant qualification, that the disabled person concerned is or may be such an applicant, or, in any case, that the disabled person has a disability and is likely to be affected in the way mentioned.[805]

6.269 The provisions addressing general qualifications bodies are not in force at the time of writing.[806]

H. The Equal Pay Act 1970

(1) Introduction

6.270 The Equal Pay Act 1970 (EPA) addresses discrimination in pay rather differently when compared with the other main anti-discrimination enactments. Its scheme

---

803 DDA, s 31AD(1), (2).

804 Ibid, s 31AD(3).

805 Ibid, s 31AD(4).

806 There is a regulation making power, with a duty to consult, allowing for regulations addressing lease premises and agreements.

is rather simple. Instead of creating a series of unlawful acts wherein (including in relation to pay) discrimination as defined is outlawed, the EPA regulates gender discrimination in pay and other benefits by the implication of an 'equality clause' into contracts of employment.[807] The equality clause has the effect of securing equality in pay and other terms for women employed on like work with a man, work rated as equivalent with that of a man, or work of equal value to that of a man in the same employment, save where the employer concerned can show that any variation between the woman's contract and the man's contract is genuinely due to a material factor which is not the difference of sex.

The EPA is a short Act. Its size and simplicity in form, however, belie its complexity. It has produced a voluminous amount of case law and has not proved successful in achieving its aim of closing the pay gap. Whilst there has been some improvement, the pay gap remains significant. Women who work full time earn 13 per cent less than men who work full time, based on median hourly earnings, and 17 per cent less based on mean hourly earnings.[808] The pay gap as between full-time male workers and part-time female workers is even starker—41 per cent using median hourly pay rates and 38 per cent using mean hourly pay rates. Despite the EPA, the pay gap 'stubbornly persists'.[809] **6.271**

The difficulties with the EPA are manifold, as referred to in Chapter 2. It does not impose any positive obligations on employers to introduce or maintain non-discriminatory pay systems; instead it relies on individual complaints which are complex to bring and often difficult to identify in the first place. There is no obligation to make pay systems transparent or to audit pay. This might be contrasted with the position in some other jurisdictions.[810] **6.272**

807 EPA, s 1(1). Discrimination in relation to pay and other terms regulated by a contract is employment therefore excluded from the SDA and regulated by the EPA, SDA, s 6(6).

808 'Women and Work Commission: Shaping a Fairer Future' (2006) Department of Trade and Industry, vii.

809 Ibid, 2.

810 See, eg, the proactive equal pay legislation in Ontario and Quebec, covering both public and private sector employers (excepting some small employers). Ontario's Pay Equity Act (Pay Equity Act, RSO 1990, c p 7) 'was perhaps the most progressive pay equity statute of its time' ('Pay Equity: A New Approach to a Fundamental Right, (Canadian) Pay Equity Task Force Final Report' (2004), ISBN 0-662-34045-0, p 68). Its s 7(1) provides that, 'Every employer shall establish and maintain compensation practices that provide for pay equity [defined in terms of comparisons between male and female job classes] in every establishment of the employer.' The statute imposes a positive obligation on each employer who has more than 10 employees to ensure that its own remuneration policies are not discriminatory. It sets out clear methodological and procedural requirements for attaining a non-discriminatory wage structure. The unit of comparison—the 'establishment'—is all employees of an employer in a geographic division. The statute also permits the joining together of different employers as a single establishment by agreement. The Pay Equity Act provides that a pay equity plan must be negotiated with any trade union representing employees. Where there is no trade union, there is no obligation for an employer to discuss the pay equity plan with the employees, although they are entitled to comment on the posted plan, and to raise objections with the Pay Equity Commission if they disagree with it. There are statutory bodies supporting the

6.273 As mentioned in Chapter 2, a key defect in the EPA is that it is predicated on the legal assumption that there will be a male comparator employed in the same employment against whose pay the woman's pay can be measured. This makes securing equal pay in pregnancy cases problematic.[811] In addition, it sometimes makes addressing occupational segregation impossible. 'Women's' jobs are often simply undervalued,[812] and challenging that under the EPA is very difficult. There are structural forces which cause pay disadvantage: gender stereotyping in schools; the undervaluing of women's work; the nature of women's lives which are often characterized by caring and other home responsibilities; and women's patterns of work which are more likely to be interrupted by childcare and other responsibilities, and punctuated by part-time work,[813] as well as individual incidents of discrimination against women. The EPA is an inadequate tool for addressing these issues. As will be seen below, the impact of EC law has mitigated some of the effects of the restrictions in the EPA, but equal pay cases remain technically complex and not wholly effective.

6.274 The EPA has been amended several times, in the main to give effect to EC law which has proved a very compelling context for understanding and applying the EPA. Article 141 of the EC Treaty, discussed in Chapter 4, lays down the principle that men and women should receive equal pay for the same work or for work deemed to be of equal value. That principle is one of the foundations of the Community.[814] As discussed in Chapter 4, the Equal Pay Directive[815] also lays

legislative framework. The Pay Equity Commission is composed of two separate bodies—the Ontario Pay Equity Office and the Ontario Pay Equity Hearings Tribunal. The Ontario Pay Equity Office performs various functions, including educational and advisory functions; the provision of materials and templates for use in the pay equity process; the provision of non-partisan advice about entitlements and responsibilities under the Act; the provision of assistance, through its review services branch, for employers and employee representatives engaged in job evaluation; and the formulation of pay equity plans ('Pay Equity: A New Approach to a Fundamental Right, (Canadian) Pay Equity Task Force Final Report' (2004), ISBN 0-662-34045-0, p 69). The review officers of the Pay Equity Office also have power to investigate complaints, facilitate 'discussion', and issue compliance orders, as well as to monitor and audit pay equity plans. Ontario's Pay Equity Hearings Tribunal adjudicates upon cases where a compliance order of the Pay Equity Office is appealed, or where it is referred by the Pay Equity Office for enforcement. Quebec's Pay Equity Act (Pay Equity Act, RSQ, c E-12.001), passed in 1996, adopts many of the characteristics of the Ontario model including the imposition of a positive obligation on employers in the public and private sectors. Whilst such models are not wholly successful, 'it does appear that the level of compliance is higher under this kind of system than it is under complaint-based regimes or those which rely exclusively on an audit system. The caveat attached to this is that there must be adequate support from the regulatory agency' ('Pay Equity: A New Approach to a Fundamental Right, (Canadian) Pay Equity Task Force Final Report' (2004), ISBN 0-662-34045-0, p 155).

811 See discussion at para 6.51, above.

812 'Women and Work Commission: Shaping a Fairer Future' (2006) Department of Trade and Industry, 3.

813 'Women and Work Commission: Shaping a Fairer Future' (2006) Department of Trade and Industry, 3–4.

814 *Defrenne v Sabena (Defrenne No 2)* (Case 43/75) [1976] ECR 455, para 12.

815 Which in no way alters the scope or content of the principle defined in Article 141; *Jenkins v Kingsgate* (Case 96/80) [1981] IRLR 228.

down a framework for the implementation of the principle of equal pay into national legal systems. Article 141, as mentioned in Chapter 4, is directly effective against State and non-State actors.[816] The Equal Pay Directive is directly effective against the State and emanations of it. In applying the EPA, a court or tribunal must therefore interpret it consistently with Article 141 and the Directive, and in any case disapply any provision incompatible with Article 141, and in a case against the State or an emanation of it also disapply any provision incompatible with the Equal Pay Directive.[817]

The Equal Pay Directive in fact turned out to be a 'Trojan horse'.[818] The UK agreed to it on the basis that the EPA met the obligations under it. However, that proved to be very wrong. Early on in its life the EPA was found to be incompatible with EC law. In *Commission of the European Communities v United Kingdom*[819] the ECJ held that the UK was in breach of its obligations under Article 141 and the Equal Pay Directive in that, under section 1 of the Equal Pay Act 1970 as originally enacted, a woman could only claim equal pay for work of equal value to that done by a man if a job evaluation study had been undertaken, in circumstances where such could only occur with the employer's consent. This amounted to a denial of the right to equal pay for work of equal value conferred by Article 141 and Article 1 of the Equal Pay Directive. This led to the first significant amendment to the EPA, introducing explicit *equal value* provisions, discussed below.[820] Specific provision is now also made, in consequence of EC law, to address some forms of pregnancy discrimination in pay.[821] In addition, rights arise implicitly from the EPA in consequence of EC law, which, as mentioned, significantly informs its contents.[822] For example, no express provision is made in the EPA for indirect discrimination. However, case law giving effect to EC law demonstrates that indirect discrimination in pay will breach the equality clause in certain circumstances. **6.275**

The content of the equality clause and the forms of discrimination it regulates are discussed below. The equality clause and references to it below assume that it will be a woman who has suffered pay discrimination. However, the EPA applies equally to a man who is not paid equally compared to a woman.[823] **6.276**

816 *Defrenne v Sabena (Defrenne No 2)* (Case 43/75) [1976] ECR 455, with effect from the date of the judgment, namely 8 April 1976.

817 See Chap 4. Domestic law will, therefore, defer to any higher standards in EC law, *Barber v Guardian Royal Exchange Assurance Group* (C-262/88) [1990] ICR 616; [1990] IRLR 240. An employment tribunal has no jurisdiction to hear free-standing Article 11 claims and accordingly any claim to equal pay arising under Article 141 must be brought under the EPA (or, where not regulated by contract, the SDA see chapter 8); *Biggs v Somerset County Council* [1996] ICR 364; [1996] IRLR 203.

818 A McColgan, *Discrimination Law: Text, Cases and Materials* (2005, Hart), 421.

819 [1982] ICR 578.

820 The Equal Pay (Amendment) Regulations 1983 SI 1983/1794.

821 EPA, s 1(1)(d)–(f), (5A)–(B).

822 See too, Equal Opportunities Commission Code of Practice on Equal Pay (2003, EOC), para 9.

823 EPA, s 11(2).

Nevertheless, experience and research show that it is predominantly women who suffer pay discrimination.

6.277 There has been much case law emanating from the ECJ on the extent to which Article 141 applies to occupational pensions, discussed below. The position has been resolved domestically by the enactment of the Pensions Act 1995 which contains provision which is materially identical to the EPA, applicable to occupational pension schemes (by the implication of an equal treatment rule), and this must be 'construed as one' with the EPA.[824] There are temporal limitations in the Pensions Act 1995, reflecting the impact of the decision in *Barber v Guardian Royal Exchange Assurance Group*, discussed below at paragraph 6.282.[825] Otherwise the observations below about the meaning and impact of the equality clause apply equally.

(2) The equality clause

6.278 The 'equality clause' is a provision which is implied into a contract under which a woman is employed if not already included directly or by reference to a collective agreement or otherwise.[826] It has the effect that any term in a contract under which a woman is employed which is less favourable than that contained in the contract of a comparable man is treated as modified so as not to be less favourable, and, where her contract does not include a term corresponding to a term benefiting that man, it has the effect of treating as included in her contract a corresponding term .[827] This applies to the original contractual position as well as circumstances where the woman's position *becomes* less favourable.[828]

6.279 As to the identification of the proper comparator, he is:

(a) a man employed in like work in the same employment;
(b) a man employed in work rated as equivalent in the same employment; or
(c) a man employed in work of equal value in the same employment.

Each of these expressions is considered below. In addition, and as addressed below, the EPA makes provision relating to maternity-related pay, bonuses, and pay increases referable to periods whilst absent on maternity leave.

(a) The clause's coverage

6.280 The equality clause addresses any provision which relates to terms, whether concerned with pay or not. The coverage of the equality clause has been informed

---

824 *Allonby v Accrington and Rossendale College and Others* [2001] EWCA 529; [2001] IRLR 364, para 49.

825 (C-262/88) [1990] ECR 1889; [1990] ICR 616; [1990] IRLR 240.

826 EPA, s 1(1).

827 Ibid, s 1(2)(a)–(c). For exceptions, see EPA, s 6. For comparable provision in relation to the armed forces, see EPA, s 7.

828 Ibid.

by EC law, and in light of that it has been held to cover a very wide range of benefits. The equality clause will cover all remuneration, whether contractual or non-contractual,[829] made pursuant to a collective agreement[830] or otherwise, in respect of work, provided that the worker receives it, directly or indirectly, in respect of her employment from her employer,[831] including elements of maternity pay (including statutory maternity pay),[832] sick pay,[833] bonuses, and other one-off or ad hoc payments, in whether for retrospective performance or for future loyalty,[834] pay, any consideration whether in cash or in kind, whether immediate or future,[835] occupational pensions,[836] contributions to pension schemes,[837] access to pension schemes,[838] bonuses,[839] severance pay,[840] travel concessions,[841] statutory and non-statutory redundancy pay,[842] and statutory unfair dismissal compensation.[843]

The concept of pay is an autonomous one in EC law and so does not defer to domestic nomenclature or legal form. The fact that some consideration is paid pursuant to statute (for example, statutory redundancy pay or earnings related maternity pay[844]) **6.281**

829 If regulated by a contract. Otherwise, any discrimination will fall to be considered under SDA, s 6.

830 *Kowalska v Freie und Handestadt Hamburg* (Case C33/89) [1990] ECR I-2591; [1992] ICR 29; [1990] IRLR 447.

831 *Defrenne v Sabena (Defrenne No 2)* (Case 43/75) [1976] ECR 455; *Barber v Guardian Royal Exchange Assurance Group* (C-262/88) [1990] ICR 616; [1990] IRLR 240.

832 *Gillespie and o'rs v Northern Health and Social Services Board and o'rs* (Case C-342/93) [1996] ICR 498; *Alabaster v Woolwich and A'or* (Case C-147/02) [2005] ICR 695; [2004] IRLR 486.

833 *Rinner-Kuhn v FWW Spezial-Gebaudereinigung GmbH & Co KG* [1989] ECR 2743; [1989] IRLR 493.

834 *Lewen v Denda* (Case C-333/97) [2000] ICR 648.

835 *Hammersmith and Queen Charlotte's Special Health Authority v Cato* [1988] ICR 132; [1987] IRLR 483.

836 *Bilka-Kaufhaus GmbH v Weber von Hartz* (Case 170/84) [1986] ECR 1607. As to further provision in relation to pensions, see the Pensions Act 1995, referred to above. As to pensions, *Griffin v London Pensions Fund Authority* [1993] IRLR 248 can be regarded as wrongly decided as against the weight of authority from the ECJ; *Bestuur van het Algemeen Burgerlijk Pensioenfonds v Beune* (C-7/93) [1995] IRLR 103; *Griesmar v Ministre de l'Economie, des Finances et de l'Industrie* (C-366/99) (1999) (unreported); *Barber v Guardian Royal Exchange Assurance Group* (C-262/88) [1990] ICR 616; [1990] IRLR 240.

837 *Worringham and Humphreys v Lloyds Bank Ltd* (C-69/80) [1981] IRLR 178.

838 *Vroege v NCIV Institut voor Volkshuisvesting BV* (Case C-57/93) [1994] ECR I-4541.

839 *Lewen v Denda* (C-333/97) [2000] IRLR 67.

840 *Kowalska v Freie and Hansestadt Hamburg* (C-33/89) [1992] ICR 29; [1990] IRLR 447.

841 Even those enjoyed after retirement, *Garland v British Rail Engineering Ltd* [1982] IRLR 111.

842 *European Commission v Belgium* (C-173/91) [1993] IRLR 404; *R v Secretary of State for Employment ex p Seymour-Smith and Perez* (C-167/97) [1999] ICR 447; [1999] IRLR 253; *Rutherford and another v Secretary of State for Trade and Industry (No 2)* [2006] UKHL 19; [2006] IRLR 551.

843 *R v Secretary of State for Employment, ex p Equal Opportunities Commission* [1994] ICR 317; [1994] IRLR 176; *R v Secretary of State for Employment ex p Seymour-Smith and Perez* C-167/97 [1999] ICR 447; [1999] IRLR 253.

844 *Gillespie v Northern Health and Social Services Board* (Case C-342/93) [1996] ICR 499; [1996] IRLR 214, whatever or whenever the reference period is for calculating maternity pay; *Alabaster v Woolwich* (Case C-147/02) [2005] ICR 695; *Boyle v Equal Opportunities Commission* (Case C-411/96) [1998] IRLR 717.

or by order of the State (as in statutory compensation for unfair dismissal) or, as mentioned, after the employment relationship has terminated, is immaterial. Pay, therefore, will cover any pecuniary or tangible consideration arising out of an employment relationship, whether it is to be enjoyed in the present or future.

6.282 The extent to which Article 141 and therefore the EPA covers pensions has been controversial.[845] In the monumental decision of *Barber v Guardian Royal Exchange Assurance Group*[846] (described by one commentator as '[i]n terms of its practical implications for employers and employees . . . the most far-reaching judicial decision of our time'[847]) the ECJ held categorically that Article 141 extended to occupational pensions so that pension benefits which discriminate on grounds of sex, or pension schemes which include any condition which makes differential provision according to sex, contravenes Article 141. This applied to payments made by an employer in consequence of a statutory obligation,[848] just as it did to those payments arising from contractual obligations (as indeed it applied to voluntary payments). This had the very important effect too of equalizing pension ages for women and men so that, despite the continuing difference in the State pension age, the *Barber* decision required equalization of pension ages under occupational schemes. Because of the wide-ranging implications of the ECJ decision in *Barber*,[849] the Court temporally limited the impact of its decision so that it applied only from the date of the decision (17 May 1990), from which date men acquired the right to obtain an occupational pension at age 60 without loss of benefit where (as was most common) that is the pensionable age for women.[850] An exception was created in respect of those workers who had before

845 *Newstead v Department of Transport and HM Treasury* (Case 192/85) [1988] ICR 332; [1988] IRLR 66 (deduction of a contribution to an occupational pension scheme which was a substitute for the statutory scheme, like a contribution to a statutory social security scheme, did not fall within the scope of Article 141) can be regarded as inconsistent with *Barber* and does not represent the proper position in law.

846 (C-262/88) [1990] ECR 1889; [1990] ICR 616; [1990] IRLR 240.

847 'Highlights' [1990] IRLR 209.

848 The decision also means, as was expressly acknowledged by the court, that Article 7 of the EEC Social Security Directive 79/7 and Article 9(a) Social Security Directive 86/378, which permitted the implementation of equal treatment in occupational pension schemes to be deferred, are overridden. The EC Treaty takes precedence, even though in consequence parts of the Social Security Directives were unnecessary.

849 And the fact that Member States had been encouraged to assume that discriminatory occupational pension schemes fell within the derogation in Article 7(1) of the Social Security Directive 79/7/EEC which authorized the Member States to defer the compulsory implementation of the principle of equal treatment with regard to the determination of pensionable age for the purposes of granting old-age pensions with the possible consequences thereof for other benefits. That exception has been incorporated in to Art 9 (a) of Directive 86/378/EEC on the implementation of the principle of equal treatment for men and women in occupational social security schemes which may apply to contracted-out schemes such as the one at issue in the *Barber* case.

850 *Barber v Guardian Royal Exchange Assurance Group* (C-162/88) [1990] ECR 1889; [1990] ICR 616; [1990] IRLR 240, para 42.

that date initiated legal proceedings or raised an equivalent claim under the applicable national law.[851] The extent of this temporal restriction was the subject of further case law[852] but the position is now regularized domestically by the Pensions Act 1995.

A distinction had been drawn between the applicability of the Equal Treatment Directive and the Equal Pay Directive to work related benefits. This has had the effect that certain benefits, for example subsidized nursery places, have been held to fall outside the Equal Pay Diirective,[853] but instead within the Equal Treatment Directive. The fact that pay now falls within the Equal Treatment Directive, by reason of the Equal Treatment Amendment Directive, makes this distinction less significant, as discussed in paragraph 6.304 below. **6.283**

Further, a distinction is drawn between pay for Article 141 purposes and payments made pursuant to social security schemes (which are not covered by Article 141), and such a distinction is not always easy to draw. But in general terms where a payment is made, directly or indirectly, by an employer referable to work it will fall within Article 141.[854] **6.284**

(3) The proper comparator and the relevant circumstances

(a) Comparable pay

Article 141 and, accordingly, the EPA requires that there be comparability between each of the elements of a pay package.[855] This means that discrimination in one area cannot be set off by discrimination in another area.[856] **6.285**

---

851 Ibid, para 45.

852 See, for example, *Vroege v NCIV Institut voor Volkshuisvesting BV* (Case C-57/93) [1994] ECR I-4541; *Preston v Wolverhampton Healthcare NHS Trust* (Case C-78/98) [2000] ECR I-03201. And a Protocol to the Maastricht Treaty (Protocol 2 to the Treaty of Maastricht 1992); *Quirk v Burton Hospitals NHS Trust* [2002] EWCA Civ 149.

853 *Lommers v Minister van Landbouw, Natuurbeheer en Visserji* (Case C-476/99) [2002] IRLR 430, para 40.

854 Including, for example, civil service pension schemes regulated by statute and maternity pay regulated by statute: *Bestuur van het Algemeen Burgerlijk Pensioenfonds v Beune* (C-7/93) [1995] IRLR 103; *Griesmar v Ministre de l'Economie, des Finances et de l'Industrie* (C-366/99) (1999) (unreported); *Gillespie v Northern Health and Social Services Board* (Case C-342/93) [1996] ICR 499; [1996] IRLR 214, whatever or whenever the reference period is for calculating maternity pay; *Alabaster v Woolwich* (Case C-147/02) [2005] ICR 695.

855 *Hayward v Cammell Laird Shipbuilders Ltd (No 2)* [1988] 1 AC 894; *Jämställdhetsombudsmannen v Örebro Läns Landsting* (C-236/98) [2000] IRLR 421 ('genuine transparency, permitting effective review, is assured only if the principle of equal pay applies to each of the elements of remuneration granted to men or women', para 43); *Brunnhofer v Bank der Osterreichischen Postparkasse AG* (381/99) [2001] IRLR 571.

856 For the limits of this approach, see *Degnan v Redcar and Cleveland BC* [2005] IRLR 615.

(b) Characteristics of the comparator

6.286 As seen, the EPA on its face requires that there be an actual comparator. The position in relation to hypothetical comparators is discussed below. As to the characteristics of any comparator, they must be employed 'in the same employment'.[857] Section 1(6) defines 'employed' as 'employed under a contract of service or of apprenticeship or a contract personally to execute any work or labour, and related expressions shall be construed accordingly'.[858] As to whether a comparator is in the *same employment*, the EPA provides that:

> men shall be treated as in the same employment with a woman if they are men employed by her employer or any associated employer at the same establishment or at establishments in Great Britain which include that one and at which common terms and conditions of employment are observed either generally or for employees of the relevant classes.[859]

Two employers are to be treated as 'associated', 'if one is a company of which the other (directly or indirectly) has control, or if both are companies of which a third person (directly or indirectly) has control'.[860] To this extent, the EPA allows expressly for cross-establishment comparisons but only within limited parameters. The EPA requires that the male comparator be employed by the same employer or an associated employer and *either* he is employed at the *same establishment* as the woman, or that he is employed at a *different establishment* belonging to that employer (or an associated employer) where *common terms and conditions of employment* are laid down for the two establishments, either for employees generally or for the class of employees concerned. As to whether conditions of employment are 'common' for these purposes, terms and conditions of employment governed by the same collective agreement 'represent the paradigm, though not necessarily the only example, of the common terms and conditions of employment contemplated'.[861] Adopting a purposive construction, according to Lord Bridge,[862] 'it cannot . . . possibly have been the intention of Parliament to require a woman claiming equality with a man in another establishment to prove an undefined sub-stratum of similarity between the particular terms of her contract and his as the basis of her entitlement to eliminate any discriminatory differences between those terms'.[863] A similarly broad approach was adopted by the House of Lords in *British Coal Corporation v Smith and Others*,[864] where again the House of Lords adopted a purposive approach requiring only 'broadly

857 EPA, s 1(2)(a)–(d).
858 Ibid, s 1(6)(a).
859 Ibid, s 1(6)(c).
860 Ibid, s 1(6)(c).
861 *Leverton v Clwyd County Council* [1989] 1AC 706; [1989] IRLR 28, para 7.
862 Who delivered an opinion with which all their Lordships agreed.
863 Para 8.
864 [1996] ICR 515; [1996] IRLR 404.

similar terms'[865] and rejecting the suggestion that 'common in the sense of identical' was required,[866] that being 'far too restrictive a test'.[867]

Whilst some cross-establishment comparisons are permitted, cross-employer comparisons, save in the case of associated employers, are not expressly permitted under the EPA. This has caused very significant disadvantage for women employed in local authority services which are then 'contracted out' to private contractors.[868] The impact of contracting out was to depress pay and conditions more generally, but that had a particular impact on women.[869] Article 141, however, is not so restrictive. Article 141 requires equal pay 'for equal work which is carried out in the same establishment *or service* whether private or public'.[870] This has meant that the EPA has been read so as to permit cross-employer comparisons where employed 'in the same establishment *or service*' in certain.[871] In this way the focus, of Article 141, is less on legal form and moreon the substantive reality.[872] In *Lawrence v Regent Office Care Limited*,[873] the ECJ ruled definitively that Article 141 is not limited to situations in which men and women work for the same employer. As mentioned in Chapter 4, Article 141 allows for comparisons to be made between women and men employed at different establishments and by different employers so long as there is a *single source* regulating terms and conditions, whether that is a single legislative or quasi-legislative source, or a collective agreement, or some other cross-establishment agreement.[874] This is likely to have an impact on contracting out. Contracting out by local authorities is now governed by the 'best value' regime,[875] and the Government's guidance provides that local authorities should enter into binding agreements with incoming contractors requiring them to guarantee terms and conditions for transferring employees and 'new joiners', that is employees who join the workforce later.[876] Such agreements 6.287

865 Ibid, para 44.

866 Ibid, para 45.

867 Ibid, para 45.

868 See the discussion in A McColgan, *Discrimination Law: Text, Cases and Materials* (2005, Hart), 436–7, even after the amendments to and then revocation of the Transfer of Undertakings (Protection of Employment) Regulations 1981 (see now Transfer of Undertakings (Protection of Employment) Regulations 2006 SI 2006/246).

869 A McColgan, *Discrimination Law: Text, Cases and Materials* (2005, Hart), 436.

870 *Defrenne (No 2)* (Case-43/75) [1976] ECR 455; [1976] ICR 547, para 22.

871 *Scullard v Knowles and Southern Regional Council for Education and Training* [1996] ICR 399, 405; [1996] IRLR 344.

872 Ibid, 403.

873 (Case-320/00) [2002] ECR 1-07325; [2002] IRLR 822.

874 *Lawrence v Regent Office Care Limited & Others* (Case C-320/00) [2002] ECR 1-07325; [2003] ICR 1092; [2002] IRLR 822; *Allonby v Accrington & Rossendale College and Others* (Case C-256/01) [2004] ICR 1328; [2004] IRLR 224; *South Ayrshire Council v Morton* [2002] IRLR 256.

875 Local Government Act 1989, s 19. See further Chap 15.

876 'Local Government Act 1999: Part 1 Best Value and Performance Improvement' (2003) ODPM Circular 03/2003, which in material parts constitutes statutory guidance to which a local authority must have regard, see paras 1 and 28 *et seq*.

may in future found claims under Article 141 for equal pay as between women in contracted out services and men directly employed in local authority employment.

6.288 The expansive approach taken by EC law and in *Lawrence*, in particular, allows for unequal pay caused by structural forces to be addressed. However, it has also had the bizarre result, notwithstanding the clear words of the EPA (a man in the *same employment* being *men employed by her employer at the same establishment*[877]), that men working for the same employer have been held not to be comparable to a woman where a workplace has been subdivided. This is so, according to the case law, where control over pay and conditions has been delegated to those separate subdivisions so that there is not a *single source* for pay or conditions. In a skewing of a test which was intended to be expansive, it has been held, then, that it is not enough for women to show that they have the same employer as their comparators, but they must show too that the employer was also the body responsible for setting the terms for both groups of employees. Whether this is the case depends on an evaluation of all the evidence.[878] This turns a condition for extending coverage to one which limits it. This approach has been heavily criticized.[879] Apart from anything else it encourages a fragmenting of workforces to evade the provisions of the EPA with the risk that that increases the likelihood of pay differentials becoming entrenched and perhaps more stark.

6.289 A woman may compare herself to a male predecessor[880] and a person employed subsequently.[881] Certainly nothing in Article 141 requires that a male comparator be contemporaneously employed.

6.290 As to the comparators otherwise, as seen they must be in 'like work', 'work rated as equivalent', or work of 'equal value'. Further, again because of the impact of Article 141, the EPA addresses indirect discrimination and this is addressed below.

(c) Like work

6.291 'Like work' is defined by section 1(4) of the EPA as:

> work . . . of the same or a broadly similar nature, and the differences (if any) between the things she does and the things they do are not of practical importance in relation to terms and conditions of employment; and accordingly in comparing her work with theirs regard should be had to the frequency or otherwise with which any such differences occur in practice as well as to the nature and extent of the differences.

---

877 EPA, s 1(2) and s 1(6).

878 *Robertson v Department for Environment, Food and Rural Affairs* [2005] IRLR 363; *Armstrong v Newcastle upon Tyne NHS Hospital Trust* [2006] IRLR 124.

879 S Fredman, 'Marginalising Equal Pay Laws' (2004) 33, ILJ, 281.

880 *Macarthys Limited v Smith* (Case 129/79) [1980] ICR 672; [1980] IRLR 210.

881 *Diocese of Hallam Trustees v Connaughton* [1996] ICR 860.

In its early years, the concept of 'like work' was given a narrow reading.[882] The position now is that 'trivial differences or differences not likely in the real world to be reflected in the terms and conditions of employment'[883] will be ignored for the purposes of determining whether the work done by a woman and her chosen male comparator constitutes 'like work'.[884] In determining whether or not there are any material differences between the work done by the woman and her comparator, the focus will be on the things that are actually required to be done as opposed to those which might theoretically be required.[885] By the same token, the fact that a man does more than his contract requires of him will not make him non-comparable for the purposes of a 'like work' claim. In such circumstances the focus will be on what the job requires as opposed to any 'special personal skill or merit'.[886] There is some suggestion in the case law from the ECJ that a requirement for different training or qualifications is a differentiating feature such as to make the work non—alike.[887] However, this cannot be regarded as a proposition of general application. Each case will turn on its own facts, and the question must be whether or not any differences are material.[888]

(d) Work rated as equivalent

As seen, the EPA allows a woman to compare herself to a man employed on work rated as equivalent.[889] By section 1(5), a woman is to be regarded on work rated as equivalent to that of a man: **6.292**

> if, but only if, her job and their job have been given an equal value, in terms of the demand made on a worker under various headings (for instance, effort, skill, decision), on a study undertaken with a view to evaluating in those terms the jobs to be done by all or any of the employees in an undertaking or group of undertakings, or would have been given an equal value but for the evaluation being made on a system setting different values for men and women on the same demand under any heading.

The job evaluation scheme must therefore rate the woman's work as equivalent to that of her male comparator, disregarding any discriminatory criteria or measurements adopted. As mentioned, however, there is no obligation on an employer

882 *Eaton Limited v Nuttall* [1977] ICR 272; *Waddington v Leicester Council for Voluntary Service* [1977] 1 WLR 544.

883 *Capper Pass Limited v Lawton* [1977] QB 852.

884 See too, *Shields v E Coomes (Holdings) Limited* [1978] ICR 1159; and *Bromley v H&J Quick Ltd* [1988] ICR 47.

885 *Electrolux Limited v Hutchinson* [1976] IRLR 410; [1977] ICR 252; *Capper Pass Limited v Lawton* [1977] QB 852.

886 *Shields v E Coomes (Holdings) Limited* [1978] ICR 1159, 1169; [1978] IRLR 263, 266.

887 *Angestelltenbetriebsrat der Wiener Gebietskrankenkasse v Wiener Gebietskrankenkasse* (Case C-309/97) [1999] ECR 1-02865.

888 *Glasgow City Council v Marshall* [2000] ICR 196, 206, *per* Lord Nicholls with whom their Lordships agreed.

889 EPA, s 1(2)(b).

to undertake a job evaluation study and no rights conferred on any other body to undertake such a study. Enforcing a right to equal pay for work of equal value through this route (the only route in the original enactment of the EPA), therefore, depended entirely on voluntary action by an employer.[890]

6.293 For section 1(5) to apply, for the purposes of meeting the obligation that the woman's work qualifies as rated as equivalent, any job evaluation study must be:

> thorough in analysis and capable of impartial application [and i]t should be possible by applying the study to arrive at the position of a particular employee at a particular point in a particular salary grade without taking other matters into account except those unconnected with the nature of the work.[891]

The particular job in question and that of the male comparator must be evaluated in accordance with the requirements under section 1(5) so that the study must value the woman's job and that of her male comparator analytically. It is not enough that a study has ordered each job as a whole by benchmarking against other jobs which have been evaluated analytically. The job in question and the job of the comparator must themselves have been subject to a detailed evaluation, measuring the demands of each of the jobs, if the requirements of section 1(5) are to be satisfied.[892]

6.294 The equality that is arrived at by a job evaluation study includes the determination of an appropriate salary grade, by the conversion of any points arrived at by the evaluation undertaken. In *Springboard Sunderland Trust v Robson*,[893] it was argued by an employer that a woman was not entitled to claim that her work had been rated as equivalent with that of her chosen male comparator in circumstances where her job was assessed as giving 410 points whilst her male comparator's job was assessed as giving 428 points in a scheme which placed all jobs scoring between 360 and 409 points on Grade III and those rated 410–449 on Grade IV. The claimant had been awarded a Grade IV salary and her employers contended that she was not entitled to compare herself to a man awarded a Grade III salary with 429 points. This argument was rejected. In determining whether a woman's job was rated as equivalent to that of a man, the final results of the study could be had regard to, including the final allocation of the grade.

---

890 And as mentioned above, prior to the enactment of the equal value provisions, discussed below, the 'work rated as equivalent' provisions were considered an inadequate mode of implementing Art 141 and its obligation to secure equal pay for work of equal value, by the ECJ in *Commission of the European Communities v United Kingdom* [1982] ICR 578.

891 *Eaton Limited v Nuttall* [1977] ICR 272, 277 to 278; [1977] IRLR 71, para 13. The Equal Opportunities Commission has issued guidance on non-discriminatory job evaluation schemes, 'Good Practice Guide—Job Evaluation Schemes Free of Sex Bias' (2005), EOC, available at <http://www.eoc.org.uk/Default.aspx?page=15381>.

892 *Bromley v H & J Quick Limited* [1988] ICR 623; [1988] IRLR 249.

893 [1992] ICR 554; [1992] IRLR 261.

In addition to meeting the requirements of section 1(5) in the evaluation process, the job evaluation study must itself be free from any sex discrimination, and a study may fail to meet the requirements of section 1(5) even where there is no intention to discriminate.[894] This means that if a study rates a woman's job differently to that of a man, the equality clause will nevertheless operate where the jobs would have been rated the same but for sex bias in the study. In *Rummler v Dato-Druck GmbH*,[895] the ECJ considered the inclusion of 'muscular effort' as a criterion for determining pay grades, and concluded that whilst the use of criteria relating to muscle demand, muscular effort, and the heaviness of the work was not precluded by the Equal Pay Directive, where the nature of the tasks involved required the use of physical strength, for the study to be non-discriminatory, the system as a whole should preclude any discrimination on grounds of sex by taking into account other criteria, for example, the movements of small muscle groups characteristic of manual dexterity. **6.295**

The wording of section 1(2)(b) of the EPA, which triggers the operation of an equality clause where work is rated as equivalent, may on a non-purposive reading suggest that any less favourable term is only modified where the term itself has been determined by the job evaluation study (*any term of the woman's contract determined by the rating of the work is or becomes less favourable*). This would suggest that an employer who simply failed to implement a job evaluation study could defeat the impact of it and, more particularly, evade the operation of an equality clause. However, unsurprisingly, the courts have held that such is not the proper approach. In *O'Brien v Sim-Chem Limited*[896] the House of Lords concluded that it was not necessary to wait until an employer had implemented the results of the job evaluation study for section 1(2)(b) to become engaged. Instead: **6.296**

> [o]nce a job evaluation study has been undertaken and has resulted in a conclusion that the job of the woman has been evaluated under Section 1(5) as of equal value with the job of the man, then the comparison of the respective terms of their contracts of employment is made feasible and a decision can be made . . . [A]t that stage when comparison becomes first feasible, and discrimination can first be detected, . . . the provisions of paragraph (b) would be intended to bite, and bite at once.[897]

---

894 *Bromley v H&J Quick Limited* [1988] ICR 623; [1988] IRLR 249.

895 (237/85) [1987] ICR 774; [1987] IRLR 32.

896 [1980] ICR 573; [1980] IRLR 373. Some authority indicates that a job evaluation study does not bind an employer before he accepts it as a valid study (*Arnold v Beecham Group Limited* [1982] ICR 744; [1982] IRLR 307) but this must be regarded as doubtful authority in the light of *O'Brien v Sim-Chem* and would, if correct, allow an employer to cherry-pick so that if a job evaluation study produced a result he was unhappy with he could disregard it. This would seem inconsistent with the purpose of the EPA and in particular its provisions addressing work rated as equivalent.

897 Ibid, at 597, *per* Lord Russell.

The fact that the undertaking of a job evaluation study is a voluntary exercise does not mean that an employer is not under any compulsion to implement it or, at least, to give effect to any equality clause implied in consequence.[898]

(e) Work of equal value

6.297 As mentioned above, the equal value provisions were introduced only in consequence of a ruling by the ECJ that the UK was in breach of its obligations under Article 141 in failing to make provision for equal value claims under the original enactment of the EPA. Section 1(2)(c) of the EPA was therefore introduced, apparently to fill the lacuna found to exist by the ECJ. It provides, however, that an equality clause will operate only 'where a woman is employed on work which, *not being work in relation to which paragraph (a) or (b) above applies*, is, in terms of the demands made on her (for instance under such headings as effort, skill and decision), of equal value to that of a man in the same employment'. This indicates that a woman cannot rely on the equal value provisions if there is a man employed on like work or employed on work rated as equivalent. Instead she would be bound to treat as the proper comparator that man or those men employed in like work or work rated as equivalent. However, if that reading were to be given to the equal value provisions it would have the effect that an employer could easily avoid them by the simple device of placing a single man in a job otherwise exclusively done by women. The devastating impact on the provisions that such a construction would have was easily recognized, and in *Pickstone v Freemans plc*[899] the House of Lords concluded that, having regard to the UK's obligations in EC law, a woman could bring a claim relying on the equal value claims notwithstanding the presence of a man in the same job (or one which has been rated as equivalent). As Lord Keith observed, the alternative:

> would leave a large gap in the equal pay provision, enabling an employer to evade it by employing one token man on the same work as a group of potential women claimants who were deliberately paid less than a group of men employed on work of equal value with that of the women. This would mean that the United Kingdom had failed yet again fully to implement its obligations under Article [141] . . . and the Equal Pay Directive, and had not given full effect to the decision of the European Court in *Commission v United Kingdom* . . . It is plain that Parliament cannot possibly have intended such a failure.[900]

It has to be said that it appears from the very clear wording that Parliament may very well have intended the meaning resisted by the House of Lords in *Pickstone v Freemans*, but in any event it does not survive. A woman is therefore permitted to choose her own comparator but that is not an easy exercise. Success might be

---

898 Ibid, 580.

899 [1988] 1 AC 66; [1988] ICR 697; [1988] IRLR 357.

900 Ibid, para 7.

more likely to be guaranteed if a man in an obviously less valuable job were to be selected, but to do so might be to undersell the woman and her job. On the other hand, selecting a variety of comparators, ranging from those in low value work to those in high value work, carries the danger that a tribunal or court will be unconvinced by the claim.[901] However, a woman could barely be criticized for selecting a range of comparators across work of varying value when, as indicated, there is no exact science about measuring value, making the assessment of value in a particular case very unpredictable indeed. Nevertheless, choosing a comparator remains tactically and legally problematical.

Apart from the difficulties in identifying a comparator, the procedures applicable to equal value claims have proved 'lengthy, elaborate and . . . expensive'.[902] As has been seen, in determining whether or not a woman is employed in work of equal value, an evaluation has to be undertaken by the tribunal, having regard, in particular, to effort, skill, and decision amongst other things.[903] That evaluation had required the appointment of an independent expert to advise tribunals on the issue of value. This process itself was often extremely complex, resulting in preliminary hearings as to the expert to be appointed, and depriving a tribunal of the right to consider a claim in relation to equal value until it had received the report of the independent expert. This complexity, amongst other things, led the Equal Opportunities Commission to remark in 1986 that the EPA 'serves individuals badly, groups of workers hardly at all, and does little to encourage voluntary progress towards equality'.[904] **6.298**

The position has changed so that tribunals might now consider the question of equal value without the report of an independent expert, and rules permit the appointment of tribunal panels with specialist knowledge of equal value cases, amongst other things, with the purpose of removing some of the complexity and procedural difficulties.[905] Other amendments have been made to the procedures with the aim of making the resolution of equal value claims easier and more speedy. **6.299**

However, the difficulties in establishing equal pay for work of equal value are unlikely to be completely eliminated by the new procedures. Firstly, it is often the case that non-transparent pay systems will simply conceal disparities in pay from women workers so that equal value claims are just not identified. Until 2003, **6.300**

901 *Leverton v Clwyd County Council* [1989] AC 706, 751–2; [1989] ICR 33, 65; [1989] IRLR 28, para 22, *per* Lord Bridge.

902 *Leverton v Clwyd County Council* [1989] AC 706; [1989] ICR 33; [1989] IRLR 28, para 22.

903 EPA, s 1(2)(c).

904 'Annual Report for 1986' (1986) EOC, 6.

905 Sex Discrimination and Equal Pay (Miscellaneous Amendments) Regulations 1996 SI 1996/438; and see Employment Tribunals (Constitution and Rules of Procedure) (Amendment) Regulations 2004 SI 2004/1861 and Equal Pay Act 1970 (Amendment) Regulations 2004 SI 2004/2352.

there was no questionnaire procedure provided for under the EPA comparable to that available under the other main anti-discrimination enactments.[906] That position has changed,[907] making it at least possible for a woman who has cause to be concerned about her pay to ask questions about it. However, the absence of any obligation to make transparent pay schemes, by publishing and explaining them, does mean that the incidence and causes of unequal pay most likely just go unnoticed.

6.301 Secondly, equal value claims are likely to remain expensive and therefore the province of the very rich or those supported by a trade union, leaving many of the most vulnerable women effectively outside the protection of the EPA. An equal value claim will now go through either two or three stages, depending on whether an independent expert is appointed. The likelihood is that in many cases an independent expert will still be appointed, and it remains to be seen how well the new procedures will operate. However, there is reason to believe that resolving equal value claims, save in the most obvious cases, will remain complex. Under the new procedure, a tribunal will hold an initial hearing to determine whether the woman's job and that of her comparator have been rated as unequal by a job evaluation scheme and, if so, whether there are reasonable grounds for suspecting that the evaluation contained in the study was itself discriminatory or otherwise unsuitable.[908] An evaluation contained in a job evaluation study will be regarded as discriminatory where a difference, or coincidence, between values set by that system on different demands under the same or different headings is not justifiable irrespective of the sex of the person on whom those demands are made.[909] If the claim is not barred by reason of a valid job evaluation study, the tribunal will then have to determine whether to appoint an independent expert or to determine the question of equal value itself.[910] If the tribunal decides to appoint an expert, a hearing will be conducted for the purposes of determining those matters necessary for the preparation of the report, and thereafter a third hearing will determine whether the claim for equal value is well founded and whether a 'material factor' defence under section 1(3) of the EPA (see paragraph 6.306 below) succeeds. A job evaluation study which is not 'analytical' in nature would not bar a claim in respect of equal value (see above). Some authority indicates that where a job evaluation study does not exist at the time of the claim, it may nevertheless become relevant if conducted by an employer after institution of the claim, for the purposes of defeating a claim.[911] The parties themselves may, of course, obtain

906 See Chap 14.
907 EPA, s 7B and the Equal Pay (Questions and Replies) Order 2003, SI 2003/722.
908 EPA, s 2A(2A).
909 Ibid, s 2A(2A) and 2A(3).
910 Ibid, s 2A(1).
911 *Dibro Limited v Hore* [1990] ICR 370; [1990] IRLR 129.

their own expert evidence anyway. Indeed, the fact that a tribunal might now decide the question of equal value without the assistance of an expert itself recognizes that the assessment of value is not a matter of objective certainty.[912] This procedural complexity, as well as the substantive legal complexity, still makes equal value claims very difficult indeed.

(f) Hypothetical comparators

As seen, and as mentioned above, the EPA is entirely predicated on the assumption and the legal requirement that there be an actual comparator of a different sex for the purposes of establishing that the equality clause operates in a particular case and in respect of a particular term. This had appeared to be the position in EC law[913] but the requirement for an actual comparator as a condition of proceeding under the EPA is probably not now compatible with EC law. **6.302**

As already mentioned, the requirement causes very real problems in bringing pregnancy cases, and this has been addressed by specific amendments to the EPA[914] in consequence of case law from the ECJ indicating that equal pay rights extend to maternity and related benefits. In those pregnancy cases which do not fall within the express provisions governing maternity pay and in other cases, a hypothetical comparator cannot be relied upon, at least without doing very severe damage to the EPA. In *Alabaster v Barclays Bank plc and Secretary of State for Social Security (No 2)*[915] the Court of Appeal held that a woman was entitled to bring a claim under the EPA in respect of the earnings related element of her statutory maternity pay, which, contrary to Article 141, had not taken account of a pay rise awarded before the end of her maternity leave.[916] To ensure such a right was effective, the provisions of section 1 to the extent that they impose a requirement for a male comparator were to be simply disapplied. According to the Court of Appeal, that followed the example set by the House of Lords in *Webb v EMO Air Cargo (UK) Limited (No 2)*[917] so that Ms Alabaster could succeed in her claim without the need for a comparator 'just as she would have done automatically if her claim had not related to the payment of an amount of money that was regulated by her contract of employment and had fallen within the SDA **6.303**

912 A Plummer, 'Equal Value Judgments: Objective Assessment or Lottery?' Industrial Research Unit, School of Business Studies, University of Warwick, cited in A McColgan, *Discrimination Law: Text, Cases and Materials* (2005, Hart), 60 which demonstrated that there was 'remarkable little consistency' in the approach taken to the assessment of value.

913 *Macarthys Limited v Smith* (Case 129/79) [1980] ICR 672; [1980] IRLR 210, para 15.

914 Discussed below at para 6.316.

915 [2005] EWCA Civ 508; [2005] IRLR 576.

916 Before the material amendments made to s 1 of the EPA which now allow for such a claim under s 1(2)(d), discussed below.

917 [1995] ICR 1021; [1995] IRLR 645.

regime instead'.[918] The *Alabaster* approach would apply in other pregnancy discrimination claims relating to pay and other terms falling within the scope of the EPA, not expressly addressed by the amendments made dealing with maternity related pay discrimination.[919]

6.304 Importantly, too, it is highly doubtful that EC law now requires, as a matter of law, that in any case a comparator is required for the purposes of establishing a breach of Article 141, and accordingly the imposition of such a requirement under the EPA may well contravene EC law. The point is as yet untested, save in respect of indirect discrimination where a specific comparator need not be identified (see paragraph 6.313 below).[920] However, whilst it was controversial until recently, the position seems much clearer since the enactment of the Equal Treatment Amendment Directive. As mentioned in Chapter 4, the Equal Treatment Amendment Directive amends the Equal Treatment Directive and, in so doing, requires Member States to outlaw direct and indirect sex discrimination (amongst other things) in relation to work and work related conditions, including 'pay' as provided for in the Equal Pay Directive.[921] Direct discrimination is defined as occurring where one person is treated less favourably on grounds of sex than another is, has been, or *would be* treated in a comparable situation, and, as is uncontroversial, this allows for a comparison with a hypothetical comparator.[922] According to EC law, therefore, a woman might bring a claim in relation to directly, or for that matter indirectly, discriminatory pay relying on a hypothetical comparator. The UK has not given effect to this aspect of the Equal Treatment Amendment Directive but it seems likely that in due course a challenge will be made to the requirements imposed by the EPA, either by bringing a case under the EPA and seeking to have the comparator requirements disapplied in an appropriate case, or by bringing a claim under the SDA and seeking to have the exemption which prohibits most equal pay claims being brought under its terms disapplied.[923]

6.305 The advantage of reliance upon a hypothetical comparator is that it allows for challenges to stereotyping around the valuing of jobs where there are not direct male comparators. This is particularly likely in cases of occupational segregation. A company which provides domestic home helps may only employ women (or mainly women) and employ them on very low pay, perhaps very consciously

---

918 As to the relationship between the SDA and the EPA see para 8.46.

919 Addressed below under para 6.316.

920 *Allonby v Accrington and Rossendale College and Others* [2001] EWCA 529; [2001] IRLR 364; *Bilka-Kaufhaus GmbH v Weber von Hartz* (Case C-170/84) [1986] ECR 1607; *Kowalska v Freie und Hansestadt Hamburg* (Case No 33/89) [1992] ICR 29; [1990] IRLR 447.

921 Equal Pay Directive, Art 3(1)(c).

922 See the discussion above and see para 6.46.

923 SDA, s 6(6).

recognizing that women will work for lower pay in such jobs and perhaps deliberately employing women so as to ensure wages are kept deflated. A woman in such a circumstance would not have a claim for sex discrimination in relation to her pay under the SDA, because of the exemption referred to above (and described in Chapter 8, paragraph 8.46) and nor would she, absent a disapplication of the comparator provisions, have a claim under the EPA for want of a male comparator. This would appear to contravene the very clear provisions of the Equal Treatment Amendment Directive. As mentioned, the exception to this is in indirect discrimination claims which operate somewhat differently and these are addressed below (paragraph 6.313).

(4) Genuine material factor defence

In section 1(3) of the EPA, a defence is afforded an employer against *prima facie* discrimination alleged to arise under section 1(2) (that is, that there is like work, work rated as equivalent, or work of equal value). An equality clause will not operate even where like work, work rated as equivalent, or work of equal value is shown, in relation to a variation between the woman's contract and the man's contract, if the employer proves that the variation is genuinely due to a material factor which is not the difference of sex. That 'factor' (a) in the case of an equality clause falling within sub-section (2)(a) or (b) (like work and work rated as equivalent) must be a material difference between the woman's case and the man's, and (b) in the case of an equality clause falling within sub-section (2)(c) (equal value) may be such a material difference. The same factors may be used as in the context of denying 'like work' or 'equal value',[924] though it is not necessary, before the factor may be relied upon to support a section 1(3) defence, that it has actually been raised in determining that equal value (or like work) exists.[925] **6.306**

However, firstly, the genuine material factor defence will not apply where the difference arises because of direct discrimination. Observations to the contrary cannot be regarded as good law because they are inconsistent with the plain words of the statute and have no foundation in EC law.[926] Whilst there is sometimes some obscuring of the type of discrimination being addressed by certain of the rulings in the ECJ, particularly where they arise from non-transparent pay systems, there is no decision of the ECJ holding that direct discrimination might be justified, and such would be inconsistent with the approach taken by all the EC anti-discrimination instruments. Accordingly, the *genuine material factor* defence will not assist an employer where the difference in pay is attributable **6.307**

924 *Davies v McCartneys* [1989] IRLR 439.

925 *Christie v John F. Haith Ltd* [2003] IRLR 670.

926 *Strathclyde Regional Council v Wallace* [1998] ICR 205; [1998] IRLR 26, para 18; *Armstrong v Newcastle upon Tyne NHS Hospital Trust* [2006] IRLR 124. It can be noted that every EU instrument addressing direct gender discrimination does not permit of justification.

to sex.[927] Secondly, the genuine material factor must explain the whole differential if it is to be justified in its totality, and accordingly the principle of proportionality must be applied in determining whether the defence is satisfied.[928]

6.308 As can be seen, section 1(3) imposes a different test in equal value cases by requiring that the material factor may be (but need not be) 'a material difference'. In either case the burden of proof is on the employer to show that the material factor defence applies. In the early years of the Act the 'material difference' defence (applicable to 'like work' and 'work rated as equivalent') was limited to circumstances peculiar or personal to the worker concerned, such as length of service, superior skill or qualifications, or red circling,[929] and regard could not be had to any 'extrinsic forces'.[930] As Lord Denning observed in *Clay Cross (Quarry Services) Limited v Fletcher*:

> An employer cannot avoid his obligations under the Act by saying: 'I paid him more because he asked for more', or 'I paid her less because she was willing to come for less'. If any such excuse were permitted, the Act would be a dead letter. Those are the very reasons why there was unequal pay before the statute. They are the very circumstances in which the statute was intended to operate.[931]

This imposed a rigorous test upon an employer to justify differences in pay in a particular case. When the equal value provisions were introduced,[932] as seen, a broader *genuine material factor* defence was introduced so that it is only necessary to show that the variation is genuinely due to a material factor which *may* be a material difference. This was intended to increase the opportunity for extraneous matters to be had regard to in determining the material factor defence. However, in *Rainey v Greater Glasgow Health Board*,[933] the House of Lords in any event concluded that the test imposed by *Clay Cross* was unduly restrictive, and that a relevant difference for the purposes of section 1(3) may relate to circumstances other than the personal qualifications or merits of the male and female workers who are the subject of comparison. For the difference to be 'material', it must be 'significant and relevant', and it must be between 'her case and his'. According to the House of Lords, consideration of a person's case must necessarily involve consideration of all the circumstances of that case. These may go beyond the personal qualities by way of skill, experience, or training which the individual brings to the job. This means that 'market forces' and other extraneous factors,

---

927 See, too, *Ratcliffe v North Yorkshire County Council* [1995] IRLR 439, where some doubt was thrown upon the difference between direct and indirect discrimination again.

928 *Enderby v Frenchay Health Authority* (Case C-127/92) [1993] ECR I-5535; [1993] IRLR 591; *Barry v Midland Bank Plc* [1999] ICR 859; [1999] IRLR 581.

929 *Clay Cross (Quarry Services) Limited v Fletcher* [1979] ICR 1.

930 Ibid, 5.

931 Ibid, 5.

932 Equal Pay (Amendment) Regulations 1983, SI 1983/1794.

933 [1987] 1 AC 224; [1987] ICR 129; [1987] IRLR 26.

subject to arguments on indirect discrimination referred to below, may be sufficient to constitute a material difference.

Importantly, the EPA is not a 'fair wage' statute but is directed at remedying gender-based discrimination so that its scheme is such that it creates 'a rebuttable presumption of sex discrimination . . . once the gender-based comparison shows that a woman, doing like work or work rated as equivalent or work of equal value to that of a man, is being paid or treated less favourably than the man'.[934] The burden then passes to the employer to show that the explanation for the variation is not tainted with sex. In order to discharge this burden it has ben held that the employer need only show that the proffered explanation, or reason, is genuine, and not a sham or pretence; that the less favourable treatment is due to this reason—the factor relied upon must be the cause of the disparity; that the reason is not 'the difference of sex', whether direct or indirect; and that the factor relied upon is or, in a case within section 1(2)(c), may be a 'material' difference, that is, a significant and relevant difference, between the woman's case and the man's case.[935] In this way the test under section 1(3) requires only that the material factor is causally relevant, not that it objectively justifies the difference in pay. The accuracy of this approach has been doubted.[936] It would mean that a mistaken belief in the value of a job, even if honestly held, would be sufficient to deprive a woman of equal pay. **6.309**

EC law would seem to require much more. There is authority indicating that any difference in pay must be objectively justified.[937] This means that there is a burden on an employer seeking to establish a material factor defence to prove that: **6.310**

- there were objective reasons for a difference in pay;
- those reasons were unrelated to sex;
- those reasons corresponded to a real need on the part of the undertaking;
- the discrimination was appropriate to achieving the objective pursued and that it was necessary to that end;
- the difference conformed to the principle of proportionality; and
- that was the case throughout the period during which the differential existed.[938]

This view, however, has not been consistently endorsed by the courts, and recent authorities indicate that only where a *prima facie* case of indirect discrimination

934 *Glasgow CC and others v Marshall and others* [2000] ICR 196; [2000] IRLR 272, para 18, *per* Lord Nicholls with whom their other Lordships agreed.

935 Ibid, paras 18-20, *per* Lord Nicholls with whom their other Lordships agreed.

936 'Highlights' (2000), April, 221.

937 *Brunnhofer v Bank der Osterreichischen Postparkasse AG* (Case C-381/99) [2001] ECR I-04961.

938 *Barton v Investec Henderson Crosthwaite Securities Ltd* [2003] IRLR 332. See too, *Sharp v Caledonia Group Services Ltd* [2006] IRLR 4.

is established by a complainant will there be any requirement to show objective justification.[939]

6.311 As to what constitutes a 'material difference' otherwise, it may be attributable to some personal differences, for example seniority, greater experience, or greater merit or skill and 'red circling',[940] or some extraneous factor, like market forces, though in each case the factor must not itself be tainted with sex[941] and, as described below, if indirectly discriminatory, the higher standard of justification is imposed. Where pay is non-transparent, it is less likely that an employer will discharge the burden of showing a non-discriminatory reason.[942]

6.312 As to those material factors which do not constitute a material difference, these might constitute a defence to an equal value claim (see paragraph 6.306 above). As mentioned, the requirement that any material factor constitute a material difference was not enacted in the equal value provisions to deal with the impact of *Clay Cross* and in particular the availability of a 'market forces' defence. However, post-*Rainey* the difference has become less significant. As mentioned above, a wide range of factors may justify a differential in pay or conditions but they must not be themselves tainted by sex, and, if indirectly discriminatory, they will be subject to the more onerous justification defence.

(5) Indirect discrimination

6.313 Article 141 prohibits indirect discrimination, as well as direct discrimination, in pay.[943] In *Rainey v Greater Glasgow Health Board*,[944] the House of Lords ruled that in a case of indirect pay discrimination, an employer must show 'objectively justified grounds' for the difference in pay.[945] The test of justification was that required by EC law.[946] The *Rainey* decision then put beyond doubt that the

939 *Nelson v Carillion Services Ltd* [2003] ICR 1256; [2003] IRLR 428; *Home Office v Bailey* [2004] IRLR 921; *Parliamentary Com'r for Administration and the Health Com'r v Fernandez* (2003) EAT 0137/03; *Armstrong v Newcastle upon Tyne NHS Hospital Trust* [2006] IRLR 124; *Tyldesley v TML Plastics Ltd* [1996] ICR 356; *Villalba v Merrill Lynch & Co Inc* [2006] IRLR 437.

940 *McGregor v General Municipal Boilermakers and Allied Trades Union* [1987] ICR 505; *Forex Neptune (Overseas) Ltd v Miller* [1987] ICR 170.

941 *Ratcliffe v North Yorkshire CC* [1995] ICR 833; [1995] IRLR 439.

942 *Barton v Investec Henderson Crosthwaite Securities Ltd* [2003] IRLR 332 (though see para 6.310 above, suggesting the approach taken to the burden of proof was wrong); *Handels -Og Kontorfunktionaerernes Forbund i Danmark v Dansk Arbejdsgiverforening (acting for Danfoss)*, 109/88 [1989] IRLR 532 ECJ.

943 *Jenkins v Kingsgate* (Case C-96/80) [1981] ECR 1-00911; [1981] ICR 592 and put beyond doubt in *Bilka-Kaufhaus GmbH v Webber von Hartz* [1987] ICR 110. See too *Rinner-Kühn v FWW Spezial-Gebäudereinigung GmbH & Co KG* [1989] ECR 274; [1989] IRLR 493; *Nimz v Freie und Hansestadt Hamburg* (C-184/89) [1991] IRLR 222.

944 [1987] 1 AC 224; [1987] ICR 129; [1987] IRLR 26.

945 Though the outcome of the decision calls into question the extent to which they applied the test properly themselves. In particular, the disadvantaged group were all women and no regard seems to have been paid to the impact of the discriminatory rule upon women in determining whether justification was made out.

946 *Bilka-Kaufhaus v Weber von Hartz* [1987] ICR 110.

EPA would not mandate indirect discrimination unless such discrimination was justified. This imposed a more rigorous test than the 'genuine material factor' defence which must now be read as incorporating the justification defence in cases of indirect discrimination. Later cases confirm that categorizing employees in one way or another, by reference to collective bargaining units, pay structures, red circling etc, will not be sufficient by themselves to make out the genuine material factor defence if there is a disparate impact on women.[947] Disparate impact is discussed above (paragraph 6.122). It is not necessary to identify an actual comparator for a claim in indirect pay discrimination.[948] Instead it is necessary to show only that there 'is a much higher percentage of women than of men' disadvantaged by the pay practice in issue.[949]

Importantly, the Court of Appeal recently referred to the ECJ the question whether length of service alone may justify differences in pay where that disadvantages women workers. In *Cadman v Health and Safety Executive*[950] a band 2 principal inspector employed in the Health and Safety Executive (HSE) was paid substantially less than her comparators who carried out work rated as equivalent to hers under a job evaluation study. The principal reason for the difference in pay was that the HSE had operated a pay scale based on annual increments over a number of years. Although this system was altered in 1995, existing pay differentials were preserved, with the result that the men received higher pay by reason of their longer service. Ms Cadman was able to show that the length of service criterion had a disproportionate adverse impact on comparable women workers because they tended to have shorter service. The differential in pay, as between her and her male comparators, was substantial. According to the Advocate-General in his Opinion,[951] where an employer uses length of service to determine pay, and this has a disparate impact as between men and women workers, the employer should be required to show that the use of a length of service criterion takes into account the business needs of the undertaking, and is applied proportionately so as to minimize its disadvantageous impact on women. Where an employer cannot justify the use of a length of service criterion as a in general, it should provide specific justification for the difference 6.314

947 *Enderby v Frenchay Health Authority* (Case C-127/92) [1993] ECR I-5535; [1993] IRLR 591.

948 *Allonby v Accrington & Rossendale College and Others* (Case C-256/01) [2004] ICR 1328; [2004] IRLR 224.

949 *Allonby v Accrington & Rossendale College and Others* (Case C-256/01) [2004] ICR 1328; [2004] IRLR 224, para 75. This case arose in the context of a statutory scheme, as have other cases falling under EU equal pay law; see, eg, *R v Secretary of State for Employment ex p Seymour-Smith and Perez*, C-167/97 [1999] ICR 447; [1999] IRLR 253; *Rutherford and another v Secretary of State for Trade and Industry* (No 2) [2006] UKHL 19; [2006] IRLR 551, but the same would apply equally to indirect discrimination arising under a collective agreement, contractual terms etc.

950 [2005] ICR 1546. Now see, Case C-17/05 (not reported at the time of writing).

951 C-17/05, Advocate-General Poiares Maduro delivered on 18 May 2006.

in pay levels between the woman worker and her comparator. Given the uncertainty created by the earlier judgments of the ECJ[952] and the potential economic effect of a ruling in such terms, the Advocate-General agreed with the UK and Irish Governments that the temporal effects of the judgment should be limited. His recommendation was that the ECJ should hold that the judgment could not be relied upon to support claims of indirect discrimination arising prior to the date of judgment unless the complainant had brought proceedings before that date. In a surprising judgment, but one which reflects earlier case law, the ECJ ruled that, as a general rule, determining pay by length of service will be appropriate 'to attain the legitimate objective of rewarding experience acquired which enables the worker to perform his duties better'. It is not necessary therefore for an employer to establish specifically that recourse to that criterion is appropriate in a particular case or in respect of a particular job.[953] Exceptionally, however, where a worker provides evidence capable of raising serious doubts as to whether length of service attains the objectives just described (where, for example, length of service after a certain period can make no difference at all to skill or competence in the performance of duties), an employer will be required to prove 'that which is true as a general rule, namely that length of service goes hand in hand with experience and that experience enables the worker to perform his duties better, is also true as regards the job in question'.[954] Further, where a job classification system based on an evaluation of the work to be carried out is used in determining pay, there is no need to show that an individual worker has acquired experience during the relevant period which has enabled him to perform his duties better. Instead the position is to be judged objectively (that is, without specific reference to the individual worker).[955] The judgment is surprising, firstly, because it suggests that the burden of proof is differently placed where length of service is the alleged discriminatory criterion. In such a case, it is for the claimant to prove the absence of an otherwise presumed justification. This is different to the position that usually pertains[956] and against the trend in EU law of imposing the burden of disproving discrimination, where the facts are such that discrimination might otherwise

952 *Cadman v Health & Safety Executive* C-19/05, paras 67 *et seq*. In particular the case of *Handels-og Kontorfunktionêrernes Forbund I Danmark v Dansk Arbejdsgiverforening ('Danfoss')* (Case 109/88) [1989] ECR 3199 in which it had been held by the ECJ that use of length of service as a criterion in a pay system need not be justified by the employer, even if it works to the disadvantage of women, since 'length of service goes hand in hand with experience and since experience generally enables the employee to perform his duties better' (para 24). See too, Case C-184/89 *Nimz* [1991] ECR I-297, Case C-1/95 *Gerster* [1997] ECR I-5253, and Case C-243/95 *Hill and Stapleton* [1998] ECR I-3739.

953 *Cadman v Health & Safety Executive* C-19/05, paras 35–36.

954 Ibid, para 38.

955 Ibid, para 39.

956 See paras 6.306 and 6.310.

be presumed, on an employer.[957] Secondly, service-based criteria are especially likely to be objectionable on grounds not only of sex (which the ECJ recognized),[958] but also race,[959] and, necessarily, age.

Outside of length of service, however, an objective basis for any indirectly discriminatory measure in a particular case must be shown. A mere non-discriminatory explanation (which will suffice for the genuine material factor defence) will not be adequate. **6.315**

(6) Pregnancy

The equality clause does not operate (in favour of a man) in relation to terms affording special treatment to women in connection with pregnancy or childbirth. EPA, s6(1)(b), except where a woman is relying on those terms to assert rights she has under the EPA in respect of earnings related maternity pay etc., EPA s6(1AA). Further, the EPA now makes specific, but limited, provision addressing discrimination in pay related to pregnancy and maternity leave.[960] These provisions give effect to the ECJ decisions in *Gillespie and others v Northern Health and Social Services Board*[961] and *Alabaster v Barclays Bank plc and Secretary of State for Social Security (No 2)*,[962] so that a pay increase which a woman would have received but for pregnancy or maternity leave must be had regard to in calculating any earnings related maternity pay and pay on her return to work. The 'equality clause' implies such an entitlement if such is not expressly provided for in the contract of employment. Further the equality clause guarantees the right to the benefit of any pay increase or bonus referable to periods before or after maternity leave and during the two weeks of compulsory leave[963] at the time they would ordinarily fall due for payment. The provisions do not deal with circumstances where bonuses are reduced pro rata to take account of absence on maternity leave (outside the two weeks compulsory leave) or for pregnancy related reasons.[964] If an entitlement to the same can be proved as a matter of EU law, the comparator requirements in the EPA would have to be disapplied (see paragraph 6.303 above). **6.316**

---

957 See, para 6.310.

958 *Cadman v Health & Safety Executive* C-19/05, para 22.

959 Because newer entrants to the UK will have reduced opportunities to build up long service. See, by analogy, *Perera v The Civil Service Commission and the Department of Customs & Excise (No 2)* [1983] ICR 428; [1983] IRLR 166.

960 EPA, s 1(2)(d)–(f).

961 (Case C-342/93)[1996] ICR 499; [1996] IRLR 214.

962 [2005] EWCA Civ 508; [2005] IRLR 576.

963 Employment Rights Act 1996, s 72(1).

964 *GUS v Home Shopping Ltd v Green and McLaughlin* [2001] IRLR 75; *Lewen v Denda* [2000] IRLR 67; *Hoyland v Asda Stores Ltd* [2006] CSIH 21; [2006] IRLR 468.

I. Victimization

6.317 Victimization is a quite different form of discrimination from those forms described above. It is not concerned with protecting against adverse treatment connected to the personal characteristics, and nor is it concerned with an individual's status (and in the case of the DDA, protects disabled as well as non-disabled people[965]). The victimization provisions protect those people involved in enforcing the anti-discrimination enactments, either as complainants or witnesses, and those assisting them.

6.318 All the main anti-discrimination enactments define and outlaw victimization within their scope.[966] Different formulations are used but their effect is the same.

6.319 Section 4 of the SDA provides that:

> (1) A person ('the discriminator') discriminates against another person ('the person victimised') in any circumstances relevant for the purposes of any provision of this Act if he treats the person victimised less favourably than in those circumstances he treats or would treat other persons, and does so by reason that the person victimised has—
> (a) brought proceedings against the discriminator or any other person under this Act or the Equal Pay Act 1970 [or sections 62–65 of the Pensions Act] 1995, or
> (b) given evidence or information in connection with proceedings brought by any person against the discriminator or any other person under this Act or the Equal Pay Act 1970 [or sections 62–65 of the Pensions Act 1995], or
> (c) otherwise done anything under or by reference to this Act or the Equal Pay Act 1970 [or sections 62–65 of the Pensions Act 1995] in relation to the discriminator or any other person, or
> (d) alleged that the discriminator or any other person has committed an act which (whether or not the allegation so states) would amount to a contravention of this Act or give rise to a claim under the Equal Pay Act 1970 [or under sections 62–65 of the Pensions Act 1995],
>
> or by reason that the discriminator knows the person victimised intends to do any of those things, or suspects the person victimised has done, or intends to do, any of them.
>
> (2) Sub-section (1) does not apply to treatment of a person by reason of any allegation made by him if the allegation was false and not made in good faith.[967]

[965] DDA, s 55.

[966] SDA, s 4; RRA, s 2; DDA, s 55; Religion or Belief Regulations, Sexual Orientation Regulations, and Age Regulations, regulations 4; EA, s 45(4).

[967] Words in square brackets inserted by Pensions Act 1995, s 66(2).

Section 2 of the RRA is in materially identical terms.[968] Section 55 of the DDA deals with victimization for the purposes of the DDA. It is drafted in somewhat different terms, though its meaning and effect is now (following amendment) substantially the same. Section 55 of the DDA provides that: 6.320

> (1) For the purposes of Part II[[969]][Part 3[970] or Part 4[971]], a person ('A') discriminates against another person ('B') if—
> (a) he treats B less favourably than he treats or would treat other persons whose circumstances are the same as B's; and
> (b) he does so for a reason mentioned in subsection (2).
>
> (2) The reasons are that—
> (a) B has—
> (i) brought proceedings against A or any other person under this Act; or
> (ii) given evidence or information in connection with such proceedings brought by any person; or
> (iii) otherwise done anything under [, or by reference to,[972]] this Act in relation to A or any other person; or
> (iv) alleged that A or any other person has (whether or not the allegation so states) contravened this Act; or
> (b) A believes or suspects that B has done or intends to do any of those things.
>
> . . .
>
> (4) Subsection (1) does not apply to treatment of a person because of an allegation made by him if the allegation was false and not made in good faith.[973]

The acts set out under section 4(1) of the SDA and section 55(2) of the DDA and the equivalent provisions of the main anti-discrimination enactments are usually described in shorthand as the 'protected acts'. The protected acts are defined in materially the same way under the other main anti-discrimination enactments. 6.321

The victimization provisions do not make any act unlawful by themselves. The victimization provisions merely define one form of discrimination for the purposes of the other parts of the main anti-discrimination enactments. This is plain from the terms of the legislation itself, and has been confirmed by case law.[974] 6.322

---

968 Except that reference is made to the RRA rather than the SDA, EPA, and Pensions Act 1995.

969 Discrimination in the employment field, see Chap 8.

970 Discrimination in the provision of goods and services, housing and public authorities, see Chaps 10 and 11.

971 Discrimination in the field of education, see Chap 9.

972 Added by the DDA 2005. Prior to the DDA 2005, s 55(2)(a)(iii) read 'otherwise done anything under this Act in relation to A or any other person' and s 55(6) read '[f]or the purposes of Part 2 [employment and related fields] and, to the extent that it relates to the provision of employment services, Part 3, subsection 2(a)(iii) has the effect as if there were inserted after "under" or "by reference to"'. S 55(6) was itself inserted to give effect to the Framework Directive by the Disability Discrimination Act 1995 (Amendment) Regulations, SI 2003/1673.

973 DDA, s 55(4).

974 *Nagarajan v Agnew & Ors* [1995] ICR 520; [1994] IRLR 61.

The victimization provisions in the DDA, unlike the other discrimination provisions of the DDA, protect all persons who have done a protected act whether or not they are disabled.[975]

6.323 'Less favourable treatment', for the purposes of the victimization provisions, has the same meaning as in direct discrimination and the observations above (paragraph 6.27 *et seq*) apply equally.

6.324 As with direct discrimination, the victimization provisions depend upon a comparison between the treatment afforded the complainant and another person, who may be a real or hypothetical comparator. As with the direct discrimination provisions, the proper comparator and the relevant circumstances for this purpose have proved controversial. As mentioned, the personal status (sex, racial group etc) of the person victimized is irrelevant to any comparison which must be undertaken. A white person who is less favourably treated for complaining about towards race discrimination a black person has the protection of the victimization provisions under the RRA; the complainant's racial group is irrelevant. This is implicit in the wording of the victimization provisions in the SDA and the RRA, and it is made explicit by the DDA.[976] In the case of the DDA, the disability status of the person victimized is expressly irrelevant to the comparison exercise and must be disregarded.[977] Otherwise, and in all cases, the proper comparison is between a person who has done one of the protected acts and a person who has not done one of the protected acts. The circumstances must otherwise be the same.[978]

6.325 There has been considerable controversy about the relevant circumstances for the purposes of the comparison required. Case law had held that the proper comparator was a person who had done the act which the complainant had done and which caused the less favourable treatment, but otherwise than in circumstances protected by the victimization provisions.[979] This meant that a person

[975] DDA, ss 55(5), 19(4), 21B(6), 21F(7), 22(7), 28A(6), 28R(4). See modification in the context of education, addressed at para 6.330 below (in respect of the provisions affecting schools and education, references to 'B' in (2) above include references to B's parent and a sibling of B. This means that a child's parents and siblings are equally protected but only in respect of protected acts done in the context of the education provisions, DDA, s 55(3A) and (3A)(b)).

[976] DDA, ss 4(5), 12(4), 13(3), 19(4), and 22(7), which state that the unlawful acts concerned apply to non-disabled people where the complaint is of victimization, and s 55(3), which states that where a person victimized has any present or past disability this is to be disregarded in undertaking any comparison for the purposes of the victimization provisions.

[977] DDA, s 55(3).

[978] Ibid, s 55(1)(a); SDA, s 4(1); RRA, s 2(1); Religion or Belief Regulations, Sexual Orientation Regulations, and Age Regulations, regulations 4(1). EA, s 45(4) does not require that the circumstances be the same expressly but the comparison analysis will necessarily require such.

[979] *Kirby v Manpower Services Commission* [1980] ICR 420; [1980] 1 WLR 725; [1980] 3 All ER 334; [1980] IRLR 229.

dismissed for acting as a witness in race discrimination proceedings against her employer was to be compared to a person who had given evidence against her employer in non-discrimination proceedings. This obviously narrowed the reach of the victimization provisions. The issue has now been settled otherwise by the decision of the House of Lords in *Chief Constable of West Yorkshire v Khan*, referred to above for its guidance as to the meaning of less favourable treatment.[980] Detective Sergeant Khan had complained of race discrimination when he was refused promotion over a number of years because of assessments made by his managers. The promotion assessments identified weaknesses in Detective Sergeant Khan which made him unsuitable for promotion to a more senior post. While Detective Sergeant Khan was awaiting a hearing of his race discrimination complaints, he had applied to a different police force for a more senior post . The second police force requested a reference from the Chief Constable of West Yorkshire, Detective Sergeant Khan's employer. Any reference would have been based on the promotion assessments about which Detective Sergeant Khan complained in his race discrimination case. The Chief Constable took advice and refused to provide a reference because of the outstanding proceedings. He responded to the reference request to the effect that there was an outstanding claim in respect of his failure to support Detective Sergeant Khan's application for promotion and that he would make no further comment for fear of prejudicing his own case. Detective Sergeant Khan commenced proceedings for victimization arising out of the refusal to provide him with a reference. The question in the victimization proceedings was then whether the treatment of him should be compared to that afforded a person who had brought proceedings against the Chief Constable other than under the RRA, or whether he should be compared to a person who had not brought proceedings at all. The evidence before the employment tribunal was that the Chief Constable would have refused a reference to any person who had brought proceedings against him where the accuracy of the reference was going to be the subject matter of dispute in the proceedings, whether or not the proceedings were brought under the RRA. Identifying the proper comparator was therefore very important. The House of Lords held that the proper comparator was a person who had not brought proceedings against the Chief Constable at all:

> The statute is to be regarded as calling for a simple comparison between the treatment afforded to the complainant who has done a protected act and the treatment which was or would be afforded to other employees who have not done the protected act. Applying this approach, Sergeant Khan was treated less favourably than other employees. Ordinarily West Yorkshire provides references for members of the force who are seeking new employment.[981]

---

980 Para 6.28.

981 *Chief Constable of West Yorkshire Police v Khan* [2001] UKHL 48; [2001] 1WLR 1947, paras 27–8, *per* Lord Nicholls.

The proper comparator in a victimization complaint is then a person who has not done the act which gave rise to the less favourable treatment. It is not someone who has done the same act, but in circumstances unconnected with the main anti-discrimination enactments. As to constructing a hypothetical comparator, the observations above apply (paragraph 6.46).

6.326 The less favourable treatment must be 'by reason' that the person victimized has done a protected act.[982] As with direct discrimination, it is not necessary that the discriminator was *consciously* motivated or influenced by the fact that the person victimized had done the protected act,[983] so that although victimization 'has a ring of conscious targeting, this is an insufficient basis for excluding cases of unrecognized prejudice'[984] from the victimization provisions. The relevant question is 'why did the alleged discriminator act as he did? What, consciously or unconsciously, was his reason?'[985]

6.327 As with direct discrimination, some case law suggests that whilst the fact that the complainant had done a protected act need not be the sole cause of the less favourable treatment, it must have had a 'significant influence'[986] or be the 'principal' or 'important' cause.[987] This must be regarded as superseded by the Directives which define the principle of equal treatment as prohibiting any discrimination *whatsoever*.[988] Whilst victimization does not expressly form part of the principle of equal treatment, it is covered by the Directives,[989] and the burden of proof provisions will operate upon this form of discrimination in precisely the same way as with direct discrimination (see paragraph 6.72 above). However, a subjective analysis of why the discriminator treated the complainant less favourably is required. Where the protected act has caused the less favourable treatment, it will usually mean that the less favourable treatment was 'by reason' of it. But this will not always be the case, particularly where proceedings are pending. This is an important distinction, because the fact that a complainant has done a protected act will frequently cause another person to act in a particular way, although the latter may have a reason unconnected with the main anti-discrimination enactments for so acting. In *Khan* the House of Lords held that, although

---

982 Or A believes or suspects that B has done or intends to do a protected act: DDA, s 55(2)(b).

983 *Nagarajan v London Regional Transport* [2000] 1 AC 501, [1999] ICR 877, [1999] IRLR 572, para 14, *per* Lord Nicholls.

984 Ibid, *per* Lord Nicholls, para 18.

985 *Chief Constable of West Yorkshire Police v Khan* [2001] UKHL 48; [2001] 1WLR 1947, *per* Lord Nicholls, para 29.

986 *Nagarajan v London Regional Transport* [2000] 1 AC 501, [1999] ICR 877, [1999] IRLR 572, para 14, *per* Lord Nicholls, para 19.

987 Ibid, *per* Lord Steyn, para 34.

988 See para 6.72 above.

989 *Coote v Granada Hospitality Ltd* (Case C-185/97) [1998] IRLR 656; Race Directive, Art 9; Framework Directive, Art 11.

the fact that Detective Sergeant Khan had brought proceedings caused the Chief Constable to refuse a reference, this did not establish that the refusal was 'by reason' of the fact that he had brought proceedings:

> Employers, acting honestly and reasonably, ought to be able to take steps to preserve their position in pending discrimination proceedings without laying themselves open to a charge of victimisation. This accords with the spirit and purpose of the Act. Moreover, the statute accommodates this approach without any straining of the language. An employer who conducts himself in this way is not doing so because of the fact that the complainant has brought discrimination proceedings. He is doing so because, currently and temporarily, he needs to take steps to preserve his position in the outstanding proceedings. Protected act (a) ('by reason that the person victimised has—(a) brought proceedings against the discriminator . . . under this Act'[990]) cannot have been intended to prejudice an employer's proper conduct of his defence, so long as he acts honestly and reasonably. Acting within this limit, he cannot be regarded as discriminating by way of victimisation against the employee who brought the proceedings.[991]

Importantly, the House of Lords in *Khan* was influenced by the fact that Detective Sergeant Khan's complaint of race discrimination was outstanding. Their Lordships held that the pending proceedings had the effect of changing the relationship between Detective Sergeant Khan and the Chief Constable. Once proceedings had been commenced they were not just employer and employee, but also adversaries in litigation. The Chief Constable was entitled to protect himself in respect of that litigation. Indeed he could have been roundly criticized and ordered to pay more compensation if he provided a reference based on the promotion assessments when Detective Sergeant Khan was complaining that they were racially discriminatory, and that issue had not been decided. According to Lord Hoffman: **6.328**

> A test which is likely in most cases to give the right answer is to ask whether the employer would have refused the request if the litigation had been concluded, whatever the outcome. If the answer is no, it will usually follow that the reason for refusal was the existence of the proceedings and not the fact that the employee had commenced them. On the other hand, if the fact that the employee had commenced proceedings under the Act was a real reason why he received less favourable treatment, it is no answer that the employer would have behaved in the same way to an employee who had done some non-protected act, such as commencing proceedings otherwise than under the Act.[992]

In many cases where proceedings are outstanding, alleged discriminators must take steps in connection with those proceedings which are *less favourable* to the **6.329**

990 DDA, s 55(a)(i).

991 *Chief Constable of West Yorkshire Police v Khan* [2001] UKHL 48; [2001] 1WLR 1947, *per* Lord Nicholls, para 31.

992 Ibid, para 60.

person who has brought the proceedings (by, for example, collecting evidence against an employee; making statements which are adverse to an employee, etc) and a prohibition on allowing them to do so might interfere with their right to a fair resolution of those proceedings. But a discriminator will need to show, as in *Khan*, that there was a reason apart from the fact that proceedings were commenced which caused the less favourable treatment. A court or tribunal is likely to be satisfied that any less favourable treatment was caused by the bringing of the proceedings where the less favourable treatment complained of is unreasonable, unconnected with the proceedings, or dishonest. In *IRC v Morgan*,[993] for example, the Employment Appeal Tribunal upheld a finding of victimization made by an employment tribunal arising out of a memo sent by a manager to staff addressing a race discrimination claim brought by one of their colleagues. The memo gave 'a general warning' that, because of the complainant's complaints of race discrimination, details of personnel records might possibly become public knowledge. The Employment Appeal Tribunal concluded that the employment tribunal were entitled to find that the circulation of the memo constituted less favourable treatment of the complainant and victimization.

6.330 As mentioned above the protected acts are those set out in the enactments themselves, and a complainant must identify which applies, though often (because of their overlap) more than one will be relied upon[994]. In relation to the first protected act ('brought proceedings against A or any other person under this Act'), as can be seen from *Khan* and the discussion above, where the protected act relied upon is the bringing of proceedings, the less favourable treatment must be something other than an honest and reasonable step in the proceedings, taken to preserve the alleged discriminator's position in outstanding proceedings. As to the second protected act ('given evidence or information in connection with such proceedings brought by any person'), this is self-explanatory. The proceedings in respect of which evidence or information have been given must be proceedings under the main anti-discrimination enactments, as the provisions make clear. There is some case law indicating that this protected act cannot be relied upon where proceedings have not yet been brought at the time of the less favourable treatment (even if they are brought thereafter).[995] The third protected act ('otherwise done anything under or by reference to this Act in relation to A or any other person') is a 'catch-all' and protects a person who does anything under or by refer-

[993] *Commissioners of Inland Revenue and another v Morgan* [2002] IRLR 776. See to similar effect, *St Helens MBC v J E Derbyshire & 38 Ors* (2004) Appeal No. UKEAT/0952/03/ILB.

[994] *Nagarajan v London Regional Transport* [2000] 1 AC 501, [1999] ICR 877, [1999] IRLR 572.

[995] *Kirby v Manpower Services Commission* [1980] ICR 420; [1980] 1 WLR 725; [1980] 3 All ER 334; [1980] IRLR 229, para 15.

ence to the main anti-discrimination enactments, for example, serving a questionnaire.[996] Where a complainant relies on something done *under* the main anti-discrimination enactments, case law indicates that a specific provision (under which the act is done) must be capable of identification and must be identified.[997] The words 'by reference to' import a wider reach. Thus, for example, a report made to the Community Relations Council by an employee of a Job Centre about racially discriminatory client employers was something done *by reference to* the RRA.[998] Similarly, attending an employment tribunal to offer support to a complainant in proceedings under the main anti-discrimination enactments would be protected, because this would be something which is done by reference to the Act.[999] As the fourth protected act 'alleged that A or any other person has (whether or not the allegation so states) contravened this Act', this requires that, though the allegation need not identify the enactments at all, the facts founding the allegation must be capable of constituting a contravention of the enactment in issue.[1000] This is a rather narrow approach, particularly given the technical complexities of the main anti-discrimination enactments. Similarly, however, a generalized complaint that there has been some unspecified discrimination may be insufficient.[1001] If an allegation proves not to be capable of constituting an unlawful act, the making of it might still be protected as done 'by reference' to the main anti-discrimination enactments especially if they are referred to in terms.[1002] The protected acts must be done by the complainant, except that in the case of claims of victimization made under the schools provisions, where the protected acts concern

996 *National Probation Service for England and Wales (Cumbria Area) v Kirby* [2006] IRLR 508 (holding that the protection, which applies where the victimization is 'by reason that the person victimised has . . . otherwise done anything under or by reference to this Act in relation to the discriminator or any other person', is a 'catch-all' which is necessarily wider than the more restricted circumstances set out in s 2(1)(a), (b), and (d) of the RRA (and the directly parallel provisions of the other discrimination statutes). In this case, that covered the claimant's participation in an interview by the employers' assistant chief officer concerning an allegation by one of the claimant's work colleagues of race discrimination against a manager, even though the claimant herself during the interview made no suggestion that she had witnessed race discrimination. 'That was otherwise doing something by reference to the Act in relation to another person', says Judge Peter Clark, 'construing s.2(1)(c) generically with the circumstances set out in s.2(1)(a), (b) and (d).' See Chap 14 for questionnaires.

997 *Kirby v Manpower Services Commission* [1980] ICR 420; [1980] 1 WLR 725; [1980] 3 All ER 334; [1980] IRLR 229.

998 Ibid.

999 Employment Code of Practice of Practice, para 4.33.

1000 *Waters v Commissioner of Police for the Metropolis* [1997] ICR 1073[1997] IRLR 589.

1001 In *Benn v London Borough of Hackney* (Case No 22956/91 DCLD 19), an employment tribunal held that allegations of a racist or sexist 'culture' did not amount to an allegation that the SDA and RRA had been contravened.

1002 *Kirby v Manpower Services Commission* [1980] ICR 420; [1980] 1 WLR 725; [1980] 3 All ER 334; [1980] IRLR 229, in which the overlap between these provisions in sub-ss (iii) and (iv) in the RRA was acknowledged, see para 18.

the schools provisions of the DDA, they may be done by the complainant's parent or sibling.[1003]

6.331 There is a statutory defence available in respect of a complaint of victimization. The victimization provisions do not apply to treatment of a person because of an 'allegation made by him if the allegation was false and not made in good faith'.[1004] These requirements are conjunctive and accordingly both elements must be satisfied. A person who makes an allegation in good faith which turns out to be false will be protected, as will a person who makes an allegation of discrimination which is true, but which is made for some improper motive. In practice this defence is very rarely relied upon.

6.332 As mentioned above, there are specific provisions addressing the burden of proof and the shifting of it in certain circumstances, and these apply equally to victimization as to direct discrimination. This is described at Chapter 14 below. As with direct discrimination, a court or tribunal is entitled to infer that the less favourable treatment of a person who has done one of the protected acts was by reason of his or her having done the protected act, without proof of intent, motive, or otherwise, where there is an otherwise inadequate explanation by the discriminator.[1005]

1003 DDA, s 55(3A).

1004 SDA, s 4(2); RRA, s 2(2); and DDA, s 55(4). EA, s 45(5); Regulations 4(2) of the Religion or Belief Regulations, the Sexual Orientation Regulations, and the Age Regulations, are to the same effect.

1005 *Nagarajan v London Regional Transport* [2000] 1 AC 501, [1999] ICR 877, [1999] IRLR 572, *per* Lord Nicholls at paras 17–19.

Part III

THE UNLAWFUL ACTS AND ENFORCEMENT

7

THE UNLAWFUL ACTS: AN INTRODUCTION

> The most beautiful and enriching trait of human life is diversity—a diversity that can never be used to justify inequality. Repressing diversity will impoverish the human race. We must facilitate and strengthen diversity in order to reach a more equitable world for us all. For equality to exist, we must avoid standards that define what a normal human life should be or the normal way of achieving success and happiness. The only normal quality that can exist among human beings is life itself.[1]

As mentioned in previous chapters, the main anti-discrimination enactments do not create any broad equality guarantees, but instead create a series of statutory torts outlawing discrimination as defined in the context of certain activities. The provision made is now very full indeed, and, whilst earlier case law suggested that the anti-discrimination enactments did not create 'a comprehensive anti-discrimination scheme',[2] many of the lacunae have since been filled. **7.01**

The meaning given to 'discrimination' by the main anti-discrimination enactments is explained in Chapter 6. Discrimination, for the purposes of the unlawful acts, may occur, depending on the unlawful act concerned, because of direct or indirect discrimination, disability-related discrimination, harassment or victimization, or because of a breach of the reasonable adjustments duties.[3] This can mean that in certain circumstances a failure to take positive action may give rise to liability, in particular where such a failure amounts to a breach of a reasonable adjustments duty, or where the maintenance of a particular practice constitutes indirect discrimination. **7.02**

---

[1] Dr Oscar Arias, President, Costa Rica, cited in 'From Exclusion to Inclusion, Final Report of the Disability Rights Taskforce', December 1999 at <http://www.dft.gov.uk/stellent/groups/dft_mobility/documents/divisionhomepage/611413.hcsp>.

[2] *Rhys-Harper v Relaxion Group plc & others* [2003] UKHL 33; [2003] ICR 867; [2003] IRLR 484, para 133.

[3] See Chap 6.

7.03 As to the unlawful acts, these create a series of statutory torts,[4] enforceable by individuals in the courts and tribunals in the usual way.[5] The number of unlawful acts has increased over time, by amendments to the main anti-discrimination enactments. Their coverage, however, differs as between the main anti-discrimination enactments, as discussed in Chapter 2. The coverage of the Sex Discrimination Act 1975 (SDA), the Race Relations Act 1976 (RRA), and the Disability Discrimination Act 1995 (DDA) is now wide. All three enactments have been fairly recently amended so as to outlaw discrimination by public authorities in the exercising of their public functions. The impetus for these amendments came, in the first place, from the findings of the Stephen Lawrence Inquiry,[6] and accordingly the first amendments were seen in the RRA. All the activities of public authorities are now caught by the unlawful acts created by the SDA, RRA, and DDA, save where specifically exempted. The Religion or Belief Regulations, the Sexual Orientation Regulations, and the Age Regulations, on the other hand, address only discrimination in the employment and related fields, including, in certain contexts, education. The Equality Act 2006 (EA) fills many of the gaps in protection against discrimination connected with religion or belief by creating unlawful acts comparable to those made under the SDA, RRA, and DDA.[7] The provisions in the EA are expected to be brought into force in April 2007. The specific unlawful acts created are described below.

7.04 Importantly, sexual orientation discrimination outside the employment and related fields is not yet outlawed by the anti-discrimination enactments. However, as mentioned in Chapter 2, in the course of the EA's progress through Parliament, following significant lobbying from, in particular, Stonewall, at the third reading stage the Government accepted an amendment to the Bill, giving the Secretary of State broad powers to make Regulations which prohibit sexual orientation discrimination in the field of non-employment (mirroring the provision made in respect of religion, belief, and other strands). The Government has since issued a consultation paper 'Getting Equal: Proposals to Outlaw Sexual Orientation Discrimination in the Provision of Goods & Services'[8] which sought views on specific points about the range of activities that should be covered by the Regulations, and on whether any exceptions should be provided from them to ensure that the protection from sexual orientation discrimination that is introduced is effective

4 *Hall v Woolston Hall Leisure Ltd* [2001] ICR 99.

5 As to remedies and enforcement, see Chap 14.

6 *The Stephen Lawrence Inquiry: Report of an Inquiry by Sir William MacPherson of Cluny advised by Tom Cook, the Rt Rev Dr John Sentamu, Dr Richard Stone*, Cm4262-I, as discussed in Chap 2.

7 Except in the employment and related fields and in further and higher education which is addressed by the Religion or Belief Regulations.

8 (2006) Women and Equality Unit.

and appropriately targeted. The Government intends to introduce and implement the Regulations addressing sexual orientation in those fields, broadly, covered by the EA in the context of religion or belief in around April 2007, and at the same time as the provisions in the EA addressing religion or belief discrimination are brought into force.

There are numerous exemptions to the unlawful acts created by the main anti- **7.05** discrimination enactments. Many of those exemptions limit their operation considerably. Some exemptions are of general application and others are specific to certain of the unlawful acts. The generic exemptions are discussed in Chapter 13, and the activity-specific exemptions are discussed as they arise in relation to each of the unlawful acts. Further, as explained in Chapter 6, there are exceptions[9] embedded in certain of the concepts of discrimination themselves.

The RRA now creates a complex scheme both for identifying discrimination, as **7.06** described in Chapter 6, and in the creation of its unlawful acts. Some of the unlawful acts only apply to discrimination connected to race, ethnic, and national origins reflecting the origin of these acts in the Race Directive.[10] These are identified below, but in summary include those statutory torts which outlaw harassment;[11] discrimination against office holders;[12] discrimination occurring after a relevant relationship has ended;[13] and certain of the exemptions apply only to such discrimination.[14] Conversely, some exemptions apply only to discrimination connected to grounds *other* than race, ethnicity, and national origins, reflecting the requirements of the Race Directive.[15]

Discrimination in the context of employment and in other work relationships falls **7.07** under Part 2 of each of the main anti-discrimination enactments. Discrimination in the provision of goods, facilities, and services, and in relation to the disposal and management of premises and by public authorities in the exercising of their public functions, falls within Part 3 of the SDA, RRA, and DDA, and Part 2 of the EA.[16] Discrimination by educational institutions and related bodies falls within

---

9 For example, by way of a 'justification' defence.

10 See Chap 4.

11 Eg, RRA, s 4(2A). See Chap 8 below.

12 RRA, s 76ZA.

13 Ibid, s 27A, see Chap 12.

14 See, RRA, s 4A (genuine occupational requirement).

15 Ibid, ss 10(1A) (exemption for small partnerships), 21(3) (exemption relating to home sales), 22(1) and 24(2) (small premises exemptions), 34(2)(b) (exception in relation to acts done to give effect to a provision in a charitable instrument), 36 (provision of education and training for persons not ordinarily resident in Great Britain), 41(1A) (acts done under statutory authority). See too the burden of proof provisions which are limited to discriminatory acts connected to race, ethnicity, or national origins (s 54A), Chap 14.

16 Part 3 of the EA gives the Secretary of State power to make regulations outlawing sexual orientation discrimination in the same fields, as mentioned in para 7.04.

Part 3 of the SDA and RRA, Part 4 of the DDA, Part 2 of the EA, and Part 2 of the Religion or Belief Regulations, the Sexual Orientation Regulations, and the Age Regulations. In broad terms, the order followed by the main anti-discrimination enactments is followed below in addressing the unlawful acts created by them.

7.08 The main anti-discrimination enactments provide for the taking of strategic action, in particular by the statutory equality Commissions.[17] The statutory Commissions have exclusive powers to take proceedings in respect of certain unlawful acts (for example, discriminatory advertisements and pressure to discriminate) where there may be potentially multiple victims (or none). They may also bring proceedings in judicial review. Certain public authorities are now also required to take strategic action because of the imposition of statutory equality duties upon them. The statutory Commissions have power to take enforcement action in respect of non-compliance with those duties. The Commissions also have important powers to undertake formal investigations and to take action in respect of any findings of discrimination which emerge.[18] These powers and obligations are of a more strategic nature than the individually enforceable unlawful acts addressed in Chapters 8 to 12. These strategic powers and obligations are considered and explained in Chapter 15.

[17] The Equal Opportunities Commission, the Commission for Racial Equality, the Disability Rights Commission, and, from October 2007, the Commission for Equality and Human Rights and the Northern Ireland Equality Commission (see Chap 15), may all take action which does not depend upon an individual complainant, or in certain circumstances, even an individual wrong. Strategic action is addressed in Chap 15.

[18] The anticipatory reasonable adjustment duties imposed on service providers, *inter alia*, explained in Chap 6 might also be described as a form of strategic action, but these create individually enforceable rights where a breach of a duty is made unlawful, as described in Chap 6.

8

EMPLOYMENT AND OCCUPATION

A. Introduction

All the main anti-discrimination enactments outlaw discrimination in the context of employment and occupation widely. The provision made regulates discrimination against prospective employees and other workers, existing employees and other workers, and ex-employees and other workers.[1] In the Disability Discrimination Act 1995 (DDA) full protection is afforded to disabled people only.[2] **8.01**

Amendments made to the Sex Discrimination Act 1975 (SDA), the Race Relations Act 1976 (RRA), and the DDA to give effect to EU law[3] have extended the scope of the enactments. EU law has also resulted in the enactment of the Religion or Belief Regulations, the Sexual Orientation Regulations, and the Age Regulations. In consequence protection against discrimination in the context of employment and **8.02**

[1] SDA, ss 6, 9, 10B, 11, 12, 13, 14, 15, 16, 17, and 20A; RRA, ss 4, 7, 10, 11, 12, 13, 14, 15, and 27A; DDA, ss 4, 4D, 6A, 7A, 7C, 13, 14A, 14C, 15B, and 16A; regulations 6, 8, 10, 11, 11A, 12, 13, 14, 15, 16, 17, 18, 19, and 21 of the Religion or Belief Regulations and the Sexual Orientation Regulations; and regulations 7, 9, 12, 13, 14, 15, 16, 17, 18, 19, 20, 21, 22, and 24 of the Age Regulations.

[2] The only protection afforded disabled people relates to victimization, see Chap 6.

[3] In particular, the Race Directive and Framework Directive, see Chap 4.

occupation is fairly comprehensive so that most discrimination will be outlawed, save where a specific exemption applies. Importantly, the new provisions addressing certain discriminatory acts (office holders, discrimination against ex-employees and workers, and harassment[4]) and exemptions (genuine occupational requirements) introduced into the RRA to give effect to the Race Directive[5] apply only to discrimination connected to race or ethnic or national origins. These reflect the limitations in the Race Directive discussed in Chapter 4.

8.03 There remain some lacunae caused by the breadth of exemptions in certain areas, as described below,[6] and because certain forms of discrimination are not outlawed at all or do not give rise to individually enforceable rights, as is discussed in Chapter 2.[7]

B. Employment

8.04 Discrimination by employers is outlawed specifically. The main anti-discrimination enactments make it unlawful for an employer, in relation to employment by him at an establishment in Great Britain,[8] to discriminate in the arrangements[9] he makes for the purpose of determining who should be offered employment, or in the terms on which he offers employment, or by refusing or deliberately omitting to offer employment.[10] As to existing employees it is unlawful for a person, in the case of a person employed by him at an establishment in Great Britain,[11] to discriminate against an employee in the terms of employment which he affords; or in the way he affords access to opportunities for promotion, transfer, or training, or to any other benefits, facilities, or services, or by refusing or deliberately omitting to afford access to them; or by dismissing, or subjecting

[4] RRA, ss 3A, 76ZA, and 27A. See too, Chap 6 for the different forms of indirect discrimination applicable under the RRA, reflecting again the impact of the Race Directive.

[5] Race Relations Act 1976 (Amendment) Regulations 2003 SI 2003/1626.

[6] 'Age' being the most stark example, see para 8.49.

[7] As with, eg, 'instructions to discriminate' and disability.

[8] For territorial jurisdiction, see Chap 8.

[9] Given the significant change to the meaning of indirect discrimination, and in particular to the concept of disparate impact so that only 'particular disadvantage' needs now to be shown, the result in *Lord Chancellor v Coker & Osamor* [2001] EWCA Civ 1756; [2002] ICR 321; [2002] IRLR 80 might be different. Word of mouth recruitment, warned against by the Court of Appeal in that case in a bemusing postscript, might arguably now found a claim in indirect discrimination, having regard to its new meaning (see Chap 6) (see the observations of Mummery LJ, at ICR 321, 339–40 and IRLR paras 53–7).

[10] SDA, s 6(1). RRA, s 4(1), DDA, s 4(1), and regulations 6(1) of the Religion or Belief and Sexual Orientation Regulations are in materially identical terms.

[11] For territorial jurisdiction, see Chap 13.

an employee to any other 'detriment'.[12] It is also unlawful for an employer to subject to harassment a person whom he employs or a person who has applied to him for employment.[13]

Further, discrimination and harassment against ex-employees is outlawed, where it subjects an ex-employee to a detriment and the discrimination or harassment 'arises out of and is closely connected to the relevant relationship'. A 'relevant relationship' is an employment or other relationship caught by Part 2 of the enactments.[14] Examples include discriminatory refusals to provide references; discrimination in the handling of an internal appeal against dismissal; and a discriminatory failure to reinstate.[15] The Framework Directive specifically addresses discrimination occurring after a relevant relationship. It provides that Member States must ensure that appropriate measures are in place for the enforcement of obligations under the Directive to all persons 'who consider themselves wronged by failure to apply the principle of equal treatment to them, even after the relationship in which the discrimination is alleged to have occurred has ended'.[16] The Race Directive and the amended Equal Treatment Directive contain identical provisions.[17] To give effect to this requirement, all the main anti-discrimination enactments now contain express provision addressing discrimination after a relevant relationship has ended.[18] **8.05**

There are differences in the way that the SDA regulates discrimination in relation to existing employees because pay is dealt with separately under the Equal Pay Act 1970 (EPA), as discussed in Chapter 6.[19] For this reason, the SDA does not make **8.06**

12 RRA, s 4(2); DDA, s 4(2) (which is in materially identical terms); s 6(2) of the Religion or Belief, Sexual Orientation, and Age Regulations, which are also in materially identical terms).

13 SDA, s 6(2A); RRA, s 4(2A); DDA, s 4(3); Religion or Belief Regulations and Sexual Orientation Regulations, regulation 6 and Age Regulations, regulation 7.

14 SDA, s 20A; RRA, s 27A (which applies only to discrimination connected to race, ethnic, or national origins but extends beyond relationships found in Part 2, see Chap 12); DDA, s 16A (and importantly, in addition, s 16A imposes a duty to make reasonable adjustments in the same circumstances as would apply were the relevant relationship still in place but this does not apply to councillors and members of other relevant authorities under s 15B, see para 8.18 below); Religion or Belief Regulations and Sexual Orientation Regulations, regulations 21, and Age Regulations, regulation 24 (which also apply to further and higher education).

15 *Coote v Granada Hospitality Limited (No 2)* [1999] ICR 942; [1999] IRLR 452; *Kirker v British Sugar plc* [2003] UKHL 33, [2003] ICR 867; [2003] IRLR 484; *Adekeye v The Post Office (No 2)* [1997] ICR 110; [1997] IRLR 105; *D'Souza v London Borough of Lambeth* [2003] UKHL 33, [2003] ICR 867; [2003] IRLR 484, though in each of these cases the law at the time precluded action being taken. Following *Rhys-Harper v Relaxion Group plc & others* [2003] UKHL 33; [2003] ICR 867; [2003] IRLR 484 and then the express provision made following amendments to the enactments, these cases would be decided differently.

16 Framework Directive, Art 9(1).

17 Article 7(1) and Article 6(1) respectively.

18 Giving statutory effect to the holding in *Rhys-Harper v Relaxion Group plc & others* [2003] UKHL 33; [2003] ICR 867; [2003] IRLR 484. See, further, Chap 12.

19 And further below at para 8.19.

it unlawful for an employer to discriminate against a woman in relation to the 'terms of employment which he affords her'. Otherwise the unlawful acts are the same.[20]

8.07 The unlawful acts are very widely drawn. The concept of 'detriment', for the purposes of the employment provisions, is particularly expansive. As already referred to,[21] it has the same meaning as 'less favourable treatment', an expression seen in various of the definitions of discrimination. It will protect against any 'disadvantage',[22] whether or not the person subjected to the discriminatory treatment was aware of it at the time.[23] In particular, it is not necessary to establish any tangible disadvantage, for example pecuniary losses, but instead a mere loss of opportunity, even if only valued by the claimant, will be sufficient.[24] The concept of 'detriment' was wide enough to cover harassment, and much of the case law developed under the main anti-discrimination enactments in relation to harassment[25] developed under the 'detriment' provisions. However, since the amendments made to the main anti-discrimination enactments to give effect to the Race Directive, the Framework Directive, and the amended Equal Treatments Directive[26] special provision is made so as to ensure that there is no overlap between the new harassment provisions and the provisions outlawing discriminatory 'detriments'. Each of the main anti-discrimination enactments now provides that 'detriment' 'does not include conduct of a nature such as to constitute harassment' under the express provisions addressing the same.[27] Detriment covers a wide range of conduct nevertheless, and might be regarded as a residual provision in that any disadvantageous conduct which does not fall within the scope of one of the other unlawful acts is likely to fall within the concept of 'detriment'. This means that any discriminatory treatment within the employment and related fields is likely to be unlawful unless subject to a specific exemption. The meaning given to 'dismissal' is also wide and includes a termination of employment by the expiration of notice and a constructive dismissal.[28]

---

20 SDA, s 6(2). See further SDA, s 6(6), addressed below at para 8.46.

21 Chap 6.

22 *Jeremiah v Ministry of Defence* [1980] ICR 13; [1980] QB 87; [1979] IRLR 436.

23 *Garry v London Borough of Ealing* [2001] IRLR 681.

24 *Chief Constable of West Yorkshire Police v Khan* [2001] UKHL 48; [2001] 1 WLR 1947; [2001] ICR 1065; [2001] IRLR 830. See, too, *Gill v El Vino Co Limited* [1983] QB 425; *R v Birmingham City Council ex p Equal Opportunities Commission* [1989] AC 1155; [1989] IRLR 173; *Simon v Brimham Associates* [1987] ICR 596; [1987] IRLR 307 (though the result in this case is somewhat unfathomable, see 'Highlights' [1987] IRLR 305–306).

25 See Chap 6.

26 See Chap 4.

27 RRA, s 78(1) and to materially identical effect; SDA, s 82; DDA, s 18D (except in relation to s 16(2)(b), instructions and pressure to discriminate), and Religion or Belief Regulations, Sexual Orientation Regulations, and Age Regulations, regulations 2(3).

28 SDA, s 82(1A); RRA, s 4(4A); DDA, s 4(5) (and importantly, as mentioned in Chap 6, the duty to make reasonable adjustments now applies in relation to dismissals, cf DDA, s 6(2) of the unamended DDA); Religion or Belief Regulations and Sexual Orientation Regulations, regulation 6(5), and Age Regulations, regulation 7(7).

Each of the main anti-discrimination enactments defines 'employment' and related terms broadly, so that 'employment' 'means employment under a contract of service or of apprenticeship or a contract personally to execute any work or labour', and related expressions are to be construed accordingly.[29] This means that the unlawful acts relating to employment apply to a wide range of working relationships and, in particular, their application is not limited to those engaged under a 'contract of service' which certain of the other employment enactments require for their protection.[30] In addition to apprentices, persons working under a contract, where that contract is personally to do work or where the dominant purpose of that contract is to do work personally, will be protected.[31] This means that the relationship between employer and employee need not be solely for the provision of labour for a wage, but that there must be some obligation to personally perform work or labour, and the contract must contemplate that as its dominant purpose.[32] The fact that work undertaken personally pursuant to a contractual arrangement is provided to a third party is not inconsistent with an employment relationship between worker and 'employer'.[33] Persons 'on the books' of an employment agency who were engaged under a contract described as a 'temporary workers contract' and sent to clients to provide work were 'employed' by the employment agency for the purposes of the DDA.[34] Temporary workers engaged by an employment agency to provide work for third parties will not, however, always be employed by the employment agency.[35] In some circumstances, agency workers will instead be treated as employed by the third party clients, depending upon whether or not it can be said that the relationship between the client third party and the agency worker satisfies the irreducible minimum necessary to establish a contractual relationship.[36] The reality of the situation must be considered in 8.08

29 SDA, s 82; RRA, s 78, RRA; DDA,s 68(1) (the DDA provides, too, that such meaning is 'subject to any prescribed provision', but none has been made); Religion or Belief Regulations and Sexual Orientation Regulations, regulations 2(3) and Age Regulations, regulation 2(3).

30 See, eg, Employment Rights Act 1996, s 230.

31 *Mirror Group Newspapers Limited v Gunning* [1986] ICR 145; [1986] IRLR 27.

32 Ibid. And see *Hugh-Jones v St John's College Cambridge* [1979] ICR 848; *Byrne Brothers (Formwork) Limited v Baird* [2002] ICR 667; [2002] IRLR 96 (in respect of claims brought under the analogous definition of 'worker' in the Working Time Regulations 1998); *Loughran & Kelly v Northern Ireland Housing Executive* [1998] ICR 828; [1998] IRLR 70 (under the analogous provisions in the Fair Employment (Northern Ireland) Act 1976); and, conversely *Patterson v Legal Services Commission* [2004] EWCA Civ 1558; [2004] ICR 312; [2004] IRLR 153 and *Commissioners of Inland Revenue & Others v Post Office Limited* [2003] ICR 546; [2003] IRLR 199.

33 *Burton v Higham t/a Ace Appointments* [2003] IRLR 257 (falling under the, now repealed, small-employer exemption in DDA, s 7 but which remains good law for the purposes of DDA, s 68(1)).

34 Ibid.

35 *Bunce v Postworth Limited t/a Slyblue* [2005] IRLR 557.

36 *Dacas v Brook Street Bureau (UK) Limited* [2004] ICR 1437; [2004] IRLR 358.

all cases. An employment relationship may be inferred,[37] and the fact that an express provision in a written agreement purports to preclude a contract of employment is not by itself conclusive.[38]

8.09 The wide meaning given to the concept of 'employment' in the main anti-discrimination enactments nevertheless requires a contractual relationship at its core. This requires that there be some mutuality of obligation. However, it does not require that any obligation be enforceable as a matter of common law. This is important in the context of contracts tainted with illegality, for example where an employee is implicated in tax evasion. In such circumstances a claim will still lie under the main anti-discrimination enactments, notwithstanding that as a matter of common law such a contract would be unenforceable.[39] This is because:

> the anti-discrimination Acts are not really concerned with employees' rights under their contracts of employment. So, for instance, where a contract of employment is tainted by illegality, an employee may nonetheless complain that her employer discriminated against her . . . since [the legislation is] designed to provide effective relief in respect of discriminatory conduct 'rather than relief which reflects any contractual entitlement which may or may not exist'.[40]
>
> It is the . . . discrimination that is the core of the complaint, the fact of employment and the dismissal being the particular factual circumstances which parliament has prescribed for the . . . discrimination complaint to be capable of being made'.[41] Accordingly a complaint of discrimination under the main anti-discrimination enactments 'does not involve enforcing, relying on or founding a claim on the contract of employment'.[42]

8.10 The position might be different if there is active participation in the illegality[43] or if the contract itself was entered into for an illegal purpose. However, mere illegality

---

37 Ibid. And see *Cotswold Developments Construction Limited v Williams* [2006] IRLR 181; *Cable & Wireless plc v Muscat* [2006] IRLR 354; [2006] ICR 975 (a contract could be inferred between client and agency worker where it was necessary to give business reality to the relationship between the parties and where both the irreducible minimum requirements of mutuality and control—in the case of a contract of employment—by the end user were present, but it did not matter that payment was made through the agency, indirectly). See also *James v Greenwich Council* [2006] UKEAT 6/06.

38 Ibid.

39 *Hall v Woolston Hall Leisure Limited* [2001] ICR 99; [2000] IRLR 578, at 586, para 67, *per* Lord Justice Mance. This case was referred to approvingly in *Rhys-Harper v Relaxion Group plc & others* [2003] UKHL; [2003] ICR 867; [2003] IRLR 484, para 210.

40 *Rhys-Harper v Relaxion Group plc & others* [2003] UKHL 33; [2003] ICR 867; [2003] IRLR 484, para 210.

41 *Hall v Woolston Hall Leisure Limited* [2000] IRLR 578, 584, *per* Peter Gibson LJ.

42 *Leighton v Michael* [1995] ICR 1091; [1996] IRLR 67, 69, para 29, *per* Mummery J. This is important not just for the employment and related fields but also for discriminatory acts occurring outside the employment field which may suppose the existence of a contract underpinning a relevant relationship between the parties, as, for example, between landlord and tenant, see Chap 10.

43 *Hall v Woolston Hall Leisure Limited* [2000] IRLR 578, paras 46, 47, and 80.

in performance will not deprive a complainant of the benefit of the protection afforded by the main anti-discrimination enactments.

Volunteers are not covered by the employment provisions. This is because in the case of a pure volunteer there is no mutuality of obligation and accordingly no contract in existence, and as such there is no protection under the employment provisions of the main anti-discrimination enactments. This may be so even where there is some degree of commitment required by the volunteering arrangement and where expenses are paid.[44] In determining whether an arrangement really is a volunteering arrangement: **8.11**

> at least one test which may help in this identification exercise is to consider whether, if the volunteer should decline without prior notice to perform any work for the employer, the latter would have any legal remedy against him; and similarly to consider whether, if the volunteer attends to do work and there is none, he has any legal remedy against the employer.[45]

In the absence of any contractual relationship, there is not an employment relationship even within the extended meaning given to that expression under the main anti-discrimination enactments. The fact that such a meaning excludes volunteers has proved particularly significant in the context of disability discrimination because volunteering has proved an important means of helping disabled people enter the labour market.[46]

As to other workers covered by the employment provisions, they include police officers who, because of their peculiar constitutional position (that is, that they are office holders with an original jurisdiction and not employees at common law), are **8.12**

44 *South East Sheffield Citizens Advice Bureaux v Grayson* [2004] ICR 1138; [2004] IRLR 353 (this case concerned a small employer exemption in the DDA—now repealed—and the question therefore was whether volunteers could be included for the purposes of the small employer calculation. The case however remains good law for the purposes of the employment provisions more broadly); *Melhuish v Redbridge Citizens Advice Bureaux* [2005] IRLR 419.

45 *South East Sheffield Citizens Advice Bureaux v Grayson* [2004] IRLR 353, para 13.

46 The Joint Committee on the Draft Disability Bill recommended before the enactment of the DDA 2005 that volunteers be brought within the scope of the DDA. Firstly, they recommended that the Government should consult on and produce an employment code on volunteers. Secondly, they recommended that the Disability Discrimination Bill should include a regulation-making power, enabling volunteers to be brought within the coverage of the DDA, should a code prove ineffective. Thirdly, they recommended that alongside a voluntary code the Disability Discrimination Bill should include a provision protecting disabled people who are volunteers, or who apply to volunteer, from direct discrimination. In so recommending, the joint committee drew attention to the real importance of volunteering to disabled people (Joint Committee on the Draft Disability Discrimination Bill, First Report (May 2004), paras 353–61). The Government did not accept those recommendations, taking the view that it was not right to legislate in relation to volunteers at that stage: the Government's Response to the Report of the Joint Committee on the Draft Disability Discrimination Bill (July 2004), DWP, Response to Recommendation 63 and 64.

made subject to a statutory deeming provision. For the purposes of the main anti-discrimination enactments, police officers are treated as employees and are therefore protected by the employment provisions, and the vicarious liability provisions are modified so that vicarious liability arises in respect of the acts of police officers as against the Chief Constable of Police.[47]

8.13 The employment provisions of the main anti-discrimination enactments also apply to service in a government department, for a minister of the Crown and to service on behalf of the Crown, to the holding of a statutory office, and for purposes of a statutory body in the same way as they apply to employment by a private person.[48] The employment provisions also apply to staff at the House of Commons and the House of Lords.[49]

8.14 Members of the armed forces are expressly protected by the employment provisions of the main anti-discrimination enactments,[50] except in the case of the DDA and the Age Regulations. Both provide that the employment and related provisions do not apply to service in 'any of the naval, military or air forces of the crown'.[51] As to disability, the Joint Committee on the Draft Disability Discrimination Bill, before the enactment of the DDA 2005, recommended that the Bill should include a regulation-making power enabling the Government to delete the exemption but the Government did not accept that recommendation.[52] The exemptions are, as the Government has observed, consistent with the Framework Directive.[53]

---

47 SDA, s 17; RRA, s 76A; DDA, s 64A; EA, s 75; and Religion or Belief Regulations and Sexual Orientation Regulations, regulations 11, and the Age Regulations, regulation 13. This addresses the difficulties that otherwise would arise, in particular, with vicarious liability, see *Farah v Metropolitan Police Commissioner* [1998] QB 65; *Chief Constable of Kent Constabulary v Baskerville* [2003] EWCA Civ 1354; [2003] ICR 1463, both of which are now addressed by the amendments made deeming police officers to be employees both for the protection under the employment provisions and the vicarious liability provisions. All the main anti-discrimination enactments under the same provisions make consequential provision to deal with the payment of compensation, costs and expenses, and related issues.

48 SDA, s 85(2); RRA s 75(2); DDA s 64; Religion or Belief Regulations and Sexual Orientation Regulations, regulations 36, and Age Regulations, regulation 44.

49 SDA, s 85A–B; RRA, s 75A–B; DDA, s 65; Religion or Belief Regulations and Sexual Orientation Regulations, regulations 37–8, and Age Regulations, regulations 45–6.

50 SDA, s 85(2)(c); RRA, s 75(2)(c); Religion or Belief and Sexual Orientation Regulations, regulations 36(2)(c).

51 DDA, s 64(7), and Age Regulations, regulation 44(4).

52 Joint Committee on the Draft Disability Discrimination Bill, First Report (May 2004), para 121 and recommendation 18; 'The Government's Response to the Report of the Joint Committee on the Draft Disability Discrimination Bill' (July 2004), DWP, Recommendation 18.

53 Art 3(4) ('Member States may provide that this Directive, in so far as it relates to discrimination on the grounds of disability and age, shall not apply to the armed forces').

C. Other Workers

8.15 In addition to the provision made in relation to employees, comparable provision is made by the main anti-discrimination enactments outlawing discrimination against contract workers,[54] including applicants for contract work; office holders, including applicants for office;[55] partners, including applicants for partnership;[56] pupil barristers and tenants or applicants for pupillage and tenancy;[57] members, including applicants for membership of trade unions and trade organizations;[58] and against those upon whom authorizations or qualifications, needed for or facilitating engagement in a particular profession or trade, have been conferred or those who are seeking the conferment of such authorizations or qualifications, by qualifying bodies.[59] These unlawful acts reflect closely those made in relation to employees and applicants for employment. In addition, in the DDA only, comparable protection is afforded for those seeking or undertaking a work placement, that is, practical work experience.[60] All the unlawful acts just described outlaw harassment within the relationships addressed by them. As with the unlawful acts created in the employment field, in the DDA protection is provided for 'disabled' people only.[61]

8.16 A number of observations can be made about these unlawful acts. As to contract workers, the unlawful acts regulate discrimination by a 'principal' against contract workers. A 'principal' is a person who makes work available for individuals who are employed by another person who supplies them under a contract made with the principal. A 'contract worker' means any individual who is supplied to the principal under such a contract. The effect of the contract worker provisions is that the contract worker is treated for all effective purposes as if he were employed

54 SDA, s 9; RRA, s 7; DDA, s 4B;, Religion or Belief Regulations and Sexual Orientation Regulations, regulations 8; and Age Regulations, regulation 9.

55 SDA, s 10B; RRA, s 76ZA; DDA, s 4D, DDA; Religion or Belief Regulations and Sexual Orientation Regulations, regulations 10; and Age Regulations, regulation 12.

56 SDA, s 11; RRA, s 10; DDA, s 6A; Religion or Belief Regulations and Sexual Orientation Regulations, regulations 14; and Age Regulations, regulation 17.

57 SDA, s 35A (35B in respect of advocates in Scotland); RRA, s 26A (26B, in relation to advocates in Scotland); DDA, s 7A (7C, in relation to advocates in Scotland); Religion or Belief Regulations and Sexual Orientation Regulations, regulations 12 (regulations 13, in relation to advocates in Scotland); and Age Regulations, regulation 15 (regulation 16, in relation to advocates in Scotland).

58 SDA, s 12; RRA, s 11; DDA, s 13; Religion or Belief Regulations and Sexual Orientation Regulations, regulation 15; and Age Regulations, regulation 18.

59 SDA, s 13; RRA, s 12; DDA, s 14A; Religion or Belief Regulations and Sexual Orientation Regulations, regulation 16; and Age Regulations, Regulation 19.

60 DDA, s 14C.

61 As to the meaning of disability see Chap 5.

by the principal. This means that, in relation to disabled contract workers, the duty to make reasonable adjustment applies in the same way.[62] The unlawful acts protecting contract workers apply where there is in existence a contractual obligation to supply individuals to do what can properly be described as 'work for' the principal. There is no requirement that the supply of workers should be the dominant purpose of the contract between the principal and the employer.[63] In addition, the contract worker provisions do not require a direct contractual relationship between the employer and the principal. They apply equally where there is no direct contract between the person making the work available and the employer of the individual who was supplied to do that work. The statutory definition only requires that the supply of the individual be 'under a contract' with the principal. It does not expressly stipulate who must be the party who contracts with the principal. Although in many cases the contract with the end-user will be made by the employer who supplies the individual, the definition does not require this.[64] The prohibition of discrimination against a contract worker is not restricted to discrimination against a contract worker who is actually working. It prohibits discrimination in the selection by the principal from among all workers supplied under an agency arrangement. Accordingly, a complaint might be brought under the SDA by a contract worker against a principal where she is refused permission to return to work after absence due to maternity.[65]

8.17 New provision is now made in all the main anti-discrimination enactments in consequence of the Race Directive, the Framework Directive, and the amended Equal Treatment Directive, outlawing discrimination against 'office holders'.[66] Office holders include some company directors, judges, and chairmen or members of non-departmental public bodies. In each case the key characteristic is that they are not regarded as employees at common law or under the broad interpretation given to that concept by the main anti-discrimination enactments.[67]

---

62 Chap 6. This will have particular significance for the 'work step scheme' (formerly known as the supportive placement scheme) operated by JobCentre Plus for severely disabled people. The 'contractor' under the scheme (usually a local authority or voluntary body) is the equivalent of the contract worker's own employer, and the 'host employer' is the equivalent of the principal. A local authority might even be the contractor and the host employer at the same time (as can a voluntary body), see Code of Practice on Employment and Occupation (2004) DRC, para 9.13.

63 *Harrods Limited v Remick* [1998] ICR 156; [1997] IRLR 583.

64 *Abbey Life Assurance Co Limited v Tansell* [2000] ICR 789; [2000] IRLR 387.

65 *BP Chemicals Limited v Gillick* [1995] IRLR 128.

66 EPA, s 1(6A); SDA, s 10A(1); RRA, ss 76ZA(7) and 76(10); DDA, s 4C(3); Religion or Belief Regulations and Sexual Orientation Regulations, regulation 10(8); and Age Regulations, regulation 12(8).

67 The 'office holder provisions' do not apply if the relationship falls within one of the other unlawful acts provided for under Part 2; SDA, s 10A; RRA, s 76ZA(7); DDA, s 4C(1)(a); Religion or Belief Regulations and Sexual Orientation Regulations, regulations 10(8); and Age Regulations, regulation 12(12).

An office holder is the holder of an office or post which requires the office or post holder to discharge functions personally under the direction of another in return for remuneration, or is one to which appointments are made by a Minister of the Crown, a government department, the National Assembly for Wales, or any part of the Scottish administration (or on the recommendation of, or subject to the approval of, such a person).[68] A 'relevant' person for the purposes of determining against whom proceedings should be brought, in relation to discrimination against an office holder, is defined by the main anti-discrimination enactments. In summary, the 'relevant' person is the person with power to make or approve the appointment or determine the material term or condition, or with power to terminate the appointment.[69] The RRA alone also outlaws discrimination in the conferring of honours, including peerages by the Queen, made on the recommendation of a Minister.[70]

The provision made in relation to office holders excludes the holding of political office.[71] However, the DDA, alone and in consequence of amendments made by the DDA 2005, covers discrimination against local authority councillors. This was in response in particular to the recommendation of the Disability Rights Taskforce that 'local councils should be placed under a duty not to discriminate against disabled councillors, including a duty to make reasonable adjustments'.[72] The authorities covered include the Greater London Authority, a county council in England or Wales, a county borough council in Wales, a district council in England, and a London borough council.[73] The unlawful acts, with appropriate modifications, closely match those found in the employment and related fields, and outlaw harassment as well as imposing a duty to make adjustments.[74] The unlawful acts relate to treatment in the course of a member 'carrying out . . . official business'.[75] **8.18**

68 SDA, s 10A(1); RRA, ss 76Z(7) and 76(10); DDA, s 4C(3); Religion or Belief Regulations and Sexual Orientation Regulations, regulation 10(8); and Age Regulations, regulation 12(8).

69 SDA, s 10B(9); RRA, s 76ZA(9)(c); DDA, s 4F(2); Religion or Belief Regulations and Sexual Orientation Regulations, regulation 10(10)(c); and RAge Regulations, regulation 12(10)(c).

70 RRA, s 76, enforceable by judicial review, RRA, s 76(12), and in the case of discrimination on the grounds of race, ethnic or national origins, or harassment, in the employment tribunal, s 76(14). The RRA permits certain prescribed public bodies, such as the Bank of England and the British Council, to restrict employment on grounds of birth, nationality, descent, or residence, but not race or colour, Race Relations (Prescribed Public Bodies) (No 2) Regulations 1994 SI 1994/1986).

71 SDA, s 10A(3); RRA, s 76ZA(9); DDA, s 4C(5); Religion or Belief Regulations and Sexual Orientation Regulations, regulation 10(10); and Age Regulations, regulation 12(10). Though the process of selecting candidates for political office by a political party may fall within the 'clubs' provisions (see Chap 10): *Triesman v Ali and A'or* [2002] IRLR 489. And see SDA, s 42A for provision addressing women-only shortlists.

72 'From Exclusion to Inclusion, Final Report of the Disability Rights Taskforce', December 1999 at <http://www.dft.gov.uk/stellent/groups/dft_mobility/documents/divisionhomepage/ 611413.hcsp>.

73 DDA, ss 15A and 15B.

74 See Chap 6.

75 DDA, s 15B.

D. Equal Pay Act 1970

8.19 As explained in Chapter 6, the EPA operates rather differently compared with the other main anti-discrimination enactments. It implies an 'equality clause' into all employment contracts, so creating a contractual right to equal pay. The EPA protects employees who are widely defined, reflecting the same broad definition of employment and related expressions found in the other main anti-discrimination enactments and explained above.[76] For the purposes of the equality clause the EPA also treats a wide range of occupations as 'employment', reflecting closely the approach of the other main anti-discrimination enactments.[77]

E. Pensions

8.20 Special provision is made in relation to pensions insofar as they affect members of particular classes. As mentioned in Chapter 6, the Pensions Act 1995 makes materially the same provision as is made in the EPA in respect of occupational pension schemes, broadly reflecting the position that has been reached in EC law.[78] The Pensions Act 1995 treats every occupational pension scheme as containing an 'equal treatment rule'.[79] An 'equal treatment rule' relates to the terms on which persons become members of the scheme and the way in which members of the scheme are treated.[80] It has the effect that for a woman employed on like work,

---

76 EPA, s 1(6). See para 8.08.

77 EPA, s 1(8) (service in a Government department, for a Minister of the Crown and service on behalf of the Crown, the holding of a statutory office and for purposes of a statutory body); EPA, s 1(6A) (the holding of an office or post to discharge functions personally under the direction of another in return for remuneration (excluding expenses or compensation for loss of income) or an office to which appointments are made by a Minister of the Crown, a government department, the National Assembly for Wales, or any part of the Scottish administration, or on the recommendation of, or subject to the approval of, such a person, excluding the holding of political office, EPA, s 1(6C)); EPA, s 1(10A) and (10B) (staff at the House of Commons and the House of Lords).

78 See Pensions Act 1995, s 62: (1) an occupational pension scheme which does not contain an equal treatment rule shall be treated as including one; (2) an equal treatment rule is a rule which relates to the terms on which (a) persons become members of the scheme and (b) members of the scheme are treated; subject to sub-s (6), an equal treatment rule has the effect that where—(a) a woman is employed on light work with a man in the same employment, (b) a woman is employed on work rated as equivalent with that of a man in the same employment, or (c) a woman is employed on work which, not being work in relation to which para (a) or (b) applies, is, in terms of the demands made on her (for instance under such headings as effort, skill, and decision) of equal value to that of a man in the same employment, but (apart from the rule) any of the terms referred to in sub-s (2) is or becomes less favourable to the woman than it is to the man, the term shall be treated as so modified as not to be less favourable. See too Occupational Pension Schemes (Equal Treatment) Regulations 1995 SI 1995/3183. For a full discussion, see Palmer, et al in A McColgan (ed), *Discrimination Law Handbook* (2007, LAG).

79 Pensions Act 1995, s 62(1).

80 Ibid, s 62(2).

work rated as equivalent, or work of equal value[81] any less favourable term relating to access or treatment is modified so as not to be less favourable.[82] These terms are to be construed 'as one' with section 1 of the EPA.[83] Variations are permitted in certain circumstances where based upon actuarial factors.[84] Further, as with the EPA, the genuine material factor defence applies where the difference in treatment between the woman and her comparator is genuinely due to a material factor which is not the difference of sex and is a material difference between the woman's case and the man's.[85] In certain circumstances, differences in pension provision may be exempt where they constitute *bridging* arrangements, such as a pension designed to equalize the overall payments to men and women of equal age when differential State pensionable ages are taken into account.[86] This exception applies where a man[87] has not reached State pensionable age, but would have done so if he were a woman, is in receipt of an occupational pension and receives an additional amount of pension (not exceeding the amount of Category A retirement pension) which is no more than a woman with the same earnings would receive from the State scheme.

Provision is also made in the DDA 2003,[88] the Religion or Belief Regulations,[89] the Sexual Orientation Regulations,[90] and the Age Regulations[91] (but not the RRA) inserting a non-discrimination rule, subject to temporal limitations, into every occupational pension scheme. The DDA also imposes duties upon the trustees and managers of occupational schemes to make reasonable adjustments.[92] The DDA, the Religion or Belief Regulations, the Sexual Orientation Regulations, and the Age Regulations make it unlawful for a trustee or manager of an occupational scheme to discriminate against a member or prospective member of an occupational pension scheme or harass such a member.[93] There are wide exemptions in **8.21**

81 All described in the same way as under s 1(2) of the EPA.

82 Pensions Act 1995, s 62(3).

83 *Allonby v Accrington and Rossendale College and Others* [2001] EWCA 529; [2001] IRLR 364, para 49. Pensions Act 1995, s 63(4) and the procedures applicable to determine equal pay claims apply equally; s 63(4).

84 Pensions Act 1995, s 64(3) and regulation 15, Occupational Pension Schemes (Equal Treatment) Regulations 1995; *Neath v Hugh Steeper Ltd*, Case C-152/91 [1994] ECR I-6935, [1994] IRLR 91.

85 Pensions Act 1995, s 62(4). See too, the temporal limitations applicable to the terms on which members are treated, Pensions Act 1995, s 63(6).

86 Ibid, s 64(2).

87 Occupational Pension Schemes (Equal Treatment) Regulations 1995, regulations 13 and 14.

88 Disability Discrimination Act 1995 (Pensions) Regulations 2003, SI 2003/2770.

89 Religion or Belief Regulations, Sch 1A.

90 Ibid.

91 Age Regulations, Sch 2, Part 1, para 2.

92 See Chap 6. For a full discussion see K Monaghan, *Blackstone's Guide to the Disability Discrimination Legislation* (2005, OUP) 272–4.

93 DDA, s 4G–H; Religion or Belief Regulations and Sexual Orientation Regulations, regulations 9A; and Age Regulations, regulation 11.

the Age Regulations, reflecting the exemptions in the Framework Directive[94] which permit Member States to:

> provide that the fixing for occupational social security schemes of ages for admission or entitlement to retirement or invalidity benefits, including the fixing under those schemes of different ages for employees or groups or categories of employees, and the use, in the context of such schemes, of age criteria in actuarial calculations, does not constitute discrimination on the grounds of age, provided this does not result in discrimination on grounds of sex.[95]

The Directive also allows for differences in treatment on grounds of age 'where they are objectively and reasonably justified by a legitimate aim, including legitimate employment policy, labour market and vocational training objectives, and if the means of achieving that are appropriate and necessary'.[96] Accordingly, the Age Regulations exempt a number of rules, practices, actions, and decisions which rely directly or indirectly upon age criteria (including minimum and maximum age for admission, age criteria in actuarial calculations, amongst other matters).[97] Many of these rules come within the above exception in Article 6(2). In their explanatory notes to the Age Regulations, the Government suggests that others can be objectively justified under Article 6(1).[98]

8.22 The RRA, alone, makes no special provision. However, all discrimination in access to or the enjoyment of pension benefits, except under the SDA and EPA,[99] is likely to be unlawful under the employment provisions of the main anti-discrimination enactments.[100] The provisions described above are *in addition* to the protection afforded by the employment provisions, except in the case of the Pensions Act 1995 which provides exclusive protection for gender-based discrimination in pensions.[101]

F. Trade Organizations and Qualifying Bodies

8.23 The main anti-discrimination enactments all outlaw discrimination by trade organizations, whether organizations of employees (as in the case of trade unions)

94 See Chap 4.

95 Art 6(2).

96 Art 6(1).

97 Age Regulations, Sch 2, Parts 2 and 3.

98 Draft Employment Equality (Age) Regulations 2006, Notes on Regulations, DTI, para 191.

99 Because of the exemptions under SDA, s 6(6) and EPA, s 6(1B).

100 RRA, s 4(2)(b) covers any other 'benefit' and s 4(2)(c) covers any 'detriment', which as described above is likely to cover any disadvantage. See too, *Barclays Bank plc v Kapur* [1991] ICR 208 and *Barclays Bank Plc v Kapur (No 2)* [1995] IRLR 87. The same applies to the other main anti-discrimination enactments.

101 EPA, s 6(1B).

or employers.[102] The provisions will include organizations that have regulatory functions like the Bar Council and the Law Society. An organization need not have a membership comprised exclusively of employers or workers in order to fall within the provisions addressing discrimination by trade organizations. In *National Federation of Self Employers and Small Businesses Limited v Philpott*,[103] the Employment Appeal Tribunal concluded that the federation whose membership included individual self-employed people who had no employees, as well as employers, was a trade organization for the purposes of section 12 of the SDA, and the same will apply in relation to the other main anti-discrimination enactments.

The prohibitions on discrimination by qualifications bodies are now found in all the main anti-discrimination enactments.[104] A qualifications body is one which can confer an authorization or qualification which is needed for, or facilitates engagement in, a particular profession or trade, and an authorization or qualification includes recognition, registration, enrolment, approval, and certification.[105] **8.24**

The courts have in general given a narrow meaning to the expression 'qualifications bodies'. In *Tattari v Private Patients Plan Limited*[106] the Court of Appeal held that a commercial provider of medical and health insurance, which stipulated in its commercial agreements that particular qualifications were necessary in order for doctors to be included on its list of specialist practitioners, was not a 'qualifying body' for the purposes of the RRA. The Court of Appeal held that the insurance company did not confer any authorization or qualification itself, but merely stated what qualifications were required in order to include practitioners on its list. In *Arthur v Attorney-General*,[107] the Attorney-General was held not to be a qualifying body for the purposes of the RRA when carrying out functions relating to the appointment of magistrates. According to the Employment Appeal Tribunal, section 12 of the RRA 'is directed to circumstances in which A confers on B a qualification which will enable B to render services for C. Where A and C are the same entity, the section would appear to be inapplicable, otherwise it would apply to every selection panel'. In *Triesman (sued on his own behalf and on behalf of all other members of the Labour Party) v Ali*,[108] **8.25**

102 SDA, s 12; RRA, s 11; DDA, s 13; Religion or Belief Regulations and Sexual Orientation Regulations, regulations 15, and Age Regulations, regulation 18.

103 [1997] ICR 518; [1997] IRLR 340.

104 Following amendment to the DDA by the Disability Discrimination Act 1995 (Amendment) Regulations 2003 SI 2003/1673.

105 SDA, s 13; RRA, s 12; DDA, s 14A; Religion or Belief Regulations and Sexual Orientation Regulations, regulations 16; and Age Regulations, Regulation 19. Those bodies falling within the scope of the education provisions of the main anti-discrimination enactments are not covered by the provisions addressed in qualifications bodies, ibid.

106 [1998] ICR 106; [1997] IRLR 586.

107 [1999] ICR 631 at 637.

108 [2002] EWCA Civ 93, [2002] ICR 1026; [2002] IRLR 489.

the Court of Appeal concluded that section 12 of the RRA did not extend to the Labour Party's selection procedures in respect of candidates for political office, so that in failing to select and re-select applicants as candidates for election as local councillors, the Labour Party were not acting as a 'qualifying body'. According to the Court of Appeal, the proper application of section 12 of the RRA was in relation to:

> the employment field . . . in a wide or loose sense. The obvious application of the section is to cases where a body has among its functions that of granting some qualification to, or authorising, a person who has satisfied appropriate standards of competence, to practise a profession, calling or trade.[109]

8.26 On the other hand, in *Patterson v Legal Services Commission*,[110] the Court of Appeal concluded that the franchising arrangements imposed by the Legal Services Commission upon solicitors seeking contracts to provide legal services fell within the scope of section 12 of the RRA. In *Patterson* the Court of Appeal accepted that in granting a franchise and, in effect, the right to do publicly funded work on behalf of her clients, the Commission conferred an authorization on an applicant which facilitated her engagement in the solicitor's profession, within the meaning of section 12 of the RRA.[111] The Court of Appeal noted that the Commission was quite a different body from either Private Patients Plan Ltd (in *Tattari*) or the Labour Party (in *Triesman*), and was charged with specific public functions under its establishing Act.[112] The Court of Appeal noted that:

> [w]hen it grants a franchise to a solicitor on the ground that LAFQAS has been satisfied and thus enables the franchisee to display the logo, it seems to us to grant an authorization to do so. Further, since the grant of the franchise is an essential precondition to the making of a three year contract it can in our opinion again fairly be said to be conferring on the franchisee an authorization to perform publicly funded legal services for its clients.[113]

In addition, such a franchise is sufficiently personal to constitute the 'conferring' of an authorization upon an applicant,[114] for purposes of section 12 of the RRA.

8.27 The 'professional or trade qualifications' covered by the provisions addressing 'qualifications bodies' are widely defined, so as to cover an authorization, qualification,

---

109 Ibid, para 28. In so holding they overruled the earlier case of *Sawyer v Ahsan* [2000] ICR 1; [1999] IRLR 609. The complainant was nevertheless entitled to bring his claim under RRA, s 25 (clubs, see Chap 10). As to sex, see now Sex Discrimination (Election Candidates) Act 2002, and SDA, s 42A.

110 [2004] EWCA Civ 1558; [2004] ICR 312; [2004] IRLR 153.

111 Ibid, paras 62 and 63.

112 Access to Justice Act 1999, see *Patterson v Legal Services Commission* [2004] EWCA Civ 1558; [2004] ICR 312; [2004] IRLR 153, para 71.

113 *Patterson v Legal Services Commission* [2004] EWCA Civ 1558; [2004] ICR 312; [2004] IRLR 153, para 72.

114 Ibid, para 79.

recognition, registration, enrolment, approval, or certification which is needed for, or facilitates the engagement in, a particular profession or trade.[115] These expressions have a wide reach, but the courts have not given them an unrestricted meaning. Instead it has been held that the expressions:

> convey with reasonable clarity the idea of (a) some sort of status conferred on an employee or self-employed person in relation to his work, or the work which he proposes to do; and as respects the self-employed person, in relation to his trade, profession or calling or what he proposes to be his trade, profession or calling; (b) a status which relates only to a person carrying on that work or trade, profession or calling; and (c) is either necessary for the lawful carrying on thereof or making that carrying on more advantageous.[116]

Whilst Lord Slynn has remarked that this emphasis on 'status' 'may be subject to further argument', the word 'status' may give some indication of the essence of a 'qualification'.[117] Some caution must be expressed about the emphasis on status because, as has been observed:

> the reference . . . to the conferring of some sort of status may be dangerous as distracting one from the statutory requirement. A professional qualification within the section may give status, but the fact that status may follow upon an appointment does not necessarily mean that the appointment is one to which the section relates.[118]

Some dicta indicate that the expressions 'professions' and 'trades' suggest an engagement in remunerative occupation[119] and a link between that and the conferral of the relevant authorization or qualification, but there is nothing in the provisions that requires the same. In *British Judo Association v Petty*,[120] the Employment Appeal Tribunal concluded that the granting or withholding of certificate-conferring status as a qualified referee by the British Judo Association fell within the scope of the 'qualifications bodies' provisions of the SDA. This was so notwithstanding that referees were not remunerated. This was because the National Referee Certificate facilitated the engagement of Miss Petty in her occupation as a paid instructor in judo. It was not necessary that the purpose of the certifying body in issuing the certificate was to facilitate the certificate

115 See too SDA, s 82; RRA, s 78(1); DDA, s 68(1); Religion or Belief Regulations and Sexual Orientation Regulations, regulations 16(3) with 15(4); and Age Regulations, regulation 19(3) with regulation 18(4), which all define 'profession' as including any 'vocation or occupation' and 'trade' as including any business.

116 *Department of the Environment for Northern Ireland v Bone* [1993] 8NIJB 41 at 46 (Fair Employment (Northern Ireland) Act 1976, s 23).

117 In *Kelly v Northern Ireland Housing Executive* [1998] ICR 828; [1998] IRLR 593 at para 34.

118 Ibid, para 73, *per* Lord Clyde.

119 *Triesman (sued on his own behalf and on behalf of all other members of the Labour Party) v Ali* [2002] EWCA Civ 93, [2002] ICR 1026; [2002] IRLR 489, para 33.

120 [1981] ICR 660; [1981] IRLR 484.

holder's engagement in a particular profession or trade, if that were its effect. The words 'is needed for' and 'facilitates' are disjunctive and therefore if the particular authorization 'facilitates engagement in' a particular profession or trade then that is sufficient.[121]

8.28 Section 13(2) of the SDA, uniquely, provides that:

> [w]here an authority or body is required by law to satisfy itself as to his good character before conferring on a person an authorization or qualification which is needed for, or facilitates, his engagement in any profession or trade then, without prejudice to any other duty to which it is subject, that requirement shall be taken to impose on the authority or body a duty to have regard to any evidence tending to show that he, or any of his employees, or agents (whether past or present), has practised unlawful discrimination in, or in connection with, the carrying on of any profession or trade.

Whilst no analogous provision is made under the other main anti-discrimination enactments, for those 'qualifications bodies' which are subject to the equality duties (described in Chapter 15), an obligation to have due regard to such matters in exercising their functions relating to the granting of authorizations or qualifications is likely to be implicit in the duties.

G. Employment Services, Careers Guidance, and Vocational Training

8.29 All the main anti-discrimination enactments regulate discrimination by employment agencies,[122] and in relation to the provision of vocational training,[123] and, in the case of the SDA and RRA, by the Training Commission and other statutory training providers.[124]

---

[121] *Patterson v Legal Services Commission* [2004] EWCA Civ 1558; [2004] ICR 312; [2004] IRLR 153, para 75.

[122] SDA, s 15; RRA, s 14; Religion or Belief Regulations and Sexual Orientation Regulations, regulations 18; Age Regulations, regulation 21.

[123] SDA, s 14 (note too, that to the extent that any vocational training falls within the reach of the 'goods, facilities or services' provisions—described in Chap 10—such will cover gender reassignment discrimination too (SDA, s 29(4)), although generally gender reassignment discrimination is only prohibited under Part 2 (employment and related fields) of the SDA); RRA, s 13; Age Regulations, regulation 20.

[124] SDA, s 16; RRA, s 15, except where the vocational training provisions apply or the Secretary of State is acting as an employment agency: SDA, s 16(2); RRA, s 15(2). Such discrimination will usually fall within the vocational training provisions of the anti-discrimination enactments, and where it does not, the absence of specific protection under the other enactments is unlikely to be significant because it will fall within the goods, facilities or services or public functions or education provisions discussed in Chaps 9–11.

H. Contracts, Collective Agreements, and Rules of Undertaking[125]

8.30 Discriminatory provisions in contracts, collective agreements, and rules of undertakings are made void or unenforceable by the main anti-discrimination enactments in certain circumstances. In summary, a term of a contract will be void where the making of the contract is, by reasons of the inclusion of the term, unlawful under the enactments, where it is included in furtherance of an act which is unlawful under the enactments, or where it provides for the doing of an act which is unlawful under the enactments.[126]

8.31 As to collective agreements and rules of undertakings, in the first place the SDA 1986 makes void any discriminatory terms (including those which would fall to be modified under the EPA)[127] in collective agreements, employers' rules, and rules made by trade organizations and qualifications bodies.[128] Exceptionally, however, the rights of the person to be discriminated against and any contractual rights of a person treated more favourably under the contract are preserved. This means that any rights a victim has under the discriminatory rule can be relied upon by her, and a person who has some contractual benefit under the rule cannot be deprived of it (except in so far as they enable any person to require another person to be treated less favourably than himself).[129] The RRA[130] and DDA[131] now[132] make similar provision, as do the Religion or Belief, Sexual Orientation, and Age Regulations.[133]

I. Exemptions and Limitations: Employment and Related Fields

8.32 In addition to the generic exemptions described in Chapter 13, there are a number of exemptions and limitations applicable to the unlawful acts created by the

125 For contracts purporting to oust the jurisdiction of the courts or tribunals, see Chap 14.

126 SDA, s 77; RRA, s 72; Religion or Belief Regulations, Sch 4, Part 1, para 1; Sexual Orientation Regulations, Sch 4, Part 1, para 1; Age Regulations, Sch 5, Part 1.

127 SDA 1986, s 69(3). Note too that the EPA will apply to terms incorporated into individual contracts by collective agreements in the same way as any other terms.

128 SDA 1986, s 6, with SDA 1975, s 77. For the impact of EC law on collective agreements, see *Kowalska v Frie und Hansestadt Hamburg* (Case 33/89) [1990] ECR I-2591; [1990] IRLR 447; *Nimz v Frie und Hansestadt Hamburg*, Case 184/89 [1991] ECR I-297; [19991] IRLR 222.

129 SDA, s 6(5).

130 RRA, s 72A, with s 72, applicable to race, ethnicity, and national origins discrimination only, and only in relation to those unlawful acts falling within RRA, s 1(1B), reflecting the limits of the Race Directive (see s 72A2).

131 DDA, Sch 3A, Parts 1 and 2, read with DDA, s 17C.

132 After amendment to give effect to the Race and Framework Directives, see Chap 4.

133 Religion or Belief Regulations, Sch 4, Part 2; Sexual Orientation Regulations, Sch 4, Part 2; Age Regulations, Sch 5, Part 2.

main anti-discrimination enactments in the employment and related fields. Some are applicable to certain of the enactments only and others apply across all the main anti-discrimination enactments in the same, or broadly the same, way.

8.33 The main exemptions[134] which apply to all, or mainly all, the main anti-discrimination enactments are addressed first, followed by those ground-specific exemptions.

(1) Genuine occupational requirements and qualifications

8.34 All the main anti-discrimination enactments, except the DDA, exempt discriminatory recruitment, including promotion, transfer, and training and, sometimes, dismissal, where being of a particular sex, race, religion or belief, sexual orientation, or age is a 'genuine occupational requirement'. Additional provision is made, as described below, to address some such racially discriminatory decisions where they constitute a 'genuine occupational qualification'. No such exemption appears in the DDA.[135]

8.35 In broad terms, the *genuine occupational requirement* or *qualifications* defences are designed to address those circumstances where being a woman, or a man, or black, etc is a real requirement for the post in question. Such is very unusual but does arise where there are intimate or culturally sensitive tasks to be performed in the post, or where an actor of a particular sex or race is required for reasons of authenticity, and in limited other circumstances. The breadth of the exceptions vary across the enactments and the approach taken differs. The exemptions apply to employment and the other employment-related provisions,[136] and, in the case of the Religion or Belief Regulations, the Sexual Orientation Regulations, and the Age Regulations, to discrimination by further and higher education institutions where the discrimination only concerns training which would help fit a person for employment which the employer could lawfully refuse to offer the person in question because of the genuine occupational requirement defence.[137] None of the genuine occupational

---

[134] Other exemptions and limitations include SDA, s 18 (employment provisions do not render unlawful any discrimination between male and female prison officers as to requirements relating to height (the lawfulness of which exemption must be seriously doubted having regard to EC law); SDA, s 18 (midwives until 1 Sept 1983); SDA, s 19 (ministers of religion), as modified by the Employment Equality (Sex Discrimination) Regulations 2005, SI 2005/2467; RRA, s 9 (exception for seamen recruited abroad); Religion or Belief Regulations, regulation 26(2) (exemption for Sikhs relating to wearing of safety helmets).

[135] However, the meaning given to 'discrimination' will often permit discrimination where the absence of the particular disability (or absence of such 'inability') is a key requirement for the job, see Chap 6.

[136] SDA, s 7; RRA, ss 4A and 5; Religion or Belief Regulations and Sexual Orientation Regulations, regulation 7 and Age Regulations, regulation 8.

[137] Religion or Belief Regulations and Sexual Orientation Regulations, regulation 20(3) and the Age Regulations, regulation 23(3).

requirement or qualifications exemptions apply to the terms on which a person is employed, and in the case of the SDA do not apply to a dismissal.

The SDA sets out an exhaustive list of circumstances in which being a man or a woman constitutes a 'genuine occupational qualification'.[138] These include circumstances where the essential nature of the job calls for a man or a woman for reasons of physiology (excluding physical strength or stamina); or, in the case of dramatic performances or other entertainment, for reasons of authenticity; or to preserve decency or privacy; or because the job is to be performed in a particular place (particularly if a residential job) and a man is required for that reason; or the job involves providing individuals with personal services promoting their welfare or education, or similar personal services, and those services can *most effectively*[139] be provided by a woman or a man, as the case may be.[140] Such applies, even if only some of the duties of the job involve the tasks just described.[141] In any case, the exemption does not apply where there are adequate employees of the sex required already in post who could reasonably undertake the work in question.[142] Nevertheless, there is some doubt as to whether the genuine occupational qualifications are sufficiently tightly drawn to comply with EC law. The amended Equal Treatment Directive provides that: **8.36**

> as regards access to employment including the training leading thereto, . . . a difference of treatment which is based on a characteristic related to sex shall not constitute discrimination where, by reason of the nature of the particular occupational activities concerned or of the context in which they are carried out, such a characteristic constitutes a genuine and *determining* occupational requirement, provided that the objective is legitimate and the requirement is *proportionate*.[143]

The Explanatory Notes[144] to the proposal for the Equal Treatment Amendment Directive made clear that ECJ case law requires that 'the derogation must be interpreted strictly and applied in accordance with the principle of proportionality; that principle requires that derogations remain within the limits of what is *appropriate and necessary* for achieving the aim in view',[145] and that the term 'genuine occupational qualification' should cover 'only those occupational requirements where a particular sex is *necessary* for the performance of the activities concerned'.[146] Not all

138 SDA, s 7.

139 *Lambeth LBC v CRE* [1990] ICR 768; *Tottenham Green Under Fives' Centre v Marshall* [1989] ICR 214; [1989] IRLR 147; *Tottenham Green Under Fives' Centre v Marshall (No 2)* [1991] ICR 320; [1991] IRLR 162. See SDA, s 7(2)(e).

140 For a critique, see D Pannick, *Sex Discrimination Law* (1985, OUP), 250.

141 SDA, s 7(3).

142 Ibid, s 7(4).

143 Equal Treatment Amendment Directive, Art 2(6).

144 OJ C 337 E, 28/11/2000, paras 19–27.

145 Ibid, para 21.

146 Ibid, para 27.

the present genuine occupational qualifications found in the SDA require that it is 'necessary' for the post to be held by a man. Some only require that it be 'impracticable' and 'unreasonable' for an employer to employ a woman,[147] or that services can 'most effectively be provided by a man'.[148] This falls short of the amended Equal Treatment Directive demand that sex be a 'determining' requirement and that the means be 'proportionate', that is 'appropriate and necessary'. Arguably, too, the deeming of certain aims as, in all cases, 'legitimate' without requiring any scrutiny in a particular case does not give full effect to the Directive.[149]

8.37 The RRA (where the discrimination concerns race or ethnic or national origins[150]), the Religion or Belief Regulations, the Sexual Orientation Regulations, and the Age Regulations, on the other hand, exempt discriminatory decisions on recruitment, promotion, transfer, training, and dismissal only where:

> having regard to the nature of the employment or the context in which it is carried out—
>
> (a) [being of a particular race or of particular ethnic or national origins, religion or belief, sexual orientation or possessing a characteristic related to age] is a *genuine and determining occupational requirement*;
>
> (b) it is *proportionate*[151] to apply that requirement in the particular case; and
>
> (c) either—
>
> (i) the person to whom that requirement is applied does not meet it, or
>
> (ii) the employer is not satisfied, and in all the circumstances it is reasonable for him not to be satisfied, that that person meets it.[152]

This requires proof in each case that the discriminatory requirement is 'genuine and determining' *and* that it is proportionate to apply that requirement in the particular case. In this way it imposes a more rigorous test than those found in the SDA, but it does extend beyond closely dilineated circumstances. As seen, the exemption applies where the employee or prospective employee concerned *meets* the requirement to be gay, straight, a Muslim, as the case may be, but the employer is not satisfied, and it is reasonable for him not to be satisfied, that that person meets it. This permissive provision has been held to be compliant with the Directives[153] which permit a difference of treatment '*based* on a characteristic

147 SDA, ss 7(2)(c), (d).

148 SDA, s 7(2)(e).

149 Art s 2(6). See also *Moyhing v Barts and London NHS Trust* [2006] IRLR 860.

150 Reflecting the origins of the exemption in the Race Directive and then the regulations implementing it: the Race Relations Act 1976 (Amendment) Regulations 2003 SI 2003/1626.

151 Emphasis added.

152 RRA, s 4A; Religion or Belief Regulations and Sexual Orientation Regulations, regulation 7, and Age Regulations, regulation 8.

153 Race and Framework Directives. See Chap 4.

related to' race, religion or belief, sexual orientation, or age where such is a genuine requirement of the job.[154] The requirement of reasonableness ensures, as is required, that decisions cannot lawfully be based on mere assumptions or social stereotyping.[155]

In addition to the general genuine occupational requirement exemption, the RRA, the Religion or Belief Regulations, and the Sexual Orientation Regulations make further related provision. As seen, the RRA applies this exemption only to discrimination connected to race and ethnic or national origin. In other cases, a genuine occupational *qualifications* defence applies.[156] This provides that where the genuine occupational requirement defence 'does not apply' discriminatory acts relating to recruitment, promotion, transfer, and training are exempt where: 8.38

> [b]eing of a particular racial group is a genuine occupational qualification for a job [that is] only where—
> (a) the job involves participation in a dramatic performance or other entertainment in a capacity for which a person of that racial group is required for reasons of authenticity; or
> (b) the job involves participation as an artist's or photographic model in the production of a work of art, visual image or sequence of visual images for which a person of that racial group is required for reasons of authenticity; or
> (c) the job involves working in a place where food or drink is (for payment or not) provided to and consumed by members of the public or a section of the public in a particular setting for which, in that job, a person of that racial group is required for reasons of authenticity; or
> (d) the holder of the job provides persons of that racial group with personal services promoting their welfare, and those services can most effectively be provided by a person of that racial group.[157]

Such applies where only some of the duties of the job fall within the preceding paragraphs but does not apply in relation to the filling of a vacancy at a time when the employer already has employees of the racial group in question who could reasonably carry out these duties.[158] Although on a plain reading, this genuine occupational qualification exemption might seem to apply to discrimination connected with race and ethnic or national origin where the genuine occupational

154 Art 4 Race Directive and Art 4(1) Framework Directive. See, *R (on the application of Amicus-MSF section and others) v Secretary of State for Trade and Industry and Christian Action Research Education and others (Interveners)* [2004] EWHC 860 (Admin); [2004] IRLR 430, para 84–6.

155 *R (on the application of Amicus-MSF section and others) v Secretary of State for Trade and Industry and Christian Action Research Education and others (Interveners)* [2004] EWHC 860 (Admin); [2004] IRLR 430, para 81.

156 RRA, s 5.

157 Ibid, s 5(2).

158 Ibid, s 5(3) and (4).

requirement exemption *does not apply*, the genuine occupational qualification exemption cannot apply to discrimination connected to race, ethnic, or national origin. This is because the Race Directive, which led to the introduction of the genuine occupational requirement exemption, and which provides a relevant interpretative context,[159] *only permits* discrimination connected with race, ethnic, and national origins where such a characteristic 'constitutes a genuine and determining occupational requirement, provided that the objective is legitimate and the requirement is proportionate'.[160] This means that in practical terms the genuine occupational qualification exemption is a residual exemption applying only to discrimination connected to nationality (which is explicitly exempted from the Race Directive[161]). Some of its terms are unlikely ever now to be relevant. For example, it is difficult to see how a requirement as to nationality (indeed, even ethnicity) would ever be relevant to work in a place where food or drink is provided, for example. The breadth of the genuine occupational qualification defence has in any event been criticized as anachronistic.[162] The 'food and drink' exemption would seem to have no contemporary relevance but, on the other hand, none of the genuine occupational qualifications exemptions leave much room for innovative measures directed at meeting the needs of a diverse community,[163] so satisfying very few.

8.39 As to the Religion or Belief Regulations and the Sexual Orientation Regulations, they controversially contain a provision addressing religious organizations specifically. The origins of these particular provisions are found in the Framework Directive; Article 4(2) provides that:

> Member States may maintain national legislation in force at the date of adoption of this Directive or provide for future legislation incorporating national practices existing at the date of adoption of this Directive pursuant to which, in the case of occupational activities within churches and other public or private organisations the ethos of which is based on religion or belief, *a difference of treatment based on a person's religion or belief* shall not constitute discrimination where, by reason of the nature of these activities or of the context in which they are carried out, a person's religion or belief constitute a *genuine, legitimate and justified occupational requirement*, having regard to the organisation's ethos. This difference of treatment shall be implemented taking account of Member States' constitutional provisions and principles, as well as the general principles of Community law, and *should not justify discrimination on another ground.*

159 See Chap 4.

160 Race Directive, Art 4.

161 See discussion in Chap 4.

162 'First review of the Race Relations Act 1976: proposals For Change' (1998, CRE).

163 *Lambeth LBC v CRE* [1990] ICR 768; *Tottenham Green Under Fives' Centre v Marshall* [1989] ICR 214; [1989] IRLR 147; *Tottenham Green Under Fives' Centre v Marshall (No 2)* [1991] ICR 320; [1991] IRLR 162.

> Provided that its provisions are otherwise complied with, this Directive shall thus not prejudice the right of churches and other public or private organizations, the ethos of which is based on religion or belief, acting in conformity with national constitutions and laws, to require individuals working for them to act in good faith and with loyalty to the organization's ethos.[164]

As can be seen, this exemption requires that religion or belief be a genuine, legitimate, and justified occupational requirement. The requirement need not be *determining*, and there is no test of proportionality, as imposed by the standard genuine occupational requirement exemption provided for by the Framework Directive.[165] Apparently in reliance upon this, regulation 7(3) of the Religion or Belief Regulations and regulation 7(3) of the Sexual Orientation Regulations make special provision in relation to religious employers. Regulation 7(3) of the Religion or Belief Regulations exempts discrimination: **8.40**

> where an employer has an ethos based on religion or belief and, having regard to that ethos and to the nature of the employment or the context in which it is carried out—
> (a) being of a particular religion or belief is a genuine occupational requirement for the job;
> (b) it is proportionate to apply that requirement in the particular case; and
> (c) either—
> (i) the person to whom that requirement is applied does not meet it, or
> (ii) the employer is not satisfied, and in all the circumstances it is reasonable for him not to be satisfied, that that person meets it.

Though this exemption imposes a test of proportionality, it does not require that being of a particular religion or belief is a *determining* condition, reducing the threshold required for the exemption to apply, as compared to the standard genuine occupational requirement defence. This provision and Article 4(2) to which it gives effect is not uncontroversial,[166] but more controversial is the parallel provision made in the Sexual Orientation Regulations. Regulation 7(3) of the Sexual Orientation Regulations provides that discrimination is exempt:

> where—
> (a) the employment is for purposes of an organized religion;
> (b) the employer applies a requirement related to sexual orientation—
> (i) so as to comply with the doctrines of the religion, or
> (ii) because of the nature of the employment and the context in which it is carried out, so as to avoid conflicting with the strongly held religious convictions of a significant number of the religion's followers; and

164 Emphasis added.
165 Art 4(1).
166 A McColgan, *Discrimination Law, Text, Cases and Materials* (2005, Hart) 663–8.

(c) either—
  (i) the person to whom that requirement is applied does not meet it, or
  (ii) the employer is not satisfied, and in all the circumstances it is reasonable for him not to be satisfied, that that person meets it.

This cannot fall within Article 4(2) because that mandates discrimination based on religion or belief only (not sexual orientation), and nor does it meet the exacting standards of the standard genuine occupational requirement exemption in the Framework Directive which requires that any discrimination pursue a legitimate objective, constitute a genuine and determining occupational requirement and be legitimate and proportionate.[167] A challenge to the *vires* of regulation 7(3) of the Sexual Orientation Regulations has been unsuccessful but on the basis that on its proper construction, regulation 7(3) is of very narrow application. It must be construed strictly because it is a derogation from the principle of equal treatment, and it has to be construed purposively so as to ensure, so far as possible, compatibility with the Framework Directive, so that it affords an exception only in very limited circumstances. The fact that the exception applies 'for the purposes of an organized religion' operates as an important initial limitation, and it is a narrower expression than 'for the purposes of a religious organisation' or 'an ethos based on religion or belief', in the latter case as used in the Religion or Belief Regulations. This means that employment as a teacher in a faith school is likely to be for the 'purposes of a religious organisation' but not for the 'purposes of an organised religion'. Further, the condition in regulation 7(3)(b)(i) that the employer must apply the requirement 'so as to comply with the doctrines of the religion' is an objective test so that it must be shown that employment of a person not meeting the requirement would be incompatible with the doctrines of the religion. That is very narrow in scope. The alternative in regulation 7(3)(b)(ii), which refers to an employer applying a requirement related to sexual orientation 'because of the nature of the employment and the context in which it is carried out, so as to avoid conflicting with the strongly held religious convictions of a significant number of the religion's followers', will also be a 'very far from easy test to satisfy in practice'.[168] Furthermore, although regulation 7(3)(b), which refers to an employer applying 'a requirement related to sexual orientation', may be wider in scope than regulation 7(2), which refers to 'being of a particular sexual orientation', in that it covers sexual behaviour, the protection against discrimination on grounds of sexual orientation relates as much to the manifestation of that orientation in the form of sexual behaviour as it does to sexuality as such. Sexual orientation and its manifestation in sexual

167 Framework Directive, Art 4(1).

168 *R (on the application of Amicus-MSF section and others) v Secretary of State for Trade and Industry and Christian Action Research Education and others (Interveners)* [2004] EWHC 860 (Admin); [2004] IRLR 430, para 117.

behaviour are both inextricably connected with a person's private life and identity so that a person discriminated against because of a manifestation of sexual orientation in behaviour is protected unless the narrow exemption applies. The wording of the derogation in Article 4(1) of the Directive, which refers to a difference of treatment 'which is based on a characteristic related to' sexual orientation, conversely, is wide enough to embrace a difference of treatment based on sexual behaviour related to sexual orientation. This gives a potentially wide reach to the exemption, but given the restrictions placed upon its reach by the interpretation given to it by the court on the *vires* challenge, regulation 7(3) is unlikely to have much practical impact. The challenge, then, was unsuccessful but described by a commentator as 'a good loss'.[169]

Although not properly a genuine occupational requirement, the unlawful acts created by the Religion or Belief Regulations are made without prejudice to sections 58 to 60 and 124A of the School Standards and Framework Act 1988. Sections 58 and 60 allow for the recruitment of 'reserve' teachers for the purposes of teaching religious education where they are selected for their fitness and competence to give religious education as is required by the school's arrangements for religious education, in accordance with the school's trust deed, or with the tenets of the school's specified religion or religious denomination, subject to certain limitations. Sections 60 and 124A allow for independent schools and voluntary aided schools which have a religious character to give preference, in connection with the appointment, promotion, or remuneration of teachers at the school, to persons whose religious opinions are in accordance with the tenets of the religion or the religious denomination specified in relation to the school, or who attend religious worship in accordance with those tenets, or who give, or are willing to give, religious education at the school in accordance with those tenets. Provision is also made allowing for regard to be had to any conduct on the part of a teacher which is incompatible with the precepts, or with the upholding of the tenets, of the religion or religious denomination so specified, in connection with the termination of the employment or engagement of any teacher at the school. Section 59 gives teachers in certain schools the right not to teach religious education and protects them against any disadvantageous treatment in consequence of a refusal to teach religious education or in consequence of their religious opinions or of their attending or omitting to attend religious worship. **8.41**

The SDA makes specific provision in relation to gender reassignment and genuine occupational qualifications, but these do not apply if an employee has become the acquired gender under the Gender Recognition Act 2004.[170] In addition, the SDA makes provision addressing appointments to the clergy in which case discrimination **8.42**

169 '*A Good Loss: R v (Amicus-MSF Section) v Secretary of State for Trade and Industry*' (2004) EOR 130.

170 See too *A v Chief Constable of West Yorkshire Police* [2005] AC 51.

on the ground of sex, gender reassignment, civil partnership, or married status may be exempt.[171]

8.43 Importantly, the occupational qualifications defences do not apply to secure diversity for its own sake. Instead any requirement as to sex, race etc must be linked to the tasks of a particular post. They do not, then, allow for positive action directed at addressing disadvantage in the labour market or under-representation.

(2) Pregnancy and the Sex Discrimination Act 1975

8.44 As seen in Chapter 6, a new section 3A of the SDA now addresses pregnancy and maternity discrimination. In addition, section 6A of the SDA creates a number of exceptions from the protection afforded by the employment provisions, as they may apply to discrimination regulated by section 3A. These provide that the unlawful acts created in the employment field do not make it unlawful to deprive a woman who is on ordinary maternity leave of any benefit from the terms and conditions of her employment relating to non-maternity-related remuneration. Nor do they make it unlawful to deprive a woman who is on additional maternity leave of any benefit from the terms and conditions of her employment except benefit by way of maternity-related remuneration, the benefit of her employer's implied obligation to her of trust and confidence, the benefit of any notice provisions,[172] the benefit of any terms relating to compensation in the event of redundancy and relating to disciplinary or grievance procedures, and membership of a pension scheme. These exemptions do not apply to benefit by way of remuneration in respect of times when the woman is not on ordinary or additional maternity leave, including increase-related remuneration in respect of such times or benefit by way of maternity-related remuneration that is increase-related. This deals with the issue in *Alabaster v Woolwich and A'or*,[173] namely, that a woman is entitled to the benefit of any increase she would have received had she not been absent on maternity leave, for the purposes of calculating earnings related maternity pay. As to the remainder of section 6A, the provisions described above bring the protection afforded by the SDA in line with the protection afforded by the Maternity and Parental Leave Regulations 1999[174] which guarantee some rights to women on maternity leave. However, prior to the enactment of section 6A there was no such limitation in the SDA. Section 6A was enacted by the Employment Equality (Sex Discrimination) Regulations 2005,[175] made under

171 SDA, s 19.

172 In respect of termination of employment.

173 (Case C-147/02) [2005] ICR 695; [2004] IRLR 486. See SDA, s 6 A(5).

174 SI 1999/3312, regulations 9 and 17.

175 SI 2005/ 2467, in force from 1 Oct 2005.

the European Communities Act 1972.[176] These Regulations were made purportedly to give effect to the Equal Treatment Amendment Directive. However, whilst EU law, as seen,[177] restricts the scope of the equal treatment guarantees, in particular as regards pay, in their application to women on maternity leave, there is no *requirement* in the Equal Treatment Amendment Directive to statutorily limit any equal treatment entitlements to women on maternity leave. This raises the question whether the Regulations, to the extent that they enact section 6A, are *ultra vires* section 2 of the European Communities Act 1972 and unlawful having regard to the non-regression provision in the Directive.[178] Further, section 6A goes further than the limitation in EU law relating to pay in excluding the right to claim in respect of entitlements guaranteed by EU law. EU law makes no distinction between periods of maternity leave,[179] and accordingly ordinary and additional maternity leave are subject to the same EU requirements. EU law guarantees all the benefits to women on maternity leave that they would have enjoyed if at work (for example, consultation rights, appraisal rights, promotion opportunities, loyalty bonuses etc), except full pay.[180] These, therefore, must be guaranteed and, until the enactment of section 6A, this has been achieved through the SDA (and, in respect of benefits regulated by contract, through the EPA[181]). The lawfulness of section 6A must therefore be doubted.[182]

The new section 6A does not repeal section 6(6) and this is discussed below (paragraph 8.46). **8.45**

---

176 European Communities Act 1972, s 2, see Chap 4.

177 Chaps 4 and 6.

178 Equal Treatment Amendment Directive, 2002/73/EC, see Art 8(e)(2).

179 *Land Brandenburg v Sass* (Case C-284/02) [2005] IRLR 147, assuming the objective and purpose of both periods of leave are the protection of women as regards pregnancy and maternity, which must be taken to be so in the case of both ordinary and additional maternity leave, because if additional maternity leave was directed at some other objective, it would necessarily have to be available to men (or otherwise it would breach the principle of equal treatment).

180 See Chaps 4 and 6 and *Land Brandenburg v Sass* (Case C-284/02) [2005] IRLR 147; EC law makes it clear that less favourable treatment at work connected to pregnancy or maternity leave is contrary to EC law and in particular the Equal Treatment Directive 76/207; *Dekker v Stichting Vormingsentrion voor Jong Volwassenen (VJV-Centrum Plus)* (Case C-177/88) [1992] ICR 325; *Gillespie and Others v Northern Health and Social Security Board and Others* (Case C-342/93) [1996] ICR 498, ECJ; *Alabaster v Woolwich PLC and A'er* (Case C-147/02) [2004] IRLR 486; *Caisse Nationale D'Assurance Vieillesse Des Travailleurs Salaries (CNAVTS) v Thibault* (Case C-136/95) [1999] ICR 160; *Handels-og Kontorfunktionaerernes Forbund I Danmark, acting on behalf of Berit Hoj Pedersen v Faellesforeningen for Danmarks Brugsforeninger and others* (Case C-C66/96) [1999] IRLR 55); *Lewen v Denda*, C-333/97 [2000] IRLR 67; *Alabaster v Woolwich and A'or* (Case C-147/02) [2005] ICR 695; [2004] IRLR 486; *Sarkatzis Herrero v Instituto Madrileno de la Salud*, Case C-294/04 [2006] IRLR 296.

181 Even if damage had to be caused to it in consequence: *Alabaster v Barclays Bank plc and Secretary of State for Social Security (No 2)* [2005] EWCA Civ 508; [2005] IRLR 576.

182 As to remedies, see Chap 4.

(3) Pay, benefits, and pensions

8.46 The SDA excludes from the coverage provided by its employment provisions (only) benefits consisting of the payment of money when the provision of those benefits is regulated by the woman's contract of employment.[183] Such claims fall instead to be determined under the EPA, discussed above. Case law indicates that this exemption extends beyond benefits to which a person is contractually entitled, to benefits which are 'discretionary' but regulated by some contractual provision, in the sense that they arise out of the contract of employment and 'but for the existence of the contract of employment the [benefit] would not be paid, and it is therefore being paid as a consequence of its very existence'.[184] The exemption does not apply to the other unlawful acts created by the SDA in relation to workers, for example contract workers, who may bring claims in respect of pay under the SDA.[185]

8.47 Further, the unlawful acts in the employment and related fields do not cover benefits of any description if the employer is concerned with the provision (for payment or not) of benefits of that description to the public, or to a section of the public which includes the employee in question, unless the provision to the employee differs in a material respect, or the provision of the benefits to the employee in question is regulated by his contract of employment, or they relate to training. This means that if an employee works for a car mechanic and she takes her car in to be repaired in the same way as any other customer, any remedy for discrimination in the service she is provided is not actionable under the employment provisions, just because she happens to be employed by the mechanic. Such would be actionable under the goods, facilities, and services provisions instead (see Chapter 10 below).

8.48 Regulation 25 of the Sexual Orientation Regulations also provides that:

> [n]othing in Parts II or III shall render unlawful anything which prevents or restricts access to a benefit by reference to marital status where the right to the benefit accrued or the benefit is payable in respect of periods of service prior to the coming into force of the Civil Partnership Act 2004; the conferring of a benefit on married persons and civil partners to the exclusion of all other persons.

This allows employers to discriminate against same-sex partners, in favour of married persons, in respect of benefits accrued or due before the coming into force of the Civil Partnership Act 2004, and thereafter allows employers to discriminate against unmarried people and those who are not civil partners, in favour of married persons and civil partners. It does not permit discrimination after the coming

183 SDA, s 6(6).

184 *Hoyland v Asda* [2006] CSIH 21; [2006] IRLR 468, para 14.

185 *Allonby v Accrington and Rossendale College and Others* [2001] EWCA 529; [2001] IRLR 364.

into force of the Civil Partnership Act 2004 in favour of married persons to the exclusion of civil partners.[186] To this extent it treats civil partners and married persons as equivalent and does not permit discrimination as between them.

(4) Age

The Age Regulations uniquely contain exemptions relating to the National Minimum Wage and retirement, amongst other things, entrenching discrimination against young people as well as older people. The scope of the exemptions is controversial as discussed below. **8.49**

Firstly, regulations 7(4) and (5) of the Age Regulations contain a very wide-ranging exemption in relation to those who have reached or are near to reaching the employer's 'normal retirement age'. This is said to derive from the permitted exemptions in the Framework Directive to which the Age Regulations are intended to give effect. The Framework Directive provides that Member States may provide that differences of treatment on grounds of age shall not constitute discrimination, if, within the context of national law, they are objectively and reasonably justified by a legitimate aim, including legitimate employment policy, labour market, and vocational training objectives, and if the means of achieving that aim are appropriate and necessary.[187] Regulation 7(4) provides that the unlawful acts relating to recruitment (except those relating to the terms on which employment is offered) do not apply in relation to a person: **8.50**

> whose age is greater than the employer's normal retirement age or, if the employer does not have a normal retirement age, the age of 65 or who would, within a period of six months from the date of his application to the employer, reach the employer's normal retirement age or, if the employer does not have a normal retirement age, the age of 65.

This exception applies only to a person to whom regulation 30 would apply if he was recruited by the employer.[188] Regulation 30 is discussed below, but applies only to employees within the meaning of section 230 of the Employment Rights Act 1996 (that is, those employed under a contract of employment, namely a contract of service or apprenticeship, whether express or implied, and whether oral or in writing).[189] The blanket exclusion in regulation 7(4) is said to be justified, by

186 See *R (on the application of Amicus-MSF section and others) v Secretary of State for Trade and Industry and Christian Action Research Education and others (Interveners)* [2004] EWHC 860 (Admin); [2004] IRLR 430, for a discussion on the lawfulness of an earlier, unamended, version of regulation 25.

187 Framework Directive, Art 6. See Art 6(2) for a permitted exemption in occupational pension schemes. See Chap 4.

188 Ibid, regulation 7(5).

189 See Employment Rights Act 1996, s 230(1) and (2).

the Government, to be justified because of the exception in regulation 30 which allows for the dismissal of a person at or over the age of 65, where the reason for the dismissal is retirement. The 'rationale' for the exclusion in regulation 7(4), then, 'flows from the rationale for regulation 30 . . . There is little point in requiring an employer not to discriminate at the point of receiving an application from a prospective employee when, if he were to employ the person, that person would be retired (without it amounting to discrimination to do so) within six months of their appointment'.[190] However, whilst the Framework Directive, as has been seen, permits broad exemptions in the context of age discrimination, recent case law suggests that blanket exclusions may not meet the requirements of Article 6. In *Mangold v Helm*,[191] the ECJ considered an exclusion in German law of those aged 52 and over from protection in relation to fixed term work. The object of the exclusion was to promote the vocational integration of unemployed older workers, which the ECJ held was a legitimate public interest objective. However, the Court held that the means used to achieve that objective could not be regarded as appropriate and necessary and thus justified under the Framework Directive. According to the ECJ:

> Observance of the principle of proportionality requires every derogation from an individual right to reconcile, so far as is possible, the requirements of the principle of equal treatment with those of the aim pursued.[192]

It is doubtful, then, whether the blanket exclusion in regulation 7(4) will meet the requirements of Article 6. This is particularly so where the justification relied upon is the justification for a different regulation that is not necessarily coincidental with or mutually dependent upon regulation 7(4). Whilst it may be likely in some circumstances, it is not necessarily so that an employee recruited after the default retirement age would then be dismissed by reason of retirement, as the rationale for regulation 7(4) seems to suppose. A reference has been made to the ECJ, from Spain, as a result of which the ECJ will be asked whether the Framework Directive precludes a national law which makes lawful compulsory retirement clauses in collective agreements, in circumstances where they apply to workers who have reached normal retirement age and meet the conditions set out in the social security legislation of the Spanish State relating to the drawing of certain retirement pensions.[193] The decision of the ECJ is awaited, but if the Spanish

---

190 See 'Employment Equality (Age) Regulations 2006, Notes on Regulations' DTI (available at <http://www.dti.gov.uk/files/file27136.pdf>), para 30.

191 (Case C-144/04) [2005] ECR I-9981; [2006] IRLR 143.

192 Ibid, para 65.

193 *Palacios de la Villa v Cortefiel Servicios SA* (C-411/05) referred on 14 Nov 2005. And at the time of writing, the High Court of England and Wales has just decided to refer the lawfulness of the exclusion in relation to retirement ages to the ECJ, reportedly without objection by the Government, on an application by Age Concern. At the time of writing no official reports have been published,

law in issue is found incompatible with the Framework Directive, it is unlikely that regulation 7(4) can survive.

Secondly, regulation 31 makes an exception to the application of the minimum wage. The National Minimum Wage Act 1998 and regulations thereunder[194] prescribe a minimum wage which differentiates between age groups. The exemption in regulation 31 permits employers to base their pay structures on the national minimum wage legislation, although it does not allow for persons within the same age category (for the purposes of the national minimum wage) to be paid different rates. Further, the exemption only applies where the lower paid worker is remunerated below the single hourly rate for the national minimum wage. If an employer chooses to pay above the single hourly rate, then it cannot differentiate between its employees on the grounds of age. Regulation 31(2) allows an employer to pay an apprentice who is not entitled to the minimum wage—because certain conditions are met—less than an apprentice who is entitled to the national minimum wage. The justification for this is that the treatment of apprentices under the National Minimum Wage legislation is designed to encourage employers to offer apprenticeships to young workers, so the exception is said to be 'intended to ensure that this design is not defeated because employers fear the threat of legal challenge on the grounds of age discrimination'.[195] 8.51

Thirdly, regulation 32 of the Age Regulations makes provision, by way of a general exemption to the unlawful acts created under the Regulations, in respect of service-related benefits. Regulation 32 provides an exemption so that it is not unlawful for a person (A), in relation to the award of any benefit by him, to put a worker (B) at a disadvantage when compared with another worker (C) if and to the extent that the disadvantage suffered by B is because B's length of service is less than that of C. This broad exemption is limited where B's length of service exceeds five years, in which case it must reasonably appear to A that the way in which he uses the criterion of length of service, in relation to the award in respect of which B is put at a disadvantage, fulfils a business need of his undertaking (for example, by encouraging loyalty or motivation, or rewarding the experience of some or 8.52

---

but see <http://www.heyday.org.uk/wps/portal/!ut/p/kcxml/04_Sj9SPykssy0xPLMnMz0vM0Y_QjzKLN4g3cjMESYGZrsH6kRhiphhijgiRIH1vfV-P_NxU_QD9gtzQ0IhyR0UAH5joqA!!/delta/base64xml/L0lDU0lKQ1RPN29na21BISEvb0VvUUFBSVFnakZJQUFRaENFSVFqR0VBLzRKRmlDbzBlaDFpY29uUVZHaGQtc0lRIS83XzBfOU4xLzI2MzE1Mg!!?PC_7_0_9N1_WCM_CONTEXT=/content/home/community/community_campaigns_mra_6+dec+announcement&bodyfield=2&WCM_DOC_ID=com.ibm.workplace.wcm.api.WCM_Content/community_campaigns_mra_6%20dec%20announcement/e57b66457284cdf>.

194 National Minimum Wage Regulations 1999 SI 1999/ 584.

195 'Employment Equality (Age) Regulations 2006, Notes on Regulations' DTI (available at <http://www.dti.gov.uk/files/file27136.pdf>), para 109.

all of his workers), if the exemption is to apply.[196] Regulation 32, then, completely excludes persons with less than five years' service from any claim in age discrimination arising out of service-related benefits.[197] As to those with more than five years' service, it is only necessary for an employer to show that it '*reasonably appears*' to him that the criterion of length of service challenged fulfils a business need. This sets a lower threshold than the justification defence found in EU anti-discrimination law. The notes to the Regulations issued by the Government suggest that the rationale for regulation 32 derives from Article 6(1), described above.[198] However, given the discussion above in relation to blanket exclusions, the lawfulness of this provision must also be doubted. In addition, the complex formula for calculating length of service allows an employer to discount service where an employee was absent from work or present at work where that period preceded a period during which the worker was absent from work if it is *reasonable* for him so to do.[199] This raises the question as to what period of service, whether arising otherwise during absence from or attendance at work, it would be reasonable for an employer to discount. This obviously raises questions about the relationship between the Age Regulations and other anti-discrimination laws, including the SDA (and, in particular, its protection against disadvantage associated with pregnancy and maternity leave), the RRA (which may protect workers from certain minority groups from disadvantage associated with absence related to the membership of that group), and the DDA (which may protect a worker against disadvantage associated with absence caused by disability).[200]

8.53 Fourthly, in regulation 33 there is a complex exemption allowing employers to discriminate on the grounds of age in the awarding of redundancy payments which are linked to the statutory redundancy provisions:

> The principal object of this provision is to assist those employers who base their redundancy schemes on the statutory scheme but who are more generous than the statutory scheme requires them to be. It would be ironic if employers who did the minimum necessary did not run the risk of a successful challenge under these regulations, yet a more generous employer—because he was doing more than he was

[196] Age Regulations, regulations 32(3)–(6) makes provision for determining *length of service* for these purposes.

[197] And such would otherwise be indirectly discriminatory in many cases.

[198] 'Employment Equality (Age) Regulations 2006, Notes on Regulations' DTI (available at <http://www.dti.gov.uk/files/file27136.pdf>), para 112.

[199] Regulation 32(4). Certain service is deemed by regulation 32(5) but may then be discounted under regulation 32(4)(b) and (c), Age Regulations.

[200] Importantly, the exemption in relation to service-related benefits described above and contained within regulation 32 does not apply to termination payments. Regulation 33 makes special provision for enhanced redundancy payments that are based on the statutory redundancy payment multipliers, as described below.

required to do—could be challenged. If this were the position, there is a real risk that more generous would simply 'level down'. This would benefit no one.[201]

It is true that penalizing an employer who provided a more generous but statutorily linked redundancy payment scheme might be counter-productive. However, the Government originally took the view that the statutory redundancy scheme, which depends, in part, on the age of the employee concerned, was directly discriminatory and would require removal. This was controversial on both sides of industry, with the TUC arguing that a multiplier of one week would be contrary to the Framework Directive's principle of non-regression,[202] and the CBI opposing a levelling up. The Government therefore shied away from addressing the discrimination in the statutory redundancy scheme and left matters as they were, but, recognizing that this would have an impact on those redundancy schemes which were linked to the statutory scheme, introduced regulation 33. The exemption is fairly limited, but its lawfulness again must be doubted given that it does result in a broad exemption to the principle of equal treatment contained in the Framework Directive.

The most controversial exemption in the Age Regulations, however, relates to termination of employment, in particular retirement, as alluded to above. Recital 14 of the Framework Directive provides that 'this Directive shall be without prejudice to national provisions laying down retirement ages'. Apparently relying on this and the special provision made in the Directive under Article 6(1), described above, regulation 30 has been enacted. It provides[203] as is material that '[n]othing in part 2 or 3 shall render unlawful the dismissal of a person to whom this regulation applies at or over the age of 65 where the reason for the dismissal is retirement'. Amendments are made to the unfair dismissal provisions of the Employment Rights Act 1996 bolstering the exemption in relation to age discrimination under regulation 30, by providing a context for determining whether a dismissal is for retirement and for deeming dismissals for retirement fair in circumstances where the statutory procedure described below is complied with.[204] It is not at all clear that such a blanket exemption will be compliant with the Framework Directive, having regard to the observations above.[205] A complex set of provisions in the Schedules to the Age Regulations address the procedure which must be followed if any dismissal is to be 8.54

201 'Employment Equality (Age) Regulations 2006, Notes on Regulations' DTI (available at <http://www.dti.gov.uk/files/file27136.pdf>), para 129.

202 Found in Article 8(2). See Chap 4.

203 The regulation applies in relation to an employee within the meaning of s 230(1) of the Employment Rights Act, a person in Crown employment, a relevant member of the House of Commons staff, and a relevant member of the House of Lords staff, regulation 30(1).

204 Employment Rights Act 1996, ss 98, 98ZA–98ZF.

205 At the time of writing, the High Court has just decided to refer the lawfulness of the exclusion in relation to retirement ages to the ECJ, reportedly without objection by the Government, on an application by Age Concern. At the time of writing no official reports have been published,

automatically fair. By paragraph 2 of Schedule 6 to the Age Regulations, an employer who intends to retire an employee must inform her or him in writing of the intended date of retirement and the right to make a request to continue working past that date. This requirement must be complied with no more than one year and no less than six months before the intended retirement date, and applies irrespective of whether the date has been specified elsewhere. If an employer fails to notify an employee at least six months before the intended retirement date, he is subject to a continuing duty to inform and of the right to request to work on past the retirement date.[206] This continuing duty lasts until two weeks before the employee's employment is due to terminate. Irrespective of the effect on the fairness of the dismissal of a failure to notify in accordance with the procedure, such a failure can form the subject of an employment tribunal claim by the employee affected, by itself.[207] If a tribunal finds such a complaint to be well founded, it must order compensation of an amount not exceeding eight weeks' pay.[208]

8.55 Any employee who an employer proposes to retire has the right to request not to retire on the intended date of retirement.[209] To take advantage of this *right*, an employee must meet certain conditions.[210] Once an employee has made such a request, the employer must *consider* such request.[211] These requirements include a requirement to hold a meeting to discuss the request with the employee within a reasonable period after receiving it. The Regulations do not require that an employer accede to an employee's request, and nor do they define the circumstances in which it would be proper to do so. This rather minimizes the impact of the duty to inform and the right to request. The employer's decision must be notified to the employee in writing and must be dated, and, in the case of a positive decision, the employer must state that the employee's request has been accepted and whether, if requested, the employment is to continue indefinitely or for a particular period, and then the length of the period. Where an employer refuses any request, the employer must also state the same in writing, confirming the date

but see <http://www.heyday.org.uk/wps/portal/!ut/p/kcxml/04_Sj9SPykssy0xPLMnMz0vM0Y_QjzKLN4g3cjMESYGZrsH6kRhiphhijgiRIH1vfV-P_NxU_QD9gtzQ0IhyR0UAH5joqA!!/delta/base64xml/L0lDU0lKQ1RPN29na21BISEvb0VvUUFBSVFnakZJQUFRaENFSVFqR0VBLzRKRmlDbzBlaDFpY29uUVZHaGQtc0lRIS83XzBfOU4xLzI2MzE1Mg!!?PC_7_0_9N1_WCM_CONTEXT=/content/home/community/community_campaigns_mra_6+dec+announcement&bodyfield=2&WCM_DOC_ID=com.ibm.workplace.wcm.api.WCM_Content/community_campaigns_mra_6%20dec%20announcement/e57b66457284cdf>.

206 Schedule 6, para 4.

207 Schedule 6, para 11.

208 A week's pay for these purposes is to be determined in accordance with the provisions under the Employment Rights Act 1996.

209 Schedule 6, para 5.

210 See para 5(2) for where an employer has failed to notify an employee of the intended retirement date altogether.

211 Schedule 6, paras 7–9.

upon which the dismissal is to take effect. The Regulations do not require that an employer give reasons for its refusal. The Regulations provide an employee with the right to appeal a refusal to grant his request to continue working or to continue working for a particular period.[212] An employee has the right to be accompanied to any initial meeting to consider his request not to retire, and the same applies during any appeal meeting.[213] A failure to allow an employee to be accompanied gives rise to a complaint itself and if successful may result in an award of no more than two weeks' pay.[214] The Regulations also provide protection against a *detriment* and *dismissal* in favour of the employee making the request and any employee accompanying him to the initial meeting or the appeal meeting.[215] An employer who fails to comply with the procedures described above is at risk of a finding of unfair dismissal.[216]

As seen, there is a blanket exemption in relation to employees aged 65 or over, **8.56** so long as the procedures are complied with, in which case a dismissal will be fair. Where an employee has a normal retirement age below 65 and that lower retirement age is objectively justified, the same will apply.[217] It is likely to be difficult, however, to justify retirement ages below 65, particularly given that in accordance with EU law, justification will have to be shown in each case. The blanket exemption in regulation 30 is said, by Government, to be justified so as to meet the legitimate social policy aim of meeting employers' concerns in relation to (a) workforce planning, and (b) avoiding an adverse impact on the provision of occupational pensions and other work-related benefits.[218] Given the discussion above in relation to blanket exclusions it is difficult to see how this broad exemption can be justified in EU law. It is also difficult to see how it is consistent with an anti-age discrimination agenda. The Spanish reference described above (paragraph 8.50) is likely to be influential on developments in age discrimination law domestically.

As seen above, the regulation 30 exemption applies only to employees and other **8.57** defined categories of workers. Agency workers and independent contractors, for example, who would be covered by the Regulations, do not fall within the exemption. These workers cannot, of course, claim unfair dismissal but do have the

212 Schedule 6, para 8.

213 Schedule 6, para 9.

214 Again calculated in accordance with the Employment Rights Act 1996.

215 Schedule 6, para 13 and see amended s 108 of the Employment Rights Act 1996.

216 Certain transitional arrangements are made in Sch 7 of the Regulations providing for a situation where the dismissal for retirement takes place after commencement of the regulations and before 1 April 2007.

217 Direct as well as indirect discrimination being capable of justification under the Age Regulations, see Chap 6.

218 Employment Equality (Age) Regulations 2006, Notes on Regulations' DTI (available at <http://www.dti.gov.uk/files/file27136.pdf>), para 99.

rights provided under the Age Regulations and therefore any dismissal based on age would need to be justified if it were not to be unlawful.

8.58 As to other age discriminatory dismissals, that is, those not based on retirement, these will be unlawful unless justified. This is particularly important having regard to stereotyping around age. Redundancy dismissals too, for example, particularly where based on a 'last in first out' policy, may also be indirectly discriminatory.

9

EDUCATION AND COMMUNITY SERVICES

A. Introduction

All the main anti-discrimination enactments to some extent make provision regulating discrimination by educational institutions. The widest coverage is provided by the Sex Discrimination Act 1975 (SDA), the Race Relations Act 1976 (RRA), the Disability Discrimination Act 1995 (DDA), and the Equality Act 2006 (EA) (in the case of religion or belief discrimination[1]), with the Religion or Belief Regulations, the Sexual Orientation Regulations, and the Age Regulations providing very limited protection. **9.01**

The SDA and the RRA contained provisions addressing discrimination by schools and in further and higher education in their original enactments. The EA makes similar provision in relation to schools.[2] The DDA, on the other hand, as originally enacted did not outlaw discrimination in educational provision, and excluded 'education' from the goods, facilities, and services provisions.[3] No individual rights were conferred upon disabled pupils and students. Instead the DDA **9.02**

---

[1] When read with the Religion or Belief Regulations and when in force. These provisions are expected to be brought into force in April 2007.

[2] Though with significant exemptions discussed below.

[3] DDA, s 19(5)(a) and (6) as unamended.

in its original form introduced reporting obligations on educational institutions and local education authorities, requiring them to publish information annually regarding their admission and other arrangements for disabled pupils and students and the like.[4] With the enactment of the Special Educational Needs and Disability Act 2001 (SENDA), the DDA was amended so as to outlaw discrimination in the field of education. Part IV, Chapter 1 of the DDA now regulates discrimination in relation to schools and education authorities in relation to schooling, and Part IV, Chapter 2 of the DDA regulates discrimination in further and higher education. The Religion or Belief Regulations, the Sexual Orientation Regulations, and the Age Regulations all outlaw discrimination by further and higher education institutions only.

9.03 The education provisions are of particular importance. The contemporary significance of equality and integration in education cannot be overstated. The relationship between segregation in education and broader social cohesion is well reported. In particular, in the report which followed the disturbances in Oldham, Bradford, and elsewhere in the spring and summer of 2001, the Independent Review Team chaired by Ted Cantle was particularly struck by the depth of polarization in towns and cities, and:

> the extent to which these physical divisions were compounded by so many other aspects of our daily lives . . . Separate educational arrangements, community and voluntary bodies, employment, places of worship, language, social and cultural networks, means that many communities operate on the basis of a series of parallel lives. These lives often do not seem to touch at any point, let alone overlap and promote any meaningful interchanges . . . There is little wonder that ignorance about each other's communities can easily grow into fear; especially where this is exploited by extremist groups determined to undermine community harmony and foster divisions.[5]

In particular, the Cantle Report identified that '[i]n terms of community cohesion . . . a significant problem is posed by existing and future monocultural schools, which can add significantly to the separation of communities described above'. The Report recommended that schools should not limit their intake to one culture

4 Ibid, ss 29–31, as unamended.

5 'Community Cohesion: A Report of the Independent Review Team chaired by Ted Cantle' (2001, Home Office) (The Cantle Report), paras 2.1 and 2.3. Whilst recent research indicates that 'segregation' may not be as marked as some commentators have suggested so that 'Segregation by ethnicity has fallen. It declined between 1991 and 2001 in 48 out of 56 cities' (para 5.8.15); cities in the North, including Burnley and Bradford, 'dominate the group of places with the highest levels of segregation. The top eight cities on White/Non-White segregation are all from here. All the places with high or very high segregation are Pennine towns crossing from West Yorkshire into Lancashire, north of Greater Manchester. Five of the top 10 most segregated places are small cities in the north and west. Seventeen of the top 20 most segregated cities are in the north and west' (para 5.85), 'State of the English Cities, A Research Study' (Vol 1) (2006, ODPM).

or ethnicity, and should take steps to make themselves 'attractive to other cultures and ethnicities from a wider area'.[6] The Report made other recommendations to address the problems of mono-cultural schools, the tendency towards Eurocentric curricula and pervasive Christian worship.[7] It noted that most people the researchers spoke to felt that more faith schools would add to the lack of contact and understanding between communities and that 'we need to break that down'.[8] It also recorded the paradoxical position that, as Christian faith-based schools were already supported, 'fairness demanded that the same facility should be available to the Muslim and other communities'.[9] Notwithstanding the concerns expressed in the Report, the Education Act 2002[10] (in line with the White Paper, *Schools—Achieving Success*[11]) encourages the provision of education through faith-based schools. The 2005 White Paper, *Higher Standards, Better Schools for All, More Choice for Parents and Pupils*[12] proposes 'diversity' in school provision and sees faith groups as forming part of that diverse provision.[13] These aspirations are reflected in the Education and Inspection Bill (2006) and the enactment of the EA does nothing to undermine them (see Chapter 13, paragraph 13.21 below). All State schools in England and Wales are required to provide religious education for their pupils,[14] although parents can opt for their children not to attend these classes.[15] The content of the school curriculum and collective worship, or other religious observance organized by the school, are therefore exempt from protection from the prohibition against discrimination connected to religion or belief in the EA, whether or not the school is a faith school.[16]

Gender segregation in education through discriminatory stereotyping remains **9.04**
prevalent. The Equal Opportunities Commission has found, for example, that, notwithstanding the introduction of the national curriculum, decisions on optional subjects remains 'strongly influenced by gender'.[17] In particular, choices on vocational subjects 'generally reflect the traditional pattern of the labour market'.[18] 'In this way certain pathways through employment are immediately closed down'[19] and existing patterns of pay disadvantage are replicated. Gender differences permeate all

6 'Community Cohesion' (see note 5), paras 5.8.6 and 5.8.7.
7 Ibid, para 5.8.13.
8 Ibid, para 5.8.8.
9 Ibid.
10 Amending and supplementing the School Standards and Framework Act 1998.
11 CM 6677 (2001).
12 Cm 6677 (2005).
13 Ibid, para 1.30.
14 Education Act 2002, ss 80 and 101, and School Standards and Framework Act 1998, Sch 19.
15 School Standards and Framework Act 1998, s 71.
16 Equality Act 2006, s 50(2).
17 'Women and Men in Britain: Sex Stereotyping: from School to Work' (2001, EOC).
18 Ibid.
19 Ibid.

levels of the education system, so that gender stereotyping is as prevalent at degree level as at other levels.[20] Boys, too, suffer specific disadvantage in the education system. They generally perform less well than girls in most subjects, and have higher exclusion rates than girls.[21]

9.05 Importantly, education is an area that is highly regulated outside the main anti-discrimination enactments, and in all cases close attention must be paid to that regulatory regime. In particular, in the case of disability discrimination, the 'special educational needs framework' addresses the specific needs of children where they have particular educational requirements. The special educational needs framework is complex and is provided for in statute, a statutory Code of Practice, and a number of Statutory Instruments and Department for Education and Skills (DfES) Circulars and Guidance. In England and Wales, the Education Act 1996[22] is the main legislative source of the provision made in relation to special educational needs.[23] It has been amended by SENDA. The Education Act 1996[24] gives the Secretary of State for Education the power to issue and revise a Code of Practice giving practical advice and guidance to all those who have a responsibility to discharge legal functions regarding special educational needs. The new 'Special Educational Needs Code of Practice' became effective in England on 1 January 2002[25] and in Wales on 1 April 2002,[26] and this addresses certain of the amendments made by SENDA.[27] The Code of Practice gives detailed guidance which is informed by certain general principles and the guidance must 'be read with them clearly in mind'.[28] The general principles are as follows: a child with special educational needs should have their needs met; the special educational needs of children will normally be met in mainstream schools or settings; the views of the child should be sought and taken into account; parents have a vital role

---

20 Ibid and EOC, 'Research Findings: Gender and Differential Achievement in Education and Training: A Research Review' (1998, EOC) also available at <http://www.eoc.org.uk>.

21 Ibid.

22 Similar provision is made in Scotland through the Education (Scotland) Act 1980; the Standards in Scotland's Schools etc. Act 2000. See too, the Education (Additional Support for Learning) (Scotland) Act 2004. Guidance from the Scottish Office Education and Industry Department, *Circular 4/96, Children and Young Persons with Special Educational Needs: Assessment and Recording* (SOEID, 1996) and guidance in the *A Manual of Good Practice* (SOEID, 1998).

23 Part 4.

24 S 313.

25 The Special Educational Needs Code of Practice (Appointed Day) (England) Order 2001, SI 2001/3943.

26 The Special Educational Needs Code of Practice (Appointed Day) (Wales) Order 2002, SI 2002/156.

27 Sec, too, DfES 581/2001, foreword, paras 7 and 13. And see 'Disability Discrimination Act 1995 Part IV, Code of Practice for Schools', Disability Rights Commission, COPSH July 2002.

28 Code of Practice, para 1.5.

to play in supporting their child's education; children with special educational needs should be offered full access to a broad, balanced, and relevant education, including an appropriate curriculum for the foundation stage and national curriculum.

The Code gives detailed guidance on the identification and assessment of special educational needs.[29] It makes clear that most special educational needs will be met effectively within mainstream settings and without the need for a statutory assessment. However, in some cases a statutory assessment will be required, and the obligation for securing the same is on the local education authority. Where a local education authority is of the opinion that a child for whom they are responsible has special educational needs, and it is necessary for the authority to determine the special educational provision for which any learning difficulty he may have calls for, they must serve a notice on the child's parents informing them that they are considering whether to make an assessment and the procedure to be followed.[30] Having served the notice and having taken into account any representations made, where they remain of the opinion that the child has special educational needs and it is necessary for the authority to determine the special educational provision for which any learning difficulty he may have calls for, they must make an assessment of his educational needs. If in the light of such assessment it is necessary for the local education authority to determine the special educational provision which any learning difficulty he may have calls for, the authority must make and maintain a 'statement of his special educational needs'. As the Code of Practice makes clear, where a school requests such a statutory assessment, the child will have demonstrated significant cause for concern.[31] A statutory assessment should only be undertaken if the local education authority believes that the child probably has special educational needs and that it needs or probably needs to determine the child's special educational provision itself by making a statement.[32] Further, a statutory assessment itself will not always lead to a statement.[33] Where a statement is made it will give details of the authority's assessment of the child's special educational needs, and specify the special educational provision to be made for the purpose of meeting those needs, including specifying the type of school which the local education authority consider would be appropriate.[34] 9.06

A child has 'special educational needs' for the purpose of the special education needs framework if he has 'a learning difficulty which calls for special educational 9.07

29 Ibid, Chap 4.
30 Education Act 1996, s 323.
31 Code of Practice, para 5.62 and para 6.71.
32 Ibid, para 7.4.
33 Ibid, para 7.6.
34 Education Act 1996, s 324.

provision to be made for him'.[35] A child[36] has a 'learning difficulty' if he has a significantly greater difficulty in learning than the majority of children of his age, he has a disability which either prevents or hinders him from making use of educational facilities of a kind generally provided for children of his age in schools, or he is under compulsory school age and would have such difficulties if provision were not made.[37]

9.08 Provision is made by the Education Act 1996 (in respect of England and Wales) permitting parents of a child for whom a local education authority has undertaken an assessment to appeal to the Special Educational Needs and Disability Tribunal (which also hears certain education claims under the DDA[38]) in relation to a decision not to make a statement or in relation to the contents of a statement.[39] There is then a close relationship between the DDA and the provision made by the special educational needs framework. However, the fact that a child has a 'special educational need' for the purposes of the special educational needs framework does not mean that they will be 'disabled' for the purposes of the DDA. A child may have special needs and be disabled but similarly may have special needs and no disability, or a disability and no special educational needs.

9.09 Some 'educational provision' may not fall within the education provisions of the main anti-discrimination enactments (for example, early years, youth clubs, scouts etc), but in such a case it is likely to fall within the 'goods, facilities and services provisions', described below.[40]

9.10 Whilst there are compelling grounds for strong and effective legislation against discrimination in the education field, there have been very few cases brought under the education provisions outside the DDA.[41] The DDA creates different enforcement procedures, discussed below, and it is likely that the relative informality seen in those procedures has encouraged greater confidence in exercising

---

35 Ibid, s 312.

36 A child for the purposes of the special educational needs provisions includes any person who has not attained the age of 19 and is a registered pupil at a school: Education Act 1996, s 312(5).

37 Education Act 1996, s 312(2).

38 DDA, s 28.

39 Education Act 1996, ss 325, 326, 333, and 336ZA.

40 See, eg, Schools Code of Practice, 'Disability Discrimination Act 1995 Part IV, Code of Practice for Schools' (2002) DRC (Disability Discrimination Codes of Practice (Education) (Appointed Day) Order 2002, SI 2002/2216), para 10.7.

41 Though discriminatory uniform requirements remain a typical area of challenge: *Mandla v Dowell Lee* [1983] 2 AC 548 and *R (on the application of Begum, by her litigation friend, Rahman) v Headteacher and Governors of Denbigh High School* [2006] UKHL 15. There have also been some formal investigations into education provision (the meaning of which is explained in Chap 15), eg, 'Teaching English as a Second Language: Report of a Formal Investigation in Calderdale LEA' (1996, CRE).

rights under the DDA. In addition, the education provisions under the DDA are supported by other strategic measures (see section 28D of the DDA) and this may have assisted in creating awareness around disability rights.

None of the main anti-discrimination enactments outlaw discrimination in education connected to sexual orientation. This is so despite the fact that gay and lesbian young people suffer significant discrimination in schools. For example, homophobic bullying is 'endemic' in British schools, making it more likely that lesbian and gay pupils will leave school at 16 despite achieving marks that merit continuing with their education.[42] The EA gives the Secretary of State power to make provision about discrimination and harassment connected to sexual orientation in education.[43] The Government has published a Consultation document indicating that they propose to make regulations outlawing, amongst other things, sexual orientation discrimination by schools.[44] **9.11**

There are certain statutory duties imposed on local education authorities and others in respect of education provision and these are addressed in Chapter 15. **9.12**

B. Schools

Parts 3 of the SDA and the RRA, Chapter 1 of Part 4 of the DDA,[45] and section 49 of the EA outlaw discrimination in education. Section 22(1) of the SDA, section 17 of the RRA, and section 49(1) of the EA make it unlawful for a person specified in relation to an educational establishment ('the responsible body'[46]) to discriminate against prospective pupils in the terms on which it offers admissions, or by refusing or deliberately omitting to accept an application for admission, or, in relation to existing pupils, in the way it affords them access to any benefits, facilities, or services, or by refusing or deliberately omitting to afford access to benefits, facilities, or services, or by excluding[47] them from the establishment or subjecting them to any other detriment. **9.13**

Section 28A of the DDA makes similar provision, though protecting 'disabled' pupils only, but outlaws discrimination also in the arrangements made for determining **9.14**

42 'Education For All, Tackling Homophobia in Schools' (2006, Stonewall), 2 (at <http://www.stonewall.org.uk/documents/cornerstone.pdf>).

43 EA, s 81(1).

44 'Getting Equal: Proposals to Outlaw Sexual Orientation Discrimination in the Provision of Goods & Services' (2006) Women and Equality Unit, 34. Regulations are expected to be made in April 2007.

45 As inserted by the Special Educational Needs and Disability Act 2001, and amended regularly since.

46 SDA, s 22; RRA, s 17; DDA, Sch 4A; and EA, s 49.

47 See 'Exclusion from School and Racial Equality: A Good Practice Guide' (1997, CRE) for guidance.

admission to a school, such arrangements being subject (along with the other acts covered) to the reasonable adjustments duties described in Chapter 6. As to existing pupils, the DDA makes more limited provision as is discussed in Chapter 6. The DDA makes it unlawful to discriminate against existing pupils in the education or associated services provided for, or offered to, pupils at the school, or by permanently or temporarily excluding a disabled person from the school, only. There are, too, important exemptions and defences available in relation to a claim of discrimination under section 28A of the DDA and these are discussed in Chapter 6.

9.15 The RRA makes it unlawful for a responsible body to subject pupils and prospective pupils to harassment.[48]

9.16 A 'pupil' is defined by the SDA, RRA, and DDA as, broadly, a person receiving education at an institution to which the schools provisions apply;[49] and a 'disabled pupil' is a pupil who is a disabled person within the meaning of the DDA.[50] The body responsible for a school for the purposes of these provisions is identified by each of the Acts.[51] Except in respect of independent schools and special schools not maintained by a local authority, in which case the proprietor is the responsible body, the local education authority or governing body will be the responsible body according to which has the function in question. In the case of a claim under the DDA, where the school is a pupil referral unit or a maintained nursery school it will always be the local education authority. As to Scotland, the education authority will be the responsible body in the case of a school managed by an education authority; the proprietor in the case of an independent school; the Board of Management in the case of a self-governing school; and the managers of the school where the school is one in respect of which the managers are for the time being receiving grants under section 73(c) or (d) of the Education (Scotland) Act 1980.[52]

9.17 The unlawful acts in relation to schools provided for under the SDA, RRA, and EA are widely drawn and, subject to any specific exemption (see paragraph 9.20 below), any discrimination which causes a disadvantage in the context of schooling is likely to be unlawful. This is so particularly having regard to the wide meaning given to the concept of 'detriment', described above.

9.18 However, segregation is not outlawed in terms in the SDA.[53] It is therefore potentially lawful to provide separate lessons in single-sex groups for boys and girls in a

---

48 RRA, s 17(2), reflecting the requirements of the Race Directive, see Chap 4.

49 SDA, s 22A; RRA, s 17A; DDA, s 28Q(3).

50 DDA, s 28Q(2).

51 SDA, s 22, table; RRA, s 17, table; DDA, Sch 4A table.

52 'Local Education Authority'; 'Proprietor'; 'Board of Management'; 'Education Authority'; 'Managers' are all defined by SDA, s 82: RRA, s 78; DDA, Sch 4A.

53 See Chap 6.

mixed school provided that one sex does not receive *less favourable treatment* in consequence. Any facilities, benefits, or services provided must ordinarily be available to both sexes and provide equal opportunities. Provided that this test is met, segregated classes on, for example, sex education are likely to be lawful.

The unlawful acts under the DDA, applicable to existing disabled pupils, are more narrowly drawn. As described above, the DDA covers discrimination against existing pupils in the 'education or associated services provided for, or offered to, pupils at the school', or by permanently or temporarily excluding a disabled person from the school, only.[54] As discussed in Chapter 6, it is nevertheless intended that the expressions 'education' and 'associated services' are given a broad reach so as to cover all aspects of school life.[55] The expressions are unlikely to convey a meaning as wide as that conveyed by the concept of 'detriment', and so, for example, uniform requirements and other matters only tangential to the provision of education may not be covered.[56] The Statutory Schools Code of Practice issued by the Disability Rights Commission provides a list of what 'exemplifies the range of activities that may be covered' by the expression.[57] The list includes preparation for entry to the school; the curriculum; teaching and learning; classroom organization; timetabling; grouping of pupils; homework; access to school facilities; activities to supplement the curriculum, for example, a drama group visiting the school; school sports; school policies; breaks and lunch times; interaction with peers; assessment and exam arrangements; school discipline and sanctions; though as the Schools Code of Practice makes clear, the list is not exhaustive.[58] 9.19

C. Exemptions: Schools

Section 26 of the SDA exempts single-sex establishments from the unlawful acts relating to the admission of pupils. Single-sex establishments are establishments 9.20

54 DDA, s 28A(2).

55 'Disability Discrimination Act 1995 Part IV, Code of Practice for Schools' (2002, DRC) (Disability Discrimination Codes of Practice (Education) (Appointed Day) Order 2002, SI 2002/2216), para 4.23.

56 Though some tangential services and some educational provision not made by schools (for example, early years, youth clubs, scouts etc) may fall within the 'goods, facilities and services provisions' of the DDA as well as the SDA and RRA, described below (see, Schools Code of Practice, 'Disability Discrimination Act 1995 Part IV, Code of Practice for Schools' (2002) DRC (Disability Discrimination Codes of Practice (Education) (Appointed Day) Order 2002, SI 2002/2216), para 10.7).

57 'Disability Discrimination Act 1995 Part IV, Code of Practice for Schools' (2002, DRC) (Disability Discrimination Codes of Practice (Education) (Appointed Day) Order 2002, SI 2002/2216), para 4.23.

58 Ibid, para 4.24. DDA, s 28A(3) provides the Secretary of State with power to prescribe services (by regulation) which are, or services which are not, to be regarded for the purposes of DDA, s 28A as being education or an associated service. So far, no such regulations have been made.

which admit pupils of one sex only, or which admit pupils of the opposite sex only exceptionally or in comparatively small numbers to particular courses of instruction or teaching classes.[59] A similar exception is made in respect of schools which permit only one sex to board but which are otherwise not single-sex establishments.[60]

9.21 Where a school is a 'single-sex establishment', notwithstanding that it takes pupils of the opposite sex in comparatively small numbers for particular courses of instruction or teaching classes, the fact that pupils of one sex are confined to particular courses of instruction or teaching classes is not unlawful.[61] Provision is made for single-sex establishments which are becoming co-educational to maintain discriminatory admissions during a transitional period.[62]

9.22 The selection of children for admission to faith schools[63] and, where they are pupils, the terms on which they are afforded access to benefits, facilities, and services, and in relation to exclusions are exempted from the unlawful acts provided for in relation to schools. This means that faith schools can lawfully continue to prioritize the admission of children of a particular religion or belief and refuse to take pupils of a different religion, or even non-observant pupils of their own religion, on school trips or other visits, for example.[64] This is addressed further in Chapter 13.

D. Further and Higher Education

9.23 All the main anti-discrimination enactments outlaw discrimination and harassment in the context of further and higher education. They all make it unlawful for a person specified in relation to a further and higher educational establishment (described in the SDA, the RRA, and the DDA as 'the responsible body'[65]) to discriminate against prospective and existing students.[66] The provision made varies materially. All the main anti-discrimination enactments outlaw discrimination by further and higher educational establishments against prospective students in the terms on which they offer admissions, or by refusing or deliberately omitting to accept an application for admission. Further, all the main anti-discrimination enactments, except the DDA, outlaw discrimination by further and higher educational

59 SDA, s 26(1).

60 Ibid, s 26(2). The exemption in relation to physical education was repealed by the Employment Equality (Sex Discrimination) Act 2005, SI 2005/2467.

61 SDA, s 25A.

62 Ibid, s 27.

63 EA, s 50(1) describes the particular schools affected.

64 EA 2006, s 50(1).

65 The bodies covered and the bodies responsible for them are defined in SDA, s 22, RRA, s 17, and DDA, s 28R(6)–(8) and Sch 4B; Religion or Belief Regulations and Sexual Orientation Regulations, regulation 20(4), and Age Regulations, regulation 23(4).

66 Described as pupils in the SDA and RRA and given the meaning above, para 9.16.

establishments against existing pupils, in the way they afford access to any benefits, facilities, or services, or by refusing or deliberately omitting to afford access to them, or by excluding a student from the establishment or by subjecting him or her to any other detriment.[67] As with schools, these unlawful acts will cover a wide range of discriminatory acts.

The SDA, the RRA, the DDA,[68] the Religion or Belief Regulations, the Sexual Orientation Regulations and the Age Regulations also outlaw harassment against prospective, existing, and former students.[69] **9.24**

The DDA outlaws discrimination against prospective students[70] in the same way, but also outlaws discrimination in the arrangements it makes for determining admissions to the institution (and a duty to make adjustments therefore arises in respect of the same, as with the other unlawful acts under the DDA, see Chapter 6).[71] As to existing students, it is unlawful for an educational institution to discriminate against a disabled student in the student services it provides, or offers to provide, or by excluding him or her from the institution, whether permanently or temporarily.[72] 'Student services' mean services of any description that are provided wholly or mainly for students,[73] and these cover a whole range of student services including, for example, teaching, including classes, lectures, seminars, practical sessions; curriculum design; examinations and assessments; field trips and outdoor education; arranging study abroad or work placements; outings and trips; distance learning; learning facilities such as classrooms, lecture theatres, laboratories, studios, dark rooms, amongst other things.[74] **9.25**

---

67 SDA, s 2(3); RRA, s 17(2); Religion or Belief Regulations and Sexual Orientation Regulations, regulations 20(2); and Age Regulations, regulation 23(2). The Religion or Belief Regulations, the Sexual Orientation Regulations, and the Age Regulations do not outlaw discrimination in the provision of facilities or services in terms, but they do outlaw discrimination in the provision of benefits and in the subjection to a detriment, and those expressions are sufficiently wide to catch discrimination in the provision of facilities and services.

68 As a result of amendments made by the Disability Discrimination Act 1995 (Amendment) (Further and Higher Education) Regulations 2006 SI 2006/1721, to give effect to the Framework Directive, see para 9.26 below.

69 SDA, s 22(3); RRA, ss 17(2) and 27A (in the case of race, ethnic, or national origins only); Religion or Belief Regulations and Sexual Orientation Regulations, regulations 20(2) and 21(2); and Age Regulations, regulation 23(2) and 24(2).

70 A 'student' means a person who is attending, or undertaking a course of study at, an educational institution. A 'disabled student' means a student who is a disabled person (DDA, s 31A). See, eg, *Ford-Shubrook v St. Dominic's Sixth Form College* 'Legal Bulletin' (April 2004), DRC, Issue 5, 21.

71 DDA, s 28R(1).

72 Ibid, s 28R(2) and (3).

73 Ibid, s 28R(11). By s 28R(12) regulations may make provision as to services which are, or are not, to be regarded for these purposes as student services. However, no such regulations have been made, to date.

74 'Code of Practice: Post-16 Education' (2006) DRC, in force from 1 Sept 2006.

9.26 The protection provided by the DDA has recently been significantly amended to give effect to the Framework Directive. The Disability Discrimination Act 1995 (Amendment) (Further and Higher Education) Regulations 2006[75] create new unlawful acts in addition to those described above by inserting a new section 28R(3A) and (3B). Section 28R(3A) outlaws discrimination against a disabled person in the arrangements made by a further or higher educational institution for the purpose of determining upon whom to confer a qualification; in the terms on which it is prepared to confer a qualification on him; by refusing or deliberately omitting to grant any application for a qualification; or by withdrawing a qualification or varying the terms on which it is held by the disabled person. Section 28R(3B) outlaws harassment by a further or higher educational institution of a disabled person who holds or applies for a qualification conferred by the institution; is a student at the institution; or seeks admission as a student to the institution.

E. General Qualifications Bodies

9.27 The DDA, alone amongst the main anti-discrimination enactments, makes provision outlawing discrimination by general qualifications bodies, following amendments made to it by the DDA 2005.[76] It is intended that these bodies will be those bodies which award qualifications but which do not fall within the educational provisions described above or the 'qualifications bodies' provisions described at Chapter 8 above[77]—bodies which award, for example, GCSEs, 'A' Levels etc. The bodies covered, however, are yet to be prescribed.[78]

9.28 The provisions addressing general qualifications bodies are not in force at the time of writing. However, when in force they will outlaw disability discrimination[79] by general qualifications bodies in the arrangements which they make for the purpose of determining upon whom to confer a relevant qualification;[80] in the terms on which they are prepared to confer a relevant qualification; by refusing or deliberately omitting to grant any application for such a qualification; or by withdrawing such a qualification or varying the terms on which it is held. The provisions also make it unlawful for a general qualifications body, in relation to a relevant qualification conferred by it, to subject to harassment a disabled person who holds or applies for such a qualification.

---

75 SI 2006/1721.

76 DDA, s 31AA.

77 Ibid, s 31AA(5) and (6).

78 Ibid, s 31AA(6)(a).

79 See Chap 6.

80 Including the renewal or extension of a qualification or authentication of a qualification, DDA, s 31AA(6)(b).

F. Youth and Community Services

9.29 Section 28U of the DDA read with Schedule 4C of the DDA specifically outlaws discrimination by youth and community services. These will include clubs and activities; one-to-one counselling or guidance work; off site and outreach work; outings and trips; facilitated work with groups of people, such as support for a residents' association.[81] The unlawful acts created are almost identical to those created under the further and higher education provisions. Section 28R(1)(b) is modified so that it is unlawful for an educational institution to discriminate against a disabled person in the terms on which it offers to *admit* him or her to the institution. Section 28U[82] makes it unlawful for a local education authority or governing body to discriminate against a disabled person in the terms on which they offer to *enrol* him or her on the course.[83] The duty to make adjustments is also modified.[84]

9.30 The responsible body in the case of statutory youth and community services is the local education authority or the governing body of a maintained school depending on the particular provision,[85] and in Scotland the responsible body will be the education authority.[86]

9.31 No comparable provision is made in the other main anti-discrimination enactments, but to the extent that any activities described above fall outside the education provisions, they are likely, subject to any exemption, to fall within the 'goods, facilities and services' provisions (see Chapter 10).

G. Local Education Authorities

9.32 There are specific duties imposed on local education authorities which are considered in Chapter 15. Further, the SDA, RRA, DDA, and EA make it unlawful for local education authorities and certain other bodies with responsibilities in relation to education provision to discriminate in the exercising of their functions.[87] These provisions allow for challenges to education provision between educational institutions or between, for example, sexes across institutions. For example, differential

81 Post 16 Code of Practice, para 3.16.
82 Read with DDA, s 28R as modified by Sch 4C.
83 DDA, Sch 4C.
84 See Chap 6.
85 DDA, s 28R(6) as substituted by Sch 4C, Part 1, para 1.
86 Ibid, s 28R(6) as substituted by Sch 4C, Part 2.
87 SDA, ss 25 (local education authorities), 23A (discrimination by further education and higher education funding councils), 23BA (discrimination by Scottish Further and Higher Education

provision by a local authority of grammar school places for girls and boys respectively will fall within the local education provisions of the SDA.[88] The EA exempts discrimination in relation to the provision of schools so that in the case of the discriminatory *provision* of schools (for example, by providing certain faith schools but not others), this cannot be challenged under these provisions.[89]

Funding Council), 23D (discrimination by Training and Development Agency for Schools); RRA, ss 18 (local education authorities), 18A (discrimination by further education and higher education funding councils), 18BA (discrimination by Scottish Further and Higher Education Funding Council), 18D (discrimination by Training and Development Agency for Schools); DDA, s 28F; and EA, s 51(1) (with certain exceptions).

[88] *Equal Opportunities Commission v Birmingham City Council* [1989] 1 AC 1155. See, too, *R v Secretary of State for Education and Science ex p Keating* [1985] LGR 469.

[89] EA, s 51(2)(a). Nor does it apply to the provision of transport (EA, s 51(2)(b)). This means, *inter alia,* that although many education authorities provide transport to faith schools for those who live a distance away from them, they will not be required to make similar provision for pupils at another faith or non-faith school.

10

GOODS, FACILITIES, SERVICES, PLANNING, HOUSING, PREMISES, AND CLUBS

A. Introduction

The Sex Discrimination Act 1975 (SDA), the Race Relations Act 1976 (RRA), the Disability Discrimination Act 1995 (DDA),[1] and the Equality Act 2006 (EA)[2] outlaw discrimination connected to sex, race, disability, and religion and belief in the provision of goods, facilities, services, premises, and clubs. There is presently no protection against discrimination connected with sexual orientation in these areas. However, the EA gives the Secretary of State power to make regulations addressing sexual orientation in these areas,[3] and the Government has published proposals for the same.[4] 10.01

1 In the case of clubs and more broadly in relation to premises, in consequence of amendments made by the DDA 2005.

2 The material provisions of the EA are expected to come into force in April 2007.

3 EA, s 81.

4 'Getting Equal: Proposals to Outlaw Sexual Orientation Discrimination in the Provision of Goods & Services' (2006) Women and Equality Unit. Regulations are expected to be made and brought into force in April 2007, at the same time as the material parts of the EA, addressing religion or belief discrimination, come into force.

10.02 The scope of these provisions requires careful identification, in particular because the unlawful acts in relation to the exercising of public functions described below will only operate where there is no other provision in the relevant anti-discrimination enactment which, ignoring any exemption, would apply.[5] The scope of the goods, facilities, and services provisions in particular has proved controversial, as discussed below, and they are particularly likely to overlap with the functions of public authorities which might otherwise fall within the public functions provisions described below.

B. Goods, Facilities, and Services

10.03 The SDA, RRA, DDA, and EA outlaw discrimination in the provision of goods, facilities, and services.[6] Each of these enactments makes it unlawful for any person concerned with the provision (for payment or not) of goods, facilities, or services to the public or a section of the public to discriminate against a person who seeks to obtain or use those goods, facilities, or services by refusing or deliberately omitting to provide him with any of them; or by refusing or deliberately omitting to provide him with goods, facilities, or services of the like quality, in the like manner, and on the like terms as are normal in the first-mentioned person's case in relation to other members of the public or (where the person so seeking belongs to a section of the public) to other members of that section.[7] The provision in the DDA is slightly differently expressed but is materially to the same effect.[8] The RRA also makes it unlawful for any person concerned with the provision of goods, facilities, and services to harass a person to whom he provides them.[9]

10.04 As seen, the service provider must be 'concerned' with the provision of goods, facilities, or services to the public or a section of the public. The fact of goods, facilities, or services actually having been provided to members of the public, or a section thereof, is not material. The service provider simply must be 'concerned' with providing them. The unsuccessful service provider and the first time service provider are covered equally. It is irrelevant whether any goods, facilities, or services are is provided on payment (for example, a restaurant) or without payment (for

---

5 See Chap 11 below.

6 SDA, s 29; RRA, 20; DDA, s 19; EA, s 46.

7 SDA, s 29; RRA, s 20; DDA, s 19; and EA, s 46. By SDA, ss 29(4), s 29(1) of the SDA, to the extent that it addresses vocational training, applies to gender reassignment discrimination.

8 DDA, s 19.

9 RRA, s 20(5).

example, access to a park). The public, to whom the provisions apply, include children as well as adults, so children's services are therefore covered. This means that all service providers, whether in the voluntary, statutory, or commercial sector, are covered.

Providers of goods, facilities, and services are only caught by these provisions where the particular service is truly provided to (or is one which the service provider is truly prepared to provide to) members of the public or a section of it. The main anti-discrimination enactments are not, therefore, concerned with purely private or one-off arrangements. In *Dockers Labour Club & Institute Limited v Race Relations Board*,[10] under comparable provisions in the RRA 1968, the Race Relations Board[11] sought a declaration that the Dockers Labour Club, which operated a colour bar such that only white people were admitted into its club, was acting unlawfully.[12] The House of Lords upheld an earlier decision of the House[13] in holding that the club did not provide facilities or services to the public, or a section of it. The club elected its members, adopting a genuine process of selection, and thus was not accessible to the public or a section of it but properly operated within the private sphere. The House of Lords also held that the same principle applied where clubs, operating under reciprocal arrangements with other clubs, offered hospitality or temporary membership to members of the other club. Even in such circumstances, so long as *each* club exercised 'a rigorous choice in electing their members', there would be no discrimination within the meaning of the goods, facilities, and services provisions because the clubs would be operating only within the private sphere.[14] **10.05**

Prisoners have been held to constitute a section of the public.[15] Children in the care of a local authority have also been held to constitute a section of the public to whom foster parents provide services or facilities for the purposes of the RRA,[16] though foster arrangements have now been taken outside the scope of the Act.[17] **10.06**

---

10 [1976] AC 285.

11 The predecessor of the Commission for Racial Equality.

12 This claim was brought under the RRA 1968, s 2(1) but the existing provisions are in materially the same terms.

13 *Race Relations Board v Charter* [1973] AC 868.

14 The effect of the decision in the *Dockers Labour Club* case has been limited by changes introduced by the RRA 1976. Discrimination by private members' clubs is now made expressly unlawful under the RRA. However, the same does not apply under the SDA.

15 *Alexander v Home Office* [1988] 1 WLR 968; [1998] ICR 685; [1988] IRLR 190, though apparently this point was not taken, at least on appeal.

16 *Applin v Race Relations Board* [1975] AC 259.

17 RRA, s 23(2).

10.07 The SDA, RRA, and EA contain express provision addressing services which are indirectly provided. Section 50 of the SDA provides that:

> references in this Act to the affording by any persons of access to benefits, facilities or services are not limited to benefits, facilities or services provided by that person himself, but include any means by which it is in that person's power to facilitate access to benefits, facilities or services provided by any other person (the 'actual provider').

Section 40 RRA is in the same terms and section 76 of the EA is in materially identical terms.[18] The DDA contains no such provision but given the wide meaning given to the provision of services, described below, such might be implied.

10.08 The SDA, RRA, DDA, and EA give a non-exhaustive list of examples of 'facilities and services' to which the 'goods, facilities and services' provisions apply.[19] They differ slightly as between the enactments, but the examples are in any event illustrative only and, in particular, the DDA identifies examples which concern accessibility (means of communication, access to information services). All the enactments give as examples access to and use of any place which members of the public are permitted to enter; accommodation in a hotel, boarding house, or other similar establishment; facilities by way of banking or insurance, or for grants, loans, credit, or finance; facilities for entertainment, recreation, or refreshment; the services of any profession, trade, or public authority. It is not necessary, then, that any tangible benefit is to be enjoyed. Instead, mere access to a place (including streets, pathways etc) to which the public have access is adequate. 'Profession' includes any vocation or occupation and 'trade' includes any business.[20]

10.09 The words 'goods, facilities or services' are not otherwise described, but they will be given their ordinary and natural meaning so that 'goods' will refer to any movable property, including merchandise or wares; 'facilities' will include any opportunity for obtaining some benefit or for doing something, and 'services' will refer to any conduct tending to the welfare or advantage of other people, especially conduct which supplies their needs.[21] Each of these expressions is deliberately vague and general; taken together, they cover a very wide range of human activity.[22]

10.10 Whether particular services are caught will depend upon the particular circumstances. Some organizations may be providing services covered by the goods, facilities, and services provisions for the purposes of certain of their activities but

18 'A reference in this Part to providing a service, facility or benefit of any kind includes a reference to facilitating access to the service, facility or benefit'.

19 SDA, s 29(2); RRA, s 20(2); DDA, s 19, and EA, s 46(2).

20 SDA, s 82; RRA s 78(1); DDA, s 68(1).

21 A Lester and G Bindman, *Race and Law* (1972, Penguin), 260.

22 Ibid.

not others. This may be so with membership clubs (see paragraph 10.29 below) where on an 'open day' to which the public are invited, they will be covered by these provisions, but when providing services exclusively to members, they will not. Similarly, the police will be providing a service for these purposes when giving advice and information about crime prevention, but are unlikely to be providing a service when arresting someone[23] (as to which, see Chapter 11 below).

10.11 The key controversy that has arisen under the 'goods, facilities and services' provisions has arisen in relation to their application to the exercising of public functions. This controversy has become less important because those main anti-discrimination enactments which address discrimination in the provision of goods, facilities, and services now also expressly address discrimination by public authorities in the exercising of public functions. However, it is still necessary to be aware of the limits of the 'goods, facilities and services' provisions because the unlawful acts regulating discrimination by public authorities will not apply to discrimination regulated by another provision. If the complaint falls within the goods, facilities, and services provisions, therefore, it will not also fall within the scope of the 'public functions' provisions.[24]

10.12 The SDA, the RRA, and the DDA all expressly apply to at least some of the functions of public authorities by providing in their non-exhaustive list of examples of facilities and services 'the services of any . . . local or other public authority'.[25] However, notwithstanding the ordinary and natural meaning of these words, the courts have given a narrow meaning to them in a series of decisions in cases arising in the immigration field. Thus according to the Court of Appeal, read in their 'natural and ordinary meaning', these words were not aimed at the Secretary of State when he was exercising powers concerned with giving leave to enter or remain under the Immigration Act 1971, instead:

> [t]he word 'facilities' in that section is flanked on one side by the word 'goods' and on the other 'services'. This suggests . . . that the word 'facilities' is not to be given a wholly unrestricted meaning but must be limited or confined to facilities that are akin to goods or services . . . When the Secretary of State allows an immigrant to enter and stay in this country, he is granting a permission, he is not providing a facility.[26]

---

23 Revised Code of Practice on Right of Access, Goods, Facilities, Services, and Premises (2002) DRC, para 2.14.

24 SDA, s 21A(9), paras 15–16; RRA, s 19B(6); DDA, s 21B(7); and EA, s 52(4)(m).

25 SDA, s 29(2)(g); RRA, s 20(2)(g); and DDA, s 19(3)(h). The EA does not expressly refer to the same under its s 46.

26 *R v Immigration Appeal Tribunal ex parte Kassam* [1980] 1 WLR 1037, *per* Stevenson LJ, 1044. See, for a non-controversial example of a facility or service provided by a local authority, *James v Eastleigh Borough Council* [1990] 2 AC 751 (local authority swimming facilities).

10.13 In *Re Amin*[27] the House of Lords were concerned with a special voucher scheme under which certain Commonwealth citizens could apply to settle in the UK, so long as they were the head of a household. Ms Amin complained that this indirectly discriminated against women, and, in judicial review proceedings, relied upon section 29 of the SDA. The House of Lords concluded that section 29 was concerned with facilities and services that might be done by a private person[28] and 'market place activities'. Read as a whole, according to the House of Lords, it applied to the direct provision of facilities and services and not to the mere grant of permission to use those facilities, and that the entry clearance officer who had refused Ms Amin's application for a special voucher had not been providing a service for would-be immigrants, but performing his duty of controlling immigration. The special voucher scheme was, then, outside the scope of section 29, as are any decisions involving the exercise of executive discretion, according to the House of Lords. The same would apply equally to the parallel provisions under the RRA, DDA, and EA.

10.14 Outside of immigration decision making, the courts have generally given a more generous meaning to the 'goods, facilities and services' provisions, resulting in some inconsistency in approach. In *Savjani v Inland Revenue Commissioners*[29] the Court of Appeal distinguished the case law described above in holding that the Inland Revenue provided a service to taxpayers when performing their statutory duties, for the purposes of the 'goods, facilities and services' provisions. The Inland Revenue provided such services by the provision, dissemination, and implementation of regulations which enabled the taxpayer to know that he was entitled to a deduction or a repayment of tax, and which might entitle him to know how to satisfy the Inspector or the Board if he was so entitled, and which would enable him to obtain the actual deduction or repayment which Parliament said he was to have.[30] Similarly, in *Alexander v The Home Office*[31] a prisoner complained about the allocation of work to him on racial grounds. He succeeded in his claim before a County Court and no point was taken, at least at the Court of Appeal, that his claim fell outside the 'goods, facilities and services' provisions.

10.15 In the context of policing, the courts have taken an increasingly expansive view of the 'goods, facilities and services' provisions as compared to that seen in the immigration cases. In *Farah v Commissioner of Police of the Metropolis*[32] the Court of

27 [1983] 2 AC 818.
28 At 835, in particular.
29 [1981] QB 458.
30 Ibid, at 467 *per* Templeman LJ.
31 [1988] 1 WLR 968.
32 [1998] QB 65.

Appeal concluded that section 20 of the RRA (which, as is material, has the same meaning as section 29 of the SDA, section 19 of the DDA, and section 46 of the EA) was wide enough to cover some of the activities of the police, in particular those parts of a police officer's duties involving assistance to or protection of members of the public which amounted to the provision of services to the public:

> What is said is that the service sought by the plaintiff was that of protection and that she did not, because of her race, obtain the protection that others would have been afforded. It seems to me that that is no less the provision of a service than is the giving of directions or other information to a member of the public who seeks them.[33]

The Court of Appeal were particularly influenced by the words of Lord Fraser in *Re Amin*[34] that having regard to the Act as a whole it applies to acts done on behalf of the Crown but only where they are of a kind similar to acts that might be done by a private person:

> Lord Fraser . . . drew a distinction between acts done on behalf of the Crown which are of a kind similar to acts that might be done by a private person and acts done by a person holding statutory office in the course of formulating or carrying out government policy, the latter being quite different in kind from any act that would ever be done by a private person. The assertion in the pleading is that officers failed to react to the plaintiff's emergency telephone call, to investigate her account at the scene, and to afford her protection—all on account of her colour: 'These acts (or services) which the plaintiff sought from the police were, to my mind, acts which might have been done by a private person.' The second category envisaged by Lord Fraser covers those acts which a private person would never do, and would normally only ever be performed by the police, eg gaining forcible entry into a suspected drugs warehouse. Here the officers would be carrying out government policy to which the Act would not apply. Moreover, they would be performing duties in order to prevent and detect crime and exercising their powers to enable them to perform those duties.[35]

In *Brooks v Commissioner of Police for the Metropolis & Others*,[36] in a case brought by Duwanye Brooks arising out of the murder of his best friend, Stephen Lawrence, in a racist attack, the Court of Appeal went further. Mr Brooks brought a claim against various police officers alleging that they had discriminated against him under section 20 of the RRA. The numerous allegations of discrimination fell into two broad categories namely (1) allegations of failing to protect, assist, and support, and (2) allegations of failure to investigate crime with appropriate **10.16**

33 Ibid, at 78.
34 *Re Amin* [1983] 2 AC 818, 834–5.
35 [1998] QB 65, 85, *per* Otton LJ.
36 [2002] EWCA Civ 407.

competence and vigour.[37] The judge at first instance struck out parts of Mr Brooks' claim, in particular those parts which related to the investigation of the crime. The Court of Appeal allowed an appeal by Mr Brooks and permitted the complaints made regarding the investigation of the crime to proceed on the grounds that they were capable of falling within the scope of section 20. This followed a concession by counsel for the police officers that 'it would be "technically possible" for an individual police officer to be asked to provide investigatory services by a member of the public, and to respond in a way which would fall foul of section 20(1)(a) or (b)'.[38]

10.17 Accordingly, outside of the immigration field, the 'goods, facilities and services' provisions have been given a wider reach and, in particular, have applied to instances of discrimination done pursuant to a statutory duty or a statutory power.[39] Extensive functions of public authorities will, then, fall within the scope of the 'goods, facilities and services' provisions, including the provision of health services, certain functions of highway authorities, police forces, and, perhaps in respect of non-judicial decision making at least, the courts.[40] In any event, where the acts done are such that they might have been done by a private person, they are likely to fall within section 29 of the SDA, section 20 of the RRA, section 19 of the DDA, and section 46 of the EA. It is not necessary that an express request for services is made for the 'goods, facilities and services' provisions to apply[41] so that, for example, a police officer who passes by a victim of crime without stopping to assist, protect, or investigate, on racial grounds, will be guilty of unlawful discrimination even in circumstances where the victim did not make a request for help.

10.18 The 'goods, facilities and services' provisions will also apply to transport services. 'Facilities for transport or travel' are given as a specific example of the services to which the provisions may apply under the SDA, the RRA, and the EA.[42] The DDA does not in terms refer to such services in its illustrative list of services

---

37 Ibid, at para 817.

38 Ibid, at para 36.

39 *Savjani v Inland Revenue Commissioners* [1981] QB 458; *Farah v Commissioner of Police of the Metropolis* [1998] QB 65; *Brooks v Commissioner of Police for the Metropolis & Others* [2002] EWCA Civ 407; *Alexander v The Home Office* [1988] 1 WLR 968. See also *Alder v Chief Constable of Humberside Police and Others* [2006] EWCA Civ 1741.

40 Though *obiter dicta* in *Woodrup v London Borough of Southwark* [2002] EWCA Civ 1716, [2003] IRLR 111 suggests otherwise (Simon-Browne LJ described the submission that an employment tribunal was 'providing a service to the public under Part III' 'far-fetched' and Clarke LJ was 'not at present persuaded' of the same at paragraphs 16 and 24). See Chap 10 below for an exemption in relation to judicial decision making applicable under the public functions provisions.

41 *Brooks v Commissioner of Police for the Metropolis & Others* [2002] EWCA Civ 407, para 39. This is so, notwithstanding that SDA, s 29, RRA, s 20, and EA, s 46 (though not DDA, s 19) require that a person 'seeks to obtain or use' goods, facilities, or services.

42 SDA, s 29(2)(f); RRA, s 20(2)(f); and EA, s 46(2)(e).

to which its 'goods, facilities and services provisions' apply.[43] This reflects the fact that in its original enactment, 'transport' services were largely excluded from the unlawful acts and regulated instead by the imposition of accessibility requirements on public transport providers,[44] licensing requirements, and the like. Transport *related* activities (as opposed to services consisting of the *use* of transport[45]) have always fallen within the scope of all the goods, facilities, and services provisions, including those in the DDA, and that position is unaltered. Such services include the provision of customer services (for example, assistance to transport users) and infrastructure services (for example, stations and airports).[46] However, 'the use of any means of transport' was expressly excluded from the 'goods, facilities, and services' provisions in the DDA.[47] The position has now changed as a result of the enactment of the DDA 2005 and the making of regulations under it.[48]

In summary, the DDA excludes from the 'goods, facilities, and services' provisions the provision of vehicles[49] and services when travelling in a vehicle, and excludes any duty to make adjustments involving the alteration or removal of a physical feature of a vehicle, amongst other things.[50] However, by regulations made under the DDA, certain vehicles are excluded from this exemption so providing coverage in respect of them.[51] In consequence, the DDA now applies to the providers of transport services[52] who provide such services through the use of specified vehicles. The extent to which the duties apply depends on the type of vehicle involved. As mentioned in Chapter 6, the goods, facilities, and services provisions apply to certain hire vehicles; private hire vehicles; public service vehicles; rail vehicles; taxis; vehicles deployed by a breakdown or recovery operator, whether or not through a third party, the sole or partial purpose of which is to transport the driver and occupants of a broken down vehicle from the scene of an accident or breakdown; and vehicles deployed on a system using a mode of **10.19**

43 DDA, s 19(3).

44 Under Part V, DDA, see Chap 15.

45 DDA, s 19(5).

46 *Ross v Ryanair and Another* [2004] EWCA Civ 1751; 'Code of Practice: Provision and Use of Transport Vehicles' (Disability Discrimination Code of Practice (Supplement to Part 3 Code of Practice) (Provision and Use of Transport Vehicles) (Appointed Day) Order 2006 2006 No 1094), para 2.2.

47 DDA, s 19(5).

48 See s 21ZA, DDA and the Disability Discrimination (Transport Vehicles) Regulations 2005 SI 2005/3190 and the Disability Discrimination (Northern Ireland) Order 2006, SI 2006/312.

49 'Vehicles' are defined by DDA, s 21ZA(4).

50 DDA, s 21ZA(2).

51 Disability Discrimination (Transport Vehicles) Regulations 2005 SI 2005/3190 and the Disability Discrimination (Northern Ireland) Order 2006, SI 2006/312. See Chap 6, for the duties in respect of physical features and auxiliary aids.

52 Defined in DDA, s 21ZA(4).

guided transport.[53] The Disability Rights Commission have issued a statutory Code of Practice,[54] explaining the impact of the new provisions in the DDA addressing transport: *Provision and Use of Transport Vehicle: Supplement to Part 3 Code of Practice* (2006).[55]

C. Contracts

10.20 As to discriminatory terms in contracts, see Chapter 8, paragraph 8.30. The provisions there described apply equally to contractual terms operable outside the employment and related fields.

D. Exemptions

10.21 There are a number of exemptions to the 'goods, facilities and services' provisions, some of which apply generally,[56] but some are specific to the goods, facilities, and services provisions. The SDA excludes services or facilities restricted to one sex where they are provided at certain places.[57] Services provided at hospitals or establishments providing special care, supervision, or attention are excluded.[58] Such would apply to nursing homes or other psychiatric institutions. Women's refuges might fall within this exception if they were providing 'special care, supervision and attention' comparable to that provided at a hospital, as would rape crisis centres if they were providing medical or psychiatric care. Services provided at a place occupied or used for purposes of an organized religion, where they are restricted to men to comply with the doctrines of that religion or to avoid offending the religious susceptibilities of a significant number of its followers, are excluded.[59] Services provided at a place such that two or more persons are likely to be using the services at the same time, and the presence of the other sex would be that those persons would be likely to suffer serious embarrassment at the presence

53 Regulation 3, Disability Discrimination (Transport Vehicles) Regulations 2005 SI 2005/3190 (all these expressions are defined by regulation 2).

54 See Chap 15, for the impact of the same.

55 DRC, ISBN 978 0 11 703632 1; Disability Discrimination Code of Practice (Supplement to Part 3 Code of Practice) (Provision and Use of Transport Vehicles) (Appointed Day) Order 2006 SI 2006/1094.

56 See Chap 13.

57 SDA, s 35.

58 Ibid, s 35(1)(a), including a resettlement unit provided for under Sch 5 of the Supplementary Benefits Act 1976. 'Gender Equality Duty, Code of Practice' (2006, EOC). Laid before Parliament a the time of writing.

59 SDA, s 35(1)(b).

of the other sex, are excluded.[60] This exception potentially covers services such as group counselling or advice about matters such as sexual health, sexual offences, or intimate personal health or hygiene. Rape crisis centres and women's refuges may fall within this exception if they involve group provision of services involving intimate personal matters. Services provided in places where the users are likely to be in a state of undress or where physical contact is likely and users might reasonably object to the presence of the opposite sex, such as facilities for separate male and female changing rooms, and any group service involving intimate personal health and hygiene, are excluded.[61] These exceptions will cover changing rooms and sports sessions involving a high degree of physical contact, for example.[62]

E. Planning

The RRA, alone, makes specific provision in relation to discrimination by planning authorities. Section 19A of the RRA makes it 'unlawful for a planning authority to discriminate against a person in carrying out their planning functions'.[63] All authorities in England, Wales, and Scotland are covered,[64] as are all planning functions under the Town and Country Planning Act 1990[65] and related planning statutes.[66] Though planning regulation raises very significant issues for certain minority groups (travellers in particular), there have been very few cases indeed under these provisions.[67] **10.22**

60 Ibid, s 35(1)(c)(i). 'Gender Equality Duty, Code of Practice' (2007, EOC).

61 SDA, s 35(1)(ii) and (2). 'Gender Equality Duty, Code of Practice' (2007, EOC).

62 These exceptions apply equally to discrimination falling within the 'premises' provisions.

63 This provision was inserted by s 55 of the Housing and Planning Act 1986.

64 RRA, s 19A(2).

65 And the Town and Country Planning (Scotland) Act 1997.

66 RRA, s 19A(3).

67 'The Code of Practice on Racial Equality in Housing in England' (2006, CRE), gives as an example of discrimination under s 19A: 'A planning authority responds to pressure from residents objecting to an application for a Gypsy caravan site, because they do not want Gypsies or Irish Travellers living in the neighbourhood. Both Gypsies and Irish Travellers have full protection as racial groups under the RRA and the planning authority would be acting unlawfully if it succumbed to pressure and treated racist objections as material grounds for refusing planning permission. Decisions by local authorities on planning applications must be based on their merit in terms of planning; for example, the effects the proposal might have on amenities or on the local environment.' (The Code of Practice on Racial Equality in Housing in England', para 2.58 (Race Relations Code of Practice (Housing) (Appointed Day) Order 2006 SI 2006/2239)). The one case of which I am aware is *Davis v Bath and North East Somerset District Council* (Bristol County Court, claim no. 9324149) in which the County Court found that the claimant had been subject to direct race discrimination when the council's planning officers repeatedly obstructed his applications for planning permission in relation to the development of a site (following which the council paid into court the sum of £750,000 which was awarded to the claimant with costs).

10.23 Any planning functions falling outside section 19A of the RRA might fall within sections 19B[68] or 20 of the RRA and the equivalent provisions of the SDA, DDA, and EA.

F. Housing and Premises

10.24 The SDA, RRA, DDA, and EA outlaw discrimination by those disposing of or managing premises. These are usually agents and managing agents because home owners selling their own home are usually not covered, unless they use the services of an estate agent or advertise their home for sale.[69]

10.25 The SDA, RRA, DDA, and EA make it unlawful for a person, in relation to premises in Great Britain of which he has power to dispose, to discriminate in the terms on which he offers those premises, by refusing an application for those premises, or in his treatment of a person in relation to any list of persons in need of premises of that description. They also make it unlawful for a person, in relation to premises managed by him, to discriminate against a person occupying the premises in the way he affords access to any benefits or facilities, or by refusing or deliberately omitting to afford access to them, or by evicting the person, or subjecting him to a detriment. These outlaw discrimination widely in the context of housing.[70] The RRA also makes it unlawful for a landlord or manager of premises to harass a person applying for or occupying the premises.[71]

10.26 Discrimination in relation to a list of persons requiring accommodation is expressly made unlawful, and this means that, for example, nationality requirements or residence requirements for admission or priority on local authority housing lists, as well as onerous conditions (for example, repeated bidding under a 'choice based letting scheme'), may be unlawful under the RRA and DDA respectively where they disadvantage certain minority groups and disabled people.

68 RRA, s 19B will not apply if the act complained of is made unlawful by another provision: RRA, s 19B(6) (see below, for similar provision in the SDA, DDA, and EA).

69 SDA, s 30(3); RRA, s 21(3) (save that discrimination connected with race, or ethnic or racial origins is not subject to this exception and so is always unlawful); DDA, s 22(2); EA, s 48(3).

70 The Commission for Racial Equality and Disability Rights Commission have issued new statutory Codes of Practice addressing housing (for the impact of the same, see Chap 15): 'Code of Practice on Racial Equality in Housing' (2006) CRE (Race Relations Code of Practice (Housing) (Appointed Day) Order 2006 SI 2006/2239); 'Rights of Access: services to the public, public authority functions, private clubs and premises' (2006, DRC) (Disability Discrimination Code of Practice (Services, Public Functions, Private Clubs and Premises) (Appointed Day) Order 2006, SI 2006/1967).

71 RRA, s 21(2A).

The SDA, RRA, DDA, and EA also make it unlawful for a person whose licence or consent is required for the disposal of premises to discriminate by withholding his licence or consent.[72] **10.27**

The SDA, RRA,[73] DDA, and EA create exemptions for 'small premises', those being premises in which the landlord or his close family live.[74] **10.28**

G. Clubs

The RRA and DDA outlaw discrimination by membership clubs.[75] The SDA does not,[76] preserving undisturbed the phenomenon of 'gentlemen's clubs' in the UK. Similarly, the EA does not outlaw discrimination by members' clubs so that Catholic clubs and the like, whose membership is determined by reference to religious belief, are lawful. Clubs which are truly open to the public, that is that do not operate a genuine selection process, will fall within the goods, facilities, and services provisions.[77] **10.29**

The 'clubs' provisions of the RRA and DDA apply to any association of persons, whether corporate or unincorporate, and whether or not its activities are carried on for profit if it has 25 or more members and permission to membership is regulated by its constitution.[78] Discrimination against members, prospective members, associates, and prospective associates is outlawed.[79] **10.30**

The RRA creates an exception for membership clubs with certain specialist interests, based on shared experiences or interests connected to ethnicity,[80] where the main object of the association is to enable the benefits of membership (whatever they may be) to be enjoyed by persons of a particular racial group defined otherwise **10.31**

---

[72] SDA, s 31; RRA, s 24 (or in the case of race, ethnic or national origin, harass a person who applies for licence or consent); DDA, s 22(4); EA, s 47(3).

[73] Except in the case of discrimination connected to race, ethnic, or national origins (RRA, s 22(1)).

[74] SDA, s 32(2) and RRA, s 22(2). The exceptions described in para 10.21, above, apply equally to the 'premises' provisions.

[75] RRA, s 25; DDA, s 21F.

[76] Unless they are truly open to the public or a section of the public so fall within the goods, facilities, and services provisions, as in the case of most 'nightclubs' where entry is to the public generally, without personal selection, on payment of a fee.

[77] *Dockers Labour Club & Institute Limited v Race Relations Board* [1976] AC 285.

[78] And is so conducted that the members do not constitute a section of the public within the meaning of the goods, facilities, and services provisions (see para 10.03–10.05) and it is not an organization to which the trade organization provisions apply (see Chap 8 above); RRA, s 25(1)(c) and DDA, s 21F(1(c).

[79] RRA, s 25 and DDA, s 21F.

[80] RRA, s 26.

than by reference to colour.[81] In such a case, the 'clubs' provisions will not apply. The Government's proposals for regulations outlawing sexual orientation discrimination in clubs (at the time of writing) indicate that they propose to exclude clubs and associations which exist:

> in order to provide a genuine benefit or opportunity to a group linked to their sexual orientation . . . for example a gay men's social and support group which exists particularly to enable gay and bisexual men to form friendships and provide mutual support [so that they] would be allowed to require that its members be gay or bisexual.[82]

However, clubs and associations that do not and cannot, for a legitimate reason explicitly connected with their purpose, include the sexual orientation of a prospective member as a membership criterion will be prohibited from discriminating.[83]

[81] In determining whether that is the main object of an association, regard shall be had to the essential character of the association and to all relevant circumstances including, in particular, the extent to which the affairs of the association are so conducted that the persons primarily enjoying the benefits of membership are of the racial group in question, RRA, s 26(1).

[82] 'Getting Equal: Proposals to Outlaw Sexual Orientation Discrimination in the Provision of Goods & Services' (2006) Women and Equality Unit, 31, para 3.19.

[83] 'Getting Equal: Proposals to Outlaw Sexual Orientation Discrimination in the Provision of Goods & Services' (2006) Women and Equality Unit, 31, para 3.20. (For example, a golf club that existed to provide members with access to a golf course, whose only membership criterion was having a certain golfing handicap, would not be able to turn down prospective members on the grounds of their sexual orientation.)

11

PUBLIC AUTHORITIES

The Sex Discrimination Act 1975 (SDA),[1] the Race Relations Act 1976 (RRA),[2] the Disability Discrimination Act 1995 (DDA),[3] and the Equality Act 2006 (EA)[4] outlaw discrimination by public authorities in the exercising of their public functions. These provisions represent the most important changes to discrimination law in a generation. Their effect is to constitutionalize discrimination law so that the actions of the State may now be called to account against discrimination law standards. Their effect is wide-reaching.[5] The origins of these provisions have been described in Chapter 2. The fact that the impetus for these provisions came from the recommendations in the Stephen Lawrence Inquiry Report[6] means that their impact is most commonly associated with the functions of the criminal justice system. They have indeed proved important for policing and prosecutorial decision-making but their impact is wider than that,[7] as is described below. The statutory equality duties enacted alongside these provisions are addressed in Chapter 15. **11.01**

The SDA, the RRA, the DDA, and the EA each provide that it is unlawful for a public authority in carrying out any functions of the authority to do any act which constitutes discrimination.[8] It is also unlawful for a public authority to sexually harass a person in the carrying out of their functions,[9] or to racially harass a **11.02**

---

1 SDA, s 21A, in force from 6 April 2007 (SI 2006/1082, Art 4(a)).

2 RRA, s 19B, in force from 2 April 2001 (SI 2001/566, Art 2(1)).

3 DDA, s 21B, in force from 4 December 2006 (SI 2005/2774, Art 4(a)).

4 EA, s 52, expected to come into force in April 2007.

5 See, eg, *Secretary of State for Defence v Elias* [2006] EWCA Civ 1293; *R (on the Application of Al Rawi & Others) v Secretary of State for Foreign and Commonwealth Affairs & Anor* [2006] EWCA Civ 1279.

6 *The Stephen Lawrence Inquiry: Report of an Inquiry by Sir William Macpherson of Cluny*, advised by Tom Cook, the Rt Rev Dr John Sentamu, Dr Richard Stone, Cm 4262-I.

7 See, eg, *Secretary of State for Defence v Elias* [2006] EWCA Civ 1293; *R (on the Application of Al Rawi & Others) v Secretary of State for Foreign and Commonwealth Affairs & Anor* [2006] EWCA Civ 1279.

8 SDA, s 21A; RRA, s 19B; DDA, s 21B; EA, s 52.

9 SDA, s 21A.

person[10] in the carrying out of any function which consists of the provision of any form of social security, healthcare, any other form of social protection, or any form of social advantage.[11]

11.03 These provisions create exclusive wrongs in that treatment made unlawful by any other provision of the SDA, RRA, DDA, or EA, or would be so but for an exemption, will not fall within the public functions provisions.[12]

11.04 'Public authorities' are defined in the same way as in the Human Rights Act 1998 (HRA).[13] Accordingly, a 'public authority' includes any person 'certain of whose functions are functions of a public nature',[14] namely, private bodies carrying out public functions, or 'hybrid bodies', as they are usually known. A 'core' public authority will be caught by the 'public function' provisions in respect of all their activities, subject to any exemption.[15] A core public authority is:

> a body whose nature is governmental in a broad sense of that expression . . . The most obvious examples are government departments, local authorities, the police and the armed forces. Behind the instinctive classification of these organisations as bodies whose nature is governmental lie factors such as the possession of special powers, democratic accountability, public funding in whole or in part, an obligation to act only in the public interest, and a statutory constitution.[16]

Core public authorities will include, in addition to those just identified, NHS trusts and boards; the Crown Prosecution Service and Crown Office; courts and tribunals;[17] and inspection and audit agencies such as the National Audit Office, Audit Scotland, Audit Commission, Her Majesty's Inspectorate of Constabulary (HMIC), and the Healthcare Commission.[18]

11.05 A 'hybrid' body is,[19] on the other hand, a private body that exercises both public functions and non-public functions. In relation to a particular act, a 'hybrid' body is not a public authority by virtue only of the fact that certain of its functions are

---

10 On the grounds of race, ethnic, or national origins only.

11 RRA, s 19B(1A), reflecting the scope of the Race Directive, see Chap 4.

12 SDA, s 21A(9), paras 15–16; RRA, s 19B(6); DDA, s 21B(7); EA, s 52(4)(m).

13 See Chap 4.

14 SDA, s 21A(2); RRA, s 19B(2); DDA, s 21B(2)(a), and EA, s 52(2)(a). The formulations vary slightly but they are to materially the same effect.

15 *Aston Cantlow and Wilmcote with Billesley Parochial Church Council v Wallbank and another* [2003] UKHL 37; [2004] 1 AC 546.

16 Ibid, para 7.

17 Though see exception in relation to judicial decision making (para 11.10 below).

18 'Code of Practice—Rights of Access: Services to Public, Public Authority Functions, Private Clubs and Premises' (2006) DRC (Disability Discrimination Code of Practice (Services, Public Functions, Private Clubs and Premises) (Appointed Day) Order 2006 SI 2006/1967, bringing the code into force on 4 December 2006), para 11.5.

19 *Aston Cantlow and Wilmcote with Billesley Parochial Church Council v Wallbank and another* [2003] UKHL 37; [2004] 1 AC 546, para 11.

functions of a public nature if the nature of the particular act under challenge is private (for example, selecting employees, opening bank accounts, purchasing stationery).[20] The inclusion of 'hybrid bodies' is intended to be expansive and to cover, for example, private security companies running a prison in respect of functions relating to the running of the prison.[21]

Certain public authorities are expressly excluded from the scope of these unlawful acts. They are both Houses of Parliament; the Security Service; the Secret Intelligence Service; the Government Communications Headquarters; and a unit or part of a unit of any of the naval, military, or air forces of the Crown, which is required by the Secretary of State to assist the Government Communications Headquarters in carrying out its functions.[22] **11.06**

The RRA and DDA do not define what is a 'public function' (as contrasted with a 'private act'). The Commission for Racial Equality's statutory Code of Practice on the race equality duty[23] defines them as: **11.07**

> functions that affect, or are likely to affect, the public or a section of the public. While only the courts can decide this, public functions would normally not include internal management or contractual matters such as employing staff; purchasing goods, works or services; or buying or selling premises. This term is used to refer to those authorities that are bound by the duties only in relation to their public functions (for example professional representative organizations, such as the Royal College of Surgeons, or broadcasting authorities).[24]

The SDA and EA define a 'function' as a 'function of a public nature',[25] and this is implicit in the RRA and DDA because all functions of 'core' authorities will be public functions and private acts done by 'hybrid' bodies are excluded.[26] In discerning the distinction between a public function and a private act regard should be had to the fact that 'essentially the contrast being drawn is between functions

---

20 SDA, s 21A(2)(b); RRA, s 19B(4); DDA, s 49B(4); EA, s 52(2)(b).

21 See, for example, 'Code of Practice—Rights of Access: Services to Public, Public Authority Functions, Private Clubs and Premises' (2006, DRC) (Disability Discrimination Code of Practice (Services, Public Functions, Private Clubs and Premises) (Appointed Day) Order 2006 SI 2006/1967, bringing the code into force on 4 December 2006), para 11.5.

22 SDA, s 21A(3); RRA, s 19B(3) (including a person exercising functions in connection with proceedings in Parliament); DDA, s 21B(3) (including a person exercising functions in connection with proceedings in Parliament); EA, s 52(3) (including the authorities of either House of Parliament).

23 Code of Practice on the Duty to Promote Race Equality (2002, CRE), ISBN 1 85442 430 0.

24 Ibid, 5.

25 SDA, s 21A(2)(b) and EA, s 52(2)(b). It is understood that in the drafting stages, the decision to define public functions was not intended to introduce any difference between the public function provisions found in these Acts and those found in the HRA, RRA, and DDA.

26 RRA, s 19B(4) and DDA, s 21B(2).

of a governmental nature and functions, or acts, which are not of that nature'.[27] Factors to be taken into account in deciding whether a function is a 'public function' include 'the extent to which in carrying out the relevant function the body is publicly funded, or is exercising statutory powers, or is taking the place of central government or local authorities, or is providing a public service'.[28] There is some case law indicating that a narrow approach will be taken to the circumstances in which a private body will be treated as performing public functions for the purposes of the HRA.[29] However, these 'hybrid' body provisions are intended to ensure that equality is properly mainstreamed[30] through the work of public authorities whether or not that work is performed through the services of a private provider. Those aspirations would be undermined if too narrow a reach were given to the provisions addressing 'hybrid' bodies.

11.08 The public functions covered by these unlawful acts cover a wide range of conduct not otherwise falling within the scope of the SDA, RRA, DDA, or EA. They will include arrests made by the police; the charging and prosecution of alleged offenders;[31] the preparation of pre-sentence reports; the regulatory and law enforcement functions of bodies such as HM Revenue and Customs; local authority licensing functions; tax inspection and collection; trading standards activities;[32] decisions by highway authorities;[33] prison disciplinary and allocation decisions; the formulating or carrying out of public policy (for example, devising policies and priorities in health, education, and transport etc, or making decisions on the allocation of public money); and the exercise of a statutory duty

27 *Aston Cantlow and Wilmcote with Billesley Parochial Church Council v Wallbank and another* [2003] UKHL 37; [2004] 1 AC 546, para 10.

28 Ibid,, para 12.

29 See *Poplar Housing and Regeneration Community Association Ltd v Donoghue* (2002) QB 48 (esp paras 58–9); *R (on the application of Heather and others) v Leonard Cheshire Foundation and another* (2002) 2 All ER 936, removing from the reach of the HRA and the DDA public functions provisions care provided by privately run care homes even though the care is funded by a local authority pursuant to its powers under duties under the National Assistance Act 1948. The Leonard Cheshire Foundation case has been subject to challenge in *Johnson & Ors (R on the application of) v London Borough of Havering* [2006] EWHC 1714 (Admin), which was unsuccessful at first instance and it is to be heard by the Court of Appeal in January 2007.

30 They were enacted at the same time as the statutory equality duties described in Chap X as part of a package of measures designed to achieve that aim. See para 11.10 below.

31 They do not apply to decisions not to prosecute. See para 11.10.

32 Code of Practice on the Gender Equality Duty for England and Wales (2006) (Laid before Parliament at the time of writing).

33 'Code of Practice—Rights of Access: Services to Public, Public Authority Functions, Private Clubs and Premises' (2006, DRC) (Disability Discrimination Code of Practice (Services, Public Functions, Private Clubs and Premises) (Appointed Day) Order 2006 SI 2006/1967, bringing the code into force on 4 Dec 2006), para 11.21.

or statutory powers or discretion in certain circumstances (for example, a Secretary of State refusing to give leave to enter or remain under immigration provisions).[34]

The DDA, alone, expressly provides that the outlawing of discrimination in the exercising of 'public functions' applies to appointments to offices or posts, which, but for the fact that they do not meet any of the conditions prescribed (that is, remunerated posts or appointments, or recommended by a specified body), would fall within the office holder provisions under Part 2 of the DDA (described in Chapter 8).[35] This provision is directed at, in particular, voluntary office holders (for example, school governors or those on the Board of Governors of NHS Foundation Trusts).[36] In such cases, the duties under the public authority function provisions apply. The provisions cover both the appointment of a person to a post and functions of the public authority in relation to the person whilst in post. Further, the DDA also expressly covers certain elected office or post holders (other than councillors, who are already covered by the DDA; see Chapter 8). In summary, where Part 2 of the DDA (the employment-related provisions, see Chapter 8) does not apply to the office or post in question, and it is not an excluded office or post, the public authority function provisions will apply to functions of the relevant public authority in relation to a candidate or prospective candidate for these public offices. These provisions also apply to functions of the authority in relation to the elected office holder once he holds office. For example, the functions of a local education authority in organizing an election of parent school governors would be covered by the public authority provisions, as would the authority's functions in relation to the parent governor once elected. The provisions, in relation to candidates or prospective candidates for election in the DDA, do not apply where the office or post is membership of either House of Parliament, the Scottish Parliament, the National Assembly for Wales, or any of the authorities specified in the provisions addressing councillors described in Chapter 8. Although the SDA, RRA, and EA make no comparable provision, if the particular office or post is not covered by the office holder provisions (or any other provisions), or would be covered but for an exemption, then the public functions provisions will apply, absent an express exemption. 11.09

34 See 'Gender Equality Duty, Code of Practice' (2006, EOC); *Secretary of State for Defence v Elias* [2006] EWCA Civ 1293; *R (on the Application of Al Rawi & Others) v Secretary of State for Foreign and Commonwealth Affairs & Anor* [2006] EWCA Civ 1279.

35 DDA, s 21B(8).

36 'Code of Practice—Rights of Access: Services to Public, Public Authority Functions, Private Clubs and Premises' (2006, DRC) (Disability Discrimination Code of Practice (Services, Public Functions, Private Clubs and Premises) (Appointed Day) Order 2006 SI 2006/1967, bringing the code into force on 4 Dec 2006), para 11.17.

11.10 There are a large number of exceptions to the unlawful acts addressing the functions of public authorities. All the enactments exclude:

- acts which are made unlawful by any other provision of the SDA, RRA, DDA, or EA, or which would be so but for an exemption;[37]
- the exercise of a judicial function or anything done on behalf of or on the instructions of a person exercising a judicial function (respecting the constitutional independence of the judiciary);[38]
- the preparing, passing, confirming, approving, or considering of any enactment (including enactments of the General Synod of the Church of England[39]);
- the making of a statutory instrument by a Minister of the Crown or by a Scottish Minister or member of the Scottish Executive;
- certain immigration decisions together with guidance issued about the making of such decisions (see further below at paragraph 11.12); and
- decisions not to institute or continue criminal proceedings, or anything done for the purposes of reaching, or in pursuance of, such a decision (but not *to* institute criminal proceedings).[40]

11.11 The SDA makes important provision addressing separate services for men and women. Section 21A(9) exempts the provision of a service for one sex only where persons only of that sex require the service (for example, certain forms of health care); where a joint service would or might be less effective; where the service is also provided jointly for both sexes and if the service were provided only jointly it would or might be insufficiently effective; or where if the service were provided jointly it would or might be less effective; and the extent to which the service is required by the other sex makes it not reasonably practicable to provide separate services for that sex. Similarly, the provision of separate services for each sex in different ways or to different extents where, if the service were provided for both sexes jointly, it would or might be less effective, and the extent to which the service is required by one sex makes it not reasonably practicable to provide the service for that sex in the same way or to the same extent as for the other sex, is exempt. Further, actions taken for the purpose of assisting one sex to overcome a disadvantage (as compared with the other sex) or to overcome the effects of discrimination are exempt.[41] These exemptions, therefore, do recognize the need for some forms of positive action, and that different treatment may be required to

[37] SDA, s 21A(9), para 15–16; RRA, s 19B(6); DDA, s 21B(7); EA, s 52(4)(m).

[38] SDA, s 21A(9); RRA, s 19C(1); DDA, s 21C(1); EA, s 52(4).

[39] Though no exemption in relation to the General Synod is made under the RRA.

[40] See *Alder v Chief Constable of Humberside Police and O'rs* [2006] EWCA Civ 1741 for the limits of this exemption.

[41] S 21A(9) also exempts the exercise of a function of the Charity Commissioners for England and Wales or the holder of the Office of the Scottish Charity Regulator in relation to an instrument in relation to which s 43 applies.

secure effective equality in service provision. Positive action is discussed further below (Chapter 13) but the explicit provisions addressing it are rather limited in the main anti-discrimination enactments (outside of the DDA). The exemptions in the SDA in relation to the exercising of public functions do allow for innovative action by public authorities (pursuant to the general equality duty under the SDA, discussed in Chapter 15, or otherwise) to address the specific needs of women, including needs which arise because of instances of discrimination. These might include, for example, rape crisis centres; domestic violence support facilities; Sexual Assault Referral Centres (SARCs); hygiene provision at police stations, etc.[42]

The RRA makes specific provision in relation to immigration functions. Outside of these specific exemptions, immigration functions, like all functions, are covered.[43] Section 19C(4) of the RRA provides that section 19B of the RRA does not apply 'to any act of, or relating to, imposing a requirement, or giving an express authorization . . . in relation to the carrying out of immigration functions' of a kind mentioned in section 19D(3) of the RRA. This includes a requirement imposed or express authorization given with respect to a particular case or class of case by a Minister of the Crown, or with respect to a particular class of case by certain enactments or by any instrument made under or by virtue of those enactments.[44] Section 19D of the RRA provides, in particular, that section 19B does not make it unlawful for a relevant person to discriminate against another person on grounds of nationality or ethnic or national origins in carrying out immigration functions. A 'relevant person', for these purposes, is a Minister of the Crown acting personally or any other person acting in accordance with a relevant authorization.[45] A 'relevant authorisation' is 'a requirement imposed or express authorisation given with respect to a particular case or class of case, by a Minister of the Crown acting personally or with respect to a particular class of case' by specified enactments[46] or by any instrument made under or by virtue of those enactments. 'Immigration functions' are the functions which may be exercised **11.12**

[42] See, for guidance, H Dustin, *Understanding your duty. Report on the gender equality duty and criminal justice system* (2006, Fawcett Society) and *Doing your duty. Guide to the gender equality duty. A guide for criminal justice agencies working with adult women accused or convicted of offences in England and Wales* (2006, Fawcett Society).

[43] *R (European Roma Rights Centre and others) v Immigration Officer at Prague Airport and another (United Nations High Commissioner for Refugees intervening)* [2004] UKHL 55; [2005] 2 AC 1; *R (European Roma Rights Centre and others) v Immigration Officer at Prague Airport and another (United Nations High Commissioner for Refugees intervening)* [2003] EWCA Civ 666; [2004] QB 811.

[44] The enactments concerned are the main immigration statutes.

[45] RRA, s 19D(2).

[46] The main immigration statutes.

under the main immigration statutes.[47] Section 19D of the RRA permits the relevant Minister to discriminate on grounds of nationality or ethnic or national origins (but not colour or race), and provides that any other person may also do so, so long as he or she is acting in accordance with a relevant authorization. This obviously permits widespread discrimination in the exercising of immigration functions, subject only to the making of a relevant authorization. The apparent rationale behind the authorizations made is that groups subject to the authorizations are considered more likely to be bogus asylum seekers or illegal immigrants. However, any authorization which goes beyond the limits permitted, in particular by allowing discrimination on grounds of colour or race, will not operate to exempt any race discrimination done in consequence.[48]

11.13 Section 19E of the RRA requires that a monitor be appointed by the Secretary of State to oversee the exceptions provided by sections 19C and D of the Act in relation to immigration and nationality cases. The monitor, who is not to be a member of the Secretary of State's staff, is to monitor 'the likely effect on the operation of the exception in Section 19D of any relevant authorisation relating to the carrying out of immigration which has been given by a minister acting personally and the operation of that exception in relation to acts which have been done by a person acting in accordance with such an authorisation'.[49] She or he is obliged to make an annual report on the discharge of his or her functions.[50,51]

11.14 The EA also enacts specific exemptions to the public functions provisions.[52] The EA excludes actions in relation to a school curriculum, admission to a faith school, acts of collective worship in schools, the governing body of a faith school, transport to or from a faith school (permitting education authorities to continue to provide school transport to faith schools but to remain under no obligation to make similar provision for those seeking to go to non-faith schools), and any decision to establish, alter, or close any school, and the exercise by the local authority of its powers to promote the economic, social, and environmental well-being

---

47 RRA, s 19D(4) and (5).

48 See discussion in *R (European Roma Rights Centre and others) v Immigration Officer at Prague Airport and another (United Nations High Commissioner for Refugees intervening)* [2004] UKHL 55; [2005] 2 AC 1; *R (European Roma Rights Centre and others) v Immigration Officer at Prague Airport and another (United Nations High Commissioner for Refugees intervening)* [2003] EWCA Civ 666; [2004] QB 811.

49 RRA, s 19E(1) and (3).

50 Ibid, s 19E(4).

51 Mary Coussey is the present monitor. See Mary Coussey, 'Annual Report 2004–5: Independent Race Monitor' (2005). Available at <http://www.ind.homeoffice.gov.uk/6353/aboutus/independantracemonitor.pdf#search=%22independent%20race%20monitor%22>.

52 EA, s 52(4)(f)–(l).

of their area.[53] Provision is also made exempting certain immigration functions. As with the RRA, the exemptions are apparently wide. Firstly, a wide exception permits the immigration and nationality department to discriminate in connection with a decision to refuse entry or refuse or vary leave to enter or remain in the UK on the grounds that such exclusion is 'conducive to the public good' or that 'it is undesirable to permit the person to remain in the UK'.[54] These exceptions mean that the Immigration and Nationality Department have wide powers to discriminate on grounds of a person's actual or presumed religion or belief when making decisions on entry clearance and leave to remain, whether related to actual behaviour or not. However, this must be read subject to the Convention rights and the terms of the HRA.[55] Secondly, the EA permits immigration officers to discriminate in the determination of applications for entry clearance or applications for leave to enter or remain in the UK from ministers of religion and other persons who hold office or a position or who provide services in connection with a religion or belief and that religion or belief 'is not to be treated in the same way as other religions or beliefs'.[56] This provision was inserted as a positive action measure in response to a request from a number of different minority faiths in order to enable them to bring to the UK ministers of their religions who they had not been able to train or recruit within the UK. Consequently where a particular religious community has a shortage of ministers it can request that the immigration procedures are expedited in order to permit a minister of their religion to enter the UK more quickly than others. Further, however, provision is made exempting exclusions of such persons where the exclusion 'is conducive to the public good'.[57]

The Government's proposals for regulations outlawing sexual orientation discrimination by public authorities propose making the same provision in respect of public functions and sexual orientation discrimination as seen in the SDA, RRA, and EA.[58] **11.15**

53 Under Local Government Act 2000, s 2.

54 Equality Act 2006, s 52(4)(f).

55 See Chap 4.

56 Ibid, s 52(4)(g).

57 EA, s 52(4)(g).

58 'Getting Equal: Proposals to Outlaw Sexual Orientation Discrimination in the Provision of Goods & Services' (2006) Women and Equality Unit, 32–3. Regulations are expected to be made and brought into force by April 2007, to coincide with the bringing into force of the religion or belief provisions of the EA.

12

POST-RELATIONSHIP DISCRIMINATION

Sections 20A and 35C of the Sex Discrimination Act 1975 (SDA), section 27A of the Race Relations Act 1976 (RRA), section 16A of the Disability Discrimination Act 1995 (DDA), regulations 21 of the Religion or Belief Regulations and Sexual Orientation Regulations, and regulation 24 of the Age Regulations address discrimination after termination of certain relationships caught by the unlawful acts. In all cases they are concerned with discrimination arising out of and closely connected to the relevant relationship. Section 20C of the SDA and section 16A of the DDA cover relationships falling within Part 2 of the Acts (employment and related fields),[1] and make it unlawful to discriminate against or harass a person in such circumstances. Section 27A of the RRA covers relationships falling within the scope of section 1(1B) or 3A of the RRA[2] and makes it unlawful to discriminate against or harass a person in such circumstances. Regulations 21 of the Religion or Belief Regulations and Sexual Orientation Regulations and regulation 24 of the Age Regulations cover relationships falling within the scope of the Regulations (employment and related fields and further and higher education). **12.01**

The origins of these provisions lie in the Race and Framework Directives and in the amended Equal Treatment Directive.[3] All three Directives make express provision addressing discrimination after termination of a relationship falling within their scope.[4] Even before express provision was made in the Equal Treatment Directive, the ECJ held that retaliatory action by an employer after termination of an employment relationship, where that was motivated by a woman exercising her non-discrimination rights during the currency of the relationship, was outlawed **12.02**

[1] And in the SDA, the provisions of Part 3 addressing barristers and advocates and vocational training and in the DDA, excluding the provisions addressing councillors in Part 2 but including employment services in Part 3.

[2] See Chap 6.

[3] See Chap 4.

[4] Art 6 of the amended Equal Treatment Directive; Race Directive, Art 7; Framework Directive, Art 9.

by the Directive.[5] This resulted in domestic decisions holding that victimization after termination of employment, by, for example, a refusal to provide references amongst other things, was contrary to the SDA.[6] Later, the House of Lords in *Rhys-Harper v Relaxion Group plc & others* concluded that the employment provisions of the SDA, RRA, and DDA were broad enough to capture incidences of discrimination occurring after the termination of employment where there was a substantive connection between the discriminatory conduct and the relationship of employer and employee, or where the relationship between employer and employee was still continuing, notwithstanding the termination of the employment, in that transactions attributable to a continuation of the relationship remained to be completed.[7]

12.03 Whilst the express provisions outlawing discrimination after termination of specified relationships are not comprehensive, relying on the House of Lords decision in *Rhys-Harper v Relaxion Group plc & others*, it is possible to argue that discrimination occurring after termination of other relationships caught by the main anti-discrimination enactments might give rise to justiciable complaints.

5 *Coote v Granada Hospitality Ltd* (Case C-185/97) [1998] ECR I-5199; [1999] ICR 100; [1998] IRLR 656.

6 *Coote v Granada Hospitality Ltd (No 2)* [1999] ICR 942; [1999] IRLR 452.

7 [2003] UKHL 33; [2003] ICR 867; [2003] IRLR 484, paras 34, 37, 44, 45, 114–16, 137, 139, 140, 149, 197, 200, 204, 206, 215, 220, 221).

13

GENERAL EXEMPTIONS, TERRITORIAL LIMITATIONS, EXTENT, AND LIABILITY

A. Introduction

13.01 All the main anti-discrimination enactments contain a large number of exemptions. Many of those have been addressed as they have arisen under the particular unlawful acts described above. The remaining important[1] exemptions are dealt with under thematic headings below. Further, all the enactments expressly address

[1] Other exemptions are found in SDA, ss 32 (exception for small dwellings), 33 (exception for political parties, so allowing for, *inter alia*, women only short lists—note, no comparable provision is found in the other enactments), 34 (voluntary bodies, allowing voluntary bodies to restrict membership and benefits to one sex), 35 (facilities or services restricted to one sex in hospitals etc), 45 (insurance—this will require modification when the Gender Goods and Services Directive is implemented, see Art 5 and see Chap 4), 46 (sex-specific facilities and communal accommodation), 35(3) (goods, facilities, services, and premises provisions do not apply to acts made unlawful by Part 2 (the employment and related provisions) or the education provisions), 42A (selection of candidates for political office), 43 (charities, see further below), 44 (sport, see further below), 45 (insurance, see further below), 46 (communal accommodation), 47–8 (positive action and training and encouragement, see further below), 49 (reserve seats and trade unions); s 51 and 51 A (statutory authority, see further below), 52 (national security, see further below); RRA, ss 9 (exception for nationality

secondary forms of liability (vicarious liability, agency, and aiding) and this is addressed below, under paragraph 13.42 onwards.

B. Exemptions

(1) Positive action

(a) Introduction

13.02 Each of the main anti-discrimination enactments contain express provision addressing positive action. However, as alluded to in earlier chapters, the main anti-discrimination enactments, excepting the Disability Discrimination Act 1995 (DDA), make very limited provision addressing positive action.[2] The DDA operates somewhat differently because its duties to make reasonable adjustments require positive action.[3] Outside of the DDA, the express positive or affirmative action measures in the main anti-discrimination enactments are so narrowly drawn as to have had very little impact indeed. Positive action is permitted only within limited spheres and there are no *obligations* imposed in any of our anti-discrimination statutes (outside the duties to make reasonable adjustments) to take

discrimination and seamen recruited abroad), 22 (small dwellings), 23(1) (SDA (goods, facilities, services and premises provisions do not apply to acts made unlawful by Part 2 (the employment and related provisions) or the education provisions); RRA, ss 23(2) (foster carers), 26 (clubs with objects directed at specific racial groups, save where defined by reference to colour), 34 (charities, see further below), 35 (special needs of racial groups, see further below), 36 (training and education for persons not ordinarily resident in Great Britain, on grounds other than race, ethnicity or national origins), 37–8 (discriminatory training and encouragement, see further below), 39 (sports and competitions, see further below), 41 (statutory authority, see further below), 42 (national security, see further below); DDA, ss 23 and 24H (small dwellings), 59 (statutory authority and national security, see below), 24M (premises provisions do not apply to acts made unlawful by other provisions); EA, ss 47 (small premises), 50 and 59 (faith schools, see further below), 56 (statutory requirements, see further below), 57 (organizations relating to religion or belief, see further below), 58 and 6 (charities, see further below), 61 (special needs, see further below), 62 (foster care), 63 (national security, see below), 64 (the power to create exceptions or amend existing exceptions by order); regulation 24, Religion and Belief Regulations (exception for national security, see further below); regulation 25, Religion and Belief Regulations (positive action, see further below); regulation 26, Religion and Belief Regulations (Sikhs and the wearing of safety helmets); regulation 24, Sexual Orientation Regulations (national security, see below); regulation 25, Sexual Orientation Regulations (benefits dependent on marital status); regulation 26, Sexual Orientation Regulations (positive action, see further below); regulation 27, Age Regulations (statutory authority, see further below); regulation 28, Age Regulations (national security, see further below); regulation 29 (positive action, see further below).

[2] The indirect discrimination provisions can operate so as to require affirmative action in some cases, eg, by requiring employers to allow part time working or to change shift arrangements so as to accommodate women in certain circumstances, because failure to do so may be indirectly discriminatory as disadvantaging women who are still the primary child carers: see, eg, *London Underground Limited v Edwards (No 2)* [1999] ICR 494; [1998] IRLR 364 and Chap 6. See also the statutory duties discussed in Chap 15.

[3] See Chap 6.

positive or affirmative action in a particular case to address disadvantage and historic discrimination in a particylar case. The positive action provisions that do exist are treated as exceptions to the prohibitions on discrimination.

Northern Ireland is exceptional in this regard because its Fair Employment and Treatment Order 1988[4] requires affirmative action in certain circumstances, recognizing that a mere obligation not to treat like cases differently, or not to impose neutral rules which disadvantage one group or another (as in the British legislation), would be inadequate to address the very marked differences that existed as between the Catholic and Protestant communities, in employment and related areas.[5] The Fair Employment and Treatment Order 1988 has as its expressed aim 'fair participation in employment'.[6] Consistent with the more substantive approach it adopts to addressing inequality, it allows for affirmative action to secure fair participation in employment by members either of the Protestant, or of the Roman Catholic community in Northern Ireland. This includes the adoption of practices aimed at encouraging such participation, and the modification or abandonment of practices that have or may have the effect of restricting or discouraging such participation.[7] The Order addresses structural barriers ('practices'); it does not define 'fair participation' and nor does it allow for 'positive discrimination', that is, the preferring of a person in a particular case because she or he is part of a disadvantaged group. This is underscored by the fact that the Order has as a central aim the promotion of equality of opportunity, described as having 'the same opportunity' for employment and employment-related benefits, due allowance being made for any material difference in their suitability, but a person is not to be treated as not having the same opportunity as another person has or would have by reason only of anything lawfully done in pursuance of affirmative action.[8] This has been the subject of some criticism, particularly because it prioritizes what is usually described as the 'merit principle' (which usually means that the starting position of any candidate is ignored) and: 13.03

> [w]e know . . . that there is a connection between lack of educational and skilled qualifications and belonging to the Catholic community. The appeal to 'merit' must appear disingenuous to members of the disadvantaged community who are rejected as 'unsuitable'.[9]

---

4 Fair Employment and Treatment (Northern Ireland) Order 1998, SI 1998/3162 (NI 21), as amended in 2003 to give effect to the Framework Directive.

5 Catholics were more than twice as likely to be unemployed as Protestants with the same educational qualifications in 1991: Fair Employment Commission, 'The Key Facts: Religion and Community Background in Northern Ireland' (1995).

6 Fair Employment and Treatment Order 1988, Art 4.

7 Ibid, Art 4.

8 Ibid, Art 5.

9 B Hepple, 'Discrimination and Equality of Opportunity—Northern Irish Lessons' [1990] 10 OJLS 408. See also, B Parekh, 'The Case for Positive Discrimination' in B Hepple and E Szyszczak (ed), *Discrimination: The Limits of the Law* (1992, Mansell), 261–80.

13.04 However, the Order allows for broad affirmative action measures and includes auditing obligations,[10] requiring employers to 'review the composition of those employed and ceasing to be employed in' their concerns 'and the employment practices of' their concerns 'for the purposes of determining whether members of each community are enjoying, and are likely to continue to enjoy, fair participation in employment' in their concerns. Where such a review indicates that a particular community is not enjoying fair participation, then an employer is obliged to 'determine the affirmative action (if any) which would be reasonable and appropriate'. In certain circumstances the Northern Ireland Equality Commission can extract an undertaking or direct that affirmative action be taken to address under-representation.[11]

13.05 The more substantive approach to equality adopted by the Northern Ireland Fair Employment and Treatment Order appears to have worked. Results demonstrate that there is greater participation of the disadvantaged Catholic community in employment across sectors, and 'there can be little doubt that the change that these data reflect does not come about by accident. It was the product of legislation, effort, endeavour, and not least, of the work of the Commission and its predecessor bodies'.[12] According to one commentator:

> There is virtually no comparison with how things were over a quarter of a century ago. There has been a substantial improvement in the employment profile of Catholics, most marked in the public sector but not confined to it. Catholics are now well represented in managerial, professional and senior administrative posts. There are some areas of under-representation such as local government and security but the overall picture is a positive one. Catholics are still more likely than Protestants to be unemployed. As unemployment levels have fallen, lack of employment is a contributory factor to disadvantage and poverty, but not its main determinant . . . There has been a considerable increase in the numbers of people who work in integrated workplaces. At a time when public housing for example is virtually completely segregated, this represents another positive trend in the assessment of the implementation of the legislation . . . Strong legislation has played its part. Employers have indicated that it has helped change practices. Evidence also suggests that affirmative action agreements between the Equality Commission and employers have helped redress both Catholic and Protestant under-representation as a vital part of the process of change . . . [R]eal social change [has been measured] over the past generation and the existence and use of the fair employment legislation has played a vital part in this.[13]

10 Fair Employment and Treatment Order 1988, Art 55.

11 Ibid, Arts 11–14, 56–8.

12 *2004, Monitoring Report: Monitoring Report No.15, A Profile of the Northern Ireland Workforce, Summary of Monitoring Returns 2004* (2004), Equality Commission, 1.

13 Summary by Professor Bob Osborne of some conclusions contained within 'Fair Employment in Northern Ireland: A Generation On', published for the Equality Commission by Blackstaff Press, ed Bob Osborne of the University of Ulster and Ian Shuttleworth of Queen's University.

Other jurisdictions also adopt affirmative action obligations, particularly those which adopt a substantive approach to equality. In South Africa, for example, the concept of 'unfair discrimination',[14] for the purposes of the prohibitions contained in their law, excludes affirmative action measures. This means that 'legislative and other measures that properly fall within the requirements of section 9(2)[[15]] are not presumptively unfair. Remedial measures are not a derogation from, but a substantive and composite part of, the equality protection envisaged by the provisions of section 9'.[16] South Africa's main anti-discrimination statute—the Promotion of Equality and Prevention of Unfair Discrimination Act 2000—similarly provides that the concept of 'unfair' discrimination does not extend to 'measures designed to protect or advance persons or categories of persons disadvantaged by unfair discrimination or the members of such groups or categories of such persons'.[17] These provisions are bolstered by statutory duties and these are discussed further in Chapter 15. South Africa's Employment Equity Act, consistent with the other equality measures, defines 'unfair discrimination' as excluding affirmative action measures.[18] Section 13 requires employers caught by its provisions to implement affirmative action measures for people from designated groups.[19] These must include 'measures to identify and eliminate employment barriers, including unfair discrimination, which adversely affect people from designated groups; measures designed to further diversity in the workplace based on equal dignity in respect of all people [and] making reasonable accommodation for people from designated groups in order to ensure that they enjoy equal opportunities and are equitably represented in the workforce'.[20] **13.06**

(b) EC law

The Equal Treatment Amendment Directive, the Race Directive, and the Framework Directive all contain positive action provisions. Article 5 of the Race Directive, under the heading 'Positive Action', provides that: **13.07**

> with a view to ensuring full equality in practice, the principle of equal treatment shall not prevent any Member State from maintaining or adopting specific measures to prevent or compensate for disadvantages linked to racial or ethnic origin.

This expressly contemplates positive action as consistent with the principle of equal treatment, and contemplates it as material to 'ensuring full equality in practice'.

---

14 See Chap 6.

15 'To promote the achievement of equality, legislative and other measures designed to protect or advance persons or categories of persons, disadvantaged by unfair discrimination may be taken'.

16 *Minister of Finance and Another v Frederik Yacobus van Heerden* CCT 63/03.

17 Promotion of Equality and Prevention of Unfair Discrimination Act 2000, s 14(1).

18 Employment Equity Act, s 6.

19 Ibid, s 13, for *designated employers* and *designated groups.*

20 Ibid, s 15.

Similar provision is made in Article 7 of the Framework Directive, and comparable provision is made in Article 2(8) of the amended Equal Treatment Directive.[21]

13.08 Further, in 1984 the European Council promulgated the Recommendation on the Promotion of Positive Action for Women.[22] In the Preamble the Council recognized that:

> existing legal provisions on equal treatment, which are designed to afford rights to individuals, are inadequate for the elimination of all existing inequalities unless parallel action is taken by governments, both sides of industry and other bodies concerned, to counteract the prejudicial effects on women in employment which arise from social attitudes, behaviour and structures.

In the operative paragraphs, the Council made several recommendations regarding positive action in the public and private sectors, and in particular recommended that Member States:

> adopt a positive action policy designed to eliminate existing inequalities affecting women in working life, and to promote a better balance between the sexes in employment, comprising appropriate general and specific measures, within the framework of national policies and practices, while fully respecting the spheres of competence of the two sides of industry, in order: (a) to eliminate or counteract the prejudicial effects on women in employment or seeking employment which arise from existing attitudes, behaviour and structures based on the idea of a traditional division of roles in society between men and women; (b) to encourage the participation of women in various occupations in those sectors of working life where they are at present under-represented, particularly in the sectors of the future, and at higher levels of responsibility in order to achieve better use of all human resources.[23]

13.09 The lawfulness of positive action measures under EU discrimination law has been the subject of a good deal of controversy. In summary, where a particular protected group is under-represented in any particular field or otherwise disadvantaged then proportionate positive action measures (including those which would otherwise amount to unlawful discrimination) are likely to be regarded as lawful.

13.10 In the controversial case of *Kalanke v Freie Hansestadt Bremen*[24] the ECJ for the first time addressed the legitimacy of positive action within the framework of EC law. The ECJ held that a 'tie-break' positive action scheme which gave priority to a female job candidate over an equally qualified male candidate, in an

---

21 ex Art 2(4) (ex Art 2(4) which was slightly differently phrased but apparently intended to be to the same effect) and see Art 141, EC Treaty. See too, Art 6 of the Gender Goods and Services Directive.

22 84/0635/EEC OJ L 331, 19/12/1984.

23 Para 1.

24 (Case C-450/93) [1995] ECR I-3051.

employment sector where women were under-represented, was contrary to the terms of the Equal Treatment Directive.[25] This was because the law in question aimed to ensure the 'result' of actual employment, by according 'absolute and unconditional priority' to women applicants. This, according to the ECJ, went beyond the scope of the positive action provisions of the Directive, the focus of which was on equality of 'opportunities'. The positive action scheme in issue, according to the ECJ, infringed the male candidate's (Kalanke's) individual right to non-discriminatory treatment.

However, since *Kalanke* the ECJ has 'beat a hasty retreat' from that position.[26] In *Marschall v Land Nordrhein-Westfalen*[27] the ECJ took a more favourable approach to positive action. Similar to *Kalanke*, the case concerned a German provision which provided that an employer should, where there were two applicants of equal merit, choose the female one; however, the provision contained a 'saving clause' under which the male candidate might still be appointed, in preference to a woman, where reasons specific to an individual equally qualified male candidate tilted the balance in his favour. The ECJ held that the existence of 'secondary criteria of selection' under the saving clause eliminated the automatic gender preference, and ensured a personalized assessment of candidates' qualities; as such it was sufficient to bring the law within the scope of the positive action provision of the Equal Treatment Directive and was accordingly lawful. Similarly, in *Badeck et al v Hessische Ministerpräsident*,[28] the ECJ held lawful certain positive discrimination measures. *Badeck* again concerned a local German law which aimed to provide equal access for men and women to public sector posts. The law in issue required public sector departments to adopt an 'advancement plan' to eliminate the under-representation of women. Women were regarded as being under-represented if fewer women than men were employed in a particular pay grade in a career group. The legislation set out the general principle that a women's advancement plan must provide that more than half of the posts to be filled in a sector in which they were under-represented must be given to women. Where women were under-represented, a tie-break rule operated in their favour. However, the legislation did not require that women should be automatically selected over men where the candidates had equal qualifications. There were five types of situation which were regarded as justifying an overriding of the rule. These included giving priority to promoting disabled persons, to the long-term unemployed, or to those wishing to return to full-time working after a period of part-time work. Nevertheless, this was a significant positive action programme, 13.11

25 76/207/EC, see Chap 4.
26 Highlights [1998] IRLR 3.
27 (Case C-490/95) [2001] ICR 45; [1998] IRLR 39.
28 (Case C-158/97) [2000] ECR I-1875; [2000] IRLR 432.

and the ECJ rejected a challenge to the legislation, following *Marschall*, holding that:

> a measure which is intended to give priority in promotion to women in sectors of the public service where they are underrepresented is compatible with Community law if it does not automatically and unconditionally give priority to women when women and men are equally qualified, and the candidatures are the subject of an objective assessment which takes account of the specific personal situations of all candidates.

13.12 By the time the ECJ decided *Badeck*, the Treaty of Amsterdam, amending the Treaty on the European Union and the Treaties establishing the European Communities, had been agreed. Pursuant to the same, Article 119 of the Treaty of Rome (the jurisprudential basis for the Equal Treatment Directive[29]) had been renumbered Article 141 and amended to include a new Article 141(4) expressly endorsing positive action measures in the field of gender equality ('With a view to ensuring full equality in practice between men and women in working life, the principle of equal treatment shall not prevent any Member State from maintaining or adopting measures providing for specific advantages in order to make it easier for the underrepresented sex to pursue a vocational activity or to prevent or compensate for disadvantages in professional careers'). This is closely similar to the provision made in Article 5 of the Race Directive and Article 7 of the Framework Directive. It is likely that all positive action (connected with any protected ground) will be tested against the same threshold, and the gender cases are thus instructive.

13.13 In *Abrahamsson et al v Fogelqvist*[30] the ECJ drew a line around lawful positive action measures by holding that a rule which required the appointment of a less well qualified woman, where women were under-represented, was not permissible under the Equal Treatment Directive. The case concerned an appointment system in a Swedish university which provided that a candidate from an under-represented sex possessing sufficient qualifications must be granted preference over a candidate of the opposite sex who would otherwise have been chosen, unless the difference between the qualifications of each were so great that it would render the appointment of the woman no longer objective. Importantly, the ECJ concluded that the provision was unlawful because it was not proportionate, and did not provide for consideration of the individual situations of the candidates. The ECJ did not appear to consider that Article 141(4) was significant in that it did not require any different view to be taken as to the limits on lawful positive action under the Directive. This suggests that there is no *greater* scope for positive

---

[29] See Chap 4.

[30] (Case C-407/98) [2000] ECR I-5539; [2002] ICR 932; [2000] IRLR 732.

action in the field of gender than in race, and thus, as mentioned, all the case law under the Equal Treatment Directive is likely to be compelling in so far as the Race and Framework Directives are concerned.

The ECJ, then, in *Abrahamsson* indicated that a test of 'proportionality' should apply in determining the lawfulness of positive action measures. This was made more explicit by the ECJ in *Lommers v Minister Van Landbouw, Natuurbeheer En Visserij*.[31] In *Lommers*, the ECJ was concerned with provision of subsidized nursery places by an employer only to women members of staff where the scheme had been set up by the employer to tackle extensive under-representation of women, and in a context characterized by a proven insufficiency of proper, affordable childcare facilities. The ECJ held that such a scheme was allowed in principle so long as male employees who took care of their children by themselves were allowed to have access to the scheme on the same conditions as female employees. The ECJ concluded that the Equal Treatment Directive authorizes measures which are intended to eliminate or reduce actual instances of inequality which may exist in the reality of social life. It authorizes national measures relating to access to employment, including promotion, which give a specific advantage to women with a view to improving their ability to compete on the labour market and to pursue a career on an equal footing with men. Accordingly, and importantly, the fact that the policy did not guarantee access to nursery places to employees of both sexes on an equal footing was not contrary to the principle of proportionality. Account had to be taken of the fact that the number of nursery places was limited, and there were waiting lists for female employees to obtain a place. Moreover, the scheme did not deprive male employees of all access to nursery places for their children, since such places were accessible in the market generally. **13.14**

Finally, in *Serge Briheche v Ministre de l'Intérieur, Ministre de l'Éducation Nationale et Ministre de la Justice*[32] the ECJ confirmed that proportionality was the measure against which the lawfulness of any positive discrimination was to be determined, observing as follows: **13.15**

> Those conditions are guided by the fact that, in determining the scope of any derogation from an individual right such as the equal treatment of men and women laid down by the Directive, due regard must be had to the principle of proportionality, which requires that derogations must remain within the limits of what is appropriate and necessary in order to achieve the aim in view and that the principle of equal treatment be reconciled as far as possible with the requirements of the aim thus pursued.

31 (Case C- 476/99) [2002] ECR I-2891; [2002] IRLR 430.
32 (Case C-319/2003) [2004] ECR I-8807, para 24.

The test for determining the lawfulness of positive and affirmative measures is therefore one of proportionality.[33] Presently the ECJ case law would suggest that if a positive action measure has the effect of barring completely a person from access to some benefit or opportunity, it is likely to be regarded as disproportionate and unlawful.

(c) *The main anti-discrimination enactments*

13.16 All the main anti-discrimination enactments permit positive action in training for employment. Under those provisions in the Sex Discrimination Act 1975 (SDA) and the Race Relations Act 1976 (RRA), it is permissible to restrict access to training to a particular protected class (one sex or another or a particular racial group), to help fit them for particular work, and it is permissible to encourage one protected class to take advantage of opportunities for doing that work, where nationally the numbers of the particular class doing such work were comparatively small at any time during the preceding 12 months. Where the numbers undertaking particular work in a local area are comparatively small, such training may also be provided where it is likely that those undertaking the training are likely to take up that work in that area to help fit them for that work.[34] Such provision covers training bodies and employers, and comparable provision is made in relation to training and encouragement by trade organizations, directed at membership and office holding.[35]

13.17 The Religion or Belief Regulations, the Sexual Orientation Regulations, and the Age Regulations make the same provision, except that it is not necessary to show an actual under-representation for training and encouragement to be lawful. Instead such is lawful where 'it reasonably appears to the person doing the act that it prevents or compensates for disadvantages linked to' religion or belief, sexual orientation or age, as the case may be.[36]

13.18 The RRA and the Equality Act 2006 (EA) also exclude any act done in affording persons of a particular racial group or religion or belief access to facilities or services to meet the special needs of persons of that group in regard to their education, training or welfare, or any ancillary benefits.[37] Such provision in the RRA has been

---

33 As to which, see Chap 4.

34 SDA, s 47 and RRA, s 37. RRA, s 36 also excludes training to persons not ordinarily resident in GB where it appears they do not intend to remain in GB.

35 SDA, ss 47–49; RRA, ss 37–38.

36 Religion or Belief Regulations, regulation 25, Sexual Orientation Regulations, regulation 26, and of the Age Regulations, regulation 29.

37 RRA, s 35 and EA, s 61.

rarely used but might cover language classes, or training or education in basic work skills, available for people from a particular racial group, or groups, who would otherwise be excluded from opportunities.[38]

None of the positive action provisions extend to positive action in recruitment (outside of encouragement), and any training must be genuinely just training, and no more than that. The training or encouragement provided as a form of positive action must not constitute employment, or lead automatically to employment; for example, 'on-the-job' training or apprenticeships, which are defined as employment, and not training, cannot form part of a positive action programme.[39] **13.19**

The provisions, then, permit positive action in a limited range of circumstances. Their impact has been minimal in consequence. **13.20**

C. Faith Schools and Other Faith-Based Organizations

The Religion or Belief Regulations and the Sexual Orientation Regulations make specific provision in relation to genuine occupational requirements and religious employers discussed above (Chapter 8). Further, the EA contains wide exemptions from the unlawful acts it creates in relation to faith schools and other faith-based organizations. **13.21**

As described above, the EA makes provision allowing faith schools to discriminate in respect of education provision, in certain circumstances. Further, faith-based educational institutions and schools may restrict the (non-educational) services they provide and discriminate in the disposal of premises, where such restrictions are imposed for reasons connected to the purpose of the institution or in order to avoid causing offence on the grounds of the religion or belief to which the institution relates to persons connected with the organization.[40] **13.22**

Discrimination by other, non-commercial, religious organizations is subject to wide exemptions. These exemptions cover non-commercial organizations whose purpose is to practise a religion or belief, to advance a religion or belief, to teach the practice or principles of a religion or belief, to enable persons of a religion or belief to receive any benefit, or to engage in any activity, within the framework of that religion or belief, or to improve relations, or maintain good relations, **13.23**

38 Code of Practice on Racial Equality Employment (2006, CRE), para 3.43–4.
39 Ibid. However, see SDA, s 42A per women-only shortlists for political office.
40 EA, s 59, see comments below as to the test.

between persons of different religions or beliefs.[41] Non-commercial organizations are those whose sole or main purpose is not commercial.[42] Such organizations may restrict membership or participation in their activities. They may also restrict the provision of goods, facilities, or services in the course of their activities, and they may restrict the use or disposal of their premises.[43] Additionally a minister or other person with a similar function in such an organization[44] may restrict participation in activities carried on in the performance of his or her functions in relation to the organization. She or he may also restrict the provision of goods, facilities, or services in the course of those activities.[45] Such restrictions are, however, permitted only where they are imposed by reason of, or on grounds of, the purpose of the organization, or in order to avoid causing offence, on the grounds of the religion or belief to which the organization relates, to persons of that religion or belief.[46] These exemptions do not apply to discrimination on grounds other than religion or belief (for example, gender or sexual orientation), and in determining whether they apply at all an objective assessment must be undertaken to determine whether the prescribed conditions are in fact met.

D. Charities

13.24 Section 34 of the RRA has the effect of making any provision in a charitable instrument void whenever the instrument took or takes effect, insofar as it provides for the conferring of benefits on persons of a class defined by reference to colour. Where such provision is made, the instrument is to be read as if it provided for the conferring of such benefits on persons of the class which results if the restriction by reference to colour is removed or, where the original class is defined by reference to colour only, on persons generally.[47] Otherwise, section 43 of the SDA and section 34 of the RRA generally exempt from the unlawful acts created in both the employment and non-employment fields anything done pursuant to provisions contained in charitable instruments conferring benefits on persons of one sex or racial group (apart from one defined by reference to colour) only (disregarding any benefits to persons of the opposite sex which are exceptional or

41 Ibid, s 57(1).

42 Ibid, s 57(2).

43 Ibid, s 57(3).

44 Ibid, s 57(4). A minister is defined as a minister of religion or other person who performs functions linked to a religion or belief to which an organization, to which this section applies, relates and she or he holds an office or appointment in relation to that organization—see s 57(6).

45 Ibid, s 57(4).

46 Ibid, s 57(5).

47 RRA, s 34(1).

are relatively insignificant).[48] The exemption does not apply to any discriminatory act done on the grounds of race, ethnic, or national origins which is unlawful by reason of the employment or contract worker provisions.[49]

The EA allows charities that have been set up with the intention of providing a benefit to members of a particular religion or belief community to continue to do so, where the charitable instrument of the charity requires or permits it to do so.[50] Further, the EA makes specific provision permitting charities to require members or people seeking to become members to 'make a statement which asserts or implies membership or acceptance of a religion or belief'. However, the latter exemption applies where the charity imposed the requirement before 18 May 2005 and it has continued to do so ever since. This exception was inserted in order to ensure that organizations such as the Scouts Association and the Girl Guides Association can retain a requirement for its members to assert a belief in God. **13.25**

E. Sport and Competition

The SDA exempts from both the employment and the non-employment provisions any acts related to the participation of a person as a competitor in events involving any sport, game, or other activity of a competitive nature where the physical strengths, stamina, or physique of the average woman puts her at a disadvantage to the average man, where the activities are confined to competitors of one sex.[51] **13.26**

The RRA exempts any acts done which discriminate against another on the basis of that other's nationality or place of birth or the length of time for which he has been resident in a particular area or place, if the act is done in selecting one or more persons to represent a country, place, or area, or any related association, in any sport or game or in pursuance of the rules of any competition so far as they relate to eligibility to compete in any sport or game.[52] **13.27**

---

48 SDA, ss 78 and 79 provide a means by which charitable instruments in the educational field might be altered in England and Wales and Scotland respectively.

49 EA, s 34(3A) and RRA, s 4 and 7.

50 EA, s 58(1).

51 SDA, s 44. This is a broad exemption and one which the Equal Opportunities Commission has recommended should be changed, particularly for young people, because though girls are unlikely to be at a physical disadvantage to boys pre-puberty, case law has established that this exception applies to children as well as adults: 'Sex Equality in Sport (2000, EOC). See too, *GLC v Farrar* [1980] ICR 266 and *British Judo Association v Petty* [1981] ICR 660.

52 RRA, s 39.

F. National Security

13.28 All the main anti-discrimination enactments exempt any acts done for the purposes of safeguarding national security.[53] However, such exemption only applies (except in the case of discrimination under the SDA) if the doing of the act was justified by that purpose. Though there is no express requirement under the SDA to show justification for discrimination done purportedly for the purposes of safeguarding national security, such a requirement is implied in the context of any complaint falling within the employment and related spheres to ensure compliance with EC law.[54]

G. Statutory Authority

13.29 The SDA, RRA, DDA, the Age Regulations, and the EA make provision for acts done under statutory authority.

13.30 The provision made by the SDA in relation to the exercising of public functions is explained at Chapter 11. Further, section 51A of the SDA provides that none of the unlawful acts (except those under Part 2[55] or those applicable to vocational training) render unlawful any act done by a person if it was necessary for that person to do it in order to comply with the requirement of an existing statutory provision within the meaning of section 51. An 'existing statutory provision' is any provision of an Act passed before the SDA, or an instrument approved or made by or under an Act passed before the SDA (including one approved or made after the passing of the SDA), and any Act passed after the SDA which re-enacts with or

[53] SDA, s 52; RRA, s 42; DDA, s 59(2A) (which provides that DDA, Part II and the employment services provisions do not make unlawful any act done 'for the purpose of safeguarding national security if the doing of the act was justified by that purpose'. However, discriminatory acts falling under DDA, Part III (save for those falling under the employment services provisions), are subject to the blanket exclusion in DDA, s 59(3) matching the SDA, that is without the need to show justification); Religion or Belief Regulations and Sexual Orientation Regulations, regulations 24 and Age Regulations, regulation 28.

[54] *Sirdar v Army Board and Secretary of State for Defence* (Case C-273/97) [2000] IRLR 47; *Johnston v Chief Constable of the RUC* [1987] QB 129 [1987] ICR 83; *Devenney v UK* (2002) 35 EHRR 24; *Tinnelly and McElduff v UK* (1999) 27 EHRR 249. SDA, s 52, RRA, s 69, and DDA, Sch 3, para 8(1)(b) for the issuing of 'certificates' by the Secretary of State in certain circumstances which are to be treated as conclusive evidence of their contents. The effectiveness of any such certificate must be judged having regard to EC and ECHR law: *Johnston v Chief Constable of the RUC* [1987] QB 129; *Devenney v UK* (2002) 35 EHRR 24; *Tinnelly and McElduff v UK* (1998) 27 EHRR 249; and see discussion in *Barracks v (1) Chief Superintendent Coles (2) Commissioner of Police of the Metropolis* [2006] EWCA Civ 1041.

[55] Employment and related fields, see Chap 8.

without modification a provision of an Act passed before the SDA, insofar as the re-enacted provision is concerned.[56]

The RRA,[57] the DDA,[58] the Age Regulations,[59] and the EA[60] exempt discriminatory acts done in necessary compliance[61] with any enactment or Order in Council; any instrument made under any enactment by a Minister of the Crown; or necessarily to comply with any condition or requirement imposed by a Minister of the Crown by virtue of any enactment. In the case of the EA, the same applies in respect of any measure of the General Synod of the Church of England. These provisions mean that the RRA,[62] the DDA,[63] the Age Regulations,[64] and the EA[65] are not prioritized over other legislative measures. Importantly, the exemption in the RRA does not apply to discriminatory acts done on grounds of race, ethnicity, or national origin falling within the scope of the provisions identified in section 1(1B) of the RRA.[66] Similar provision is made in the SDA but in respect of statutory measures existing at the time of the enactment of the SDA only and applicable only to discriminatory acts outside the employment and related fields.[67] **13.31**

The RRA makes express provision in relation to nationality and residence conditions under section 41(2). It exempts certain discriminatory acts done on the basis of nationality or place of ordinary residence, or the length of time a person has been present in or resident in or outside the UK, or in an area within the UK. The exemption applies where such an act is done in necessary[68] pursuance of an enactment or Order in Council or of any instrument made under any enactment by a Minister of the Crown, or in order to comply with any requirement imposed by a Minister of the Crown[69] by virtue of any enactment or in pursuance of any arrangements made[70] by or with the approval of, or for the time being approved by, a Minister of the Crown, or in order to comply with any condition imposed[71] **13.32**

---

56 SDA, s 51(3).

57 RRA, s 41.

58 DDA, s 59.

59 Age Regulations, regulation 27.

60 EA, s 56.

61 See *Hampson v Department of Education and Science* [1991] 1 AC 171; [1990] ICR 511; [1990] IRLR 302.

62 RRA, s 41.

63 DDA, s 59.

64 Age Regulations, regulation 27.

65 EA, s 56.

66 Reflecting the impact of the Race Directive.

67 SDA, s 51A.

68 *Hampson v Department of Education and Science* [1991] 1 AC 171; [1990] ICR 511; [1990] IRLR 302.

69 Whether before or after the passing of the RRA.

70 Whether before or after the passing of the RRA.

71 Whether before or after the passing of the RRA.

by a Minister of the Crown.[72] So far, this exemption has been held to be compliant with the Race Directive,[73] though to the extent that it might exempt acts done on the grounds of race, ethnicity, or national origins falling within the scope of the Directive, this must be doubted. Further, the existence of exemptions pertaining to nationality has been criticized by the Committee on the Elimination of Racial Discrimination (the supervisory body for the International Convention on the Elimination of All Forms of Racial Discrimination (CERD)[74]) which has observed that:

> the emerging situation may lead to inconsistencies in discrimination laws and differential levels of protection according to the categorization of discrimination (ie race, ethnic origin, colour, nationality, etc), and create difficulties for the general public as well as law enforcement agencies.[75]

13.33 As to what might constitute 'arrangements' for these purposes, the courts appear likely to give this a very narrow reach. In *R (on the Application of Al Rawi & Others) v Secretary of State for Foreign and Commonwealth Affairs & Anor*,[76] the Court of Appeal, though not having to rule on the issue, indicated that the term required something more concrete than 'policies of the government having no special, or formal, characteristics'. Instead the term 'contemplates something altogether tighter, less fluid: a code of some kind, such as one might find in a statutory instrument, but made in a context where legislation is not required'.[77]

H. Territorial Limitations, Extent, and Northern Ireland

(1) Extent, Northern Ireland, and devolution

13.34 All the main anti-discrimination enactments, except the DDA, apply to Great Britain only and separate provision is made for Northern Ireland (see paragraph 13.38 below).[78]

---

[72] So far, this has been held compliant with the Race Directive (*Couronne & O'rs v Crawley BC and O'rs* [2006] EWHC 1514), though to the extent that it exempts acts done on the grounds of race, ethnicity, or national origins falling within the scope of the Directive, this must be doubted. See also *Gingi v Secretary of State for Work and Pensions* [2001] EWCA Civ 1685. The existence of the exemption has been criticized by the Committee on the Elimination of Racial Discrimination (the supervisory body for CERD, see Chap 4).

[73] *Couronne & O'rs v Crawley BC and O'rs* [2006] EWHC 1514. See, too, *Gingi v Secretary of State for Work and Pensions* [2001] EWCA Civ 1685.

[74] See Chap 4.

[75] Concluding observations of the Committee on the Elimination of Racial Discrimination: United Kingdom of Great Britain and Northern Ireland. 10/12/2003, *CERD/C/63/CO/11. Concluding Observations/Comments*, para 15.

[76] [2006] EWCA Civ 1279.

[77] Ibid, para 82.

[78] SDA, s 87; RRA, s 80. The Government's proposals to outlaw discrimination connected to sexual orientation under the EA indicate that the provisions will not extend to Northern Ireland;

Generally, the DDA applies to the UK, including, therefore, Northern Ireland.[79] The provisions of the DDA in their application to Northern Ireland are subject to the modifications set out in Schedule 8 of the DDA. These modifications are concerned with acknowledging and accommodating the particular bodies, constitutional arrangements,[80] and legislative contexts that exist in Northern Ireland. Amendments now made to the DDA by Parliament do not extend to Northern Ireland (see paragraph 13.38 below, for the effect of devolution), and accordingly new law under the DDA[81] does not apply to Northern Ireland.[82] **13.35**

Otherwise, in broad terms, substantively the same provision as is found in the SDA, RRA, the Sexual Orientation Regulations, and the Age Regulations is made for Northern Ireland.[83] Religion or belief is separately protected. **13.36**

The Fair Employment and Treatment (Northern Ireland) Order 1998 (FETO)[84] regulates discrimination connected to religious belief and political opinion. FETO has material similarities to some of the main anti-discrimination enactments, and it has been amended to reflect the obligations contained in the Framework Directive;[85] however, there are significant differences both in terms of the substantive grounds it covers and the obligations it creates. First, FETO prohibits **13.37**

'Getting Equal: Proposals to Outlaw Sexual Orientation Discrimination in the Provision of Goods & Services' (2006) Women and Equality Unit. And EA, s 82 gives power to the Office of First Minister and Deputy Minister to make provision addressing sexual orientation discrimination outside the employment fields.

79 DDA, s 70(6). See, for an exception, DDA, s 70(5A) and (5B).

80 See, in particular, the Northern Ireland Act 1998 and the Northern Ireland Assembly.

81 See, eg, regulation 1(4), Disability Discrimination Act 1995 (Amendment) Regulations 2003, SI 2003/1673, though the Disability Discrimination Act 1995 (Amendment) Regulations (Northern Ireland) 2004, SR No 55 make substantially the same provision.

82 Further, the Special Education Needs and Disability Act 2001 only applies to Northern Ireland to the extent that it does not encroach upon the powers of the Assembly, and accordingly its substantive provisions do not apply to Northern Ireland (s 43(12) Parts 2 and 3 of the Act do not apply to Northern Ireland), but see Special Educational Needs and Disability (Northern Ireland) Order 2005 SI 2005/1117.

83 The Sex Discrimination (Northern Ireland) Order 1976 SI 1976/1042 (NI 15); as amended by the Employment Equality (Sex Discrimination) Regulations (Northern Ireland) 2005 SR No 426; the Race Relations (Northern Ireland) Order 1997 SI No 869 (NI 6), as amended by the Race Relations Order (Amendment) Regulations (Northern Ireland) 2003 SR No 341; the Employment Equality (Sexual Orientation) Regulations (Northern Ireland) 2003 SR No 497; and the Employment Equality (Age) Regulations (Northern Ireland) 2006 SR No 261.

84 SI No 3162, as amended by the Fair Employment and Treatment Order (Amendment) Regulations (Northern Ireland) 2003 SR 2003 No 520. FETO amends and consolidates the previous Fair Employment Acts of 1976 and 1989. See Chap 15 for s 75 of the Northern Ireland Act 1998.

85 Although beyond the minimum required, so as to cover political opinion in addition to religion or belief: Fair Employment and Treatment Order (Amendment) Regulations (Northern Ireland) 2003 SR 2003 No 520.

discrimination on the ground of religious belief *and* political opinion.[86] This encompasses a person's actual or perceived religious belief or political opinion, and the absence of any, or any particular, religious belief or political opinion.[87] There is no equivalent protection in Great Britain in relation to 'political belief'. 'Political opinion' includes 'left' and 'right' politics,[88] essentially encompassing those views which relate to the conduct of the Government or matters of public policy.[89] However, FETO explicitly states:

> . . . any reference to a person's political opinion does not include an opinion which consists of or includes approval or acceptance of the use of violence for political ends connected with the affairs of Northern Ireland, including the use of violence for the purpose of putting the public or any section of the public in fear.[90]

Secondly, FETO imposes obligations on employers, which are not found in the main anti-discrimination enactments applicable to Great Britain. These include requiring employers to register with the Equality Commission; submission of an annual monitoring return detailing the community background of the workforce; and reviews of employment procedures such as recruitment, training, and promotion practices at least tri-annually to examine fair participation from both sides of the community.[91]

13.38 The Scotland, Wales, and Northern Ireland legislative and political bodies now each have varying competence in relation to equal opportunities measures or policies. The Scottish[92] and Welsh[93] devolved bodies have limited legislative powers in relation to anti-discrimination. The Northern Ireland Assembly, on the other hand, has broad powers to enact anti-discrimination law (treated as 'transferred

---

86 FETO, s 3.

87 Ibid, s 2(3).

88 *McKay v Northern Ireland Public Service Alliance* [1994] NI 103.

89 *Gill v Northern Ireland Council for Ethnic Minorities* [2002] IRLR 74.

90 FETO, s 2(3).

91 Ibid, Part IV.

92 Under the Scotland Act 1998 'reserved matters', on which the Scottish Parliament is not empowered to legislate, include equal opportunities, and in particular the EPA, SDA, RRA, and DDA (Sch 5 Part 2, L.2), although the Parliament can encourage (without prohibiting or regulation) equal opportunities; the equal opportunity being defined as 'the prevention, elimination or regulation of discrimination between persons on grounds of sex or marital status, on racial grounds, or on grounds of disability, age, sexual orientation, language or social origin, or of other personal attributes, including beliefs or opinions, such as religious beliefs or political opinions' (Sch 5 Part 2, L.2).

93 The Welsh Assembly, which has more limited legislative scope than the Scottish Parliament, is under a duty to '. . . make appropriate arrangements with a view to securing that its business is conducted with due regard to the principle that there should be equality of opportunity for all people' (s 48 Government of Wales Act 1998).

matters' under the Northern Ireland Act 1998).[94] Specifically, the Northern Ireland Assembly has direct legislative responsibility for laws on fair employment, sex, race, and disability discrimination.[95]

(2) Territorial limitations

In general, the main anti-discrimination enactments limit the application of the unlawful acts to Great Britain. **13.39**

The employment and related provisions protect employees employed at an establishment in Great Britain; those are employees who do their work wholly or partly in Great Britain.[96] In certain circumstances a person is to be treated as employed at an establishment in Great Britain, namely where she or he does her or his work outside Great Britain but in circumstances where the employer has a place of business at an establishment in Great Britain; the work is for the purposes of the business carried on at that establishment; and the employee is ordinarily resident in Great Britain either at the time when she or he applies for or is offered the employment, or at any time during the course of the employment.[97] **13.40**

The provisions addressing discrimination in the provision of goods, services, and facilities,[98] in relation to premises,[99] in education,[100] and in the exercising of public functions[101] in all the main anti-discrimination enactments, except the DDA (otherwise than in relation to education), apply to Great Britain only.[102] The provision of goods, facilities, and services will generally be within the scope if they are provided within Great Britain, although there are some particular modifications to this general rule.[103] **13.41**

---

94 Ie, matters which are within the legislative competence of the Assembly, Northern Ireland Act 1998, s 4.

95 Whilst the Northern Ireland Assembly remains suspended at the time of writing, specific provision is made to ensure that required legislative measures are being enacted; Northern Ireland Act 2000 and see Northern Ireland Act 2006.

96 RRA, s 8; SDA, s 10; DDA, s 68; Sexual Orientation Regulations, regulation 9; and Religion and Belief Regulations, regulation 9 and Age Regulations, regulation 10.

97 RRA, s 8(1A); SDA, s 10(1A); DDA, s 68(2A); Sexual Orientation Regulations, regulation 9(2); and Religion and Belief Regulations, regulation 9(2); Age Regulations, regulation 10; *Carver v Saudi Arabian Airlines* [1999] IRLR 370 CA; *Saggar v Ministry of Defence* [2005] EWCA Civ 413; [2005] IRLR 618. For the impact of EC law and free movement rights, in particular, see *Bossa v Nordstress Ltd* [1998] IRLR 284.

98 SDA, s 36; RRA, s 27; EA, s 80 (see further for exceptions in relation to ships).

99 SDA, s 30; RRA, s 21(1); EA, s 47(4).

100 SDA, s 36; RRA, s 27; EA, s 80.

101 SDA, s 36; RRA, s 27; EA, s 80.

102 DDA, s 70(6). See paras 13.37 and 13.38 in relation to discrimination under the FETO and Northern Ireland Act 1998.

103 RRA, s 27; EA, s 80, for ships; see SDA, s 36; RRA, s 27; EA, s 80, for immigration decisions (entry clearance) outside the UK. See SDA, s 36 for limitations.

I. Vicarious Liability

13.42 All the main anti-discrimination enactments expressly provide for vicarious liability in materially identical terms.[104] Section 41(1) of the SDA provides that:

> Anything done by a person in the course of his employment shall be treated for the purposes of this Act as done by his employer as well as by him, whether or not it was done with the employer's knowledge or approval.

This has the effect of making employers liable for those discriminatory acts of their employees[105] which are done in the course of their employment, whether or not they are done with the employer's knowledge or approval.[106] Special provision is made in relation to police officers so that police officers[107] are now treated as employees of the Chief Constable and anything done in the performance or purported performance of their functions is treated as done in the course of that employment. However, the amendment creating vicarious liability under the RRA in respect of police officers has effect only from 1 April 2001;[108] the amendment creating vicarious liability in respect of police officers under the SDA[109] has effect only from 19 July 2003, and the amendment creating vicarious liability under the DDA has effect only from 1 October 2004.[110] In respect of claims arising before these amendments came into effect, no vicarious liability will arise, and accordingly the individual police officer or police officers responsible for any discriminatory acts must be proceeded against in their own names.[111]

---

104 SDA, s 41(1); RRA, s 32(1) (which, alone, in terms provides that it does not apply in respect of offences under the RRA); DDA, s 58(1); EA, s 74(1); Religion or Belief and Sexual Orientation Regulations, regulations 22(1) and Age Regulations regulation 25(1).

105 And such expression is to be interpreted widely, see DDA, s 68(1) and Chap 8.

106 And whatever the status (managerial or not) of the employee, *De Souza v Automobile Association* [1986] IRLR 103.

107 SDA, s 17; RRA, s 76A; DDA, s 64A; EA, s 75 and Religion or Belief Regulations and the Sexual Orientation Regulations, regulations 11, and Age Regulations, regulation 13. This addresses the difficulties that would otherwise arise, in particular, with vicarious liability, see *Farah v Metropolitan Police Commissioner* [1998] QB 65; *Chief Constable of Kent Constabulary v Baskerville* [2003] EWCA Civ 1354; [2003] ICR 1463, both of which are now addressed by the amendments made deeming police officers to be employees both for the protection under the employment provisions and the vicarious liability provisions. All the main anti-discrimination enactments under the same provisions make consequential provision to deal with the payment of compensation, costs and expenses, and related issues. Constables seconded to serve in the Serious Organised Crime Agency are to be treated as employees of the Serious Organised Crime Agency, Religion or Belief Regulations and Sexual Orientation Regulations, regulations 11A; Age Regulations, regulation 14.

108 Race Relations (Amendment) Act 2000 (Commencement) Order 2001 SI 2001/556.

109 Sex Discrimination Act 1975 (Amendment) Regulations 2003 SI 2003/1657.

110 Disability Discrimination Act 1995 (Amendment) Regulations 2003 SI 2003/1673.

111 *Farah v Metropolitan Police Commissioner* [1998] QB 65; *Chief Constable of Kent Constabulary v Baskerville* [2003] EWCA Civ 1354; [2003] ICR 1463.

A statutory defence is available to an employer in a claim against him based on vicarious liability where the employer can prove that it took such steps as were reasonably practicable to prevent the employee from doing the discriminatory act or from doing, in the course of his or her employment, acts of that description.[112] This defence is explained below (paragraph 13.49). **13.43**

An employer will only be liable for discriminatory acts done by its employees *in the course of their employment*. This expression is given a wide reach. In *Jones v Tower Boot Co Ltd*[113] the Court of Appeal was concerned with a complaint of race discrimination from a 16-year-old boy, subjected to horrific physical and verbal racial abuse. This included coemployees burning his arm with a hot screwdriver, whipping him on the legs with a welt, throwing bolts at him, and trying to put his arm in a lasting machine. The Employment Appeal Tribunal adopted the test of vicarious liability which at that time applied at common law—namely whether the employees concerned were acting in a way which was authorized by the employer or acting in a way which could be described as a mode, albeit an improper mode, of acting in an authorized way. The Employment Appeal Tribunal concluded (by a majority) that the employer was not liable because the acts could not be described as an improper mode of performing authorized tasks. The Court of Appeal robustly rejected this test together with the implicit assumption that the more heinous the acts of harassment, the less likely the employer would be liable under the discrimination legislation. According to the Court of Appeal, the vicarious liability provisions were intended: **13.44**

> to deter racial and sexual harassment in the workplace through a widening of the net of responsibility beyond the guilty employees themselves by making all employers additionally liable for such harassment, and then supplying them with the reasonable steps defence [described below] which will exonerate the conscientious employer who has used his best endeavour to prevent such harassment, and will encourage all employers who have not yet undertaken such endeavour to take the steps necessary to make the same defence available in their own workplace.[114]

The effect of the Court of Appeal's decision in *Jones v Tower Boot* is to make employers liable for a wide range of discriminatory actions even if they do not occur as part of work duties, or indeed occur in the context of the working environment (subject only to the employer making out the statutory defence).

---

112 SDA, s 41(3); RRA, s 32(3); DDA, s 58(5); Religion or Belief and Sexual Orientation Regulations, regulation 22(3); Age Regulations, regulation 25(3); and EA, s 74(4).

113 [1997] ICR 254; [1997] IRLR 168. *Irving v The Post Office* [1981] IRLR 289, CA must now be wrong. See the comments in *Waters v Commissioner of Police of the Metropolis* [1997] IRLR 589, CA.

114 *Jones v Tower Boot Ltd* [1997] ICR 254, 263–4, [1997] IRLR 168, para 38.

13.45 The House of Lords in *Lister v Helsey Hall*[115] have now brought the common law test of vicarious liability closer to the *Tower Boot* definition. In *Lister* the warden of a boarders' house in a school sexually abused a number of pupils who brought a County Court action some years later. On appeal the House of Lords held that the respondent school was vicariously liable for the warden's actions, ruling that the correct approach to vicarious liability was to concentrate on the relative closeness of the connection between the nature of the employment and the employee's wrongdoing, and to ask whether it would be fair and just to hold the employer vicariously liable. The House of Lords concluded that the fact that the warden's actions were an abuse of his position did not sever the connection with his employment.[116] This means that in cases in which more than one cause of action is relied upon (particularly outside the employment field, where disability-related discrimination claims will often be pursued alongside other complaints), questions of vicarious liability which arise under the main anti-discrimination and at common law are likely to be determined on similar principles.

13.46 In the context of discrimination occurring in the employment field, the vicarious liability provisions anticipate that discrimination may occur as between persons employed by the same employer in circumstances where their mutual employer is not liable for it. The 'in the course of employment' requirement draws the line between those incidents for which an employer will be liable and those for which he will not. However, that line is sometimes difficult to discern. Discrimination for which an employer is vicariously liable may occur in a rest break, just before going home, or outside the workplace altogether. There are, as the Court of Appeal said in *Jones v Tower Boot*, an infinite variety of circumstances, and in each case it will be a question of fact for each court or tribunal to resolve, having regard to the broad test set now appliable. A court or tribunal might find an employer liable for acts of discrimination notwithstanding that they were done outside working hours and outside the workplace altogether. Each case will, however, turn very much on its own facts.[117]

13.47 An employee who does a discriminatory act made unlawful by the main anti-discrimination enactments 'in the course of his employment' such that his employer is liable for it (or would be but for the statutory defence described below) is also personally liable.[118] This is because the perpetrator is deemed to 'aid'

---

115 [2001] UKHL 22; [2001] IRLR 472.

116 See, too, *Mattis v Pollock (t/a Flamingo's Nightclub)* [2003] EWCA Civ 887; [2003] 1 WLR 2158; [2003] IRLR 603.

117 See *Sidhu v Aerospace Composite Technology* [2000] ICR167; [2000] IRLR 602; *Chief Constable of the Lincolnshire Police v Stubbs* [1999] ICR 547; [1999] IRLR 81.

118 Whichever of the unlawful acts apply; that is, employment, education, goods, facilities and services, public functions etc.

his or her employer, who is treated as having done that unlawful act by reason of the vicarious liability provisions.[119] This applies even where the employer makes out the statutory defence (paragraph 13.49 below), in which case the guilty employee will find himself solely liable.[120] In any case where an employer might make out such defence, a claimant should the consider bringing proceedings against the employee as well as the employer.[121]

If the acts of discrimination complained of are not done in the course of employment, liability will not attach to the employee and nor will vicarious liability arise as against his employer. **13.48**

As mentioned, the main anti-discrimination enactments provide a specific defence to an employer in respect of a claim based on vicarious liability.[122] The defence is not available to an employer who is said to have himself done the discriminatory act. The defence is in materially the same terms in each of the enactments. An employer will escape liability where he can prove that he took such steps as were reasonably practicable to prevent the employee from doing the act complained of or doing, in the course of his employment, acts of that description. **13.49**

The defence depends upon an employer establishing that it took steps *before* the relevant discriminatory act occurred.[123] In *Canniffe v East Riding of Yorkshire Council*[124] the Employment Appeal Tribunal concluded that the proper approach to determining whether the defence is made out is, first, to identify whether the employer took any steps at all to prevent the employee from doing the act or acts complained of in the course of his employment; and, second (having identified what steps, if any, the employer took), to consider whether there were any further steps the employer could have taken which were reasonably practicable. Whether the taking of any such steps would have been successful in preventing the acts of discrimination in question is not determinative. An employer will not be exculpated **13.50**

---

[119] *AM v (1) WC (2) SPV* [1999] IRLR 410. An employer is vicariously liable for an employee's act of discrimination. The employee who perpetrated the act of discrimination is deemed to have aided the doing of the act by his or her employer. The same applies to agents and principals respectively (see para 13.51). See also *Gilbank v Miles* [2006] IRLR 538. Liability for knowingly aiding unlawful acts of discrimination arises under DDA, s 57(1), see para 13.52 below.

[120] For examples of the same, see *Yeboah v Crofton* [2002] EWCA Civ 794; [2002] IRLR 634 and *Gilbank v Miles* [2006] IRLR 538.

[121] Where liability is joint, the court or employment tribunal will apportion compensation between the employer and individual discriminator. Thus in *Armitage, Marsden and HM Prison Service v Johnson* [1997] ICR 275; [1997] IRLR 162, £500 was awarded against each of the individual respondents as well as £27,500 against the Prison Service.

[122] SDA, s 41(3); RRA, s 32(3); DDA, s 58(5); Religion or Belief and Sexual Orientation Regulations, regulation 22(3); Age Regulations, regulation 25(3); and EA, s 74(4).

[123] See for example *Martins v Marks & Spencer plc* [1998] ICR 1005; IRLR 326, CA. The burden is on the employer: DDA, s 58(5).

[124] [2000] IRLR 555. See, too, *Balgobin & Francis v London Borough of Tower Hamlets* [1987] ICR 829; [1987] IRLR 401.

if it has not taken reasonably practicable steps simply because, if it had done so, it would not have prevented the discrimination from occurring. In this regard, the Employment Appeal Tribunal recognized that, if it were otherwise, the more serious the act of discrimination, the more likely that the employer would escape liability.

13.51 In addition to vicarious liability for the acts of employees, principals are made liable for the discriminatory acts of their agents.[125] Where an agent has authority (either express or implied, and whether given before or after the act in question[126]) to act for the principal, both the principal and the agent will be liable for the discriminatory acts of the agent. In *Lana v Positive Action Training in Housing (London) Ltd*[127] the complainant was placed by the respondent as a trainee with another company, WM. Very soon after she announced that she was pregnant, WM informed the respondent that it wished to dispense with her services. The respondent terminated its training contract with the complainant on the basis that it did not have any work to offer her. The Employment Appeal Tribunal allowed an appeal against a finding that Ms Lana had not been discriminated against by Positive Action Training, holding that WM was the agent of the respondent and that, accordingly, the respondent was liable for any discriminatory acts done by it. The Employment Appeal Tribunal in *Lana* concluded that liability did not arise only where authority had been given to do a discriminatory act (which will rarely if ever be authorized), but also where authority had been given to do an act which was capable of being done in a discriminatory manner, as well as in a lawful manner. The agents in this case had authority to terminate the placement and, if they did so in a discriminatory way, Positive Action Training was liable.

J. Aiders

13.52 All the main anti-discrimination enactments make a person who 'knowingly aids' another to do an unlawfully discriminatory act jointly liable for those acts.[128] A person 'aids' another if he helps or assists, or cooperates or collaborates with him.[129] It is

125 SDA, s 41(2); RRA, s 32(2) (which, alone, in terms provides that it does not apply in respect of offences under the RRA); DDA, s 58(2) and (3); EA, s 74(2); Religion or Belief and Sexual Orientation Regulations, regulations 22(2) and Age Regulations, regulation 25(2).

126 Ibid (though the EA does not say so in terms).

127 [2001] IRLR 501.

128 SDA, s 42; RRA, s 33: DDA, s 58; Religion or Belief and Sexual Orientation Regulations, regulation 23; Age Regulations, regulation 26; and EA, s 73. See para 13.47 for employee 'aiders', and agents.

129 *Anyanwu and another v South Bank Students' Union and South Bank University* [2001] ICR 391; 1 WLR 638, [2001] IRLR 305, *per* Lord Steyn.

not necessary for the person's help to be substantial or productive, so long as it is not so insignificant as to be negligible.[130] The aid must be 'knowingly' given and accordingly a general attitude of helpfulness and cooperation will not be enough. An 'aider' must know that the person he is aiding is doing an act made unlawful, or that he is about to do so, or is thinking of doing so.[131] In most cases there will be little doubt that aid was given 'knowingly' if it is found to have been given at all.[132] A person who aids a discriminator is not liable if, in so doing, he was acting in reliance on the discriminator's claim that the act was not unlawful.[133] Such a case would be very unusual. 'Aiding' cases in which the alleged aider is not an employee are quite rare. Examples of claims include a complaint that a person has complained about a person to their professional body, on racial grounds, thereby knowingly aiding that body to bring disciplinary proceedings on racial grounds.[134]

130 Ibid, *per* Lord Bingham. See also *Gilbank v Miles* [2006] IRLR 538.

131 *Hallam v Avery* [2001] ICR 408; [2001] 1 WLR 655; [2001] IRLR 312, HL.

132 Ibid, para 11.

133 DDA, s 57(3).

134 *Herbert v (1) Bar Council (2) Lord Laming* [2004] Case No 2200381/04 and see *Anyanwu and another v South Bank Students' Union and South Bank University* [2001] ICR 391; [2001] 1 WLR 638, [2001] IRLR 305.

14

PRACTICE, PROCEDURE, AND REMEDIES

A. Introduction

In general, the anti-discrimination enactments are self-contained codes, and proceedings in respect of the unlawful acts created might only be brought in accordance with the enforcement mechanisms provided for in the enactments themselves.[1] The enforcement mechanisms differ, as do the remedies available, according to the class of unlawful act concerned. The unlawful acts are statutory torts and in general terms the courts and tribunals have addressed issues relating to enforcement and remedies in relation to them in much the same way as any other statutory tort.[2] Where an award of compensation is made in respect of joint **14.01**

1 SDA, s 62(1); RRA, s 53(1); DDA, Sch 3, paras 2, 5, 9, and 12; EA, s 65(1); Religion or Belief, regulation 27(1); Sexual Orientation Regulations, regulation 27(1), and Age Regulations, regulation 35(1) (though these provisions do not prevent applications for judicial review, proceedings under specified immigration enactments or applications to the pensions ombudsman; SDA, s 62(2); RRA, s 53(2); DDA, Sch 3, paras 2 and 5; EA, s 65(2); Religion or Belief, regulation 27(2); Sexual Orientation Regulations, regulation 27(2), and Age Regulations, regulation 35(2)). The EPA is less restrictive, see para 14.08 below. For claims that might be raised in immigration proceedings, see RRA, ss 57A and 68(2A) and EA, ss 67 and 69(2).

2 For claims by members of the Armed Forces under the employment provisions, see EPA, s 7A; SDA, s 85(9A); RRA, s 75(8); Race Relations (Complaints to Employment Tribunals (Armed Forces) Regulations 1997 SI 1997/2161; Equal Pay (Complaints to Employment Tribunals)

tortfeasors, therefore, the award will be distributed according to what is just and equitable having regard to the extent of that person's responsibility for the damage in question.[3] Further, where a person has a cause of action under the main anti-discrimination enactments, that cause of action survives his death for the benefit of his estate.[4] As to those unlawful acts which arise in the context of contractual relationships (for example, employment or tenancy relationships), their enforcement, importantly, does not depend upon the validity of the contract. Instead, the contractual relationship provides the occasion for the unlawful discriminatory act but not the condition for it.[5] Enforcement by the statutory Commissions and judicial review are addressed in Chapter 15.

B. Proceedings

14.02 In summary, proceedings under Part 2 of the enactments and in respect of other unlawful acts in the employment and related fields created under Part 3[6] are instituted and heard in the employment tribunals.[7]

14.03 However, where an appeal, or proceedings in the nature of an appeal, may be brought under 'any enactment' in respect of an act falling within the 'qualifications bodies' provisions,[8] proceedings may not be brought in an employment tribunal.[9]

(Armed Forces) Regulations 1997 SI 1997/2162; Sex Discrimination (Complaints to Employment Tribunals (Armed Forces) Regulations 1997 SI 1997/2163; Religion or Belief Regulations, regulations 36(7)–(11); and Sexual Orientation Regulations, regulations 36(7)–(11). The DDA and the Age Regulations exempt the armed forces from the protections afforded by their employment provisions: DDA, s 64(7) and Age Regulations, regulation 44(4).

3 Civil Liability (Contribution) Act 1978 and see *Prison Service and Others v Johnson* [1997] ICR 275; [1997] IRLR 162; *Gilbank v Miles* [2006] IRLR 538.

4 Law Reform (Miscellaneous) Act 1934; *Lewisham and Guys Mental Health NHS Trust v Harris (Personal Representative of Andrews (Deceased)* [2000] ICR 707; [2000] IRLR 320.

5 *Hall v Woolston Hall Leisure Limited* [2001] ICR 99; [2000] IRLR 578, at 586, para 67, *per* Lord Justice Mance (referred to approvingly in *Rhys-Harper v Relaxion Group plc & Others* [2003] UKHL 33; [2003] ICR 867; [2003] IRLR 484, para 210).

6 Variously, barristers, advocates, office holders, and employment services.

7 SDA, s 63; RRA, s 54; DDA, ss 17A and 25(7)–(9); Religion or Belief Regulations, regulation 28; Sexual Orientation Regulations, regulation 28; and Age Regulations, regulation 36. The rules relating to the institution, management, and hearing of such claims are dealt with by the Employment Tribunals (Constitution and Rules of Procedure) Regulations 2004 SI 2004/1861. Certain conditions now apply to the instituting of proceedings, as contained in the Employment Tribunals (Constitution and Rules of Procedure) Regulations 2004 read with the Employment Act 2002 and the Employment Act 2002 (Dispute Resolution) Regulations 2004 SI 2004/752.

8 See Chap 8.

9 SDA, s 63(2); RRA, s 54(2); DDA, s 17A(1A); Religion or Belief Regulations, regulation 28(2)(a); Sexual Orientation Regulations, regulation 28(2)(a); Age Regulations, regulation 36(2)(a).

'Enactment' for these purposes includes an enactment comprised in, or in an instrument made under, an Act of the Scottish Parliament.[10] Many professions are now regulated by statutory schemes. Some have statutory arrangements (either in primary or secondary legislation) addressing entry and practice in the professions with the provision of appeals against decisions affecting access to or continuation in a particular profession. This is most particularly so in relation to the medical profession, where a number of claims of discrimination have failed because appeals lie in respect of relevant decisions pursuant to statutory arrangements.[11] On the face of it, this restriction would appear to apply even where the appeal process is limited and does not extend to reversing the original decision, and where the appeal process itself is allegedly tainted by discrimination.[12] However, it is certainly arguable that if the appeal process concerned does not allow for a proper investigation of the merits of any decision against the threshold of the statutory torts within the main anti-discrimination enactments, with the facility to overturn any discriminatory decision, then it will not provide for a sufficiently effective process. In such a case, any appeal should not be regarded as such for the purpose of ousting the jurisdiction of the employment tribunal because otherwise such would not comply with the reqiurements of amended Equal Treatment Directive, the Race Directive, and the Framework Directive[13] to provide for the effective enforcement of the obligations created by the Directives. Further, it might be possible to argue in an appropriate case that a statutory appeal which does not provide for a merits-based review of any alleged discriminatory decision with power to overturn it does not give proper effect to the obligations under Article 6 of the European Convention on Human Rights (ECHR).[14] Importantly too, this exclusion of the employment tribunal's jurisdiction extends only to arrangements made under an 'enactment'. This covers subordinate legislation but not, for example, articles of association or other sets

---

[10] SDA, s 82; RRA, s 78; DDA, s 17A(1B); Religion or Belief Regulations, regulation 28(4); Sexual Orientation Regulations, regulation 28(4); Age Regulations, regulation 36(4).

[11] *Khan v General Medical Council* [1993] ICR 1032; [1993] IRLR 378.

[12] Ibid.

[13] See Chap 4.

[14] HRA, Sch 1 which provides that 'in the determination of his civil rights and obligations . . . , everyone is entitled to a fair and public hearing within a reasonable time by an independent and impartial tribunal established by law'. In *R v Department of Health ex p Gandhi* [1991] ICR 805; [1991] IRLR 431 the Divisional Court ruled that the Health Secretary, in exercising an appellate function in respect of the Medical Practices Committee of the NHS, was bound to consider the allegations of race discrimination upon which the appeal rested. However, even in that case, the obligations imposed by the Divisional Court as to the requirements of natural justice were not onerous. Thus the Secretary of State was not required to give reasons in respect of the dismissal of complaints of race discrimination made in the course of the appeal and nor was an oral hearing necessarily required. This case, of course, preceded the HRA.

of non-statutory rules.[15] Further, it does not affect any right to bring proceedings in judicial review.[16]

14.04 Claims under Part 3 of the Sex Discrimination Act 1975 (SDA), the Race Relations Act 1976 (RRA), the Disability Discrimination Act 1995 (DDA), and under Part 2 of the Equality Act 2006 (EA) (education,[17] goods, facilities and services, premises, clubs, public functions), and under the further and higher education provisions of the Religion or Belief Regulations and the Sexual Orientation Regulations must be instituted in the County Court, in England and Wales, and in the Sheriff Court, in Scotland.[18] This may be done by way of a claim or by way of counter-claim (as, for example, in possession proceedings where a landlord seeks to evict a tenant in breach of the enactments[19]). The RRA requires that proceedings be issued in a County Court designated by the Lord Chancellor for the purposes of hearing such claims.[20] The County Courts therefore have exclusive jurisdiction over claims of discrimination outside the employment and related fields, without, however, affecting any rights in judicial review.[21] Such claims are commenced in the ordinary way using a claim form.

14.05 Claims of race discrimination must be heard by a judge sitting with two assessors, unless the parties consent otherwise.[22] These assessors are appointed from a list of persons prepared and maintained by the Secretary of State, 'being persons appearing to the Secretary of State to have special knowledge and experience of problems connected with relations between persons of different racial groups'.[23] Such a requirement was first seen in the RRA 1968 and as to that provision:

> During the parliamentary debates, the Lord Chancellor explained the purpose of this provision. He conceded that it was a matter on which there were three

---

15 *Zaidi Financial Intermediaries Managers and Brokers Regulatory Association (FIMBRA)* [1995] ICR 876.

16 SDA, s 62(2); RRA, s 53(2); DDA, Sch 3, paras 2 and 5; EA, s 65(2); Religion or Belief regulation 27(2); Sexual Orientation Regulations, regulation 27(2); and Age Regulations, regulation 35(2)).

17 Except in the case of the DDA. See para 14.09 below.

18 SDA, s 66; RRA, s 57; DDA, s 25; Religion or Belief and Sexual Orientation Regulations, regulation 31; Age Regulations, regulation 39; and EA, s 66. See 'Practice Direction—Proceedings Under Enactments Relating to Discrimination', CPR, available at <http://www.dca.gov.uk/civil/procrules_fin/contents/practice_directions/proceedings_under_enactments.htm>.

19 *Council of the City of Manchester v (1) Romano (2) Samari* [2004] EWCA Civ 834.

20 RRA, ss 57(2) and 67(1).

21 SDA, s 62(2); RRA, s 53(2); DDA, Sch 3, paras 2 and 5; EA, s 65(2); Religion or Belief Regulations, regulation 27(2); Sexual Orientation Regulations, regulation 27(2); and Age Regulations, regulation 35(2)).

22 RRA, s 67(4).

23 Ibid, s 67(4).

> perfectly rational views which anyone might take. 'The first view, strongly put forward by the Street Report, was that there ought to be special race relations tribunals; and many people agreed with that view. The second view, taken by the lawyers mainly, was that they did not like the idea of special tribunals; that being lawyers they liked the ordinary courts . . . The third view is . . . a compromise . . . That was that there should be selected County Courts but that, while the judge should be the only person to decide the case, he should have assessors consisting of people with special experience in race relations to advise him.' (Hansard (HL Debates), 15 October 1968, vol 296, col 1260.) The Government had adopted the third view because it was 'most anxious that this Bill . . . should receive the largest measure of support possible'. And although the Lord Chancellor later confessed that it was not his favourite clause in the Bill, he pointed out that many people 'feel strongly that race relations is such a sensitive subject that it ought to be dealt with by special race relations courts and not left to a judge who may have nothing at all to do with race relations or with coloured people' (Hansard (HL Debates), 24 October 1968, vol 296, col 1572).[24]

The White Paper preceding the RRA 1976 indicated the Government's intention to retain provision for assessors, noting that the provisions in the 1968 Act: **14.06**

> enable the courts (like the industrial tribunals) to have the benefit of lay expertise and minority representation in dealing with cases under the race relations legislation . . . The Government intends to ensure that members of racial minorities and others with relevant knowledge and experience are substantially represented in these lists. For example, those who have had experience of the work of the conciliation committees would have a valuable contribution to make.[25]

The assessors continue to have a very important role, and the observations made above about the constitution in the judiciary and confidence in the process remain apposite.[26]

The SDA makes provision for the appointment of assessors[27] but does not require that they sit in any particular case. The DDA and the Religion or Belief Regulations, Sexual Orientation Regulations, and Age Regulations make no such provision. Where assessors sit in claims brought under the RRA (and presumably therefore the SDA), they have a full role in evaluating the evidence. For this reason it is not possible to have both a jury and assessors. Where there is a serious difference in view as between the judge and the assessors, this should be disclosed in the judgment.[28] **14.07**

---

24 G Bindman and A Lester, *Race and the Law* (1972, Penguin), 328.

25 'Racial Discrimination' (1975), Cmnd 6234, para 96.

26 For a discussion on the absence of specialist tribunals, which continues to be the subject of controversy, see B Hepple, M Coussey, T Choudhury, 'Equality: A New Framework: report of the Independent Review of the Enforcement of the UK Anti-Discrimination Legislation' (2000, Hart), Chap 4.

27 SDA, s 66(6).

28 *Ahmed v Governing Body of Oxford University* [2003] 1 WLR 195.

14.08 The Equal Pay Act 1970 (EPA) is less restrictive than the other enactments in that it allows for claims to be brought both in the employment tribunals[29] and in the High Court or in the County Courts, reflecting the contractual nature of the rights arising from its provisions.[30] However, where proceedings are issued in the High Court or in a County Court and it appears to the court that a claim or counter-claim under the EPA 'could more conveniently be disposed of separately by an employment tribunal, the court may direct that the claim or counter-claim shall be struck out'.[31] Alternatively, where in proceedings before any court a question arises as to the operation of an equality clause under the EPA, the court may on the application of any party to the proceedings or on its own motion refer that question, or direct it to be referred by a party to the proceedings, to an employment tribunal for determination by the tribunal, and may stay the proceedings in the meantime.[32] It is likely that, except in the simplest of EPA cases and in equal value cases in particular, any claims instituted in the High Court or a County Court will be referred to the employment tribunals. This is because they have particular experience in adjudicating such claims, and there are special procedural rules in place addressing the management (including by the provision of experts) of equal pay claims in employment tribunals.[33]

14.09 Claims under Chapter 1 of Part 4 of the DDA (schools and local authorities' residual duties[34]), in England and Wales, must be brought in the Special Educational Needs and Disability Tribunals[35] (SENDIST) (for England and Wales [36]), subject to the exceptions described below. Claims may only be brought against the responsible body[37] and may only be brought by the child's parent.[38] The Special Educational Needs and Disability Tribunal (General Provisions and Disability Claims Procedure) Regulations 2002[39] govern the procedure in relation to such claims.

---

29 And proceedings may be commenced in the employment tribunal by a reference by the Secretary of State where it appears to him that there may be a question whether the employer of any woman or women is or has been contravening a term modified or included by virtue of their equality clauses, but that it is not reasonable to expect them to take steps to have the question determined. Such a reference must be dealt with as if the reference were of a claim by the women, or woman, against the employer (EPA, s 2(2)).

30 EPA, s 2(1).

31 Ibid, s 2(3).

32 Ibid, s 2(3). And a court is bound to treat as conclusive any finding by an employment tribunal under the EPA (or the SDA) unless that finding is still subject to appeal (SDA, s 73(3)).

33 Employment Tribunals (Constitution and Rules of Procedure) Regulations 2004 SI 2004/1861, Sch 6.

34 See Chap 9.

35 DDA, s 28I(1).

36 Ibid, s 28I(5).

37 That is, not the individual for whom a responsible body might be liable: DDA, s 28I(1).

38 Ibid.

39 SI 2002/1985 (as amended by the Special Educational Needs Tribunal (Amendment) Regulations 2002 SI 2002/2787).

C. Time Limits

The main anti-discrimination enactments prescribe the time limits for instituting proceedings under them.[40] Proceedings in the employment tribunal must be instituted within three months beginning when the act complained of was done,[41] subject to the operation of the Employment Act 2002 (Dispute Resolution) Regulations 2004.[42] Proceedings in the County or Sheriff Court (except in education cases) must be instituted within six months beginning when the act complained of was done.[43] Proceedings under the education provisions of the EA, the Religion or Belief Regulations, the Sexual Orientation Regulations, and the Age Regulations must be instituted within six months beginning when the act complained of was done.[44] However, in certain circumstances, the time limits applicable to proceedings under the education provisions of the SDA, the RRA, and the DDA may be extended to within eight months beginning when the act complained of was done.[45] 14.10

As to when time begins to run, as mentioned, that is when the 'act complained of was done'. In the usual case, this is self-explanatory. Specific provision is made in all the enactments, except the EA, for cases which are less obvious so that where an unlawful act of discrimination is attributable to a term in a contract, that act is to be treated as extending throughout the duration of the contract; any act extending over a period shall be treated as done at the end of that period; and a deliberate omission shall be treated as done when the person in question decided upon it.[46] 14.11

40 Discriminatory acts occurring outside the time limits may nevertheless be relied upon in proceedings relating to acts in time where probative (as they often will be), as might acts occurring after the discriminatory act in issue: *Chattopadhyay v Headmaster of Holloway School* [1981] IRLR 487. *Qureshi v Victoria University of Manchester and Another* [2001] ICR 863.

41 SDA, s 76(1) (see the same for the extended period in relation to proceedings brought by members of the armed forces); RRA, s 68(1) (see the same for the extended period in relation to proceedings brought by members of the armed forces); DDA, Sch 3, Part 1, para 3(1); Religion or Belief Regulations, regulation 34 (see the same for the extended period in relation to proceedings brought by members of the armed forces); Sexual Orientation Regulations, regulation 34 (see the same for the extended period in relation to proceedings brought by members of the armed forces); Age Regulations, regulation 42.

42 SI 2004/752, which extends the time limits for bringing proceedings in the employment tribunals in certain circumstances where the statutory grievance and disciplinary procedures apply.

43 SDA, s 76(2); RRA, s 68(2); DDA, Sch 3, Part 2, para 6; EA, s 69; Religion or Belief Regulations, regulation 34(3); Sexual Orientation Regulations, regulation 34(3), Age Regulations, regulation 42(2).

44 EA, s 69; Religion or Belief Regulations, regulation 34(2); Sexual Orientation Regulations, regulation 34(2); Age Regulations, regulation 42(2).

45 SDA, s 76(2) and (2A) and RRA, s 68(3A); DDA, Sch 3, Part 4, para 13(2).

46 SDA, s 76(6); RRA, s 68(7); DDA, Sch 3, Part 1, para 3(3); Part II, para 6(4); Part 3, para 10(5); Part 4, para 13(4); Religion or Belief Regulations, regulation 34(4); Sexual Orientation Regulations, regulation 34(4), and Age Regulations, regulation 42(4).

A person is to be taken to have decided upon an omission when he does an act inconsistent with doing the omitted act; or if he has done no such inconsistent act, when the period expires within which he might reasonably have been expected to do the omitted act if it was to be done.[47] Identifying the circumstances in which an act might be said to 'extend over a period' for the purposes of the time limit has proved problematic and controversial. A policy, rule, or practice, in accordance with which decisions are taken from time to time, might constitute a 'continuing act' for these purposes, even where such policy is unwritten and informal.[48] Likewise a continuing state of affairs may constitute a continuing act for these purposes,[49] even where the individual acts relied upon are done by different persons, so capturing instances of institutional discrimination.[50]

14.12 A claim instituted outside the time limits for so doing may nevertheless be considered if a court or tribunal considers it 'just and equitable' to do so.[51] This confers a wide discretion to hear a claim notwithstanding that it has been presented out of time. In determining whether to exercise a discretion to hear a claim instituted outside the time limits, relevant factors will usually include the length of time and the reasons for the delay; the extent to which the cogency of the evidence is likely to be affected by the delay; the extent to which the party sued had cooperated with any requests for information; the promptness with which the claimant acted once she or he knew of the facts giving rise to the cause of action; and the steps taken by the claimant to obtain the appropriate professional advice once he or she knew of the possibility of taking action.[52] In all cases, in determining whether to exercise its discretion to extend time, a court or tribunal will consider the general justice of a decision either way,[53] and the fact that proceedings have been instituted very far outside of the statutory time limits will not necessarily mean that it will be inappropriate to extend time.[54]

---

47 SDA, s 76(6)(c); RRA, s 687)(c); DDA, Sch 3, Part I, para 3(4); Part II, para 6(5); Part 3I, para 10(6); Part IV, para 13(5); Religion or Belief Regulations, regulation 34(4)(c); Sexual Orientation Regulations, regulation 34(4)(c), and Age Regulations, regulation 42(4)(c).

48 *Owusu v London Fire and Civil Defence Authority* [1995] IRLR 574; *Cast v Croydon College* [1998] ICR 500; [1998] IRLR 318.

49 *Hendricks v MPC* [2003] IRLR 96.

50 *Hendricks v MPC* [2003] IRLR 96; *Rihal v London Borough of Ealing* [2004] IRLR 642.

51 SDA, ss 76(5); RRA, s 68(6); DDA, Sch 3, Part 1, para 3(2); Part 2, para 6(3); Part 3I, para 10(3); Part 4, para 13(3); Religion or Belief Regulations, regulation 34(3); Sexual Orientation Regulations, regulation 34(3) and Age Regulations, regulation 42(3).

52 *Anderson v Rover Group (1999) 1426/99 EAT*; and *British Coal Corporation v Keeble and Others* [1997] IRLR 336 at 338.

53 *Anderson v Rover Group* (1999) 1426/99 EAT.

54 See, eg, *London Borough of Southwark v Afolabi* [2003] IRLR 220 presented nearly nine years after the expiry of the statutory time limit.

The EA addresses time limits somewhat differently as compared to the other main anti-discrimination enactments. It provides that proceedings under Part 2 (religion and belief discrimination outside the employment and related fields) must be instituted within six months 'beginning with the date of the act (or last act) to which the proceedings relate' or 'with the permission of the court in which the proceedings are brought'.[55] No further restrictions are specified. It is likely that these provisions, particularly in so far as they confer discretion to hear claims instituted with 'permission' outside the time limits, will be construed broadly in line with the limitation provisions in the other main anti-discrimination enactments.[56] However, the requirement in the other main anti-discrimination enactments that any acts occurring outside the primary time limit and preceding the date of the last act must, with the last act (assuming that has occurred within the time limit), form part of a 'continuing act' if the court or tribunal is to have automatic jurisdiction conferred upon it is not seen in the EA. Instead, it is 'the last act to which the proceedings relate' which will start the limitation period running. This is more generous than the provision made in the other main anti-discrimination enactments, and will avoid many of the tortuous efforts sometimes seen in the case law to link events so as to obtain the benefit of the 'continuing act' provisions. 14.13

The EPA also addresses limitation differently, reflecting the contractual jurisdiction it confers. The time limits for instituting proceedings in the High Court or County Courts are prescribed by the ordinary limitation periods affecting contractual disputes.[57] However, in respect of claims in the employment tribunals, or referred to the employment tribunals,[58] the time limits are considerably shorter.[59] In relation to a continuing contract of employment, proceedings may be issued at any time.[60] However, where the claimant is no longer working for the employer, proceedings must be instituted in general within six months of the last day of her employment.[61] 'Employed' in this context means employed under a contract of employment in which the equality clause relied on for the purpose of the claim 14.14

55 EA, s 69.

56 See the observations in para 14.12.

57 Limitation Act 1980, s 6. As to the limitation on awards of back pay by the courts or tribunals, see EPA, s 2(5)(b).

58 See para 14.08 above.

59 And with certain modifications in specific cases, apparently compliant with EU law: *Preston v Wolverhampton Healthcare NHS Trust and Secretary of State for Health*; *Fletcher v Midland Bank plc* [2000] IRLR 506, ECJ. See, for the modifications, discussed below, the Equal Pay Act 1970 (Amendment) Regulations 2002, SI 2003/1656.

60 *British Railways Board v Paul* [1988] IRLR 20.

61 EPA, s 2(4)) read with s 2ZA(3).

applied, and consequently a period during which the employee is receiving pay in lieu of notice (but where termination of her contract has not yet taken place) is still regarded as employment for these purposes.[62] Modifications apply to this time limit in certain circumstances.[63] In particular, they apply where there is a deliberate concealment of facts relevant to a failure to comply with the equality clause in the woman's contract by the employer, in which case the six-month period only begins to run from the date when the woman discovered (or might reasonably have been expected to discover) the facts in question;[64] where there is a qualifying disability, in which case the six-month period does not start to run until the woman has ceased to be under a disability;[65] where there is both concealment and disability, in which case the six-month period starts to run from whichever is the later of the dates;[66] and in a 'stable employment case', namely one in which a woman is employed under a series of individual contracts linked by the existence of an ongoing relationship between the contracts, even if not employed under a contract of employment during all such times, when she is entitled to bring a claim either during the period of the relationship, or within six months of it ending.[67]

14.15 In certain cases, the time limits may be extended where conciliation has been attempted or where an application to one of the statutory Commissions has been made.[68]

14.16 Time limits in discrimination claims outside the employment and related fields are considerably shorter than those applicable in comparable common law actions. The extent to which the time limits are consistent with the principles of effectiveness and non-discrimination in EU law has been the subject of consideration in the context of equal pay claims.[69] However, particularly in relation to

---

62 *HQ Service Children's Education (MOD) v Davitt* [1999] ICR 978.

63 In consequence of amendments made by the Equal Pay Act 1970 (Amendment) Regulations 2003, SI 2003/1656, enacted to give effect to the requirements of EU law.

64 EPA, s 2ZA(5). For the meaning of 'concealment', see EPA, s 2ZA(2).

65 Ibid, s 2ZA(6). For the meaning of 'disability', see ibid, s 2ZA(2).

66 Ibid, s 2ZA(7).

67 Ibid, s 2ZA(4). For the meaning of 'stable employment case', see ibid, s 2ZA(2). As to where there has been a transfer falling within Transfer of Undertakings (Protection of Employment) Regulations 1981, see *Powerhouse Retail Ltd v Burroughs* [2006] UKHL 13; *Armstrong v Newcastle upon Tyne NHS Hospital Trust* UKEAT/0158/04, 22 November 2004.

68 SDA, s 76(2C), when the material provisions of the EA are brought into force; RRA, s 68(3); RRA, s 68(3C) when the material provisions of the EA are brought into force; DDA, Sch 3, Part 2, para 6(2), Part 3, para 10(2), and Part 4, para 13(2).

69 See, *Levez v T H Jennings (Harlow Pools) Ltd*, Case C-326/96 [1999] ICR 521; [1999] IRLR 36.

County Court claims, it is arguable that the very short time limits are not consistent with the EU law.[70] Whilst time limits themselves are not *per se* incompatible with EU law,[71] where they are likely to render the bringing of a claim falling within the scope of EU law virtually impossible or excessively difficult, or where they entail procedural rules or other conditions which are less favourable than those applicable to similar domestic actions, then they may breach the EU law principles of equality, equivalence, and effectiveness.[72] The time limits applicable to claims under the main anti-discrimination enactments falling within the jurisdiction of the County Courts are very much shorter than the time limits applicable to other common law and statutory torts,[73] and there is no obvious justification for that distinction. Many claims justiciable in the County Courts now fall within the scope of EU law (particularly race discrimination claims falling within the scope of the Race Directive[74]) and it is at least arguable that the time limits applicable to them are challengeable under EU law.

D. Burden of Proof

In general, it has been for the claimant who complains of discrimination to prove her or his case. The position has altered in relation to many claims under the main anti-discrimination enactments because of the impact of EU law, discussed below.[75] However, the older guidance on discharging the burden of proof remains relevant to all cases, including those now affected by the changes made to the incidence of the burden of proof, because it illustrates when the burden might shift, as is discussed further below. **14.17**

The courts have long acknowledged that proving direct discrimination (absent an admission, which will be most unusual) is peculiarly problematic. This is reflected in such statistical data as exists, which indicates that discrimination, particularly race discrimination, cases have lower prospects of success than any **14.18**

70 See Chap 4 and see *Alabaster v Barclays Bank Plc (formerly Woolwich plc) and Secretary of State for Social Security (No 2)* [2005] EWCA Civ 508; [2005] ICR 1246; [2005] IRLR 576; *Marshall v Southampton and South West Area Health Authority II* (Case C-271/91) [1993] ECR I-4367; [1993] ICR 893; [1993] IRLR 445.

71 *Levez v T H Jennings (Harlow Pools) Ltd* (Case C-326/96) [1999] ICR 521; [1999] IRLR 36.

72 Ibid, *Alabaster v Barclays Bank Plc (formerly Woolwich plc) and Secretary of State for Social Security (No 2)* [2005] EWCA Civ 508; [2005] ICR 1246.

73 Limitation Act 1980, ss 2–4A.

74 See Chap 4. See too, the Gender Goods and Services Directive (Chap 4) the scope of which covers many sex discrimination claims in the County Courts.

75 Para 14.20.

other comparable claims.[76] At an early stage, recognizing the difficulties in proving an existing state of mind in a discriminator, as would be required for direct discrimination and victimization, the Employment Appeal Tribunal suggested that where a claimant proved a *prima facie* case, the burden would shift to the discriminator to show the absence of unlawful discrimination.[77]

14.19 That position did not pertain for long, but guidance was given in a number of cases by the Court of Appeal and the House of Lords directed at ensuring the burden on a claimant was not placed impossibly high.[78] In summary, the position is that it is for the claimant who complains of discrimination to make out his or her case, unless the specific provisions addressing the burden of proof in certain cases apply.[79] Courts and tribunals must nevertheless bear in mind that it is unusual to find direct evidence of unlawful discrimination. Few discriminators will be prepared to admit such discrimination even to themselves. In some cases discrimination will not be ill-intentioned but merely based on an assumption that the claimant 'would not have fitted in'. Discrimination need not be 'conscious' or intentional.[80] The outcome of a case will therefore usually depend on what inferences it is proper to draw from the primary facts found by a court or tribunal. Though there will be some cases where, for example, treatment of a claimant is clearly not on protected grounds, a finding of discrimination (that is, a difference in treatment), and a finding of a difference in race, sex, disability status, religion or belief, sexual orientation, or age etc will often point to the possibility of discrimination on those grounds. In such circumstances the court or tribunal should look to the alleged discriminator for an *explanation* for the treatment complained about. If no explanation is then put forward, or if the court or tribunal considers the explanation to be inadequate or unsatisfactory, it will be legitimate for it to infer that the discrimination was on one of the prohibited grounds. This is not a matter of law but 'almost common sense'.[81] It is not, however, sufficient to show merely that there has been *unreasonable* treatment.[82] There must be proved *less favourable* treatment. It is therefore

76 Recent research indicates that only 16% of race discrimination cases win at employment tribunals ('Claims of race bias fall by the wayside', Labour Research Department (LRD), April 2002 and <www.lrd.org.uk>). This figure compares extremely poorly with the success rate of other cases, eg, redundancy (43%) and the success rate of cases across all jurisdictions in the employment tribunals (43%) (LRD, ibid).

77 *Chattopadhyay v Headmaster of Holloway School* [1982] ICR 132, CA.

78 *Zafar v Glasgow CC* [1998] ICR 120; [1998] IRLR 36; *King v Great Britain-China Centre* [1992] ICR 516; and *Anya v University of Oxford* [2001] ICR 847; [2001] IRLR 377, paras 8, 9, 10, 11, 14.

79 As to which, see para 14.20 below.

80 *Nagarajan v London Regional Transport* [2000] AC 1 501.

81 *North West Thames Regional Health Authority v Noone* [1988] ICR 813, 822, *per* May LJ.

82 *Zafar v Glasgow CC* [1998] ICR 120; [1998] IRLR 36; *Bahl v The Law Society* [2004] IRLR 799.

necessary to ask whether the claimant was treated less favourably than the alleged discriminator treated or would have treated other persons of a different status in the same, or not materially different, relevant circumstances, and whether that treatment was on protected grounds. However, where an alleged discriminator relies on a contention that he treats all persons *unreasonably*, or the treatment complained of was by reason of mistake, it is for him to *prove* the same on evidence: 'whether there is such an explanation . . . will depend not on a theoretical possibility that the employer behaves equally badly to employees of all races, but on evidence that he does'.[83] This at least addresses what is colloquially known amongst discrimination law practitioners as the 'bastard defence' ('I treated the claimant badly but I am a bastard and treat everyone equally badly, irrespective of race, gender etc'), the defence of last resort, which can be very difficult to rebut. In relation to each of the issues just described the court must make findings of fact, either on the basis of direct (or positive) evidence or by inference from circumstantial evidence (or evidentiary facts; these might include whether there were good equal opportunities policies in place; the discriminator's attitudes and understanding of discrimination;[84] and relevant events before or since). It is not necessary for the court to ask itself, in relation to each piece of such circumstantial evidence, whether it was itself explicable on protected grounds or on innocent grounds. That would be to misapprehend the nature and purpose of evidentiary facts. Hostility may justify an inference of discrimination if there is nothing else to explain it. The fact that equal opportunities procedures are not used when they should be may point to the possibility of protected discrimination. A court or tribunal should have regard to all its findings of fact before deciding whether to draw an inference of discrimination on prohibited grounds in respect of a particular complaint.[85] The outcome of a case will, therefore, usually depend on the inferences which it is proper to draw from the primary facts. These inferences can include, in appropriate cases, any inferences that it is just and equitable to draw in accordance with the questionnaire provisions.[86]

---

[83] *Anya v University of Oxford* [2001] ICR 847; [2001] IRLR 377,and see *Yeboah v Crofton* [2002] EWCA Civ 794; [2002] IRLR 634, *per* Mummery LJ: 'In principle the onus of proving a fact is on the person who asserts it. Thus, in an action for defamation, if the defendant pleads justification, it is for him to prove that the words used are true. It is not for the claimant to prove that they are untrue.'

[84] *Anya v University of Oxford* [2001] ICR 847; [2001] IRLR 377.

[85] *Qureshi v Victoria University of Manchester and another* (1996) [2001] ICR 863.

[86] As to which, see below, and see *King v Great Britain-China Centre* [1992] ICR 516, 528.

14.20 As a result of EU law, changes have now been made such that in certain circumstances the burden of proof will formally shift to an alleged discriminator to demonstrate that there has been no unlawful discrimination. The origins of these provisions can be found, in the first place,[87] in the Burden of Proof Directive,[88] applicable only to gender discrimination, which provided, importantly, that its aim was to:

> ensure that the measures taken by the Member States to implement the principle of equal treatment are made more effective, in order to enable all persons who consider themselves wronged because the principle of equal treatment has not been applied to them to have their rights asserted by judicial process.[89]

To this end,[90] its Article 4 provided that:

> Member States shall take such measures as are necessary, in accordance with their national judicial systems, to ensure that, when persons who consider themselves wronged because the principle of equal treatment has not been applied to them establish, before a court or other competent authority, facts from which it may be presumed that there has been direct or indirect discrimination, it shall be for the respondent to prove that there has been no breach of the principle of equal treatment.

This led to amendments to the SDA addressing the burden of proof within the scope of the areas covered by EU gender discrimination law (employment and related fields).[91] The Race and Framework Directives[92] contained similar provision. All the main anti-discrimination enactments[93] now contain measures shifting the burden of proof in certain circumstances. Section 57ZA of the RRA provides that:[94]

> Where, on the hearing of the claim, the claimant proves facts from which the court could, apart from this section, conclude in the absence of an adequate explanation that the respondent—
>
> (a) has committed . . . an act of discrimination or harassment against the claimant, or

87 No doubt inspired by certain of the ECJ case law in the field of equal pay (eg, *Enderby v Frenchay Health Authority and A'or* (Case C-127/92) [1994] ICR 112; [1993] IRLR 591.

88 97/80/EC, extended to the UK (which had not at the time of its enactment signed the European Social Charter, see Recital (1)) by Directive 98/52/EC.

89 Burden of Proof Directive, Art 1.

90 It also provided for a more liberal meaning of indirect discrimination than that which had been found in the original SDA, see Chap 4.

91 Chap 4.

92 Arts 8 and 10, respectively and see Gender Goods and Services Directive, Art 9; see Chap 4.

93 Except the EPA, in which the presumption of discrimination is implicit in the operation of the equality clause.

94 As inserted by the Race Relations Act 1976 (Amendment) Regulations 2003 (which implements the directive).

(b) is by virtue of section 32[95] or 33[96] to be treated as having committed such an act of discrimination or harassment against the claimant,

the court shall uphold the claim unless the respondent proves that he did not commit or, as the case may be, is not to be treated as having committed that act.

Similar provision is made in the RRA in relation to employment tribunal claims.[97] The other main anti-discrimination enactments contain materially the same provision applicable to those unlawful acts falling within the scope of the amended Equal Treatment Directive, and the Framework Directive.[98] The specific provision made applies only to employment tribunal and County Court claims falling within the purview of the Directives, but these provisions should be read as applying equally to judicial review and any other proceedings in which discrimination claims are made falling within the scope of the Directives to ensure proper effect is given to the Directives.[99] As seen, then, the burden of proof shifts when the claimant proves such facts from which the court *could* (not *would*) conclude in the absence of an adequate explanation from the alleged discriminator that discrimination or harassment has occured. The burden on an alleged discriminator is compelling and requires that he show no discrimination 'whatsoever'.[100] The Court of Appeal gave guidance on the operation of the burden of proof changes in the important case of *Igen Ltd and O'rs v Wong and O'rs*,[101] as follows: **14.21**

(1) Pursuant to section 63A of the 1975 Act, it is for the claimant who complains of sex discrimination to prove on the balance of probabilities facts from which the tribunal could conclude, in the absence of an adequate explanation, that the employer has committed an act of discrimination against the claimant which is unlawful by virtue of Part 2, or which, by virtue of section 41 or section 42

95 The vicarious liability provision, see Chap 13.

96 The 'aiding' provision, making those who 'knowingly aid' a discriminatory act liable, see and *Anyanwu v South Bank Students' Union and Another* [2001] IRLR 305 HL, see Chap 13.

97 RRA, s 54A, the RRA applicable to all claims not determined before 19 July 2003, whenever the claim was instituted, and whenever the cause of action arose, regulation 2(2), Race Relations Act 1976 (Amendment) Regulations 2003, SI 2003/1626.

98 SDA, ss 63A and 66A; DDA, s 17A(1C) (applicable to all claims not determined before 12 Oct 2001 and 1 Oct 2004, respectively, whenever the claim was instituted and whenever the cause of action arose, regulation by reason of regulation 2(2) of the Sex Discrimination (Indirect Discrimination and Burden of Proof) Regulations 2001, SI 2001/2660 and regulations 2(1) and (4) of the Disability Discrimination Act 1995 (Amendment) Regulations 2003, SI 2003/1673; regulation 29, Religion or Belief Regulations; regulation 29, Sexual Orientation Regulations; and regulation 40, Age Regulations. See too, EA, s 65(5).

99 There is no material limitation on their application in the Directives.

100 Burden of Proof Directive 97/80/EC, Art 2(1); Framework Directive, Art 2(1)—not said in terms in the Race Directive but which has the same effect.

101 [2005] ICR 931; [2005] IRLR 258.

of the 1975 Act, is to be treated as having been committed against the claimant. These are referred to below as 'such facts'.

(2) If the claimant does not prove such facts he or she will fail.

(3) It is important to bear in mind in deciding whether the claimant has proved such facts that it is unusual to find direct evidence of sex discrimination. Few employers would be prepared to admit such discrimination, even to themselves. In some cases the discrimination will not be an intention but merely based on the assumption that 'he or she would not have fitted in'.

(4) In deciding whether the claimant has proved such facts, it is important to remember that the outcome at this stage of the analysis by the tribunal will therefore usually depend on what inferences it is proper to draw from the primary facts found by the tribunal.

(5) It is important to note the word 'could' in section 63A(2). At this stage the tribunal does not have to reach a definitive determination that such facts would lead it to the conclusion that there was an act of unlawful discrimination. At this stage a tribunal is looking at the primary facts before it to see what inferences of secondary fact could be drawn from them.

(6) In considering what inferences or conclusions can be drawn from the primary facts, the tribunal must assume that there is no adequate explanation for those facts.

(7) These inferences can include, in appropriate cases, any inferences that it is just and equitable to draw in accordance with section 74(2)(b) of the 1975 Act from an evasive or equivocal reply to a questionnaire or any other questions that fall within section 74(2) of the 1975 Act.

(8) Likewise, the tribunal must decide whether any provision of any relevant code of practice is relevant and, if so, take it into account in determining such facts pursuant to section 56A(10) of the 1975 Act. This means that inferences may also be drawn from any failure to comply with any relevant code of practice.

(9) Where the claimant has proved facts from which conclusions could be drawn that the employer has treated the claimant less favourably on the ground of sex, then the burden of proof moves to the employer.

(10) It is then for the employer to prove that he did not commit, or as the case may be, is not to be treated as having committed, that act.

(11) To discharge that burden it is necessary for the employer to prove, on the balance of probabilities, that the treatment was in no sense whatsoever on the grounds of sex, since 'no discrimination whatsoever' is compatible with the Burden of Proof Directive.

(12) That requires a tribunal to assess not merely whether the employer has proved an explanation for the facts from which such inferences can be drawn, but further that it is adequate to discharge the burden of proof on the balance of probabilities that sex was not a ground for the treatment in question.[102]

102 In one of the appeals heard in *Igen* (*Webster v Brunel University*), the EAT had held that the burden of proof went to the question of the identity of the discriminator so that where, in a

(13) Since the facts necessary to prove an explanation would normally be in the possession of the respondent, a tribunal would normally expect cogent evidence to discharge that burden of proof. In particular, the tribunal will need to examine carefully explanations for failure to deal with the questionnaire procedure and/or code of practice.[103]

This requires that 'a two-stage process [is followed] if the complaint of the complainant is to be upheld'.[104] Importantly, although any *exculpatory* explanation is to be ignored at the first stage, a court or tribunal should take into account any *inculpatory* explanation, so that the claimant is entitled to benefit from any incriminating explanation at the first stage but the alleged discriminator is not to benefit from any innocent explanation at that stage. This does not mean that any evidence from the alleged discriminator should be ignored at the first stage.[105] However, care must be taken to ensure that the burden of proof provisions are respected and that only evidence which undermines the establishment of 'such facts', as are necessary to shift the burden of proof, are had regard to at the first stage.[106] Evidence which explains *prima facie* discriminatory treatment must not be considered until the second stage when the burden of proving those matters rests firmly on the alleged discriminator.[107] The '... the distinction between fact **14.22**

crowded room, racist abuse was shouted at the complainant but he was unable to prove that it was an employee of his employer who had shouted it, the burden of proof would assist him as follows: having proved that the abuse was shouted in the first place, the burden would then shift to the employer to disprove that it was a person for whom he was legally responsible who had shouted it. The Court of Appeal disapproved of this analysis: the claimant retains the obligation of proving on ordinary principles that the respondent committed the act in question. The shift in the burden of proof is for the purposes of establishing the ground for the act, not the identity of the actor (paras 25–33): 'The scheme of the statutory amendments appears to us simple and to make good sense given that a complainant can be expected to know how he or she has been treated by the respondent whereas the respondent can be expected to explain why the complainant has been so treated. Of course there may be cases where the complainant will have difficulty in proving that it was the employer who committed the unlawful act. But that is a difficulty faced by many who feel aggrieved and would wish to obtain redress through the courts or the tribunals. The complainant may have no less difficulty in establishing others of the essential facts, but that does not mean that it is sufficient for the complainant to prove only the possibility rather than the probability of those other facts at the first stage', *Igen Ltd and O'rs v Wong and O'rs* [2005] ICR 931; [2005] IRLR 258, at para 31.

[103] *Igen Ltd and O'rs v Wong and O'rs* [2005] ICR 931; [2005] IRLR 258, Annex.

[104] Ibid, at para 17.

[105] *Laing v Manchester City Council* [2006] IRLR 748; *Mohmed v West Coast Trains Ltd* UKEAT/0682/05/DA.

[106] In *Laing v Manchester City Council* [2006] IRLR 748, the Employment Appeal Tribunal appeared to suggest that evidence going to the *explanation* might be had regard to, but this cannot be right because it would render the burden of proof provisions nugatory.

[107] *EB v BA* [2006] IRLR 471. *EB* is not cited in either *Laing v Manchester City Council* [2006] IRLR 748 or *Mohmed v West Coast Trains Ltd* UKEAT/0682/05/DA and their authority must therefore be doubted.

and explanation' has been said to be 'tolerably clear'; [108] however, the courts have not always respected that distinction.[109]

14.23 At the first stage, the claimant need only prove on the balance of probabilities facts from which the tribunal could conclude, in the absence of an adequate explanation, that the alleged discriminator has committed an act of discrimination against the claimant. As seen, she or he may use evidence of non-compliance with a relevant provision of a Code of Practice,[110] or a failure to respond without adequate explanation to a question in a statutory questionnaire,[111] to discharge the burden of proving 'such facts'.[112] Where a comparator is relied upon, that comparator's circumstances must be the same or not materially different if the comparative treatment is to shift the burden of proof.[113]

14.24 Once the burden has shifted, and since the facts necessary to prove an explanation would normally be in the possession of the respondent, a court or tribunal will expect cogent evidence to discharge that burden of proof and:

> If an employer takes the stance . . . "You prove it"—then claimants, particularly those with limited or no means, who challenge large corporations in cases of this kind would be at a great disadvantage. Such an approach may well render the reverse burden of proof provision of little or no use to a claimant. The stance taken by the

---

108 *Laing v Manchester City Council* [2006] IRLR 748.

109 See *Laing v Manchester City Council* [2006] IRLR 748 where factual evidence of widespread non-discriminatory misbehaviour by the alleged discriminator was said to be relevant at the first stage, though plainly indivisible from the employer's explanation. See, too, the even more surprising *Mohmed v West Coast Trains Ltd* UKEAT/0682/05/DA. In both cases, the important case of *EB v BA* [2006] IRLR 471 was, mystifyingly, not cited, and they must be regarded as of doubtful weight for that reason alone. In *EB v BA* [2006] IRLR 471 the Court of Appeal did not directly address the fact/explanation dichotomy, but its approach is instructive nonetheless: in concluding that the burden of proof had been shifted, the Court did not consider any of the evidence that might have supported a non-discriminatory explanation by the employer.

110 See para 14.28, below, and Chap 15.

111 See para 14.28, below.

112 *Igen Ltd and O'rs v Wong and O'rs* [2005] ICR 931; [2005] IRLR 258, Annex, at (7)–(8).

113 *Dresdner Kleinwort Wasserstein Ltd v Adebayo* [2005] IRLR 514. The comments of Elias J in *Network Rail Infrastructure Ltd v Griffiths-Henry* (2006) UKEAT/0642/05/CK suggesting that at the first stage, treatment of other persons in comparable situations—not of the same sex, racial group etc as the claimant—could be had regard to rebut evidence of less favourable treatment, is wrong. This is explicatory material and is relevant only at the second stage. If the claimant is able to demonstrate less favourable treatment by comparison with an actual comparator who satisfies the statutory requirement of similarity, that ought, as a matter of law, to shift the burden. The employer is able to refer to other unsuccessful candidates, ie explain his conduct/treatment, at the second stage. This approach is itself not unproblematic: the identification of a comparator is not always simple and may itself involve consideration of the 'reason why' certain treatment was afforded, but it is a more stable platform from which to apply the statutory provisions than that obliquely suggested in *Network Rail*. See further Chap 6 for comparators.

> respondent may be suitable for commercial cases. In my view it is not suitable for a difficult discrimination case. It is important . . . that tribunals bear in mind the objectives of [the burden of proof provisions] at the prehearing and hearing stage. Employers should not be permitted to escape the provisions . . . .by leaving it to the employee to prove her case.[114]

Unreasonable conduct, where it disadvantages a person from a protected class, may now require explanation if a finding of discrimination is not to be made.[115] This recognizes, as the courts have frequently done, and as is mentioned above, that it is rare to find direct evidence of discrimination. Often, unreasonable conduct is the only evidence of discrimination.[116]

14.25 As has already been mentioned,[117] claims of direct discrimination do not require an actual comparator. Identifying when the burden shifts in a case where there is no comparator is problematic. In such a case, 'it must surely not be inappropriate for a tribunal in such cases to go straight to the second stage'.[118] It is difficult to see, in a case involving a hypothetical comparator, how one could not do so. Such would be consistent with the purpose of the burden of proof provisions. The placement of the burden of proof in a claim dependent upon a hypothetical comparator may be all-important for the claimant. If the burden of proof does not move to the alleged discriminator, he will very probably be unable to prove his claim. This is precisely the situation that the burden of proof provisions were designed to relieve.[119]

14.26 As to the impact of the burden of proof in indirect discrimination there is *obiter dicta* suggesting that the new provisions have done no more than codify the existing law so that the burden of proving disparate impact remains on a claimant in all cases.[120] However, this *dicta* is inconsistent with the thrust of the decisions in *Igen Ltd and O'rs v Wong and O'rs*.[121] Further, the Directive and the domestic provisions it make it clear that the burden of proof changes apply equally to direct and indirect discrimination.[122] This means that if a complainant can prove 'such facts' as are required, including by inferences that might be drawn including from any

114 *EB v BA* [2006] IRLR 471, para 52, *per* Hooper LJ.

115 *Anya v University of Oxford* [2001] ICR 847; [2001] IRLR 377; *Igen Ltd and O'rs v Wong and O'rs* [2005] ICR 931; [2005] IRLR 258, at para 51.

116 *Zafar v Glasgow CC* [1998] ICR 120; [1998] IRLR 36; *King v Great Britain-China Centre* [1992] ICR 516; and *Anya v University of Oxford* [2001] IRLR 377.

117 Chap 6.

118 *Laing v Manchester City Council* [2006] IRLR 748, para 74.

119 See the observations in *EB v BA* [2006] IRLR 471, paras 51–2, *per* Hooper LJ.

120 *Nelson v Carillion Services Ltd* [2003] 1 ICR 1256.

121 [2005] ICR 931 and *EB v BA* [2006] IRLR 471.

122 And harassment and victimization: Chap 4 and see *Enderby v Frenchay Health Authority and Secretary of State for Health* [1993] IRLR 591, ECJ paras 14, 18–19.

questionnaire replies (or failure to reply) and a failure to comply with a relevant Code of Practice, the burden shifts.[123] The position otherwise would be inconsistent with the Directives and the scheme of the legislation. If it were right that the complainant in all cases had the burden of proving disparate impact on the balance of probabilities, an employer seeking to avoid liability for compensation would be best advised not to comply with the Code of Practice[124] and the statutory duties which both require monitoring and the collecion of relevant statistical material.[125] These measures are designed to promote equality and eliminate discrimination, and those objectives would be frustrated by 'rewarding' a discriminator who fails to comply. Similarly, the objectives of the Directives would be undermined by placing the burden on a claimant in such circumstances.[126] Further, it would create a marked and significant distinction between the burden on claimant's in direct as compared to indirect discrimination cases, when none is envisaged by the legislation or the Directives and where that distinction is sometimes difficult to draw.[127]

14.27 As to the impact of the provisions on claims arising from an alleged breach of a duty to make reasonable adjustments, the Code of Practice on Employment and Occupation produced by the Disability Rights Commission states that:

> To prove an allegation that there has been a failure to comply with a duty to make reasonable adjustments, an employee must prove facts from which it could be inferred in the absence of an adequate explanation that such a duty has arisen, and that it has been breached. If the employee does this, the claim will succeed unless the employer can show that it did not fail to comply with its duty in this regard.[128]

This suggests that, first, the claimant does not have to prove that the duty to make reasonable adjustments has arisen, merely that it could have done; second, and assuming that the first hurdle has been overcome, the claimant need not prove that the duty has been breached, only that it could have been. There are a number of problems with this analysis. Firstly, it is unsatisfactory to regard the existence of the duty to make reasonable adjustments as an issue that is inappropriate for conclusive determination at the outset of the inquiry. The existence of the duty is triggered by the existence of a substantial disadvantage to the worker caused by a provision, criterion, or practice of the employer or by a physical feature of the premises. The existence of a substantial disadvantage does not depend in any way

123 See para 14.28.
124 Which does not give rise to liability by itself, see Chap 15.
125 Which will not give rise to a private law claim in compensation, see Chap 15.
126 Chap 4.
127 *Secretary of State for Defence v Elias* [2006] EWCA Civ 1293, para 114.
128 Para 4.43.

upon an employer's explanation for any such disadvantage and is capable of being established as a discrete question. Further, in accordance with the normal rules as to the burden of proof the burden ought to lie on the claimant. This is because the existence of the substantial disadvantage does not depend on an inquiry into the employer's reasons for acting. The introduction of the changes to the burden of proof was to counter the difficulties inherent in those parts of the discrimination analysis requiring the claimant to establish the alleged discriminator's grounds for acting in a particular way. Secondly, it is not easy to see why the claimant should even begin to demonstrate that the employer has failed to comply with his duty, except at the most basic level. For example, a disabled employee with mobility impairments who has difficulty entering and exiting his place of work would be able to prove the existence of a substantial disadvantage for the purposes of establishing the employer's duty to make reasonable adjustments. At that point, it should fall to the employer to prove: (i) that it made reasonable adjustments; or (ii) that there were no adjustments that it was reasonable to make. This information is peculiarly within the province of the employer. Requiring more of the claimant is to deprive him of the benefit of the burden of proof provisions.[129]

E. The Codes of Practice and Questionnaires

The SDA, RRA, and DDA all contain provision permitting the Equal Opportunities Commission (EOC), the Commission for Racial Equality (CRE), and the Disability Rights Commission (DRC) to issue Codes of Practice. The Commission for Equality and Human Rights (CEHR) will, when fully functional, have the same powers.[130] All Codes so issued give guidance on how discrimination can be avoided. A failure to follow such guidance will be highly relevant in determining whether in a particular case the burden of proof shifts,[131] and **14.28**

129 In *Tarbuck v Sainsbury's Supermarkets Limited* [2006] IRLR 664, the Employment Appeal Tribunal suggested that the claimant did bear some burden of showing a failure to comply but such does not leave any room for a material application of the burden of proof law in reasonable adjustment cases. Further, it ignores the proactive role that the Code of Practice specifically requires of employers and which is in any event implicit within the duty to make reasonable adjustments. The employer's duty (as with other duties) to make reasonable adjustments does not depend upon receiving a request from the employee. The employee may have communication or other difficulties. The employer is under an obligation to take such steps as, objectively viewed, it is reasonable to take in order to limit or remove the particular disadvantage from the worker. Where a worker can demonstrate the existence of the disadvantage and demonstrate that it remained present throughout the period covered by the allegations of discrimination, the burden of proof should operate so as to require the employer to explain why he did not act so as to remove that disadvantage.

130 EA, ss 14 and 15.

whether unlawful discrimination has occurred. All are admissible in proceedings under the SDA, RRA, and DDA and *shall* be taken into account when relevant to any question arising in the proceedings.[132] See further Chapter 15.

14.29 Further, provision is made for the serving of questionnaires under the main anti-discrimination enactments. This recognizes the difficulties in identifying whether discrimination has occurred, and allows for questions to be asked of an alleged discriminator, with sanctions for failures to respond or for equivocal or unsatisfactory answers.[133] Under this procedure, a potential claimant can serve a list of questions in a prescribed form on potential defendants. The questions might be used to obtain documents, statistical data, information on the normal practice in a particular situation, and a pre-claim explanation for any adverse treatment. Questionnaires are therefore very important tools and should be carefully drafted. The questionnaire and any answers given will be admissible as evidence where the questionnaire was served before proceedings have been instituted, if it was so served before expiry of the limitation period, or, after proceedings have been instituted, with the leave of the court in claims heard in the County Court, or within 21 days after proceedings have been instituted in an employment tribunal, or with leave of the tribunal thereafter.[134] If the questionnaire is admissible, then the court or tribunal will be entitled to consider the answers to the questionnaire and, importantly, draw any inference it considers just and equitable, including an inference that the defendant has committed an unlawful act, from any delay (that is, a failure to reply within eight weeks or a reasonable period, depending upon the activity[135]) in answering the

131 See para 14.20 above.

132 SDA, s 56A(10); RRA, ss 47(10), 71(C)(11); DDA, ss 3(3), 51(5) and 53A(8A); EA, s 15(4).

133 SDA, s 74; RRA, s 65 and DDA, s 56; EA, s 70; Religion or Belief Regulations, regulation 33; Sexual Orientation Regulations, regulation 33; and Age Regulations, regulation 41. The forms are prescribed under the Sex Discrimination (Questions and Replies) Order 1975 SI 1975/ 2048; the Race Relations (Questions and Replies) Order 1977 SI 1977/842; the Disability Discrimination (Questions and Replies) Order 2004 SI 2004/1168; the Disability Discrimination (Questions and Replies) Order 2005, SI 2005/2703 and the Religion or Belief Regulations, Sexual Orientation Regulations, and Age Regulations themselves; and EPA s 7B and Equal Pay (Questions and Replies) Order 2003, SI 2003/722.

134 Sex Discrimination (Questions and Replies) Order 1975 SI 1975/ 2048, Arts 4 and 5; the Race Relations (Questions and Replies) Order 1977 SI 1977/842, Arts 4 and 5; Disability Discrimination (Questions and Replies) Order 2004 SI 2004/1168, Art 4 and the Disability Discrimination (Questions and Replies) Order 2005, SI 2005/2703, Art 3; Religion or Belief Regulations, regulation 33(3) and (4); Sexual Orientation Regulations, regulation 33(3) and (4); and Age Regulations, regulation 41(3) and (4).

135 In summary, the eight-week threshold applies to discrimination in the employment and related fields (except in the case of race discrimination where it applies to all claims of discrimination connected to race, ethnicity, or national origins, and except in the case of disability, where the eight-week threshold always applies) otherwise the period prescribed is a 'reasonable' period; SDA,

questionnaire, or from evasive or equivocal answers.[136] A court is unlikely to draw such an inference if the questions are oppressive or irrelevant.

F. Remedies

Remedies for claims of discrimination closely match the remedies available in other claims for breach of a statutory tort.[137] Compensation may be awarded, including compensation for injury to feelings[138] and aggravated damages.[139] Compensation is otherwise generally to be assessed in the same way as with any other statutory tort.[140] Exemplary damages may be awarded in an appropriate case.[141] Exemplary damages may be awarded where there has been oppressive, **14.30**

s 74(2)(b) and (2A); RRA, s 65(2)(b); DDA, s 56(3)(b); Religion or Belief Regulations, regulation 33(2)(b); Sexual Orientation Regulations, regulation 33(2)(b); and Age Regulations, regulation 41(2)(b). Exceptions are made in relation to claims relating to prosecutorial functions where the person to whom the question is addressed reasonably believes that an answer or a particular answer might prejudice a criminal investigation (SDA, s 21A(7); RRA, s 65(4A)–(c); DDA, s 56(6)).

[136] SDA, s 74(2)(b); RRA, s 65(2)(b); DDA, s 56(3)(b); Religion or Belief Regulations, regulation 33(2)(b); Sexual Orientation Regulations, regulation 33(2)(b); and Age Regulations, regulation 41(2)(b). Exceptions are made in relation to claims relating to prosecutorial functions where the person to whom the question is addressed reasonably believes that an answer or a particular answer might prejudice a criminal investigation (SDA, s 21A(7); RRA, s 65(4A)–(c); DDA, s 56(6)).

[137] SDA, ss 65(1) and 66(1); RRA, ss 56(1) and 57(1); DDA, ss 17A(2) and 25(1)–(2); EA, s 68(2); Religion or Belief Regulations, regulation 30; Sexual Orientation Regulations, regulation 30; and Age Regulations, regulation 38(1). See *Essa v Laing Ltd* [2004] ICR 746; [2004] IRLR 313; *Atos Origin IT Services Ltd v Haddock* [2005] IRLR 20 (the same rules apply on payments from third parties as a court will apply in a PI action); *Aon Training Ltd v Dore* [2005] IRLR 891 (normal rules of mitigation apply); *HM Prison Service v Beart (No 2)* [2005] EWCA Civ 467, [2005] IRLR 568 (defendant cannot rely on its own further wrong to break the chain of causation). Awards of interest in the County Court are regulated by s 69 of the County Courts Act 1984 and in Scotland by the Act of Sederunt (Interest in Sheriff Court Decrees or Extracts) 1975 (And, Act of Sederunt (Interest in Sheriff Court Decrees and Extracts) 1993); Employment Tribunals (Interest on Awards in Discrimination Cases) Regulations 1996, SI 1996/2803.

[138] SDA, s 66(4); RRA, s 57(4); DDA, ss 17A(4) and 25(2); EA, s 68(4); Religion or Belief Regulations, regulation 30(1)(b) and 31(3); Sexual Orientation Regulations, regulation 30(1)(b) and 31(3); and Age Regulations, regulation 38(1). See *Vento v Chief Constable of West Yorkshire (No 2)* [2003] ICR 31; [2003] IRLR 102; *HM Prison Service v Johnson* [1997] ICR 275, 283B.

[139] *HM Prison Service v Beart (No 2)* [2005] EWCA Civ 467; [2005] ICR 1206; [2005] IRLR 568; *Atos Origin IT Services Ltd v Haddock* [2005] IRLR 20; *HM Prison Service v Johnson* [1997] ICR 275; *British Telecommunications v Reid* [2004] IRLR 327 CA; *HM Prison Service v Salmon* [2001] IRLR 125; *Ministry of Defence v Meredith* [1995] IRLR 539; *Virgo Fidelis Senior School v Boyle* [2003] IRLR 268.

[140] *Hurley v Mustoe (No 2)* [1983] ICR 422; *Essa v Laing Ltd* [2004] ICR 746.

[141] Exemplary damages may be awarded in discrimination claims in principle, if the other conditions for such an award are made out: *Virgo Fidelis Senior School v Boyle* [2003] IRLR 268. Until recently they were not available (*Broome v Cassell & Co* [1972] AC 1027; *Deane v London Borough of Ealing* [1993] IRLR 209) but the decision of the House of Lords in *Kuddus (AP) v Chief Constable of Leicestershire Constabulary* [2001] UKHL 29; [2002] 2 AC 122 changes the position.

arbitrary, or unconstitutional action by servants of the Government, or where the defendant's conduct has been calculated by him to make a profit for himself which may well exceed the compensation payable to the claimant.[142] The requirements of 'oppressive, arbitrary or unconstitutional' action are disjunctive: only one need be established to make good a claim for exemplary damages.[143] The facility to award such damages gives effect to the normative, deterrent, and punitive objectives[144] of the main anti-discrimination enactments and would meet the requirements of 'equivalence' found in EU law,[145] at least in respect of claims in the County Court.[146] The remedial powers directed at pecuniary sanctions in the employment tribunals (unlike the County Court) are limited to awards of 'compensation' and exemplary damages do not constitute 'compensation' as the expression is usually understood. Exemplary damages are not primarily focused on compensating a victim but instead on punishing a tortfeasor. Nevertheless, the power to award 'compensation' under the main anti-discrimination enactments is described as extending to 'an amount corresponding to any damages' that could be awarded in the County Court, and accordingly exemplary damages are probably available in both the employment tribunals and County Courts.

14.31 The only exception to the general power to award compensation relates to claims of indirect discrimination, outside the areas covered by the amended Equal Treatment Directive, the Race Directive, and the Framework Directive. In such cases, no compensation will be awarded where the discriminator proves that the offending requirement or condition was not applied with the intention of treating the claimant unfavourably on grounds of sex, race, or religion or belief, as the case may be.[147] These exceptions do not apply to those areas falling within the scope of the Directives because, as is implicit in their repeal in those areas, they would constitute a breach of the EU principle of effectiveness and the requirement for an

142 *Kuddus (AP) v Chief Constable of Leicestershire Constabulary* [2001] UKHL 29; [2002] 2 AC 122; Diana.

143 *Holden v Chief Constable of Lancashire* [1987] QB 380.

144 *Jones v Tower Boot Ltd* [1997] ICR 254 at 262, [1997] IRLR 168 at para 31, *per* Waite LJ.

145 *Levez v TH Jennings (Harlow Pools) Ltd* C-326/96 [1999] IRLR 36; *Alabaster v Barclays Bank Plc (formerly Woolwich plc) and Secretary of State for Social Security (No 2)* [2005] EWCA Civ 508; [2005] ICR 1246; [2005] IRLR 576, see further Chap 4.

146 Other statutory torts may result in awards of exemplary damages, *Kuddus (AP) v Chief Constable of Leicestershire Constabulary* [2001] UKHL 29; [2002] 2 AC 122.

147 SDA, s 66(3); RRA, s 57(3); EA, s 68(3). Other remedies, including declaratory relief and recommendations, may be granted. There is a further limitation in SDA, s 65(1B); Religion or Belief Regulations, regulation 30(2); Sexual Orientation Regulations, regulation 30(2); and Age Regulations, regulation 38(2), applicable to cases within the scope of the amended Equal Treatment Directive and the Framework Directive, but the limitation is minimal and it has had no practical effect.

effective remedy contained within the Directives.[148] The exceptions should in any event be read strictly[149] and, particularly given the extensive statutory guidance that exists to help prevent inadvertent discrimination, should rarely be applicable. Intention for the purposes of these exceptions:

> signifies the state of mind of a person who, at the time when he does the relevant act (ie, the application of the requirement or condition resulting in indirect discrimination) (a) wants to bring about the state of affairs which constitutes the prohibited result of unfavourable treatment on racial grounds; and (b) knows that that prohibited result will follow from his acts.[150]

The 'intention' condition does not require any particular motivation on the part of a discriminator. It is not necessary for the discriminator to have a reason connected with the main anti-discrimination enactments which causes him to act as he does. It is concerned only with the state of mind of the discriminator in relation to the consequences of his acts. A discriminator intends the consequences to follow from his acts if he knew when he did them that those consequences would follow and if he wanted those consequences to follow, and relevant intention may be inferred from that knowledge. A discriminator must show a state of non-intention to treat unfavourably on the protected ground and, adopting a purposive approach to the main anti-discrimination enactments, this will be difficult if he has ignored the relevant statutory Codes of Practice; otherwise the scheme of the enactments would be undermined. The enactments provide for the publishing of statutory Codes of Practice (reflecting the normative functions of the enactments[151]), which a truly innocent discriminator should have attempted, at least, to follow.

In the employment tribunals there is an additional power to make 'recommendations'.[152] These are non-binding orders which must be directed at 'obviating or reducing the adverse effect on the complainant' of any act of discrimination or harassment to which the complaint relates.[153] This is a limited power[154] and does not extend to the making of orders directed at broader strategic change. Where **14.32**

148 See Chap 4.

149 *Hampson v Department of Education and Science* [1991] 1AC 171, at 182.

150 *JH Walker Ltd v Hussain* [1996] ICR 291, at 299.

151 *Jones v Tower Boot Ltd* [1997] ICR 254, at 262.

152 SDA, s 65(1)(c); RRA, s 56(1)(c); DDA, s 17A(2)(c); Religion or Belief Regulations, regulation 30(1)(c); Sexual Orientation Regulations, regulation 30(1)(c); and Age Regulations, regulation 38(1)(c).

153 The DDA contains a somewhat wider power to make an order 'obviating or reducing the adverse effect on the complainant of *any matter to which the complaint* relates', s 7A2)(c). *British Gas v Sharma* [1991] IRLR 101 and *Noone v North West Thames RHA (No 2)* [1988] IRLR 530 must be viewed in that light.

154 *British Gas v Sharma* [1991] IRLR 101 and *Noone v North West Thames RHA (No 2)* [1988] IRLR 530.

an employment tribunal makes a recommendation and 'without reasonable justification' the respondent fails to comply with it, then 'if it thinks it just and equitable to do so', the employment tribunal may increase the amount of any compensatory award or, if an order of compensation was not made, make such an order.[155]

14.33 Awards of interest in the County Court are regulated by section 69 of the County Courts Act 1984 and in Scotland by the Act of Sederunt (Interest in Sheriff Court Decrees or Extracts) 1975.[156] Interest on financial losses is likely to be calculated on the same basis as in the employment tribunals, though it is unclear as to what rate would apply on awards for injury to feelings.[157]

14.34 As to the remedies available to SENDIST, the DDA[158] provides that the tribunal may 'declare' that the complainant (pupil or prospective pupil) has been discriminated against and, if it does so, it may make 'such order as it considers reasonable in all the circumstances of the case'.[159] Such orders may, in particular, be exercised with a view to obviating or reducing the adverse effect on the person concerned of any matter to which the claim relates.[160] It has no power to make an award of compensation in respect of a claim under the DDA.[161] If a claim of unlawful discrimination is successful, SENDIST can make a declaration that a child has been unlawfully discriminated against, and it can order any remedy it thinks reasonable against the responsible body, with the exception of financial compensation.[162]

14.35 As for claims under the EPA, the EPA gives rise to contractual rights and as such damages for a breach of the 'equality clause' are contractual. Typically damages will be sought but declaratory and injunctive relief is also available in the High Court and County Courts.[163] Originally recovery of damages was limited to arrears in respect of the two years immediately preceding the commencement of proceedings

---

155 SDA, s 65(3); RRA, s 56(4); DDA, s 17A(5); Religion or Belief Regulations, regulation 30(3); Sexual Orientation Regulations, regulation 30(3); and Age Regulations, regulation 38(3).

156 And, Act of Sederunt (Interest in Sheriff Court Decrees and Extracts) 1993.

157 By comparison, interest is usually assessed at the rate of 2% flat per annum from the date of presentation of the claim to the date of computation on personal injury awards for pain, suffering, and loss of amenity. See Employment Tribunals (Interest on Awards in Discrmination Cases) Regulations, 1996 SI 1996/2803.

158 DDA, s 28I.

159 Ibid, s 28I(3).

160 Ibid, s 28I(4)(a).

161 Ibid, s 28I(4)(b).

162 Examples of the sorts of awards that might be made can be seen in the 'Disability Discrimination Act 1995 Part IV, Code of Practice for Schools' (2002) Disability Rights Commission, COPSH July 2002, para 9.11. The Code came into force on 1 Sept 2002: Disability Discrimination Code of Practice (Education) (Appointed Day) Order 2002 SI 2002/2216.

163 EPA, s 2.

in all cases,[164] but this limitation was found to be incompatible with EU law.[165] In consequence of this and general concerns about its compliance with EU law, the EPA was amended so that the position now is that the period in respect of which arrears of pay may be recovered is increased to six years in England and Wales, and five years in Scotland. These periods reflect the limitation period for actions for breach of contract in the two jurisdictions. In cases where there has been concealment of facts by the employer relevant to his failure to comply with the equality clause, and without knowledge of which the woman could not reasonably have been expected to institute proceedings, the period in respect of which arrears may be recovered goes back to the date of the contravention of the equality clause, and may be longer than six years (or five in Scotland), but (in Scotland) may not be more than 20 years.[166] However, proceedings must have been instituted by the woman within six years of the day on which she discovered the fact, or could with reasonable diligence have discovered it. In cases where the woman is suffering from a disability (that is, is a minor or of 'unsound mind'[167]) the same principle applies, that is, the period over which arrears of pay can be awarded may also be extended to more than six (or five) years, but (in Scotland) it may not be more than 20 years.[168] Again, proceedings must be instituted within six years of the day on which the woman ceased to be under a disability. The periods of six or five years for England and Wales and Scotland respectively reflect compliance with the principle of equivalence, these being the periods which apply in claims for breach of contract. Different rules apply in relation to a claim in respect of access to an occupational pension scheme.[169]

Specific provisions address settlement agreements the terms of which oust the jurisdiction of the courts or tribunals. Such 'compromise agreements' are exempt from the provisions rendering void contractual provisions ousting the jurisdiction of the courts and tribunals, where they meet certain conditions.[170] **14.36**

---

164 Ibid, s 2(5).

165 *Levez v TH Jennings (Harlow Pools) Ltd* C-326/96 [1999] IRLR 36.

166 EPA, ss 2ZB(1)–(4), 2ZC(1), (3). See s 7A–C for analogous provision in relation to claims arising from service in armed forces.

167 Which has the same meaning as in s 38(2) of the Limitation Act 1980, EPA, s 11(2A)(a). Similar provision is made for Scotland, EPA, s 11(2A)(b).

168 EPA, ss 2ZB, 2ZC.

169 An individual is entitled to complain of, and secure a remedy in respect of, a denial of access going back to 1976—the date of *Defrenne v Sabena (No 2)* 43/75 [1976] ECR 455, ECJ, see Chap 4; *Preston v Wolverhampton Healthcare NHS Trust (No 2)* [2001] IRLR 237; *Magorrian and Cunningham v Eastern Health and Social Services Board and Department of Health and Social Services*: C-246/96 [1998] IRLR 86. See further and for members of schemes regulations 5(7), 6A and 7, Occupational Pension Schemes (Equal Treatment) Regulations (OPSR) 1995, SI 1996/3183.

170 SDA, s 77(4)–(4C); RRA, s 72(4)–(4C)RRA; DDA, Sch 3A, Part 1, paras 2(1)–(8); EA, s 72(4); Religion or Belief Regulations, regulation 35 and Sch 4, para 2(1)–(8); Sexual Orientation Regulations, regulation 35 and Sch 4, para 2(1)–(8); and Age Regulations, regulation 43 and Sch 5, para 2(1)–(8).

14.37 As seen, the remedial powers available to courts and tribunals are limited. They are directed at remedying damage suffered by individual victims of discrimination. In particular, the courts and tribunals have no power to direct that strategic action be taken by a discriminator directed at avoiding further acts of discrimination, following a finding of unlawful discrimination. Given the prevalence of 'repeat offenders' in the courts and tribunals, this might be regarded as a weakness in the main anti-discrimination enactments. Some other jurisdictions have broader remedial powers, some of which are directed at deterrence and some of which are directed at ensuring, by the application of proper processes, changes in procedure etc, so that objectionable discrimination does not recur.[171]

[171] See, for example, s 21 of South Africa's Promotion of Equality and Prevention of Unfair Discrimination Act 2000, which gives an 'equality court' power, *inter alia*, to direct that a respondent undergo an audit of specific policies or practices; to make 'an order to make specific opportunities and privileges unfairly denied in the circumstances, available to the complainant in question [and make] an order for the implementation of special measures to address the unfair discrimination . . . [and] an order directing the reasonable accommodation of a group or class of persons by the respondent . . . '; to direct that progress reports be made to a court or to a relevant constitutional institution (ie, a commission) in relation to the implementation of a court's order. Deterrent measures may also be directed, including by a power to make 'recommendation to the appropriate authority, to suspend or revoke the licence of a person' (s 21).

Part IV

STRATEGIC ACTION, STATUTORY DUTIES, AND COMMISSIONS

15

STRATEGIC ACTION AND THE COMMISSIONS

A. Introduction

This chapter addresses the strategic action that might be taken under the main anti-discrimination enactments, rather than individual remedial action which is described in Chapter 14. Important strategic mechanisms arise from the establishment of the statutory equality Commissions and the statutory duties imposed on public authorities, both of which are discussed below. 15.01

15.02 As to the Commissions, the Sex Discrimination Act 1975 (SDA) and the Race Relations Act 1976 (RRA) in their original enactments established the Commission for Racial Equality (CRE) and the Equal Opportunities Commission (EOC),[1] with various powers including the exclusive power to bring proceedings under certain of the unlawful acts created under the enactments, the power to undertake formal investigations, and the power to issue statutory Codes of Practice.[2] The DDA did not create for disability a body comparable to the CRE or the EOC. Instead the DDA established the National Disability Council[3] the main duty of which was to advise the Secretary of State. Whether on its own initiative or when asked to do so by the Secretary of State, the National Disability Council was expected to advise the Secretary of State on matters relevant to the elimination of discrimination against disabled people, and on matters related to the operation of the DDA and of provision made under the DDA.[4] Overall it was a much weaker institution than the EOC and the CRE. Following the election of the Labour Government in 1997 and their pre-election manifesto commitment to 'comprehensive and enforceable civil rights for disabled people',[5] the Disability Rights Task Force was established.[6] They first reported in April 1998 highlighting the problems caused by the lack of an enforcement body responsible for ensuring compliance with the DDA. In response, the Government published a White Paper in July 1998, *Promoting Disabled Peoples Rights—Creating a Disability Rights Commission Fit for the 21st Century*.[7] The White Paper identified that a Disability Rights Commission was essential if the rights of disabled people were truly to be recognized, and if business and the public and voluntary sectors were to have the consistent and central support they needed. The Disability Rights Commission Act 1999 (DRCA) was enacted shortly afterwards; this established the Disability Rights Commission (DRC). Its powers more closely match those of the EOC and CRE.[8]

---

[1] SDA, s 53; RRA, s 43.

[2] Each of which is discussed below.

[3] DDA, s 50(1).

[4] Amongst others, DDA, s 50(2). In discharging such duties, the National Disability Council was required to have regard to the extent and nature of the benefits which would be likely to result from the implementation of any recommendation it made and the likely cost of implementing any such recommendation and where reasonably practicable they were required to make an assessment of the likely cost and likely financial benefits which would result from implementing any recommendation: DDA, s 50(5) and (6).

[5] See reference to the same in the Introduction to the White Paper *Promoting Disabled Peoples Rights, Creating a Disability Rights Commission Fit for the 21st Century* (July 1998) CM 3977. See Chap 2.

[6] Discussed in Chap 2.

[7] CM 3977.

[8] In Northern Ireland a single equality body, the Equality Commission for Northern Ireland, was established by ss 73–4 of the Northern Ireland Act 1998.

The proliferation of new law addressing discrimination on grounds other than sex, race, and disability led to increasing calls for a single equality Commission. In addition, the enactment of the Human Rights Act 1998 (HRA) prompted calls for institutional support for the protection of human rights. The original architects of the HRA saw the establishment of such a Commission as an essential component of a three-pronged system for the protection of human rights in this country, together with the passing of the Act itself and the establishment of the Parliamentary Joint Committee on Human Rights (JCHR). To that extent, the setting up of the Commission was seen as 'unfinished business'.[9] Further impetus for a Commission came from research demonstrating that the human rights 'culture' expected from the enactment of the HRA had not been achieved by the HRA alone.[10] As is addressed below,[11] a single Commission for Equality and Human Rights (CEHR) has been established by the Equality Act 2006 (EA), and in due course it will assume the functions of the EOC, the CRE, and the DRC. **15.03**

The proposal for a single Commission was first trailed by the Government in its consultation paper on the implementation of the Race and Framework Directives: *Towards Equality and Diversity; Making it Happen.*[12] The CRE and EOC were **15.04**

---

[9] F Klug, 'The Commission for Equality and Human Rights: Where Now for Human Rights Protection in the UK?', (unpublished) seminar, 12 July 2005.

[10] A report by the British Institute of Human Rights in December 2002 concluded that 'there is no serious attempt from either government or the voluntary sector to use the Human Rights Act to create a human rights culture that could in turn lead to systemic change in the provision of services by public authorities', and found that: 'The Act has simply not had an impact in the [voluntary sector], leaving many vulnerable people open to abuses of their rights. Yet without an independent body of some kind to promote the Human Rights Act and the principles that it upholds this situation is unlikely to change' (British Institute for Human Rights, *Something for Everyone: The impact of the Human Rights Act and the need for a Human Rights Commission* (London, 2002), 8); the Sixth Report of the JCHR concluded that '. . . [t]here is no vision, no administrative framework and scant guidance reaching public authorities to tell them how a culture of respect for human rights might look or how it can be delivered' (JCHR, Sixth Report, *The Case for a Human Rights Commission* (2002–3 HL 67; HC 489), 29); the 2003 Audit Commission report concluded that 58% of public bodies had not adopted a strategy for human rights and had no clear corporate approach, demonstrating no improvement on the findings for 2002 (Audit Commission, *Human Rights: Improving Public Service Delivery* (London, 2003), para 12); and a report on behalf of the Institute of Public Policy Research for the Department of Constitutional Affairs concluded that '[t]he HRA has not yet been of sufficiently demonstrable value in improving standards in public services as the Government intended when the Act was passed.' In particular, there was 'insufficient awareness of the legal principle of 'positive obligations' to protect human rights' which was worsened by '. . . the current confusion about which private and voluntary organizations constitute public authorities for the purposes of legal liability under the HRA . . . ' which was '. . . perpetrating an injustice particularly experienced by vulnerable people . . . ' (Institute for Public Policy Research, *Improving Public Services: Using a Human Rights Approach* (2005, London), 4–5).

[11] Para 15.57.

[12] *Towards Equality and Diversity: Implementing the Employment and Race Directives* (2002, Cabinet Office and DTI), vii. See Chap 4 for the Directives.

initially supportive of the proposal to create a single equality body, although they stressed the need for thoroughgoing reform of the discrimination legislation,[13] a point made also by the DRC which was, however, less than enthusiastic about the prospects of amalgamation.[14]

15.05 In May 2004 the Government published the White Paper, *Fairness for All: A New Commission for Equality and Human Rights*[15] which set out detailed proposals for the creation of the new Commission, and asserted that the new body would bring benefits, amongst other things, as a single 'strong and authoritative champion for equality and human rights', that it would 'incorporate a depth of expertise on specific areas of discrimination, while also being able to cast a wide net across all equality and human rights issues', that it would, as a single body, be more user-friendly both to potential claimants and to employers and service providers, and 'be better equipped to address the reality of the many dimensions of an individual's identity, and therefore tackle discrimination on multiple grounds'.[16] The Government, however, at that stage adopted a tone which suggested they favoured a 'light touch' Commission, with a focus on 'promotional' activities over enforcement. The DRC, EOC, and CRE all expressed concerns about, amongst other things, the 'light touch' emphasis of the White Paper,[17] the adequacy of resources intended to be made available to the proposed CEHR, and the absence of any commitment to harmonized equality legislation. Concern was also raised in response to the proposals which implied that there may be some narrowing of the Commissions' powers to conduct formal investigations and to support litigation. The CRE, which had supported the proposal for a single Commission in principle, was extremely critical of the White Paper and rejected the proposals for the Commission, stating that it would be 'less a single champion enforcing strong legislation, and more a hopeful chorus of voices, which [*Fairness for All*] speculates can be made to sing in tune'.[18] The CRE went on to express its 'main concerns' with the White Paper, listing no fewer than 18 perceived instances of 'downgrading [of] powers or direct legal detriment'; and 10 'instances of clear detriment to equality, including unclear or unworkable proposals'. In particular, the CRE was extremely

[13] See for example EOC, *Towards Equality And Diversity—Making It Happen: A Response From The Equal Opportunities Commission*, paras 3–6.

[14] Disability Rights Commission Briefing on *Equality and Diversity: Making It Happen*.

[15] Cm 6185.

[16] White Paper, *Fairness for All: A New Commission for Equality and Human Rights* (2004) Cm 6185, 17.

[17] See the DRC, *Government White Paper 'Fairness for All', Response from the DRC*: <http://www.drc-gb.org/about_us/commission_for_equality_and_hu/response_from_the_disability_r.aspx>.

[18] CRE, *Fairness for All: A New Commission for Equality and Human Rights, A Response* (August 2004): <http://www.cre.gov.uk/downloads/ffa_cre_response.doc>.

concerned about the change in emphasis from enforcement: whereas, under the current provisions, the law enforcement duty, 'to work towards the elimination of discrimination' is the first for each of the Commissions, the White Paper listed it as the fourth of five duties, all the rest of which were concerned with promotion. According to the CRE '[t]his reversal suggests a downgrading of the duty', while the CRE's powers to enforce were in its view downgraded by the White Paper's categorization of law enforcement as 'complementary and secondary', to be 'used sparingly and in the last resort', rather than strategically as at present. The CRE was also very critical, as were the other Commissions, of the proposed tightening of the criteria for the direct support of litigation. Section 66(1) of the RRA and the other anti-discrimination provisions[19] give the Commissions power to support litigation, within their resources, where 'the case raises a question of principle; or it is unreasonable, having regard to the complexity of the case, or to the applicant's position in relation to the respondent or another person involved, or to any other matter, to expect the applicant to deal with the case unaided; or by reason of any other special consideration'. The White Paper suggested that cases might only be supported where they 'raise a question of principle', 'affect large numbers of people', or 'flag up the need for legislative change'. Finally, the CRE was alarmed by the apparent intention to tighten, rather than to improve and strengthen, powers to formally investigate.

The establishment of the Equalities and Discrimination Law Reviews[20] influenced the CRE's change of stance on the CEHR, as did the manifesto commitment to a Single Equality Act. In its briefing paper on the Equality Bill, however, the CRE drew attention to 'a number of issues in the legislation which [they remained] concerned about', as well as stressing the fundamental importance of the new Commission's independence from Government and of non-regression ('there must, as a minimum, be no diminution of scope, powers and resources to promote equality of opportunity and eliminate discrimination on the existing grounds of race, sex and disability [and] . . . powers and duties should be harmonized upwards'). The CRE called both for the provision to the CEHR of 'sufficient and secure resources' and for 'clarity, coherence and consistency where appropriate' in any forthcoming Single Equality Act.[21] The CRE expressed particular concern too that: **15.06**

> the CEHR will not be able to focus properly on community relations, extremism and integration issues. These will be lost within a unified body that must deal with

19 SDA, s 75(1); DRCA, s 7.
20 Chap 1.
21 June 2005.

> anti-discrimination across seven separate and distinct strands. Much of the CRE's work may be effectively 'orphaned' inside an organisation focused on legal and monitoring activities; work on integration and developing good community relations may rapidly become a poor relation. The CRE has tried to tackle issues on the ground, but is held back by a lack of funds and bureaucracy. The CEHR, with seven strands to cover, will also not have the time, the focus or the funding. There is also no guarantee that the CEHR will support the current network of local organizations, including race equality councils, which work hard with the CRE to promote integration.[22]

The CRE repeatedly expressed concern then that the CEHR would not meet the needs of black and ethnic minority communities and was otherwise 'not right for race'.[23]

15.07 Nevertheless the amendments made between the White Paper and the publication of the Equality Bill in 2004 resulted in a change of position on the part of the CRE, which in June 2005 declared that it welcomed the Equality Bill. These amendments included provision for the dissolution of the EOC, CRE, and DRC not later than 31 March 2009, thereby allowing the CRE to negotiate for its later dissolution and entry to the CEHR, in 2009.[24] The appointment of Trevor Philips, then chair of the CRE, to the position of first chair of the CEHR was announced on 8 September 2006. In what must be regarded as an historic *volte face*, the CRE decided almost immediately that the 'advantages of a simultaneous entry clearly out-weigh the disadvantages of late entry' and 'therefore unanimously agreed that the advice to the Secretary of State' 'should be a common entry date of October 2007'.[25] It seems inevitable, then, that they will not now defer their entry to the CEHR but will instead join in October 2007, with the EOC and DRC.

15.08 The Commission for Equality and Human Rights,[26] as it is known, will come into being in October 2007. At that time it will take over the functions of the EOC, the DRC, and, it now appears, the CRE.[27] It will assume new powers and

22 'The Equality Bill, the Commission for Equality and Human Rights and why we need a new body to deal with Community Relations', CRE, <http://www.cre.gov.uk/policy/newbody.html>.

23 CRE statement on the Commission for Equality and Human Rights, 16 January 2006, at <http://www.cre.gov.uk/Default.aspx.LocID-0hgnew09t.RefLocID-0hg00900c002.Lang-EN.htm>.

24 Reflected in their 'Corporate Plan' for 2006–09, available at <http://www.cre.gov.uk/policy/corporateplan.html>. See too, the CRE's statement at <http://www.cre.gov.uk/policy/newbody.html>.

25 Leaked e-mail reported by Black Information Link, at <http://www.blink.org.uk/pdescription.asp?grp=44&cat=356&key=12636> and confirmed by the CRE information office in a telephone call with the author on 9 Oct 2006.

26 Established by EA, Part 1 and Schs 1–3.

27 Which will all be dissolved, subject to any transitional functions, EA, ss 36 and 42.

duties in relation to religion and belief, sexual orientation, and age. It will also have powers to provide institutional support in relation to the promotion of human rights.

15.09 The Commissions have important functions in the overall anti-discrimination schemes found in the main anti-discrimination enactments. They have, in theory at least, the capacity and powers to secure broader remedial action and influence law reform. Both the Race Directive[29] and the amended Equal Treatment Directive[28] (but not the Framework Directive[30]) require Member States to designate a body or bodies 'for the promotion of equal treatment of all persons without discrimination on the grounds of racial or ethnic origin' and 'for the promotion of, analysis, monitoring and support of equal treatment of all persons without discrimination on the grounds of sex', respectively. The competences of such bodies must include the power to provide independent assistance to victims of discrimination in pursuing their complaints about discrimination; the power conduct independent surveys concerning discrimination, and power to publish independent reports and make recommendations on any issue relating to such discrimination.[31] Such bodies 'may form part of agencies charged at national level with the defence of human rights or the safeguard of individuals' rights'. These obligations are presently given effect to through the statutory Commissions. However, arguably a specific body (even if within a larger body) is required by the Directives to meet the obligations under them in respect of race, sex equality, and a single Commission without designated specialist provision would not meet the requirements of the Directives. This is discussed further below at paragraph 15.60.

[28] Equal Treatment Directive, Art 8a. See, also Art 6(3) ('Member States shall ensure that associations, organisations or other legal entities which have, in accordance with the criteria laid down by their national law, a legitimate interest in ensuring that the provisions of this Directive are complied with, may engage, either on behalf or in support of the complainant, with his or her approval, in any judicial and/or administrative procedure provided for the enforcement of obligations under this Directive.'). The Gender Goods and Services Directive makes the same provisions at Art 12.

[29] Article 13. See also, Article 7(2) 'Member States shall ensure that associations, organizations or other legal entities, which have, in accordance with the criteria laid down by their national law, a legitimate interest in ensuring that the provisions of this Directive are complied with, may engage, either on behalf or in support of the complainant, with his or her approval, in any judicial and/or administrative procedure provided for the enforcement of obligations under this Directive.').

[30] But see Art 9(2) ('Member States shall ensure that associations, organisations or other legal entities which have, in accordance with the criteria laid down by their national law, a legitimate interest in ensuring that the provisions of this Directive are complied with, may engage, either on behalf or in support of the complainant, with his or her approval, in any judicial and/or administrative procedure provided for the enforcement of obligations under this Directive.').

[31] Amended Equal Treatment Directive, Art 8a; Framework Directive, Art 13.

15.10 In addition to the important functions of the Commissions, the RRA,[32] SDA,[33] and DDA[34] create important statutory duties. These statutory duties are an important tool for mainstreaming equality policy and practice. Their origins lie, in the first place, in the RRA which was amended following the Stephen Lawrence Inquiry Report and its identification of 'institutional discrimination'. This led to legal reform to address such discrimination, and that included the creation of positive duties on public authorities to address race discrimination.[35] The DDA and then the SDA were amended thereafter to add similar duties in respect of disability and sex. The details of the duties are explored below (Section D). As discussed further below, the DDA also imposes statutory duties on certain private service providers with important strategic impact.

15.11 In summary, the duties fall into three groups. Firstly, general duties are imposed on public authorities requiring that they have 'due regard' to the need to achieve certain equality objectives (including the promotion of equality of opportunity and the elimination of unlawful discrimination and harassment). Secondly, specific duties are imposed on certain public authorities, requiring that they take designated action. The equality Commissions have various responsibilities and powers for securing compliance with these duties. Thirdly, specific disability duties are imposed on certain transport providers. The Commissions' powers and functions are addressed below, as are the content and impact of the statutory duties.

B. The Equal Opportunities Commission, the Commission for Racial Equality, and the Disability Rights Commission: Duties and Functions

15.12 The EOC, the CRE, and the DRC are non-departmental public bodies the members of which[36] are appointed by a designated Secretary of State,[37] to whom each

32 RRA, s 71 (as amended by the Race Relations (Amendment) Act 2000), in force from 2 April 2001, see SI 2001/566.

33 SDA, s 76A (as amended by the EA), in force from 6 April 2007, see SI 2006/1082.

34 DDA, s 49A, DDA (as amended by the DDA 2005), in force from 4 December 2006, see SI 2005/2774.

35 The Race Relations (Amendment) Act 2000.

36 EOC and CRE, 8–15 members (SDA, s 53; RRA, s 43), DRC, 10–15 members (DRCA, schedule).

37 SDA, s 53(2); RRA, s 43(2); and DRCA, Sch 1, para 2.

Commission must report annually.[38] The general duties of the Commissions are statutorily prescribed. The EOC's duties are:

> to work toward the elimination of discrimination; to work towards the elimination of harassment that is contrary to any of the provisions of this Act; to promote equality of opportunity between men and women generally; to promote equality of opportunity in the field of employment and of vocational training, for persons who intend to undergo, are undergoing or have undergone gender reassignment, and to keep under review the working of [the SDA and EPA] and, when ... required by the Secretary of State or otherwise think it necessary, draw up and submit to the Secretary of State proposals for amending them.[39]

The CRE's duties are:

> to work towards the elimination of discrimination and harassment; to promote equality of opportunity and good relations, between persons of different racial groups generally; and to keep under review the working of [the RRA] and, when they are so required by the Secretary of State or otherwise think it necessary, draw up and submit . . . proposals for amending it.[40]

The DRC's duties are:

> to work towards the elimination of discrimination against and harassment of disabled persons; to promote the equalisation of opportunities for disabled persons; to take such steps as it considers appropriate with a view to encouraging good practice in the treatment of disabled persons; and to keep under review the working of the Disability Discrimination Act 1995 and [the DRCA].[41]

These general duties will inform the scope of the powers granted under the SDA, RRA, and DRCA.

As to their powers, each Commission has a number of specific powers considered below. Further, each has implied powers to do that which is necessary to give effect to their duties, so that the absence of an express power will not prevent them taking otherwise lawful action in the performance of their general duties. This will include action by way of judicial review and third party interventions,[42] discussed further below. **15.13**

---

38 SDA, s 56; RRA, s 46; DRCA, Sch 1, para 16.

39 SDA, s 53(1)SDA as amended by Sex Discrimination (Gender Reassignment) Regulations 1999, SI 1999/1102, regulation 7(1) and Employment Equality (Sex Discrimination) Regulations 2005, SI 2005/2467, regulation 27.

40 RRA, s 43(1) as amended by Race Relations Act 1976 (Amendment) Regulations 2003, SI 2003/1626, regulation 36.

41 DRCA, s 2(1) as amended by Disability Discrimination Act 1995 (Amendment) Regulations 2003, regulation 30.

42 Eg, *R v Birmingham City Council ex p EOC* [1989] IRLR 173; *R v Secretary of State for Employment ex p EOC* [1994] IRLR 176; *Essa v Laing Ltd* [2004] ICR 746; [2004] IRLR 313 (Commissions intervening); *Igen Ltd v Wong* [2005] IRLR 258 (Commissions intervening).

(1) Codes of Practice

15.14 The Commissions have express powers to issue statutory Codes of Practice.[43] All three Commissions have power to issue Codes of Practice giving practical guidance on the elimination of discrimination and harassment and the promotion of equality of opportunity in the field of employment.[44] The CRE also has power to issue a Code of Practice in the field of housing,[45] and the DRC may issue Codes of Practice[46] giving guidance to service providers, private clubs, public authorities, educational institutions, and others on how to avoid acts which are unlawful under Parts 2, 3, or 4 of the DDA and to any person with a view to promoting the equalization of opportunities for disabled people, or encouraging good practice in any field within Parts 2, 3, or 4 of the DDA.[47] The EOC, CRE, and DRC may issue Codes of Practice on the duty to promote equality under the SDA, RRA, or DDA as appropriate.[48] The DRCA specifically gives the DRC power to issue non-statutory guidance,[49] but such power is implicit in the general duties of the Commissions, and the Commissions regularly issue non-statutory guidance.[50]

15.15 The statutory Codes of Practice may be relied upon in legal proceedings, to the effect that:

> [a] failure on the part of any person to observe any provision of a code of practice shall not of itself render that person liable to any proceedings; but in any proceedings under this Act before an [employment tribunal or a County Court or, in Scotland, a Sheriff Court] any code of practice issued under this section shall be admissible in evidence in legal proceedings under this Act, and if any provision of such a code appears to the tribunal [or the court] to be relevant to any question arising in the proceedings it shall be taken into account in determining that question.[51]

A failure to comply with a provision of a Code may also be highly relevant in determining whether an inference of discrimination might be drawn from any adverse treatment, for the purposes of proving discrimination or shifting the burden of proof.[52]

---

43 Such Codes must follow consultation and receive Parliamentary approval through the negative resolution procedure; SDA, s 56A, RRA, s 47, and DDA, s 53A.

44 SDA, s 56A(1); DDA, ss 47(1)(a) and (b), 53A(1)(a).

45 RRA, s 47(1)(c) and (d).

46 And the Secretary of State may issue statutory Guidance on the meaning of 'disability'; DDA, s 3.

47 DDA, s 53A(1).

48 SDA, s 76E; RRA, s 71C; and DDA, s 53A(1C).

49 DRCA, s 9(3).

50 Available on their websites at <http://www.cre.gov.uk/>; <http://www.eoc.org.uk/>; <http://www.drc-gb.org/>.

51 RRA, s 47(10) and in materially the same terms, RRA, s 71C(11); SDA, s 56A(10); and DDA, s 53A(8A).

52 See Chap 14.

Numerous statutory Codes have been issued and they have proved important in affecting awareness and practice.[53] The important Codes include the CRE's Code of Practice on Racial Equality in Employment (2005);[54] the CRE's Code of Practice on Racial Equality in Housing (2006);[55] the CRE's Code of Practice on the Duty to Promote Race Equality (2002);[56] the EOC's Code of Practice on Equal Pay (2003);[57] the EOC's Code of Practice on Sex Discrimination, Equal Opportunity Policies, Procedures and Practices in Employment (1985);[58] the DRC's Code of Practice on Employment and Occupation (2004);[59] the DRC's Code of Practice on Trade Organisations and Qualifications Bodies (2004);[60] the DRC's Code of Practice on Rights of Access: Services to Public, Public Authority Functions, Private Clubs and Premises (2006);[61] and the DRC's Code of Practice on the Provision and Use of Transport Vehicles (2006).[62] 15.16

(2) Formal investigations

All three Commissions[63] have power to conduct 'formal investigations' for any purpose connected with the carrying out of their duties.[64] They must carry out such investigations if required to do so by the Secretary of State.[65] 15.17

---

53 M Coussey, 'The Effectiveness of Strategic Enforcement of the Race Relations Act 1976', in B Hepple and E Szyszczak (eds), *Discrimination: the Limits of Law* (1992, Mansell) 35–49.

54 Race Relations Code of Practice Relating to Employment (Appointed Day) Order 2006 SI 2006/630.

55 Race Relations Code of Practice (Housing) (Appointed Day) Order 2006, SI 2006/2239.

56 CRE, ISBN 1 85442 430 0. Race Relations Act 1976 (General Statutory Duty: Code of Practice) Order 2002, SI 2002/1435.

57 Code of Practice on Equal Pay Order 2003, SI 2003/ 2865.

58 Sex Discrimination Code of Practice Order 1985, SI 1985/ 387. At the time of writing a new Code of Practice is expected from the EOC on the gender equality duty (which has been laid before Parliament, see <http://www.eoc.org.uk/Default.aspx?page=15016>).

59 (2004) DRC ISBN 0 11 703419 3; Disability Discrimination Codes of Practice (Employment and Occupation, and Trade Organisations and Qualifications Bodies) Appointed Day Order 2004, SI 2004/2302.

60 (2004) DRC ISBN 0 11 703418 5; Disability Discrimination Codes of Practice (Employment and Occupation, and Trade Organisations and Qualifications Bodies) Appointed Day Order 2004, SI 2004/2302.

61 (2006) DRC (Disability Discrimination Code of Practice (Services, Public Functions, Private Clubs and Premises) (Appointed Day) Order 2006 SI 2006/1967), bringing the code into force on 4 Dec 2006.

62 Disability Discrimination Code of Practice (Supplement to Part 3 Code of Practice) (Provision and Use of Transport Vehicles) (Appointed Day) Order 2006, SI 2006/1094.

63 The Commissions may delegate all or some of aspects of the investigation to its staff: *R v CRE ex p Cottrell and Rothon* [1980]IRLR 279.

64 SDA, s 57(1); RRA, s 48(1); DRCA, s 3(1) and (2). See *Home Office v CRE* [1981] 1 All ER 1042 (where there was not said to be of unlawful discrimination, but CRE were able to carry out an investigation for the purposes of its duty to promote equality of opportunity and good race relations).

65 Where a formal investigation is requested by the Secretary of State, then the SDA, RRA, and DRCA require the Commissions to involve the Secretary of State at various stages through the investigation process.

The formal investigation powers are very important indeed for the Commissions' work and were intended to be so. The White Papers which preceded the enactment of the SDA, RRA, and DRCA envisaged that the formal investigation powers would account for much of the law enforcement work of the EOC and the CRE.[66]

15.18 In fact, the powers have been used more sparingly than was expected, most particularly in recent years.[67] There are a number of possible explanations for this, but it is likely that a key reason concerns the courts' approach to the formal investigation powers in the early years of the RRA, in particular when the judiciary demonstrated considerable hostility to the deliberately widely drawn powers and construed them narrowly.[68] The provisions of the RRA and SDA provided the EOC and CRE with apparently unconditional power to instigate formal investigations (subject only to the usual public law duties of rationality and the like).[69] These powers were regarded with suspicion by the courts so that Lord Denning, for example, observed in an infamous passage that the powers of the Commissions were 'immense', noting in particular the powers to conduct formal investigations:

> by which they can interrogate employers and educational authorities up to the hilt and compel disclosure of documents on a massive scale. They can take up the cause of any complainant who has a grievance and, in his name, issue a questionnaire to his employers or educational authorities. They can use his name to sue them, and demand full particulars in the course of it. They can compel discovery of documents from them to the same extent as in the High Court. No plea is available to the accused that they are not bound to incriminate themselves. You might think that we were back in the days of the Inquisition. Now we come to the most presumptuous claim of all. They demand to see documents made in confidence, and to compel breaches of good faith—which is owed to persons who are not parties to the proceedings at all. You might think we were back in the days of the General Warrants.[70]

---

[66] 'Equality for Women' (1974, Home Office), Cmnd 5724; 'Race Discrimination' (1975, Home Office) Cmnd 6234, para 109. By the time of the DRCA, Government was less enthusiastic, regarding such powers as limited to 'serious or complex situations and issues'; *Promoting Disabled Peoples Rights—Creating a Disability Rights Commission fit for the 21st Century* (July 1998) CM 3977, para 4.23.

[67] See, 'Teeth and Their Use-Enforcement by the Three Equality Commissions' (2006, PIRU), in which the outcome of a research study indicated that there was a lack of use by the Commissions of their enforcement powers more generally.

[68] See 'Unnatural Justice for Discriminators' (1984) 47 MLR 334; *Hillingdon London Borough Council v Commission for Racial Equality* [1982] AC 779; and *R v CRE ex p Prestige Group plc* [1984] ICR 473.

[69] There are provisions addressing terms of reference and notice but they do not affect the general power to decide to conduct an investigation.

[70] *Science Research Council v Nassé* [1979] QB 144, 172.

In the early years of the CRE, it carried out a number of investigations into named organizations with the purpose of determining the extent of inequality in a number of representative industries located in areas with significant ethnic minority populations and of demonstrating how discrimination operates and tackling it.[71] These investigations proved very important and much of the learning gained was the basis for many of the recommendations in the Employment Code of Practice issued by the CRE in 1983[72] (since replaced by a 2006 Code[73]). However, the EOC was considerably slower in exercising its formal investigation powers and has since conducted very few. The CRE's early enthusiasm was short-lived too.[74] Following the early judicial hostility referred to above, the simple formal investigation powers became infected with bureaucratic complexity and fewer were seen.[75] 15.19

Section 57 of the SDA and section 48 of the RRA provide that: 15.20

> [w]ithout prejudice to their general powers to do anything requisite for the performance of their duties . . . , the Commission[s] may if they think fit, and shall if required by the Secretary of State, conduct a formal investigation for any purpose connected with the carrying out of those duties.

Section 3 of the DRCA provides that '[t]he Commission may decide to conduct a formal investigation for any purpose connected with the performance of its duties . . . '.

As to the scope of any formal investigation, they 'may either be wide-ranging or confined to a particular organization or individual'.[76] The Commissions may therefore formally investigate the smallest of organizations in the private sector as well as the largest, in the private or public sector. The formal investigation powers have obvious benefits for the Commissions because they allow them to be pro-active in selecting issues for investigation, in accordance with their own priorities, and they allow for focused scrutiny of a business, industry, or sector. 15.21

---

71 M Coussey, 'The Effectiveness of Strategic Enforcement of the Race Relations Act 1976', in B Hepple and E Szyszczak (eds), *Discrimination: the Limits of Law* (1992, Mansell) 35–49.

72 Commission for Racial Equality: Code of Practice for the Elimination of Racial Discrimination and the Promotion of Equality of Opportunity in Employment (1983) (Race Relations Code of practice Order 1983, SI 1983/1081).

73 Referred to at para 15.16 above.

74 The last full investigation conducted by the CRE in respect of the private sector was in the mid-1990s and this was a general investigation into the equal opportunities policies and practice among large companies in Britain ('Large Companies and Racial Equality' (1995) ISBN185442162X); there were very few in the period, in particular, commencing in the mid-1980s and ending in the mid-1990s.

75 The Institute for Public Policy Research, have recommended that the CRE conduct more general investigations, 'Race Equality: The Benefits for Responsible Business, Task Force on Race Equality and Diversity in the Private Sector' (2004, IPPR).

76 Race Discrimination (1975, Home Office) Cmnd 6234, para 111.

15.22 The specific powers differ slightly, but importantly, as between the CRE, the EOC, and the DRC. The SDA and RRA distinguish between non-accusatory 'general' formal investigations and those based on a suspicion that a named organization has been, or is, acting unlawfully. The latter 'belief', 'named person', or 'accusatory' investigations, as they are variously but usually known, require that the EOC or CRE believe that the organization may have committed or may be committing an unlawful act of discrimination or harassment, a contravention of section 37 of the SDA or of section 28 of the RRA (discriminatory practices),[77] or a contravention of sections 38 to 40 of the SDA or 29 to 31 of the RRA[78] (prohibition of discriminatory advertisements, pressure, and instructions to discriminate).[79] Whilst there is no such express (or obviously implied) restriction on the powers to conduct formal investigations, two House of Lords decisions so limited the powers of the EOC and CRE to investigate 'named' organizations.[80] In *Re Prestige*, the House of Lords held that it is:

> a condition precedent to the exercise by the CRE of its power to conduct named persons investigations that the CRE should in fact have already formed a suspicion that the persons named may have committed some unlawful act of discrimination and had at any rate *some* grounds for so suspecting.[81]

The test for determining whether there are sufficient grounds to instigate a 'named person' investigation was described by the House of Lords in *R v Commission for Racial Equality, ex p Hillingdon London Borough Council*:[82]

> To entitle the Commission to embark upon the full investigation it is enough that there should be material before the Commission sufficient to raise in the minds of reasonable men, possessed of the experience of covert racial discrimination that has been acquired by the Commission, a suspicion that there may have been acts by the person named of racial discrimination of the kind that it is proposed to investigate.[83]

According to their Lordships, before commencing a 'belief' investigation, the EOC or CRE must have formed a belief that the person concerned may have Committed or may be committing one of the unlawful acts described above. They must also have informed the 'person' of such belief and allowed him or her to make representations. The terms of reference of any such formal investigation must limit the scope of the investigation to the unlawful acts or other breaches of the SDA or RRA which have been notified. The required level

77 See para 15.34 below.

78 See para 15.33 below.

79 SDA, ss 58–9; RRA, ss 49–50.

80 *Hillingdon London Borough Council v Commission for Racial Equality* [1982] AC 779 and *R v CRE ex p Prestige Group plc* [1984] ICR 473.

81 *Per* Lord Diplock at 342 and see *R v Commission for Racial Equality, ex p Hillingdon London Borough Council* [1982] QB 276.

82 [1982] QB 276.

83 [1982] AC 779 *per* Lord Diplock at 791.

of belief is not high, but nevertheless it is a threshold which must be met if the powers can be lawfully exercised, notwithstanding the absence of any requirement for the same in the SDA or RRA. This means that all the powers flowing from the formal investigation powers, including the power to obtain information and disclosure of documents,[84] are dependent upon there first being some suspicion, based on some grounds, that an unlawful act has been committed.

The requirement that there be some evidence founding a suspicion as a precondition to the exercising of the formal investigation powers potentially frustrates important aspects of these powers. The investigative powers are there to provide the Commissions with the evidence necessary to determine whether there are any unlawful acts occurring. The requirement that there be some evidence founding a suspicion undermines the role of the Commissions in tackling particularly covert or institutional discrimination; prohibits the Commissions from uncovering and addressing unlawful acts by named persons during the course of a general investigation, and risks drawing the Commissions into prolonged and expensive litigation about whether or not a particular investigation of a named person falls within or without their powers (as exemplified by the *Hillingdon* and *Prestige* cases which both went to the House of Lords). It would appear that this interpretation of the Commissions' powers is not consistent with Parliament's intention[85] or their chosen model. **15.23**

Before embarking on any formal investigation the EOC and CRE must draw up terms of reference and give notice in the prescribed manner.[86] In a 'belief' investigation, the Commissions must inform the 'named person' of their 'belief', offer them an opportunity to make written and oral representations, and take account of any representations before finalizing any terms of reference. In any 'belief'-based formal investigation, the EOC and CRE may serve a notice[87] requiring the recipient to provide information, produce documents, or attend to be interviewed,[88] and non-compliance is enforceable by a court.[89] The EOC and CRE are required to publish a report of every formal investigation and may make **15.24**

---

84 SDA, s 59(1) and RRA, s 50(1).

85 See observations of the CRE in their first review of the Race Relations Act 1976, 'Review of the Race Relations Act 1976: Proposals for Change' (1985, CRE).

86 SDA, s 58; RRA, s 49; Sex Discrimination (Formal Investigations) Regulations 1975, SI 1975/1993; Race Relations (Formal Investigations) Regulations 1977, SI 1977/841.

87 Sex Discrimination (Formal Investigations) Regulations 1975, SI 1975/1993; Race Relations (Formal Investigations) Regulations 1977, SI 1977/841.

88 SDA, s 59; RRA, s 50.

89 SDA, s 59(6) and (7); RRA, s 50(6) and (7). It is a criminal offence wilfully to destroy any document that a person has been required by such notice to produce.

recommendations to any person either in the course of the formal investigation or after its conclusion.[90]

15.25 If, in the course of a 'belief' investigation, the EOC or CRE become satisfied that a person is committing, or has committed any of the acts described in paragraph 15.22 above, they may serve on that person a Non-Discrimination Notice.[91] The Notice may require the person not to commit such acts; and where to do so requires changes in practices to notify the EOC or CRE that such changes have been made, and to furnish such other information as the EOC or CRE may require to verify compliance with the Notice. Before serving such a Notice the EOC or CRE must give notice to the person that they are minded to do so, offering them the opportunity to make oral or written representations (or both). They must take account of any such representations. A right of appeal to the employment tribunal or County or Sheriff Court exists. The tribunal or court may quash any requirement in the Non-Discrimination Notice that they consider unreasonable because it is based on an incorrect finding of fact,[92] or for any other reason.[93] During the five years after a Non-Discrimination Notice becomes final, if it appears to the EOC or CRE that, unless restrained, the person is likely to commit an act of unlawful discrimination or harassment, or adopt any discriminatory practice, the EOC or CRE may apply to the County Court for an injunction (or to the Sheriff Court for an order) restraining him or her from doing so.[94]

15.26 The DRCA prescribes the DRC's powers to conduct formal investigations in some respects differently when compared with the SDA and RRA. The DRCA contains a broad power to conduct formal investigations in section 3(1), set out above. As with the SDA and the RRA, it is plainly envisaged that the DRC might conduct a general or a named investigation, as the DRCA provides for different forms of notice. Thus:

> [w]here the terms of reference[95] confine the investigation to activities of one or more named persons, notice of the holding of the investigation and the terms of reference shall be served on each of those persons.[96]

---

[90] SDA, s 60; RRA, s 51.

[91] SDA, s 67; RRA, s 58.

[92] *R v CRE ex p Amari Plastics* [1982] IRLR 252.

[93] SDA, s 68; RRA, s 59.

[94] SDA, s 71; RRA, s 62. This power in relation to 'persistent discrimination' is also available to the EOC or CRE where there is a finding that she or he had committed an unlawful act or (EOC only) an act in breach of an equality clause.

[95] As with the EOC and the CRE, such is a precondition to exercising any formal investigation powers: DRCA, Sch 3, para 2(1).

[96] DRCA, Sch 3, Part 1, para 2(3).

However:

> [w]here the terms of reference do not confine the investigation to activities of one or more named persons, notice of the holding of the investigation and the terms of reference shall be published in such manner as appears to the Commission appropriate to bring it to the attention of persons likely to be affected by it.[97]

Reflecting the case law described above, where the DRC proposes to investigate whether a person has committed or is committing any unlawful act[98] it may not do so unless the investigation is a named person investigation and such persons are named within the terms of reference, and the DRC 'has reason to believe that the person concerned may have committed or may be committing the acts in question'.[99] The 'unlawful acts' are those made unlawful by any provision of Parts 2, 3, or 4 of the DDA.[100] This puts the *Prestige* test described above into statutory form where an 'accusatory' investigation into a named person is to take place. In such a case the DRC must serve a notice on the person concerned offering him the opportunity to make written or oral representations about the matters being investigated.[101] The Notice must include a statement informing the named person that the DRC has reason to believe that they may have committed or may be committing an unlawful act.[102] However, importantly, where the DRC do not propose to investigate whether a person has committed or is committing an unlawful act, they are entitled nonetheless to commence a formal investigation into a named person.

15.27 Section 3(1) of the DRCA plainly envisages that a 'non-accusatory' investigation (that is, one which is not proposing to investigate whether an unlawful act has been committed and not predicated upon such belief) may take place into a named person. This means that the DRC has at its disposal powers to obtain information, documents etc[103] from a named person without any necessary precondition of the sort described in the case law above. If evidence founding an appropriate belief thereafter emerges, the requisite notice must be served before

97 Ibid, Sch 3, Part 1, para 2(4).

98 Ibid, Sch 3, para 3(10). The same applies in relation to references elsewhere to 'unlawful acts' in the context of formal investigations—for example see DRCA, s 4(5) in relation to non-discrimination notices; s 5(11) in relation to agreements in lieu.

99 Ibid, Sch 3, para 3(3) (except where that matter is to be investigated in the course of a formal investigation into the named person's compliance with any requirement of a non-discrimination notice or any undertaking given in lieu: DRCA, Sch 3, Part 1, para 3(1), (2) and (3)).

100 Save where that matter is to be investigated in the course of a formal investigation into the named person's compliance with any requirement of a non-discrimination notice or any undertaking given in lieu: DRCA, Sch 3, Part 1, para 3(1), (2) and (3).

101 DRCA, Sch 3, Part 1, para 3(4).

102 Ibid, Sch 3, Part 1, para 3(5).

103 Ibid, Sch 3, para 4.

the DRC can investigate whether an unlawful act has occurred.[104] But, as indicated, an investigation may be commenced even into a named person—with all the information-gathering powers then available—without such a belief having been formulated and notices being given. Following the decisions of the House of Lords described above, the EOC and CRE have no such power.

15.28 The DRC may also conduct a formal investigation into whether any requirement imposed by a Non-Discrimination Notice served on a person (including a requirement to take action specified in an action plan) has been or is being complied with, and whether any undertaking given by a person in an agreement made with the Commission under section 5 (see paragraph 15.52 below) is being or has been complied with but, as with 'unlawful acts', only where the investigation is a named person investigation and such persons are named within the terms of reference.[105] The DRC have power to obtain information, including documents, from persons named in a named person investigation and from others, but in the latter case only with the authority of the Secretary of State.[106] The power is enforceable by order of the County Court, or Sheriff Court, and is supported by penal measures.[107]

15.29 As with the EOC and the CRE, at the conclusion of an investigation the DRC must prepare a report of its findings.[108] However, the DRC must exclude from its report any matter which relates to an individual's private affairs or a person's business interests if, in the DRC's opinion, it might prejudicially affect that individual or person, and its exclusion is consistent with the DRC's duties and the object of the report.[109] Such a report must be published.[110]

15.30 Unlike formal investigations conducted by the EOC and CRE, there are statutory time limits for a DRC formal investigation. The DRC must publish the report of a formal investigation within 18 months (subject to the Secretary of State granting an extension) of the notice of the investigation and its terms of reference being served or published, failing which any requirement contained in a Non-Discrimination Notice served by the Commission in relation to the formal investigation ceases to have effect; any requirement contained in an information notice served in relation to the formal investigation which has not yet been complied with ceases to have effect; and no steps or further steps may be taken by the Commission

104 Ibid, s 3, Sch 3, para 3.
105 Ibid, Sch 3, Part 1, para 3.
106 Ibid, Sch 3, Part 1, para 4.
107 Ibid, Sch 3, Part 1, para 5(1) and Part 4, paras 23–24.
108 Ibid, Sch 3, Part 1, para 7.
109 Ibid.
110 Ibid.

in the conduct of the formal investigation.[111] In the light of its findings, the DRC has power to make recommendations[112] and to serve a Non-Discrimination Notice. It also has power to make recommendations to any person for changes in their policies or procedures, or as to any other matter, with a view to promoting the equalization of opportunities for disabled persons or persons who have had a disability. In addition the DRC may make recommendations to the Secretary of State for changes to the law or otherwise. This power exists before the conclusion of the investigation concerned.[113] As with the EOC and CRE, the DRC may issue a Non-Discrimination Notice[114] where in the course of a formal investigation the DRC becomes satisfied that a person has committed or is committing an unlawful act. The Notice is required to give details of the unlawful act and requires the person on whom it is served not to commit any further unlawful acts of the same kind or to cease doing so.[115] Such a notice may include a recommendation to the person concerned as to action which the DRC considers they could reasonably be expected to take so as to comply with a requirement not to commit any further unlawful acts or to cease doing so.[116] The Notice may require the person concerned to propose an adequate action plan, and once an action plan has become final to take any action specified in the plan which he has not already taken at times specified.[117] An action plan is a document drawn up by the person concerned specifying action, including action he has already taken, intended to change anything in his practice, policies, procedures, or other arrangements which caused or contributed to the commission of the unlawful act concerned or is liable to do so.[118] Such a plan is adequate if the action specified is sufficient to ensure within a reasonable time that the person concerned is not prevented from complying with a requirement not to commit any further unlawful acts or to cease doing so.[119] Inadequate action plans can be addressed by the DRC in the first place by requesting a revised plan and then by application to the County Court for an order that the person concerned provide an adequate plan.[120] Action plans become final 12 weeks after a draft is served on the DRC[121] or eight weeks after a

111 Disability Rights Commission (Time Limits) Regulations 2000, SI 2000/879.

112 DRCA, Sch 3, para 6.

113 Ibid, Sch 3, Part I, para 6(3).

114 Ibid, s 4.

115 Ibid.

116 Ibid.

117 Ibid.

118 Ibid.

119 Ibid.

120 Ibid, Sch 3, Part 3, paras 16 and 17. See Disability Rights Commission (Time Limits) Regulations 2000 SI 2000/879 for time at which such plans come into force.

121 Disability Rights Commission (Time Limits) Regulations 2000 SI 2000/879, regulation 3(1).

revised plan is served where one has been served.[122] Additional time limits apply following an order by the court.[123]

15.31 A person to whom a Non-Discrimination Notice is addressed may appeal the same to a tribunal or County or Sheriff Court (depending on the requirements imposed by it). [124] A court or tribunal may quash any requirement in a Non-Discrimination Notice if it considers it unreasonable or based on an incorrect finding of fact.[125] In addition, the court or tribunal may make such modifications as it considers appropriate.[126] Further provision is made in relation to action plans so that if within a period of five years beginning on the date on which an action plan becomes final the DRC considers that the person concerned has failed to comply with the requirement to carry out any action specified in the action plan, it may apply to the County Court or to a Sheriff Court for an order requiring the person to comply with the requirement.[127]

15.32 Once an action plan is in force, then the person concerned is bound to comply with it. This position might be distinguished from the position under the SDA and the RRA. The EOC and the CRE do not have power to require enforceable action plans. Such action plans have the obvious attribute of requiring persons subject to investigations themselves to consider and adopt plans for addressing institutionalized disability discrimination.

(3) Commission-only enforceable unlawful acts

15.33 The SDA, RRA, and DDA create a number of unlawful acts which are enforceable only by the Commissions.[128] These address discriminatory practices, discriminatory advertisements,[129] instructions to discriminate,[130] and pressure or inducement to discriminate.[131] The rationale for providing the Commissions with exclusive power to take action under these provisions, in particular in relation to

122 Ibid, regulation 3(2). Where a revised plan has been sought and not served, the original plan becomes final four weeks from the date given by the DRC for service of the revised plan or four weeks from any extended period provided by the DRC: regulation 3(3) and (4).

123 Disability Rights Commission (Time Limits) Regulations 2000, regulation 3(5) and (6) and DRCA, Sch 3, Part 3.

124 DRCA, Sch 3, Part 2, para 10.

125 Ibid.

126 Ibid.

127 Ibid, Sch 3, Part 3, para 20. The DRCA makes provision for obtaining information in relation to whether a person has complied or is complying with a requirement to take action specified, see Sch 3, Part 3, para 21.

128 In the case of the EA, the CEHR will have the relevant enforcement powers, when in place.

129 SDS, s 38; RRA, s 29; and DDA, s 16B.

130 SDA, s 39; RRA, s 30; DDA, s 16C.

131 SDA, s 40; RRA, s 31; DDA, s 16C.

advertisements, is that such acts are unlikely to result in substantial disadvantage to individuals but may result in numerous complaints, each of which would have to be individually resolved, if the Commissions were not given exclusive powers over them.[132]

The SDA and the RRA outlaw 'discriminatory practices'. In the case of the SDA and RRA, a 'discriminatory practice' occurs in the application of an indirectly discriminatory provision which results in an act of unlawful discrimination, or which would be likely to result in an act of unlawful discrimination if there were any persons of the disadvantaged group in the pool to whom the provision is applied.[133] Indirect discrimination is defined according to the unlawful act concerned, and these meanings are described in detail in Chapter 6. These provisions allow the Commissions to take action to secure the removal of discriminatory barriers which may deter women and black and ethnic minority communities from accessing employment, services, and other opportunities. 15.34

The SDA, RRA, and DDA[134] contain provisions addressing discriminatory advertisements. The SDA makes it unlawful 'to publish or cause to be published an advertisement which indicates, or might reasonably be understood as indicating, an intention by a person to do any act which is or might be unlawful' by virtue of the unlawful acts under the SDA.[135] For the purposes of this provision 'use of a job description with a sexual connotation (such as "waiter", "salesgirl", "postman" or "stewardess") shall be taken to indicate an intention to discriminate, unless the advertisement contains an indication to the contrary'.[136] These provisions do not apply to an advertisement where the intended act would not in fact be unlawful (for example sex is a genuine occupational qualification[137]). 15.35

The RRA makes it 'unlawful to publish or cause to be published an advertisement which indicates, or might reasonably be understood as indicating, an intention by a person to do an act of discrimination, whether the doing of that act by him 15.36

---

132 Race Discrimination (1975, Home Office) Cmnd 6234, para 104.

133 SDA, s 37 and RRA, s 28.

134 Since the amendments made to the DDA to give effect to the Framework Directive by the Disability Discrimination Act 1995 (Amendment) Regulations 2003, SI 2003/1673. Before then by s 11(1)–(3) of the unamended DDA, use of a discriminatory advertisement by an employer obliged an employment tribunal to assume, unless the contrary was proved, that the reason for a disabled applicant being refused a job was related to their disability. This section therefore had the effect of reversing the burden of proof in cases where a disabled applicant had been refused employment and the employer has advertised for that employment in a discriminatory way. S 11 has been repealed and replaced by the provision made by the Regulations.

135 SDA, s 38(1).

136 Ibid, s 38(3).

137 See Chap 8.

would be lawful or, by virtue of Part 2 or Part 3,[138] unlawful'.[139] This provision does not outlaw such advertisements where the intended act would be lawful under certain enumerated provisions of the RRA.[140] Unlike the SDA, however, the fact that an intended act may be lawful does not mean that an advertisement of it will necessarily be lawful. Only if the intended act would be lawful under the provisions identified will advertisement of it be lawful too. This provision does not apply to an advertisement which indicates that persons of any class defined otherwise than by reference to colour, race, or ethnic or national origins are required for employment outside Great Britain.[141]

15.37 The DDA makes an advertisement unlawful where it:

> (a) . . . invites applications for a relevant appointment or benefit; and (b) indicates, or might reasonably be understood to indicate, that an application will or may be determined to any extent by reference to, (i) the applicant not having any disability, or any particular disability, (ii) the applicant not having had any disability, or any particular disability, or (iii) any reluctance of the person determining the application to comply with a duty to make reasonable adjustments or (in relation to employment services) with the duty imposed by section 21(1)[142] as modified by section 21A(6).[143]

A relevant appointment is one for employment and other occupational opportunities under Part 2 of the DDA, except that this provision does not apply to council members in respect of any appointment or benefits to be made by, or conferred by, a local authority.[144] This provision does not apply where the intended act would in fact be lawful.[145] Similar provision is now made by the DDA in the context of further and higher education in relation to applications to any course or student service provided or offered by a responsible body, or any qualification conferred by it,[146] but otherwise the 'advertisement provisions' extend to a narrower range of unlawful acts as compared to the SDA and RRA.

---

138 See Chaps 7–12.

139 RRA, s 29.

140 If the intended act would be lawful by virtue of any of ss 5, 6, 7(3) and (4), 10(3), 26, 34(2)(b), 35–9, and 41; or if the advertisement relates to the services of an employment agency (within the meaning of s 14(1)) and the intended act only concerns employment which the employer could by virtue of s 5, 6, or 7(3) or (4) lawfully refuse to offer to persons against whom the advertisement indicates an intention to discriminate, RRA, s 29(2).

141 RRA, s 29(3).

142 See Chap 6.

143 DDA, s 16B.

144 Ibid, s 16(2C) and (3).

145 Ibid, s 16B(2). However, it is impossible to conceive of a case where reluctance of a person determining the application to comply with a duty to make reasonable adjustments or (in relation to employment services) with the duty imposed (s 16B(1)(b)(iii)) could ever be lawful.

146 DDA, s 28UC (inserted by the SI 2006/1721).

An 'advertisement' for these provisions has a wide meaning so that they include 'every form of advertisement or notice, whether to the public or not, and whether in a newspaper or other publication, by television or radio, by display of notices, signs, labels, show cards or goods, by distribution of samples, circulars, catalogues, price lists or other material, by exhibition of pictures, models or films, or in any other way'.[147] However, liability does not attach to an innocent publisher.[148] **15.38**

The SDA, RRA, DDA, and EA also outlaw 'inducements' and 'instructions' to discriminate.[149] Adverse treatment caused by an instruction to discriminate will amount to direct discrimination, as discussed in Chapter 6, under the main anti-discrimination enactments, except in the case of the SDA and DDA because of the different way in which direct discrimination is defined. As has been mentioned, the fact that no legal rights are conferred upon individuals to bring claims arising out of sexually discriminatory instructions and discriminatory instructions connected to disability probably contravenes the Framework Directive and the amended Equal Treatment Directive.[150] The 'pressure' and 'instructions' provisions in the DDA extend only to employment[151] and to further and higher education.[152] The parallel provisions in the SDA and RRA extend to all the unlawful acts. **15.39**

It is unlawful under the SDA, RRA and DDA for a person: **15.40**

> (a) who has authority over another person, or (b) in accordance with whose wishes that other person is accustomed to act, to instruct him to do any act which is unlawful . . . or to procure or attempt to procure the doing by him of any such act.[153]

This requires that there should be some relationship between the person giving the instructions or doing the procuring and the other person, and that the other person is a person who is accustomed to acting in accordance with the wishes of the first person. Since 'person', by reason of the Interpretation Act 1978,[154] includes 'a body of persons incorporate or unincorporate', if there is evidence that the other person is accustomed to acting in accordance with the wishes of an *employer*, it would not matter that the other person had never before spoken to the

147 RRA, s 78(1). SDA, s 82(1) is to materially the same effect. The DDA does not define 'advertisement' but it is likely the provisions under the DDA will be given the same meaning, see Chap 3.

148 SDA, s 38(4)–(5); RRA, s 29(4)–(5); DDA, s 16B(2A)–2(B).

149 SDA, s 39; RRA, s 30; DDA, Ss 16C(1) and 28UB (to materially the same effect).

150 See Chap 4.

151 Including employment services, under DDA, s 21A.

152 DDA, ss 16C and 28UB.

153 SDA, s 39; RRA, s 30; DDA, ss 16C(1) and 28UB (to materially the same effect).

154 Interpretation Act 1978, Sch 1.

particular individual, within the employer organization, giving the instructions. However, it is unlikely to be sufficient to show that the other person is merely accustomed to acting in accordance with the wishes of persons in the *same position* as the person giving the instructions.[155]

15.41 The words 'procure' and 'attempt to procure' have a wide meaning and include the use of words which bring about or attempt to bring about a certain course of action. Therefore, an expression of preference for applicants from a particular racial group is 'an attempt to procure applicants from a particular racial group'.[156]

15.42 Further, the SDA, RRA, and DDA make it unlawful for a person 'to induce, or attempt to induce, a person to do any act which contravenes' the enactments, in the case of the SDA and DDA (but not the RRA which is not so restricted), by '(a) providing or offering to provide him with any benefit, or (b) subjecting or threatening to subject him to any detriment'.[157] The word 'induce' by itself covers a mere request to discriminate. It does not necessarily imply an offer of some benefit or the threat of some detriment. The ordinary meaning of the word 'induce' is 'to persuade or to prevail upon or to bring about' and there is no reason to construe the word narrowly or in a restricted sense. Therefore, a request by a respondent's secretary to a head of careers at a school that 'she would rather the school did not send anyone coloured (*sic*)' to fill a job vacancy constituted an attempt to induce the head of careers not to send such applicants for interview.[158] Importantly, an attempted inducement is not prevented from falling within subsection (2) because it is not made directly to the person in question, 'if it is made in such a way that he is likely to hear of it'.[159] It appears that mere communication of information from a person other than the employer that an employer as a matter of fact operates a discriminatory policy is not likely to constitute an attempt to induce discrimination where there is no attempt to persuade another to do anything.[160]

15.43 The unlawful acts addressing advertisements, instructions, and inducements are enforced by the EOC, RRA, and DRC, and, in due course, by the CEHR.[161] Enforcement is through the employment tribunals or County Court or Sheriff Court depending upon the context. Where the unlawful acts advertised,

---

155 *Commission for Racial Equality v Imperial Society of Teachers of Dancing* [1983] ICR 473; [1983] IRLR 315, EAT.

156 Ibid.

157 SDA, s 40; RRA, s 31; DDA, ss 16C(2) and 28UB.

158 *Commission for Racial Equality v Imperial Society of Teachers of Dancing* [1983] ICR 473; [1983] IRLR 315, EAT.

159 SDA, s 40(2); RRA, s 31(2); DDA, s 16C(3).

160 *CRE v Powell and City of Birmingham District Council* (EAT, 10.9.85) EOR 7B.

161 EA, s 25.

instructed, or induced are said to be in the employment and related fields, enforcement will be in the employment tribunals, otherwise proceedings must be brought in the County or Sheriff Courts for a declaration.[162] Where it appears to the Commissions that, unless restrained, the person concerned is likely to do a further unlawful act, then they may apply to a County Court for an injunction (or to a Sheriff Court in Scotland for an interdict) restraining him from doing so.[163]

(4) Other enforcement, judicial review, and interventions

In addition to the specific enforcement mechanisms prescribed in relation to the unlawful acts described above, the Commissions may bring proceedings in judicial review, for example, to challenge a failure to comply with a general statutory duty,[164] to challenge a specific discriminatory decision or practice[165] of a body amenable to judicial review, or to challenge the *vires* of legislation made under the SDA, RRA, or DDA, or other relevant enactments, or for declaratory relief as to the State's compliance with EU equality law.[166] The main anti-discrimination enactments expressly provide that, notwithstanding that in respect of any unlawful act proceedings will lie only in accordance with the enactments, this does not preclude an application for judicial review and the making of an order of certiorari, mandamus, or prohibition.[167] **15.44**

As to interventions, it has become increasingly common for the EOC, CRE, and DRC to intervene in litigation. There is no express power in the SDA, RRA, or DRCA permitting the Commissions to intervene. However, the Commissions' powers are non-exclusively defined, and such powers as are consistent with the need to discharge their duties may be implied. The Commissions have regarded their powers as being broadly enough defined to allow them to intervene in litigation where a matter of general interest relating to the main anti-discrimination enactments is likely to be determined, or where the purpose of any proposed intervention would be connected with one or more of their duties. There is no entitlement to intervene in litigation. In each case an interest would have to be shown, **15.45**

[162] SDA, s 72; RRA, s 63; DDA, ss 17B and 28VA–B; EA, s 25.

[163] Ibid.

[164] *Birmingham CC v Equal Opportunities Commission* [1989] AC 1155; *Secretary of State for Defence v Elias* [2006] EWCA Civ 1293.

[165] *Birmingham CC v Equal Opportunities Commission* [1989] AC 1155. *Secretary of State for Defence v Elias* [2006] EWCA Civ 1293.

[166] *R v Secretary of State for Employment, ex p Equal Opportunities Commission* [1995] 1 AC 1; [1994] IRLR 176; *R v Secretary of State for Social Security, ex p Equal Opportunities Commission* (Case C-9/91) [1992] ICR 782; [1992] 3 All ER 577, ECJ; *R v Secretary of State for Defence, ex p Equal Opportunities Commission* (unreported), 20 Dec 1991, DC.

[167] SDA, s 62(2); RRA, s 53(2); DDA, Sch 3, part 1, para 2(2); Sch 3, part 2, para 5(2); Sch 3, part 3, para 9(2); Sch 3, part 4, para 12(2).

and the court retains a discretion as to whether or not to grant leave to do so. However, in general, no objection has been taken by the courts to the Commissions intervening in appropriate cases.[168]

15.46 The question whether or not interventions are appropriate is not uncontroversial.[169] Proceedings in this jurisdiction are largely adversarial, and permitting a third party to intervene to make representations has not always proved welcome. Nevertheless, interventions are now part of the jurisprudential landscape. Where the EOC, CRE, and DRC have intervened, on occasions those interventions have been expressly welcomed by the court.[170] The procedures for applying to intervene vary according to the court in which the proceedings are being heard.[171] The new CEHR has been given express powers to intervene (see paragraph 15.92 below).[172]

15.47 The SDA, RRA, and DDA[173] give the EOC, CRE, and DRC powers to enforce compliance by public authorities with the specific equality duties, described below. This is addressed further below.[174]

---

168 Examples of cases include Anyanwu v South Bank Students' Union [2000] ICR 221 and [2001] ICR 391 in the Court of Appeal and House of Lords respectively; Essa v Laing Ltd [2004] ICR 746; [2004] IRLR 313 (Court of Appeal); Igen Ltd v Wong [2005] IRLR 258 (Court of Appeal); R (A, B, X and Y) v East Sussex CC and the Disability Rights Commission (No 2) [2003] EWHC 167 (Admin), (2003) 6 CCLR 194 (see paras 178–185); R (Burke) v (1) General Medical Council (2) The Disability Rights Commission (3) The Official Solicitor [2004] EWHC 1879 (Admin) (see para 23); R (Burke) v General Medical Council and others Intervening [2005] EWCA Civ 1003 and Secretary of State for Defence v Elias [2006] EWCA Civ 1293.

169 See discussion in S Hannett, 'Third Party Interventions: in the Public Interest' (2003) PL 128.

170 *R (A, B, X and Y) v East Sussex CC and the Disability Rights Commission (No 2)* [2003] EWHC 167 (Admin), (2003) 6 CCLR 194 (see paras 178–85); *R (Burke) v (1) General Medical Council (2) The Disability Rights Commission (3) The Official Solicitor* [2004] EWHC 1879 (Admin) (see para 23).

171 A detailed survey of the various procedural rules that might be relevant is outside the scope of this work, but the most usual method is to apply to be joined as a party—albeit an intervening party. Rule 18 of the Employment Appeal Tribunal Rules (SI 1993/2854) applies in respect of the same in the Employment Appeal Tribunal; rule 19.2 and 19.2 of the Civil Procedure Rules 1998 apply in respect of the same in the County Courts, the High Court, and Court of Appeal. Rule 54.17 of the Civil Procedure Rules 1998 applies in respect of the same in relation to judicial review proceedings where a person may apply for permission to file evidence or make representations at the hearing of a judicial review. Direction 36 of the House of Lords Practice Directions and Standing Orders Applicable to Civil Appeals (November 2003) regulates interventions in the House of Lords although little guidance is given.

172 The Government having indicated that it believes this would give a positive signal to the courts about the potential value of the CEHR's involvement. It anticipates that the CEHR would be able to seek leave to intervene in support of the full breadth of its remit, covering both equality and human rights cases: White Paper, *Fairness for All: A New Commission for Equality and Human Rights* (2004) CM 6185, paras 4.11–4.13.

173 SDA, s 76D; RRA, s 71D–71E; DDA, s 49E and 49F.

174 Para 15.93 onwards.

(5) Assistance to individuals

The EOC and CRE must consider all applications for assistance from claimants in relation to proceedings or prospective proceedings under the SDA or RRA, and they may grant assistance 'if they think fit to do so' on the grounds that the case raises a question of principle, or it is unreasonable, having regard to the complexity of the case or the applicant's position in relation to the respondent or another person involved or any other matter, to expect the applicant to deal with the case unaided, or by reason of any other special consideration.[175] The DRC may grant assistance on these same grounds,[176] but it is not required as a matter of express statutory obligation to consider every application for assistance made.[177] **15.48**

The power to grant assistance extends only to proceedings brought under the SDA or EPA in the case of the EOC, under the RRA in the case of the CRE, and under the DDA in the case of the DRC. In the case of the DRC, the White Paper[178] which preceded its creation recognized that it was likely that individual disabled people would want to test their Convention rights following the enactment of the Human Rights Bill[179] by reliance on Article 14. The White Paper indicated that: **15.49**

> [g]iving the DRC powers to provide assistance in Article 14 cases where discrimination prevents individuals enjoying the other rights provided for in the ECHR would seem to fall within the DRC's duty to eliminate discrimination.[180]

The White Paper therefore proposed that the DRC should have power to assist individuals bringing cases under the HRA in cases where a breach of Article 14 was an issue.[181] However, the power to provide assistance does not reflect this recommendation. Instead regulation-making powers were included under section 7(1) of the DRCA for the purposes of authorizing support in other proceedings 'being proceedings in which an individual who has or has had a disability relies or proposes to rely on a matter relating to that disability'. No regulations have been made under this provision, and accordingly the DRC's powers remain limited.

---

175 SDA, s 75(1); RRA, s 66(1).

176 DRCA, s 7(2).

177 Though the same obligation is likely to be implied if their power to grant assistance is to be properly exercised.

178 *Promoting disabled people's rights—creating a Disability Rights Commission fit for the 21st Century* (1998) ISBN 0101397720.

179 As it was at the time of publication of the White Paper.

180 See para 4.11.

181 Ibid.

15.50 All three Commissions nevertheless regularly support complainants who have claims in proceedings in addition to discrimination, as is very common indeed, without challenge. A very narrow reading of the powers to assist individuals is unlikely to be workable because it is unusual in practice to find a discrimination claim being pursued without any other causes of action attached to it.[182] It would be disproportionate and impractical to hive off the discrimination claims from the other claims and have separate representation for each of them. A pragmatic construction of the SDA, RRA, and DRCA therefore requires a sufficiently broad meaning to be given to the powers of the EOC, CRE, and DRC so as to permit them to provide assistance at least in cases where one of the claims falls under the SDA, EPA, RRA, or DDA claim, even if other causes of action are attached.

15.51 Provision is made under the SDA, RRA, and DRCA for recouping costs and expenses incurred by the EOC, CRE, and DRC in providing assistance to an individual by the creation of a statutory charge over any costs or expenses awarded to such an individual.[183]

(6) Conciliation and binding agreements

15.52 The DRC alone has specific power to make arrangements with any other person for the provision of conciliation services. The DRC has made such arrangements for the purposes of conciliating claims under Parts 3 (goods and services) and 4 (education) of the DDA. The Disability Conciliation Service (DCS) liaises between disabled people and providers of goods and services and education providers within the meaning of Parts 3 and 4 of the DDA. The DCS is an independent service, funded by the DRC and run by Mediation UK. Its purpose is to resolve disputes by assisting those involved to reach agreement with the help of an impartial third party conciliator.[184]

15.53 Further, the DRC may enter into statutory agreements in lieu of enforcement action (unlike the EOC and the CRE). Where the DRC has reason to believe that a person has committed or is committing an unlawful act it may enter into an

---

182 For example, commonly in an employment-related discrimination claim there will be a claim for unfair dismissal, unlawful deduction from wages etc. Similarly in a goods and services claim, there may be a claim in breach of contract, or, where the claim is against, eg, the police, for unlawful arrest etc. Research indicates, eg that 51.6% of DDA claims instituted in the employment tribunal include a claim in unfair dismissal: S Leverton, 'Monitoring the Disability Discrimination Act 1995 (Phase 2), Final Report' (2001) IDS, iii.

183 SDA, s 75(3); RRA, s 66(5); DRCA, s 8.

184 DDA, ss 28 and 31B and see, <http://www.drc-gb.org/about_us/conciliation_service.aspx#whatissues>.

agreement in writing with that person on the assumption that the belief is well founded (whether or not it is admitted).[185] Such an agreement requires the DRC to undertake not to take any enforcement action, and requires the person concerned not to commit any further unlawful acts or to cease the same and take such action as may be specified in the agreement.[186] Such 'action' will be that which is intended to change anything in the policies, practices, or procedures of the person which caused or contributed to the unlawful act, or which would be likely to cause or contribute to a failure by that person to honour his undertaking not to do a similar thing.[187]

These agreements are binding so that the DRC may apply to a County Court or a Sheriff Court for an order requiring the other party to comply with the undertaking, or with directions for the purpose of ensuring compliance with the undertaking.[188] In addition, a belief that a party has failed to comply may form the basis of an 'accusatory' formal investigation (see paragraph 15.26 above). Such an agreement only stops the DRC commencing or continuing a formal investigation[189] and taking steps to issue a Non-Discrimination notice in relation to the particular unlawful act in question.[190] It does not prevent the DRC supporting individual cases, or (although probably unlikely) commencing or continuing a formal investigation on other grounds, or entering into a second agreement on a different issue. This model offers real potential for securing expeditious and cost effective strategic change. It allows the DRC to insist upon change against an agreed timetable without the need to prove harassment or discrimination, or embark upon or continue an expensive formal investigation. The EA now makes similar provision in respect of the CEHR.[191] 15.54

(7) Research and educational activities

All three Commissions have powers to undertake research and educational activities where this is necessary or expedient for the purposes of their statutory duties, and to support, financially or otherwise, such activities undertaken by others.[192] 15.55

185 DRCA, s 5(1).

186 Ibid, s 5.

187 'DRC Legal Strategy—2003–2006' (2003) DRC, para 40.

188 As in relation to non-discrimination notices, an 'unlawful act' for these purposes is one made unlawful by Part II to 4 of the DDA: DRCA, s 5(11).

189 DRCA, s 5(4)(a)–(c).

190 Ibid, s 5(4)(a)–(c).

191 EA, s 23, see para 15.97 below.

192 SDA, s 54; RRA, s 45; DRCA, s 2(2)(c).

(8) Power to fund organizations: The Commission for Racial Equality

15.56 The CRE has a power to give financial or other assistance to organizations that appear to it to be concerned with the promotion of equality of opportunity, and good relations, between persons of different racial groups.[193] It is required, however, to have the approval of the Secretary of State and the consent of the Treasury to provide such assistance out of the grant it receives from the Secretary of State.[194] These powers reflect the functions of the Community Relations Commission which the CRE partially replaced,[195] as discussed in Chapter 2. These powers are used to provide financial support to a number of local and regional Racial Equality Councils.[196]

C. The Commission for Equality and Human Rights: Duties and Functions

(1) Introduction: establishment and transition

15.57 Part 1 and Schedules 1 and 2 of the EA establish the CEHR and create its structure, duties, and powers. The EA provides for the dissolution of the EOC, CRE, and DRC not later than 31 March 2009, and for the transfer of property, rights, and liabilities.[197] Schedules 3 and 4 make consequential amendments and repeals to other legislation, including the SDA, RRA, and DDA as a consequence of the EOC, CRE, and DRC's dissolution and the establishment of the CEHR. The CEHR in many respects replicates the constitution of the EOC, CRE, and DRC. It is an executive non-departmental corporate public body[198] whose members[199] are appointed by a designated Secretary of State,[200] to whom the Commission must report annually.[201] The Commission may delegate a function to a Commissioner

---

193 RRA, s 44.

194 In February 2006 the CRE announced s 44 funding for 129 organizations and smaller grants to 41 other organizations <http://www.cre.gov.uk/about/gettingresults.html> who are identified at <http://www.cre.gov.uk/Default.aspx.LocID-0hgnew0b6.RefLocID-0hg00900c008.Lang-EN.htm>.

195 s 43(5), RRA. See Chap 2 for a discussion of the functions of the Community Relations Commission.

196 See the comparable powers under the CEHR, s 17.

197 EA, ss 36–8. Anything which was in the course of being done by one of the Commissions before such transfer (including any legal proceedings) may be continued by the CEHR, but the CEHR is not required to do so (EA, s 38(2)(b)).

198 EA, s 1.

199 Between 10 and 15 members, EA, Sch 1, Part 1, para 1(1).

200 EA, Sch 1, Part 1, para 1. At the time of writing this is the Secretary of State for Communities and Local Government.

201 EA, Sch 1, Part 2, para 32.

or to staff.[202] The general duties of CEHR are again statutorily prescribed, as explained below.

At least one commissioner of the CEHR must be, or have been, a disabled person;[203] one Commissioner must know about conditions in Scotland and one must know about conditions in Wales.[204] 15.58

The Commission may establish decision-making committees, to whom it may delegate functions, and advisory committees. Committees may include Commissioners, staff, and other non-Commissioners. The chairman of any decision-making committee must be a Commissioner.[205] 15.59

Special statutory arrangements are made for disability, so that the Commission *must* establish a decision-making Disability Committee.[206] The Chairman and at least half of the members must be, or have been, disabled. The CEHR will be treated[207] as having delegated to the Disability Committee its duties under sections 8 and 10 as they relate to *disability matters*,[208] together with its relevant powers in relation to monitoring the law, information, research, and advice, issuing Codes of Practice, providing legal assistance, conciliation, and instituting or intervening in legal proceedings. The Commission must consult the Disability Committee before exercising a power or fulfilling a duty in relation to a matter affecting disabled people, for example an inquiry or investigation, and in particular any matter within Part 2 of the DDA.[209] The CEHR must arrange for a review of the activities of the Disability Committee after five years.[210] Following the review, the CEHR will recommend to the Secretary of State how long the Disability Committee should continue in existence, and the Secretary of State will make an order dissolving the Disability Committee with effect from a specified date and repeal the provisions of the EA relating to the Disability Committee.[211] There is no comparable provision in relation to race or any other of the grounds 15.60

202 Ibid, Sch 1, Part 2, para 10, including an 'Investigating Commissioner' appointed by the Commission, with the consent of the Secretary of State, to carry out a particular function, Sch 1, Part 2, para 9.

203 Ibid, Sch 1, Part 1, para 2(3)(a).

204 Ibid, Sch 1, Part 1, para 2(3) (b) and (c): appointed with the consent of the Scottish Ministers and National Assembly for Wales, respectively.

205 Ibid, Sch 1,Part 2, paras 11–15.

206 Ibid, Sch 1, Part 5, with between 7 and 9 members.

207 Ibid, Sch 1, Part 5, para 52.

208 With the applicable powers to take action in respect of the same. 'Disability matters' are those matters provided for in Parts 1, 3, 4, 5, and 5B of the DDA, EA, ss 8 and 10 as they relate to disability, and matters addressed in EA, ss 14(3) and (4), 27(2) and (3), and 28(2) and (3).

209 EA, Sch 1, Part 5, para 53 (see too for Welsh and Scottish matters, para 52(4) and (5)).

210 Ibid, Sch 1, Part 5, paras 57–62.

211 Ibid, Sch 1, paras 57–62.

protected by the main anti-discrimination enactments (though there is a broad power to establish committees more generally[212]). As mentioned above, the Race Directive[213] and the amended Equal Treatment Directive[214] (but not the Framework Directive) require Member States to designate a specific body or bodies 'for the promotion of equal treatment of all persons without discrimination on the grounds of racial or ethnic origin' and 'for the promotion of, analysis, monitoring and support of equal treatment of all persons without discrimination on the grounds of sex', respectively. Without a specific committee designated with these functions, some doubt must exist as to whether compliance with the Directives has been achieved through the establishment of the CEHR. The CRE has observed:

> During the last eighteen months we are pleased that the government has listened and addressed many of our key concerns. Additionally, we have consistently maintained the importance of a Race Committee. If other equality strands have a committee, it stands to reason that race should too. It would also be beneficial to maintaining a link between the CEHR and local race equality organizations and ensuring the continuation of local race equality work.[215] However, we remain concerned that the CEHR will not be able to focus properly on community relations, extremism and integration issues. These will be lost within a unified body that must deal with anti-discrimination across seven separate and distinct strands. This is why we have proposed a new non-governmental public body to guide, advise and mediate on community relations, civic engagement and citizenship. This would complement the CEHR by focusing on the distinct challenges presented by community relations work.[216]

15.61 The Commission must establish a Scotland Committee and a Wales Committee as decision-making committees to advise the Commission about the exercise of its functions as they affect Scotland and Wales. Powers of the CEHR in relation to publishing information, undertaking research, providing education or training as they affect Scotland and Wales are delegated to the respective Committees, as are powers to advise devolved governments on the effects of legislation.[217]

15.62 The EA contains transitional provisions so that a 'transitional period' for the establishment of the CEHR began on 18 April 2006,[218] since when the provisions of the EA necessary to establish the CEHR are in force but with some modifications.

---

212 Ibid, Sch 1,Part 2, paras 11–15.

213 Race Directive, Art 13.

214 Amended Equal Treatment Directive, Art 8a.

215 CRE statement on the Commission for Equality and Human Rights, 16 January 2006, at <http://www.cre.gov.uk/Default.aspx.LocID-0hgnew09t.RefLocID-0hg00900c002.Lang-EN.htm>.

216 'About Us', at <http://www.cre.gov.uk/about/index.html>.

217 EA, Sch 1,Part 2, paras 21–2 and 29–30.

218 EA, s 41 and Equality Act 2006 (Commencement No 1) Order 2006, SI 2006/1082.

This means that, for example, the minimum number of Commissioners is five, and 'transition' Commissioners have been appointed comprising three in number, one from each of the Commissioners of the EOC, CRE, and DRC, nominated by the respective chairmen (who may nominate themselves). A Transition Commissioner may serve until a time specified by the Secretary of State not more than two years after the relevant Commission has ceased to exist or has lost its principal functions.[219]

(2) Functions, duties, and independence

During consultation on the White Paper *Fairness for All: a New Commission for Equality and Human Rights*[220] and during passage of the Equality Bill, concerns were expressed regarding the independence of the CEHR. Various submissions were made recommending that the CEHR should be accountable to Parliament rather than to the Executive and, more particularly, should be subject to the 'Paris Principles' applicable to human rights bodies.[221] The JCHR, in particular, stressed the need to ensure the CEHR's ability to participate in the UN reporting process in relation to international human rights treaties. The JCHR itself has done much work in this field, responding to UN treaty scrutiny reports and to the Government's own submissions to such bodies.[222] The JCHR noted that the UN Paris Principles on National Institutions for the Protection and Promotion of Human Rights[223] require that national human rights institutions shall have a responsibility to 'contribute to reports which States are required to submit to United Nations bodies and committees' and to 'co-operate with the UN and any other agency in the UN system' relating to human rights. The Government has given assurances in both Houses of Parliament that the CEHR will be able to work with the UN's Committees and contribute to their processes of examining the UK's compliance with international human rights treaties.[224] However, the submissions **15.63**

219 EA, s 41.

220 Department for Trade and Industry, May 2004.

221 'Commission for Equality and Human Rights: The Government's Response to Consultation' (2004), paras 70–3.

222 The JCHR has itself reported to the UN bodies monitoring the Convention on the Elimination of Racial Discrimination, the International Convention on Economic, Social and Cultural Rights, and the Convention on the Rights of the Child. See Joint Committee on Human Rights, Fourth Report, *Legislative Scrutiny: Equality Bill* (2005-6 HL 89; HC 766), para 6. And see Chap 4 for the relevant UN Conventions.

223 Principles relating to the status and functioning of national institutions for protection and promotion of human rights ('Paris Principles'), para A3(d) (Endorsed by the Commission on Human Rights in March 1992 (resolution 1992/54) and by the General Assembly in its resolution A/RES/48/134 of 20 December 1993).

224 Hansard, HC (SCA) cols 57–60 (Meg Munn MP, 9 Nov 2005) and HC (SCA) cols 99–100 (1 Dec 2005); Hansard, HL coL 296 (Baroness Ashton of Upholland, 11 July 2005). See for discussion, A Lester and K Beattie, 'The New Commission for Equality and Human Rights' [2006] PL Summer 197, 200–1.

made on independence from Government were not accepted.[225] Instead the EA now provides, importantly, that:

> [t]he Secretary of State shall have regard to the desirability of ensuring that the Commission is under as few constraints as reasonably possible in determining (a) its activities, (b) its timetables, and (c) its priorities.[226]

This provision has been described as 'particularly innovative' and such that it 'will have relevance for other statutory bodies'.[227] Further, the Secretary of State is required to pay to the CEHR 'such sums as appear to the Secretary of State reasonably sufficient for the purpose of enabling the Commission to perform its functions'.[228]

15.64 The EA describes the duties of the CEHR under a series of headings: general duties; equality and diversity; human rights; groups; monitoring the law; and monitoring progress.[229] In exercising its functions, the CEHR is to do so:

> with a view to encouraging and supporting the development of a society in which (a) people's ability to achieve their potential is not limited by prejudice or discrimination, (b) there is respect for and protection of each individual's human rights, (c) there is respect for the dignity and worth of each individual, (d) each individual has an equal opportunity to participate in society, and (e) there is mutual respect between groups based on understanding and valuing of diversity and on shared respect for equality and human rights.[230]

Further, the CEHR shall, by exercising its powers:

> (a) promote understanding of the importance of equality and diversity, (b) encourage good practice in relation to equality and diversity, (c) promote equality of opportunity, (d) promote awareness and understanding of rights under the equality enactments, (e) enforce the equality enactments, (f) work towards the elimination of unlawful discrimination and unlawful harassment.[231]

The CEHR has duties, too, amongst other things to:

> (a) promote understanding of the importance of human rights, (b) encourage good practice in relation to human rights, (c) promote awareness, understanding and protection of human rights, and (d) encourage public authorities to comply with section 6 of the Human Rights Act 1998[232] [and to] promote understanding of the importance

225 'Commission for Equality and Human Rights: The Government's Response to Consultation' (2004), paras 70–3.

226 EA, Sch 1, Part 4, para 42(3).

227 A Lester and K Beattie, 'The New Commission for Equality and Human Rights' [2006] PL Summer, 205.

228 EA, Sch 1, Part 3, para 38.

229 Ibid, Part 1.

230 Ibid, s 3.

231 Ibid, s 8.

232 Ibid, s 9.

of good relations between members of different groups and between members of groups and others; encourage good practice in relation to relations between members of different groups and between members of groups and others; work towards the elimination of prejudice against, hatred of and hostility towards members of groups, and work towards enabling members of groups to participate in society.[233]

A 'group' means a group or class of persons 'who share a common attribute in respect of. . . .age, disability, gender, proposed, commenced or completed reassignment of gender . . . race, religion or belief and sexual orientation'.[234] The CEHR also has monitoring functions over the law, including the duty to advise Government about the effectiveness of any of the equality and human rights enactments.[235]

Further, the CEHR has novel duties, from time to time, to identify changes in society that have occurred or are expected to occur that are relevant to its aims as identified in its general duties, to identify results at which to aim for the purpose of encouraging and supporting the development of the society described in its general duties, and to identify factors by reference to which progress towards those results may be measured.[236] **15.65**

The CEHR must prepare a strategic plan, after consultation, showing the activities or classes of activity it intends to undertake, a timetable, and priorities or principles to be applied in determining priorities, and must review the plan at least once every three years and make any appropriate revisions.[237] **15.66**

The CEHR is under a duty to monitor its own progress in achieving the aims prescribed for it and described above.[238] **15.67**

(3) General powers of the Commission for Equality and Human Rights

Many of the powers of the CEHR reflect those given to the EOC, CRE, and DRC. They include disseminating ideas, information, advice, and guidance.[239] It is given broad powers to issue Codes of Practice.[240] The CEHR is given wider powers than the EOC, CRE, or DRC to issue Codes of Practice. The CEHR may issue a Code of Practice in connection with a matter addressed by[241] the EPA; **15.68**

233 Ibid, s 10.
234 Ibid, s 10(2).
235 Ibid, s 12.
236 Ibid, s 12.
237 Ibid, ss 4 and 5.
238 Under EA, ss 3, 12.
239 EA, s 13.
240 Ibid, s 14 (as amended byAge Regulations, Sch 8, Part 2, para 38).
241 EA, s 14. The Secretary of State may vary the range of matters that a code of practice might address, EA, s 15(6). The CEHR must comply with direction by the Secretary of State to issue a code in connection with a matter she or he intends to add to this list, EA, s 14(5).

the SDA, Parts 2 to 4, and sections 76A to 76C; the RRA, Parts 2 to 4 and section 71; the DDA, Parts 2 to 4 and 5A; the EA, Part 2; regulations under the EA, Part 3; the Sexual Orientation Regulations, Parts 2 and 3; the Religion or Belief Regulations; and the Age Regulations. Such Codes will contain provisions designed to ensure or facilitate compliance with the law or to promote equality of opportunity.[242] The CEHR may also issue a Code of Practice giving practical guidance to landlords and tenants regarding the circumstances in which a tenant requires the landlord's consent to make a relevant improvement and 'reasonableness' in relation to such consent.[243]

15.69 As with the Codes issued by the EOC, CRE, and DRC, the CEHR must consult on proposals for a Code and must submit a draft to the Secretary of State which is then subject to Parliamentary approval through a negative resolution procedure. The impact of a failure to comply with a provision of a statutory Code is as with those issued by the EOC, CRE, and DRC, namely that 'a failure to comply with a provision of a code shall not of itself make a person liable to criminal or civil proceedings; but a code shall be admissible in evidence in criminal or civil proceedings, and shall be taken into account by a court or tribunal in any case in which it appears to the court or tribunal to be relevant.'[244]

15.70 The CEHR may make grants to organizations or individuals, which may be subject to conditions, including conditions as to repayment,[245] and may make, cooperate with, or assist in arrangements; for monitoring hate crime, designed to reduce crime within or affecting certain groups and for activities (social, recreational, sporting, etc) designed to involve members of groups.[245a]

15.71 Further, the CEHR may cooperate with others over human rights (but not, strictly, equality or diversity issues as such)[246, 247]. Other specific powers are addressed below.

(4) Inquiries

15.72 The EA gives the CEHR power to conduct 'inquiries'.[248] These are in addition to the formal investigation powers, described below. This is a novel power.

---

242 EA, s 14.

243 Ibid, s 14(3). S 14(4) provides parallel code making power for Scotland.

244 Ibid, s 15(4).

245 EA, s 17. During debate on the Equality Bill, Meg Munn MP, Parliamentary Under Secretary of State for Trade and Industry, announced that the Government had 'made a commitment to the continued funding of race equality councils and of others involved in local race equality work' Hansard, 16 Jan 2006, col 642.

245a EA, s 19.

246 EA, s 18.

247 Ibid, s 19.

248 Ibid, s 16, Sch 2.

The Explanatory Notes indicate that such inquiries might be 'thematic' (for example into the causes of unequal outcomes), 'sectoral' (looking at inequality in, for example, the uptake of health screening services, or at the employment of disabled people in particular sectors, for instance, such as the retail sector), or relate to one or more named parties.[249] The model derives from the existing Commissions' general investigatory powers, but in addition to sector-specific inquiries the CEHR will have power to examine issues cutting across different equality strands and human rights in a way that was not possible before.

The CEHR has an unqualified power to conduct an inquiry into any matter relating to its duties, described above (paragraph 15.64),[250] subject only to the restriction that it must relate to the CEHR's duties concerning equality and diversity, human rights, or groups. An inquiry by the CEHR may consider or report on human rights matters,[251] except in relation to an intelligence service.[252] **15.73**

The CEHR must publish the terms of reference of an inquiry and must give notice to any persons specified in the terms of reference before conducting the inquiry.[253] In carrying out an inquiry, the CEHR is explicitly prohibited from considering whether any person may have committed an unlawful act.[254] If in the course of an inquiry the CEHR 'begins to suspect that a person may have committed an unlawful act', for example, an act of unlawful discrimination or harassment, this should not form part of the *inquiry* but may form the basis of an *investigation* by the CEHR.[255] The CEHR is required to publish a report of the findings of an inquiry,[256] but must not state, whether expressly or by necessary implication, that a specified or identifiable person has committed an unlawful act, and shall not otherwise refer to the activities of an identifiable person unless it thinks that to do so would not harm the person or is necessary for the report adequately to reflect the results of the inquiry.[257] Before settling a report of an inquiry which records findings which, in the CEHR's opinion, are of an adverse nature and relate to a specified or identifiable person, the CEHR must send that person the draft report, allow at least 28 days for written representations, and consider those representations.[258] **15.74**

249 Explanatory Notes to the Equality Act 2006, para 56.
250 EA, s 16(1).
251 Ibid, s 16(4).
252 Ibid, Sch 2, para 20.
253 Ibid, Sch 2, para 2.
254 'Unlawful' means contrary to a provision of the equality enactments (excluding any statutory equality duty) see EA, s 34.
255 EA, s 16(2).
256 Ibid, Sch 2, para 15.
257 Ibid, s 16(3).
258 Ibid, s 16(5).

(5) Investigations

15.75 The CEHR also has power to conduct investigations,[259] comparable to the formal investigation powers under the SDA, RRA, and DRCA. The CEHR may investigate whether or not a person has committed an unlawful act, has complied with a requirement imposed by an unlawful act notice (see paragraph 15.78 below), or has complied with a section 23 undertaking (see paragraph 15.83 below).[260]

15.76 The CEHR may conduct an investigation into whether or not a person has committed an unlawful act only if it suspects that the person may have committed an unlawful act,[261] following the model adopted by the DRCA, and putting the case law described above on a statutory footing.[262] According to the Government this was intended to set a 'threshold test' of 'reasonable belief' (a lower threshold than that imposed by the civil burden of proof) 'when these investigations concern an allegation of unlawful discrimination or harassment'.[263] The required suspicion may be based on matters arising during or resulting from an 'inquiry', as described above.[264]

15.77 Before conducting an investigation the CEHR must prepare terms of reference specifying who is to be investigated and the grounds, including, where relevant, the unlawful acts it suspects has taken place. Any person to be investigated must be given notice of the terms of reference and an opportunity to make representations. The CEHR must consider any representations made and must publish the terms of reference once they are settled.[265] The CEHR must publish a report of an investigation. If the report records a finding that a person has committed an unlawful act or has failed to comply with a requirement or undertaking, the CEHR must send a draft of the report to that person and specify a period of 28 days in which the person may make representations which the CEHR must consider.[266]

15.78 If the CEHR is satisfied that a person who is or has been the subject of an investigation has committed an unlawful act, the CEHR may serve an Unlawful Act Notice (similar to a Non-Discrimination Notice, described above at paragraph 5.25)

---

259 Ibid, ss 20–22 and Sch 2.

260 Ibid, s 20(1).

261 Ibid, s 20(2).

262 Paras 15.22 and 15.26.

263 'Commission for Equality and Human Rights: The Government's Response to Consultation' (2004), para 38.

264 EA, s 20(3).

265 Ibid, Sch 2, para 3.

266 Ibid, s 20(4).

specifying the unlawful act alleged and the provisions of the equality enactments by virtue of which it is unlawful. The Notice must notify the recipient of his right to appeal, the CEHR's powers to investigate non-compliance, and the CEHR's powers to seek an injunction (see paragraph 15.84 below).[267] The Unlawful Act Notice may require the person to prepare an 'action plan' or may recommend action to avoid repetition or continuation of the unlawful act.[268]

(6) Assessments

The CEHR may assess the extent to which or manner in which a public authority has complied with a general or specific equality duty under the SDA, RRA, or DDA (see paragraph 15.93 below).[269] Before carrying out an assessment the CEHR must give notice to the authority of the proposed terms of reference, give the authority an opportunity to make representations, consider any representations, and publish the terms of reference once they have been settled.[270] The CEHR must publish a report of its findings on an assessment.[271] **15.79**

(7) Recommendations

The CEHR may make recommendations to any person as part of its report of an inquiry, investigation, or assessment, or in respect of a matter arising in the course of an inquiry, investigation, or assessment. A person to whom such a recommendation is addressed is required to have regard to it.[272] **15.80**

(8) Evidence

The CEHR has compelling evidence collection powers.[273] In the course of an inquiry, investigation, or assessment the CEHR may serve a notice on any person requiring them to provide information in her or his possession, produce documents in her or his possession, or give oral evidence. A person to whom such notice is addressed can apply to a County or Sheriff Court to have the notice cancelled on grounds that the requirement is unnecessary having regard to the inquiry, investigation, or assessment, or is otherwise unreasonable.[274] The CEHR may apply to a County or Sheriff Court for an order that the recipient comply with **15.81**

267 Ibid, ss 21 (1)–(3).
268 Ibid, ss 21(4).
269 Ibid, s 31.
270 Ibid, Sch 2, para 4.
271 Ibid, Sch 2, para 15.
272 Ibid, Sch 2, paras 16 and 18.
273 Ibid, Sch 2, paras 9–14.
274 Ibid, Sch 2, para 11.

the notice.[275] A person must disregard a notice and inform the CEHR that she or he is doing so, in so far as she or he thinks that it would require her or him to disclose information that is sensitive (as defined) or that includes information relating to individuals or processes of an intelligence service.[276]

15.82 A court or tribunal may have regard to a finding within a CEHR inquiry, investigation, or assessment but shall not treat it as conclusive.[277]

(9) Binding agreements, conciliation, and injunctions

15.83 As with the DRC, the CEHR may enter into binding agreements and make arrangements for conciliation.[278]

15.84 If the CEHR thinks that a person is likely to commit an unlawful act, or fail to comply with an undertaking under an 'agreement',[279] it may apply to the County Court for an injunction prohibiting the person from committing the act.[280]

(10) Unlawful acts

15.85 As with the SDA, RRA, and DDA, the EA makes provision for certain unlawful acts which are enforceable by the CEHR only. Firstly, the EA makes provision with the effect that the CEHR will assume the power to bring proceedings in relation to those unlawful acts which are enforceable presently by the EOC, CRE, and DRC.[281] Secondly, the EA makes unlawful any practice 'which would be likely to result in unlawful discrimination if applied to persons of any religion or belief',[282] extending somewhat further than the 'discriminatory practices' provisions of the SDA and the RRA.[283] The adoption and maintenance of a practice or arrangement in accordance with which, in certain circumstances, an unlawful practice would be operated is also outlawed.[284] Discriminatory practices are only actionable by the CEHR, on an application for an injunction, by the making of a binding 'agreement', or by the issuing of an Unlawful Act Notice following an investigation, as described above.[285]

---

275 With criminal sanctions where a person fails to comply with a notice or order, or falsifies any information or document provided or produced, or makes a false statement in giving oral evidence.

276 EA, Sch 2, para 14.

277 Ibid, Sch 2, para 17.

278 Ibid, ss 23 and 27. The parameters of these powers are prescribed by EA, ss 23 and 27.

279 See para 15.83 above.

280 EA, s 24.

281 See para 15.83 above and see EA, s 25 and amendments to each of the provisions therein referred to after the coming into force of the material provisions of the EA.

282 EA, s 53(1).

283 See para 15.34 above.

284 EA, s 53(2).

285 Ibid, s 53(4)(a) and (b).

The EA makes materially the same provision in respect of discriminatory advertisements in relation to religion or belief discrimination as is made in the other main anti-discrimination enactments.[286] Again the CEHR has the exclusive power to bring proceedings in respect of the same.[287] 15.86

The EA makes it unlawful for a person to cause or attempt to cause another to unlawfully discriminate or induce or attempt to induce (directly or indirectly) another to discriminate, making similar provision to the other main anti-discrimination enactments.[288] Again the CEHR has exclusive power to take proceedings in respect of the same.[289] 15.87

(11) Assistance to individuals

The CEHR has power to assist an individual who is or may become a party to legal proceedings if the proceedings relate wholly or partly to a provision of the equality enactments,[290] and the individual alleges that she or he has been the victim of unlawful discrimination or harassment.[291] Unlike the SDA, RRA, or DRCA, the EA does not prescribe the grounds on which the CEHR may grant legal assistance, though the factors above (paragraph 15.48) are likely to be relevant. Further, unlike the SDA and RRA, the EA does not require that all applications for assistance be 'considered',[292] though such may be implied if their power to grant assistance is to be properly exercised. 15.88

'Assistance' from the CEHR may take the form of legal advice, legal representation, facilities for settlement of a dispute, or any other form of assistance.[293] The 'equality enactments' include provisions of EC law relating to discrimination on grounds of sex, racial origin, ethnic origin, religion, belief, disability, age, or sexual orientation which confer rights on individuals.[294] The CEHR may assist an individual who alleges that she or he is disadvantaged by UK legislation that is contrary to a provision of EC law or by the failure of the UK to implement a right required by EC law.[295] 15.89

286 Ibid, s 54.

287 Ibid, ss 54(3) and 25.

288 Ibid, s 55.

289 Ibid, ss 55(6) and 25.

290 Defined in EA, s 33.

291 EA, s 28(1). Assistance may also be provided in relation to proceedings which concern or may concern the question of a landlord's reasonableness in relation to consent to the making of an improvement to a dwelling where the improvement would be likely to facilitate the enjoyment of the premises by the tenant or another lawful occupier having regard to a disability (EA, s 28(2)–(3)).

292 See para 15.48 above.

293 EA, s 28(4).

294 Ibid, s 28(12).

295 Ibid, s 28(13).

15.90 Specific provision is made addressing proceedings relating both to a provision of the equality enactments and to other matters, in which case the CEHR may grant assistance in respect of any aspect of the proceedings while they continue to relate to a provision of the equality enactments, but such assistance must not be continued if the proceedings cease to relate to any provision of the equality enactments.[296] The Government sought views on whether the CEHR should be able to continue to support cases involving both discrimination and human rights after the discrimination arguments fall away and '[a] majority of respondents felt the legitimacy of the CEHR would be undermined if it were not able [to do so] . . . '.[297] However, instead of expressly providing for the same, the EA makes provision allowing the Lord Chancellor by order to enable the CEHR to continue to assist an individual where, after proceedings cease to relate to a provision of the equality enactments, they relate wholly or partly to any ECHR rights within the HRA.[298] Given that analogous powers in the DDA were never used (see paragraph 15.49 above), this may be a rather weak response to the views expressed during the consultation exercise.

15.91 Provision is made under the EA for recouping costs and expenses incurred by the CEHR in providing assistance to an individual by the creation of a statutory charge over any costs or expenses awarded to such an individual.[299]

(12) Judicial review and interventions

15.92 The CEHR has the capacity to institute or intervene in legal proceedings, including judicial review, if it appears to the CEHR that the proceedings are relevant to a matter in connection with which the CEHR has a function.[300] In judicial review proceedings, which it institutes or in which it intervenes, the CEHR may rely on section 7(1)(b) of the HRA,[301] and for this purpose the CEHR need not be a victim or potential victim. However, the CEHR may act only if there is or would be one or more victims of the unlawful act.[302] Sections 7(3) and 7(4) of the HRA (the victim condition) do not then apply to such proceedings and no award of damages may be made to the CEHR.[303]

---

296 Ibid, s 28(6).

297 'Commission for Equality and Human Rights: The Government's Response to Consultation' (2004), paras 44–5.

298 EA, s 28 (7).

299 Ibid, s 29.

300 Ibid, s 30(1).

301 In claiming that a public authority has acted in a way that is incompatible with a ECHR right (HRA, s 6(1)), a person may rely on the ECHR right in any legal proceedings.

302 EA, s 30(3)(b).

303 Ibid, s 30(3)(c) and (d).

D. Statutory Duties

(1) Introduction

The SDA, RRA, and DDA now all impose important statutory duties on public authorities.[304] As mentioned,[305] those duties fall into three groups: the general duties (to have 'due regard' to the need to achieve certain equality objectives); specific duties imposed on certain public authorities, requiring them to take designated action; and specific disability duties imposed on certain transport providers. The disability transport duties are addressed discretely below (paragraph 15.133). **15.93**

These duties are extremely important. The RRA in its original enactment contained a broad statutory duty imposed upon local authorities: **15.94**

> to make appropriate arrangements with a view to securing that their various functions are carried out with due regard to the need (a) to eliminate unlawful racial discrimination; and (b) to promote equality of opportunity, and good relations, between persons of different racial groups.[306]

However, this duty was of little practical impact, in part because of the courts' approach to it, and in part because of the absence of any institutional framework to support and enforce it.[307]

Following the report of the Stephen Lawrence Inquiry,[308] the RRA was first amended to introduce more compelling statutory duties. Similar duties have now been enacted in the SDA and DDA. In broad terms, these duties are directed at addressing institutional and structural discrimination. Institutional discrimination[309] in this context refers to the practices and processes, sometimes informal, invisible, or attitudinal, of organizations that have the effect of disadvantaging certain groups. These phenomena are almost impossible to address through the statutory torts by individual enforcement,[310] and require pro-active action to identify them and address them. Structural discrimination refers to entrenched social disadvantage associated with membership of a particular class that might **15.95**

---

304 SDA, ss 76A–E (in force from April 2007); RRA, ss 71–71E (in force from April 2001); DDA, Ss 49A–F (in force from December 2005). See, too, Northern Ireland Act 1998, s 75; Greater London Authority Act 1999, ss 33 and 404.

305 Para 15.11.

306 RRA, s 71.

307 *Wheeler v Leicester CC* [1985] AC 1054. The SDA, s 25 (which remains in force) imposed a general statutory duty on education authorities but with rare exceptions this was of little use for the same reason (see *R v Birmingham city Council ex Parte* EOC [1989] IRLR 173 for an example of its use).

308 *The Stephen Lawrence Inquiry: Report of an Inquiry by Sir William Macpherson of Cluny*, advised by Tom Cook, the Rt Rev Dr John Sentamu, Dr Richard Stone, Cm 4262-I. See Chap 2.

309 See further Chap 2.

310 *Commissioners of Inland Revenue v Morgan* [2002] IRLR 776, para 38.

include segregation and social exclusion.[311] Structural discrimination often has the effect of reinforcing and replicating disadvantage through sometimes negative practices and policies, and again it may be very difficult to identify a particular discriminatory act causing disadvantage. Remedying these patterns of disadvantage requires positive intervention. The statutory duties now in the SDA, RRA, and DDA go some way to achieving this, though, as discussed below, the duties as presently crafted are flawed. They do, however, have the capacity to mainstream equality norms and create a statutory basis for securing change to organizational practices. They are explored in detail below.

15.96 As alluded to above, criticisms can be made of the model adopted for the statutory duties under the SDA, RRA, and DDA. Other jurisdictions have enacted more compelling statutory duties directed at remedying disadvantage and increasing fair representation and participation.[312] The content of the duties varies, but in general the more compelling duties are outcome-focused. This approach might be contrasted with the explicit approach taken in the main anti-discrimination enactments, which, as will be seen below, on their face are arguably concerned principally with the formalities of process and procedure (though some greater substance has been achieved through their innovative interpretation and use, as is discussed below). As will be seen below, the statutory duties imposed by the SDA, RRA, and DDA all require public authorities (only) to have 'due regard' to a series of specified 'needs' ('to eliminate unlawful discrimination', for example). As such bureaucratic obligations are imposed but without any express obligations to achieve substantive results. Specific statutory duties enacted under the SDA, RRA, and DDA impose further bureaucratic obligations (to create race equality schemes and to undertake ethnic monitoring, for example[313]). These are important obligations but suffer from the same weaknesses. If significant change is to be achieved, it might be argued that such duties must support a programme of change and not be regarded as an end in themselves. The difficulty of introducing such duties without any obligation to achieve change, measurable by rates of participation, pay, or other appropriate outcomes, is that they may appear disproportionately bureaucratic, and, absent real political will, may be unlikely to achieve change by themselves. The race equality scheme obligations require, for example, that a body subject to the obligation to prepare one must state 'those of its functions

[311] A classic example can be seen in *DH and others v Czech Republic* (2006) (Application No 57325/00).

[312] Including within limited areas, Northern Ireland: Fair Employment and Treatment Order 1998, SI 1998/3162.

[313] Race Relations Act 1976 (Statutory Duties) Order 2001 SI 2001/3458 and see SI 2002/62; SI 2003/3006; SI 2003/3007; SI 2004/3125, and SI 2004/3127. See para 15.109 below for an albeit limited but more substantive content to the specific disability duties; and see the disability 'transport duties' at para 15.133 which are again more substantive.

and policies, or proposed policies, which that person has assessed as relevant to its performance of the duty imposed by section 71(1) [the general statutory duty] of the Race Relations Act'. As will be seen below, having identified what policies might be relevant to the performance of the general race equality duty, such a body must then state what arrangements it has for assessing and consulting on the likely impact of its proposed policies, amongst other things. Nothing is said which imposes any obligation to *actually* promote race equality or to change policies to achieve substantive race equality outcomes, and the impact of the duties has been less significant than many would have hoped.[314]

Positive duties have the benefit of removing the obligation to effect change from individuals who are least able to make change to those institutions. Where a body is politically committed to achieving change, the race equality duties can help as a context for legitimizing race equality policies (on procurement for example).[315] However, there is no compulsion to achieve results and there is widespread bureaucratic compliance (and widespread non-compliance)[316] without significant substantive effect. **15.97**

As referred to above, some other jurisdictions adopt more substantive statutory duties. South Africa provides a useful illustration of how statutory duties may sit comfortably with a substantive approach to addressing equality and bolster both affirmative action and non-discrimination guarantees. In South Africa's Promotion of Equality and Prevention of Unfair Discrimination Acts[317] broad obligations are imposed on the State to 'achieve equality'.[318] Specific obligations are imposed requiring the State to 'develop awareness of fundamental rights', 'take measures to develop and implement programmes in order to promote equality', and 'where necessary or appropriate' 'develop action plans to address any unfair discrimination, hate speech or harassment'.[319] Ministers are required to implement measures which are aimed at the achievement of equality including by the preparation and implementation of equality plans. As to persons operating in the public domain (which might, it appears, include 'hybrid' bodies),[320] they are under an obligation to adopt 'appropriate equality plans' and other measures for the 'effective promotion of equality', amongst other things. Specific obligations are imposed in relation to certain strands (race, gender, and disability).[321] In the **15.98**

---

314 K Godwin, 'Race Equality: An Ongoing Obligation' (2006) EOR 154, though there is now some promising case law; *Secretary of State for Defence v Elias* [2006] EWCA Civ 1293.

315 See further below, para 15.119.

316 K Godwin, 'Race Equality: An Ongoing Obligation' (2006) EOR 154.

317 Promotion of Equality and Prevention of Unfair Discrimination Acts, 2000 and 2002.

318 Ibid, s 24(1).

319 Ibid, s 25.

320 As would be caught under HRA, s 6(3)(b).

321 Promotion of Equality and Prevention of Unfair Discrimination Acts, s 28, see Part 2 above.

employment sphere, the Employment Equity Act imposes duties on both private and public sector employers. Employers who employ more than 50 employees or have an annual turnover above a specified amount, as well as State employers,[322] must 'implement affirmative action measures for people from designated groups'.[323] Affirmative action measures must include measures 'to identify and eliminate employment barriers' amongst other things. Designated employers must also prepare an employment equity plan which must identify the objectives to be achieved in each particular year of the plan; what affirmative action measures are to be implemented; where under-representation from designated groups has been identified, the numerical goals to achieve equitable representation and timetables for the achievement of goals and objectives.[324] There will, of course, be bureaucratic obligations deriving from the duties imposed but these will be reflective of the outcomes to be achieved rather than ends in their own right.

15.99 Canada, too, imposes statutory duties to achieve change. The Employment Equity Act, for example, requires that employers identify and eliminate employment barriers and institute 'such positive policies and practices' and make 'such reasonable accommodations as will ensure that persons in designated groups achieve a degree of representation in each occupational group'.[325]

15.100 As to the duties under the RRA, which are the oldest of the duties amongst the new statutory duties, whilst the CRE Code of Practice[326] and case law,[327] discussed below, have provided some substance to the duties, the lack of legislative precision and goal-orientated focus is problematic, particularly where there is an absence of political support.[328] The Hepple Report[329] recommended that 'every employer (including an associated employer) with more than 10 employees should be required to conduct a periodical review' of its employment practices, and that if an employer finds following such a review 'that there is significant under-representation of any group, it should be under a duty to draw up and

---

322 With some exceptions being the National Defence Force, the National Intelligence Agency, and the South African Secret Service.

323 Designated groups being black people, women, and people with disabilities.

324 Employment Equity Act, ss 15 and 20.

325 Employment Equity Act, s 5. 'Designated groups' is defined to include women, aboriginal peoples, persons with disabilities, and members of visible minorities, as referred to above.

326 CRE, Statutory Code of Practice on the Duty to Promote Race Equality (2002, CRE).

327 *Secretary of State for Defence v Elias* [2006] EWCA Civ 1293.

328 C O'Cinneide, *Taking Equal Opportunities Seriously: The Extension of Positive Duties to Promote Equality* (2003, Equality and Diversity Forum/Equal Opportunities Commission), 59.

329 B Hepple, M Coussey, and T Choudhury, *Equality: A New Framework, Report of the Independent Review of the Enforcement of UK Anti Discrimination Legislation* (2000, Hart), 71.

implement an employment equity plan to identify and remove barriers to the recruitment, training and promotion of members of' protected groups. The plan, the Hepple Report recommended, should include provision for such reasonable adjustments as may be necessary (subject to 'undue hardship') with a power in the hands of a Commission to enforce compliance. Sandra Fredman, in her work, has advocated the fuller use of statutory duties.[330] As she has observed:

> the imposition of positive duties changes the whole landscape of discrimination law. The focus is no longer on the perpetrator of a discriminatory act. Instead, the spotlight is on the body in the best position to promote equality. Individual fault becomes irrelevant.[331]

There are no plans in place, however, to make the statutory duties more compelling. Nor are there any proposals to extend the duties to the private sector. Notwithstanding the inadequacies of the present scheme, the statutory duties are extremely important and mark a shift in the focus of the main anti-discrimination enactments from individual remedial action to the mainstreaming of equality objectives.[332] **15.101**

(2) The race equality duties

Section 71(1) of the RRA, as substituted by the Race Relations (Amendment) Act 2000, requires all public authorities listed in Schedule 1A to the RRA, in carrying out their functions, to have due regard to the need 'to eliminate unlawful racial discrimination; and to promote equality of opportunity and good relations between persons of different racial groups'. No express reference is made to harassment, no doubt because the express harassment provisions post-dated the enactment of the new section 71.[333] However, on a purposive construction, section 71 can be read as implicitly covering harassment, under either the limbs just described. **15.102**

Schedule 1A of the RRA lists, either by description or by name, bodies within central government, local government, the National Health Service, police, public museums and galleries, regulatory bodies, as well as the governing bodies of all maintained schools, and of all colleges and universities. The total number of authorities subject to the general duty is more than 43,000.[334] The Secretary of **15.103**

330 S Fredman, 'The Future of Equality in Britain', Working Paper Series No 5, (2002, Equal Opportunities Commission) ISBN 1 842060384, 32; S Fredman, *Discrimination Law* (2002, OUP), 176 *et seq*.

331 S. Fredman, *Discrimination Law* (2002, OUP) 177.

332 See *Secretary of State for Defence v Elias* [2006] EWCA Civ 1293.

333 See Chap 6.

334 K Godwin, 'Race Equality: An Ongoing Obligation' (2006) EOR 154.

State has power to amend Schedule 1A to add or remove listed public authorities[335] and that power has been exercised.[336]

15.104 Notwithstanding the criticisms made above about the formulation of the duties,[337] they have shown themselves through case law to have real substantive value.[338] The duties are extremely important and a failure to comply with of any of them may give rise to an actionable public law breach in judicial review, as is discussed further below.[339]

15.105 A number of specific duties are also imposed by Order[340] on the main public authorities (listed in a Schedule to the Order) including to publish a Race Equality Scheme. A Race Equality Scheme should state which of its functions and policies the authority has assessed as relevant to meeting the general duty, how it intends to fulfil its general duty under section 71(1) of the RRA, and the duties under the Order.[341] A Race Equality Scheme must set out the authority's arrangements for assessing and consulting on the likely impact of its proposed policies on the promotion of race equality; monitoring its policies for any adverse impact on the promotion of race equality; publishing the results of assessments and monitoring; ensuring public access to information and services which it provides; and training staff in connection with the general and specific duties.[342]

15.106 The Order does not require in terms that the steps identified actually be undertaken, merely that the arrangements in respect of them be identified.[343] However, such is likely to be required if compliance with the general duty is to be secured.

15.107 Specific duties on schools and on colleges and universities require them to prepare and maintain a Race Equality Policy; assess the impact of their policies, including the Race Equality Policy on pupils, students, staff, and parents of different racial groups; and monitor the operation of those policies by reference to their impact on pupils and students, staff, and parents of different racial groups.[344] Obligations

---

335 RRA, s 71(5).

336 See Race Relations Act 1976 (General Statutory Duty) Orders 2001, SI 2001/3457 and SI 2004/3127.

337 Para 15.96.

338 *Secretary of State for Defence v Elias* [2006] EWCA Civ 1293.

339 *R (on the application of Diana Elias) v Secretary of State (Commission for Racial Equality Intervening)* [2005] EWHC 1435 (Admin) Case No: CO/5181/2004.

340 RRA 1976 (Statutory Duties) Orders 2001, SI 2001/3458 and SI 2004/3125; the RRA 1976 (Statutory Duties) (Scotland) Order 2002, Scottish SI 2002/62, made by the Scottish Ministers, include similar but not identical specific duties for Scottish public authorities with devolved powers, including Scottish local councils, health boards, chief constables, and police authorities.

341 Ibid, Art 2.

342 Ibid, Art 2.

343 Reflecting the weaknesses in the scheme.

344 RRA 1976 (Statutory Duties) Orders 2001, SI 2001/3458 and SI 2004/3125, Art 3.

to monitor staff in post and applicants for employment, training, promotion, and the numbers who receive training, benefit or suffer a detriment as a result of a performance assessment, are involved in grievance procedures or are the subject of disciplinary procedures, or cease to be employed by that employer, are imposed on specified authorities.[345]

(3) The disability equality duties

Section 49A of the DDA[346] makes it a duty of every public authority in carrying out its functions to have due regard to the need to eliminate unlawful disability discrimination; eliminate harassment of disabled people; promote equality of opportunity between disabled persons and others; take steps to take account of disabled people's disabilities, even where that involves treating disabled people more favourably; promote positive attitudes towards disabled people; and encourage participation of disabled people in public life. The general disability equality duty, then, is more broadly framed than the general duty under the RRA. Further, it applies to public authorities generally—that is, to 'every public authority'[347]—rather than applying to an exclusive list (albeit a very long one) of public authorities, as in the case of the RRA.[348] Public authorities, for these purposes, include bodies '... certain of whose functions are functions of a public nature'.[349] The provisions will therefore embrace certain commercial and voluntary sector bodies which, whether under contract or other arrangements, are 'in effect exercising a function which would otherwise be exercised by the state—and where individuals have to rely upon that person for the exercise of the governmental function'.[350] In relation to a particular act, a body will not be a public authority by application of this definition if the nature of the act is private. Whether particular functions carried out by a private or voluntary sector organization are 'functions of a public nature' is ultimately a matter for the courts but it is likely to prove controversial.[350a] **15.108**

Specific disability equality duties are imposed by regulations under the DDA.[351] **15.109**
Public authorities listed in Schedule 1 to the Regulations (which include the main

345 Ibid, Art 4 and 5.

346 As inserted by the DDA 2005. See DDA s28 D for the duties on local education authorities.

347 DDA, s 49A(1).

348 RRA, Sch 1A.

349 DDA, s 49B. See Chap 11.

350 'The Duty to Promote Disability Equality DRC Statutory Code of Practice (England and Wales)' (2005), DRC, para 5.4 and see para 5.5 and see further, Chap 11.

350a See *R (on the application of Heather) v Leonard Cheshire Foundation* [2002] EWCA Civ 366; [2002] UKHRR 883 and see *R (on the application of Johnson) v Secretary of state for constitutional Affairs and O'rs* CI/06/1693 and to be heard by the court of Appeal in January 2007.

351 Disability Discrimination (Public Authorities) (Statutory Duties) Regulations 2005, SI 2005/2966. See also Disability Discrimination (Public Authorities) (Statutory Duties) (Scotland) 2005, Scottish SI 2005/565.

bodies within central and local government, the National Health Service, police authorities etc) are required to publish a Disability Equality Scheme.[352] This must state the steps the authority will take towards fulfilment of their general duty; the ways in which disabled people have been involved in its development; the authority's methods for assessing the impact or likely impact of their policies and practices on equality for disabled people; the authority's arrangements for gathering information about the effect of their policies and practices on disabled people in employment (including recruitment, development, and retention), education, service provision, and public functions more generally and its arrangement for duties making use of such information in complying with the general duty. Unlike the duties under the RRA, the specific disability duties require that within three years of publishing their scheme, an authority must take the steps identified in its scheme for the fulfilment of the general equality duties and for gathering information.[353] This creates a more, albeit limited, outcome-focused obligation requiring the taking of steps directed at the 'fulfilment' of the general statutory duty. This change apparently followed criticisms of the very process driven race equality duties, as is discussed above (paragraph 15.96).

15.110 The Regulations[354] also require every Secretary of State listed in Schedule 2 and the National Assembly for Wales (and the Scottish Ministers)[355] to publish a report every three years giving an overview of progress towards equality of opportunity between disabled people and others in the sector covered by her or his department, or in Wales (or Scotland respectively), and setting out proposals for the coordination of action by public authorities within that sector so as to bring about further progress towards disability equality.

(4) The gender equality duties

15.111 The last set of statutory duties are those introduced by the EA which amends the SDA to introduce a general gender equality duty, requiring public authorities in carrying out their functions to have due regard to the need to eliminate unlawful discrimination and harassment, and to promote equality of opportunity between men and women.[356] 'Unlawful discrimination', for these purposes, means the acts made unlawful under the SDA and a contravention of terms of contracts having

---

352 Regulation 2(6) requires national and local public authorities and most educational establishments to publish their disability equality scheme by 4 Dec 2006; governing bodies of primary schools and maintained special schools must do so by 3 Dec 2007.

353 Regulation 3, Disability Discrimination (Public Authorities) (Statutory Duties) Regulations 2005, SI 2005/2966. For the limits of the obligation, see Regulation 3(2).

354 Regulation 5, Disability Discrimination (Public Authorities) (Statutory Duties) Regulations 2005, SI 2005/2966.

355 Regulation 6, Disability Discrimination (Public Authorities) (Statutory Duties) (Scotland) 2005, Scottish SI 2005/565.

356 SDA, s 76A(1). In force from 6 April 2007

effect in accordance with an equality clause (under the EPA).[357] This falls short of the auditing obligations that are seen in other jurisdictions addressing pay,[358] but it is likely to prove significant nonetheless.

As with the DDA, the SDA defines 'public authority' as including 'any person who has functions of a public nature', and the duty applies to any public functions, namely 'functions of a public nature'.[359] Accordingly, as with the disability equality duty, the scope of application is potentially very wide, applying not only to 'pure' public authorities,[360] but also to voluntary bodies and private sector actors when, and to the extent that, they are carrying out public functions. **15.112**

Specific gender equality duties[361] have now been enacted.[362] The new duties are somewhat different to those proposed. This is explained by the Explanatory Memorandum, as follows: **15.113**

> In October 2005, the Government published 'Advancing Equality for Men and Women', a consultation inviting views on how the order making powers in what is now section 76B of the SDA should be exercised to ensure the better performance of the general duty in what is now section 76A. These centred around three main requirements, for public authorities to:
>
> - draw up and publish a gender equality scheme;
> - develop and publish a policy on their equal pay arrangements; and
> - ensure that they assess the impact of new legislation, policies, employment and service delivery changes.
>
> The proposals were designed to mainstream gender equality considerations in policy-making and service provision, and allow for flexibility so that public authorities could comply with their gender equality duties while performing their functions as public authorities . . . Overall there was a very broad welcome for the Government's proposals and especially for a statutory duty to take proactive steps in promoting gender equality with an emphasis on outcomes . . . After the consultation, Government has given further detailed consideration as to how to ensure that any requirements in respect of handling gender pay gap issues could be made workable, effective, outcome focussed and within the scope of the general gender equality duty. The Government also wanted to take account of the fact that many public authorities had, since 2003, undertaken pay reviews and are working on the findings arising from them. In particular, it considered how best to ensure that the specific duties require public authorities to address all the various causes of the gender pay gap and

---

357 Ibid, s 76A(2)(c). See Chap 6 for the 'equality clause'.

358 Eg, South Africa's Promotion of Equality and Prevention of Unfair Discrimination Act 2000 and Employment Equity Act 1998; Manitoba's Pay Equity Act, SM 1985–86, c 21, CCSM, c P13; Ontario's Pay Equity Act, RSO 1990, c P 7.

359 SDA, s 76A(2).

360 See Chap 11.

361 SDA, ss 76B and 76C.

362 The Sex Discrimination Act 1975 (Public Authorities) (Statutory Duties) Order 2006, SI 2006/2930. See also 'Advancing Equality for Men and Women: Government proposals to introduce a public sector duty to promote gender equality' (2005, DTI), for the proposed duties.

not just equal pay as covered by the Equal Pay Act 1970. This consideration has resulted in the wording that currently appears in Article 2(5) of the Order.

The specific gender equality duties are imposed upon public authorities listed in the Schedule to the Order (including government departments, local authorities etc) and require those authorities to prepare and publish a Gender Equality Scheme by 30 April 2007, that being a scheme showing how they intend to fulfil its section 76A(1) duty and its duties under the Order. In preparing a scheme, a listed authority is required to consult its employees, service users, and others (including trade unions) who appear to it to have an interest in the way it carries out its functions; take into account any information it has gathered and any other information it considers to be relevant to the performance of its general duty; and ensure that its scheme sets out the overall objectives which it has identified as being necessary for it to perform its section 76A(1) duty and its duties under the Order. Importantly, too, a listed authority is required to, when formulating its objectives, consider the need to have objectives that address the causes of any differences between the pay of men and women that are related to their sex. A listed authority is also required to set out in its scheme the actions which it has taken or intends to take to—

(a) gather information on the effect of its policies and practices on men and women and in particular—
  (i) the extent to which they promote equality between its male and female staff, and
  (ii) the extent to which the services it provides and the functions it performs take account of the needs of men and women; and
(b) make use of such information and any other information the authority considers to be relevant.

It is also required to assess the impact of its policies and practices, or the likely impact of its proposed policies and practices, on equality between women and men, and to consult relevant employees, service users, and others (including trade unions). As with the DDA, the specific gender equality duties require that a listed authority achieve the fulfilment of the objectives which it has identified as being necessary for it to fulfil its general duty within three years and take information-gathering steps within the same period. The comments above (paragraph 15.109) apply equally.

(5) Implementing and testing compliance with the duties

15.114 The Commissions have issued much statutory and non-statutory guidance on the implementation of the duties.[363] This guidance provides practical advice on

363 Available on the Commissions' websites: <http://www.cre.gov.uk/>; <http://www.eoc.org.uk/>, and <http://www.drc-gb.org/>.

implementing the duties and aids the understanding of the meaning of the duties and their impact.

As has been seen, the general duties require that public authorities have 'due regard' to achieving certain objectives. Statutory guidance has been given on the implementation of that obligation and, notwithstanding the criticism that might be made of its formalistic focus, that guidance indicates that the obligation has some significant substantive content. The CRE's statutory Code of Practice on the Duty to Promote Race Equality[364] advises that: 15.115

> [f]our principles should govern public authorities' efforts to meet their duty to promote race equality:
>
> a. Promoting race equality is obligatory for all public authorities listed in schedule 1A to the Act . . .
> b. Public authorities must meet the duty to promote race equality in all relevant functions.
> c. The weight given to race equality should be proportionate to its relevance.
>
> The elements of the duty are complementary (which means they are all necessary to meet the whole duty).[365]

As the Code makes clear, race equality will be more relevant to some functions than others. Relevance is about how much a function affects people, as members of the public or as employees of the authority. For example, a local authority may decide that race equality is more relevant to raising educational standards than to its work on highway maintenance. Public authorities should therefore assess whether, and how, race equality is relevant to each of their functions. A public authority may decide that the general duty does not apply to some of its functions, for example those that are purely technical, such as traffic control or weather forecasting. 'Due regard', therefore: 15.116

> requires that the weight given to race equality should be proportionate to its relevance to a particular function. In practice, this approach may mean giving greater consideration and resources to functions or policies that have most effect on the public, or on the authority's employees. The authority's concern should be to ask whether particular policies could affect different racial groups in different ways, and whether the policies will promote good race relations.[366]

This proportionality analysis gives substance to the general duty. Where a policy or practice is likely in fact to impact adversely on particular racial groups, or the failure to adopt a policy or practice is likely to result in an adverse impact on particular racial groups, then a public authority subject to the duty will be

364 (2002, CRE) available at <http://www.cre.gov.uk/downloads/duty_code.rtf>.
365 Ibid, para 3.2.
366 Ibid, paras 3.4 and 3.5.

required to prioritize action to ameliorate the effects of that policy, or the absence of such a policy, by changing it or introducing a new policy or practice.

15.117 Further, the requirement on public authorities, under the specific duties, to have in place arrangements for assessing the impact of their policies on people from different racial groups, people with disabilities, and on women and men, also imposes a significant obligation. A formal structured approach to assessing the impact of proposed policies on equality grounds was developed in Northern Ireland in relation to the equality duty contained in the Northern Ireland Act 1998.[367] The CRE has also published a step-by-step guide to undertaking race equality impact assessments.[368] The DRC Code of Practice on the Duty to Promote Disability Equality[369] gives some guidance on disability impact assessments, and the EOC Code of Practice on the Gender Equality Duty, when approved and published, will do the same. An equality impact assessment is a systematic method for assessing how a policy or practice, or primary or secondary legislation, affects, or is likely to affect, different groups. The object is to ensure that policies or legislation do not result in unlawful discrimination, but go some way to promoting equality. Where an assessment indicates potential adverse impact, then to comply with the general equality duty the authority will either need to change the policy, consider an alternative, or justify the adverse impact in the context of the overall aim.[370] Consultation with relevant stakeholders should form a central part of impact assessments, thereby introducing some degree of transparency into the content and process of policy-making across the public sector. Further, the results of equality impact assessments should be publicly available.

15.118 In *R (on the application of Diana Elias) v Secretary of State*,[371] containing the first authoritative judicial observations on the meaning of the general equality duties, the Administrative Court found a breach of the general statutory duty under the RRA. The Court of Appeal upheld the decision of the Administrative Court quashing a racially discriminatory scheme adopted by the Secretary of State. Mrs Elias challenged, through judicial review proceedings, the Compensation Scheme, announced by the Parliamentary Under-Secretary of State for Defence in Parliament on 7 November 2000, 'to repay the debt of honour' owed by the UK

---

367 Detailed guidance has been published by the Equality Commission for Northern Ireland (ECNI): 'S 75 of NI Act 1998—Practical Guidance on Equality Impact Assessment', (Feb 2005, ECNI).

368 In consultation with the Home Office; <http://www.cre.gov.uk/duty/reia/index.html>.

369 (2005, DRC), paras 3.28–3.42.

370 CRE guidance on race equality impact assessments; <http://www.cre.gov.uk/duty/reia/what.html>.

371 *(Commission for Racial Equality Intervening)* [2005] EWHC 1435 (Admin) Case No CO/5181/2004. The decision on the statutory duties was not the subject of appeal to the Court of Appeal (see the Court of Appeal decision at [2006] EWCA Civ 1293).

to 'British civilians' who were interned by the Japanese during the Second World War. There was no definition of 'British' and there was no reference at that time to the need to demonstrate any other links with the UK, to 'belonging to Britain', or to any other defined eligibility criteria. Thereafter, the Government decided that being a British citizen was not sufficient to entitle a person to an award under the scheme, but instead a person must have been born in the UK, or have one or more parents, or grandparents, born in the UK. Ms Elias challenged the scheme on the grounds that it directly or indirectly discriminated against her on grounds of national origins (a protected ground under the RRA). Ms Elias challenged the lawfulness of the compensation scheme on several grounds, including that in formulating the scheme the Government failed to comply with the general duty under section 71 of the RRA. Elias J (no relation) found a breach of section 71 of the RRA, holding that:

> It is nowhere suggested that there was any careful attempt to assess whether the scheme raised issues relating to racial equality, although the possibility was raised; nor was there any attempt to assess the extent of any adverse impact, nor other possible ways of eliminating or minimizing such impact. I accept that even after considering these matters the minister may have adopted precisely the same scheme, but he would then have done so after having due regard to the obligations under the section.
>
> Given the obvious discriminatory effect of this scheme, I do not see how in this case the Secretary of State could possibly have properly considered the potentially discriminatory nature of this scheme and assumed that there was no issue which needed at least to be addressed . . .
>
> . . . I accept . . . that the purpose of this section is to ensure that the body subject to the duty pays due regard at the time the policy is being considered—that is, when the relevant function is being exercised—and not when it has become the subject of challenge.[372]

(6) Public procurement

The equality duties have the potential to be very significant in the field of public procurement.[373] The expression *public procurement* refers to the State's purchasing of goods and services from the private sector. The State, of course, expends many, many millions of pounds on the purchasing of goods and services from the private sector, and it has long been understood that this presents an opportunity for 15.119

372 Ibid, paras 97, 98, and 99, judgment of Elias, J. See too, *Secretary of State for Defence v Elias* [2006] EWCA Civ 1293, para 133 (for the impact of a failure to comply on the establishing of justification for indirect discrimination) and para 274 (for the need for consideration of the statutory duties *before* any policy is formulated).

373 'Ethnic Minorities in the Labour Market, Final Report' (March 2003, Cabinet Office Strategy Unit) 119–126.

securing equality in the private sector by ensuring that the State uses its purchasing power to compel equality action by private sector actors with whom it contracts.[374]

15.120 The extent to which equality objectives might be promoted through the public procurement process has attracted some controversy. The Local Government Act 1988, for example, specifies that local authorities and certain other public bodies are precluded from taking into account 'non-commercial matters' in the award of contracts.[375] However, section 19 of the Local Government Act 1999 (which establishes the 'Best Value' regime) provides that the Secretary of State may by order provide, in relation to Best Value authorities, for a specified matter to cease to be a non-commercial matter for the purposes of the Local Government Act 1988.

15.121 The Local Government Best Value (Exclusion of non-commercial considerations) Order[376] provides that in respect of Best Value authorities, workforce matters have ceased to be defined as 'non-commercial' matters for the purposes of the Local Government Act 1988 to the extent that they are relevant to the achievement of best value.[377] In particular, the terms and conditions of employment by contractors of their workers, or the composition of, the arrangements for the promotion, transfer, or training of, or the other opportunities afforded to, their workforces and the conduct of contractors or workers in industrial disputes between them, or any involvement of the business activities of contractors in industrial disputes between other persons, are not to be regarded as non-commercial matters for the purposes of the Local Government Act 1988. But for this change, there would have been a significant limitation on the operation of the statutory equality duties in relation to outsourced workforce matters through the public procurement process. The change, however, operates so as to allow Best Value authorities to impose requirements in the procurement process relating to equality of opportunity in the employment context 'to the extent that a Best Value authority considers it necessary or expedient in order to permit or facilitate compliance with the requirements of Part I [of the Local Government Act 1999]'. Importantly, Part I of the Local Government Act 1999 includes the general duty upon a Best Value authority to 'make arrangements to secure continuous improvement in

374 Known as 'contract compliance' in the US (for early measures in the US, see Executive Order 11246, which as amended (by Executive Order 11375) intended 'to correct the effects of past and present discrimination' by, *inter alia*, prohibiting federal contractors and federally-assisted construction contractors and subcontractors, who generate over $10,000 annually from government contracts, from discriminating in employment decisions on the basis of race, colour, religion, sex, or national origin.).

375 Local Government Act 1988, s 17.

376 2001 SI 2001/909.

377 Ibid, Art 3.

the way in which its functions are exercised, having regard to a combination of economy, efficiency and effectiveness'.[378]

'Efficiency' and 'effectiveness' must be construed consistently with the obligations upon a Best Value authority (and that includes local authorities and other significant authorities) by reason of other legal requirements, including the statutory equality duties. This is consistent with the performance indicators and standards in relation to Best Value as specified in the orders made under section 4 of the Local Government Act 1999. These include, for example, in the case of the 'general corporate performance indicators', the 'equality standard' found in the 'Equality Standard for Local Government'[379] which is to be used as one of the measures of performance of specified Best Value authorities, including District Councils, London Borough Councils, County Councils, and a number of others.[380] The 'Equality Standard' is designed to mainstream equality issues and provides a framework for assessing and monitoring the achievement of this aim.[381] **15.122**

Further, and as to central government, *Government Accounting 2000* (as amended) identifies that in any procurement project, the Government policy is to achieve 'value for money having regard to propriety and regularity' (and this guidance applies to non-departmental public bodies in addition to central Government).[382] 'Value for money', for these purposes, 'is the optimum combination of whole-life cost and quality (or fitness for purpose) to meet the user's requirement'.[383] The 'user's requirement' may include a 'specific level of quality or standard of service'.[384] This self-evidently may include compliance with the 'user's' own legal obligations, and in the case of a public authority this would include its obligations to comply with the statutory equality duties. **15.123**

Such an approach is consistent with EU and domestic law on public procurement. The EC Public Procurement Directives[385] are concerned with giving effect to the **15.124**

---

378 Local Government Act 1999, s 3.

379 2001.

380 Local Government (Best Value) Performance Indictors and Performance Standards (England) Order 2005, SI 2005/598.

381 And see ODPM Circular 03/03 *Local Government Act 1999: Best Value and Performance Improvement* and the Annexed statutory Code of Practice indicating that Best Value should not be achieved at the cost of the workforce, and that a high quality workforce is required whether services are delivered directly or by a contractor (para 30) which may be relevant in seeking to secure high employment standards.

382 See *Government Accounting 2000*, Chap 22, 'Procurement Policy Guidelines'.

383 Annex 22.2, para 2.1, *Government Accounting 2000*, Chap 22, available at <http://www.government-accounting.gov.uk/current/frames.htm>.

384 Ibid.

385 See <http://ec.europa.eu/internal_market/publicprocurement/legislation_en.htm> for a full list. The Procurement Directives (Council Directives 93/37, 93/36, 92/50, and 93/38) have been transposed into UK law by, respectively, the Public Works Contracts Regulations 1991, SI 1991/2678;

principle of free movement of goods and services. The Directives and EC Regulations addressing public procurement prescribe procedures for most contracts above certain value thresholds. The Public Procurement Directives guarantee equal treatment on grounds of nationality in the contracting process in relation to, works, supplies, services, and utilities. They apply to contracts which exceed specified financial thresholds, and require that a tendering process be transparent and that the selection of candidates in the award of tenders be based on objective criteria. They provide a complex regime for meeting the aims of the Directives. They do not make specific reference to social considerations.[386] However, they must be read consistently with the provisions of the EC Treaty, and in this regard Article 2 of the EC Treaty identifies the Community's tasks as including the promotion of 'a high level of employment and of social protection . . . , sustainable and non-inflationary growth, . . . , the raising of the standard of living and quality of life, and economic and social cohesion'. Article 13 of the EC Treaty now empowers the Community to take appropriate action to combat discrimination on enumerated grounds, as discussed in Chapter 4.[387]

15.125 These provisions provide an important backdrop to the Public Procurement Directives which will be interpreted with the general tasks of the Community and fundamental rights in mind.[388] In *Gebroeders Beentjes BV v the State (Netherlands)*[389] (the *Beentjes* case), the ECJ considered, among other things, whether a tender could be rejected on the ground that the tenderer was not

---

the Public Supply Contracts Regulations 1995, SI 1995/2010; the Public Service Contracts Regulations 1993, SI 1993/3228; and the Utility Supply and Works Contracts Regulations 1992, SI 1992/3279). Recast Directives have been enacted by the European Council (2004/17/EC and 2004/18/EC) and these reflect the objectives of the previous Directives but make it clear that there is scope to take account of social issues in the procurement process where such issues are relevant, subject to the contract and do not undermine value for money for the taxpayer. Given the broad meaning of value for money which includes longer term impact on the communities being served, this does provide continued scope for using the equality duties to promote equality through procurement policies.

386 The one exception relates to employment and working conditions which is relevant where works or services may be performed in a different country to the one in which the contractor is actually based. Regulation 27 of the Public Works Contracts Regulations 1991, SI 1991/2680 (as amended) (transposing Article 23 of Directive 93/37 into domestic law) provides that: 'A contracting authority which includes in the contract documents relating to a public works contract information as to where a contractor may obtain information about obligations relating to employment protection and working conditions which will apply to the works to be carried out under the contract, shall request contractors to indicate that they have taken account of those obligations in preparing their tender or in negotiating the contract.' This wording is also found in the Public Services Contracts Regulations 1993, SI 1993/3228 (as amended) at regulation 26.

387 And see Art 6, Treaty on European Union (TEU), Chap 4.

388 As to which see Chap 4.

389 (Case 31/87) [1990] 1 CMLR 287; [1988] ECR 4635.

prepared to accept a contract condition requiring the employment of long-term unemployed persons. The Court noted that such a condition bore no relation to the checking of the contractor's suitability having regard to their economic and financial standing, their technical knowledge and ability, or to the contract award criteria as mentioned in the Directive. The Court further ruled[390] that:

> [t]he obligation to employ long-term unemployed persons could *inter alia* infringe the prohibition of discrimination on grounds of nationality laid down in Article 7(1) of the Treaty if it became apparent that such a condition could be satisfied only by tenderers from the State concerned or indeed that tenderers from other Member States would have difficulty complying with it.[391]

Even if the condition was found to be compatible with the Directive, according to the ECJ, it must be applied in conformity with all the procedural rules laid down in the Directive, in particular the rules on advertising.[392] However so long as the non-discriminatory (as between Member States) aim of the Directives were not undermined and the procedural conditions on notice were complied with, a wide range of social considerations might be had regard to in the procurement process. In its analysis of the *Beentjes* judgment the Commission stated that, provided the principles laid down by the Court are followed in relation to non-discrimination and notice, there is:

> . . . no reason to suppose that objectives other than the reduction of long-term unemployment would fall outside the area of liberty left to the Member States. Other categories of unemployment, for example of the young, would appear to be an equally legitimate concern. The same probably applies to a broad range of social matters including, for example, professional training, health and safety, labour relations, and the suppression of racial, religious discrimination or discrimination on the grounds of sex.[393]

In response to this Commission communication, local authorities were advised of **15.126** the UK's views by Department of Employment Circular 16/90 which provided that:

> Following discussions in the Advisory Committee for Public Procurement on the basis of a paper prepared by the Commission, it was agreed that certain conditions, which had to be distinguished from the verification of contractor's aptitudes and

[390] Having had regard to its judgment in *Constructions et Enterprises Industrielles SA (CEI) v Association Intercommunale pour les Autoroutes* (Case C2729/86) [1989] 2 CMLR 224 (the *CEI* case).

[391] Ibid, para 30.

[392] Ibid, paras 31 and 36: 'A condition such as the employment of long-term unemployed persons is an additional specific condition and must therefore be mentioned in the notice, so that contractors may become aware of its existence'.

[393] COM (89) 400 Final, para 46. The Commission's communication gives some examples of potentially discriminatory conditions, see paras 52 and 56, for example.

> from the criteria for award, could be acceptable in awarding contracts covered by the EC Directives provided they were capable of being fulfilled by contractors from other Member States. However, such conditions must be compatible with Community law and must be mentioned in contract notices published in the Official Journal.[394]

Thereafter and as to the performance of a contract, the Commission's communication on social issues[395] states:

> Contract conditions are obligations which must be accepted by the successful tenderer and which relate to the performance of the contract. It is therefore sufficient, in principle, for tenderers to undertake, when submitting their bids, to meet such conditions if the contract is awarded to them. A bid from a tenderer who has not accepted such conditions would not comply with the contract documents and could not therefore be accepted. However, the contract conditions need not be met at the time of submitting the tender.[396]

The Commission gives several examples of contract conditions in the social field that might be included in contracts, including 'the obligation to implement, during the execution of the contract, measures that are designed to promote equality between men and women or ethnic or racial diversity'.

15.127 In *Commission v France*[397] (the *Nord-Pas de Calais* case), decided in late 2000, the ECJ appeared to broaden the scope for considering social matters by ruling that 'additional criteria' relating to such matters may be taken into account at contract award stage. The case concerned a contract for the construction and maintenance of secondary schools in the Nord-Pas de Calais region. In the contract notices for the school refurbishment programme mention was made of participation in the local campaign against unemployment. A tenderer was then rejected for not complying with this provision and complained to the Commission. In proceedings before the ECJ brought by the Commission, the Commission maintained its position that whilst such a provision could *prima facie* be a performance requirement within the contract conditions, it could not be a contract award criterion. The Court considered the relevant provision within the Works Directive (Article 30(1) of Directive 93/37) and considered that a condition linked to the campaign against unemployment could feature as an award criterion, provided the condition was consistent with basic Treaty provisions, for example those of non-discrimination (as between Member States) and freedom to provide services. The Court also confirmed that the criterion would have to be advertised in

394 Para 64.
395 Com (2001) 466 Final.
396 Ibid, 17.
397 Case C225/97; (2000) 2 CMLR 996.

advance in the Official Journal of the European Union (OJEU) (as it had been in that case). As the Commission had not raised the possibility that the provision was in breach of Treaty provisions, and the criterion had been mentioned in the relevant notice, the Court found in favour of the French Government. It would seem therefore that non-discriminatory social provisions may comprise not only a contract condition which relates to the performance of the contract, but also an *award* criterion, provided that it has been published in advance and meets the requirement of transparency.[398]

As to the awarding of a contract, the Directives list examples of the criteria that may be applied in order to define the economically most advantageous offer. Other criteria 'according to the contract'[399] may be applied. Domestic law is clearer that this relates to the economically most advantageous *to the contracting authority*.[400] The ECJ case law establishes, then, that environmental (and therefore social) contract award criteria can be applied provided that the criteria are linked to the subject-matter of the contract; do not confer an unrestricted freedom of choice on the authority; are expressly mentioned in the contract documents or the tender notice; and comply with all the fundamental principles of Community law, in particular the principle of non-discrimination.[401] Further, any supplier can be rejected who has committed an act of grave misconduct in the course of his business or profession, which could include acts of unlawful discrimination, can be rejected.[402] This is consistent with the new recast Directives on public procurement which expressly provide that 'non-observance of national provisions implementing the Council Directives 2000/78/EC[403] and 76/207/EEC[404] concerning equal treatment of workers, which has been the subject of a final judgment or a decision having equivalent effect, may be considered an offence concerning the professional conduct of the economic operator concerned or grave misconduct'.[405] For reasons which are unclear, the Race Directive is not mentioned in terms, but the same must apply. **15.128**

The practical impact of the equality duties in relation to the procurement process is most effectively and usefully set out in the CRE's publication *The Duty to Promote* **15.129**

---

[398] See too, *Concordia Bus Finland Oy v City of Helsinki* (Case C-513/99) (the *Helsinki Buses* case) [2003] 3 CMLR 20.

[399] Eg, Art 26(1) of Directive 93/36.

[400] Eg, regulation 21(1)(a) of the Public Service Contracts Regulations 1993, SI 1993/3228.

[401] *Concordia Bus Finland Oy v City of Helsinki* (Case C-513/99) (the *Helsinki Buses* case).

[402] See for a fuller discussion see Digings and Bennett, *EC Public Procurement Law and Practice* (2004, Sweet and Maxwell), para C2.24.

[403] The Framework Directive.

[404] The Equal Treatment Directive.

[405] Recital 54, Directive 2004/17 and Recital 43 2004/18/EC.

Race Equality: Race Equality and Public Procurement, A Guide for Public Authorities and Contractors.[406] This sets out a framework for determining when race equality (but the same approach might properly be adopted for disability and gender equality) might be relevant and how, in exercising its functions in relation to procurement, a public authority should give effect to its equality duties. It identifies the relevant legal framework, though since the drafting of it the recast Directives mentioned above have been enacted. However, these do not in any way detract from the guidance. Instead they clarify that social aims are permissible where they are linked to the subject matter of the contract and do not confer an unrestricted freedom of choice on the contracting authority, are expressly mentioned and where they comply with the fundamental principles of free movement of goods, the principle of freedom of establishment and the principle of freedom to provide services, and the principle of equal treatment, the principle of non-discrimination, and the principles of proportionality and transparency.[407] Accordingly, the new Directives provide a proper legal basis for the guidance in the CRE's guide.

(7) Enforcement of the equality duties

15.130 The general and specific statutory duties may be enforced by way of judicial review, by any person or group of persons with a sufficient interest in the matter in issue, including the EOC, CRE, DRC, and, in due course, the CEHR.[408]

15.131 Further, the EOC, CRE, and DRC (and, in due course, the CEHR) have specific powers to take enforcement action to secure compliance with the specific equality duties set out in the Orders or Regulations described above.[409] Where the EOC, CRE, and DRC are satisfied that a public authority has failed or is failing to comply with a specific duty it may serve a compliance notice on the authority in question, requiring the authority to comply and to provide written information as to the steps taken to comply. If the authority fails to comply with the requirements of the compliance notice the EOC, CRE, and DRC may apply to the County or Sheriff Court for an order requiring the authority to comply.[410]

15.132 The CEHR will assume the powers of the EOC, CRE, and DRC in relation to compliance with the specific duties when they are fully functioning.[411] The threshold for intervention appears somewhat lower for the EOC and CEHR, requiring only that the EOC or the CEHR 'thinks' that a person has failed to comply with

406 (2003, CRE). See too, 'Ethnic Minorities in the Labour Market, Final Report' (March 2003, Cabinet Office Strategy Unit) 125.

407 See recitals 1 and 2.

408 *Secretary of State for Defence v Elias* [2006] EWCA Civ 1293.

409 SDA, s 76D; RRA, ss 71D and 71E; and DDA, ss 49E and 49F.

410 SDA, s 76D(6); RRA, s 71E; and DDA, s 49F.

411 EA, s 32.

a specific duty before serving a compliance notice,[412] whereas the CRE and DRC must be 'satisfied' of the same.[413] However, the EA lays down specific steps that the CEHR must take before seeking to enforce any of the duties.[414]

(8) Disability transport duties

The DDA imposes a number of duties to make reasonable adjustments on State and private actors. These are addressed in Chapter 6. The exemption relating to transport services in the context of the provision of goods, facilities, and services has also been modified in consequence of provision made by the DDA 2005, the effect which means that certain discriminatory acts by transport providers are outlawed.[415] 15.133

Further, a number of statutory duties are now placed on transport providers directed at ensuring fair access to disabled people. As is now well understood, the inaccessibility of the public transport system has a fundamental impact on the lives of disabled people.[416] In recognition of that, Part V of the DDA imposes accessibility requirements on public transport providers, and creates criminal liability in certain circumstances where there is a failure to comply with those requirements. 15.134

Section 37 of the DDA imposes duties on the drivers of regulated taxis[417] (in England and Wales) in relation to disabled passengers accompanied by guide or hearing dogs (being dogs trained to guide blind persons or dogs trained to assist deaf persons[418]). Regulated taxis have a duty to carry such passengers with their dogs and allow any dog to remain with the passenger. In addition, they are under a duty not to make an additional charge for carrying such passengers and dogs.[419] Regulations have been made extending section 37 of the DDA to include certain 15.135

412 SDA, s 76D(1); EA, s 32(1).

413 RRA, s 71D and DDA, s 49E.

414 EA, s 32 and Sch 2.

415 See Chap 10.

416 The Joint Committee on the Draft Disability Bill, First Report (May 2004), para 122; <http://www.publications.parliament.uk/pa/jt200304/jtselect/jtdisab/82/8206.htm#n134>. Not properly transcribed in the report but see evidence from Leonard Cheshire, 'Memorandum from Leonard Cheshire (DDB 11)' available at <http://www.publications.parliament.uk/pa/jt200304/jtselect/jtdisab/82/82we06.htm>. 'An Overview of the Literature on Disability and Transport' (2004) DRC, available at <http://www.drc-gb.org/uploaded_files/documents/10_548_Transport%20summary-final.pdf>.

417 Taxis to which the regulations are expressed to apply: DDA, ss 32(5) and 68(1). DDA, ss 32–9 also provide the Secretary of State with the power to make 'taxi accessibility regulations' for the purpose of securing accessible taxis. Ss 32–6 have not been brought into force so that powers designed to secure accessibility for disabled taxi users and certain duties requiring taxi drivers to carry wheelchair-using passengers have not been brought into force.

418 DDA, s 37(11).

419 Ibid, s 37(3).

disabled people with other assistance dogs, namely those assisting disabled people with epilepsy or certain physical disabilities, where those dogs have been trained by specified charities and the disabled passenger is wearing a jacket on which is prominently inscribed the name of a specified charity.[420] Provision is made for exempting drivers of taxis from these requirements on medical grounds.[421] Similar provision is made for Scotland.[422] The Private Hire Vehicles (Carriage of Guide Dogs etc) Act 2002 amends the DDA to introduce duties on operators and drivers of private hire vehicles to carry guide dogs and other assistance dogs at no additional charge.[423] Similar provision is made permitting exemptions on medical grounds.[424] These transport duties are enforced by criminal sanctions.[425]

15.136 Sections 40 to 45 of the DDA address accessibility and public service vehicles, principally by conferring regulation-making powers on the Secretary of State. Regulations have been made pursuant to these powers. The Public Service Vehicles Accessibility Regulations 2000[426] and the Public Service Vehicles (Conduct of Drivers, Inspectors, Conductors and Passengers) Regulations 1990[427] prescribe certain conduct by requiring, for example, drivers and conductors of public service vehicles to allow wheelchair users to board if there is an unoccupied wheelchair space on the vehicle. The Public Service Vehicles (Conduct of Drivers, Inspectors, Conductors and Passengers) (Amendment) Regulations 2002[428] amend the Public Service Vehicles (Conduct of Drivers, Inspectors, Conductors and Passengers) Regulations 1990 to reflect the accessibility requirements of the Public Service Vehicles Accessibility Regulations 2000.

15.137 Sections 46 to 47 of the DDA address accessibility and rail vehicles, and, as with public service vehicles, they do so principally by conferring regulation-making

420 The Disability Discrimination Act 1995 (Taxis) (Carrying of Guide Dogs etc.) (England and Wales) Regulations 2000, SI 2000/2990, as amended by the Disability Discrimination Act 1995 (Taxis) (Carrying of Guide Dogs etc) (England and Wales) (Amendment) Regulations 2006, SI 2006/1616 and SI 2006/1617.

421 DDA, s 37(3), (6), and (8) and The Disability Discrimination Act 1995 (Private Hire Vehicles) (Carriage of Guide Dogs etc.) (England and Wales) Regulations 2003, SI 2003/3122. For appeals in respect of a refusal to grant an exemption certificate, see DDA, s 38.

422 See Taxi Drivers' Licences (Carrying of Guide Dogs and Hearing Dogs) (Scotland) Regulations 2003, SI 2003/73.

423 See DDA, s 37.

424 Ibid, s 37A(5)–(7).

425 Ibid, ss 36(5), 37(4), 37A(4).

426 SI 2000/1970, as amended by the Public Service Vehicle Accessibility (Amendment) Regulations 2000, SI 2000/3318 and SI 2002/2981 and SI 2003/1818 and SI 2004/1881 (mainly in relation to the fees payable for accessibility certificates).

427 SI 1990/1020.

428 SI 2002/1724.

powers on the Secretary of State. The Rail Vehicle Accessibility Regulations 1998[429] enacted pursuant to those powers apply to rail vehicles used on railways, tramways, monorail systems, or magnetic levitation systems coming into service after 31 December 1998. They impose various accessibility requirements on these regulated rail vehicles.

The DDA 2005 amends Part 5 of the DDA and requires the Secretary of State to set an end date of no later than 2020 by which all rail vehicles will have to comply with Part 5 of the rail access standards. Other changes will affect the procedures governing the certification of rail vehicles as compliant and the way in which breaches of the regulations are penalized.[430] These provisions are not in force at the time of writing. **15.138**

E. Judicial Review[431]

The opportunity for challenging discrimination through judicial review proceedings has long since been appreciated. However, until recently most cases focused on challenges to discriminatory legislative measures or the *vires* of certain anti-discrimination legislative measures.[432] With rare exceptions[433] there was little challenge to discriminatory decision-making by public authorities under the SDA, RRA, or DDA until recently. The development of the principle of equality into a constitutional norm at common law,[434] and, therefore, a fundamental public law obligation, presents new opportunities for challenging **15.139**

429 SI 1998/2456, as amended by the Rail Vehicle Accessibility (Amendment) Regulations 2000, SI 2000/3215. And see, the Rail Vehicle (Exemption Applications) Regulations 1998 which address applications for exemption from the requirements of the Rail Vehicle Accessibility Regulations 1998.

430 DDA, ss 47A–M introduce 'compliance certificates' but these provisions are not yet in force.

431 Judicial review by the statutory Commissions is addressed in para 15.44 above.

432 As mentioned above, the original enactment of the RRA contained a broad statutory duty, and this might have founded a basis for proceedings in judicial review but for the courts' limited approach to it, amongst other things (*Wheeler v Leicester CC* [1985] AC 1054). See para 15.94 above.

433 *Equal Opportunities Commission v Birmingham City Council* [1989] 1 AC 1155.

434 Discussed in Chap 2.

435 *A v Secretary of State for the Home Department* [2005] 2 AC 68 (the context was the Government's conclusion that there was a public emergency threatening the life of the nation within the meaning of Art 15 of the ECHR and its making of the Human Rights Act 1998 (Designated Derogation) Order 2001 designating the UK's proposed derogation, under Art 15, from the right to personal liberty guaranteed by Art 5(1) of the ECHR, scheduled to the Human Rights Act 1998. The Anti-terrorism, Crime and Security Act 2001, s 23 then provided for the detention of non-nationals if the Home Secretary believed that their presence in the UK was a risk to national security and he suspected that they were terrorists who, for the time being, could not be deported because of fears for their safety or other practical consideration).

public law decision-making.[435] Further, the opportunities for challenging discriminatory decision-making by public authorities, in judicial review proceedings, have increased significantly because of the amendments made to the SDA, RRA, and DDA, and the enactment of the EA creating new statutory torts, outlawing discrimination by public authorities, and creating new general and specific statutory duties upon public authorities directed at achieving certain equality objectives, as discussed above.[436]

15.140 Importantly, whilst the SDA, RRA, DDA, and EA contain an exclusive procedural and remedial framework,[437] so that proceedings may only be brought in respect of the unlawful acts created in accordance with the procedures provided for under the Acts, this expressly does not affect any rights in judicial review.[438] The opportunities for challenging public authority decision-making through judicial review proceedings by reliance on the main anti-discrimination enactments have most recently been highlighted by the case of *Secretary of State for Defence v Elias*.[439] As *Elias* demonstrates, the unlawful acts under the main anti-discrimination enactments create a legal basis for challenging decisions by public authorities. In *Elias*, the Court of Appeal upheld the decision of the Administrative Court quashing the racially discriminatory scheme adopted by the Secretary of State, described above.[440] Mrs Elias had challenged the scheme on the grounds that it directly or indirectly discriminated against her on grounds of national origins. The Administrative Court and then the Court of Appeal, in an important judgment, concluded that the scheme was indirectly discriminatory against those of non-UK national origins and as such was unjustified, and gave declaratory relief in those terms. According to the Court of Appeal:

> Race discrimination is not the cause of action invoked by Mrs Elias in the Administrative Court. It provides the legal basis for her argument that an exercise

436 The Religion or Belief Regulations, the Sexual Orientation Regulations, and the Age Regulations create possibility for the judicial review through the unlawful acts they create, but because of their narrow reach (employment and occupation, with limited coverage in the education sphere), they are likely to prove less significant in this area.

437 SDA, s 62(1); RRA, s 53(1); DDA, Sch 3, paras 2, 5, 9, and 12; EA, s 65(1); Religion or Belief Regulations, regulation 27(1); Sexual Orientation Regulations, regulation 27(1); and Age Regulations, regulation 35(1) (though these provisions do not prevent applications for judicial review, proceedings under specified immigration enactments or applications to the pensions ombudsman; SDA, s 62(2); RRA, s 53(2); DDA, Sch 3, paras 2 and 5; EA, s 65(2); Religion or Belief Regulations, regulation 27(2); Sexual Orientation Regulations, regulation 27(2); and Age Regulations, regulation 35(2)). See Chap 14.

438 SDA, s 62(2); RRA, s 53(2); DDA, Sch 3, paras 2 and 5; EA, s 65(2); Religion or Belief Regulations, regulation 27(2); Sexual Orientation Regulations, regulation 27(2); and Age Regulations, regulation 35(2).

439 [2006] EWCA Civ 1293.

440 Para 15.118 above.

> of public power by the Secretary of State was contrary to law and should be quashed. If the power in question is re-exercised by the Secretary of State, it must not be contrary to law. In particular it must not be contrary to the 1976 Act.[441]

Further, the Administrative Court (in a decision not disturbed by the Court of Appeal) found a breach of section 71 of the RRA (imposing the general duty on public authorities[442]) and gave declaratory relief in those terms also.

Earlier cases had raised the question whether individuals had *standing* or a *sufficient interest*[443] in claims in judicial review proceedings alleging public law wrongs under the main anti-discrimination enactments or other equality provisions.[444] However, case law demonstrates that even where a remedy may lie in private law proceedings, a victim of an unlawfully discriminatory act or a person disadvantaged by a failure to comply with a statutory equality duty may bring proceedings in judicial review in respect of the same.[445] **15.141**

As to whether any claim should be brought by way of judicial review or in private law proceedings, the remedy sought will be key in determining the procedure selected. A successful judicial review may result in a quashing order or a mandatory order, either of which may be very important where, as in *Elias*, the claimant seeks to bring an end to a particular scheme (or part of it), policy, or practice. However, where the principal object of any litigation is to obtain compensation, then judicial review proceedings are less likely to be appropriate. In *Elias* the Administrative Court considered that an order for compensation was not appropriate in circumstances where, even if the offending criteria in the scheme were quashed, that would not necessarily entitle Mrs Elias to an award under the scheme. Instead a quashing order would have the effect of requiring the Government to reconsider the scheme, and any new criteria for the making of an award could, conceivably, lawfully exclude Mrs Elias.[446] Accordingly, she was not awarded compensation by the Administrative Court. In judicial review proceedings, therefore, damages for an unlawfully discriminatory measure may not be awarded in the discretion of the court (bearing in mind the entitlement to the same in a **15.142**

---

[441] [2006] EWCA Civ 1293, para 47.

[442] See para 15.102 above.

[443] Supreme Court Act 1981, s 31(2). For a full discussion see M Fordham, *Judicial Review Handbook* (2003, Hart), Part II, P38.

[444] *R v Secretary of State for Employment, ex p Equal Opportunities Commission and Another* [1994] 1ICR 317.

[445] *Secretary of State for Defence v Elias* [2006] EWCA Civ 1293; *R v Secretary of State for Employment, ex p Seymour-Smith and Another* [1997] 1 WLR 473.

[446] See reference to the same at para 219 in *Secretary of State for Defence v Elias* [2006] EWCA Civ 1293. Though the same might occur in private law proceedings, a claim based on loss of a chance is more likely to succeed, *Ministry of Defence v Cannock* [1995] ICR 918.

County Court action), particularly where declaratory relief, a quashing order, or mandatory order is more appropriate because a lawful exercise of the public power in issue may not result in damage to the claimant. This should be had regard to in deciding the forum for challenging discriminatory action by public authorities which, where there is an individual victim—absent a desire for strategic action—will usually be better litigated in the County Courts. Judicial review is more likely to be appropriate, on the other hand, where the litigation is strategic and involves large numbers of people or policies of wide impact.

INDEX